the Comprehensive Guide to

COREL® WEB.GRAPHICS SUITE

the Comprehensive Guide to

COREL® WEB.GRAPHICS SUITE

Daniel Gray
John Shanley

VENTANA

The Comprehensive Guide to CorelWEB.GRAPHICS Suite
Copyright © 1997 by Daniel Gray

Library of Congress Cataloging-in-Publication Data
Gray, Daniel, 1961–
   The comprehensive guide to CorelWEB.GRAPHICS SUITE / Daniel Gray. — 1st ed.
      p. cm.
   Includes index.
   ISBN 1-56604-614-9
   1. Computer graphics. 2. CorelDRAW! 3. HTML (Document markup language) 4. World Wide Web (Information retrieval system) I. Title.
385.G73746 1996
006.6′869—dc21   96-52032
                                  CIP

First Edition 9 8 7 6 5 4 3 2 1

Printed in the United States of America

Ventana Communications Group
P.O. Box 13964
Research Triangle Park, NC 27709-3964
919.544.9404
FAX 919.544.9472
http://www.vmedia.com

Ventana Communications Group is a division of International Thomson Publishing.

President
Michael E. Moran

**Vice President of
Content Development**
Karen A. Bluestein

**Director of Acquisitions
and Development**
Robert Kern

Managing Editor
Lois J. Principe

Production Manager
John Cotterman

Art Director
Marcia Webb

**Technology Operations
Manager**
Kerry L. B. Foster

Brand Manager
Jamie Jaeger Fiocco

Creative Services Manager
Diane Lennox

Acquisitions Editor
Neweleen A. Trebnik

Project Editor
Jessica A. Ryan

Development Editor
Sarah O'Keefe

Copy Editors
Norma Emory
Marion Laird

CD-ROM Specialist
Patrick Bragg

Technical Reviewer
Brian Little,
Imagination Workshop

Desktop Publisher
Scott Hosa

Proofreader
Marion Laird

Indexer
Ann Norcross

Cover Illustrator
Laura Stalzer

About the Authors

Daniel Gray manages the editorial content of *PrePRESS Main Street* and writes for a number of graphics and Web-related publications. His books about the computer and graphic arts fields include *Looking Good Online* and *Web Publishing With Adobe PageMill* (both published by Ventana), and the bestselling *Inside CorelDRAW!* (New Riders).

John Shanley is a veteran graphic designer and owner of Phoenix Creative Graphics. He is a long-time Corel software user and beta tester. John is a contributing author on several Corel-related books, including *Inside CorelDRAW! 4 & 5*, *The CorelDRAW! 5 Professional Reference*, and *Mastering CorelDRAW! 6*. He can be reached via the Internet at phoenix@ifu.net or on CompuServe at 76535,3443.

Acknowledgments

We'd like to thank everyone at Ventana who helped us along the way: Neweleen Trebnik for suggesting, signing, and sticking with the book; Sarah O'Keefe for her helpful development editing; Norma Emory and Marion Laird, for their deft copy edit (you made us look as if we actually passed English 101); Brian Little, for his ever-astute technical editing and great sense of humor; Patrick Bragg and company for pulling together an awesome CD-ROM; and last, but certainly never least, Jennifer Rowe and Jessica Ryan for their expert editorial skills in steering the project through shifting currents.

If it weren't for Corel putting together the WEB.GRAPHICS Suite, we wouldn't have a reason to write this book. We'd like to thank Shawn Cadeau, Manager Web Products, and Karen Kong for her patience and assistance with questions regarding CorelWEB.MOVE. Many thanks to Michael Bellefeuille and Michelle Murphy for helping to move things along.

We'd like to take note of the invaluable assistance of Leonid Kitainik and Irene Berman at Paragraph International, Inc., regarding the intricacies of CorelWEB.WORLD and VRML. Many thanks to the folks at Inner Media whose screen capture program, Collage Complete 1.1, was used extensively throughout the book. Don't forget to try out the demo version of Collage Complete included on the Companion CD-ROM. To Number Nine Video Corporation for making great video cards and stable drivers for the Windows 95 and NT platforms. Especially to Phil Parker, who, over the years has always taken the time to educate us about the "real story" behind PC video cards.

Many thanks to Kare Grams for letting us rope her into writing the chapter on CorelWEB.GALLERY.

Dedications

In the end, no one deserves more thanks than our families, who put up with us as we put in the long hours. Now can we take a few days off? ;-)
—Dan Gray

I'd like to thank all my family for putting up with a lot of inconvenience while I "hibernated" and pounded away at the keyboard. Special thanks go to my wife, Diane. Without her patience and support over the months it took to complete this project, I would never have gotten through it.
—John Shanley

Contents

Part II: CorelWEB.DRAW

Part III: CorelWEB.MOVE

Part IV: CorelWEB.WORLD

Part V: CorelWEB.Transit

Part VI: CorelWEB.Gallery

Introduction

For many, the entrance to the realm of online design can be a tollgate to the Twilight Zone. Fortunately, it doesn't have to be that way. While the World Wide Web (WWW) may seem as if it's straight out of the space age, there's no need to worry—Web page design is not rocket science. Although there are some complex issues involved, they're all conquerable, if you have the perseverance to see things through. This book's primary intent is to quickly get you acclimated to the concepts behind the WWW and to ensure your competency as a Web page designer. We'll rip apart each module of the CorelWEB.GRAPHICS Suite, as you learn how to create a dynamic Web site from scratch. We'll explain things in terms a real person can understand, and we'll provide exercises that are both educational and enjoyable.

The CorelWEB.GRAPHICS Suite holds true to the Corel tradition, in that the package contains a formidable collection of programs at a highly competitive price. In the box you'll find most of what you need to build a cutting-edge Web site. The package includes:

- CorelWEB.DESIGNER: a WYSIWYG (what you see is what you get) Web page layout program.

- CorelWEB.DRAW: a souped-up version of CorelDRAW! 5, for designing custom Web graphics.

- CorelWEB.MOVE: a GIF and Java animation program.

- CorelWEB.WORLD: an application that allows you to build awesome VRML 1.0 3D worlds.

- CorelWEB.Transit: a program that lets you automatically convert word processing to HTML.

- CorelWEB.GALLERY: a collection of more than 7,500 GIF and JPEG images.

- O'Reilly & Associates' WebSite 1.1: Web Server software.

While CorelWEB.GRAPHICS is a great value, it falls short in a few crucial places. The techniques explained herein, together with the software on *The Comprehensive Guide to Corel WEB.GRAPHICS Suite CD-ROM*, will enable you to create awesome Web page designs that look great and perform flawlessly. This book takes a module-by-module approach to building a Web site, and it provides exactly what the package is lacking. As you move through the book, you'll learn the basics behind each module while mastering the tools with hands-on exercises that are fun to do. Each section includes tips and tricks on using the application, as well as how to make the most of that particular aspect of Web page design.

Part I: Corel WEB.DESIGNER

In the early days of the World Wide Web, the only way to build a Web page was to hack out the HTML (HyperText Markup Language) coding by hand. Thankfully, we now have Corel WEB.DESIGNER, an innovative WYSIWYG Web page-layout program that insulates us from the ordeal of HTML coding while delivering powerful control over page layout. In this section, you'll learn how to:

- Design Web page layouts, from simple to complex.

- Integrate text and inline graphics.

- Create hyperlinks and image maps.

- Use HTML tables for maximum impact.

- Work with background colors and textures.

Part 2: CorelWEB.DRAW

CorelDRAW! is the bestselling drawing program on the Windows platform, with its wild special effects and cool features. CorelWEB.DRAW takes the power of the popular program to the Web by adding support for vector-based hyperlinks and image mapping. We'll show you how to get the maximum impact out of the program as you learn how to:

- Create exciting Web graphics in GIF and JPEG formats.
- Assign transparency to GIF images and fine-tune files for download speed.
- Build complete HTML Web pages.
- Create vector-based hyperlinks.
- Publish your CorelWEB.DRAW artwork as Java applets.

Part 3: CorelWEB.MOVE

It's hard to surf the Web these days without seeing Web page animation in one form or another. CorelWEB.MOVE provides you with the tools you need to quickly crank out basic animations in GIF format, and take your animations to a whole new plane with Java interactivity. While the package ships with thousands of ready-made animation elements, you can easily create your own custom designs. In this section, you'll learn how to:

- Use actors, cells, props, timelines, paths, and sounds.
- Create an animated GIF advertising banner.
- Deliver Java interactivity with cue cards.
- Design animations for maximum impact.

Part 4: CorelWEB.WORLD

Want to take your visitors into a whole new dimension? Virtual Reality Modeling Language (VRML) is the key to cool 3D walk-throughs and other-worldly experiences. CorelWEB.WORLD makes it possible for you to create your own exciting online VRML 1.0 environments for your Web site visitors to explore. We'll take a look at what Corel has provided "in the box" and learn what it takes to move your VRML environments to the next level.

In this section, you'll learn how to:

- Modify the 3D templates provided with the program.

- Build 3D custom environments for both the Internet and intranets.

- Create 3D hyperlinks to other pages on your Web site.

- Take the leap to VRML 2.0.

Part 5: CorelWEB.Transit

Oftentimes, you'll be called upon to convert word processing files into HTML Web pages from their native format. CorelWEB.Transit conveniently provides you with the ability to convert from WordPerfect, Microsoft Word, and Lotus AmiPro files, without having the native application on your computer. The program delivers powerful automation in the form of graphic conversions, hyperlinked table of contents generation, and file-splitting for Web page optimization. In this section, you'll learn how to:

- Automatically produce HTML Web pages from word processing files.

- Use CorelWEB.Transit translation templates and style names.

- Create hyperlinked tables of contents.

Part 6: CorelWEB.GALLERY

No Corel package would be truly complete without gobs of clip art and fonts! CorelWEB.GRAPHICS Suite delivers with a selection of thousands of pieces of clip art, as well as sets of Web page ornaments, such as banners, rules, bullets, and buttons. The program makes it easy for you to manage your collection of original artwork as well. In this section, you'll learn how to:

- Make the most of Corel's clip art.
- Create your own WEB.GALLERY albums.
- Convert graphics to and from different formats.
- Scan graphics with the TWAIN-compliant interface.

Moving On

It's T minus 10. We're about to blast off for the wild world of CorelWEB.GRAPHICS! As you move through this book, you'll quickly master the concepts and take charge of the tools of Web page design. Don't worry—this won't hurt a bit. Just sit down and strap in.

PART I

CorelWEB.DESIGNER

Getting to Know CorelWEB.DESIGNER

Beneath the visage of every Web page lies an intricately woven foundation of HyperText Markup Language (HTML) coding. HTML code is the glue that bonds the text and graphic files that make up a Web page. Without HTML, the World Wide Web (WWW) never would have come into existence. HTML coding is what tells the browser how all the text should look and where all the graphics should appear.

A Snippet of Syntax . . .

Every HTML tag has a beginning and an ending code. For example, when setting a word in boldface, you would use the following syntax: <B>the bold text goes here</B>.

In the beginning, all Web pages had to be coded by hand in a simple ASCII text-editing program or word processor, such as WordPad (as shown in Figure 1-1). Commercial and shareware programs specifically designed to produce HTML code for Web page production—such as SoftQuad's HoTMetaL PRO and Sausage Software's HotDog—soon followed. But most of the early Web page creation tools lacked immediate visual feedback. Instead, they relied on page designers to use Web browsers, such as Netscape Navigator and NCSA Mosaic, to preview their Web pages (as shown in Figure 1-2).

```
Sleep.htm - Notepad
File  Edit  Search  Help

<HTML>
<HEAD>
<TITLE>The Official Insomniacs Home Page</TITLE>
</HEAD>
<BODY BGCOLOR="#000000" TEXT="#FFFFFF">
<CENTER>
<IMG SRC="IMAGES/SLEEP_D.GIF" ALIGN="bottom" ALT="[ The Official Insomniacs Home Page ]"><BR>
<IMG SRC="IMAGES/SLEEP_F.GIF" ALIGN="bottom" ALT="[ Bar ]">

<P>
This Website offers solutions to you late Web surfers who can't get to sleep.
</P>
<P>
<A HREF="SLEEP_2.HTM">
<IMG SRC="IMAGES/SLEEP_E.GIF" ALIGN="bottom" ALT="[ Counting Sheep ]" BORDER="0"></A>

<A HREF="SLEEP_2.HTM">
<IMG SRC="IMAGES/SLEEP_A.GIF" ALIGN="bottom" ALT="[ Light Reading ]" BORDER="0"></A>

<A HREF="SLEEP_2.HTM">
<IMG SRC="IMAGES/SLEEP_B.GIF" ALIGN="bottom" ALT="[ Sleeping Aids ]" BORDER="0"></A>

<A HREF="SLEEP_2.HTM">
<IMG SRC="IMAGES/SLEEP_C.GIF" ALIGN="bottom" ALT="[ Sweet Dreams ]" BORDER="0"></A>
</P>
<P>
Maintained by: Sleepless Sam
</P>
</CENTER>
</BODY>
</HTML>
```

Figure 1-1: Ugh! Look at those scary codes . . .

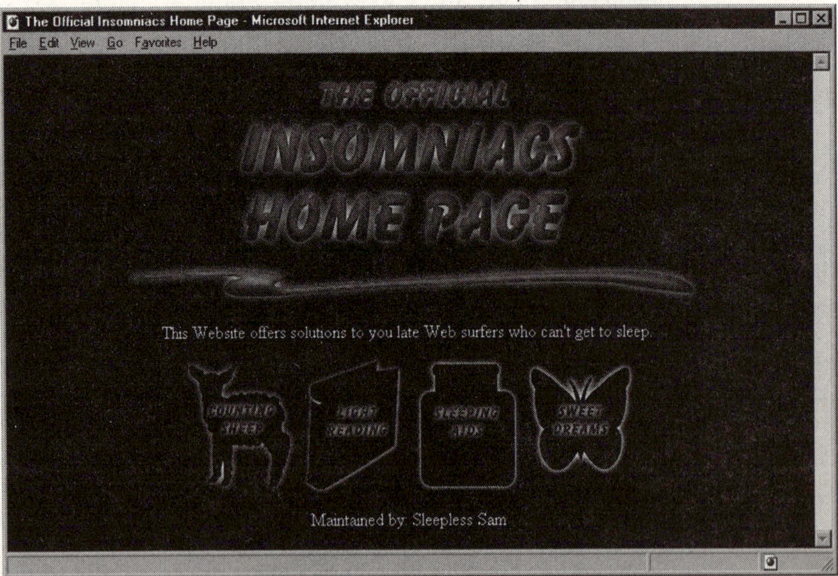

Figure 1-2: . . . but they surely make the page look nice when viewed in a Web browser, such as Microsoft's Internet Explorer.

CorelWEB.DESIGNER is your ticket to fast and easy Web page creation. The program provides a WYSIWYG (what you see is what you get) environment that allows you to build Web pages without having to hack out the code by hand. WEB.DESIGNER delivers immediate visual feedback, eliminating the need to rely on Web browsers as preview windows. When you work on a Web page in CorelWEB.DESIGNER, it appears much as it will when viewed in a browser. Figure 1-3 displays the same page as the two previous figures and demonstrates WEB.DESIGNER's powerful WYSIWYG editing prowess.

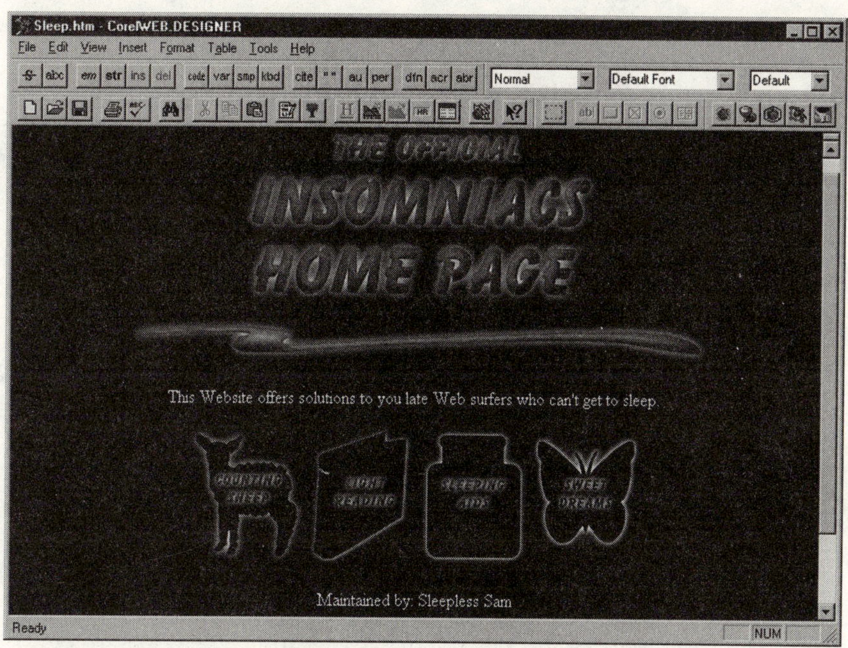

Figure 1-3: CorelWEB.DESIGNER's WYSIWYG environment closely mimics how the Web page will appear in the browser.

This chapter shows you how to produce text pages with CorelWEB.DESIGNER. Before long, you'll be churning out Web pages that include such basic text features as heading and body styles, alignment, type sizes, and linking; advanced text features, such as tables and forms, are covered in Chapter 3. As this chapter progresses, you'll learn a bit about the HTML code that underlies every Web page.

Why get into the code? Your effectiveness in building Web pages will be limited if you can't deal with some raw HTML once in a while. You need to understand the underlying structure of your HTML pages, because this will let you build more effective layouts. Throughout this (and subsequent) chapters, you'll see code examples sprinkled in to help you become familiar with the syntax.

The WEB.DESIGNER Interface

CorelWEB.DESIGNER features an interface that would do Jane Jetson proud. Talk about push buttonitis! She'd be in her glory, using (and re-arranging) all the push buttons on the program's fully customizable toolbars.

WEB.DESIGNER's toolbars can be placed almost anywhere you desire—docking at the top, bottom, or side of the window—and can be set up even as floating palettes, as shown in Figure 1-4. To move the toolbars from one position to another, just click the toolbar (not on a button) and drag it to where you want it to appear. To turn a toolbar into a floating palette, just click and drag it toward the center of the window. If you don't want to see a particular toolbar, turn it off via the View menu.

Figure 1-4: Just drag and drop to rearrange the WEB.DESIGNER window to fit your own preferences.

Figure 1-4 shows a different toolbar arrangement than that displayed in Figure 1-3. Take a gander at the style buttons running down the side of the window, the text-formatting entries at the bottom of the window, and the floating-form and program-launch palettes. This should give you an idea of the freedom you have to design your own work space in WEB.DESIGNER.

One exception worth noting: The text-formatting toolbar cannot be docked along the side of the window, because its drop-down menus use too much screen space.

The Sad Truth About HTML Text

If you've had experience working with page layout packages such as QuarkXPress, Adobe PageMaker, or CorelVENTURA, you're accustomed to rather extensive control over text. The current crop of word processors do quite an impressive job as well. Most of these programs provide a high level of control over typeface selection, type size, letter spacing, and line spacing.

The sad truth about working with Web page text is that you have practically no control over how your text will be viewed. Almost everything is browser-dependent. The HTML spec allows the browser to set individual preferences for typeface and type size on a style-by-style basis. Specifying text on a Web page you create is a leap of faith. What looks right and works well on your screen will look totally different to your audience. That having been said, HTML *does* provide a sufficient range of text styles for most situations.

While HTML forces you to give up complete typographical control, it is this lack of control that allows HTML files to be small and platform-independent. It's impossible to know what fonts may be loaded at the browser—be it running on a Windows, Macintosh, or UNIX machine—and what those fonts are named. This is in stark contrast to a typical DTP/page layout environment, where you should know *exactly* what fonts are available at the printer. HTML has become successful because it allows pages to be designed without being dependent upon a particular set of fonts. It's ambiguous yet effective.

What About FONT FACE?

Netscape Navigator 3 and Microsoft Internet Explorer 3 both support the new FONT FACE command. This allows you to take a stab at specifying typefaces, but you'll have to hack out the HTML code by hand. Chapter 4 includes a rundown on the use of this new command.

Paragraph Formats & Character Styles

HTML uses both *paragraph formats* and *character styles*. The difference between the two is that a character style affects selected characters only. A paragraph format, on the other hand, affects an entire paragraph. Character styles are used within a paragraph to style a particular word or phrase, as when the title of a book—such as *The Comprehensive Guide to CorelWEB.GRAPHICS Suite*—is set in italics.

There are three basic types of paragraph formats:

- *Heading* formats
- *Body text* formats
- *List* formats

A properly structured Web page should make efficient use of the various formats. Let's take it from the top (of the page).

Heading Formats

HTML provides six logical heading formats. WEB.DESIGNER allows you to assign each format from the Format | Heading menu or from the toolbar. Figure 1-5 illustrates the half-dozen heading style choices, while Table 1-1 shows the HTML equivalents.

Heading 1

Heading 2

Heading 3

Heading 4

Heading 5

Heading 6

Normal (Body Text)

Figure 1-5: HTML heading formats.

Size	WEB.DESIGNER	HTML Code
Largest	Heading 1	<H1>...</H1>
Larger	Heading 2	<H2>...</H2>
Large	Heading 3	<H3>...</H3>
Small	Heading 4	<H4>...</H4>
Smaller	Heading 5	<H5>...</H5>
Smallest	Heading 6	<H6>...</H6>

Table 1-1: Heading formats & their equivalents.

Because heading commands are paragraph formats, they affect everything in a text block—from one paragraph return until the next. This being so, a heading style cannot be assigned to selected words within a paragraph. All you need to do to assign a heading format is have the cursor flashing somewhere within the text block. When the style is chosen, it is assigned to the whole enchilada.

With WEB.DESIGNER up and running, type a few lines of text now; separate the lines with a return. Then go ahead and assign different heading styles to the text. Did you notice that headings 5 and 6 are actually smaller than the body text style? Although this may seem odd, you can use these tiny heading styles to great effect sometimes, such as in secondary-text navigation bars.

Body Text Formats

HTML's default paragraph format uses nonindented text, set in a plain Roman font. In practice, you'll use the paragraph format for the bulk of the text on your Web pages, although you may apply different character styles and type sizes. In addition to the default paragraph style, WEB.DESIGNER allows you to assign HTML's *preformatted text* paragraph format.

The preformatted text format is handy for displaying text in a monospaced typewriter typeface. Although HTML usually collapses word spacing—displaying only one space no matter how many spaces are actually typed in the text—the preformatted format displays everything as is. So it's often used to create crude tabular text without using table commands. Figure 1-6 displays the normal paragraph format along with some preformatted text. Paragraph formats can be assigned from the Format menu or from the toolbar.

This is a paragraph set in the normal body format. This is a paragraph set in the normal body format. This is a paragraph set in the normal body format. This is a paragraph set in the normal body format. This is a paragraph set in the normal body format. This is a paragraph set in the normal body format. It might not be exciting, but there it is. This is a paragraph set in the normal body format.

```
This is a paragraph set in the preformatted format.  Look -- Two spaces!  This is a
paragraph set in the preformatted format.  Look -- three spaces!  This is a paragraph
set in the preformatted format. This is a paragraph set in the preformatted format.

The Simple Table Truth
About Cats, Dogs & Iguana

Year      Cats      Dogs      Iguana
1997      12        18         9
1996      10        17         6
1995      14        14         4
1994      19        14         2
1993      24        12         1
```

Figure 1-6: Preformatted text allows you to create quick-and-dirty tables without invoking the HTML table commands.

List Formats

HTML provides a number of list formats for use in various situations. CorelWEB.DESIGNER includes buttons to assign the two most common list formats: unordered (bulleted) lists and ordered (numbered) lists, as shown in Figure 1-7. To use the other list formats, you must key in the codes yourself in WEB.DESIGNER's HTML source editing mode, as shown in Table 1-2. The additional list formats include:

- Directory—indented and bulleted
- Menu—indented and bulleted
- Term—used with the definition format; set flush on the left margin
- Definition—indented text, used with the term format

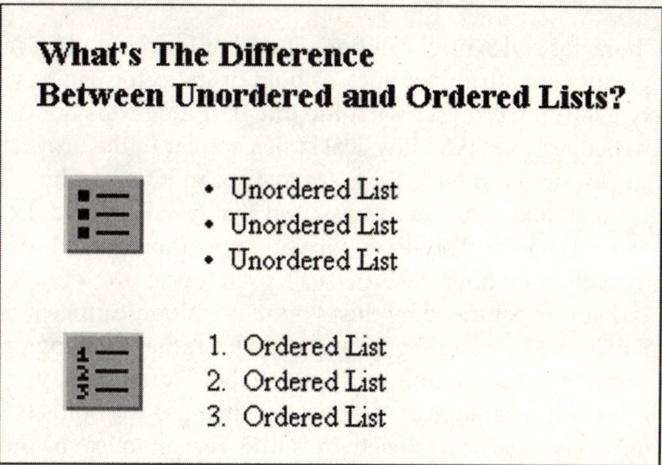

Figure 1-7: Unordered and ordered lists are just two out of a handful of HTML list formats.

While the directory and menu formats appear to be identical to the basic unordered format, the difference between them has to do with the theoretical structure of the document (and how the browser might interpret them).

Name	HTML Commands
Ordered	<OL><LI>...</OL>
Unordered	<UL><LI>...</UL>
Directory	<DIR><LI>...</DIR>
Menu	<MENU>...</MENU>
Definition	<DL><DD>...</DL>
Term	<DL><DT>...</DL>

Table 1-2: HTML list format commands.

Physical Character Styles & Logical Character Styles

Character styles can be either *physical* or *logical*. A physical style applies specific font attributes, such as bold or italic, to specific words. A logical style tells the browser what the intent of the text is but doesn't define a particular type style. Physical styles appear in the browser as the Web page designer intends for them to appear. If you assign a bold style to a chunk of text, you can rest assured that it will be bold. In contrast, text assigned a logical style can vary in appearance from browser to browser, depending on how the browser's preferences are set.

If you're confused by this, you're not alone. Suffice it to say, you can play it safe by assigning physical styles rather than logical styles. If you simply want something to appear in bold, don't rack your brain trying to figure out what logical style to use—just use the bold style. For design decisions as basic as this, there's little reason to leave your typographical decisions to the whims of the browser.

Physical Character Styles

There are four physical character styles. They can be assigned with a
keyboard shortcut, from the toolbar, or from the Style menu. Figure 1-8
displays the physical character styles along with some variations, while
Table 1-3 lists the physical character styles, HTML equivalents, and
keyboard shortcuts.

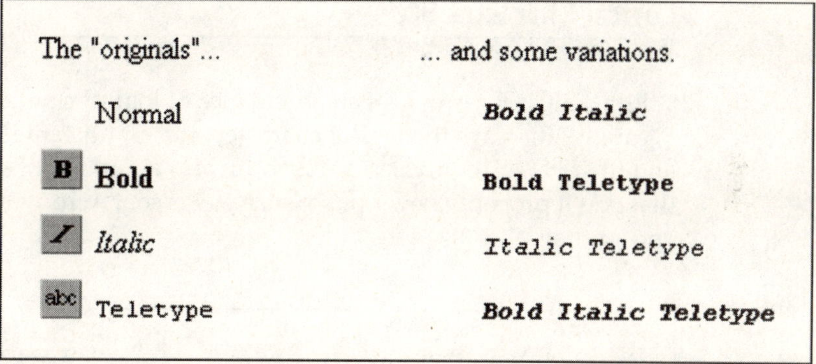

Figure 1-8: Mix-and-match physical styles.

Style	HTML Commands	Keyboard Shortcut
Plain	<P>...</P>	
Bold	<B>...</B>	Ctrl+B
Italic	<I>...</I>	Ctrl+I
Teletype	<TT>...</TT>	

Table 1-3: Physical character styles & their equivalents.

Teletype is an interesting style. It uses a monospaced (as opposed to proportionally spaced) typewriter-style font. Every character in a monospaced font takes up the same width, as opposed to a proportionally spaced font in which an *I* is much thinner than a *W* and so on. The teletype character style may seem similar to the preformatted paragraph format, but since it is a character style (as opposed to a paragraph format), it can be applied to specific passages within a paragraph (rather than the entire paragraph).

Logical Character Styles

WEB.DESIGNER provides an abundance of logical character styles. Figure 1-9 displays the logical character styles, and Table 1-4 lists them and their HTML equivalents. There are also a number of style buttons that you'll probably never push, such as Person, Acronym, Abbreviation, and Author.

s	Strikethrough	kbd	**Keyboard**
em	*Emphasis*	cite	*Citation*
str	**Strong Emphasis**	" "	Short Quotation
ins	Inserted Text	au	Author
del	Deleted Text	per	Person
code	Code	dfn	*Definition*
var	Variable	acr	Acronym
smp	Sample	abr	Abbreviation
		U	Underscore

Figure 1-9: Logical character styles.

Style	HTML Commands
Strikethrough	<S>...</S>
Emphasis	<EM>...</EM>
Strong emphasis	<STRONG>...</STRONG>
Inserted text	<INS>...</INS>
Deleted text	<DEL>...</DEL>
Code	<CODE>...</CODE>
Variable	<VAR>...</VAR>
Sample	<SAMP>...</SAMP>
Keyboard	<KBD>...</KBD>
Citation	<CITE>...</CITE>
Short quotation	<Q>...</Q>
Author	<AU>...</AU>
Person	<PERSON>...</PERSON>
Definition	<DFN>...</DFN>
Acronym	<ACRONYM>...</ACRONYM>
Abbreviation	<ABBREV>...</ABBREV>
Underscore	<U>...</U>

Table 1-4: Logical Character styles & their equivalents.

Additional Text Controls

A highly designed Web page calls for enhanced control over text attributes. WEB.DESIGNER provides the means to manipulate a variety of text attributes other than those managed via paragraph formats and character styles and allows you to more precisely define your Web page designs. These additional text controls include:

- Text alignment
- Text indent
- Text size
- Text color

Text Alignment

Web page text can be left-aligned, right-aligned, or centered (HTML does not support full justification). Text is left-aligned by default. To center a block of text, highlight it (or just click an insertion point) and click on the Align Center button. To set the text back to a left alignment, just click on the Align Left button (while text is highlighted). Right-align text the same way.

Text-alignment controls are implemented in the HTML paragraph and heading commands, as ALIGN=CENTER or ALIGN=RIGHT. CorelWEB.DESIGNER also provides extensive control over text alignment as it relates to inline graphics and text wrapping (where text appears to flow around a graphic), as you'll see in the next chapter.

Text Indent

CorelWEB.DESIGNER treats text indents in a very simple manner: The program allows you to set text on the margin or indented one level, through the use of the Block Quotation command (Format | Block Quotation) or via the Text Style drop-down menu on the toolbar.

It is possible to set up multiple indent levels, however, using iterations of the <BLOCKQUOTE>...</BLOCKQUOTE> command while in WEB.DESIGNER's HTML source editing mode (Edit | HTML Source). Multiple <BLOCKQUOTE> commands push the text around by predetermined increments, as shown by Figure 1-10. Unfortunately, there are no controls over the amount of indent provided by each iteration of the command.

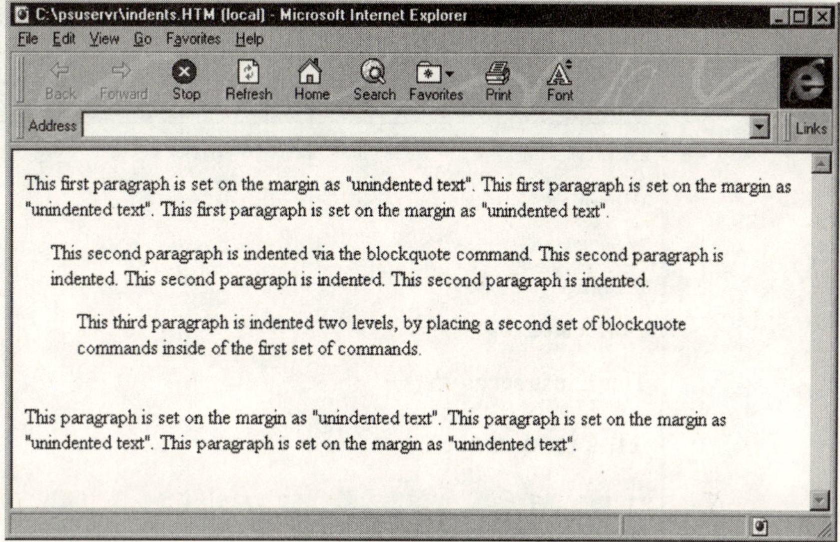

Figure 1-10: Indenting sets off passages of text.

So, the HTML coding for a second-level indent should look something like this:

```
<BLOCKQUOTE>
<BLOCKQUOTE>This third paragraph is indented two levels, by
placing a second set of blockquote commands inside of the
first set of commands.</BLOCKQUOTE>
</BLOCKQUOTE>
```

Text Size

It's not necessary to assign a heading style if all you want to do is change the type size of a selected block of text (and especially if you don't want the text to be bold). The Font Size drop-down menu on WEB.DESIGNER's toolbar affords a convenient way to change font size. It's important to note that using HTML's <FONT SIZE=X>...</FONT> command allows only seven type sizes. Figure 1-11 shows how a line of body text appears when tagged from the smallest (1) to the largest (7) of WEB.DESIGNER's seven type sizes.

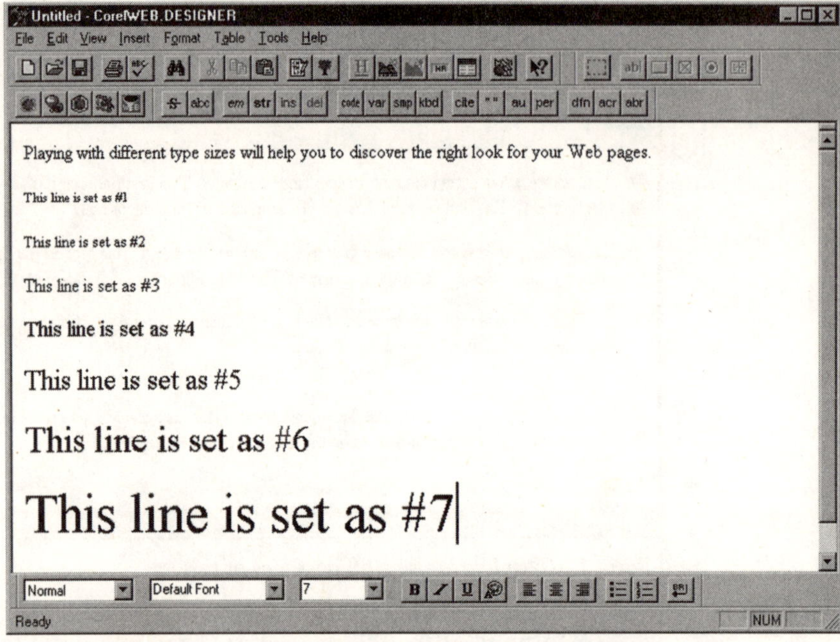

Figure 1-11: HTML's seven type sizes provide design flexibility.

CorelWEB.DESIGNER allows you to assign absolute text sizes (1, 2, 3, 4, 5, 6, 7) as well as text sizes that are relative to the page default text size (such as +1, +2, +3, +4, +5, +6, +7 and –1, –2, –3, –4, –5, –6, –7). The plus and minus settings move the text size up or down the 7-step ladder. Assigning a larger type size to a block of text within a paragraph alters the line spacing (or leading) of the lines on which the text appears. This results in a noticeably uneven look, as shown in Figure 1-12.

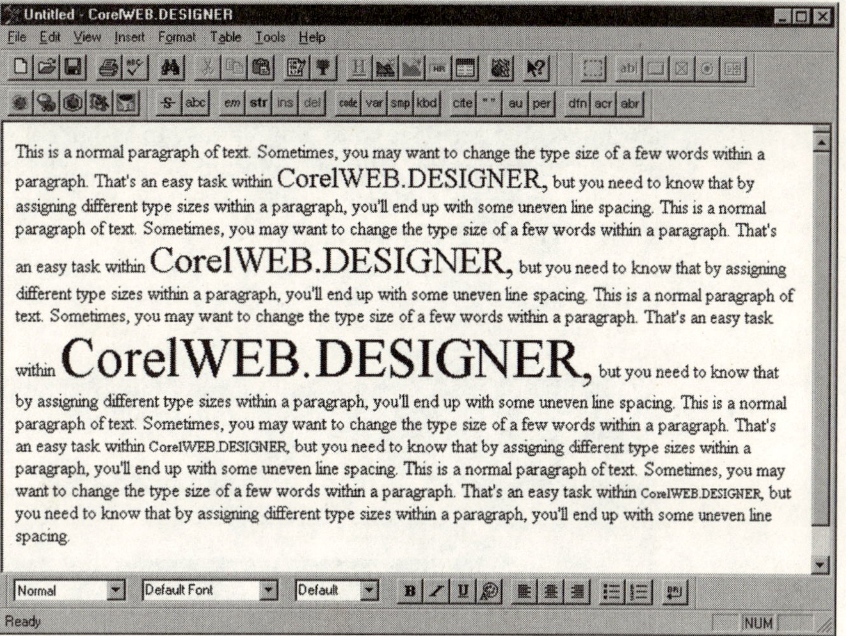

Figure 1-12: Changing the type size affects line spacing as well.

Why Is There a Font Menu?

Although CorelWEB.DESIGNER includes a font selection menu, its implementation is a tad lacking. Although the program supports the FONT FACE attribute (found in Netscape Navigator 3.0 and Microsoft Internet Explorer 3.0), it only allows you to assign one font name. To be effective, you'll need to go into HTML source edit mode to add some alternate choices. Check Chapter 4 for a full rundown on the subject of assigning typefaces.

Text Color

The Page Properties dialog box provides full control over text color attributes on a per-page basis, but it's easy to assign colors to specific text as well. To change the color of a selected block of text, highlight the text and choose the new color by clicking on the Font/Cell color button as shown in Figure 1-13. You can choose one of the 17 color selections on the drop-down menu or dial in your own colors with the Custom Color dialog box.

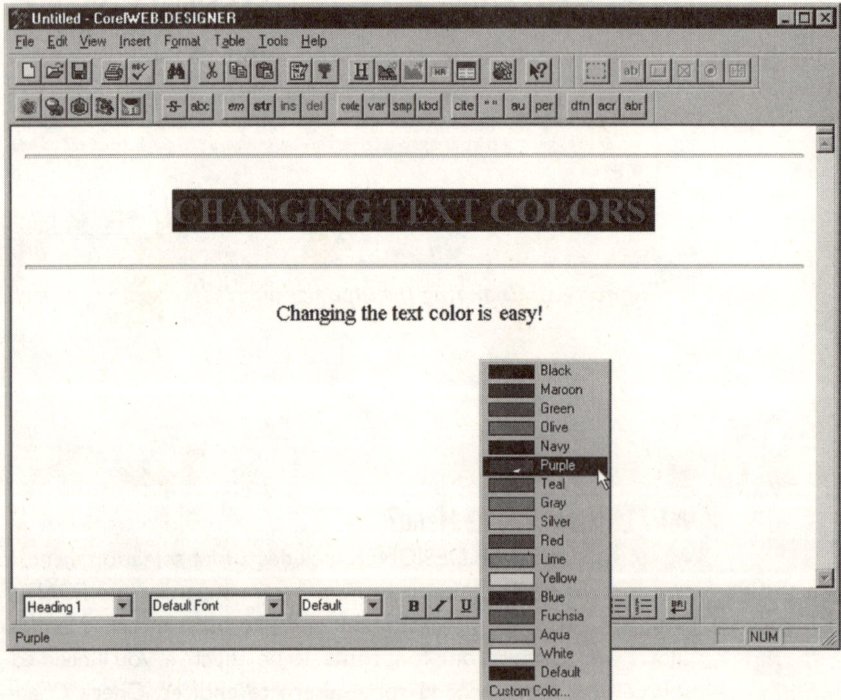

Figure 1-13: Assigning colors to text is a point-and-click procedure.

Hyperlinks—You Can Get There From Here!

Hyperlinks (or simply *links*) are at the core of the World Wide Web's allure. Some even say that they're the medium's entire reason for being. Links allow folks to jump from one spot to the next—be it from page to page or from server to server—with a single mouse click. There are three basic types of links: *internal*, *external*, and *anchored*.

Internal links are those within your Web site's directories. From a strictly navigational standpoint, they are what ties a Web site together. Visitors to your site who click on an internal link jump to one of your pages.

External (or outbound) links, conversely, tie your Web site to the World Wide Web. When visitors click on an external link, they leave your server behind as they load a new page from a different Web site.

Domain Types

There are half a dozen common domain types in the United States.

.com—commercial

.edu—educational

.gov—government

.mil—military

.net—network

.org—organization

Domains in other countries typically end with abbreviations of the name of the country, such as .ca (Canada), .uk (England), .de (Germany), and .fi (Finland).

Anchored links connect to an exact position within a page, rather than to a whole page, and can be either internal or external. They usually are internal. CorelWEB.DESIGNER refers to these links as *Bookmarks*.

What About Browser Bookmarks?

You're probably familiar with browser bookmarks—those favorite places that you've saved while surfing the Internet—consequently, WEB.DESIGNER's misguided use of the term (to refer to anchors) may be confusing.

Links can be attached to text or to graphics. In the following section, you'll learn the basics behind creating text links between your pages as well as to other Web sites. Graphic links and image maps are covered in the next chapter.

WEB.DESIGNER allows you to set up your hyperlinks via its HyperLink Properties dialog box (as shown in Figure 1-14). There are two basic ways to get at the HyperLink Properties dialog box. While the text you want to link is highlighted, choose Format | HyperLink or click on the HyperLink button (the one with the big blue *H*) on the toolbar.

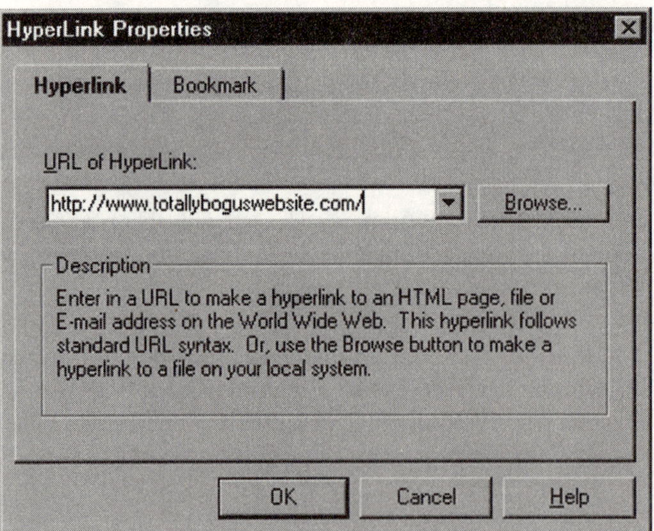

Figure 1-14: The first tab of the HyperLink Properties dialog box is used to enter the Uniform Resource Locators (URLs) of the Web pages to which you want to link.

The drop-down list (in the HyperLink Properties dialog box) allows you to instantly choose from a comprehensive list of URL prefixes (although the vast majority of your links will be to http, ftp, and mailto varieties). After you choose a prefix, type in the rest of the address, click on OK, and the text will be linked. It's that easy! The drop-down list includes the following URL prefixes:

- file—to link to a file on a local disk

- ftp—to link to a file on an FTP (File Transfer Protocol) site

- gopher—to link to a Gopher (menu-based) site

- http—to link to a file on an HTTP (HyperText Transfer Protocol) site

- mailto—to link to a specific e-mail address

- news—to link to a newsgroup

- wais—to link to a WAIS server

To link to an external page, you must include the complete URL of the page. To link to an internal page (within your own Web site), however, you don't have to include all the http://www.*yourservernamehere*.com absolute stuff—just the relative page name: /directory/subdirectory/*pagenamehere*.htm. We'll delve into directory structures in Chapter 4.

HTML provides the means to link to specific places within a Web page with anchors. Using anchors is akin to nailing up house numbers. After an anchor is dropped in the proper place, your link delivers visitors to the exact doorstep (i.e., location within a Web page).

To set an anchor, select the text to which you wish to anchor and use the Bookmark dialog box (Format | Bookmark), as shown in Figure 1-15. Once an anchor is in place, use the second tab of the HyperLink Properties dialog box to target the anchored link. Targeting an anchor is as easy as choosing the anchor from a drop-down list, as shown in Figure 1-16.

Seeing Red?

WEB.DESIGNER turns anchored text red. Don't worry . . . it's colored red only within WEB.DESIGNER itself and will appear in the default text color (or any color you tag it with) when viewed in a browser.

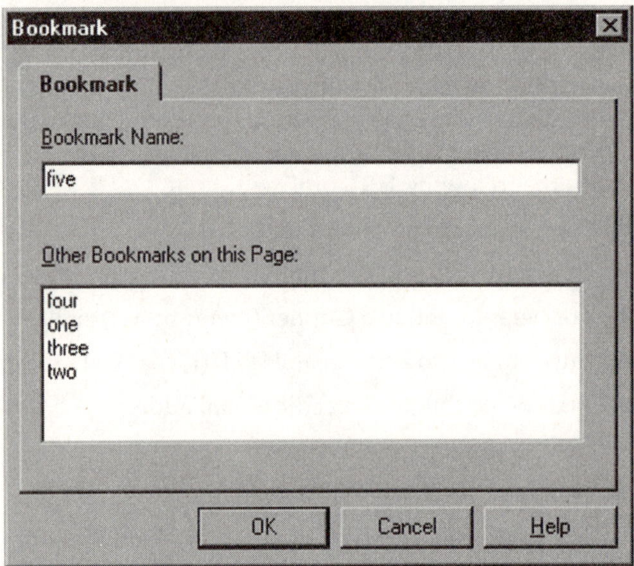

Figure 1-15: Name each anchor appropriately in the Bookmark dialog box . . .

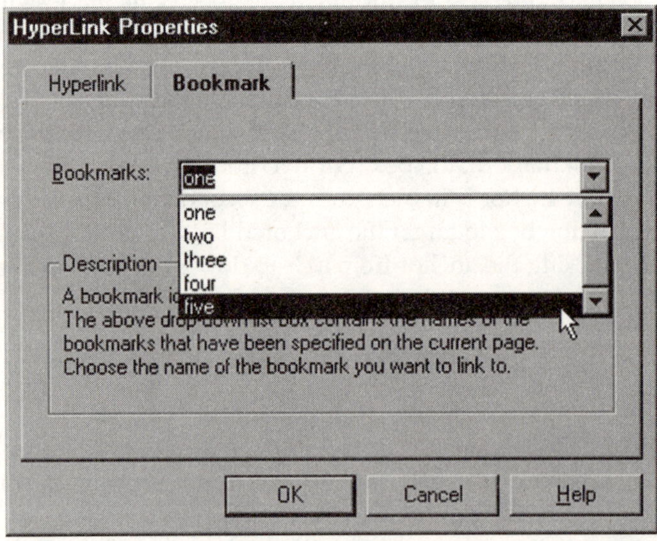

Figure 1-16: . . . then target it in the second tab of the HyperLink Properties dialog box.

Anchored jump lists often are used at the top of a long Web page, when you want to provide visitors with the ability to jump directly to their section of interest. It's also a nice touch to allow visitors to jump from one page directly to a specific anchor on another page (rather than to the top of the page).

Moving On

In this chapter you learned about the basics of CorelWEB.DESIGNER and of Web page creation in general. In the next chapter, you'll dive head-on into CorelWEB.DESIGNER's tool set as you build a simple Web page complete with hyperlinks, graphics, and image maps. Before long, you'll be integrating text and graphics like a pro! Chapter 3 takes things one step higher, delving into the advanced topics of Web design, such as tables and forms.

2

Working With Web Page Graphics

Don't bore your visitors. A Web page without graphics lacks visual interest and won't entice readers into your Web site. Even if text content contains the bulk of the site's informational value, readers may never absorb the message if it is presented poorly. A text-only page does little to entice the reader. Visually pleasing pages, on the other hand, surely attract attention and hopefully help site visitors comprehend information. As a Web page designer, you always should strive for balance between steak and sizzle.

Planning a page calls for a number of graphic-related decisions. This chapter helps you get familiar with the different types of graphics and explains how to implement each one. In practice, you may use up to seven general types of graphics when designing your Web pages. Each of these graphic types is discussed in this chapter. The images you place may include:

- Backgrounds
- Navigational aids
- Icons
- Dingbats
- Divider bars
- Illustrations
- Photographs

The greatest advantage of the CorelWEB.GRAPHICS Suite is that it provides the tools you need to create both Web page layouts (with WEB.DESIGNER) and graphics (with WEB.DRAW), along with a good selection of ready-made images. Other applications may address just one piece of the puzzle.

WWW Graphic Formats

Graphics Interchange Format (GIF) and Joint Photographic Experts Group (JPEG) are the most common graphics file formats on the World Wide Web. The GIF format should be used for solid color graphics, line art, and logos. The JPEG format is best used for photographs and continuous-tone artwork.

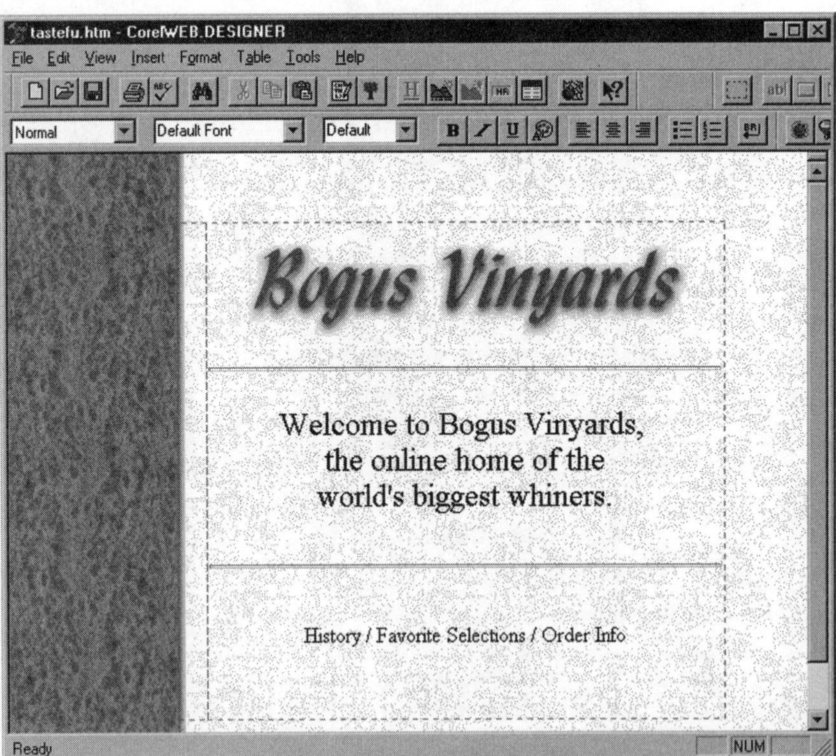

Figure 2-1: A tasteful background sets the proper mood.

Backgrounds Set the Stage

Custom backgrounds set the mood of a Web page. They let the designer replace the boring default gray of the browser window with a specific color or patterned graphic. The right background treatment sets your pages apart from the pack, as shown in Figure 2-1. The wrong background treatment, however, compromises legibility, reduces effectiveness, and irritates readers, as illustrated by Figure 2-2.

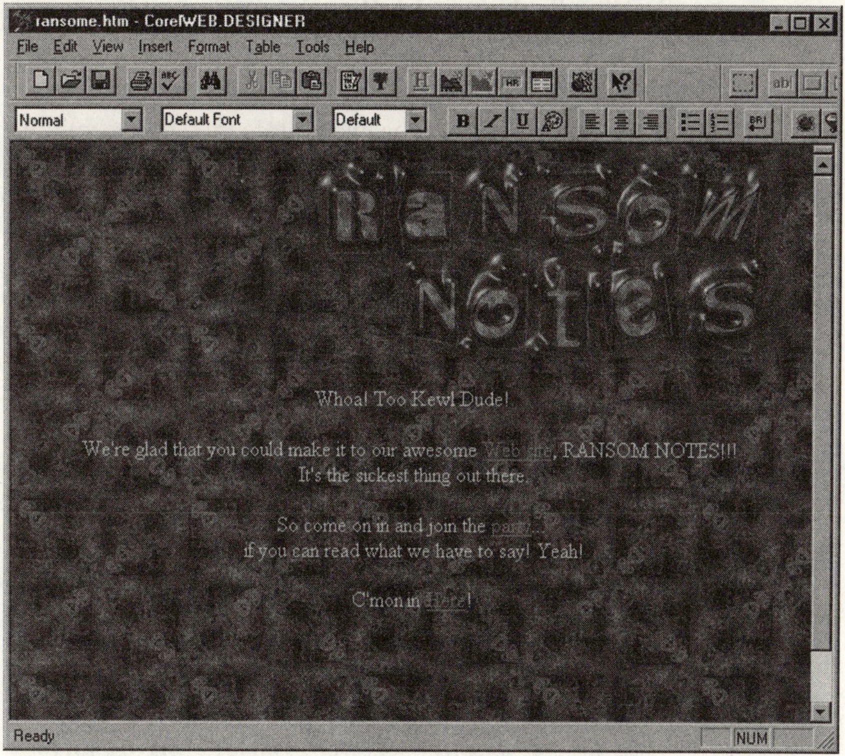

Figure 2-2: Say what? The wrong background treatment muddies a page.

Color is one of the first decisions to make when designing a Web page. Choose a background color or image that works well with your text colors. Put text legibility above all. A background color that is too close in hue to a text color makes the text difficult to read.

On the other end of the color scale, avoid combinations that present too much contrast. Wild color pairings—such as screaming yellow type on a plum purple background—can contrast and vibrate so hard that they rattle the brain. In general, try to stick to light backgrounds behind your body text. You don't have to limit yourself to pure white (R255, G255, B255), however. An off-white (R255, G255, B204) is actually easier on the eyes. Light pastel colors can be pleasing text backgrounds, as well.

Let's fire up WEB.DESIGNER and have a look around. Launch the program and open a new document.

Setting Background Colors

Assigning background colors is a snap in CorelWEB.DESIGNER. Select Page Properties from the File pull-down menu to summon the Page Properties dialog box, as shown in Figure 2-3. Using the down arrow beside Background Color, pull down a menu of 10 preset colors. Stop at Custom to summon the Custom Color dialog box, which offers a number of options: You may pick colors from a 48-color palette or mix your own either by selecting from the color chart or by directly entering color values. Once you've created a custom color, save it for later use by clicking on the Add to Custom Colors button. You can store up to 16 custom colors in WEB.DESIGNER.

Setting & Removing Background Images

Setting background images in WEB.DESIGNER is just as easy as setting colors. In the Page Properties dialog box, click on the Browse button beside the Background Image Source selection. The Select Image Source dialog box appears, prompting you to locate the desired background image (unfortunately, there's no preview, so you'll have to know the exact file name).

After you select a background image and click on Open, you may see a warning that the image exists "outside the directory in which your document is stored." Click on OK and then on Save to copy the file into the root directory. The background pattern appears on the Web page only after you click on OK in the Page Properties dialog box.

To remove a background pattern from your Web page, delete its name in the Page Properties dialog box and click on OK.

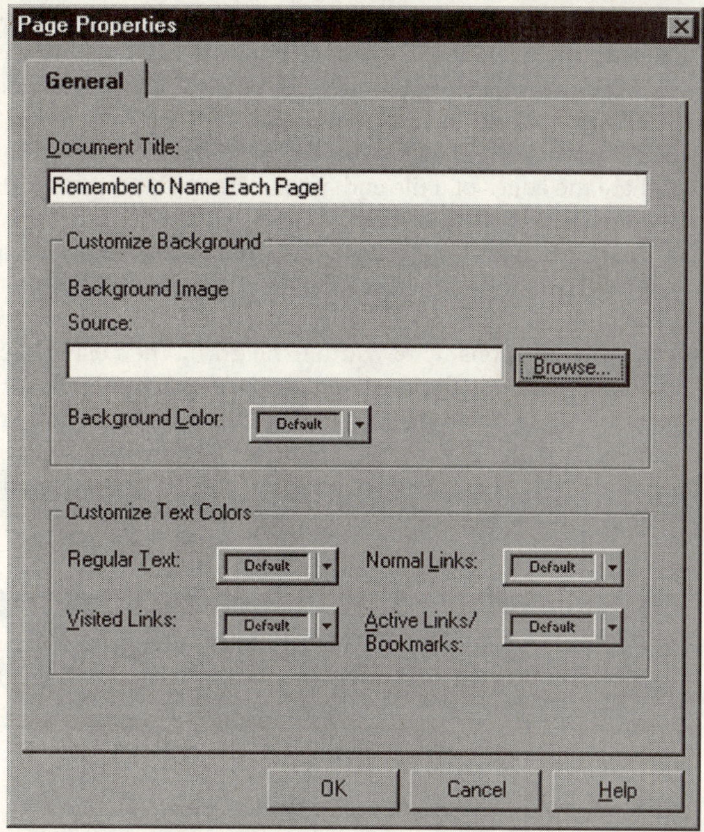

Figure 2-3: WEB.DESIGNER's Page Properties dialog box controls the overall appearance of a Web page.

Why all the Formats?

Although the Select Image Source dialog box allows you to browse GIF, JPEG, PCX, TIFF, and TARGA images, of these, GIF and JPEG are the only commonly supported Web page image formats. Thankfully, WEB.DESIGNER automatically converts the other formats for you!

Background images often are referred to as *tiles,* because the browser repeats the image to fill the open window. If the window is resized, the background image is automatically retiled. Take a look at some patterned wallpaper, fabric, or carpet, and you'll get the basic idea. While you can see the repeating pattern, you'll probably have a difficult time telling where the edges of a tile end, unlike many flooring and ceramic tiles, where the edges are distinct.

Backgrounds come in different aspect ratios and sizes, although square background images (see Figure 2-4) are among the most common. The browser automatically tiles background images, regardless of aspect ratio (the relationship of width to height). When using background tiles, you don't have to think only in terms of squares. Look at the two margin lines running down the page in Figure 2-5. This common ruled yellow notebook paper effect could not be achieved with a square texture. Instead, a short and wide rectangular tile (24 pixels high by 1024 pixels wide) was used.

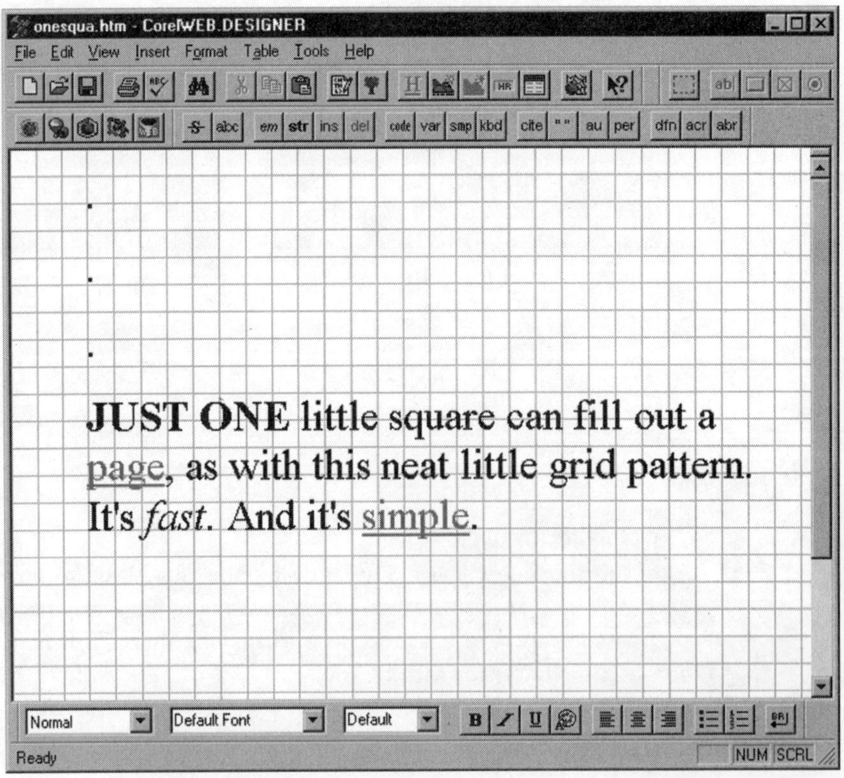

Figure 2-4: By tiling, one little square fills the window.

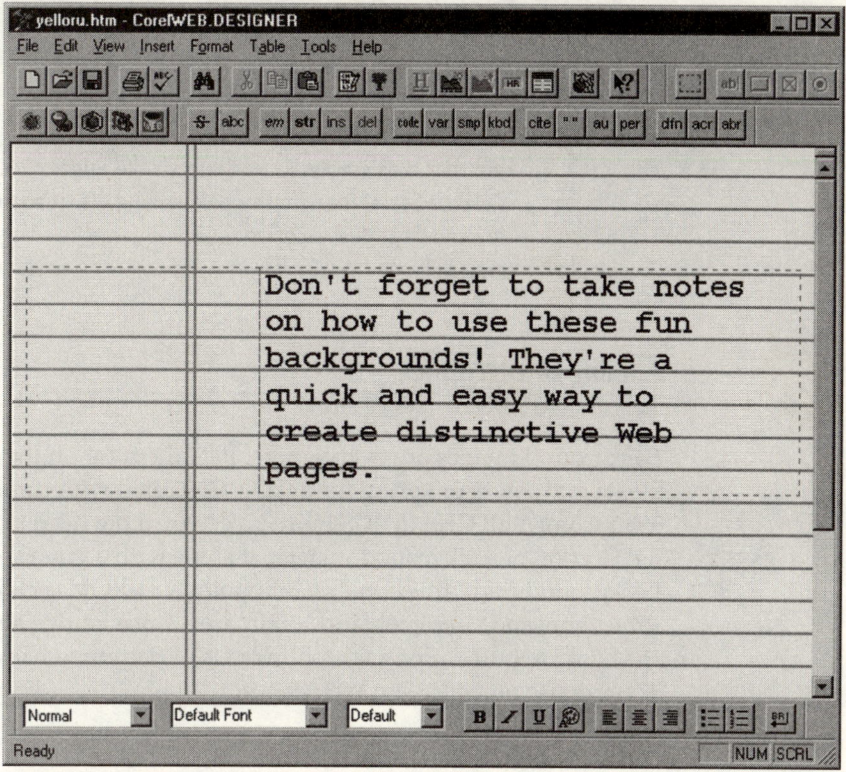

Figure 2-5: Wide patterns can be cool! And best of all, they download in a flash. You can find a bunch of patterns like this in the Backgrds/Hstripes folder on the Companion CD-ROM.

Because the browser handles the tiling, it repeats this pattern at the 1025th pixel (if the browser window is opened that far). Viewers won't notice that the pattern is repeating unless their browser windows are open all the way to the repeating margin rules. There are many uses for these short-and-wide background tiles. Square tiles work fine when using symmetrical, seamless textures. But if the background design is asymmetrical, a tiling scheme similar to the ruled yellow paper notebook paper in Figure 2-5 is better.

You are not limited to just tiles as backgrounds; you can use full-page images as well. Using a full-page image opens up your design possibilities—visualize a photograph of your town's skyline or an image of puffy clouds. A note of caution: Full-color, full-page background images can mean huge files. Use them sparingly and only when their impressive imagery makes waiting for the download well worth the viewer's time.

What Does Seamless Mean?

A seamless tile is one that tiles smoothly, with no visible edges. Creating seamless textures is not a trivial undertaking. It takes painstaking effort to achieve a result that does not look forced. Seamless texture tiles first came into vogue with three-dimensional rendering programs.

Finding Backgrounds

Background images are everywhere. Pick them up off the Web for free, create your own, or spring for a CD-ROM filled with commercial images. Your CorelWEB.GRAPHICS Suite gives you a big head start on building a collection of background images. It ships with a good selection of backgrounds, and this book's Companion CD-ROM includes more than three thousand very cool (and totally free, since you've already bought the book) textures, along with hundreds of patterned backgrounds that you can use on your own Web pages.

Check Out These Background Sites!

Bumpy: the land of textures	http://home.earthlink.net/~shaner/textures.html
Julianne's Background Textures	http://www.sfsu.edu/~jtolson/textures/textures.htm
Pattern Land	http://www.netcreations.com/patternland/index.html
Texture Land	http://www.meat.com/textures/
VBM: The Virtual Background Museum	http://www.teleport.com/~mtjans/VBM/

Don't forget to check the usage rights at each site. Many graphics on the Web are free for noncommercial use but not for commercial use.

If you want to create your own custom backgrounds, go to Part II of this book, where you'll learn how to do so with CorelWEB.DRAW.

There are scores of commercial texture collections, as well. It seems as if a new CD-ROM full of textures hits the streets every week. Many commercial texture collections on the market are targeted at print designers, who need high-resolution files for their projects. These high-resolution images contain three to four times more digital information than you for Web pages. Print files are typically 225-300 dpi (dots per inch); Web files don't need to be higher than 72 dpi. Visual Software's Textures for Professionals contains scores of seamless textures including the ever-popular wood grains and marbles. See Figure 2-6.

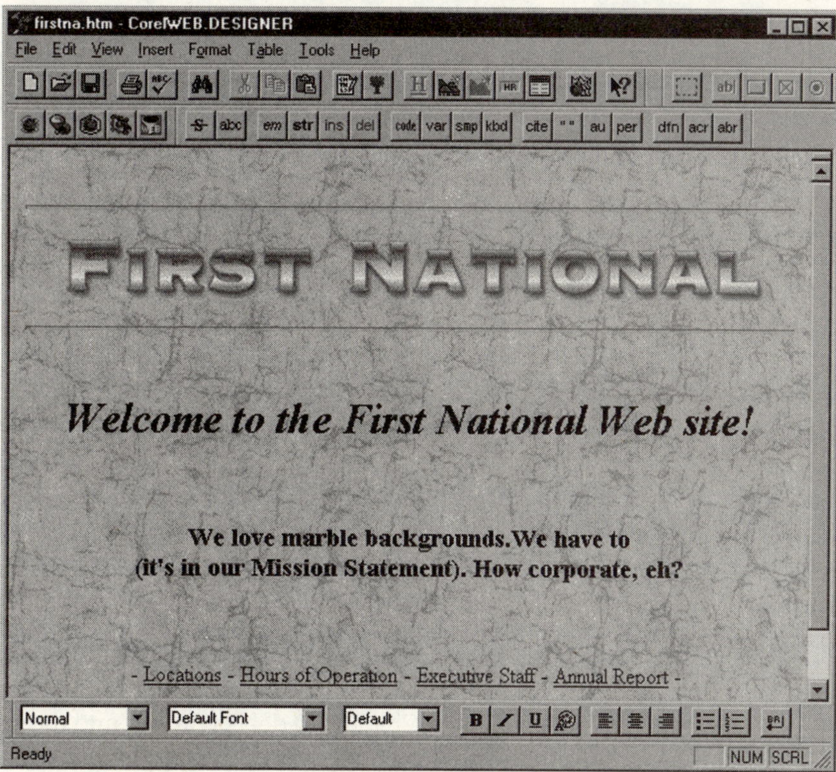

Figure 2-6: A marble background provides a corporate look.

Generate Custom Backgrounds Via the Web!
The Background Generator   http://crystal.palace.net/~dprust/Applications/Bax/

Don't overlook print-oriented selections, however. They may be more expensive, but they're often of higher quality and usually contain low-resolution as well as high-resolution images. You can always resize high-resolution images in Adobe Photoshop or other paint editors.

Speeding Up Background Images

Since background images are just that (background images), you can use some tricks to speed up loading. The basic rules of graphic loading speeds apply: The smaller an image's file size, the faster it loads. Tiles with just a handful of colors load faster than full-color tiles. The ruled yellow paper notebook paper tile shown in Figure 2-5 loads quickly, regardless of its width, because it uses a very limited color palette.

What About Converting Windows Wallpaper?
Although it's easy to convert Windows wallpaper (BMP) files to GIF format, consider whether the wallpaper image makes for a suitable Web page background.

The color palette of background images usually should be limited. The limitation depends on the image: Some images will tolerate a tight color palette; some won't. Chapter 10 delves further into the subject of palettes and palette reduction, with a specific focus on what's come to be known as the Netscape 216 Palette.

Placing Images

Once you've set the stage with a background image, think about the types of images to use on top of it. In the next section, you'll learn how images are manipulated after you've inserted them into WEB.DESIGNER. Images can be placed on your Web pages either by dragging and dropping from the desktop or via the Image Properties dialog box (summoned from the Insert Image button on the toolbar or with Insert | Image). Try bringing in a few images now, just to get the hang of it. Click on the Browse button to find an image with the Select Image Source dialog box. When an image has been selected, its filename will appear in the Image Properties dialog box's Source field. Click OK to place it on the page. To reposition an image within a page, cut and paste it to the new position.

What About Cutting & Pasting From WEB.DRAW?

Although you can cut and paste graphics directly from WEB.DRAW, avoid it for three basic reasons:

- When images come into WEB.DESIGNER in this manner, they are named arbitrarily. This is a hassle, as you may want to rename them, which also necessitates changing the image source field in the Image Properties dialog box.

- The automatic conversion to bitmap format is not of optimal quality.

- Images come in as image maps by default. If you don't want them to be image maps, you must turn off the image map attribute in the Image Properties dialog box.

In addition to deciding where you're going to place images on your Web pages, you must consider where the files reside. Otherwise, when you move them up to the Web server, you'll end up breaking links and losing files. Chapter 5 goes into creating a working directory structure in depth.

Controlling Image Properties

When you've placed an image on the page, your work is only half-done. You still need to set the alignment and other characteristics so that the image appears as it should.

The Image Properties dialog box provides precise control over a number of image *attributes*. In practice, you will use this dialog box for just about every image you place, although you won't alter all the settings for each image. The Image Properties General tab, as shown in Figure 2-7, controls the following image characteristics:

- Alignment
- Alternate text label
- Border thickness
- Horizontal and vertical spacing
- Width and height

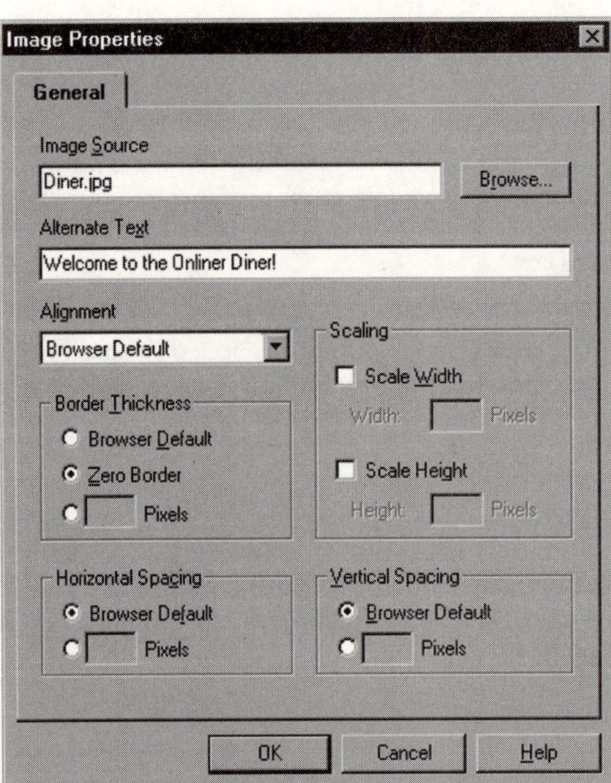

Figure 2-7: Take charge of your images with the Image Properties dialog box.

Alignment

Assigning image/text alignment is a crucial step in designing a Web page. WEB.DESIGNER provides a range of options to control how text reacts to an inline image:

- Browser default align
- Baseline align
- Top align
- Middle align
- Bottom align
- Text top align
- Absolute middle align
- Absolute bottom align
- Left align
- Right align

The top, middle, and bottom choices—along with the absolute middle and absolute bottom choices—align one line of text with the image and are used most appropriately for short captions. You're likely to use either a left or right alignment most frequently. These settings wrap text around the image. Figures 2-8 and 2-9 demonstrate the effect of five of the alignment options. More complicated alignment schemes are possible through the use of tables, which are covered in depth in the next chapter.

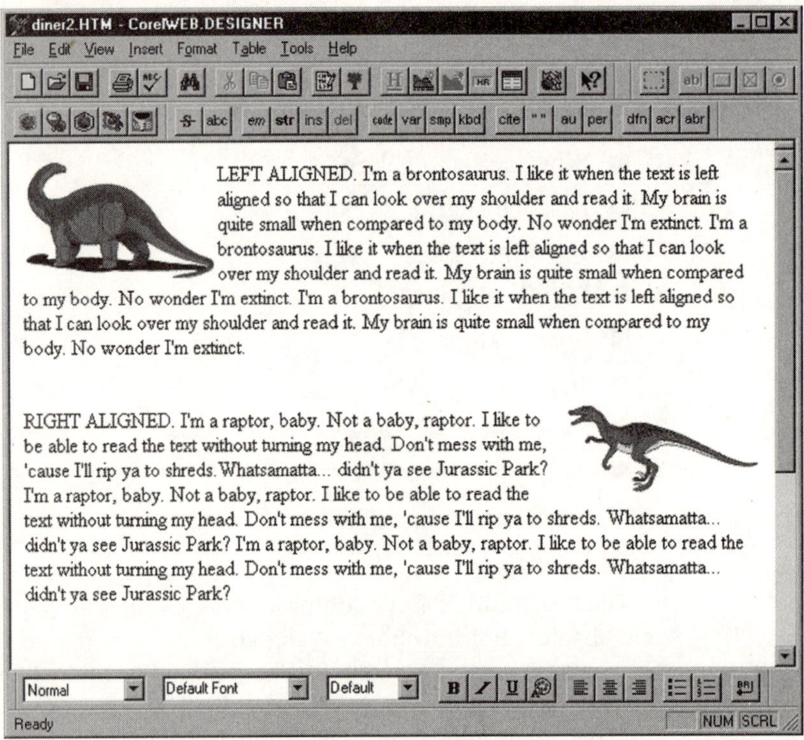

Figure 2-8: *Left or right alignment wraps text around an image.*

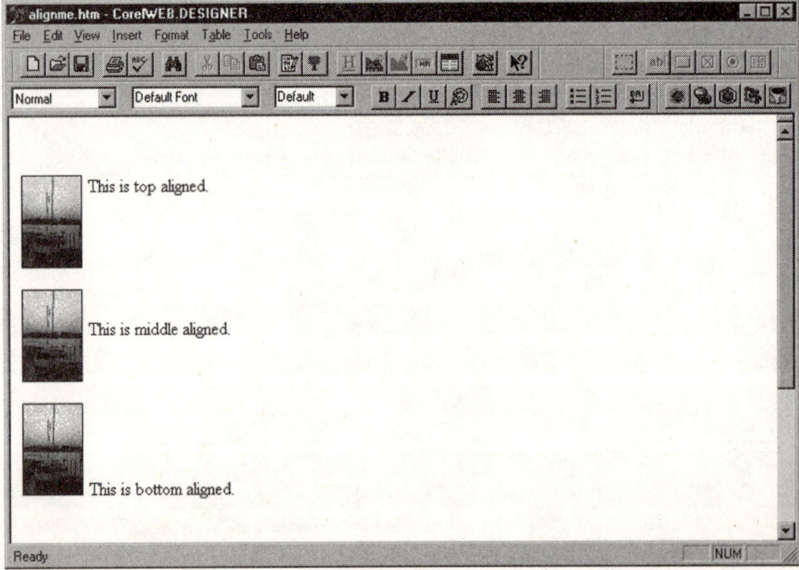

Figure 2-9: *Choose top, middle, or bottom alignment for a short caption.*

Alternate Text Label

You should specify an alternate text label for every image you place. Alternate text refers to the words shown in the browser window if an image is not displayed (such as when the browser has images turned off or when a page download is interrupted). Although naming each image may seem tedious, it's considered good Netiquette. Proper labeling helps visitors "see" what each image is, without actually downloading it. If they're enticed by the alternate text, they can reload the page to display the graphics. Figure 2-10 shows a partially loaded page that uses properly labeled images. Alternate text labels also help folks that browse with their graphics turned off.

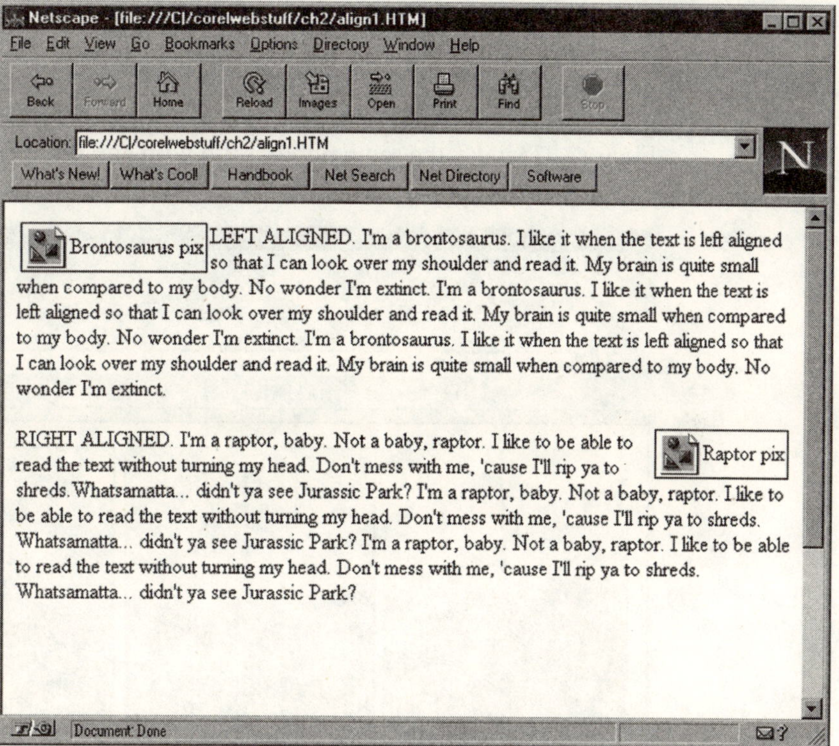

Figure 2-10: Don't leave your viewers guessing. Always specify alternate text.

Border Thickness

Images come into WEB.DESIGNER without a border (default nil). Although you can set a border as thick as you wish, it's hard to imagine one heavier than 1 or 2 pixels.

Border color is determined by object behavior. A picture uses the page's body text color, while a form button or image map uses the page's link colors (normal, active, or visited).

Links: Normal, Active & Visited

Normal links are links that have not been followed.

Active links are links that are in the midst of being clicked. Watch closely the next time you click a link!

Visited links are links that have already been followed.

Although you wouldn't want to use a border on an irregularly shaped graphic image, a rectangular photographic image looks great with one. Figure 2-11 shows the same photograph with and without borders.

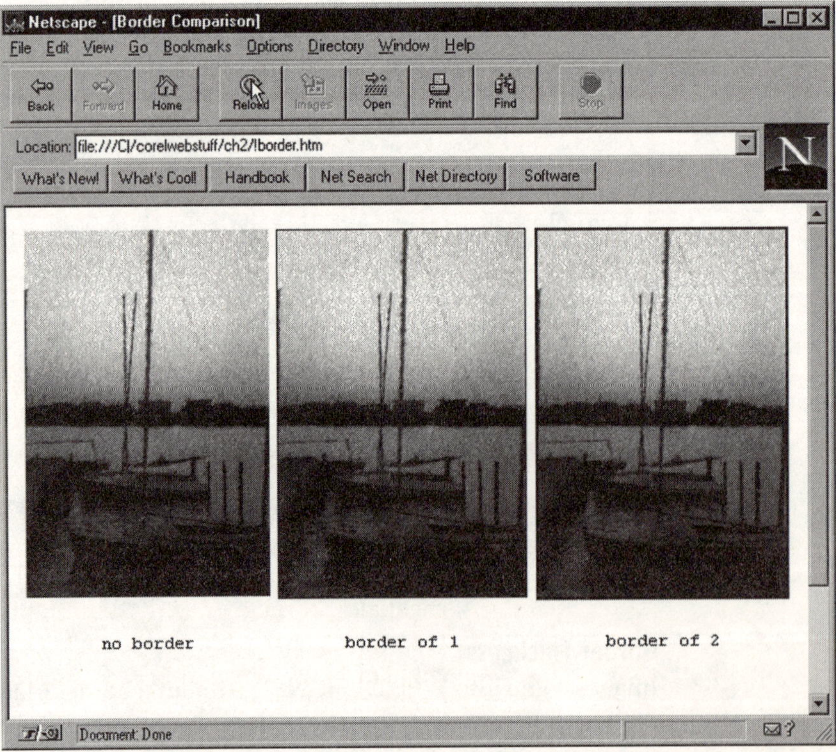

Figure 2-11: Borders make a photograph "pop."

Horizontal & Vertical Spacing

You'll also set horizontal and vertical spacing—the "air" that floats an inline image away from surrounding text. You'll want to fiddle with these settings to ensure that text and graphics are not scrunched tightly together. Figure 2-12 shows the differences achieved with different spacing settings. Notice that vertical spacing is not hard and fast—unlike horizontal spacing, which is absolute. From the value entered in the Image Properties dialog box, vertical spacing varies depending on the relationship between text line spacing and height of the graphic.

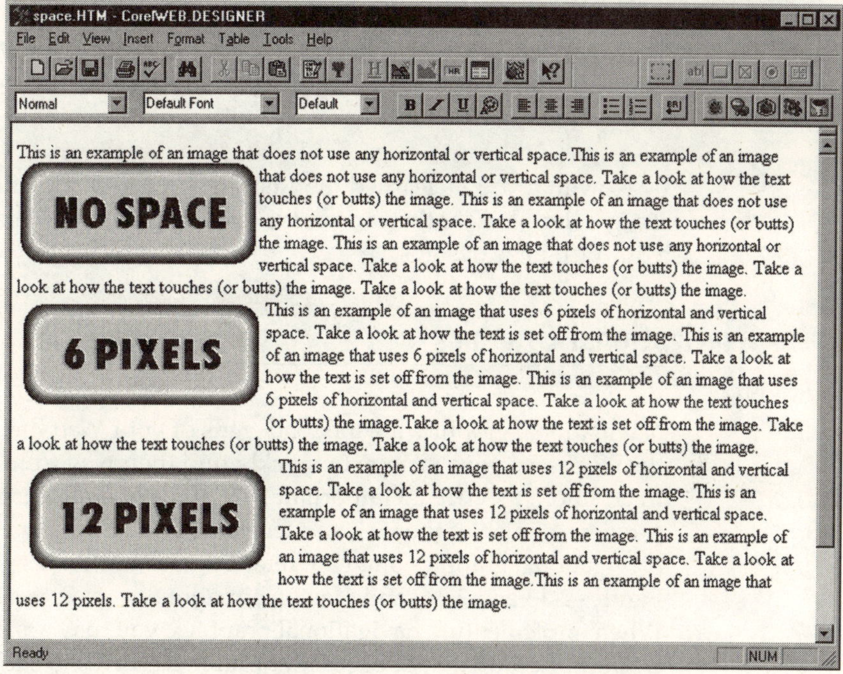

Figure 2-12: Always leave enough "air" between text and graphics.

Scaling Width & Height

Width and height can be set in exact pixel size. When an image is brought into WEB.DESIGNER, width and height default to the actual size of the image. The dialog box shows a blank field until you click the Scale Width or Scale Height check box. Then the fields will show the actual width and height of your image. Although it's easy to scale an image within WEB.DESIGNER, it's safer to change its actual size in the image editing application, such as Adobe Photoshop, before you bring it into WEB.DESIGNER. Otherwise, the image may become distorted in the browser. Even more important, scaling the image down in Photoshop will reduce file size and slash download time. One more word to the wise: always avoid scaling a bitmap image up, lest the image quality suffer.

Hot Tip: Click Those Check Boxes

There's a good (hidden) reason to click the Scale Width and Scale Height check boxes. When you do, WEB.DESIGNER places the actual width and height into the IMG SRC tag. This speeds up page display in the browser, by allowing the browser to flow text around images *before* the images have been downloaded.

Now that you've learned the basics of how to work with placed images, let's look at the various types of graphics you'll use to complete your Web page designs.

Navigational Graphics

Navigational graphics are the road signs of your Web site. They provide the means for your visitors to quickly find their way from place to place. In addition, they are an important part of the overall design scheme, providing much of the look and feel (as well as consistency) of a site. Navigational graphics often are referred to as button bars (as shown in Figures 2-13 and 2-14) and may be horizontally or vertically oriented. When implementing navigational graphics, you may assign a single Uniform Resource Locator (URL) or multiple URLs to each individual graphic (through the use of image maps, as you'll see, shortly).

Choose horizontal or vertical navigational graphics depending on the overall design of your site. Early site designs tended to horizontal schemes because of the constraints of early versions of HyperText Markup Language (HTML), specifically the lack of multiple columns. Vertical navigation devices now have come into vogue.

Whichever orientation you choose, it's always a good idea to provide a text "button bar" in addition to the navigational graphic. Text links may not look nearly as cool, but they're always faster and straight to the point. And if your visitor has their browser's graphics display turned off, the image map will not be of much use.

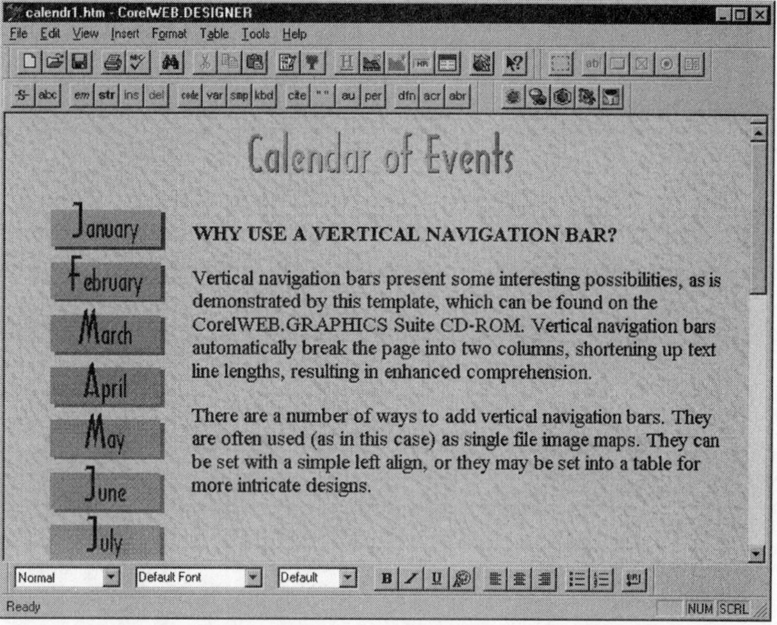

Figure 2-13: A vertical calendar button bar from the CorelWEB.GRAPHICS CD-ROM.

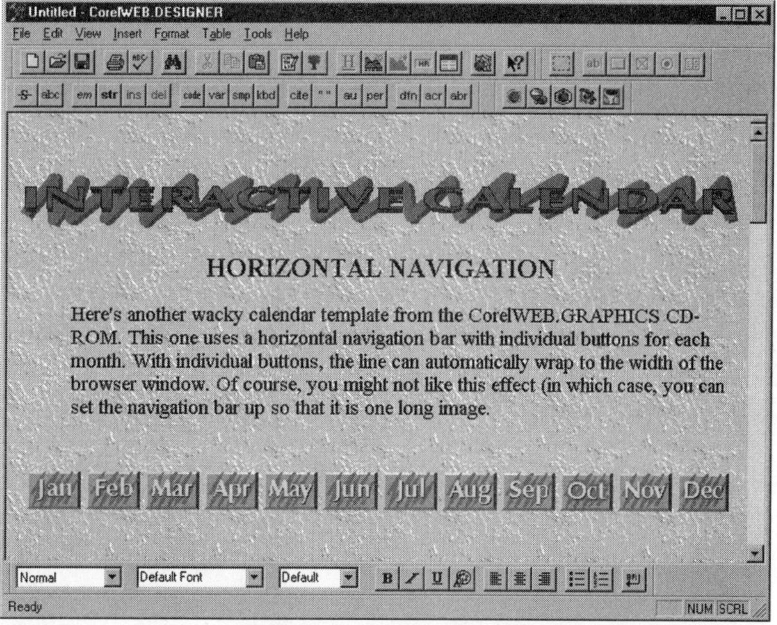

Figure 2-14: A horizontal calendar button bar from the CorelWEB.GRAPHICS CD-ROM.

Linking a Single URL to an Image

In Chapter 1 you learned how to create simple text hyperlinks. Creating graphic links is just as straightforward; assigning a URL to an image is not unlike assigning a URL to a piece of text. To link a graphic, select it and then select HyperLink from the Format pull-down menu to summon the HyperLink Properties dialog box, as shown in Figure 2-15. To link to a page on another Web site, enter its complete URL. To link to a page on your own Web site, click on the Browse button and select the file. The page you want to link to must be on your Web server and on a locally accessible drive.

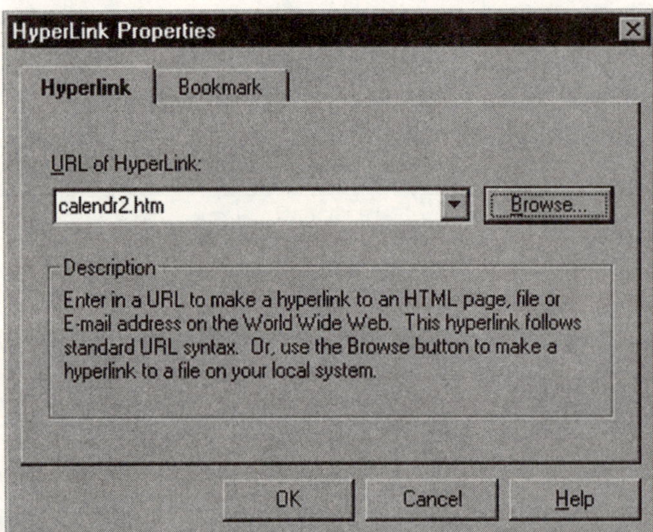

Figure 2-15: Use the HyperLink Properties dialog box to specify single URL links.

Linking to Multiple URLs With Image Maps

Image maps are coordinate sets that tell the server what page to deliver, depending on where the visitor clicks on a navigational graphic. The coordinates provide vertical and horizontal boundaries for each *hot spot* (an area that can be clicked on to call up another page). Image maps come in two flavors: server side and client side. In general, the differences between the two have to do with where the coordinates reside and how the browser reacts.

Server-Side Image Maps

Server-side image maps are separate coordinate-mapping files that must reside on the Web server. They require the use of a Common Gateway Interface (CGI) script (which also must be on the server) to tell the browser which page to fetch. When a visitor clicks on a server-side image map, the browser sends the coordinates to the server, which then runs the CGI and consequently coughs up the appropriate page.

Server-side maps are the original method, but not the method of choice these days. They're slower for the visitor, more taxing on the server, and can be a nuisance to maintain. Also, many Internet service providers (ISPs) require that your page be part of a commercial-level account if you want to use CGI scripting—a real expense if you're just setting up a personal page. Before you create a server-side map, consult with your Webmaster as to where to store the map file (and ask whether they'd really be happier with a client-side map). We'll touch on the subject of CGI scripts in the next chapter.

Client-Side Image Maps

Client-side image maps reside in the Web page itself. When a visitor clicks on a client-side image map, the browser requests a specific page. Because no CGI script is required, this reduces the load on the server. And because the page URLs are hard-coded into the page, the browser can provide feedback as to where each link leads. For these reasons, client-side image maps are considered more user friendly than server-side image maps.

Creating Image Maps

Creating an image map in either WEB.DRAW or WEB.DESIGNER is
fairly easy. If you're creating the graphic yourself in WEB.DRAW, you
may find it expedient to handle image mapping within that program. It
lets you assign hot spots to individual objects, which is extremely handy
when it comes time to rearrange an image-mapped graphic. We'll delve
into image mapping with WEB.DRAW in Chapter 8.

You'll want to create your image maps within WEB.DESIGNER when
using graphics from sources other than WEB.DRAW. Creating an image
map in WEB.DESIGNER is accomplished by means of its internal Image
Map Editor. To access this feature, double-click on the image to summon
the Image Properties dialog box. Then click on the Image Map tab,
shown in Figure 2-16. Select Use Image Map, then click on Create Map to
bring up the Image Map Editor dialog box (Figure 2-17).

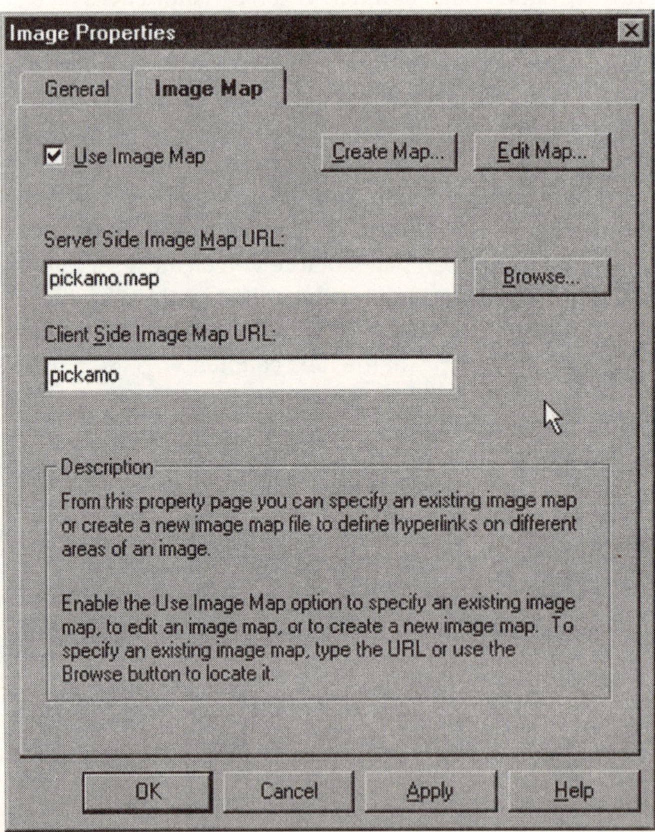

*Figure 2-16: The Image Properties dialog box allows you to create a new image
map or edit an existing one.*

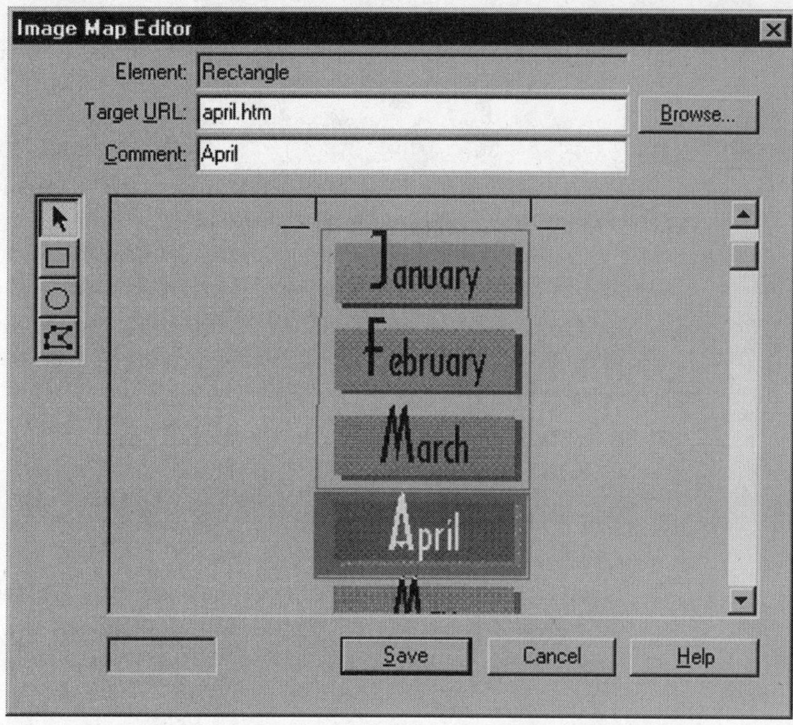

Figure 2-17: The Image Map Editor makes fast work of hot-spotting, but its not without its idiosyncrasies.

The image map tools provide the following functions:

■ Pick tool—Use to choose an existing hot spot.

■ Rectangle hot spot—Click and drag to assign rectangular hot spots.

■ Circle hot spot—Click and drag to assign oval-shaped hot spots (great for bullets!).

■ Polygon hot spot—Click-click-click around an area to assign an irregularly shaped hot spot; double-click to close the area.

Target URLs and Comments will display at the bottom of the browser window with newer browsers, such as Netscape Navigator 3.0 and later, when using client-side image maps.

To assign a hot spot, choose the appropriately shaped tool and drag out a hot spot. With the hot spot selected, enter the URL to which you want it to link in the Target URL field, along with an optional comment if you wish. Take your time: WEB.DESIGNER's Image Map Editor does not allow you to edit the shape of existing hot spots, nor does it allow you to delete a hot spot. If you mess up, you have to create a new image map from scratch.

Once you've drawn all your hot spots and assigned all the hyperlinks, save the image map: Click on Save; it'll be stored as a MAP file.

It's Not a Bug, It's a Feature Alert!

WEB.DESIGNER 1.1 Build 78 (which shipped on the original CorelWEB.GRAPHICS Suite CD-ROM) wants to save both a server-side and a client-side image map. Go ahead and save both. You'll have to edit the HTML source code (Edit|HTML Source) to assign the proper map type before uploading to your Web server.

- To edit for a client-side map, remove the two codes from around the <IMG SRC> tag:

```
<A HREF="mapnamehere.map">
</A>
```

- To edit for a server-side map, remove the following code from within the <IMG SRC> tag:

```
USEMAP="#mapnamehere.map
```

Button bars aren't the only type of navigational graphics you'll use in your Web page designs. The possibilities are truly limitless. The next sections look at spicing up your pages with icons, illustrations, and photographs.

Using Icons, Dingbats & Dividers

A well-designed Web site uses a carefully crafted aggregate of images to convey its message. So far, we've covered what one might consider the "printing stock" of a site: the background and navigational graphics. Those first two image categories form a framework into which you'll pour the good stuff. It's time to look at the types of images you can use to make each Web page entice and inform readers.

Icons

Icons are pictographic objects that can convey more information than might be gleaned from a single-word text link (or graphic button). Unfortunately, great icons are not the norm. The creation of icons is too often left to chance and a clip-art book. The best icons are custom crafted specifically for the need at hand. A meaningful image will tell your story properly. Haphazardly using prebuilt clip art will confuse and frustrate your visitors. Nonetheless, the CorelWEB.GRAPHICS Suite CD-ROM contains a good variety of icons, rendered on three different styles of button. Some examples are shown in Figure 2-18.

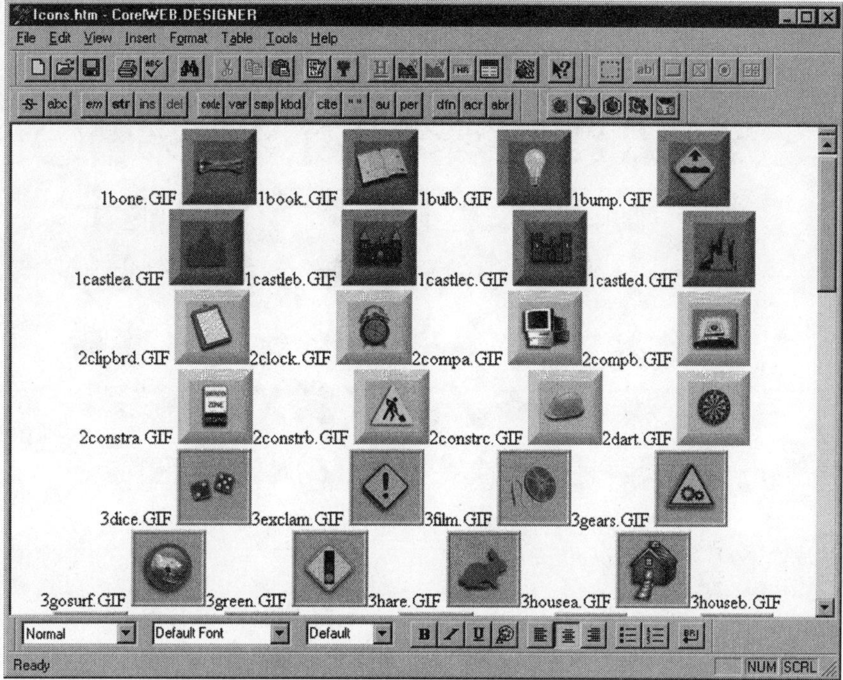

Figure 2-18: Icons are not always rendered on top of buttons, as they are on the CorelWEB.GRAPHICS Suite CD-ROM.

If you decide to use icons as links, you'll be wise to also include text links to the same URLs. These text links do not have to be placed physically next to the icons, as long as they're not buried too deeply on the page.

If you're in search of icons (or need help to create your own), check out CorelWEB.DRAW's Symbol libraries, in addition to the prebuilt icons.

Dingbats

If the only dingbat you know is Edith Bunker, you're showing your age. Any desktop publisher worth his or her weight in lead will tell you that dingbats are little typographical doodads, falling somewhere between bullets and icons. The definition can get blurry in both directions. Figures 2-19 and 2-20 display some of the dingbats in Adobe's Zapf Dingbats and Microsoft's Wingdings fonts. In all likelihood, one or both are already installed on your PC.

Figure 2-19: Adobe's Zapf Dingbats was, perhaps, the most popular dingbat font of all time, until . . .

Figure 2-20: . . . Microsoft rolled out its Wingdings. Both fonts are stuffed full of nifty little doodads.

Dingbats are wonderful replacements for the dull, boring bullets provided by HTML's list commands. In order to use a dingbat (from any font) in your designs, first size and export it to a bitmap file with WEB.DRAW. Choose to use a dingbat in basic black or colorize it to your heart's content. As you'll learn in Part II of this book, however, it's best to stick with solid colors on tiny dingbats. Blends can get "lost" when used at smaller sizes.

When using images as bullets, pay close attention to how they align with text. Depending on the image's shape, you may want to try a top, middle, or bottom alignment. This book's Companion CD-ROM contains basic round and square bullet-dingbats in a variety of sizes and 99 Netscape-safe colors. These little critters are designed to coordinate with the enclosed vertical striped backgrounds and horizontal divider bars. You'll want to look in the Bullets, Backrnds, and Hrules directories on the CD-ROM.

Divider Bars

HTML provides built-in horizontal rules (complete with control over width and weight), but you may not think they jazz up your Web page designs very much. Standard HTML rules can get a little lost on the page. Graphic horizontal dividers, on the other hand, add a nice touch by breaking pages into clearly defined sections. And to top it off, you can even use animated GIFs as bullets or dividers (should you choose to challenge the barriers of good taste). Figure 2-21 shows a few of the dividers found on the CorelWEB.GRAPHICS Suite CD-ROM, some useful, some not.

Create Cool 3D Bullets & Bars Online!

Want to create your own awesome 3D graphics? Check out Patrick J. Hennessey's insanely great Interactive Graphics Renderer (on vacation in Finland) at http://www.great.fi/phpl.cgi?IGRNEW/intro.html.

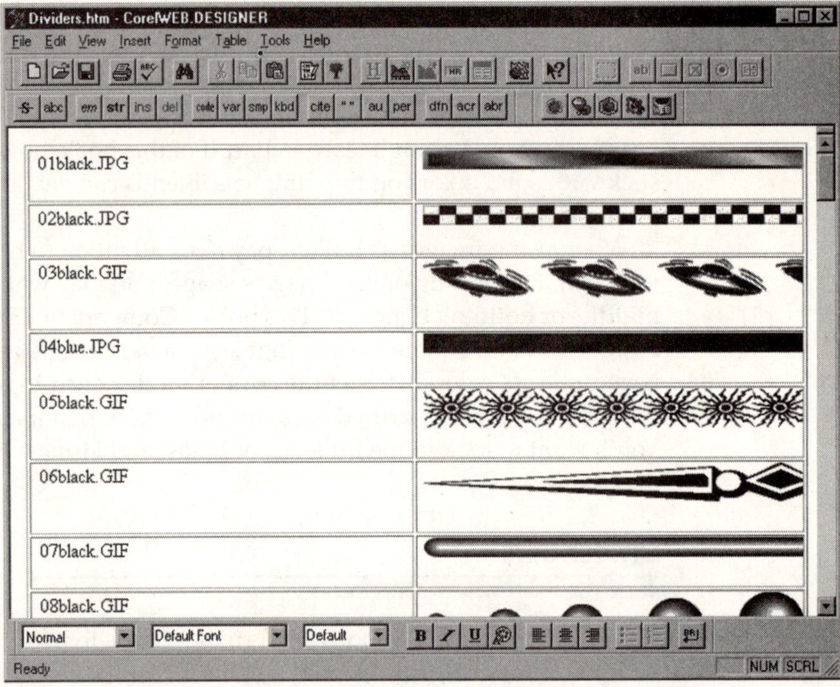

Figure 2-21: Some of the horizontal dividers on the CorelWEB.GRAPHICS CD-ROM are usable, even cute, but many are just flat-out silly.

You'll also find a nice variety of conservative horizontal dividers on this book's Companion CD-ROM. The horizontal rules on our CD-ROM are available in three convenient widths (based on the widths of the vertical striped background) but are all 2 pixels high. To change the height (or weight) of the rule, type a new height value in the Image Properties dialog box. Try adding a border to a rule for a different effect.

With the graphic appetizers out of the way, let's move on to the tastiest course: illustrations and photographs.

Using Illustrations & Photographs

An expressive illustration or an impeccable photograph can convey more in one glance than a Web page chock full of text. The old adage "A picture is worth a thousand words" is true, however, only if it's the *right* picture. Take the time to find or create the right picture, and you will be rewarded. Use what you have at hand just to fill space, and the Netizens will scoff.

Finding Illustrations & Illustrators

Illustrations can come in various forms. At the bottom of the list are commercial clip-art collections. Many of these aggregations aim to deliver a huge volume of material at a low price. While you get thousands upon thousands of images for pennies apiece, you may often find that you don't get *exactly* what you need. Rarely will you find the illustration that's in your head on a commercial disk.

CorelWEB.GALLERY also provides thousands upon thousands of images. Although, the images are stored in an undesirable bitmap format, which makes reworking them difficult if not impossible. Thankfully, CorelWEB.DRAW allows you to create your own images quickly from scratch. If you have a bit of artistic talent, you'll be able to create your own beautiful Web graphics. But if you're short on creative skills, you'd be wise to accept the fact that your Web site is your image. It's OK to look for help.

The most appropriate and effective artwork is created specifically for the need at hand. That's why it's a prudent business decision to find the right artists and have them render something according to your needs. If you have a budget to spend on real illustration, get your hands on a bunch of artists' sourcebooks or some issues of *Communication Arts* (the *Illustration Annual* is a wonderful resource) to see who's who and who does what. These books include telephone numbers (maybe even e-mail addresses) of the artists or the agents that represent them.

Looking for an Illustrator?

Here are two places to start:

- PublishersDepot   http://www.publishersdepot.com/
- Zaks Illustrators Source   http://www.zaks.com/illustrators/

A huge number of professional artists have made their way to the Internet. You can view samples and portfolios online, without ever leaving your chair. For some good places to start, check out these pages on Yahoo's Web site:

- http://www.yahoo.com/Arts/Graphic_Arts/Illustration/Artists/
- http://www.yahoo.com/Business_and_Economy/Companies/ Arts_and_Crafts/Illustration/Artists/
- http://www.yahoo.com/Business_and_Economy/Companies/ Arts_and_Crafts/Illustration/Studios/

Finding Photographs

Photographs are among the most compelling Web page graphics. More than any other type of imagery, photographs quickly tell their story. By conveying a sense of reality, photographs put the viewer right into the picture and leave little to interpretation (unless, of course, it's an abstract photo). Photographs can be brought into the computer in one of four general ways:

- Scanners
- Digital cameras
- Video frame grabs
- PhotoCD

Scanners convert either reflective or transparent art into digital form. Basic flatbed reflective scanners—used to digitize photographic prints, sketches, and the like—start in the $300 range and can run to several thousand. Transparency scanners— used to scan 35-millimeter (mm) slides, negatives, and 4- X 5-inch transparencies—start at about $1,000 and run up to more than $100,000 for a full-blown commercial drum scanner. For Web page use, however, if you're scanning from 35-mm slides, a $1,000 dollar transparency scanner will deliver all the image you need.

Digital cameras capture images directly into digital files. The most affordable digital cameras start at just a few hundred dollars but are not capable of capturing the same quality of image as the combination of a traditional camera and scanner. The most attractive aspect of the less-expensive digital cameras is that they save time by avoiding the steps of photo processing and scanning. But they won't capture the same image quality as conventional photography. High-end digital cameras, however, deliver serious image quality and are a boon to the quality-oriented, time-constrained Web publisher. As with high-end scanners, though, top-notch digital cameras still cost many thousands of dollars and are out of the reach of most budgets.

Video frame grabbers allow you to take still images from a video camcorder or VCR into your Web page designs. The most economical option is Play Inc.'s Snappy, which plugs into a PC's parallel (printer) port and delivers surprisingly good image quality for a $200 peripheral.

Kodak's *PhotoCD* is a great choice if you've shot conventional photographic film but don't have access to a scanner. A Kodak photo lab will scan your negatives onto PhotoCD media (at about a dollar a pop for 35mm images). Using PhotoCD requires a CD-ROM-equipped computer and software, such as Adobe Photoshop or CorelPHOTO-PAINT, which is capable of converting from the PhotoCD format.

Regardless of source, photographs almost always should be saved as JPEG files for Web page use. JPEG provides the highest level of detail and compression, which means that your viewers will get the juiciest shots in the shortest possible time. (See Figure 2-22.) You also can use digital stock photographs in your Web page designs, in addition to photos you've taken (or had taken) yourself. Just be sure to check copyright agreements to verify that their use is well within the constraints of the fine print!

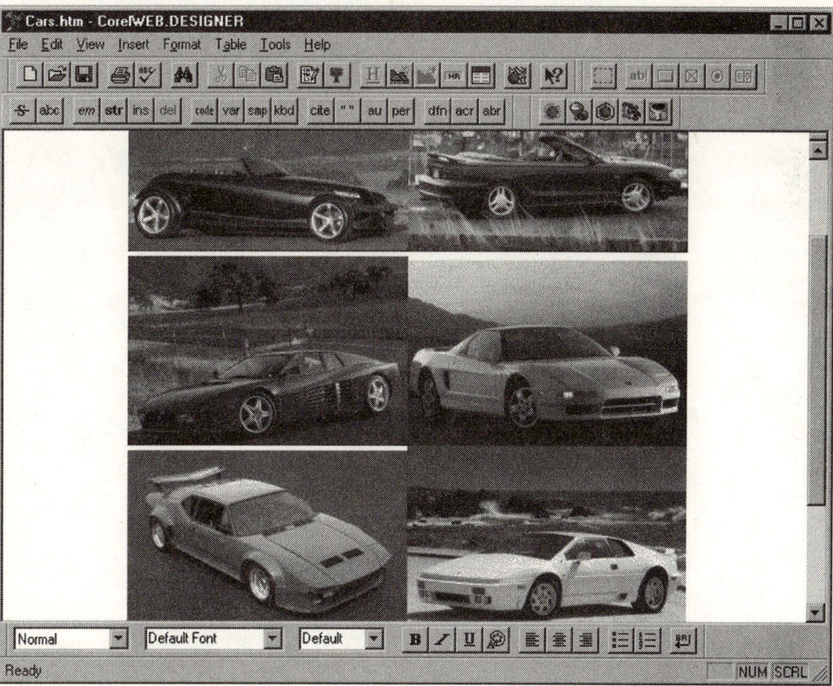

Figure 2-22: Pick your poison! The CorelWEB.GRAPHICS CD-ROM contains a nice selection of photographs that can be used in your Web page designs.

Moving On

In this chapter, you learned the basics of working with graphics in CorelWEB.DESIGNER. A successfully designed Web page includes a healthy mix of both text and graphics. We worked from the back (background and navigational graphics) of a Web page to the front (icons, illustrations, and photographs). It's good practice in page design to consider how the different layers visually interact. A haphazard collection of graphics does not make an effective Web page.

The next chapter covers some of the more advanced HTML text and layout features provided by WEB.DESIGNER, such as tables and forms.

3

Designing With Tables & Forms

Often the first-time Web page designer experiences frustration and discouragement because of the complexity involved in creating the page layout. Fortunately, CorelWEB.DESIGNER makes it easy to implement some of the most intricate features of HTML's command set, such as tables and forms. This chapter builds upon what you learned in the previous two chapters and allows you to quickly master these advanced features.

Tables and forms are the keys to the craft of advanced Web page design. With WEB.DESIGNER's visual controls, you can see exactly what you're doing, as you're doing it.

Why Use Tables?

There are three basic reasons to use HTML tables. The first reason is implied by the name of the command, while the second and third, although they are every bit as important, may not be as obvious.

- To create tables, such as spreadsheets, parts listings, statistical data, and financial reports (as shown in Figure 3-1).

- To constrain pages to a specific width.

- To create multicolumn page layouts.

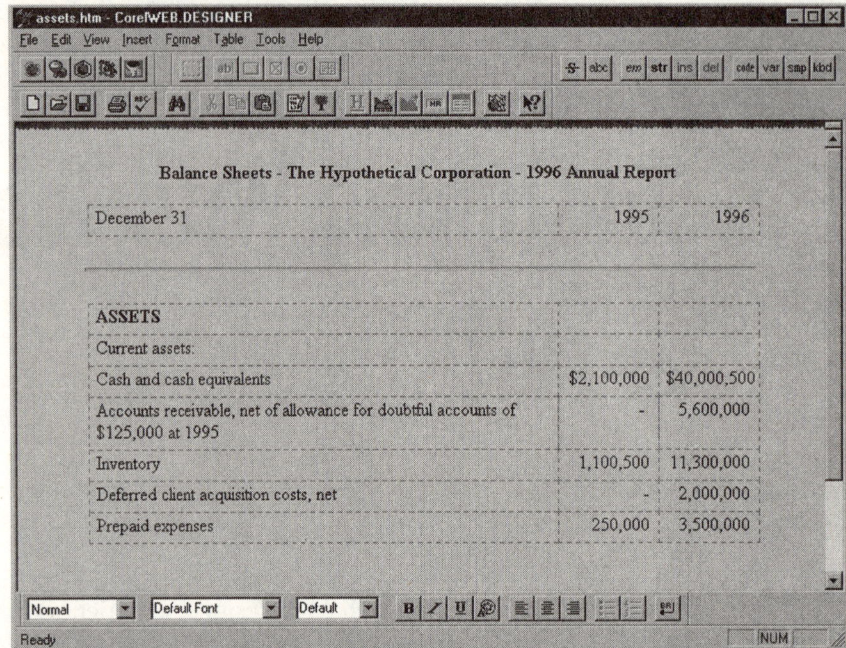

Figure 3-1: The Hypothetical Corporation uses its Web site to deliver the annual report to shareholders and the financial community.

HTML tables impart a high level of structure in your Web page designs. When tables were first implemented (back in Netscape Navigator 1.1), Web designers quickly became enthralled with their control over text alignment, individual column width, overall table width, borders, and various spacing attributes. In the early days, it was a tough hack to write out all the HTML code necessary to build a nice-looking table. Thankfully, WEB.DESIGNER's interactive design now makes it easy to control these characteristics.

Creating Tables

When you think of tables, you probably think of the many types of information commonly presented in columnar form. The first thing that might come to mind is a spreadsheet, such as those from Microsoft Excel or Lotus 1-2-3. Perhaps you might think of the asset sheet from your company's annual report (as shown in Figure 3-1). If you're a sports fan, yesterday's box scores could be the ticket.

With WEB.DESIGNER, it's easy to create HTML tables that can be customized to suit your needs. The table controls allow you to take charge over the entire table, as well as over individual cells. The Table Properties dialog box allows you to affect the following overall table characteristics (as shown in Figure 3-2).

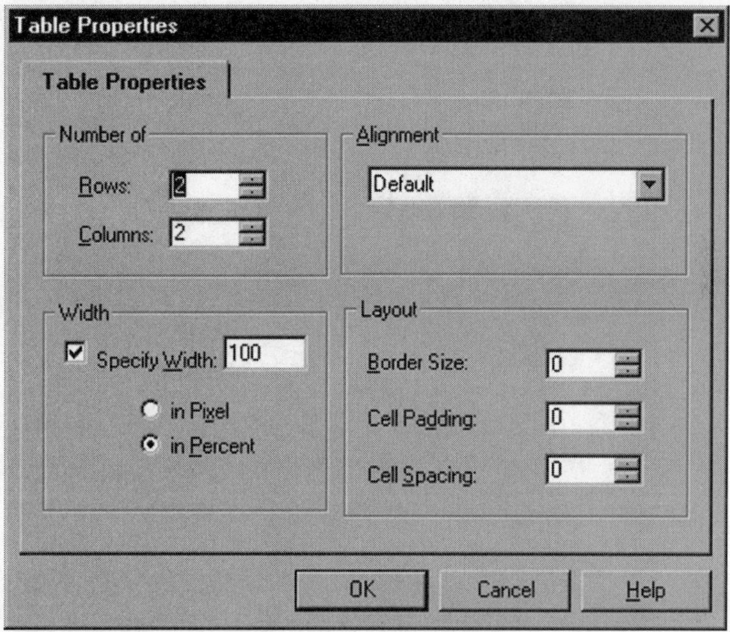

Figure 3-2: The Table Properties dialog box (shown with its default settings) is used to create new tables, as well as to modify existing tables.

- Number of rows and columns—You can set this when you first create a table. Afterward, the selection is grayed out (although you can still add or delete rows and columns via the Table menu).

- Alignment—This setting affects how the entire table is situated on the page. It can be set to left, right, center, or the browser default.

- Width—Width can be set absolutely (as pixels) or relatively (as a percentage of browser window width).

- Border—Borders that run around the outside of the table can be set anywhere from 0 (no border) to 100 (a huge, silly border). You'll rarely need to go wider than 5 (if that), although the wider the border, the more three-dimensional the table will appear.

- Cell padding—No, it's not what we need in our offices after we've been working on our Web site for too long; it's the amount of white space added *inside* each cell.

- Cell spacing—The amount of space *between* cells, which appears as visible grid lines when the table border is set to anything larger than 0 and as white space when the border is set to 0. You might think of cell spacing as individual cell borders (keeping in mind that the attributes can only be set for an entire table, not specific cells).

You can apply cell controls to individual cells or groups of cells. Here's a rundown on cell controls (as shown in Figure 3-3).

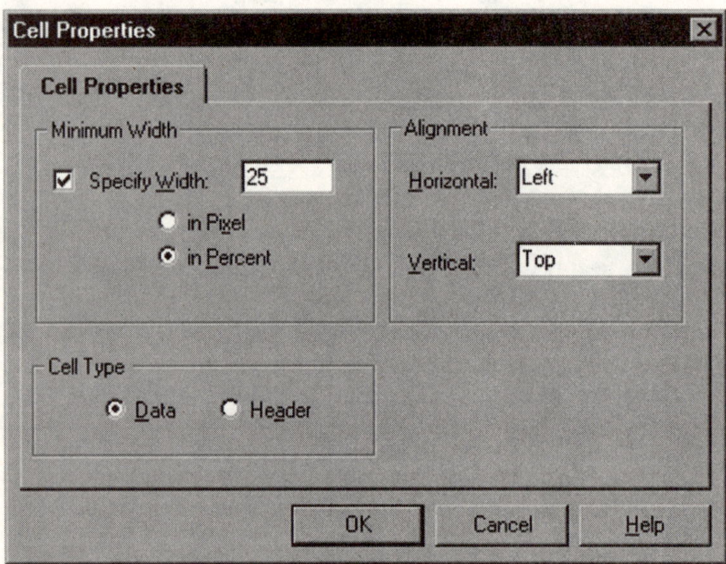

Figure 3-3: Individual cell controls are set via the Cell Properties dialog box.

- Minimum width—Can be set absolutely (as pixels) or relatively (as a percentage of table width). Only one width per column is allowed.

- Cell Type (Data or Header)—Header type is automatically set in boldface (you may want to use this attribute for the top row of a table).

- Horizontal alignment—Left, right, or center.

- Vertical alignment—Top, middle, or bottom.

You can also plug the settings directly into the table commands while in HTML source mode (as shown in Figure 3-4). HTML source mode is a great asset when you're trying to fine-tune or troubleshoot a table. You can access HTML source mode via Edit | HTML Source.

```
assets.htm - CorelWEB.DESIGNER

  Keep Changes      Discard Changes      Print Source

<HTML>
<HEAD>
<TITLE>Balance Sheets - The Hypothetical Corporation - 1996 Annual Report</TITLE>
</HEAD>

<BODY BGCOLOR="#ffffff" BACKGROUND="DECKLE.GIF">

<P ALIGN="center"><B>
<BR>
Balance Sheets - The Hypothetical Corporation - 1996 Annual Report </B></P>

<CENTER><TABLE BORDER="0" CELLSPACING="2" CELLPADDING="2" ALIGN="center" WIDTH="600">
<TR>
<TD WIDTH="420">December 31</TD>
<TD WIDTH="90" ALIGN="RIGHT">1995</TD>
<TD WIDTH="90" ALIGN="RIGHT">1996</TD>
</TR>
</TABLE></CENTER>
<HR WIDTH="600" ALIGN="CENTER">
<BR>
<CENTER><TABLE BORDER="0" CELLSPACING="2" CELLPADDING="2" ALIGN="center" WIDTH="600">
<TR>
<TD WIDTH="420"><B>ASSETS</B></TD>
<TD WIDTH="90" ALIGN="RIGHT"></TD>
<TD WIDTH="90" ALIGN="RIGHT"></TD>
</TR>
<TR>
<TD WIDTH="420">Current assets:</TD>
<TD WIDTH="90" ALIGN="RIGHT"></TD>
<TD WIDTH="90" ALIGN="RIGHT"></TD>
</TR>
<TR>

Ready                                                      NUM
```

Figure 3-4: Don't get scared! You make edits in HTML source mode only if you want to.

Working With Tables

The CorelWEB.GRAPHICS Suite lets you work with tables from a variety of sources. If your word processing program supports HTML table export, you can save time by exporting a table and then opening up the HTML file in WEB.DESIGNER to make the last few tweaks. You can use WEB.Transit to convert files, or you can create your own tables from scratch in WEB.DESIGNER.

Right now, let's see what it takes to create a table from scratch. To create a table in WEB.DESIGNER, click the Insert Table button on the button bar (it's right next to the HR button) or click Table | Insert Table. This summons the Table Properties dialog box (as shown back in Figure 3-2), which allows you to create tables up to a maximum of 100 rows by 100 columns (not that you'd ever need to create a table that large). Let's create a simple table. Specify a 10 (row) x 6 (column) table with all the default settings. When you click OK, the table will appear as in Figure 3-5. Next, try modifying your table with different border and cell spacing settings.

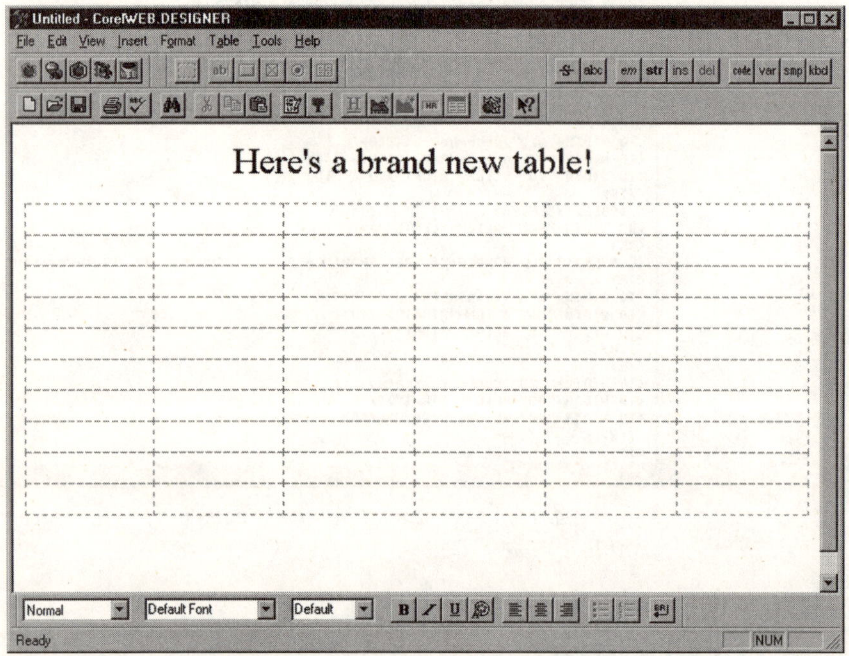

Figure 3-5: Don't worry—those dotted grid lines only show up within WEB.DESIGNER. They will not appear in the browser.

Tip

If you create a table with the wrong specifications, you can immediately delete it by clicking Edit | Undo (Ctrl+Z), or you can go back and modify a number of settings—with the exception of the number of rows and columns—by clicking Table | Table Properties. To access the Table Properties dialog box (once the table is on the page), you must have selected an insertion point within the table.

Once the table is on the page, you can proceed to enter the data or edit what's already there (if you opened up an existing HTML file). There are a handful of tricks to editing a table's contents:

- Edit the data in a cell by clicking an insertion point within the cell, by double-clicking to select a word, or by clicking and dragging to select multiple words.

- Use the Tab key to move the cursor sequentially (forward) from cell to cell. Shift+Tab will move the cursor in the opposite direction (backward).

- To change the characteristics—such as the width or alignment of a cell—click an insertion point within the cell and click Table | Cell Properties to summon the Cell Properties dialog box.

- If working in a text editor suits you better, you can always switch to the HTML source mode (as shown back in Figure 3-4).

Adding & Deleting Columns & Rows

To add a column or row, begin by selecting a cell, then click Table | Insert Columns/Rows to summon the Insert Columns/Rows dialog box (as shown in Figure 3-6). This dialog box allows you to quickly specify how many columns or rows you want to add to your table, and where you want the new columns or rows to be placed. If you want to add both columns *and* rows to a table, you'll have to visit the Insert Columns/ Rows dialog box twice; you cannot add both at the same time.

Deleting columns and rows is fairly straightforward. To delete a column, click an insertion point in the column you want to delete. Then click Table | Delete Column. To delete a row, click an insertion point in the row you want to delete. Then click Table | Delete Row. Try adding a few columns and rows to your table now, and then delete them as you see fit.

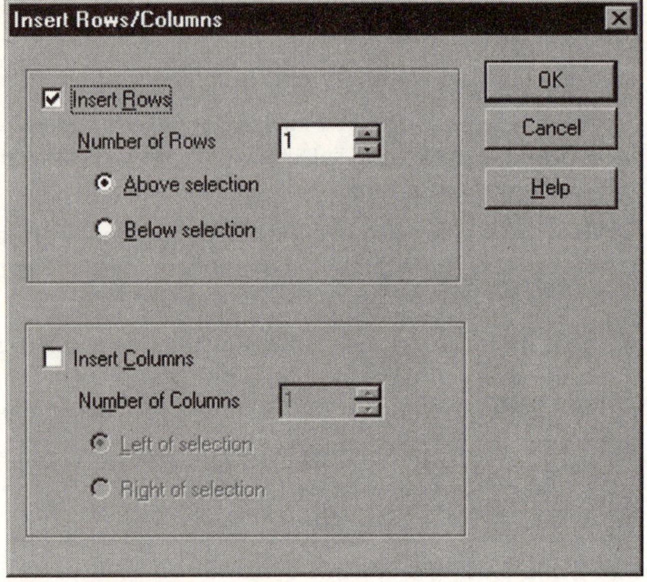

Figure 3-6: The Insert Columns/Rows dialog box makes it easy to expand a table.

Adding & Deleting Cells

As you might surmise, these two operations are straightforward as well. To add a cell, click an insertion point in the cell to the left of where you want to add the cell. Then click Table | Insert Cell. To delete a cell, click an insertion point in the cell you want to delete. Then, click Table | Delete Cell. Try adding and deleting some cells from your table, just for kicks.

OK, That's Cool, but . . . .

Unfortunately, WEB.DESIGNER doesn't provide all the niceties that you may have come to expect from your spreadsheet program. For instance, it's not possible to perform decimal alignment on columns of figures. And you can't straddle rows or columns in WEB.DESIGNER (even though HTML provides ROWSPAN and COLUMNSPAN table commands). Figures 3-7 and 3-8 demonstrate this particular shortcoming.

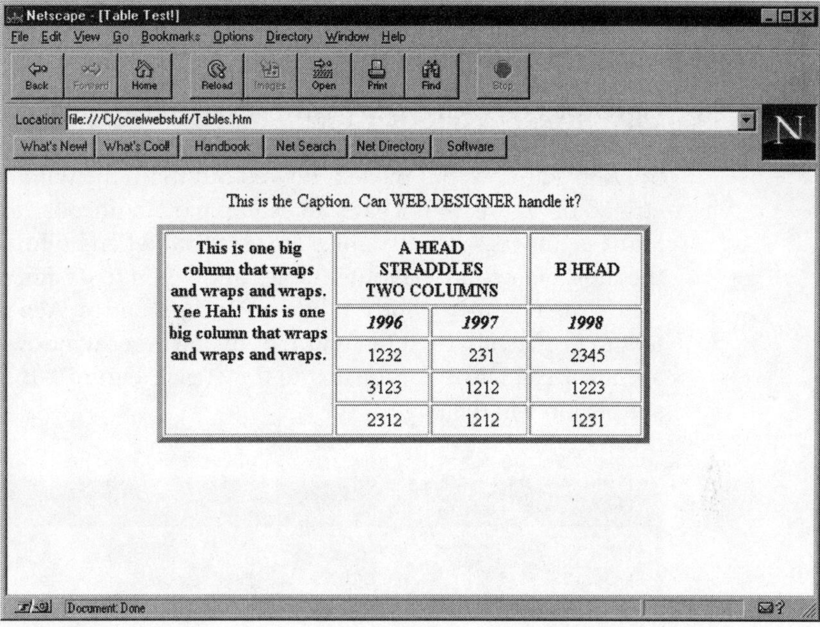

This is the Caption. Can WEB.DESIGNER handle it?

This is one big column that wraps and wraps and wraps. Yee Hah! This is one big column that wraps and wraps and wraps.	A HEAD STRADDLES TWO COLUMNS		B HEAD
	1996	*1997*	*1998*
	1232	231	2345
	3123	1212	1223
	2312	1212	1231

Figure 3-7: This table looks great in Netscape Navigator, since it uses the ROWSPAN and COLUMNSPAN modifiers. . . .

This is the Caption. Can WEB.DESIGNER handle it?

This is one big column that wraps and wraps and wraps. Yee Hah! This is one big column that wraps and wraps and wraps.	A HEAD STRADDLES TWO COLUMNS	B HEAD
1996	*1997*	*1998*
1232	231	2345
3123	1212	1223
2312	1212	1231

Figure 3-8: . . . But if you open the file up in WEB.DESIGNER, the program doesn't know how to interpret the code!

Constraining Page Width

Have you ever seen a Web page that looked totally unbalanced—one where the header graphic ended three quarters of the way across the browser window, but the text flowed out to fill the window (as demonstrated in Figure 3-9)? That's an example of an unconstrained Web page and a prime reason why tables are essential when building anything but the most elementary layouts. Tables allow you to design pages that "stick" to a defined width. While an unconstrained Web page allows its text to flow freely to fit the width of the browser window, you can set a specific pixel width for the text to flow (as in Figure 3-10), by adding a simple table to the page.

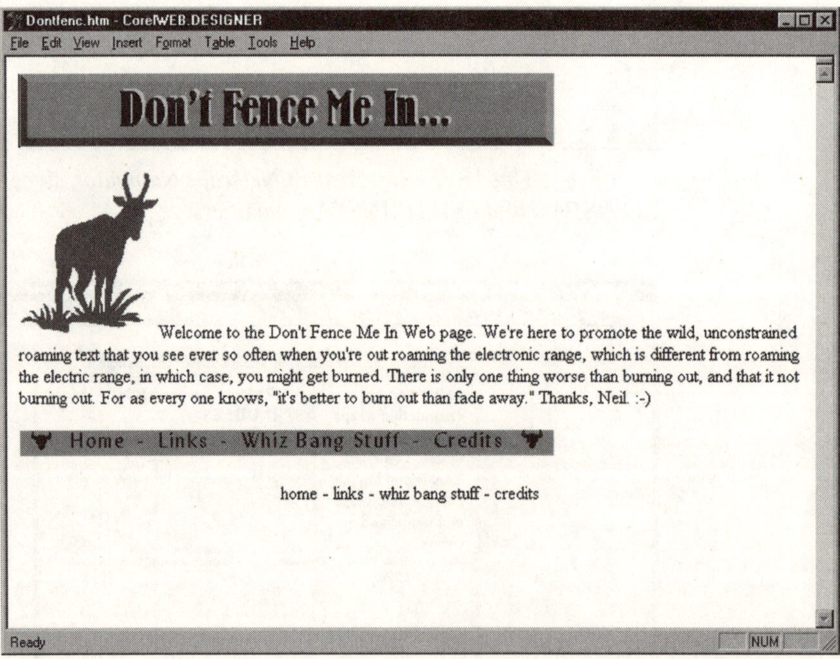

Figure 3-9: An unconstrained Web page, with text spilling all over the place.

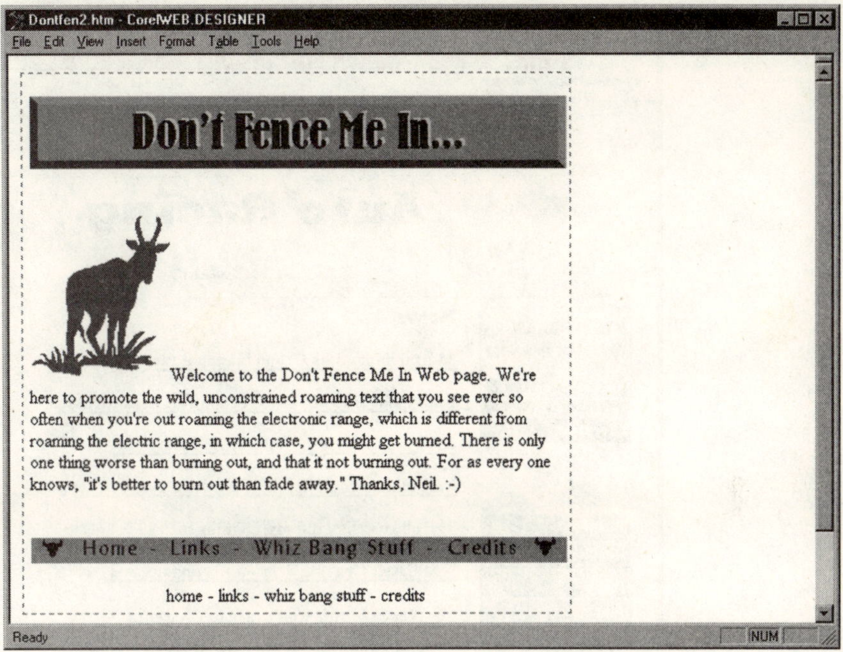

Figure 3-10: The same page, given a bit of manners with a simple table.

When creating a width-constraining table, you'll probably want to base the table width upon the width of the widest graphic on the page. It's a good strategy to have one overall page width that carries through every page on your Web site to provide a continuity of design. Otherwise, your pages will appear to be jumping all over the place. Try building some page-width-constraining tables now, using the table-building skills you've just learned.

How Wide Should Pages Be?

There are plenty of differing views as to how wide a Web page should be. The lowest common denominator is the 640 x 480 Windows display. Based on those measurements, you should make sure that your Web pages fit within 600 pixels (at the very largest) to allow for browser window borders. 500 to 525 pixels may be the safest bet, however.

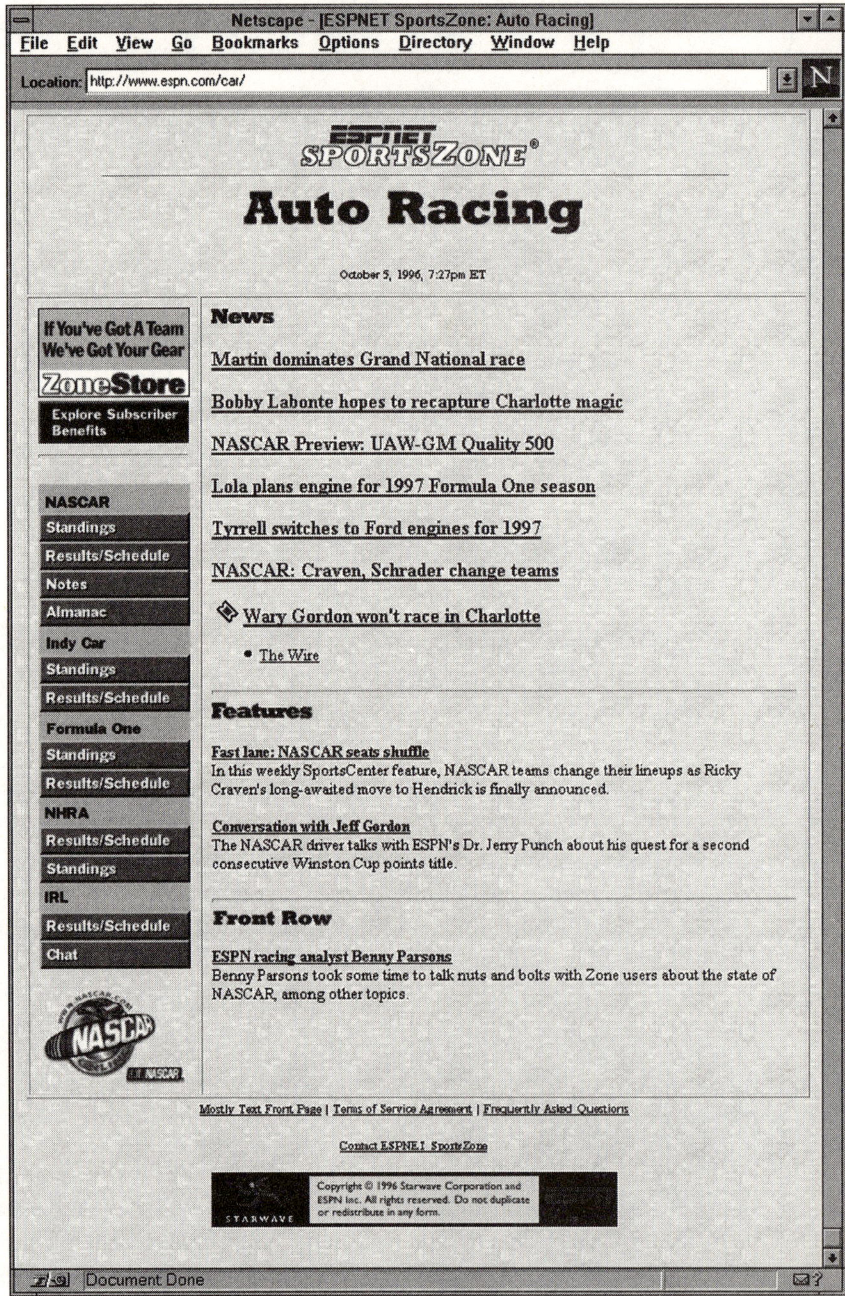

Figure 3-11: The front page of ESPN's Auto Racing Web site uses a vertical button bar in the first column.

Multicolumn Pages

The slickest Web page designs use the HTML table commands to create multiple-column layouts. While we're all accustomed to multiple-column print publications, such as newspapers and magazines, multiple-column Web page layouts are a different beast altogether. Multicolumn Web pages most often consist of two- or three-column layouts. The dynamics of good Web page design frequently demand that the first column of a multicolumn page be used for a vertical navigational bar (as shown in Figure 3-11 by the front page of the ESPN Auto Racing Web site).

ESPN uses a clean, uncluttered design on the front page of their Auto Racing Web site. The site is constantly being updated with breaking news stories, so the cleaner it is, the better. Buttons for NASCAR, Indy Car, Formula One, NHRA, and IRL standings and results line the skinny left-hand column, while the wider right-hand column contains headlines and teasers for feature stories. While most browsers cannot display the entire page without scrolling, those folks lucky enough to have a 21-inch monitor (running at a high resolution) can get it all in one glance.

The *San Jose Mercury News* Web site, Mercury Center, is a vanguard of great Web newspaper design. A lively layout, as shown in Figure 3-12, breaks the front page up into distinct sections. The info-laden page is lengthy, requiring the reader to scroll even on the largest monitor. Lead stories fill the left side, which is broken into a grid that allows the stories to span multiple columns as necessary. In contrast to the ESPN Auto Racing site, the Mercury Center site has its skinny navigational column on the right side, where it is used for short teaser lines and limited advertising spots. As you can see, Mercury Center uses COLSPAN commands to create straddled cells.

While it's doubtful that the Web sites you create will be as high-powered (or well-funded) as the ESPN and *San Jose Mercury News* sites, you can learn a lot from the way that they've built their grids. Since both of these sites are constantly changing, they've been designed so that changes can be accomplished with a minimum of hassle. Careful annotation in your HTML file can help you to keep your sanity by adding comment fields.

Figure 3-12: Mercury Center defines great newspaper Web site design through the use of a nifty table-created layout.

A Comment About Comments

Comments can be read in WEB.DESIGNER's HTML source mode but are not shown in the browser (although they will be displayed if your visitors view the source). To add a comment, switch to HTML source mode and type **<!--comment goes here-->**, placing your information between the hyphens.

Using HTML Forms

There are many reasons to add HTML forms to your Web site. If your site contains a huge amount of information, you might use a search feature to query the database. You might be building a mailing list of potential customers, or perhaps you are interested in taking a survey of visitors to gauge their opinions. Whatever the situation, you'll probably need to use a form on any page where you'd like your visitors to enter variable information for the purpose of interaction with the site.

The Form Is Only Half of the Equation

In order to use forms on your Web site, you'll need to have a program running on your Web server that knows what to do with the submitted information. These are often referred to as Common Gateway Interface (CGI) scripts.

Car Talk is a Saturday morning radio show hosted by the Tappit brothers, Click and Clack. In the real world, *Car Talk* can be found on your National Public Radio station, while on the Web, it can be found at http://www.cartalk.com. Their site is every bit as fun and informative as the radio show. Take a look at the Car Talk Classifieds ad search form, shown in Figure 3-13. This nifty form allows visitors to the Car Talk site to search for the car of their dreams through a number of criteria, including minimum and maximum price, make, body style, mileage, age, and location. When you submit your query, the database returns any vehicles that meet your specifications. This is the place to go to search for that classic set of wheels!

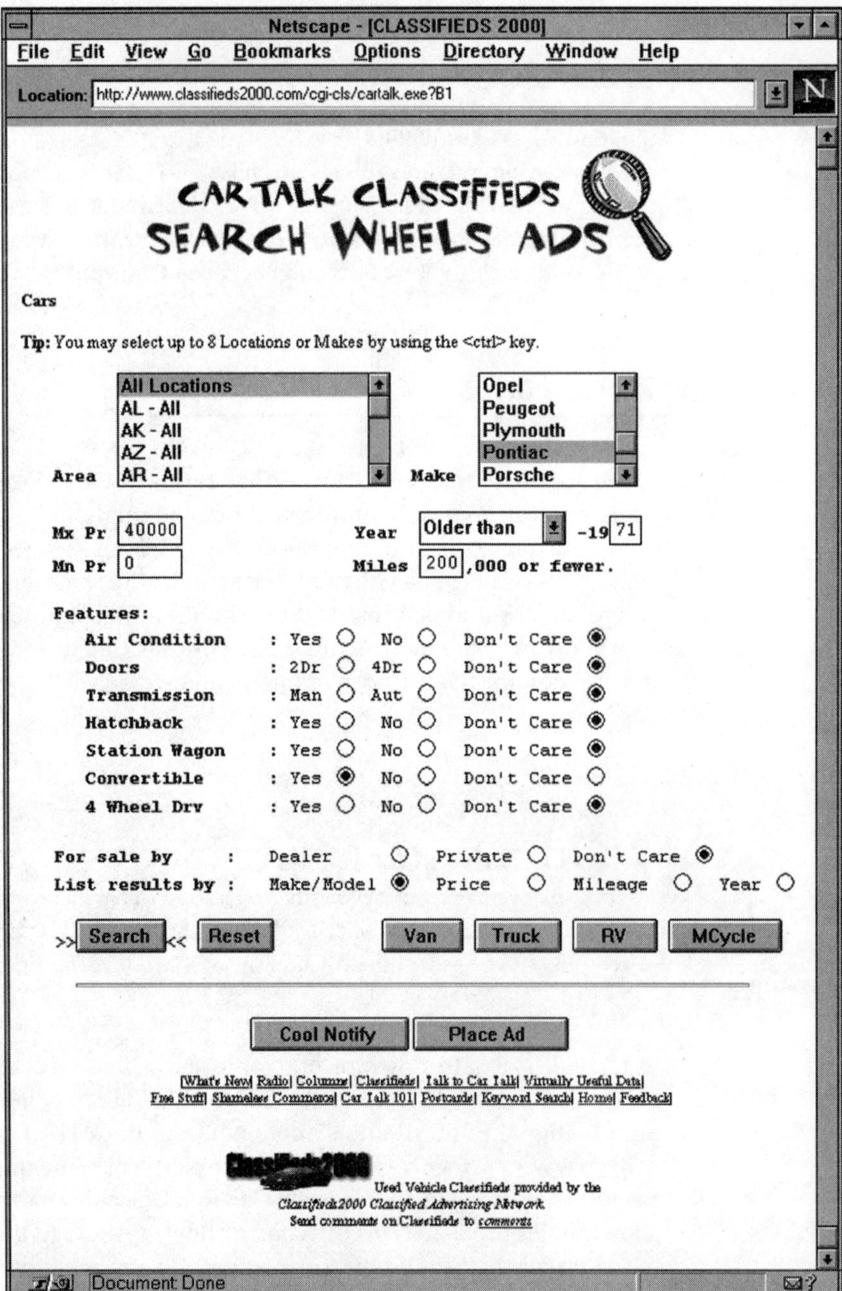

Figure 3-13: The Car Talk search form lets you look for that perfect old Pontiac convertible, just like the one you used to know and love.

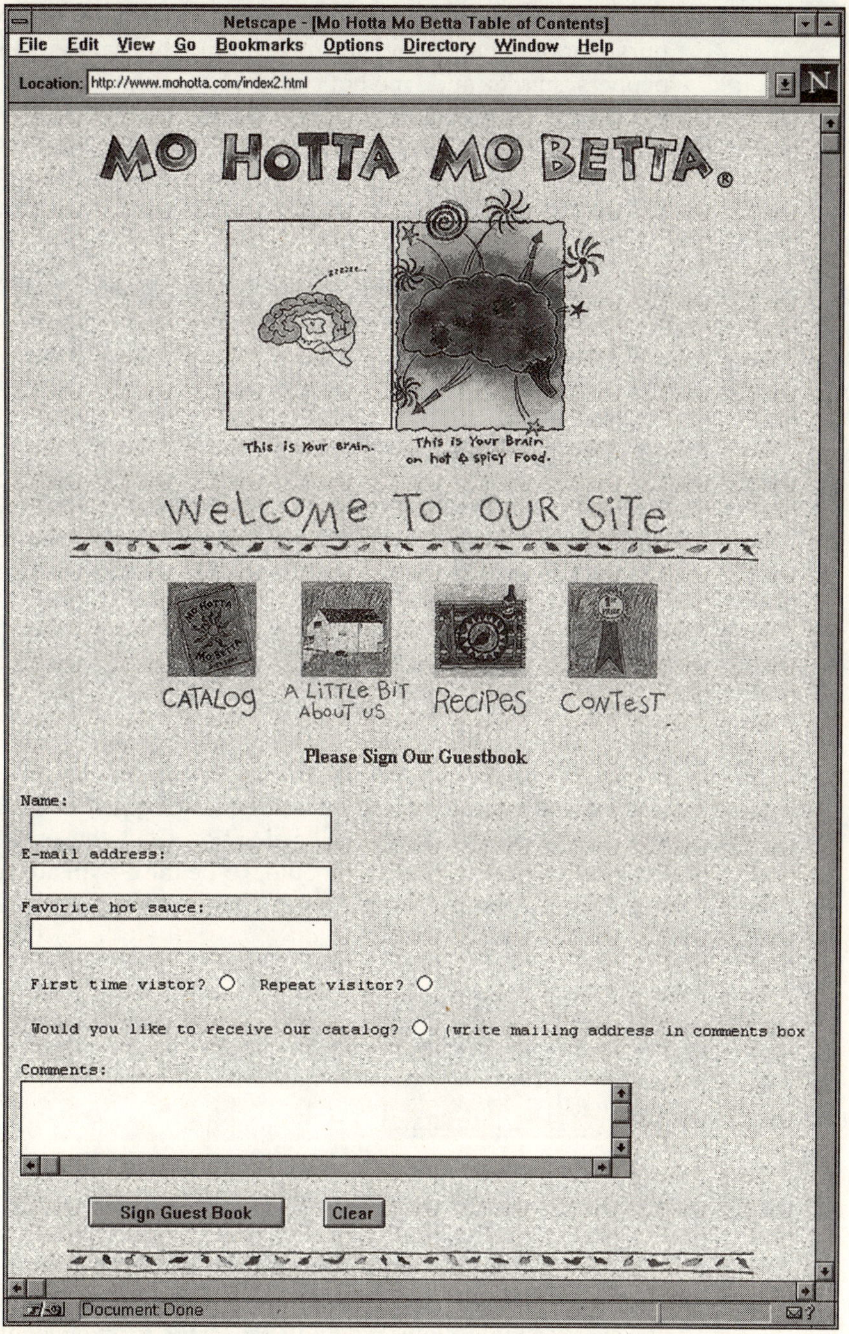

Netscape - [Mo Hotta Mo Betta Table of Contents]

File   Edit   View   Go   Bookmarks   Options   Directory   Window   Help

Location: http://www.mohotta.com/index2.html

MO HOTTA MO BETTA.®

This is Your Brain.   This is Your Brain on hot & spicy Food.

Welcome To Our Site

CATALOG   A LiTTLe BiT About us   Recipes   CONTest

Please Sign Our Guestbook

Name:

E-mail address:

Favorite hot sauce:

First time visitor? ◯   Repeat visitor? ◯

Would you like to receive our catalog? ◯   (write mailing address in comments box

Comments:

Sign Guest Book   Clear

Document Done

Figure 3-14: Hey, pepperheads, looking for some hot stuff? Go to http://www.mohotta.com/ and sign up now!

Mo Hotta Mo Betta (http://www.mohotta.com/) is a mail order purveyor of hot and spicy foods, including hot sauces, salsas, chilies, peppers, snacks, and "mo hot stuff." The San Luis Obispo, California-based firm does the majority of their sales through their whimsical printed catalog. Although their Web site contains a nice selection of goods, the catalog features an amazing array of products to entice the widest range of customers. As such, compiling a mailing list for the catalog is an important part of their Web site. Figure 3-14 demonstrates how Mo Hotta Mo Betta includes a mailing list form at the bottom of their graphic home page (the site is broken into low- and high-bandwidth tracks).

Mailto Links

If all you want to do is provide a means of visitor feedback, (rather than feeding your database), HTML's Mailto feature is the easiest type of feedback loop to implement. Although HTML forms are far more powerful, Mailto links are the fastest way to solicit e-mail from your visitors. When visitors click on a Mailto link, they are presented with a window that lets them send e-mail directly to a prespecified address. If you need more than just e-mail, however, you'll want to look into the options afforded by HTML forms and Common Gateway Interface (CGI) scripts.

WEB.DESIGNER makes it simple to create Mailto links. Just highlight the text you want to link from and click the HyperLink button to summon the HyperLink Properties dialog box. Click the arrow button to drop down the menu, click "mailto," type the e-mail address, and click OK. Bingo—you've created an instant e-mail link!

Form Creation Tools

HTML provides all the mechanisms you'll need to knock out a great-looking form. And CorelWEB.DESIGNER makes those forms relatively easy to create. The program's form creation tools allow you to build complex forms without touching any serious HTML code. Figure 3-15 illustrates the different HTML form elements within WEB.DESIGNER. In the exercise that follows, you will use all the form elements to create your own form. Figure 3-23 (toward the end of this chapter) shows how the form elements appear in Netscape Navigator.

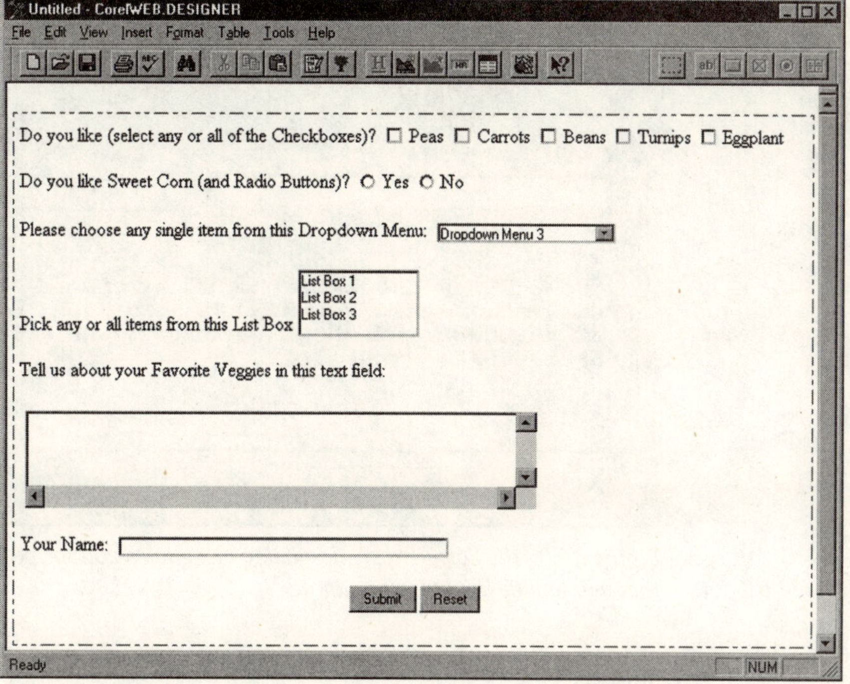

Figure 3-15: WEB.DESIGNER makes it easy to lay out forms. The real trick is making them work at the server!

Creating a Form Area

Click the Insert Form button (it's the one with the red dotted rectangle) to create a form area. The Form Properties dialog box will appear, as shown in Figure 3-16. If you know what the URL of the CGI script is, you can enter it now. If not, you can still proceed with the creation of the form by clicking the OK button. The CGI's location can be added at any time before the page goes live.

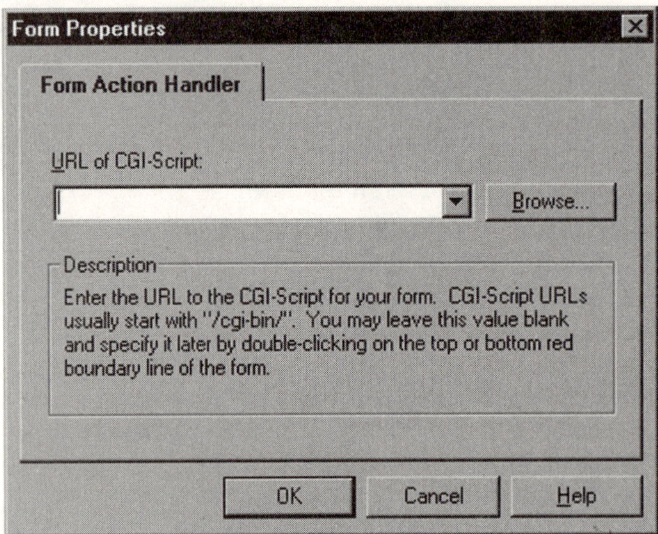

Figure 3-16: The Form Properties dialog box allows you to specify the CGI script that will handle the incoming data.

Text Fields

WEB.DESIGNER allows you to create three different types of text fields: Single Line Fields, Multi Line Fields, and Password Fields. Clicking the Text Field button places a single line field into your form by default. To change the specifications of a text field, double-click on it to summon the Text Field Properties dialog box (as shown in Figure 3-17). Here's a quick rundown of why you'll need each type of text field:

- Single Line Text Fields—Use single-line text fields when you only need your visitor to enter a single line of text, such as a name or street address. WEB.DESIGNER allows you to set the character width and maximum length of the field.

- Multi Line Text Fields—Use multiline text fields to allow your users to enter more than one line of text (such as a comment field). The Text Field Properties dialog box allows you to specify the character width and number of lines. Multiline text fields can provide automatic text wrapping in the browser. You must switch to HTML source mode and enter **WRAP="PHYSICAL"** within the text field command to allow text wrapping.

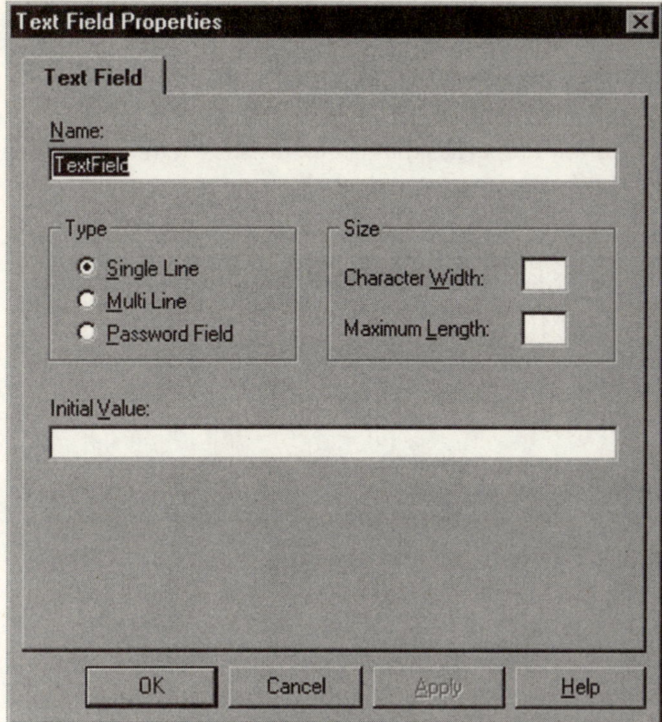

Figure 3-17: The Text Field Properties dialog box allows you to take charge of text entry areas.

- Password Fields—These are special text fields for entering passwords. When a visitor types in a password field in their browser, only bullets (or asterisks) will be displayed. You can set the character width and maximum length of the field.

The Text Field Properties dialog box also allows you to set an Initial Value for each text field. Whatever you type here will appear "as is" in the browser. By preassigning the right text in select cases, you can make your forms easier (and more pleasant) for your visitors to fill out.

Submit & Reset Buttons

You'll use the Button button (now that's a name!) to insert Submit and Reset buttons into your forms. Submit buttons send the information entered on the form to the Web server and are required on every form, while Reset buttons are a convenience feature—they allow the visitor to automatically clear the form. When you insert a new button into a form (by clicking the Button button), it comes in as a Submit button with the default label of "Button" by default. Double-clicking a button summons the Button Properties dialog box (as shown in Figure 3-18), which allows you to change its type and label.

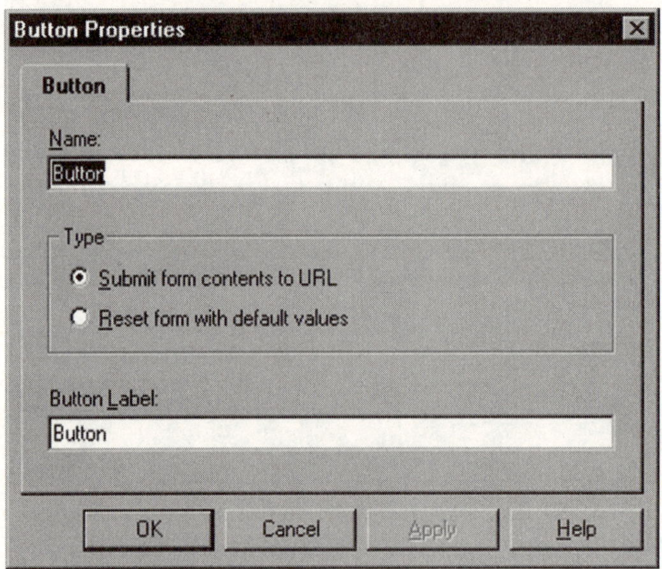

Figure 3-18: The Button Properties dialog box allows you to label a button and permits you to specify it as either a Submit or Reset button.

Check Boxes

These critters are often set as groups, which allow any, all, or none of the group to be selected. Clicking the Check Box button adds a new check box to a form. Double-clicking a check box summons the Check Box Properties dialog box (as shown in Figure 3-19). You'll use this dialog box to assign unique names and values. To set a number of check boxes as a group, such as the Peas, Carrots, Beans example shown in Figure 3-15, assign the exact same name to each of the items. Check boxes may be automatically set to be either checked or unchecked in the browser.

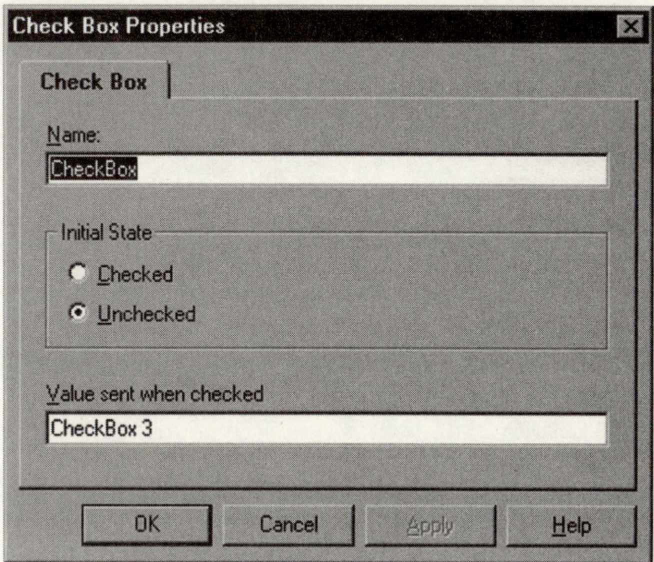

Figure 3-19: The Check Box Properties dialog box allows you to create stand-alone check boxes as well as groups of check boxes.

Radio Buttons

You'll want to use radio buttons when asking a "yes/no/maybe" type of question. While they're similar to check boxes in that they can be set as groups, radio buttons allow only one button in a group (at a time) to be selected. Take a look back at the Yes/No question in Figure 3-15 for a common example. Clicking the Radio Button button adds a new radio button to a form. Double-clicking a radio button summons the Radio Button Properties dialog box (as shown in Figure 3-20). You'll use this dialog box to assign unique names and values. To set a number of radio buttons as a group, assign the exact same name to each of the items. Radio buttons may be automatically set to be either checked or unchecked in the browser.

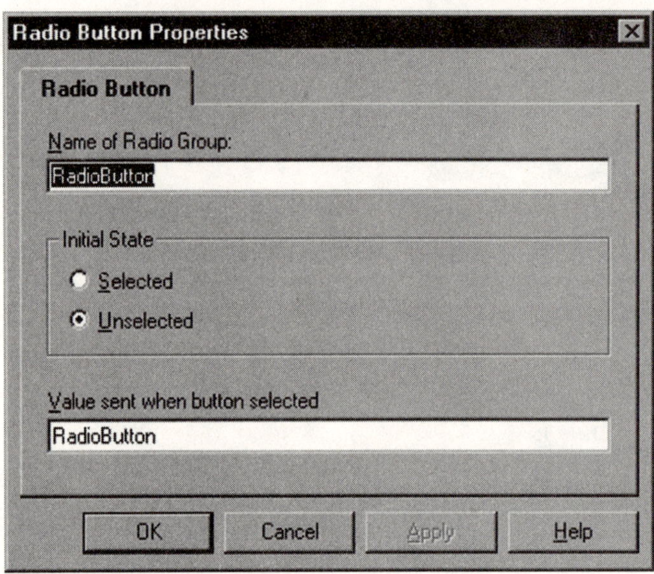

Figure 3-20: The Radio Button Properties dialog box allows you to assign the right attributes for those "one of a kind" questions.

Scrolling List Boxes & Drop-Down Menus

WEB.DESIGNER makes it easy to use scrolling list boxes and drop-down menus in your forms. Clicking the List/Menu button adds a drop-down menu. Double-clicking the drop-down menu summons the List Properties dialog box (as shown in Figure 3-21). Here, you'll name your list, assign its type, and add items to its contents. A drop-down menu allows visitors to select only one item, while the list box allows more than one item to be selected (if Allow Multiple Selections is specified). You can also assign a specific height to a list box.

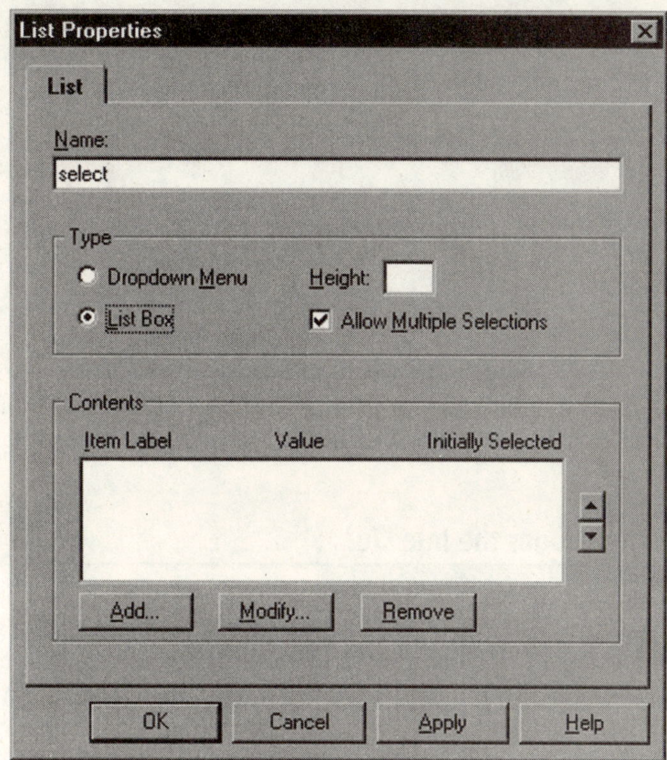

Figure 3-21: You'll use the List Properties dialog box to create both drop-down menus and list boxes.

To add contents to a drop-down menu or list box, click the Add button in the List Properties dialog. The Add Item dialog box (as shown in Figure 3-22) allows you to assign an Item Label and Value, in addition to specifying whether it is initially selected (or not). To modify an existing item, select it in the Contents list and click the Modify button to summon the Add Item dialog box. (What, you expected it to be called the Modify Item dialog box?) To delete an item, simply select it and click Remove.

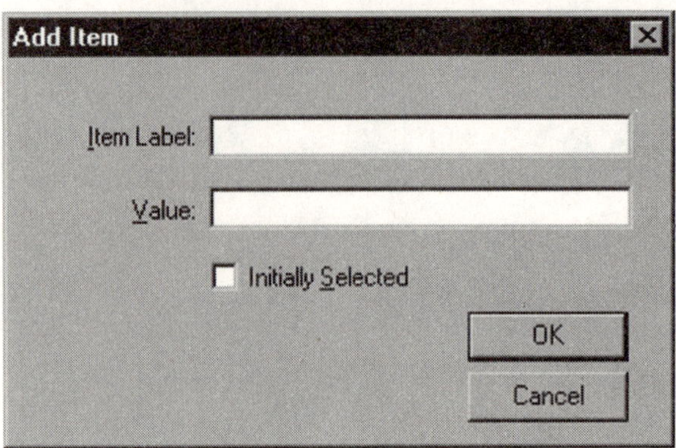

Figure 3-22: You'll have to access the Add Item dialog box for each and every item you add.

Where Does the Info Go?

Aye, here's the rub. A form merely provides the means of gathering information. You'll need to have a CGI script running on your Web server in order to do anything with the submitted data. The CGI must know what to do with this information, and it must be in synch with the form so that it understands what to do with the various names and values. In most cases, this means that you must huddle up with your Webmaster to find out what kind of support is available with regard to scripting. (Some ISP's don't allow CGI scripts at all!) It's important to note that CGI scripts are server-specific. A script written for one platform may not run on another (i.e., UNIX Perl may be useless on a Windows NT server).

In the bad old days, the only way to create a CGI script was to write it with a programming language, such as Perl. Thankfully, things have changed. Nonprogrammers will be thrilled to learn that a number of applications are now available to build scripts without writing any code. O'Reilly's PolyForm (for Windows 95/NT) is one example of an application that can be used to instantly create interactive forms without any programming whatsoever.

How does the Web server know which CGI script to use? Double-click on the red dotted outline around your form and take a quick look at the Form Properties dialog box. The Form Action Handler should be filled out with the location (URL) of the appropriate CGI, such as /cgi-bin/ blahblahblah.cgi, where /cgi-bin/ is the directory, and blahblahblah.cgi is the name of the script itself. You'll have to contact your Webmaster to determine exactly how this should be specified.

Building a Form

In this little exercise, you'll build a guestbook form for your Web site. This form will include text fields, a text area, radio buttons, a drop-down list, and a scrolling list, as shown in Figure 3-23. As you begin building the form, you'll quickly see how easy it is to create, adjust, and rearrange the different form elements. You'll want to start with a brand new page.

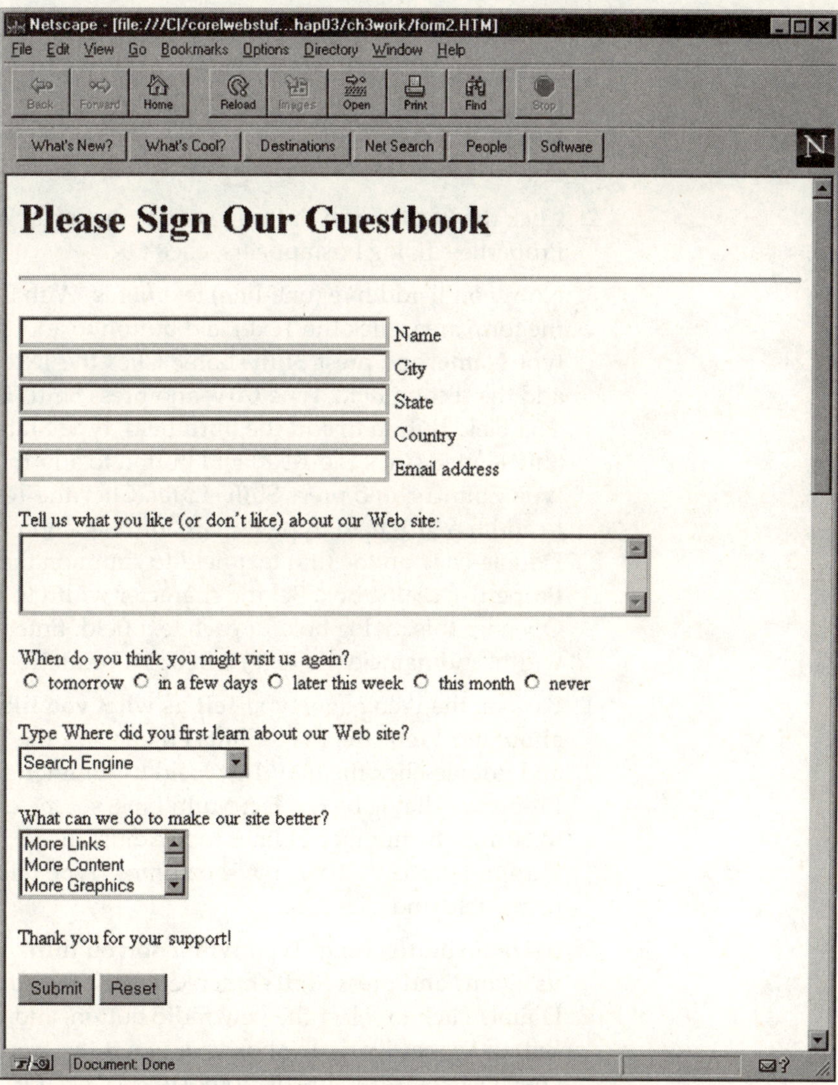

Figure 3-23: Guestbooks are among the most common Web page forms.

What's the Difference Between Enter & Shift+Enter?

Pressing Enter generates a close text style command—a <P> if you're in paragraph text—resulting in an extra line of "paragraph space." Pressing Shift+Enter, on the other hand, generates a <BR> command, which breaks to a new line without adding the extra space while maintaining the text style.

1. Let's begin by adding a simple heading. Type **Please Sign Our Guestbook**. Change the format by clicking Format | Heading | Heading 1. Press Shift+Enter. Insert a Horizontal Rule. Press Enter.

2. Click the Insert Form button to create the form. When the Form Properties dialog box appears, click OK.

3. Now, you'll add five (one-line) text fields. With the cursor inside the form area, click the Text Field button to add the first field, type **Name**, and press Shift+Enter. Click the Text Field button to add the second field, type **City**, and press Shift+Enter. Click the Text Field button to add the third field, type **State**, and press Shift+Enter. Click the Text Field button to add the fourth field, type **Country**, and press Shift+Enter. Click the Text Field button to add the fifth field, type **E-mail address**, and press Shift+Enter. Double-click on the first text field to summon the Text Field Properties dialog box. Set the character width to 40 and click OK. Open up this dialog box for each text field. Enter the character width, and name each Text Field appropriately.

4. Back on the Web page, type **Tell us what you like (or don't like) about our Web site**. Press Shift+Enter. Click the Text Field button and double-click the new Text Field to summon the Text Field Properties dialog box, select Multi Line, set the character width to **60** and the number of lines to **3**. Adjust the text area so that it is approximately 7 rows by 54 columns. Type **tellusaboutit** in the name field and click OK.

5. It's radio button time! Type **When do you think you might visit us again?** and press Shift+Enter. Click the Radio Button button. Double-click to select the new radio button, and use the Radio Button Properties dialog box to assign it the group name of "nextvisit" and a value of "tomorrow." Click OK and copy the

button with a Ctrl+C. Press Ctrl+V four times to paste in four new buttons (all with the same properties). Insert the text as shown in Figure 3-23 (**tomorrow, in a few days, later this week, this month,** and **never**) on the page and in the value field for each button.

6. Now, you'll add a drop-down menu. Type **Where did you first learn about our Web site?** and press Shift+Enter. Click the List/Menu button. Double-click the new drop-down menu to summon the List Properties dialog box. Click Add to summon the Add Item dialog box. You'll need to repeatedly access it to enter the following (with matching labels and values):
Search Engine
Banner Advertisement
Print Advertisement
Television Advertisement
Hot List

7. Let's add a scrolling list selection to the form. Type **What can we do to make our site better?** and press Shift+Enter. Click the List/Menu button. Double-click the new drop-down menu to summon the List Properties dialog box. Select the List Box option and set the height to 3 (later on, you can take the time to experiment with different sizes). Give it a name of "whatelse." Make sure that Allow Multiple Selections is checked. Click Add to summon the Add Item dialog box. You'll need to repeatedly access it to enter the following (with matching labels and values):
More Links
More Content
More Graphics
Fewer Graphics
More Shockwave

8. To finish up the form, you'll add a thank-you line and those crucial Submit and Reset buttons. Type **Thank you for your support!** and press Enter. Click the Button button, press a space, and click the Button button again. Double-click the first button to summon the Button Properties dialog box. Assign it a name and label it "Submit." The type should already be set to *Submit form contents to URL*. Click OK. Double-click the second button to summon the Button Properties dialog box. At Type, click *Reset form with default values*, then assign it a name and label it "Reset." Click OK.

9. You're done, so save your file! If this were a real working form, you'd have to set an Action in the Form Properties. This lets the server know what CGI script to use with the incoming data.

Try your new form out in your Web browser to see how it looks. You'll be able to enter text in the text fields, click the radio buttons, and choose items from the drop down menu and scrolling list. (The information cannot be submitted to a Web server without a CGI.) While some of the earlier browsers (AOL's in particular) had problems dealing with forms, just about all the browsers today support the HTML 2.0 form specification to which WEB.DESIGNER writes its forms.

Moving On

In this chapter you learned the basics of HTML table and form design. WEB.DESIGNER makes many of these chores easy, although it does come up short in some aspects of table design. In the next chapter, we'll dive into a juicy hands-on project, as we put WEB.DESIGNER's powerful tools to work in the (almost) real world.

4 Creating Web Pages

W hile conventional publishing mediums are tied to a specific event (the press run) and set size (the number of pages) of the publication, the World Wide Web provides an infinite canvas that can be revamped, rearranged, or expanded in a flash. This may be achieved, however, only when you plan your Web site carefully. As a designer, you must strive to create Web sites that are both visually compelling and inherently modular in design.

This chapter demonstrates a number of techniques that you'll use to create polished Web page designs and logically designed Web sites. The CorelWEB.GRAPHICS Suite provides a leg up for budding Web designers, as it includes a number of integrated graphic themesets, as well as prebuilt templates and scads of clip art. We begin with the all-important topic of Web site management and proper directory structure. Why start there? Because before you build your site, you need to know where to store your files.

Designing Your Site for Growth

Web sites are dynamic creatures. They live, breathe, and grow. In order for your site to mature successfully from a seedling into a sapling, you need to plan for its expansion. As it spreads its branches, you have to decide which to encourage and which to prune. A well-organized site will make your life easier and takes just a little thoughtful planning. You don't even have to be insanely compulsive to do a good job! With the right tools, organizing your Web site can be as easy as trimming the hedges.

Although Web site management is not a trivial matter, it does not have to become an all-consuming task. A sensible layout enables you to create a site that can be expanded easily. As you plan your site, you'll have to make some important decisions. The key is to conceptualize and implement an effective file hierarchy.

Some of the primary issues in site management are:

- How is the site organized?

- Where are the images stored?

- How are the links maintained?

- How are orphan files found and eliminated?

The following section will help you understand the issues that arise as a Web site grows.

How Is the Site Organized?

In addition to considering your Web site's organization from a navigational perspective, you must think about its file structure. The former often dictates the latter. When a site is small, all pages can coexist happily in one directory. As it grows, however, things may get out of hand quickly. Your site may evolve to contain many *subsites,* or "sites within a site." When the level of complexity reaches a certain point, it will make good sense to reorganize your file structure so that each of the subsites has its own directory within the main site directory. Once the number of HyperText Markup Language (HTML) and graphic files in one directory exceed what you're comfortable wading through, this will rapidly become apparent.

Savvy Web designers build their Web sites on local or internal network hard drives before putting them "out in public." This ensures that a site can be tested thoroughly and debugged *before* its audience hits a single page. If you plan your site carefully from the start, you can avoid much of the gut-wrenching that accompanies rearranging your site on the fly. It can take eons to manually change all the internal Uniform Resource Locators (URLs) on a good-sized site. An automated method can save untold time, not to mention your sanity. Programs such as Adobe SiteMill (which should appear shortly for Windows95/NT) make Web site management chores far more tolerable.

Setting a Server Root

You always should set a *server root* when creating a new Web site with
WEB.DESIGNER. The server root is a Web site's base directory, in which
all of its files and subdirectories are stored. To summon the Server Root
dialog box, as shown in Figure 4-1, select Tools | Set Server Root. This
dialog box allows you to set any directory on your computer (or on a
network drive) as the server root. The directory must already exist, since
the dialog box does not allow you to create a new directory. As you
create new pages in WEB.DESIGNER, the program always asks you if
you want to copy each file (including images, sounds, and animation)
into the server root. When it's time to *go live*, this makes it easy to move
files over to the Web server.

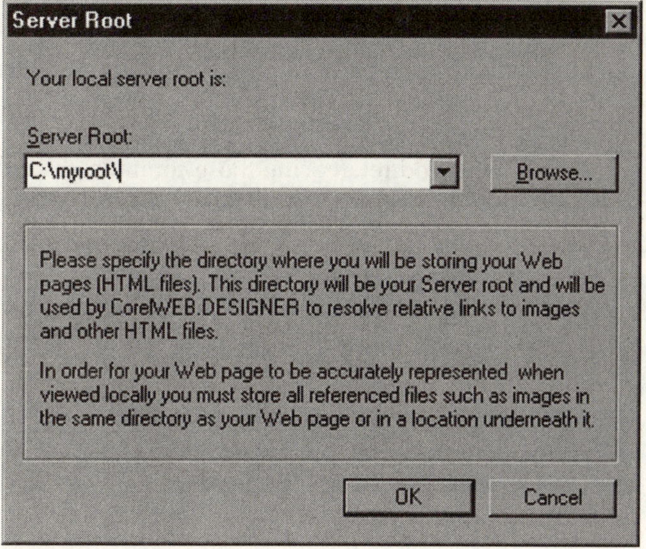

Figure 4-1: Setting a server root is a point-and-click procedure.

Building Multiple Sites?

If you create multiple Web sites, it's a good idea to have a separate root directory
for each. Using separate root directories avoids any confusion over what files
belong to which Web site.

Where Do the Images Go?

In the simplest Web sites, you can toss all of your image files in the same directory as your HTML pages. This goes only so far, however. Once your site has grown past two dozen or so files, things can get out of hand quickly. You don't want to have to wade through long lists of inter-mingled files. That's why it's a good idea to keep a separate directory (or directories) solely for images.

You may be able to get away with having one big image directory, or you may decide to break it up into smaller directories. These might be based on subject matter or perhaps by subsite. It's up to you to decide the criteria. You also have complete control over what you name the directories: Images, Graphics, Photos, Pix, or whatever suits your fancy.

In a scenario with one large (or not-so-large) site, you might create a directory for common site graphics, along with a separate image direc-tory in each of the subsite directories. This keeps the images with their subject matter and helps to trim down the size of the individual image directories. It also makes it easier to move complete directories around should the need arise. Another important reason for using a directory for common graphics (and referencing those common graphics) is to in-crease load speed for users by using the same graphic in multiple places.

A Word to the Wise . . .

If you are using separate subdirectories for your image files, you'll save your sanity by copying them into those subdirectories *before* you insert them into your WEB.DESIGNER pages. This avoids broken links and tedious file renaming.

No matter which scheme you choose, you always should keep the image directories within WEB.DESIGNER's server root directory (or within subdirectories within the server root).

Maintaining Links

You can think of links as the chains that hold your unruly Web site together. Break a link, and havoc erupts. As shown in Figure 4-2, a site will "go 404," and return a "file not found" message when someone chooses a nonexistent file. While this isn't a life-threatening event, it's an unpleasant experience for the visitor, at best. Good Webmasters strive to eliminate 404s from their site. As trivial as it may seem, it's important to test each and every link before a page goes "live."

Don't Go 404!

When a visitor has requested a nonexistent file, 404 errors are returned by the Web server. These errors often result from lackadaisical site maintenance. Some servers (such as the CERN server) will include the actual error message number; many others will not.

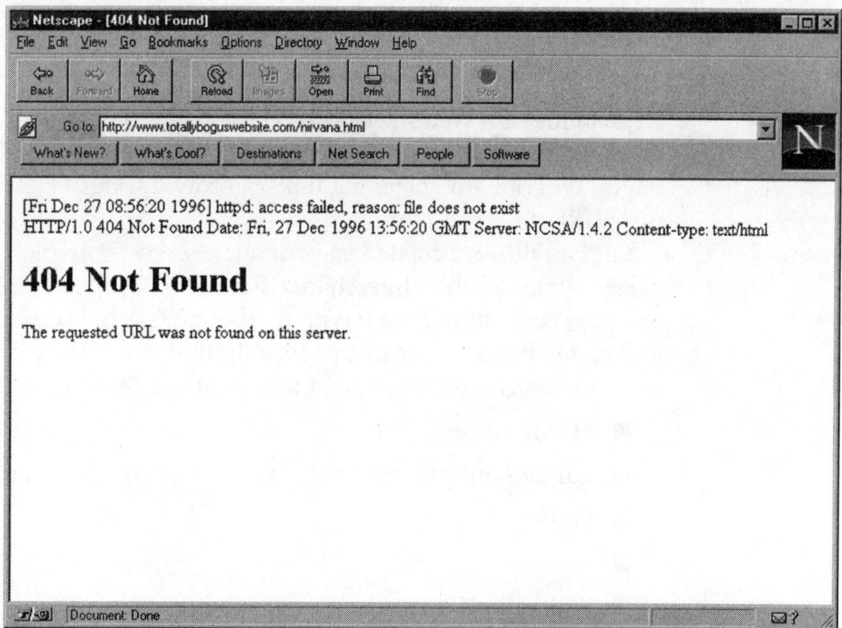

Figure 4-2: Where did the page go? If the Web server can't find a file, it returns a message like this.

A Web server sends back a 404 any time it can't find a specified file at a specific location. A 404 results when a file is on the server but is not where it's supposed to be, just as it does when the file is not on the server at all. The server looks only where the URL asks it to look. And 404s frequently happen when you've moved a file but haven't updated all of its incoming links. Anytime you move a file (or group of files) from one directory to another, you must update every occurrence of its URL within your site. Doing this manually gives a whole new meaning to the word *tedious*. Thankfully, automated methods can turn link maintenance into a simple task.

Be Careful When Deleting Pages

If you delete a Web page that's been cataloged by the search engines, visitors will continue to come to your site looking for it. If you must delete a popular page, create a forwarding page to explain where the old page went, while suggesting that visitors revise their bookmarks, as well.

Eliminating Orphan Files

Orphan files are Web site jetsam. These pages or graphics float unseen, just below the surface of your site, and are not referenced by any other pages. Without any incoming links, a browser doesn't know the orphan file's URL, thus can't find it.

Orphan files are created as your site evolves. You might have used a background Graphics Interchange Format (GIF) file in an earlier version of a page, only to replace it with a different GIF file later on. Or perhaps you eliminated all links to a page, although you left the page untouched. Orphan files can be any type of unreferenced file, including:

- HTML pages
- GIF or Joint Photographic Experts Group (JPEG) graphics
- Sounds
- Movies
- Animations
- Image maps

You'll usually want to eliminate orphan files. Even if they don't threaten the stability or navigational flow of your site, they take up server space unnecessarily. Isolating orphan files without an automated site management application is a frustrating experience, however. It's no fun sitting down with a lengthy list of files on your site, trying to discern which files are live and which are not.

A Case for Select Orphans

There is one good use for orphan files, however. You might want to have a "semisecret" page, accessible only by typing in its specific address. You might distribute this URL to a select group of people only and for a particular reason, such as to distribute semi-confidential information. This is not a secure method, however, as a dedicated individual may be able to find the hidden files as easily as typing in obvious URL combinations. If you want your information to stay hidden, you should use password protection. Even though passwords *can* be hacked, for the most part they're secure.

Rearranging Your Site: A Caveat

After your site is live, rearranging your file structure carries risks. If your site has been around for a while, its layout has been stored, analyzed, and disseminated in a number of ways. This process takes place outside your realm of control. These "runaway librarians" include:

- Search engines
- Print media citations
- Incoming links from other sites
- Individual (personal) browser bookmarks

Before you implement any site structure changes, consider how they will affect the ways that visitors are referred to the various URLs within your site. If you move a page from the URL where any of these sources expects to find it, visitors will receive a 404—File Not Found error when they use the URL. This is not a good thing! Let's take a look at how to deal with these important outside referrals.

How to Stay Out of Trouble

When you move an important page—especially the front page of a subsite, create a new page to leave in the old page's place. The new page should include some text to the tune of, "We've moved . . . ," along with a hotlink to the new location, as shown in Figure 4-3.

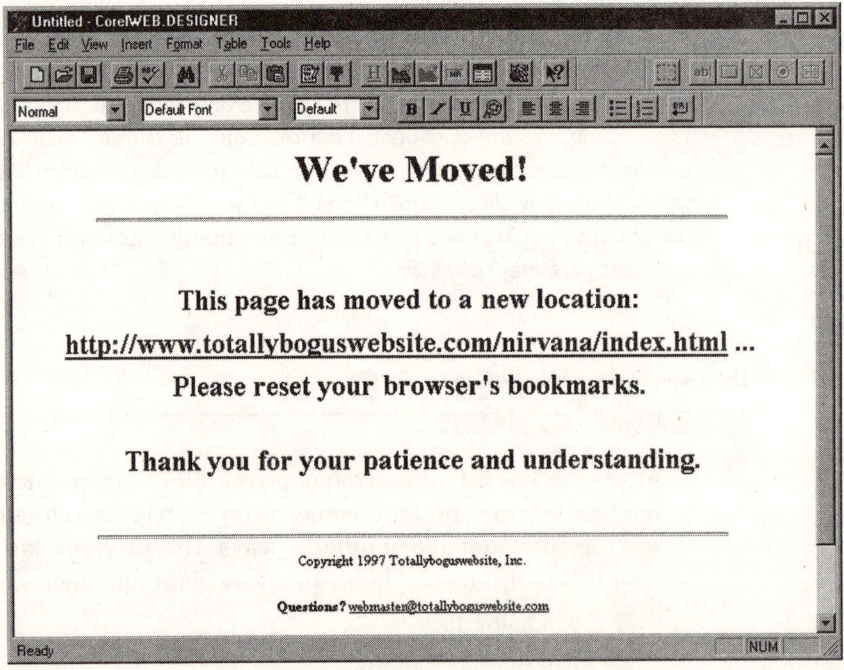

Figure 4-3: Don't forget to let them know where you moved!

What Happens With the Search Engines?

Left to their own devices, the search engines will find and catalog each and every public page on your Web site. The spiders won't catalog pages under password protection, so you needn't worry about breaking those links.

The search engines actually can help you in your efforts to rearrange your site. As the spiders revisit and recatalog your site, time heals any wounds. They'll hit your pages, follow the new links, and do their job (hopefully) without a hiccup. Some search engines appreciate notification when you make major changes. In any case, be sure to drop in linking pages in your key locations. Chapter 5 includes information on how to stay on top of the search engines.

How Should You Deal With Print Media Citations?

Everyone loves a mention in print. When a big magazine or book publishes your URL, you'll likely experience an increased hit rate. When a publication prints a URL within your site rather than your front door, the results can be indelible. Once it's in print, it's set in stone. If you move a page that's been cited in print, you'll infuriate potential visitors if they can't get to the page.

It's impossible to control the media. Instead, you have to keep a diligent watch on the pages that draw attention to your site. If you move a page, be sure to leave a linking page in its place for a certain period of time. If a publication prints the wrong URL (within your site), put a linking page (sending visitors to the correct page) at that address as soon as possible. Be considerate about how you work this page; there's no need to antagonize the publication over a simple typo. And consider it an opportunity to contact the publication and *ask* them to run a correction.

Incoming Links From Other Sites

If you've done your job well, pages within your Web site will make their way onto countless hot (and cool!) lists. While each and every one of these lists may not be huge and powerful, they're important to your Web site's success. You'll want to keep track of the referring URLs through some type of tracking program. Once you've identified which Web sites have set up hotlinks to your pages, you can notify them if you make any changes to your site, such as the locations or names of your pages. This is more than common courtesy. It's good sense. The Webmasters should be grateful for your diligence in helping them avoid broken outgoing links. If you're linked back to them, they'll be more likely to return the favor when they rearrange their Web sites.

Individual Browser Bookmarks

Visitors are likely to bookmark individual pages within your site rather than your front door. Moving or renaming a page that just goes 404 on them is bound to tick them off. You can't send e-mail to everyone who's bookmarked your pages unless you've collected their e-mail addresses. And even so, sending out a note announcing a URL change might be considered bad Netiquette. Once again, the best solution is to drop in some linking pages in key locations.

Corel's CD: Trash or Treasure?

The CorelWEB.GRAPHICS Suite is filled to the gills with many of the graphic elements you'll need when building your Web pages. Some are great, while others are merely filler. To find all the graphic elements, you need to poke around in a number of different directories on the CorelWEB.GRAPHICS distribution CD-ROM. For instance, the Designer/Template directory contains 122 templates, with corresponding subdirectories for backgrounds, bullets, horizontal dividers, and images.

Using WEB.DESIGNER's Templates (or Not)

If you've taken the time to browse through WEB.DESIGNER's templates (File | Templates), you've probably found that many are simplistic yet silly. Is there really any point to the Cool Riding Hog & Friend's Cartoon Web page shown in Figure 4-4? Can you believe someone took the time to write this less-than-lovely prose and lay out this lame page? Although you'd be wise to eschew the majority of these templates, in favor of your own designs, you still might get an idea or two by browsing.

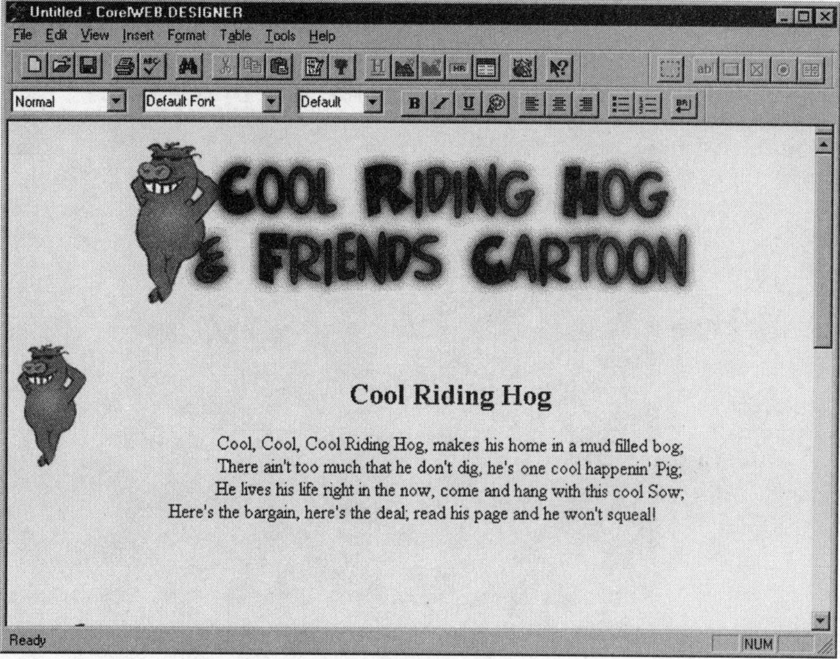

Figure 4-4: And furthermore, isn't a sow a female pig?

The Official Insomniacs Home Page, as shown in Figure 4-5, is actually one of the more coherent WEB.DESIGNER templates. While it uses a basic layout, the glowing type, horizontal separator, and icons deliver a consistent look and feel. The images appear to float above the black background. The glowing type is reminiscent of the logo for the popular Fox Television show "The X-Files." (Chapter 9 will show you how easy it is to pull off this effect.) And since we're on a slightly extraterrestrial bent, how could we resist mentioning the ever-popular Aliens Ate My Potato Chips! template illustrated in Figure 4-6?

Figure 4-5: Every successful Web designer encounters a little insomnia from time to time.

Figure 4-6: Do you think they have a link to the alien autopsy home page?

Even though the templates might be of little use, you'll find many opportunities to use the bounty of GIF and JPEG images. In the first release of the CorelWEB.GRAPHICS Suite, each of the image directories sits in the root directory of the CD-ROM. Each image directory contains an appropriately entitled HTML page that can be opened in WEB.DESIGNER or your Web browser for preview purposes. Let's review the different elements now (you can get a real look at them by thumbing through the WEB.GRAPHICS clip-art index). We'll see how CorelWEB.GALLERY can be used to quickly manage all these graphic files in Part VI of this book.

A Quiver of Arrows

Looking for direction? The ARROWS directory contains 61 sets of arrows, in both 24- and 48-pixel widths. The selections range from simple arrows through a number of three-dimensional entries and tape deck control buttons. Arrows come in handy when building linear navigation schemes. Forward and backward arrow buttons allow your visitors to move quickly from page to page.

Boffo Backgrounds

The WEB.GRAPHICS Suite CD-ROM boasts a wide variety of Web page backgrounds. Perhaps the nicest touch is its selection of photographic backgrounds in JPEG format. These textures are a wonderful resource, as long as you use them properly. The Backgrds directory includes 10 subdirectories:

- Design—26 textures, from painterly through potpourri
- Food—18 textures, from birdseed through jelly beans
- Marble—44 magnificent textures
- Metal—6 metallic-textured marvels
- Misc—101 assorted textures
- Nature—30 ultrarealistic textures
- Paper—28 textures, including a selection of gorgeous marbled paper, such as the texture used in Figure 4-7
- Stone—41 textures, from terra-cotta tile through bricks and stone walls, as shown in Figure 4-8
- Textile—29 textures, from fabrics through leathers
- Wood—22 textures so real you'll be looking for splinters

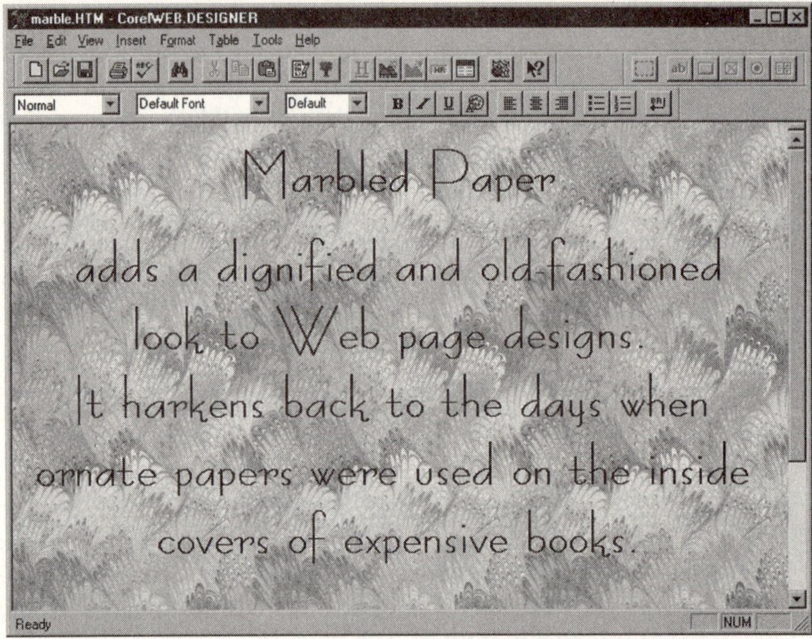

Figure 4-7: A marbled paper background delivers a rich, old-time feeling . . .

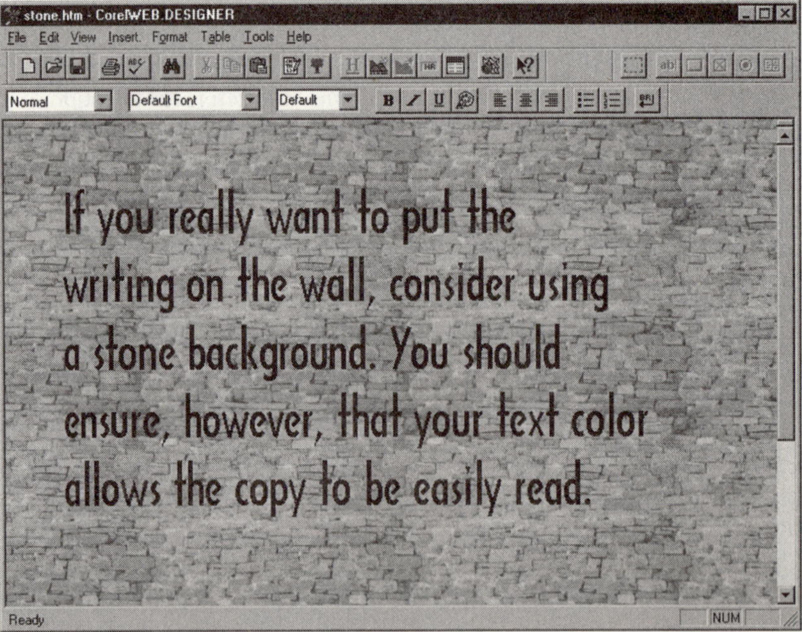

Figure 4-8: . . . while a stone wall provides a handy canvas for your Web graffiti.

Wasted Bullets

The Bullets directory is a mixed bag. The Classic subdirectory contains two more subdirectories (24 and 32), each filled with 123 useful bullets (in 24- and 32-pixel iterations). Classic bullets range from simple round examples through nifty three-dimensional designs. The Fun subdirectory is a tad disappointing. While it, too, contains two more subdirectories (24 and 32), the bullets contained therein seem to have been culled direct from the CorelWEB.DRAW Symbols roll-up. Each of these folders contains 124 symbol-bullets in red, blue, and black iterations. Some of these fun bullets look remarkably like similar objects in Microsoft's Wingdings font.

Bodacious Buttons

The Buttons directory is a treasure trove of three-dimensional button designs. There are 20 different designs, in 10 different colors. As shown in Figure 4-9, each button is presented both with and without labels, which include titles such as Information, What's New, Products, Services, Questions, Write Us, Feedback, Suggestions, Guest Book, and Help. The unlabeled buttons can be imported into WEB.DRAW, given your choice of title and font, and exported at an exact size; Chapter 8 covers the details.

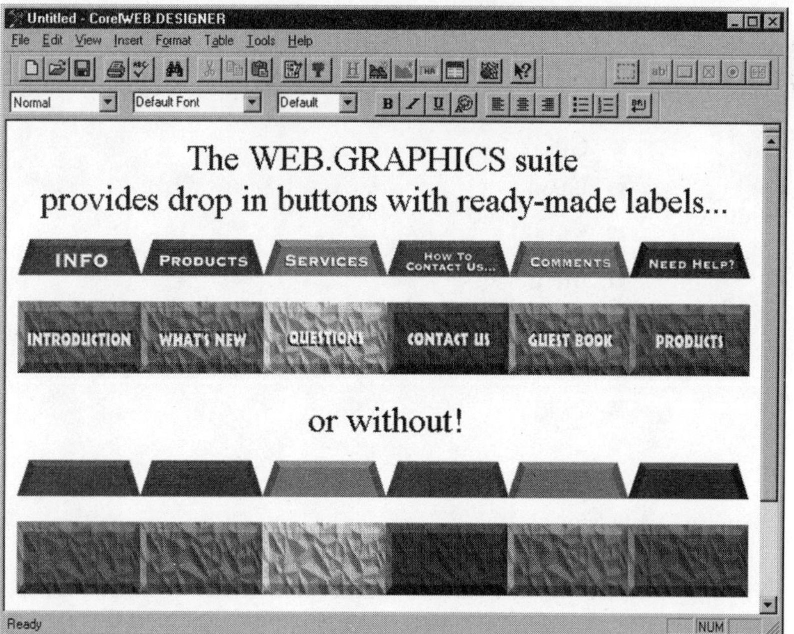

Figure 4-9: Jump-start your Web page navigational system with these nifty buttons!

Doodlicious Dividers

The 139 horizontal dividers found in the Dividers directory are fun and zany. If you're looking for a divider for a corporate Web site here, you'll probably come up dry. You will, however, find plenty of checkerboards, spaceships, neon tubes, lizards (or are they insects?), gingerbread men, palm trees, and even a zipper among the colorful entries. If you can't find what you're looking for, don't despair. Horizontal dividers are easy to knock out in CorelWEB.DRAW. In fact, you'll see just how easy it is in Chapter 8!

Colorful Drop Caps

Drop caps are the large initial caps often found at the beginning of a chapter in a book or at the start of a magazine article. The CorelWEB.GRAPHICS Suite CD-ROM contains 11 different drop cap collections, in both 48- and 64-pixel sizes. Once again, these collections are better suited to playful Web page designs than to corporate affairs. Figure 4-10 demonstrates how a handful of wild drop caps can spice up a page quickly. The collections consist of:

- Blueice
- Cosmic
- Digital
- Gold1
- Gold2
- Jagged
- Kidz
- Medieval
- Neon1
- Neon2
- Wild

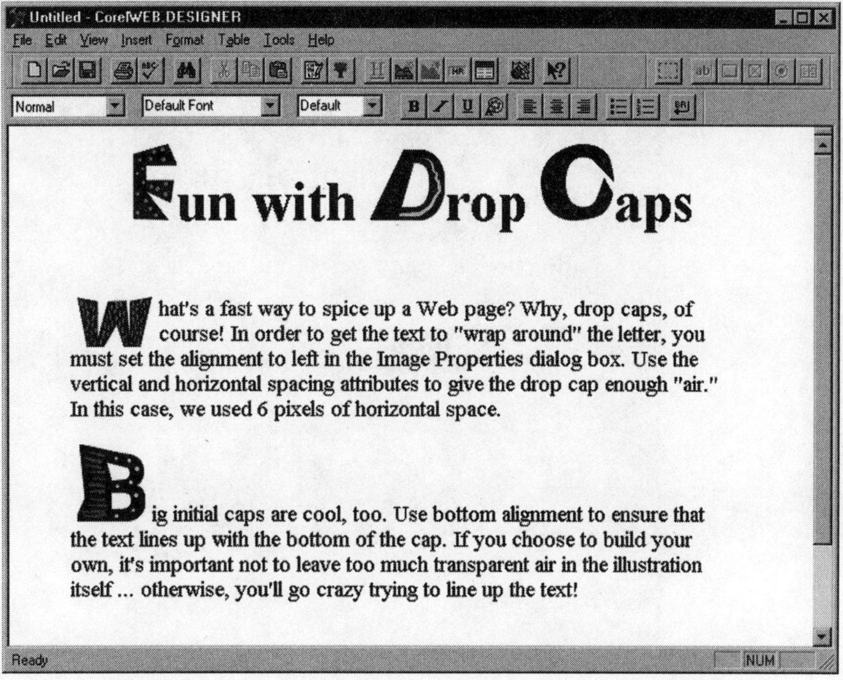

Figure 4-10: These wild drop caps lend a playful mood to this simple page.

Illustrative Icons

The Icons directory contains three sets of 81 icons each. These icons can be thought of as "icon-buttons," in that each is an icon that has been superimposed upon a square three-dimensional button. Figure 4-11 illustrates how you can use the icon-buttons to build a navigational system. It's always a good idea to follow your navigational icons with a text navigation bar, just in case your visitors are browsing with graphics turned off (or fail to comprehend the icons!).

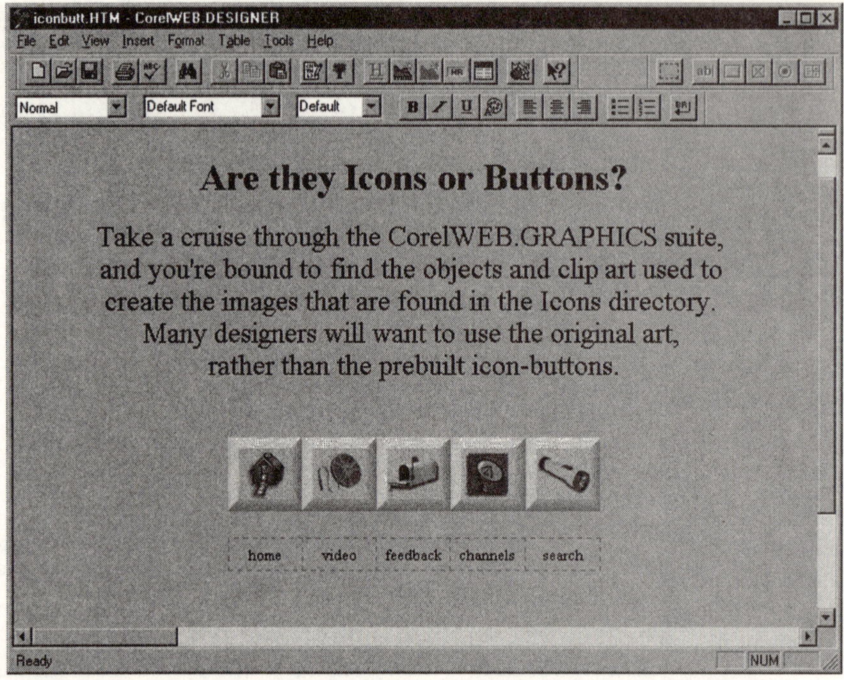

Figure 4-11: Don't forget to include a text navigation bar, along with those jazzy icons.

Opulent Objects

The Objects directory contains 105 nifty photographic objects, in both 90- and 180-pixel sizes. Each object is a transparent GIF. You can use these objects as stand-alone illustrations or as a nifty navigational bar, as shown in Figure 4-12. If you want make the objects pop off the page, you'll need to add a drop shadow in a paint editor, such as Adobe Photoshop, CorelPHOTO-PAINT, or Ulead PhotoImpact.

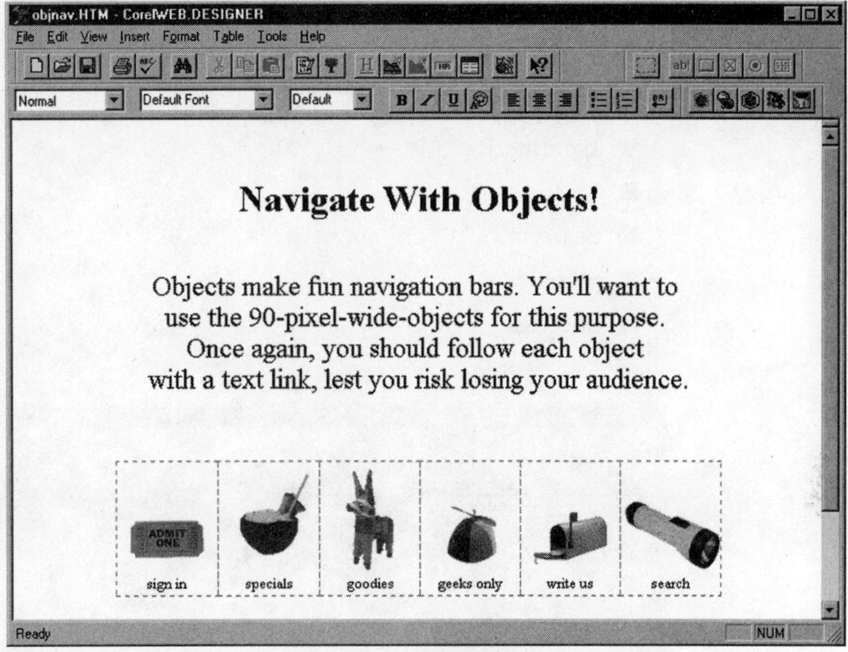

Figure 4-12: Objects provide a cute way to navigate.

Pixelicious Photographs

Corel is one of the world's largest purveyors of digital photography.
Their CD-ROM photo collections span every imaginable subject and
genre. The WEB.GRAPHICS Suite CD-ROM contains 11 sample photo
subdirectories within the Photos directory, each with 20 juicy JPEG
images in both 240- and 480-pixel widths. When carefully chosen, stock
PhotoCD images can help give your Web site a polished, professional
appearance. We created the Web page shown in Figure 4-13 with one of
our favorite images. The subjects include:

- Business
- Cars
- Design

- Fantasy
- Flags
- Industry
- Landmark
- Leisure
- Seasons
- Signs
- Success

Figure 4-13: Hey, we can dream, can't we?

Themesets

While all the aforementioned goodies are cool, in and of themselves, what if all you need is a nice integrated set of Web page design elements? CorelWEB.GRAPHICS has you covered with its *Themesets*. Themesets help add consistency to Web page designs. There are 120 themesets, each with matching banners, horizontal dividers, round buttons, and square buttons, as shown by Figure 4-14. While you'll want to customize the banners (and perhaps the square buttons) by adding text in WEB.DRAW, you can use the other elements right out of the can. Inside the Themesets directory are five subdirectories:

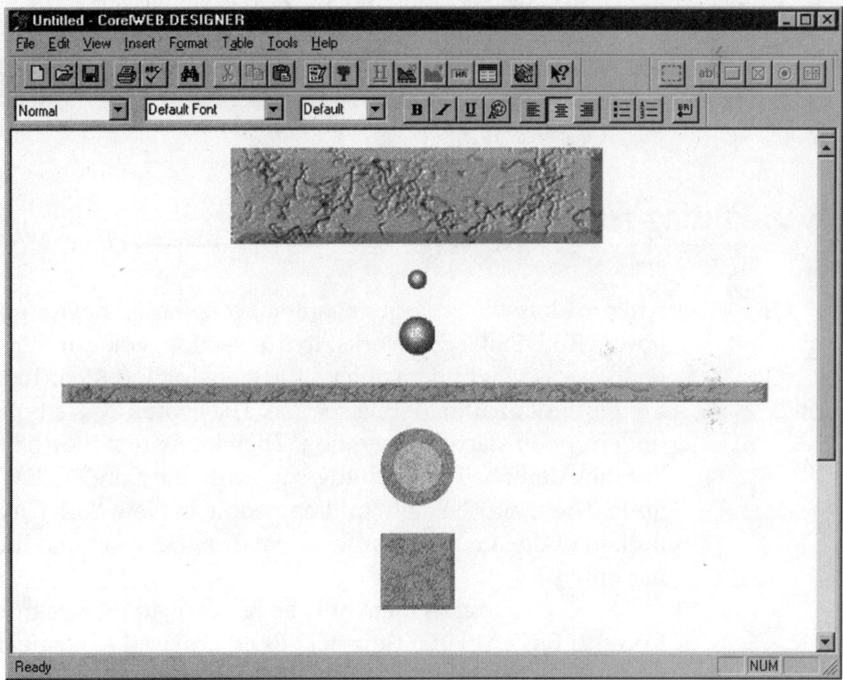

Figure 4-14: It's not modern art, folks, it's just themeset #104.

- Banners—120 JPEG images, 320 X 80 pixels
- Bullets—120 GIF images, in both 16- X 16- and 32- X 32-pixel variations

- Dividers—120 JPEG images, 608 X 16 pixels
- Rndbutt—120 GIF images, 64 X 64 pixels
- Sqabutt—42 JPEG images, 78 GIF images, 64 X 64 pixels

Has Anyone Seen My Bullets?

Although the banners, dividers, round buttons, and square buttons use a matched numbering scheme, unfortunately, the bullets do not. You may have to hunt and peck to find the correct bullet. Here's a hint: Drop the last digit before the file extension (i.e., sph0491.gif is the 32- X 32-pixel bullet for the 049 themeset). While this scheme helps to locate many bullets, you may have a tough time finding others. The best bet is to use WEB.GALLERY (or the associated HTML file) to visually browse through the entries.

Putting WEB.DESIGNER to Work

After reading the previous chapters, you should have a good feel for how WEB.DESIGNER works. In this section, you put that knowledge to good use as you build a quick little page for Too Rich, Too Thin, a mythical Manhattan dating service. The company is a typical, underfunded start-up operation. They know that they have to get online, but they don't have a big budget . . . only the CorelWEB.GRAPHICS Suite. There may be eight million people in New York City and one million of them may be professional designers, but Too Rich, Too Thin has only you.

This exercise takes them only so far; canned images from the CorelWEB.GRAPHICS Suite CD-ROM are used to create the page. In Chapter 10, you will use WEB.DRAW to customize the images and finish off the page.

Drag & Drop Images From WEB.GALLERY

To this point, we've mentioned CorelWEB.GALLERY only a handful of times. You're about to see why it's such a great convenience and a wonderful time saver. WEB.GALLERY provides a visual preview of your artwork, before you place it into WEB.DESIGNER, and lets you drag and drop the images to your Web pages. You don't even have to know the file names! When you drag and drop an image from the CD-ROM into WEB.DESIGNER, the program asks if you want to automatically copy the file into the server root, which saves untold time.

Let's start the exercise with WEB.DESIGNER running: Summon WEB.GALLERY from the toolbar.

1. Start a new page (File | New).

2. If the five-button Applications toolbar (look for the colorful Corel balloon) is not visible, click View | Applications Toolbar.

3. Click the WEB.GALLERY button (second from the right). If you're not sure which button is which, run your cursor over the buttons, and watch the status line or the fly-out definitions.

4. Select \albums\objects.gal from the Bookshelf drop-down menu, as shown in Figure 4-15, and click on the Open button (the button right next to the menu). A dialog box appears, informing you that the gallery file is read-only (since it's on the CD-ROM).

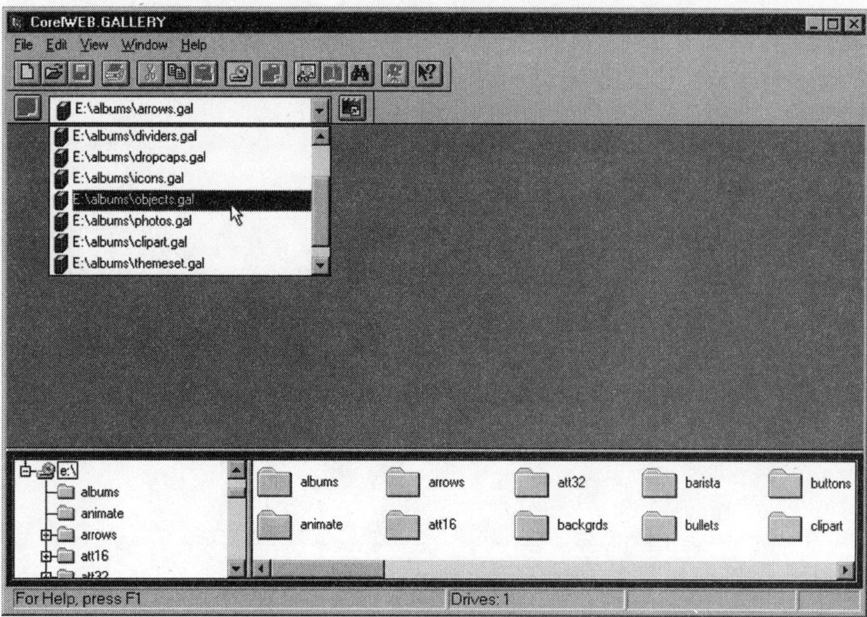

Figure 4-15: Make sure you're looking on the right Bookshelf!

5. Click on OK. Double-click on the 180 album to open it.

6. With the 180 (-pixel wide) album open, scroll over to the images named modela1.gif and modmala1.gif. Click on modela1.gif and then Ctrl+click modmala1.gif, so that both are selected. Click and drag the images into WEB.DESIGNER (even though the cursor may turn into a circle with a slash through it).

7. A dialog box appears, letting you know that the file is being copied into the server root directory. Click on OK.

8. The Copy File As dialog box appears. Click on OK (if you want to rename the file while importing it, do so before you click on OK).

9. Repeat the last two steps for the second image. As shown by Figure 4-16, our haughty-go-lucky singles are now on the page, beside a big blinking cursor. Soon they'll be bookending the header.

Figure 4-16: What a fun-lovin' pair!

10. Press Enter to move to the next line.

11. Use the drag-and-drop technique you just learned to bring the 90-pixel-wide lipstic2.gif file into WEB.DESIGNER, as shown in Figure 4-17. This image will make a dandy drop cap for the opening line of text.

12. Save the file (File | Save) as toorich.htm.

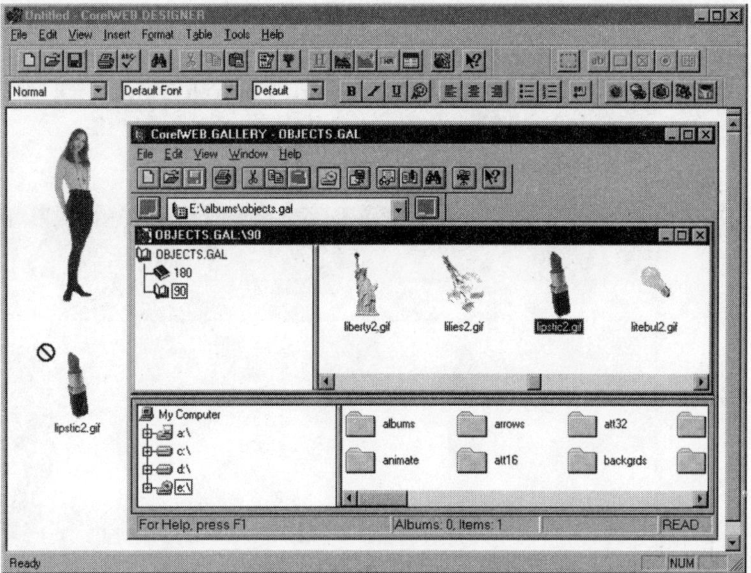

Figure 4-17: Never mind the slash icon . . . just drag and drop!

Text-Image Alignment

There are enough images on the page to begin working with some text. WEB.DESIGNER provides excellent controls over text-image alignment, via the Image Properties dialog box. The fastest way to summon this dialog box is to double-click on an image. Let's add a bit of text:

1. Click an insertion point between the lady and the gentleman. Type **Too Rich, Too Thin**. Assign it the Heading 1 format, and center the line.

2. Click an insertion point to the right of the lipstick. Type **f you're looking for just the right person, you've come to just the right place (as long as you fit our very demanding criteria). Before we accept you as a client, all we ask is that you pass a body fat percentage test and a stringent credit report. Don't worry about those poor old fat skeletons in your closet. We don't care how fat you were, or where your money came from (whether it be old, new, nouveau, or illicit).**

3. Highlight the text. Assign it a +1 size.

4. Double-click on the lipstick to summon the Image Properties dialog box. Set the alignment to left and click on OK. The page should appear as in Figure 4-18.

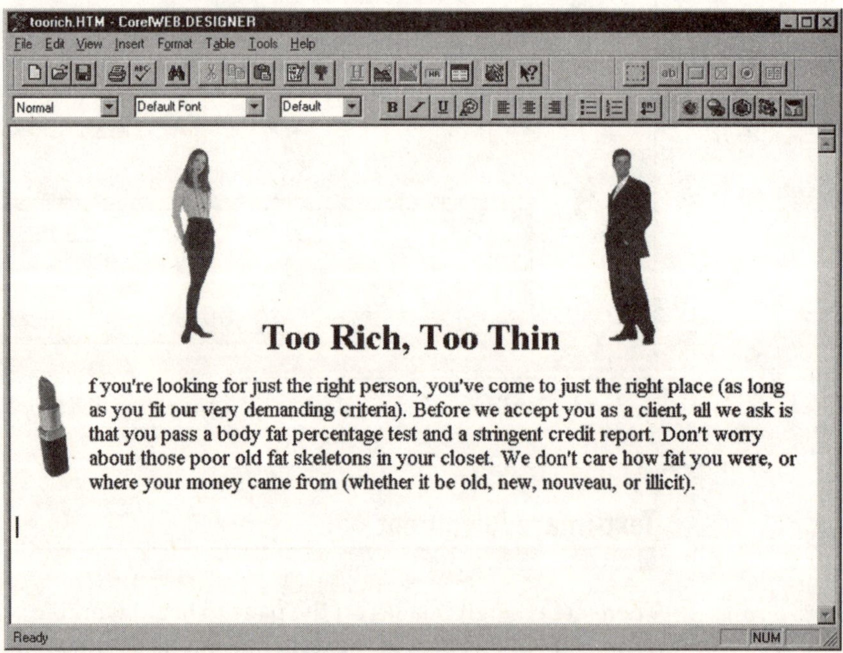

Figure 4-18: The page is starting to shape up. How about you?

While it would be nice to fiddle with the Too Rich, Too Thin headline, text alignment is problematic, since it is bookended between two inline images. Fear not . . . you'll do something special with it in Chapter 10.

Build a Simple Margin Table

Remember the wild, unconstrained Web page from the last chapter? The same phenomenon is happening here. You can whip this page into shape quickly by adding a simple margin table to constrain the width of the body copy to approximately 550 pixels. To add a one-column/one-row table:

1. Click an insertion point after the gentleman. Press Enter.

2. Click on the Insert Table button.

3. At the Table Properties dialog box:
   Set the number of rows and columns to 1.
   Set the width to 550 pixels.
   Set the alignment to center.
   Set the border size, cell padding, and cell spacing to 0.
   Click on OK.

4. Select the lipstick and the text. Cut and paste them into the new table.

5. Click an insertion point on the blank line between the table and our friends. Delete the blank line. The page should appear as in Figure 4-19. Save the file.

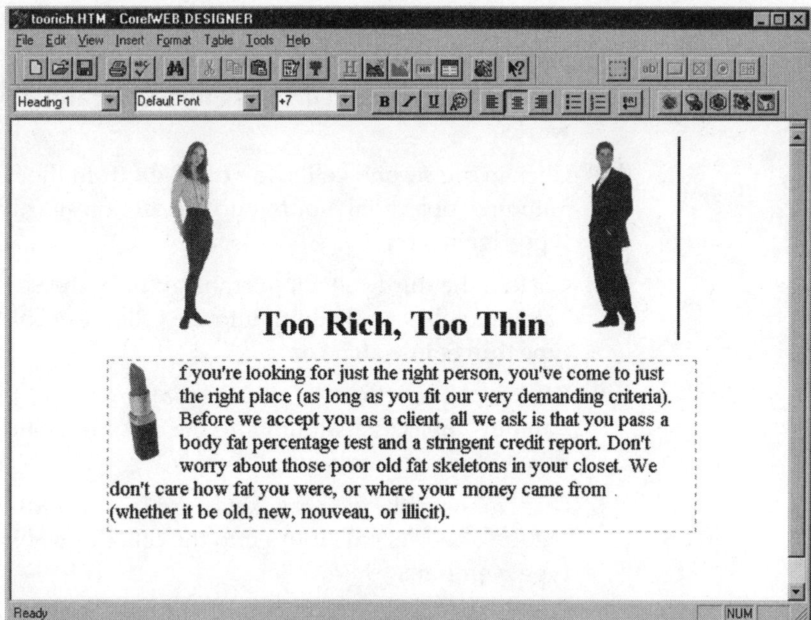

Figure 4-19: The narrower margin forces the text to wrap around the lipstick drop cap.

Build a Simple Five-Column Navbar Table

The one-column/one-row margin table is as simple as they get. In this section, a slightly more complex five-column/one-row table is used to build a snappy object navigation bar, as illustrated back in Figure 4-12. The columns space the descriptive text captions underneath the illustrative objects. In the next exercise, objects are dragged from WEB.GALLERY into specific table cells. To add the five-column navbar table:

1. Click an insertion point underneath the one-column table.

2. Click on the Insert Table button.

3. At the Table Properties dialog box:
    Set the number of rows to 1.
    Set the number of columns to 5.
    Set the width to 550 pixels.
    Set the alignment to center.
    Set the border size, cell padding, and cell spacing to 0.
    Click on OK.

4. Delete the extra line between the two tables.

5. Click in the first cell of the five-column table. This will enable you to drag the first object directly into the cell.

6. Click on the WEB.GALLERY button on the Application toolbar. Drag nutbolt2.gif from the 90-pixel-wide \albums\object.gal album into the first cell. Press Shift+Enter and type **how it works**.

7. Click in the second cell. Drag dice2.gif from the 90-pixel-wide \albums\object.gal album into the cell. Press Shift+Enter and type **give it a try**.

8. Click in the third cell. Drag crab2.gif from the 90-pixel-wide \albums\object.gal album into the cell. Press Shift+Enter and type **things to watch for**.

9. Click in the fourth cell. Drag tv2.gif from the 90-pixel-wide \albums\object.gal album into the cell. Press Shift+Enter and type **video personals**.

10. Click in the fifth cell. Drag keyb2.gif from the 90-pixel-wide \albums\object.gal album into the cell. Press Shift+Enter and type **members**.

11. To horizontally center and bottom-align the contents of each cell, click an insertion point in each cell and click on Table|Cell Properties. In the Cell Properties dialog box, set the minimum width to 20 percent, the Horizontal Alignment to center, and the Vertical Alignment to bottom. If you feel daring, you can use the HTML source mode to cut and paste the code rather than repeatedly accessing the Cell Properties dialog box. Replace the default <TD ALIGN="LEFT" VALIGN="TOP">code with <TD ALIGN="CENTER" VALIGN="BOTTOM" WIDTH="20%">.

12. Select the entire table. It's time to size the text navigation bar. Set the font size to –2. When you're done, the page should appear as in Figure 4-20. Save the file.

Figure 4-20: Not too shabby for a few minutes work, eh?

Setting Font Face

We have one more task to accomplish before we put this project away until the next part of the book. WEB.DESIGNER's Formatting toolbar provides the rudimentary means to assign a specific type face, via the FONT FACE command (supported by Netscape Navigator and Microsoft Internet Explorer versions 3 and newer). Fonts are a thorny issue, from computer to computer and from platform to platform. The crux of the problem is that one never knows what fonts might be loaded at the browser. This severely limits typographical choices. In fact, it could be considered a throwback to the early days of both the automotive industry and the desktop publishing revolution.

When asked what colors were available on the Ford Model T, at the dawn of the age of the assembly line, Henry Ford's notorious reply was "any color—so long as it's black." Likewise, with the advent of the Apple LaserWriter in 1984, you could have any font you wanted, as long as it was Times Roman or Helvetica. FONT FACE presents a similar dilemma for Web publishers. While FONT FACE allows you to specify a typeface, as well as selected alternates, you can't hope that your visitors will have more than a sans serif (Helvetica or Arial) and a serif font (Times, Times Roman, or Times New Roman).

If you want to take the leap and specify a specific typeface, all you need to do is highlight the text and select the typeface from WEB.DESIGNER's Formatting toolbar. Don't waste your time specifying anything other than these basic typefaces. And to be safe, you should go into HTML source mode and add an alternate face (or two) to the command. Specifying Bernhard Fashion and Futura Light, as shown in Figure 4-21, is a private act of typographical hara-kiri . . . only you will get to witness its beauty.

Eventually, many fonts will be portable and will travel along with electronic documents. The two most popular technologies that allow that to happen today are Adobe Acrobat and Macromedia's Shockwave for FreeHand. And once the kinks are worked out, Corel's Barista Java may hold the same promise.

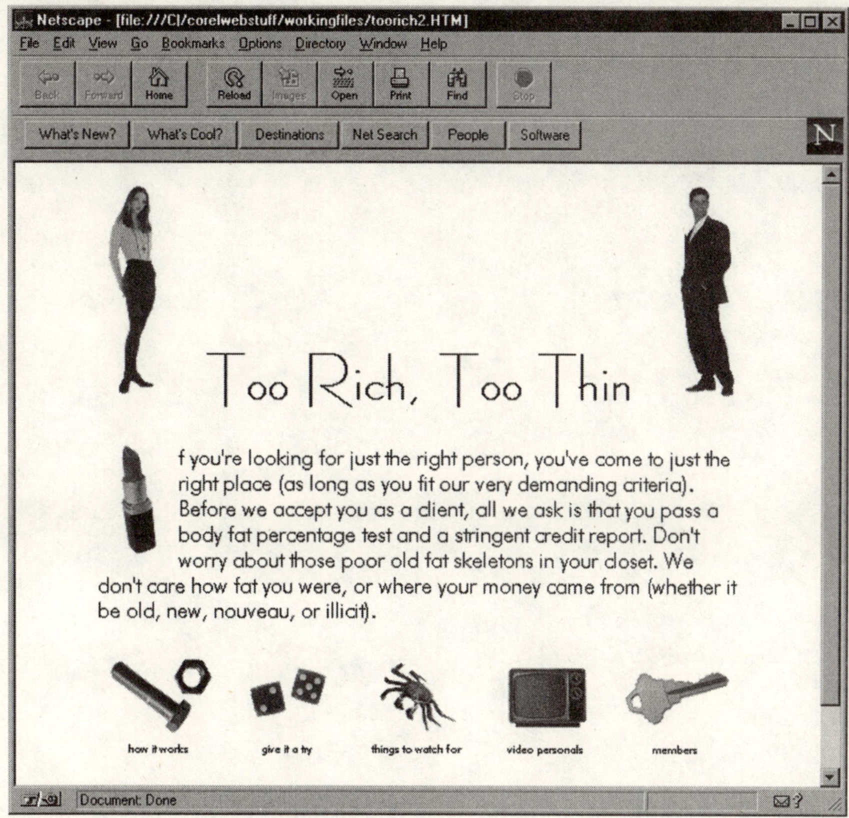

Figure 4-21: If you want to use a specific font on a Web page, the FONT FACE command will get you only so far.

Moving On

In this chapter you really got rolling with WEB.DESIGNER. We covered the importance of building a working directory structure and took a quick peek at the images you can use to create your first Web site quickly. In the Too Rich, Too Thin exercise, you learned how WEB.GALLERY can help to make your page-building sessions a more pleasant and productive experience.

The next chapter focuses on planning your Web site while discussing 13 problems commonly encountered by site developers.

5

Planning Your Web Site

The task of building a Web site can be a trivial endeavor or a monumental undertaking, and your chores can fall anywhere in between. Before you build a single page, sit down with the site sponsors and hash out what they need the site to do. What they want to accomplish and how they want to accomplish it will not always jibe.

Here's a rough outline of the initial planning stages:

- Nail down the sponsor's goals and thoughts on approach.

- Begin to assemble a rough idea of how to go about your design.

- With the site's mission in focus, think about what's needed to get the job done, considering both the creative (how it looks and feels) and logistical (how it works) aspects of the site.

- Determine what resources you have at hand and what may have to be obtained or outsourced. The clip art and fonts contained in the CorelWEB.GRAPHICS Suite will not always fit your design scheme.

- Develop a schedule and budget that both include a healthy fudge factor.

Target Your Audience

Effective Web site designers understand the wants and needs of their audience. First you capture the interest of your audience. Then you must deliver what they need (which isn't always, for your purposes, exactly what they *think* they want) in an engaging and orderly manner. Balancing the needs of the audience and the site sponsor can be tricky. Web sites, for the most part, are not altruistic endeavors . . . no matter how warm and fuzzy they make the visitor feel.

Content Is King

The first thing to understand in planning your Web site is that *content is king.* People come to your site in search of the information it provides, not for its great design. They might come back to an attractive but empty site once to show a friend how cool it looks, but they will come back to an informative site repeatedly. In the Web world, as throughout the entire Internet, steak matters far more than sizzle.

Your first task is to determine what information your audience is looking for. You must think like them and look coldly at your site from their perspective. Then you must take stock of the resources at your disposal and figure how you can use them to provide the content your audience demands.

Your organization—large corporation or small hobby group—possesses a lot of information. This information may be on paper, on computer disks, on videotape, or only in the minds of you and your cohorts. The choice of information to go up on your site is dictated by both supply and demand. If the information your audience demands exists in another form, repackage it. If the needed information doesn't exist in usable form, create it. If you can't create it for whatever reason, set up a hyperlink (as you learned back in Chapter 1) to another Web site that has it.

When you embark upon your site-building journey, try not to start with a predetermined design in mind. Stay focused on the information your audience needs, not on how you think your site should look. This is not to say that design is irrelevant to the success of your site. On the contrary, it has a great deal to do with its success. The role of the designer is to allow the Web site visitor to access quickly and easily the information a Web site provides. A clear, concise design enables visitors to get at the good stuff with just a few clicks of a mouse. A complex, dense design boggles the user's mind and leads to frustration. However, the design of your Web site—and the pages contained therein—is secondary to and dependent upon the content. Like the best designs of any type, the form of your Web site should follow its function.

Design Your Site Around Its Content

Your responsibility as a designer is akin to that of an architect. You must design the overall layout of your Web site so that visitors can find what they need quickly. When a visitor lands at your front door, you want to greet him or her warmly and provide a floor plan of your site. Don't let the first doors your visitors encounter be those leading to closets, basements, or boiler rooms.

If your most important content is in the kitchen, make sure all visitors can get there immediately from your front door. You must not expect your Web site guests to click happily away until they find what they're looking for. Since many cyberspace explorers aren't sure what they're looking for, you must provide a place where they can find *everything*.

Think about the grand old department stores. (If you've never had the pleasure of experiencing one, check out the movies *Miracle on 34th Street* or the Marx Brothers in *Big Store*.) At the elevator entrance, a friendly operator greeted shoppers and announced what they would find on each floor. Your Web site should have a central lobby, with self-service escalators to specific departments for the folks who already know where they're headed. You also should design an elevator with a friendly attendant to help other visitors quickly locate what they seek.

Provide a Site Map

An effective *site map* provides the same level of assistance as a friendly elevator attendant. A good site map enables viewers to find the information they seek at a glance.

Developing a site map is a good way to optimize the effectiveness of your Web site. There are a number of approaches to displaying a site map, but one key is to provide both graphic and text routes through your site. Figures 5-1 and 5-2 show a route to allow fast site access for both high- and low-bandwidth browsers. Those lucky folks who can download the elevator panel image map quickly through a corporate network will be pleased with the fun graphics. And those with slow modem connections should be satisfied with the slim and trim linear text directory. If this all sounds a little confusing, don't worry. We'll delve further into the concepts of browsers and bandwidth later in this chapter.

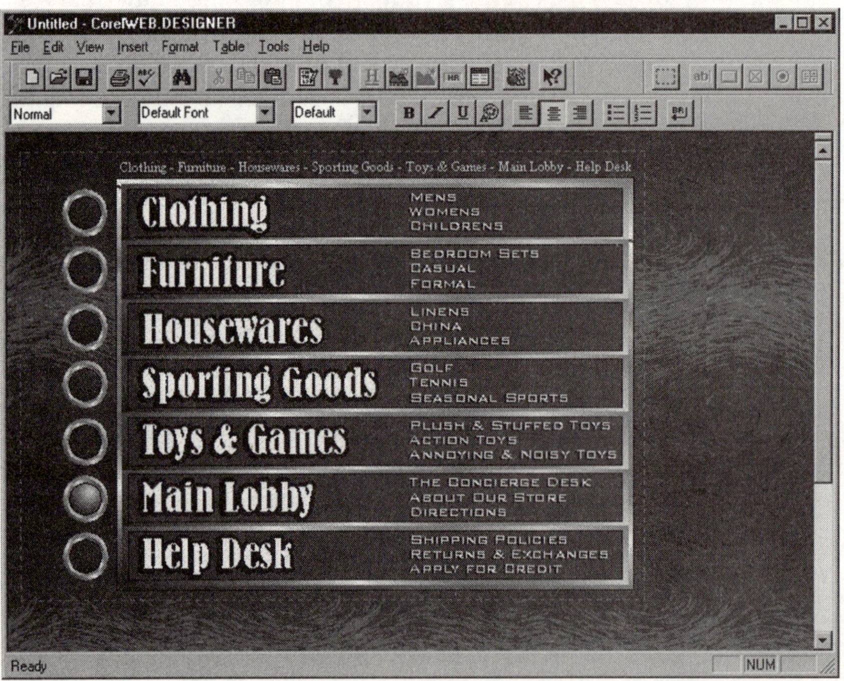

Figure 5-1: Elevator going up!

solving these common design problems. As you read along, you'll quickly notice that many of the solutions are similar. Solving one design problem often helps solve another. Take heed of this advice, and it will take care of you.

It's Too Darn Slow

This first common problem shouldn't be a surprise to anyone with more than 15 minutes exposure to the Web. It's one of the unfortunate realities of the Internet at present. Nevertheless, you always must strive to make your pages as fast as possible.

Design for the Bandwidth

Bandwidth is one of the Web buzzwords you often hear bandied about. "We don't have enough bandwidth to implement that solution" or "With a T3 line, we have all the bandwidth we need" are two hypothetical examples of how the word might be used by propellerheads. The term refers to the size of the *pipe* (capacity of the Internet hookup) being used on a Web site or browser. The more bandwidth you have, the happier you'll be, on either the server or the client side. Of course, the bigger the pipe, the bigger the price, too. For most folks, bandwidth is measured in kilobits per second (kbps). Generally, only corporate networks measure bandwidth in megabits per second (mbps).

Good Web designers always remember that the bandwidth they have at their disposal is often not the same their audience has. Your Web site may be sitting on the fastest line west of the Pecos, but it won't matter if your audience is dialing in on slow 14.4 and 28.8 modems. Bandwidth is always limited by the smallest "diameter" of inline pipe.

ISDN—What Does it Mean?

The Integrated Digital Services Network, allows you to cram a lot more data down your copper phone line, albeit at a significantly higher cost. It's no cakewalk to set up, either. You'll need to trash your trusty modem in favor of a new ISDN box or board, and make sure that your Internet Service Provider offers the service.

This is a perfect case for knowing your audience. If you are relatively certain that your target market will be coming to your site via fast T1 lines or ISDN, you can create a far more robust environment. Your graphics can be larger, and you can use such goodies as gargantuan Shockwave animations and pipe-eating QuickTime movies without the fear of bogging down. Very few folks have fast lines running to their homes, but large corporate networks typically are hooked up via T1 lines or better. Table 5-1 indicates common transmission speeds from modems to the *superfast* T3. As you can see, a double line ISDN hookup will move data at a rate better than four times the speed of a conventional 28.8 modem, and close to nine times the speed of a 14.4 modem.

Device	Speed
Modem	14.4 kbps
	28.8 kbps
	33.6 kbps
	55.6 kbps
ISDN single line	64 kbps
ISDN double line	128 kbps
DirecPC satellite dish	400 kbps
T1	1.5 mbps
T3	45 mbps

Table 5-1: Common transmission speeds.

As you can see from Table 5-1, the pipe doesn't have to be a physical wire, copper or fiber. Hughes Electronics, the General Motors division responsible for the little DirecTV home television satellite dish, has come up with a wonderful scheme to hook your computer up to the Internet via satellite. Their DirecPC package consists of a satellite dish and expansion card that combine to give you a whopping 400 kbps of throughput. It's the perfect accessory for your slopeside ski chalet, as long as you have a good clear shot to the southern sky (where the DirecPC satellites hang out). DirecPC is a hybrid system. While it downloads data through the dish at 400 kbps, requests are made to the network through a conventional modem (at conventional modem speeds).

Eventually, we'll live in a totally connected world, where we all have really fast lines coming into our homes and business, be they from the telephone company, from the cable company, or through satellite services. Once that high-tech day comes, we won't have to worry about the restrictions of limited bandwidth. Already the faster ISDN service is a residential reality in many parts of the country.

Enough Technical Nonsense; What Does It All Mean?

Easy. You always must strive to keep your pages as fast as possible. If you know that your audience is coming to you at 14.4, don't try to cram too much down the pipe. It's a common practice to offer two versions of a page, one for high-bandwidth browsers and one for our less-fortunate low-bandwidth compatriots.

Here are several ways to make your Web site move along nice and fast:

Keep your GIFs (Graphics Interchange Format files) and JPEGs (Joint Photographic Experts Group files) as small as possible.

You can easily keep graphics files small by using the lowest practical number of indexed colors in your images. The fewer the number of colors, the smaller the file. Experiment with your image editor to get the right balance between file size and appearance.

Figure 5-3 displays the difference in appearance when a button is saved with a variety of color palettes, and Table 5-2 shows file sizes. They range from 883 bytes at 3 bits per pixel to 3331 bytes at 8 bits per pixel. It's up to the Web page designer to determine where trade-offs should be made—in this case, at 1629 bytes. A 5-bits-per-pixel setting provides the best compromise of file size to image quality. Using 6 bits per pixel and higher didn't improve the image quality enough to justify increasing the file size. Using less than 5 bits per pixel lowered the image quality too far. For more details on optimizing Web graphics, be sure to check out Chapter 10.

Figure 5-3: The smaller the color palette, the smaller the GIF file, but the trade-off is in image quality.

Palette	File Size
8 bits per pixel	3331 bytes
7 bits per pixel	2755 bytes
6 bits per pixel	2143 bytes
5 bits per pixel	1629 bytes
4 bits per pixel	1213 bytes
3 bits per pixel	883 bytes

Table 5-2: Color palette size vs. file size.

When possible, consider using a composite button bar rather than individual buttons.

The more separate images on a Web page, the longer it takes to download. This has to do with the overhead that each graphic file carries. The three small individual 5-bits-per-pixel buttons shown in Figure 5-4 weigh in at 1597, 1629, and 1564 bytes, respectively, and total 4790. The composite button bar saves some space at 4004 bytes. While this doesn't sound like a dramatic savings, it adds up. When you start working with beefier files, it can make a substantial difference. Chapter 8 demonstrates how easy it is to create a composite button bar.

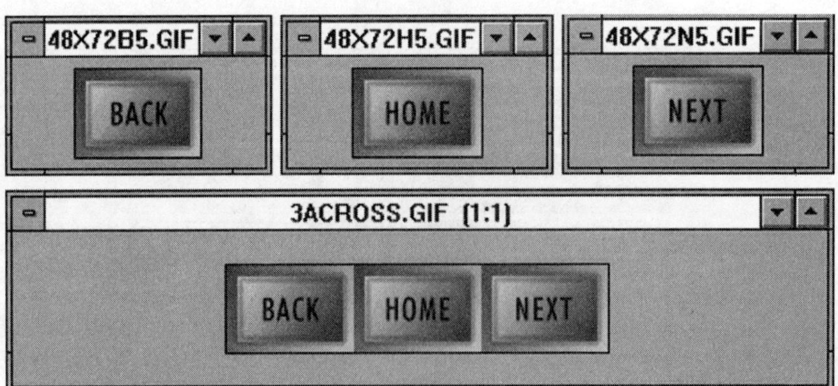

Figure 5-4: A composite button bar can save download time.

Use a repetitive button bar (or individual buttons that are identical) from page to page.

Once the browser downloads the button bar or individual button, it *caches* it (stores it in memory) and doesn't have to download it on subsequent pages. If the button bar calls a different file on each page, slower performance results. The mythical Pete's Aquatic Pets page, shown in Figure 5-5, uses a repetitive button bar that is downloaded only once. As visitors jump from page to page, the pointer moves from icon to icon through the use of a nifty little table.

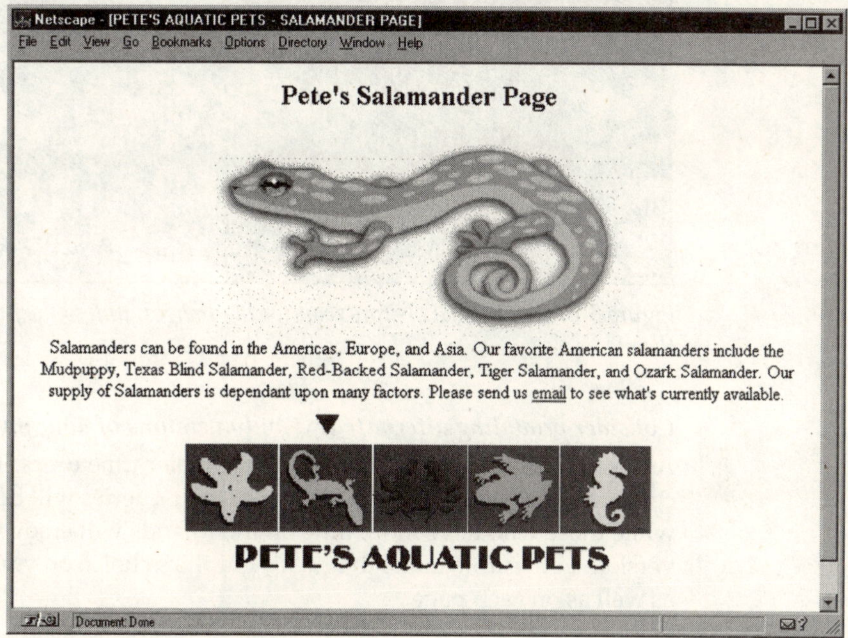

Figure 5-5: As you jump from page to page on the Pete's Aquatic Pets Web site, only the pointer moves.

Use thumbnail images and warn users about the file size of large graphics.

In other words, give folks a chance to at least think twice before they commit to downloading a great big graphic file. Figure 5-6 shows a common example of when and how you might use a thumbnail.

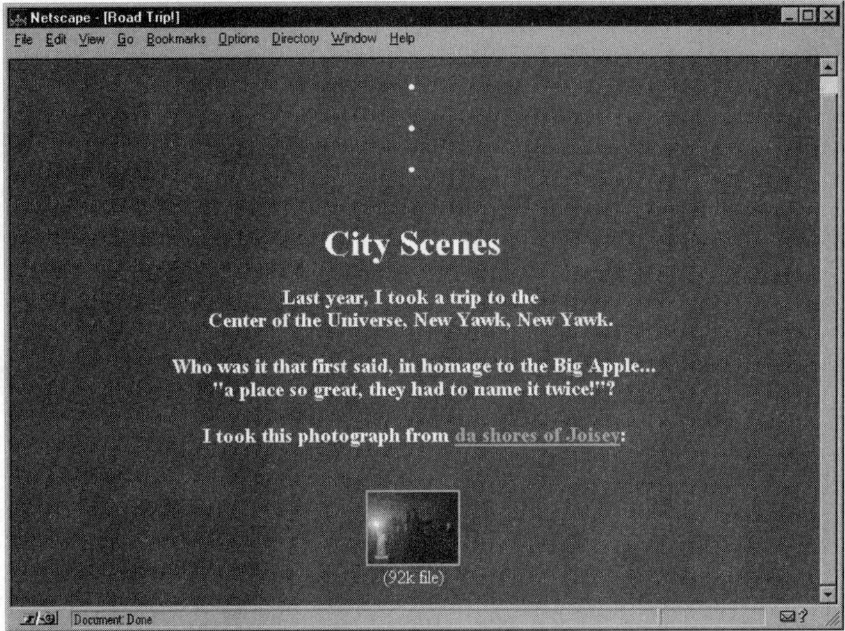

Figure 5-6: Don't make visitors wait for big images, unless they've asked for them!

Consider providing alternate text-only versions of your pages.

As creative as they are, graphics still are major time users. Those who come to your site for a quick answer to their queries will be grateful, while those who have more time on their hands will enjoy the graphics version. Let visitors make their text/graphics choice on your front page, as well as on each page.

Don't create huge text pages.

Instead, break large pages up into smaller chunks. Text pages that take what seems like a week and a half to load are just as bad as pages crammed full of graphics. Try to keep your text files under 40 kilobytes (K) or so.

Make sure you have a big enough pipe run to your server.

Look into upgrading your line if you see a high enough hit rate to justify the expenditure. The added costs are akin to making a larger press run on a printed piece. If you expect a large number of visitors, make sure that you have enough bandwidth to handle the crowd. Your systems administrator should be able to provide you with options and associated costs.

Check to see if your server is getting bogged down with requests.

If it is, find out why. If there are other busy sites running on the same server, your site's performance may suffer. Once again, talk these issues over with your systems administrator to see if there are ways to improve your site's performance without dropping a huge chunk of change to switch servers.

Consider adding a graphics server.

If your site is heavy on graphics and is running on a WebStar server, investigate the possibility of adding a Maxum RushHour graphics server. RushHour uses RAM caching to greatly accelerate site performance.

It's Hard to Read

Gee, you mean you can't read mauve type over a seafoam plaid flannel-textured background? So much of good site design is so obvious, it's amazing how some folks never give it a second thought. The bottom line is that if your audience can't read what you've got to say, you've failed in your role as a designer. Strive to make things visually interesting, not illegible. Figure 5-7 illustrates the Magnificently Obscure Page, which may not be all that magnificent but certainly is obscure. You'll have a tough time reading the text on this page without reverting to the source code.

Figure 5-7: You mean to say that you can't read this? Good Web design means site visitors can read what you have to say.

Here are some strategies to ensure that your Web site visitors actually can see what you've designed:

Lighten up your backgrounds, and choose your text colors carefully.
Stay away from heavy-handed textures and steer toward more mono-chromatic motifs. Make sure that there is enough contrast between the background pattern or color and the text color. When in doubt, always choose a lighter background. This book's Companion CD-ROM contains a number of conservative predefined color schemes that have been tweaked for maximum readability. In addition, a good number of the 3,000 textured backgrounds on the CD-ROM also have been designed with readability in mind. But fear not, zany texture aficionados, there are plenty of wacky textures there, as well!

Want to Learn More About Color?

Check out Gary Priester's *Looking Good in Color* (Ventana, 1995). It's a great reference guide. Although the book is subtitled *The Desktop Publisher's Design Guide*, most of the principles apply to online design, as well.

Use a larger text size with the <FONT SIZE="X"> command.

You don't have to resign yourself to tiny body text! WEB.DESIGNER makes it easy to ratchet your type size up with the Font Size menu. Just select and click. Figure 5-8 shows how different font sizes display within Netscape Navigator.

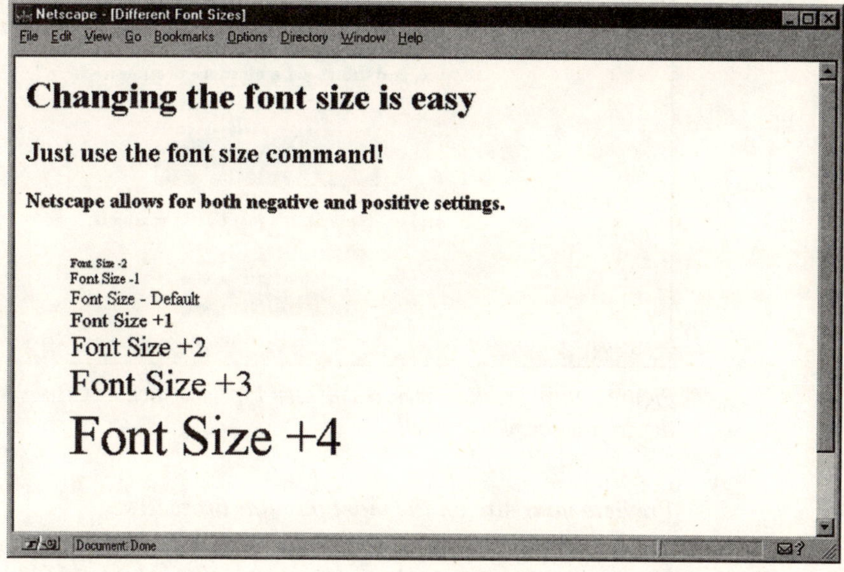

Figure 5-8: Use a larger font size when appropriate.

Use typefaces that hold up under low resolution.

When creating text graphics, such as buttons and click bars, stay away from very fine serifs and frilly faces. Stick with fonts that were designed for onscreen viewing. Figure 5-9 shows the differences between City Medium, a slab serif face, and Snell Bold, a fine script face at different point sizes. Snell actually holds up pretty well for a script!

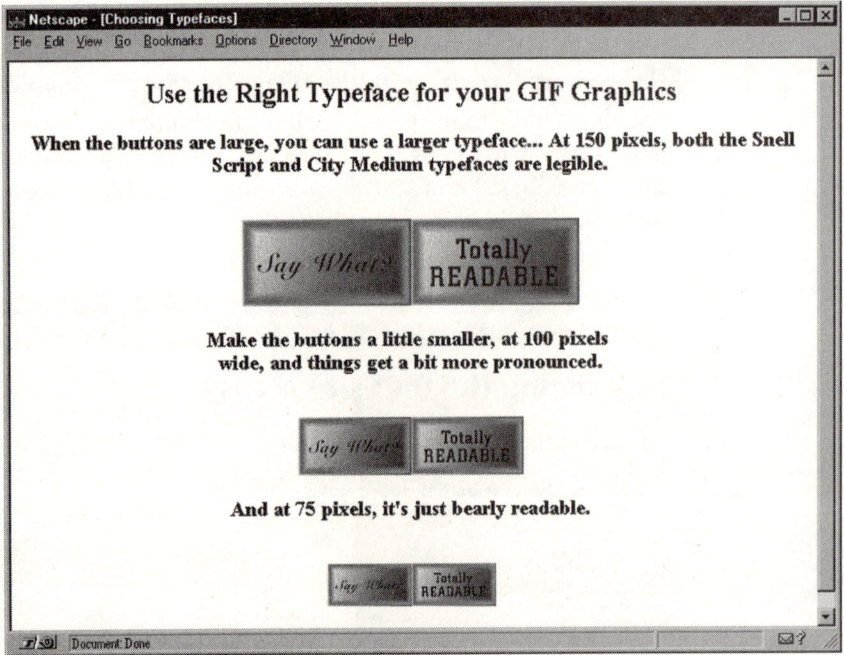

Figure 5-9: In smaller sizes, a slab serif typeface such as City will hold up better than a fine script like Snell.

Preview your site on the most popular browsers.

Take a trip to your site with Netscape Navigator, Mosaic, and Microsoft's Internet Explorer to see how it looks on each of these browsers. If you can, use the most current version of each browser, along with a previous release. Watch closely for weird things that may happen with text wraps and graphics.

Assign alternate text (ALT) tags to your inline graphics with WEB.DESIGNER's Image Properties dialog box.

This will allow users to "see" what the graphic is, even if they've turned graphics off in their browser. If the ALT description is of interest, they always can reload the page with graphics.

It's Just Plain Ugly

This Web site design problem often goes hand in hand with hard-to-read text, although it's possible to have a highly legible but very ugly site. If beauty is in the eye of the browser, consider consulting your local version of Snow White's mirror, by asking. "Who has the fairest Web site?" To which it should reply: "You have the fairest Web site of them all." If you can't get your mirror to tell you truthfully (or at least lie to you as it did to the Evil Queen), you're just going to have to roll up your sleeves, clean up your Web site, and make it truly gorgeous.

The Web page shown in Figure 5-10 displays a number of design problems that turn it into a rather unpleasant sight, even though you *can* read its bilious green text over its purple plaid background. Note the bad drop shadow (botched transparency) and unsuitable border on the headline graphic.

Figure 5-10: Well, it could have been even uglier!

Sure, WEB.DESIGNER makes it easy to crank out your own Web pages, but it doesn't turn you into an award-winning designer. If you are seriously design-challenged, give thought to hiring an experienced designer. Or at least take the advice of one. After the design of your Web site is set, you can take over the maintenance. Meanwhile, here are some helpful tips:

Start with an integrated template.

Use a template that provides matching (or complementary) bullets, bars, and accents. An integrated template makes it easy to knock out a polished site without spending a ton of time or cash. You'll find a nice selection of these on this book's Companion CD-ROM, as well as on the Corel WEB.GRAPHICS official release CD-ROM.

Remember that less is more.

Hideous backgrounds are to blame for the most offensive pages. Think twice about using that tartan plaid or busy floral print!

Use proven color schemes for backgrounds, graphics, and text.

If you're having trouble putting together a color scheme, there are a number of ways to jump-start the process. One sneaky idea is to take a trip to your local paint and home decorating store. Peruse their selection of paint chips. Often, they have chip sheets that illustrate a variety of color schemes. Take a few chip sheets back to your studio and try matching some of the combinations to see what you get. Just the thing for that Victorian, Southwestern, or Colonial look!

The Navigational System Is Confusing

Watch out! If your Web site visitors can't figure out where things are and can't get where they want to go, they'll leave your site faster than you can say, "Please don't leave! You just got here!" It's time to look at how you can make your navigational system more navigable! Nothing, after all, beats a good set of directions (Figure 5-11).

The Issaquah Online Web site makes it a snap to find your way. The site, developed by Blue World Communications, is friendly and easy to get around in. When visitors land at the Issaquah Online front door, they immediately are presented with a whimsical and graphical site image map, along with access to the site index and a handy search feature.

Figure 5-11: You can get there from here. The Issaquah Online Web site makes it easy with a solid set of directions for the visitor.

Here are some tried-and-true ways to help ensure that your Web site visitors find their way around your cyberplace with ease:

Use a consistent navigational interface.

Don't throw your visitors any spitballs. After they've plowed through a number of your pages, you've established a pattern in their minds. You don't want to undo it! It's important to establish a consistent navigational interface and maintain continuity. Avoid changing your icons midstream, and don't mix your graphical metaphors. The Issaquah Online Web site index (as shown in Figure 5-12) uses a vertical row of icons to great effect.

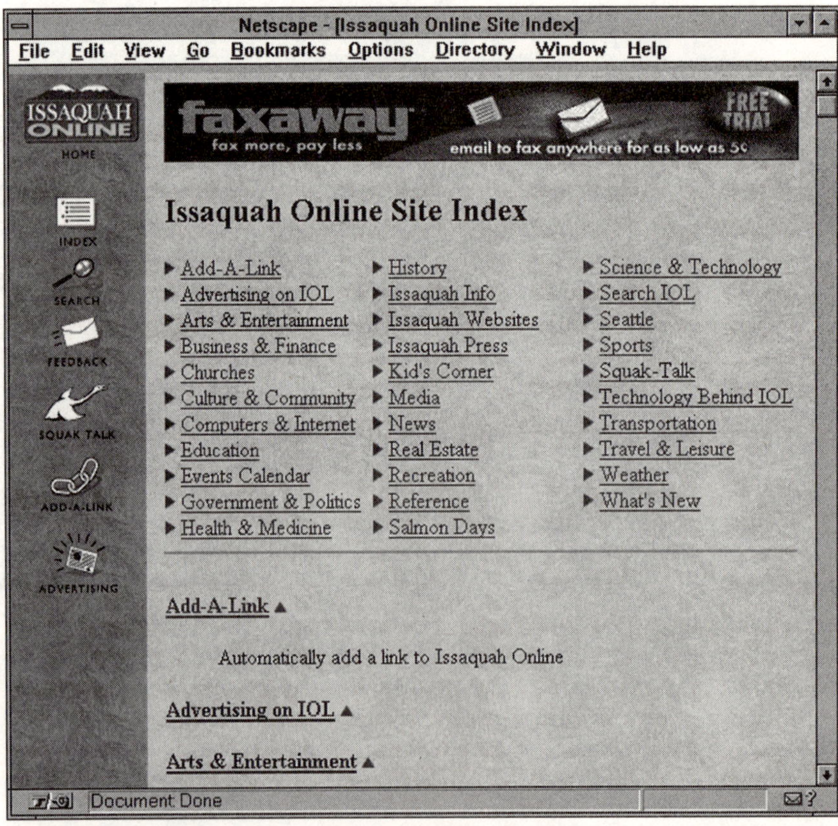

Figure 5-12: The Issaquah Online Web site index provides total access, while maintaining a consistent interface.

Always use a text navigation bar.

Use this navigation bar in addition to a graphic navigational interface. Some folks like to cruise the Web at high speed, with graphics turned off. If you have only image map navigation, you'll incur their wrath.

Stay simple, straightforward, and obvious.

Don't be seduced by way cool, overly complicated schemes. Navigation must be instantly comprehensible. Your visitors shouldn't have to figure out how to cruise your site.

It Was Designed for a Specific Browser

There are browsers other than Netscape Navigator in cyberspace. While you don't want (or need) to build a version for each browser, it's polite to have both a high- and a low-bandwidth track.

Let Them Know

If you're using Java or Shockwave animations within your Web site, be sure to let visitors know right away (just in case they're using an older browser or don't have the Shockwave plug-in). Be a courteous Web designer: Post a notice on the front door.

Here are some tips for accommodating your—perhaps browser-impaired—Web site visitors who don't happen to be using Netscape:

Preview your site on a number of platforms.

If you have the opportunity, try accessing your site from both Windows and Macintosh platforms. You'll be amazed at the difference between machines, even when running the same software on similar platforms. There are many video-related variables that will affect how your site looks.

Create a text-only version of your site.

This task might not take all that much time, but it's one of the most considerate and most important things you as a Web designer can do. Remember to use WEB.DESIGNER's Image Properties dialog box palette to label your images with an alternate text field, as mentioned earlier.

Put a Netscape Now! button on your front page!

If you've designed your site to be viewed exclusively with Netscape Navigator (or another specific browser, such as Microsoft's Internet Explorer), make it as easy as possible for the browser-impaired visitor to get a copy. Adding the Netscape Now! button is a convenience for our less-fortunate Web-browsing friends. If your site design includes features such as tables, font face commands and Java, folks using lesser browsers will never see your hard work.

It Doesn't Feel Like One Site

You don't want to boggle the minds of your Web site visitors; the Web is confusing enough as it is. As your visitors jump from one page to another, you want them to feel as if they're in the same warm fuzzy place.

Here are some easy strategies for bringing consistency to your Web site:

Keep the navigational interface consistent.

A consistent navigational interface will help unify the look and feel of your site. You don't want your visitors to have to figure out a different set of controls on each page—or even in each section—of your site.

Use your logo.

One of the easiest ways to enhance continuity is to carry a theme or motif throughout your entire Web site. If you have a nice-looking company logo, for instance, use it once on every page, if you can do so discreetly. Take a look back at the Issaquah Online pages illustrated in Figures 5-11 and 5-12 for a great example. Reuse common design elements.

You'll add to the site's continuity by reusing elements such as buttons and click bars. This will help to speed up your site, too, because the browser will have to download the graphic only once. The Issaquah Online Web site effectively implements this strategy with its vertical button bar.

Try not to vary backgrounds too widely.

Use the same background pattern or make slight variations. Change backgrounds only when you have a really good reason to do so, such as wanting to differentiate between sections of your site. An added benefit of using the same background pattern file is that it speeds up your pages, as does reusing buttons and click bars.

Use the title bar to your best advantage.

If someone bookmarks your page, you want your site and page name there. This is often overlooked and is totally unobtrusive. Page titles are picked up and used by the search engines and are an essential way to differentiate your pages. Use WEB.DESIGNER's Page Properties dialog box to perform this function.

It's Tough to Find

Hey, it's great that you've built an awesome site, but just building it doesn't mean that you'll instantly attract an audience. The Web isn't a field of dreams (except for those IPO millionaires, like the Mozillanaughts and Yahooligans we all know, love, and are envious of): If you build it, they won't come unless they know you're out there. There are a number of ways to get your site on the map, without resorting to hucksterism. See Figure 5-13.

Figure 5-13: Let everyone know where you can be found.

Promoting Your Page

For some great information on how to bring in the crowds, check out "How to Publicize Your Web Page" on Oregon State University's Web server at <http://www.orst.edu/aw/stygui/propag.htm>.

Your site will gain attention as you begin adding your Web site address (Uniform Resource Locator—URL) to everything your organization puts out: letterheads, envelopes, business cards, print advertisements (including magazine, newspaper, and yellow page ads), marketing collaterals, promotional trinkets, T-shirts, and other goodies. But don't make the address the central focus; it's just part of your contact information, like your telephone and fax numbers.

Name Your Domain

A named domain, like *mycompanynamehere.com* helps set your Web site apart. Expect to spend fifty bucks to register and fifty more on an annual basis to maintain the name. You can register the name with InterNIC (the regulatory agency) yourself, or your Internet service provider (ISP) should be able to do it for you. Expect to drop another fifty for the convenience of having your ISP do the legwork. Don't let your ISP get away with charging an exorbitant rate for the privilege of putting your named domain on their servers. Check out <http://rs.internic.net/domain-info/faq.html> for InterNIC frequently asked questions (FAQs).

It helps to get a Web site address that makes sense since most people don't enjoy typing in a URL that's as long as a football field and spells nothing. If you have the opportunity to register a suitable domain name, do so immediately. The domains won't last forever, and there could be a slew of organizations that need or want to use the same name you do.

Register With the Search Engines

The first way your audience will find your Web site is through a *search engine*. Search engines are Web sites that have been designed to catalog the contents of the entire World Wide Web. They exist because they fulfill the needs of the Web community, providing an organized way to use this wonderful resource, which draws millions of information-hungry visitors every day. In many cases, advertising revenue keeps the search engines up and running. Those little advertising banners displayed at the top and sometimes in the middle of search engine pages are easy to endure when you realize the great service they afford. Certain search engines are not financed solely through advertising revenue, however. Some charge for their searches and offer subscription plans for enhanced levels of service.

Want to Find Out Who's Linked to Your Site?

If your Web server can produce a list of referring URLs, you can identify where your visitors are finding out about your Web site. If you don't have the ability to check your site stats, however, you always can use the search engines. Just type in your Web site's name and submit the inquiry. The search engine will cough up a list of other Web sites that mention your site. Just follow these links to see what they have to say about you!

Search engines use *automated robots* to crawl around the Web on a nightly basis; they check for new pages in cyberspace and gather updated information on pages that have been cataloged already. These software robots often are referred to as spiders, crawlers, or worms. One of the busiest spiders is Digital's Scooter, which scurries from site to site, gathering up information for Digital's high-powered Alta Vista database. The information is distilled and displayed at no cost to the user.

Here's a short list of the most popular Internet search engines, along with their URLs. Each has a different approach to organizing and delivering their information. If you can't find what you're looking for on one site, keep jumping until you do!

Alta Vista	http://altavista.digital.com
CERN	http://www.w3.org/pub/DataSources/WWW/Servers.html
The Electric Library	http://www.elibrary.com
Excite	http://www.excite.com
Hot Bot	http://www.hotbot.com
Infoseek	http://www.infoseek.com
Inktomi	http://inktomi.berkeley.edu/
Lycos	http://www.lycos.com
Magellan	http://www.mckinley.com
NlightN	http://www.nlightn.com
Open Text Index	http://www.opentext.com
search.com	http://www.search.com
Web Crawler	http://www.webcrawler.com
Who Where?	http://www.whowhere.com
Yahoo!	http://www.yahoo.com
2ask	http://www.2ask.com/

The robots may find your site by chance, but you don't have to wait for them to come looking. You can (and should) ask the spiders to come crawling to your URL. This is an essential step when you launch a new Web site, as well as when you substantially revamp or move a site. Submitting your URL is akin to sending out invitations for a party. People will show up on your doorstep only if they know there's a gig. Accordingly, if you move your site and leave no forwarding address, as in the case of a hostile parting of ways with an erstwhile ISP, visitors will think your Web site has fallen off the face of the earth. Or if you open up a whole new section on your site that is thinly linked to the existing site, you can't count on a visit from the spiders unless you give them a nudge and tell them where to look.

Each engine has its own online URL submission form to fill out, and each treats this task a little differently. It can take the better part of a day going from search engine to search engine, registering your Web site's specific information. Although this may seem tedious, it's an essential step toward your site's ultimate success. Best of all, it's completely free! Figure 5-14 illustrates the Alta Vista registration form.

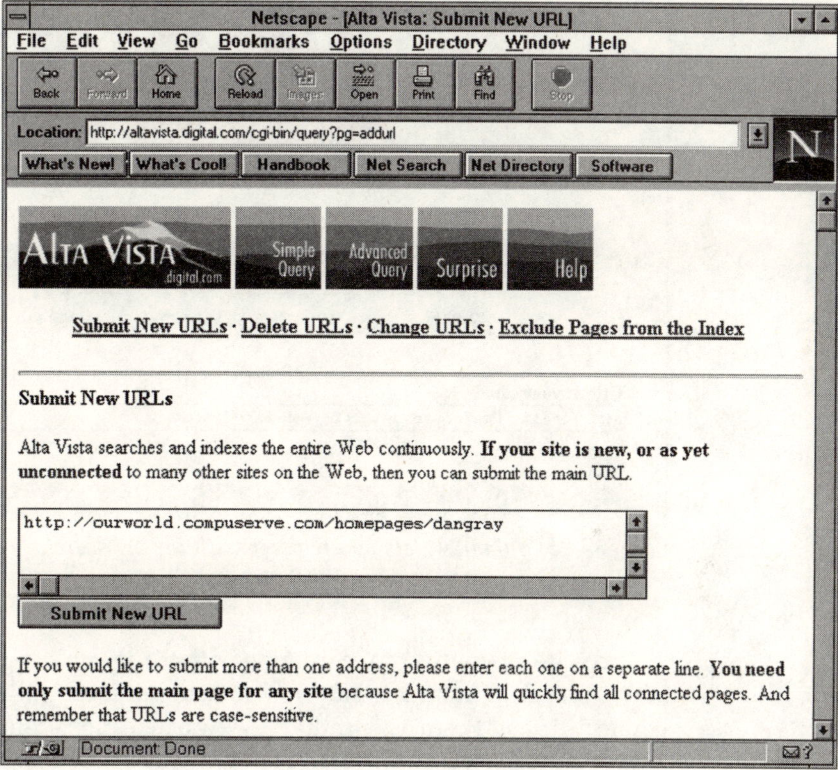

Figure 5-14: The Alta Vista registration form. Simply fill in the URL address, click on Submit New URL, and Alta Vista does the rest.

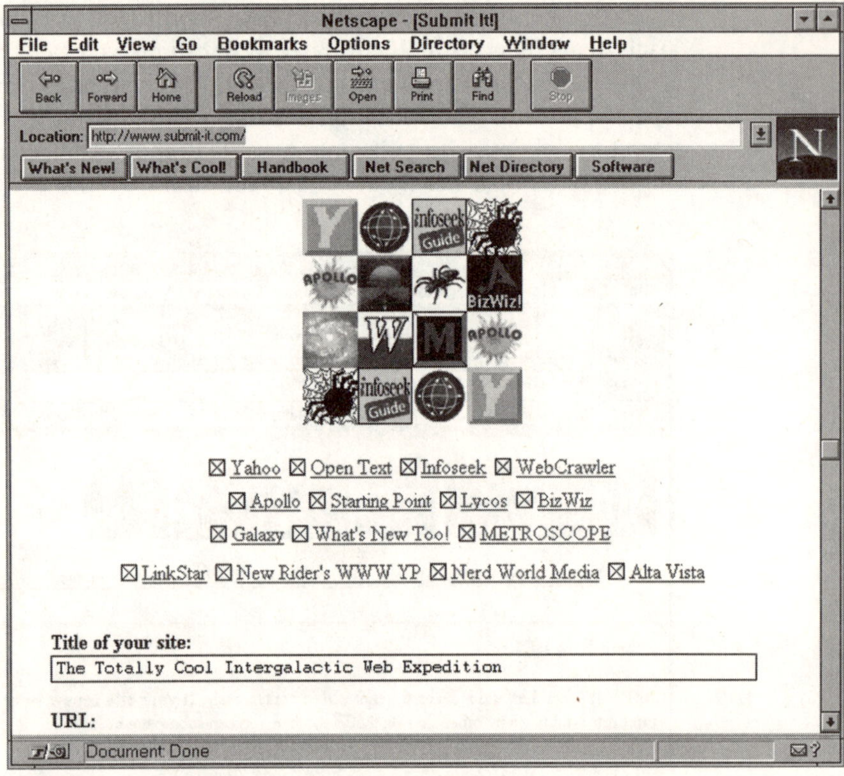

Figure 5-15: Submit-It lets you register with the big search engines in one fell swoop.

There are alternatives to registering with the search engines one by one. Services, such as Submit-It (http://www.submit-it.com/), as shown in Figure 5-15, and Postmaster (http://www.netcreations.com/postmaster/), allow you to perform a wholesale submission. These services feed your site information to the search engines. This allows you to enter your site information just once, while the site submission robots do the chump work for you.

Using a submission service can save lots of time, which is great if you don't have time to lose. But there's something to be said for *knowing* that you entered exactly the information required for each specific search engine. You might, for example, want to write a description or announcement of your site differently for one search engine in defer-ence to its particular audience. Each site also has its own indexing categories (and personality); it's very important to fill out the form as completely as possible. The more categories you can squeeze your Web site into, the better.

Some search engines, such as Excite, Magellan's McKinley, and Point offer more than just robot-gathered lists. These sites provide reviews of Web sites, complete with satirical comments and numerical ratings. A number of the hybrid print/zines do the same. You need to register your site's URL with these services and keep your fingers crossed that they like your stuff if they choose to review your site.

It's Password-Protected

Using password protection lets you monitor your visitors more closely. Unfortunately, it also lowers your hit rate and aggravates some users. On the other hand, it qualifies your visitors (Figure 5-16) to a certain extent. If they're willing to register, they're more likely to be legitimately interested in what you have to offer.

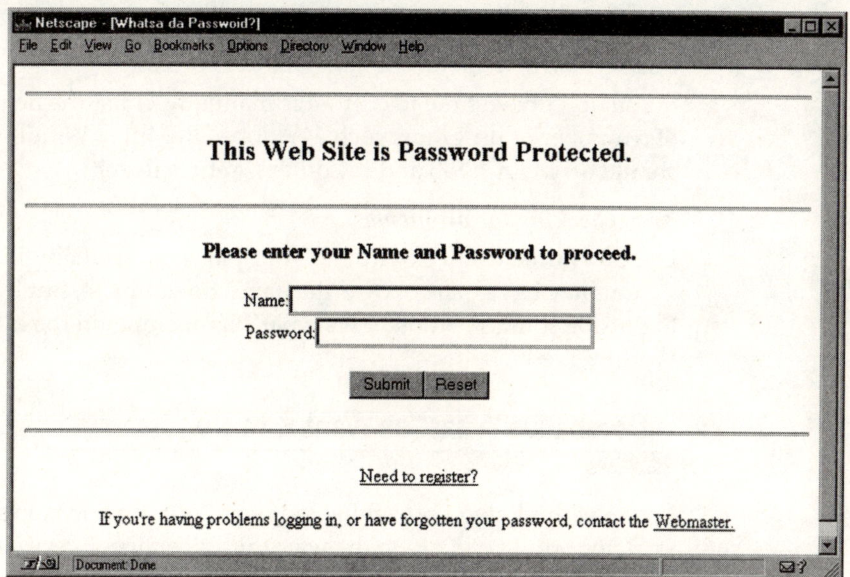

Figure 5-16: What's the password? Using password protection can both help and hurt a Web site.

You must determine the specific benefits of password protection for your site. There may be a way to achieve your end goal without putting up a big electric fence. While it's easy to create the "Please enter your password form" as shown in the last chapter, the actual password protection is done at the Web server. Consequently, you should talk this over with your site administrator to see if there are alternatives.

It Goes 404: Page Not Found

Clicking on a link to a Web site only to find that the linked page has disappeared is a big turnoff. The browser may receive a server error such as "404 - Page Not Found" message. Bad links are caused by a number of things: The linked page may have moved. The server may be unreachable. Or you may have made a typo or missed entering a character when adding the link in WEB.DESIGNER's HyperLink Properties dialog box. Here are several common pointers in Web site housekeeping:

Double-check that all links work.

Before you put a page out in the open, click through each link. It takes a little extra time, but it's worth the effort.

Don't key text in by hand.

If you're using repetitive button bars—both graphical and text—make sure that you always copy the information from the same place.

Use software "helpers."

If you don't have time to do things manually, enlist the help of any one of a number of programs such as Adobe SiteMill (a Windows version should arrive in 1997) and InContext WebAnalyzer.

Keep checking for problems.

Use downtime to check through your pages to see if anything's gone 404.

You may have control over the pages on your site, but if you're linking to outside sources, who knows what's happening on the other side of the World Wide Web.

It Doesn't Do What You Want It to Do

You may think you know what you want out of your Web site when you start your quest, yet along the way, things change. Every site is different, and the needs of the sponsoring organization (even if it's just little ol' you) must be fulfilled to make a Web project a worthwhile endeavor.

Sometimes, It's Obvious . . .

If the goal of your Web site is to sell product, for example, and your site isn't selling, then a correction is in order. You've got to find out why items are not selling, and make changes.

To get on course, take stock of your Web site on a regular schedule. Ask yourself, "Is it doing what I want it to do?" If it isn't, change course. If it is, do more of the same. Use your site statistics to fine-tune your content. The statistics will tell you which pages people are hitting. This can help you determine where to lay more bait to get them to the pages where you want them to go.

It also helps to go back to your audience, through some sort of survey mechanism, to find out what they want. Then plan your efforts so that you can give them what they need. Remember that what they want and what you are prepared to offer are not always the same thing.

Your agenda may be obvious, or it may be hidden. While your visitors may be on your Web site to glom up your freebies, you may be building a mailing list of people interested in such. They want the freebie. You want their names. Nothing in life is free.

It's a Pain in the Neck to Maintain

A Web site is not a do-it-once-and-it's-done project. By nature, a Web site requires regular maintenance. It's imperative that you design your site so that you can tend to it on a regular basis without breaking half your links with just a few keystrokes. Simply maintaining the links on your Web site can be a huge time user.

If you start by building a simple site, the maintenance aspect will remain easy. In other words, the more straightforward your site design and layout, the happier you or your Webmaster will be. That doesn't mean that you're going to make everything a straight linear path, just that the only place you want to see spaghetti is on your dinner plate.

Of course, it helps to maintain a site map on paper. Sketch out the relationships between your pages. If you can't draw it, you're bound to run into problems. Documenting your steps is especially important if you're not working alone. Your associates need to know where to go to make alterations in your absence.

Consider using a database, such as CorelWEB.DATA to publish your pages, rather than creating all of your pages manually one by one. WEB.DESIGNER does a great job of creating design-driven pages, but in certain cases, such as extensive online catalogs or informational corporate intranets, you'll need to resort to serious muscle. You can use WEB.DESIGNER to create the templates, however, and use a database to do the repetitive tasks.

Finally, use programs such as Adobe SiteMill and InContext WebAnalyzer to manage your Web site. When you move a page, SiteMill adjusts the links for you. This eliminates the chump work of manually cutting and pasting the links and saves an incredible amount of time.

It's Stale

How many Web sites have you visited that seem as if they haven't been changed since the day they were first put up? And how many times have you been back to those sites to see if they have anything new to offer? Your local bakery wouldn't survive if they didn't bake fresh goods every day. You wouldn't pick up your local newspaper if you knew it didn't contain current news. It's imperative to always have something in the proverbial oven. While your site might not require a daily change of sights and sounds, you do need to make sure that a lack of new material isn't keeping your most valuable visitors from "stopping back again soon!"

To keep your Web site fresh, start by setting a schedule for updating your site; then stick to it. If you're working with others, you'll probably need to delegate responsibility among a number of individuals so that each person has a set task.

Build Browser Muscle Memory

If you want your visitors back, day after day, think about setting up a page that *does* change on a daily basis. This can help lodge your bookmark into your visitor's daily routine.

Another way to keep your site fresh is to provide content that changes on a regular basis. Think about what you can accomplish each day or each week. You want to establish the concept of "there's always something new" for your audience so they become repeat visitors.

Finally, don't let old pages linger. If you have pages that are date-driven, such as organizational calendars, make sure you delete the old information immediately after the dates expire.

It Blinks

Blinking text was never cool. It still isn't, and it's darn close to cliché to mention blink as a no-no. There may be certain instances in which you feel you absolutely must include a blink command, but none easily comes to mind. If you're going to use flashing text, just make sure that you do so sparingly.

And Lest We Forget . . . Avoid "Under Construction" Faux Pas!

It's best not to leave any clichéd "Under Construction" signs lingering on your Web site. Yellow- and black-striped bars are tres passé. In short, if a page contains nothing more than a construction sign, there's no reason to have a link leading to it.

Moving On

There you have it. Just follow these simple directions, and you'll be a star Web site designer. Ah, if only life were that easy. Successful Web site design takes time and planning. In conventional publishing, forethought is more valuable than afterthought. This is not the case with Web publishing: If you make a mess out of your Web site design, you can always fix it (unless it was so incredibly bad that it cost you the account). By the way, you always should spend the time to beta test your Web site behind your firewall before turning it loose on your audience. Running the site through its paces in private is an essential step.

In the next section, we'll delve into the Internet-ready illustration program, CorelWEB.DRAW. You'll quickly learn the ins and outs of WEB.DRAW as you create exciting graphics that look great and download in a flash.

PART II

CorelWEB.DRAW

6

An Introduction to CorelWEB.DRAW

CorelWEB.DRAW is your ticket to creative Web page graphics. The core of the program's power is that the images you create are never set in stone. WEB.DRAW allows you to create high-impact artwork with a minimum of hassle and a high degree of "reworkability." The act of assigning colored and textured fills, for instance, is a fast, fun, and infinitely variable procedure. Even the most complex and impressive effects, such as perspectives, extrusions, and envelope warps, are easy to assign and modify.

You might be thinking, "So what's the difference between this program and most other programs designed to create images for the World Wide Web?" Although almost all Web images are *bitmap* files, which are rendered in dot-by-dot terms, CorelWEB.DRAW is a *vector-based* drawing package. Rather than relying upon absolute dots, vector (or *object-oriented*) drawing defines images in mathematical terms, which allows for the smooth reduction and enlargement of images. Each object is a mathematical statement that says something akin to "Draw a line from this point to this point, using this arc."

When Are *Real* Vector Graphics Used on Web Pages?

While they may be few and far between, vector-based images provide one of the most powerful ways to deliver graphic information on the Web. Most significantly, vector graphics can be zoomed up for a closer look at a specific part of an image. This feature is perfect for artwork such as maps and parts diagrams, when a high-level of detail is important.

As of this writing, the most prevalent method used to put actual vector-based graphics on a Web page is Macromedia's Shockwave plug-in. While Corel and Micrografx have vector graphics plug-ins, neither company can boast the huge installed base of Shockwave-enabled Web browsers.

Let's take a look at what this difference means in visual terms. Figure 6-1 shows how a bitmap image looks when zoomed up in a bitmap paint program.

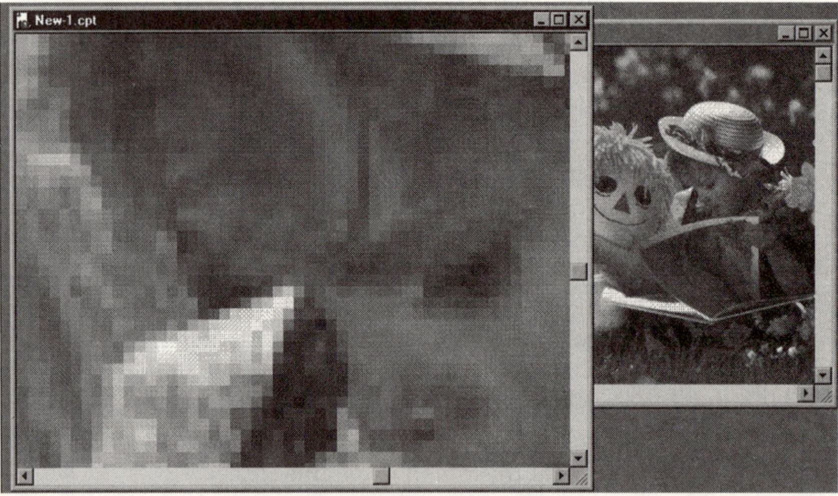

Figure 6-1: Take a closer look at this bitmap image, and you'll see the grid of dots.

If you scale up a bitmap graphic, you'll often impart the *jaggies*—a stair-stepped, chunky look—to the image. Vector graphics, on the other hand, scale up smoothly. Now look at Figure 6-2; it demonstrates how vector artwork (in this case, an interpretation of Botticelli's *Venus*, as found in the CorelDRAW! 5.0 clip-art collection) scales with nary a jaggy. This allows you to create a crisp image.

Figure 6-2: Sure, vectors are smooth, but what would Botticelli think?

To get your vector artwork from CorelWEB.DRAW to your Web page, you should export it to the proper bitmap format at an exact size. By exporting the artwork at a specific size, the result will be of the highest quality. In general, you should avoid scaling an image up or down once it's been placed on the Web page. You can export to either GIF (Graphics Interchange Format) or JPEG (Joint Photographic Experts Group) formats, with a variety of options. In Chapter 8, you'll learn how to export artwork to these formats and which format you should choose. Chapter 10 covers a number of bitmap image optimization techniques you can use to fine-tune your images for crisp display and snappy downloads.

This chapter focuses on CorelWEB.DRAW's powerful toolbox of image creation and manipulation tools. It also helps provide an overview of how the program fits into the grand scheme of Web page design.

The Basics of CorelWEB.DRAW

As a vector-based drawing package, CorelWEB.DRAW's working methodology is similar to that of Adobe Illustrator, Macromedia FreeHand, Deneba Canvas, and Micrografx Designer. If you've used one of these programs, you've already become accustomed to creating object-oriented artwork. And if you're already familiar with CorelDRAW!, you'll be right at home with CorelWEB.DRAW!

In general, you should think of vector art as electronic collages, made up of objects of different shapes and colors. Every object can be assigned an outline color and stroke width. Objects that are *closed paths* can be filled with a wide variety of colors and textures. As illustrated by Figure 6-3, *open paths*—such as simple lines—have a beginning and an end; closed paths—such as circles, squares, text, and free-form objects—form a complete loop. Composing a vector-based illustration is a process of layering objects on top of other objects. Remember the Colorforms you had as a kid? Vector illustration is a very similar principle. Just peel and stick.

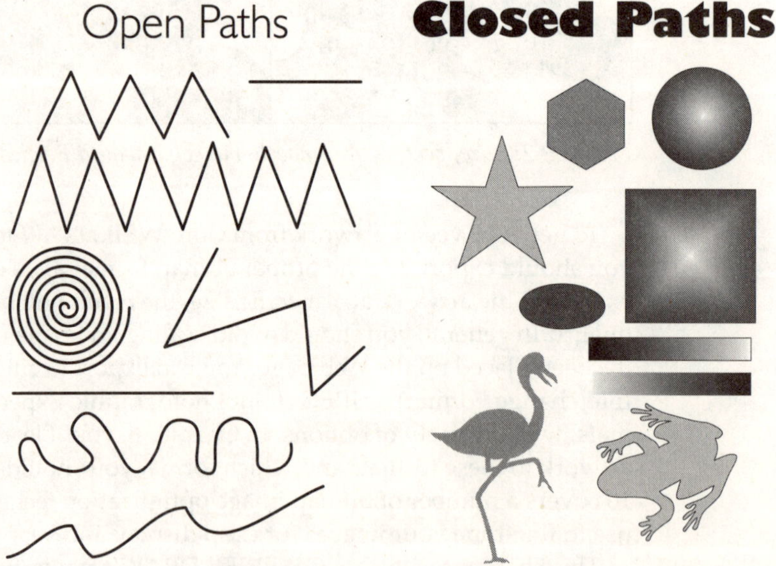

Figure 6-3: A variety of open and closed paths.

CorelWEB.DRAW provides you with the tools you need to create a wide variety of electronic artwork, from the most basic through the most complex. The program allows you to create four basic types of objects—rectangles, ovals, free-forms, and text—with ease. Figure 6-4 shows an annotated view of the floating toolbox. To choose a tool, simply click on it. When a tool is selected, the button will appear as if it is "pushed in" (like the Pointer tool in Figure 6-4). You also can select some of the tools by using keyboard shortcuts:

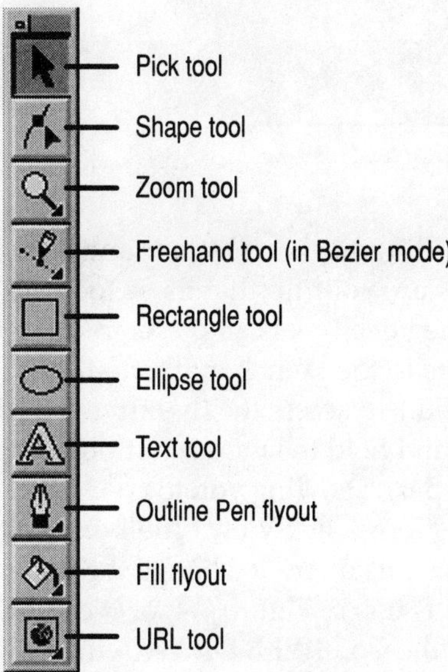

Figure 6-4: The CorelWEB.DRAW toolbox.

Action	Shortcut
Pick tool	Ctrl+Space
Shape tool	F10
Zoom in	F2
Zoom out	F3
Freehand tool	F5
Rectangle tool	F6
Ellipse tool	F7
Text tool	F8

Table 6-1: Toolbox keyboard shortcuts.

Notice that half of the 10 buttons have little triangles at their bottom right corners. The triangles are your tip that these tools feature more than one mode. For example, the Pencil tool can be set to draw freehand lines or *Bezier* lines. (Bezier refers to the French mathematician for whom the drawing method was named.) To access the fly-out menu for each of these five tools, click on the tool and hold the mouse button down. The appropriate fly-out menu will appear, allowing you to choose the correct mode.

If you can't find your toolbox, click View | Toolbox and be sure Visible is checked. You also can use this menu to change the appearance of the toolbox. It can be floating, as it is in Figure 6-4, or it can be set in a fixed position on the left side of the CorelWEB.DRAW window. Let's take a look at each of the components of the toolbox.

The Pick Tool

Pick, at the top of the Toolbox menu, selects and manipulates existing objects. This little marvel performs a multitude of functions. Click once on an object with the Pick tool to select it and display a set of eight selection handles, as shown in Figure 6-5. In this example, a Links button shows a group of four objects (inner button, outer button, and two iterations of the word). Notice how the Status Line at the bottom of the WEB.DRAW window reports on the selected object (or in this case, group).

Can't Find the Status Line?

The Status Line may be positioned at the top or the bottom of the WEB.DRAW window, or you can turn it off to gain screen space. You'll learn how to modify the appearance of the WEB.DRAW environment with the Preferences dialog box in Chapter 9.

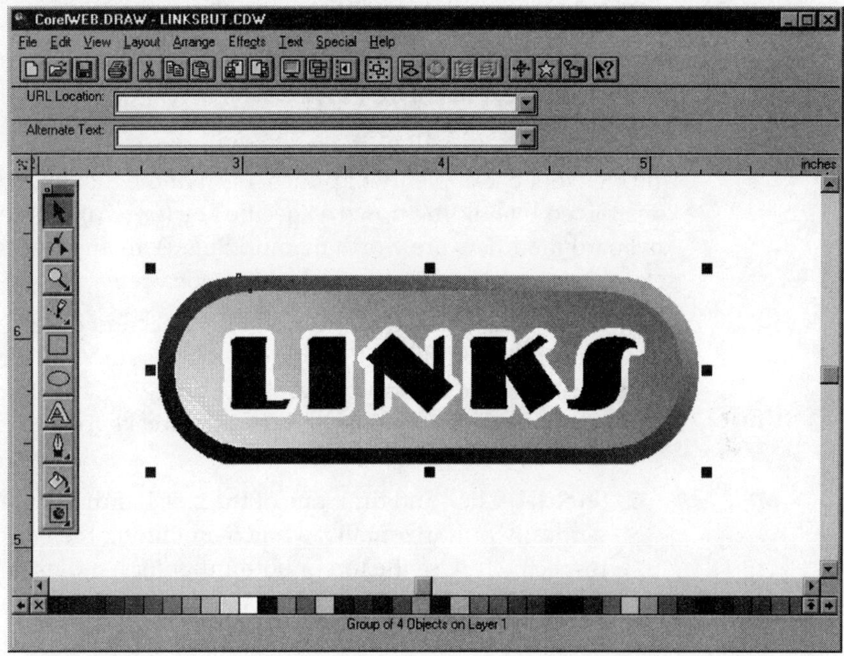

Figure 6-5: Selection handles are the key to manipulating objects.

Selecting Multiple Objects

It's easy to select multiple objects with the Pick tool. WEB.DRAW provides three handy procedures to accomplish this task:

- To select a number of specific objects, hold down the Shift key while clicking the objects.

- To select all the objects in a particular area of the screen, click and drag a *marquee* around the objects. You can think of a marquee as a big fishing net that snags every object in its path.

- Edit | Select All will select every object in the file.

- To deselect a selected object, just Shift-click it.

Stretch, Scale, Mirror & Move

The Pick tool packs plenty of punch. Each of the tool's functions can be constrained by holding down a specific key (or two). These powerful keyboard modifiers are worth memorizing. With an object (or group) selected, you can perform the following operations:

- Move—Just click anywhere on the object and drag!
  Modifier: Hold down the Ctrl key to constrain movement to a horizontal or vertical plane. While dragging, click the right mouse button or press the + key on the numeric keypad to create an exact copy of the original object.

- Stretch—Click and drag one of the side handles to stretch an object vertically or horizontally, while maintaining the width or height, respectively. Use the top or bottom center handles to stretch vertically and the left or right center handles to stretch horizontally.
  Modifiers: Hold down the Ctrl key to stretch in 100 percent increments; hold down the Shift key to stretch from the object's center. While dragging, click the right mouse button or press the + key on the numeric keypad to create an exact copy of the original object.

- Scale—Click and drag one of the corner handles to scale an object proportionally.
  Modifiers: Hold down the Ctrl key to scale in 100 percent increments; hold down the Shift key to scale from the object's center. While dragging, click the right mouse button or press the + key on the numeric keypad to create an exact copy of the original object.

- Mirror—Click and drag one of the center handles over the opposite center handle to simultaneously stretch and flop an object. *Modifiers:* Hold down the Ctrl key to maintain proportions while mirroring; hold down the Shift key to mirror from the object's center. While dragging, click the right mouse button or press the + key on the numeric keypad to create an exact copy of the original object.

But I Just Need a Duplicate!

To create an exact copy of a selected object without performing any other procedures, press the + key on the numeric keypad or press Ctrl+D.

Try a few of these maneuvers now. Notice that the cursor turns into a cross when placed over any of the eight selection handles. After you click and drag, the cursor changes, becoming a two-headed arrow when you scale or mirror and a four-headed arrow when you stretch. As you drag objects around, pay close attention to the Status Line for exact feedback on object size and location.

Rotation

Click on an object that's already selected to put it into rotation mode, denoted by the eight double-headed arrow selection handles and point of rotation shown in Figure 6-6. Rotation mode lets you rotate or skew the selected object. To rotate, click and drag on one of the four corner handles. Hold down the Ctrl key to constrain the rotation to a specified number of degrees. The default is 15 degrees; change the specified number of degrees with the Preferences dialog box.

An object being rotated spins upon its point of rotation. Alter the manner in which it rotates by moving the point of rotation: click and drag the little bull's-eye to the position you want to rotate around. Fool around with rotation mode, while experimenting with different rotation points. Chapter 9 describes how to use a little "spin-a-rama" rotation trick to create spiffy snowflakes and other radial objects.

Figure 6-6: We're in rotation mode!

Skew

Skewing allows you to push or pull one side of an object while the opposite side stays put. Use this procedure to create images that look as if they're leaning over and to create cast shadows like those shown in Figure 6-7. You'll learn more about cast shadows in Chapter 9.

To skew an object, put it in rotation mode, grab one of the double-headed arrows along the top or side, and pull in the direction you want to skew the object. Hold down the Ctrl key while you do this to skew the object in fixed increments.

Figure 6-7: Casting shadows is easy with WEB.DRAW's skew function.

To move a selected object just a tad, use the arrow keys to nudge it around. Adjust the nudge distance in the Special Preferences dialog box (for Web graphics, consider setting your Nudge amount to 1 pixel or so).

Here are additional keyboard shortcuts you can use while in Pick tool mode.

Action	Shortcut
Drop all selected objects	Esc
Cycle through objects	Tab
Cycle backward	Shift+Tab

Table 6-2: Pick tool keyboard shortcuts.

The Zoom Tool

CorelWEB.DRAW's Zoom tool allows you to move around your artwork quickly. The program gives you a range of handy zooming options. Figure 6-8 displays an annotated view of the Zoom tool fly-out menu. Crank up your operating efficiency level with the Zoom tool keyboard shortcuts to switch between different views in the blink of an eye.

Action	Shortcut
Zoom in	F2
Zoom out	F3
Zoom to selected	Shift+F2
Zoom to all objects	F4
Zoom to page view	Shift+F4

Table 6-3: Zoom tool keyboard shortcuts.

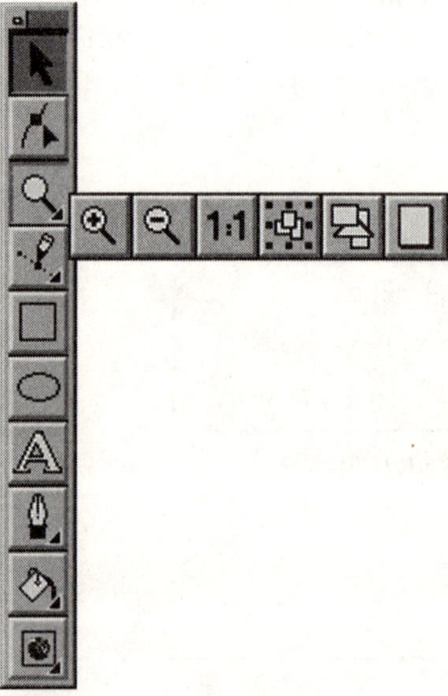

Figure 6-8: Various zoom tools.

When you select the zoom-in function, the cursor turns into a magnifying glass with a + sign. Simply clicking the page will zoom in to 2x the current setting. To zoom into a specific area, click and drag a marquee around the area.

The Pencil Tool

As mentioned earlier, CorelWEB.DRAW's Pencil tool has two different personalities: the freehand drawing mode and the Bezier drawing mode. The freehand mode acts as you would expect a "normal" drawing tool to act: the lines drawn follow the path of your mouse. The Bezier mode, on the other hand, forces you to choose your points carefully, in much the same manner as a surgeon might painstakingly stitch up a patient. CorelWEB.DRAW uses Bezier curves to define every object, regardless of the method you choose to lay down the lines.

Some Bezier Basics

CorelWEB.DRAW's Bezier curves work by means of *nodes* and *control points.* Nodes are the actual points on the line at which the curves (on either side of the node) take flight. A set of control points (which can look remarkably like a rabbit ears television antenna) projects from each curve-inducing node. There's plenty of mathematical magic at work here; thankfully, you won't have to break out the calculator! Instead the control points handle all the dirty work for you, determining the arc, distance, and shape of each curved line segment. Each curved line segment has a beginning and ending control point, as illustrated in Figure 6-9. Straight line segments, however, do not have control points.

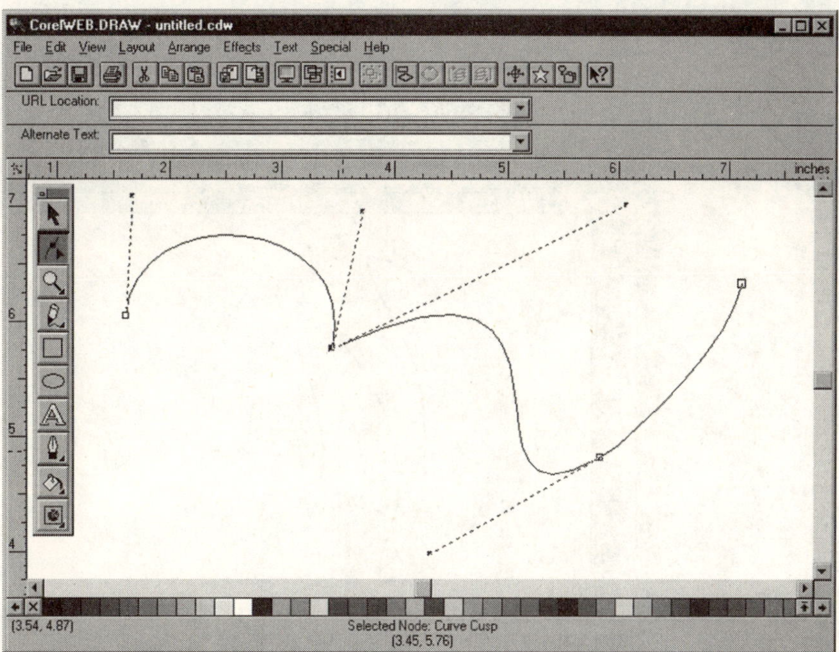

Figure 6-9: Take charge of your curves with control points.

There are three different types of curved lines: *smooth, symmetrical,* and *cusp.* Smooth curves are linked together on either side of the node; moving one control point affects the other point as well. Think of symmetrical curves as super-smooth—they're exactly the same on both sides of the node. Cusp nodes are quite the opposite: there's nothing tying these curves together but the node itself. They are best used when you want to make a sharp change of direction. While there's a brief discussion of node-tweaking in the Shape tool section later on in this chapter, you'll learn how to finesse those control points to perfection in Chapter 9.

Drawing With the Freehand Pencil Tool

To draw freehand lines, click on the Pencil tool. Move the cursor to the point from which you wish to start drawing. Then click and drag your freehand line. If things go awry while you're drawing, hold the Shift key and back up over your line to "erase" the errant portion. Release the Shift key and drag out the rest of the line. If you've drawn an open-path object, the Status Line will let you know that as well as the number of nodes in the object, as shown in Figure 6-10.

Figure 6-10: Watching the Status Line is crucial. It provides essential information on each object you draw.

To create a closed-path object, drag the cursor back to the point where you started drawing. CorelWEB.DRAW automatically closes the path for you. If you want to close an open-path object, switch to the Shape tool to select the beginning and ending nodes, double-click on one of those nodes, and click Join in the Node Edit roll-up. In fact, you'll often lay down the rough lines first, going back to tweak your objects with the Shape tool.

You'll use a different method to draw straight lines in freehand mode. Start by clicking the mouse button where you want the line to begin. Lay down the first node, to which the line will be anchored. Position the cursor where you want the line to end. Then click again to draw the line. If you want to continue drawing another connected (straight) line, double-click instead of single-clicking. Remember to keep an eye on the Status Line for important feedback while you're drawing (see Figure 6-11). Hold down the Ctrl key to constrain your straight lines to the preset number of degrees (again, the default is 15).

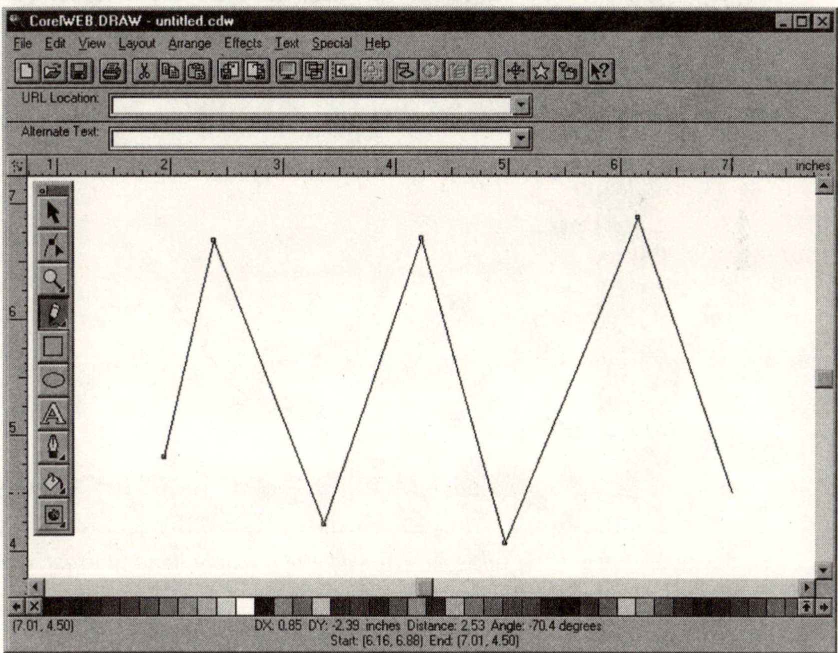

Figure 6-11: Double-click on each node to continue drawing connected straight lines.

Drawing With the Bezier Pencil Tool

Drawing with the Pencil tool's Bezier mode takes a bit more forethought and deliberate execution. When you lay down Bezier curves direct, you're creating a more "engineered" object—one that needs to be planned carefully as to where each node should be placed and how each curve should behave. Getting accustomed to creating your objects this way takes time. If you've ever drawn conventionally with a ruler and French curves (plastic templates formed in a variety of flowing arcs), you're ahead of the game. Figure 6-12 shows a fairly smooth and flowing line being created with the Bezier tool.

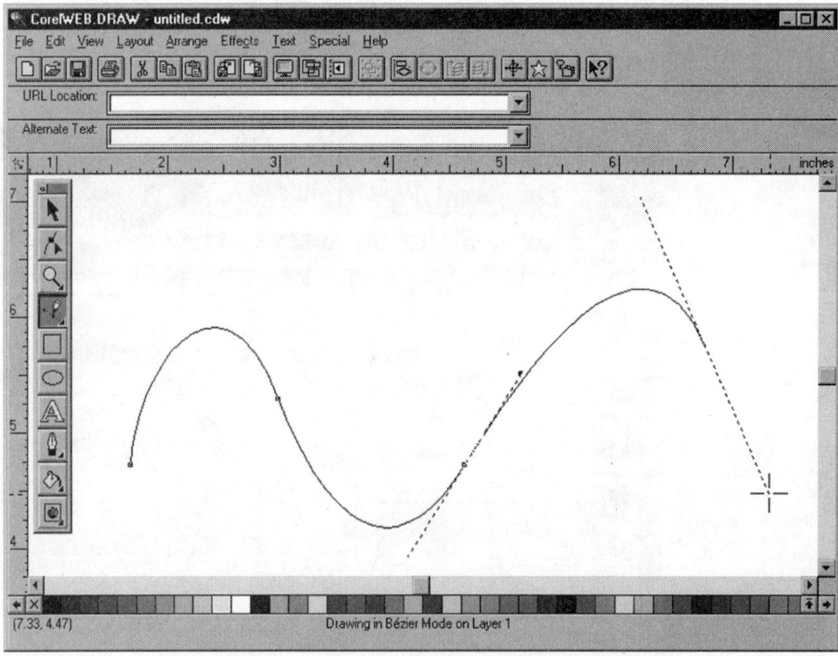

Figure 6-12: It takes a clear head and a steady hand to draw with the Bezier tool.

Think of the act of drawing in Bezier mode like lacing shoes. Just pick the positions through which you want to thread your line and carry it through. As you draw, the control points appear for each node. Click the first spot and drag the curve in the proper direction (by manipulating the control point), then click the next spot and drag again. Repeat this procedure until finished drawing the path (be it open or closed).

The Bezier tool can be used to draw straight lines as well as curved ones. The Bezier tool draws straight lines much like the freehand Pencil tool, with one important exception: you don't have to double-click at each node (as you do with the freehand Pencil tool) to draw connected straight lines; just one click does the trick. Use this method to create objects that consist of both curved and straight line segments quickly.

The Rectangle Tool

Now here's a tool that's truly easy to understand and use. The Rectangle tool's sole purpose is to create (you guessed it!) rectangles. All you do is select the Rectangle tool, then click and drag your rectangle out to the desired size and aspect ratio. Once again, watch the Status Line as you drag out your rectangle, as shown in Figure 6-13. CorelWEB.DRAW's grid feature (accessed via the Layout | Grid Setup menu) is invaluable in creating rectangles of an exact size. There are also a number of nifty keyboard modifiers to help you create perfect squares, as well as draw from a center point rather than a corner point.

Action	Shortcut
To draw from center	Hold down the Shift key
To draw a square	Hold down the Ctrl key
To draw a square from center	Hold down the Ctrl+Shift keys

Table 6-4: Rectangle tool keyboard shortcuts.

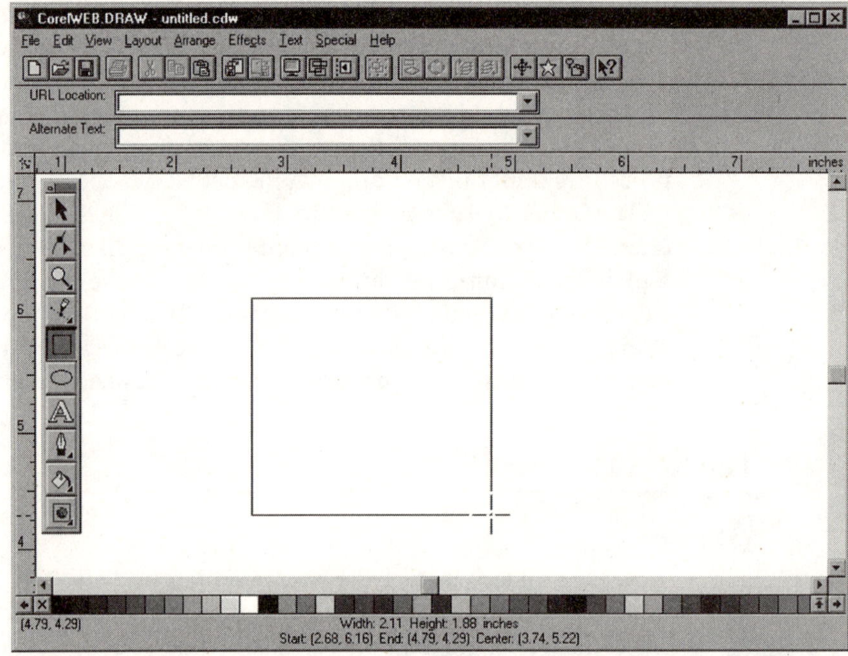

Figure 6-13: The status line provides valuable feedback while drawing rectangles.

Rectangles are special objects, which WEB.DRAW treats differently than other objects. Most important, the Shape tool can be used to quickly create rounded-corner rectangles. You'll learn how to create rounded-corner rectangles with the Shape tool later on in this chapter.

The Ellipse Tool

The Ellipse tool is similar to the rectangle tool, in that it exists for just one purpose (you guessed it again!): to draw ovals. To create an oval, select Ellipse, then click and drag your oval out to the desired size and shape. Use the grid to create ovals of a specific size. The keyboard shortcuts to draw from center or to create perfect circles are the same as those for the Rectangle tool. See Figure 6-14.

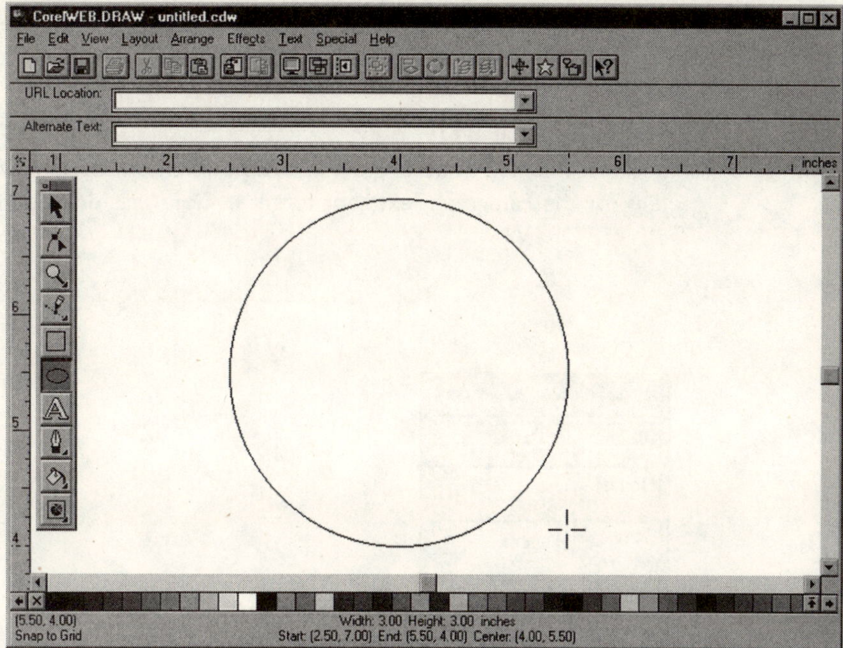

Figure 6-14: To draw a perfect circle, click and drag from its center point while holding down the Ctrl+Shift keys.

And like rectangles, ellipses are special objects that can be modified by the Shape tool in their own particular way. Stay tuned as we turn ellipses into pie slices and arcs, later on in this chapter.

The Text Tool

CorelWEB.DRAW uses what long-time Corellians refer to as the "artistic text tool." Setting text is simple: select the Text tool, then click an insertion point and type away. The text will appear onscreen in the typeface and the size you have selected in the Text roll-up. The Text roll-up (as shown in Figure 6-15) is a handy little floating palette that allows you to alter the typeface, style, size, and alignment of a selected block of text quickly. Summon the Text roll-up from the Text menu or via the Ctrl+F2 keyboard shortcut.

Whither Paragraph Text?

If you're accustomed to using the non-WEB version of CorelDRAW!, and you're looking for the Paragraph Text tool, forget it. Corel has dropped the feature in CorelWEB.DRAW.

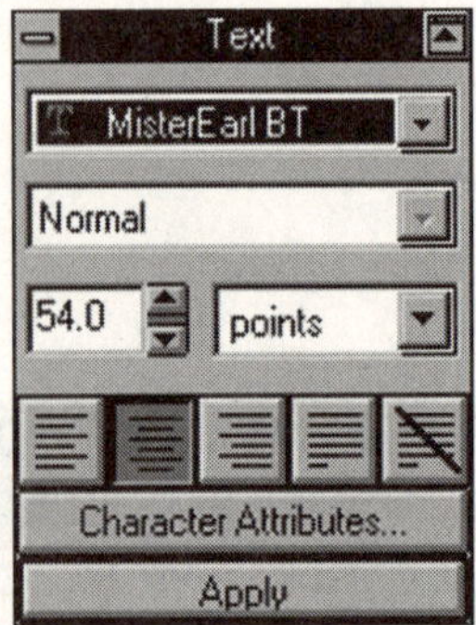

Figure 6-15: The Text roll-up lets you take charge of the most common type characteristics.

When you set a new block of text, it's easiest to type the text using the default typeface and size first, then go back and choose the typeface, style, size, and alignment. You can do it the other way around, but this is more expedient. Once the text is on the screen, select it with the Pick tool. Then scroll through the typefaces on the Text roll-up with the up and down cursor keys to get immediate visual feedback, as shown in Figure 6-16. After you choose a typeface, type style, type size, and alignment, click on the Apply button to assign those characteristics to the text.

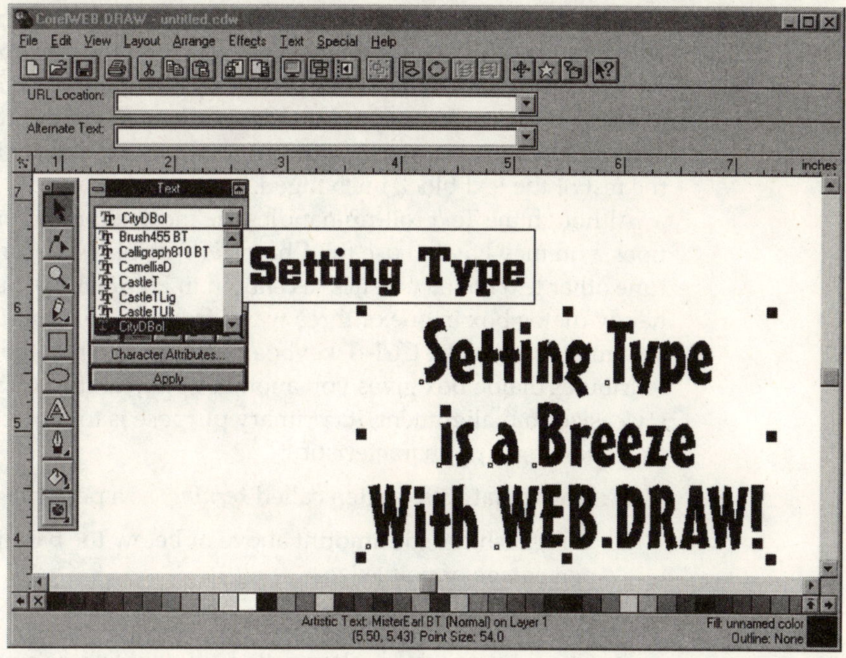

Figure 6-16: With the Text roll-up's fly-out preview, see what your type will look like before applying type characteristics.

Jump To It!

You can jump direct to a typeface by pressing the first letter of the typeface name. If you have more than one typeface with the same first letter, press the key repeatedly until you reach the typeface you want.

With the Text tool, you can apply different typefaces, sizes, and styles within a text block. Select the block of text with the pick tool. Then switch to the text tool and click and drag over the words that you want to change. Dial the new typeface, size, and style into the Text roll-up and click on Apply to change the attributes of only the selected text, leaving the rest of the text block unchanged.

Although the Text roll-up handles the most common type specifications, you may have to use the Character Attributes dialog box to fine-tune other text characteristics (as shown in Figure 6-17). Summon this handy dialog box in one of three ways: from the Text roll-up, from the Text menu, or via the Ctrl+T keyboard shortcut. While the Character Attributes dialog box gives you another opportunity to assign typeface, style, size, and alignment, its primary purpose is to provide control over the following type characteristics:

- Horizontal shift—often called *kerning;* as a percentage of point size
- Vertical shift—the amount above or below the baseline; as a percentage of point size
- Angle of rotation—in degrees
- Character spacing—often called *letter spacing;* as a percentage of space
- Word spacing—as a percentage of space
- Line spacing—often called *leading;* in points as a percentage of character height or as a percentage of point size
- Underline—single thin, single thin word, single thick, single thick word, double thin, double thin word, or none
- Overline—single thin, single thin word, single thick, single thick word, double thin, double thin word, or none
- Strikeout—single thin, single thin word, single thick, single thick word, double thin, double thin word, or none
- Placement—normal, superscript, or subscript

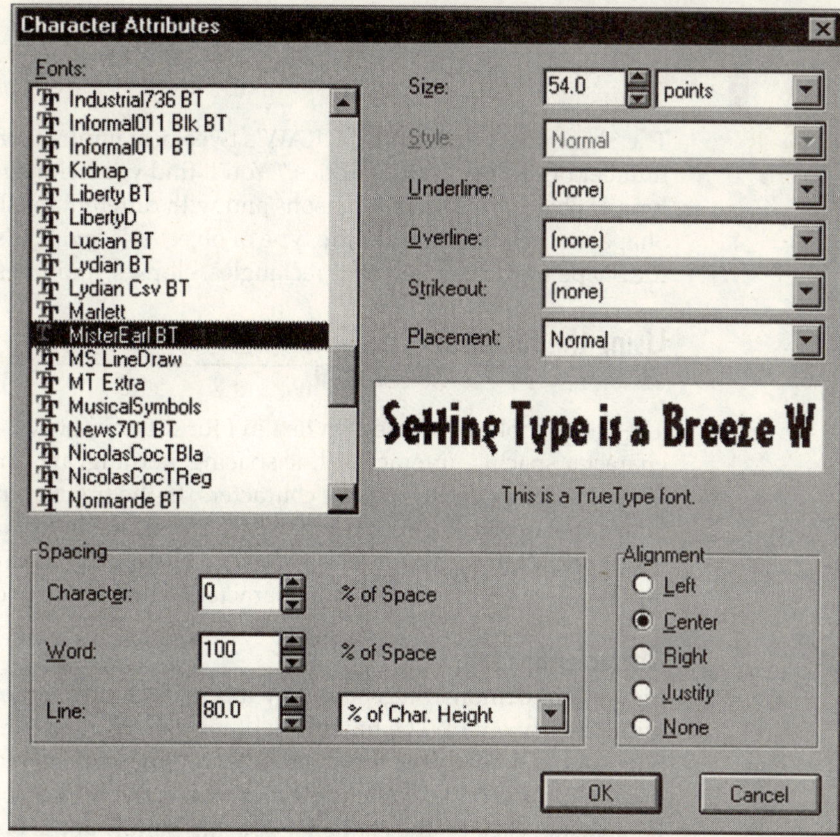

Figure 6-17: The Character Attributes dialog box provides complete control over text characteristics.

Because CorelWEB.DRAW treats all text as objects, you can use the Pick tool to interactively scale, stretch, skew, mirror, or rotate text. And in the next section, you'll learn how to use the Shape tool to change text spacing attributes interactively, as well as to change the characteristics of individual characters within a text block.

The Shape Tool

The Shape tool is CorelWEB.DRAW's tweakiest implement, with a number of distinct "personalities." You'll find yourself using it on every type of object, for different reasons and with different results. The way the Shape tool acts depends on the type of object selected. Let's look at how the Shape tool is used on text, rectangles, ellipses, and freeform objects.

Using the Shape Tool on Text

The Shape tool can be used on text in four different ways: interactive character spacing, interactive line spacing, kerning, and the application of special attributes to specific characters. In the first two methods, the Shape tool opens or closes up the space between all the characters in a text block. With the last method, you can change the spacing, rotation, and typeface on any number of characters within a text block.

Character Spacing

Figure 6-18 demonstrates how easy it is to open up character spacing with the Shape tool. The first block of text has been selected with the Shape tool and displays the character- and line-spacing handles (at the bottom right and left of the text block, respectively). To open up character spacing, click on the character-spacing handle at the bottom right corner of the text block and drag to the right. Conversely, to close up character spacing, drag to the left. A dotted line *marquee* displays as you're dragging (see the second block of text in Figure 6-18). When you reach your desired text block width, release the mouse button. The text will be spaced out like the third block of text shown in Figure 6-18.

Far and Away

OPENED UP

Far and Away

TIGHTENED & KERNED

Figure 6-20: Kerning is an esoteric procedure that, properly done, can add a finely crafted look to type.

You may have noticed that when you select a block of text with the Shape tool, each character has a single node sitting to its lower left. You can click and drag on this node and move the character around at will. Hold down the Ctrl key to constrain the movement to either a horizontal (for kerning) or a vertical (for making a character superior (superscript) or inferior (subscript)) plane. The coolest interactive kerning technique is to use the nudge (arrow) keys to push the selected characters around.

Changing Individual Character Attributes

The Shape tool is great for changing the attributes of a bunch of characters within a text block. Use this technique when you want to set off a handful of words in a different typeface, as in Figure 6-21. To select a number of characters, click on the first character node, hold down the Shift key, then click on the additional character nodes. Or you can drag a marquee around the multiple character nodes to lasso them. Once the characters are selected, use the Text roll-up to change attributes. For more intricate specifications, access the Character Attributes dialog box by double-clicking on a selected character node.

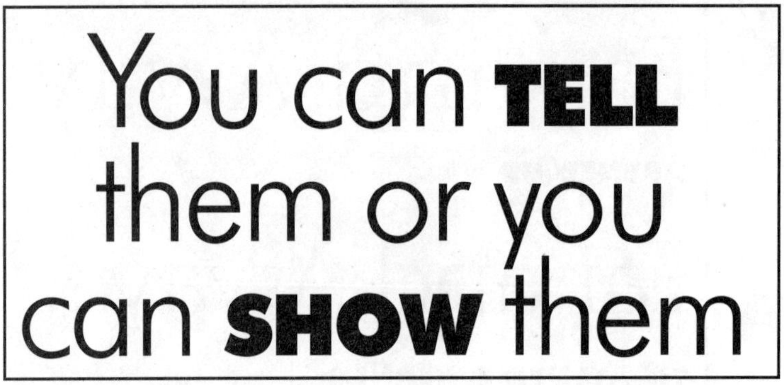

Figure 6-21: Using different typefaces and sizes within a text block can deliver a powerful effect.

Round-Corner Rectangles

Did you ever want to round the corners of a rectangle? The Shape tool makes quick work of this task. Rounded-corner rectangles often are used as navigational buttons and other Web page graphics. To create a round-corner rectangle: draw a rectangle in the desired width and height. Then switch to the Shape tool and select one of the rectangle's four nodes. As you drag the node toward the center of the rectangle, WEB.DRAW rounds the corners while reporting the corner radius on the Status Line (as shown in Figure 6-22). Dragging toward the center of the rectangle yields larger arcs; dragging outward shrinks the arcs. Constrain the corner radius to a specified size by setting the Layout | Snap to Grid feature.

Figure 6-22: To round the corners of a rectangle, just click and drag with the Shape tool.

Pie Wedges & Open-Path Arcs

The Shape tool allows you to create pie wedges and open-path arcs quickly by clicking and dragging on an ellipse's solitary node. To create a pie wedge, click and drag on the node, keeping the cursor inside the ellipse. The Status Line will report the starting and ending points, in addition to the total angle of the pie wedge, as shown in Figure 6-23. To create an open-path arc, follow the same procedure, while keeping the cursor outside the ellipse.

Figure 6-23: Keep the cursor inside the ellipse to create a pie wedge or outside the ellipse to create an open-path arc.

Basic Node Tweaking

Use the Shape tool on a freeform object to take complete control over the object's nodes and control points. In practice, you'll use the Shape tool along with the Node Edit roll-up to perform intricate maneuvers. Although we'll cover node editing in depth in Chapter 9, let's get some of the basics out of the way right now. Node tweaking is a time-consuming and sometimes frustrating endeavor. It's far more important when you're preparing vector graphics for print work than for Web work, as the differences in resolution literally blur the lines.

The two most basic ways to change the shape of an object are to move a node or to alter the way that a line radiates from a node. To move a node, all you have to do is click and drag it to a new position. When you move a node, you affect the line segments on both sides of the node (assuming it isn't the end node of an open path). To alter an individual line segment, either click and drag on the line itself, or tweak the line's control points. For more complex maneuvers, you must access the Node Edit roll-up. This handy little device (as shown in Figure 6-24) allows you to perform the following actions on a path:

- Add nodes
- Remove nodes
- Join nodes
- Break nodes apart
- Automatically reduce the number of selected nodes
- Convert a curve node to a line node
- Convert a line node to a curve node
- Stretch a number of selected nodes
- Rotate a number of selected nodes
- Convert a node to a cusp curve node
- Convert a node to a smooth curve node
- Convert a node to a symmetrical curve node
- Align two nodes

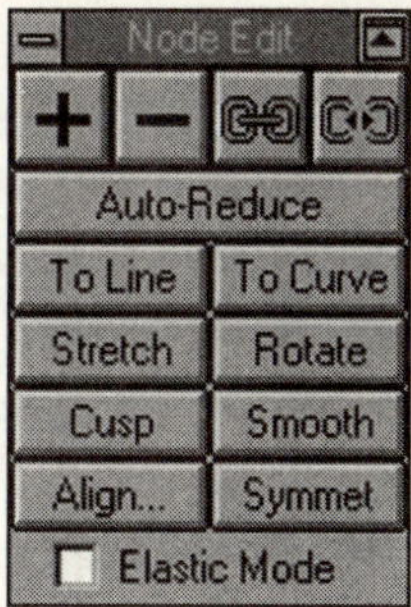

Figure 6-24: The Node Edit roll-up is your key to complete path control.

You may or may not use any or all of these functions in the process of creating your Web page graphics. You're likely to use adding, deleting, joining, and breaking apart most often.

The Outline Tool

CorelWEB.DRAW's Outline tool allows you total flexibility over an object's outline color and other attributes. The Outline tool fly-out menu, as shown in Figure 6-25, offers a variety of options. The top row features buttons for the Outline Pen dialog box, Outline Pen roll-up, and six outline width choices—from no outline or a quarter-point hairline (hardly useful for Web page work) up to a really fat 24-point outline. The bottom row includes buttons for the Outline Color dialog box, as well as one-click color choices for black, white, and tints of gray (10, 30, 50, 70, or 90 percent).

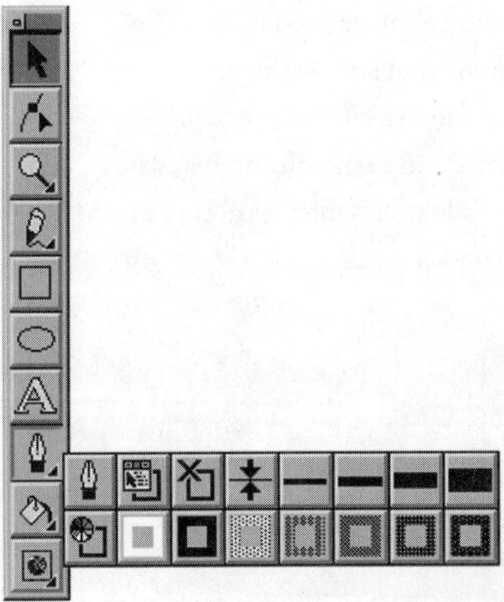

Figure 6-25: The Outline Pen fly-out menu provides access to a plethora of outline choices.

The Outline Pen roll-up, as shown in Figure 6-26, is the fastest way to make changes to the outline of a selected object. It provides control over line width, ends (such as arrowheads), style, and color. To change an outline's attributes, make your selections from the various drop-down menus and click on the Apply button. You also can copy the outline attributes from one object to another with the Update From button: Select the object you want to change. Then click on the Update From button and the object from which you want to copy the outline attributes.

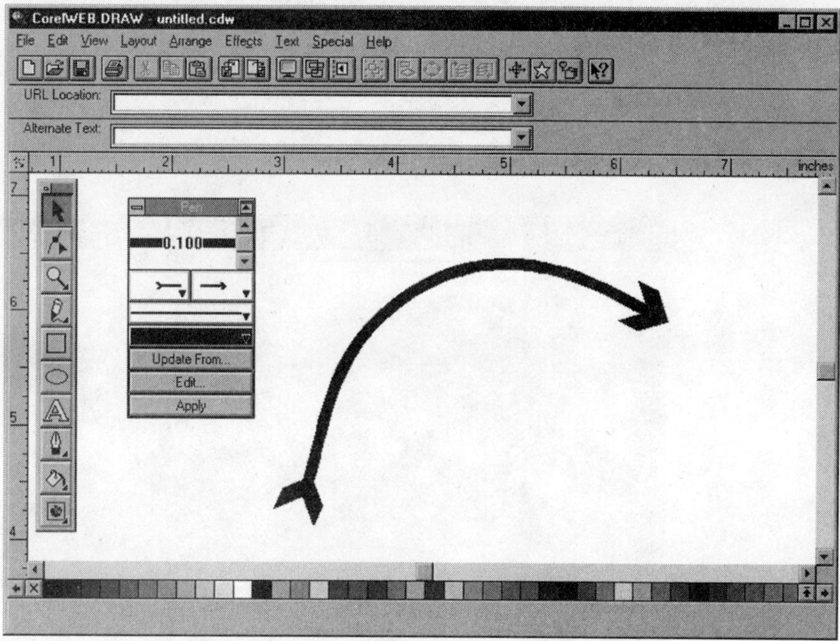

Figure 6-26: The Outline Pen roll-up makes assigning outline attributes a snap.

Outline Color

The Outline Color attributes dialog box (as shown by Figure 6-27) is summoned via the Outline Pen flyout menu, the Outline roll-up, or the Shift+F12 keyboard shortcut. This dialog box delivers an endless array of color choices that covers or maybe even exceeds what's needed for Web page graphics. In addition to the RGB (red-green-blue) color model used on the WWW, colors can be specified in CMYK (cyan-magenta-yellow-black) and HSB (hue-saturation-brightness) models. A word to the wise: Stick with RGB. Better yet, load the custom Netscape 216 color palette from this book's Companion CD-ROM for a browser-safe RGB color palette. More information on the Netscape 216 color palette and how to load and create custom palettes is in Chapter 10.

Why Bother With Anything but RGB?

HTML uses an RGB color space. The HSB and CMYK options are holdovers from CorelDRAW! 5.0's presentation and print graphic roots. For the purposes of Web page design, you should forget about using anything but RGB.

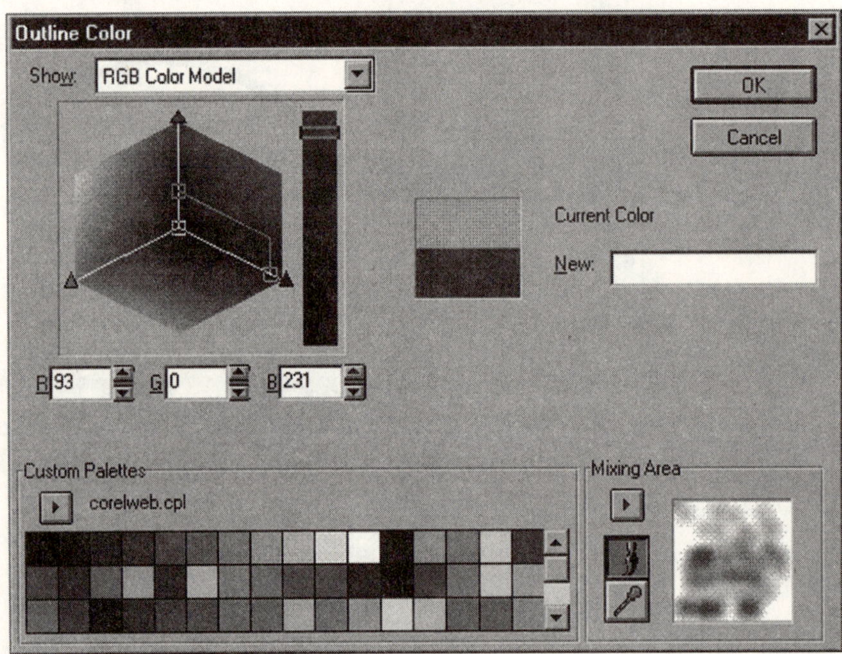

Figure 6-27: There's no end to the color rainbow!

The Outline Color dialog box provides a number of ways to specify colors. Choose according to personal preference. You may enter red, green, and blue values direct, select a color chip from the palette, click around in the color space, or blend a custom color in the mixing area. Once you find the color of your dreams, click on OK to assign the outline color to your object.

Just a warning: Corel's mysterious three-dimensional RGB color space representation is a bit odd, and may actually leave you in the dark, rather than enlightened. The points of the color cube merely signify the RGB color values, while the slider bar to the right of the color cube governs overall brightness. Pulling the slider bar to the bottom sets all the colors to identical values, which is great for assigning different gray levels. Try clicking and dragging the points of the color cube around now, to get the hang of it.

Outline Pen Attributes

The Outline Pen attributes dialog box (as shown in Figure 6-28) provides control over every possible outline characteristic. Access the Outline Pen attributes dialog box in one of three ways: from the Outline Pen fly-out menu, from the Edit button on the Outline Pen roll-up, or via the F12 keyboard shortcut. The dialog box allows you to change:

- Outline color

- Outline width—in your choice of inches, millimeters, picas and points, points, ciceros and didots, didots, or pixels

- Corners—square, rounded, or beveled

- Line caps—flat, rounded, or square

- Starting and ending arrowheads

- Line style—solid (default) or dotted

- Calligraphy—stretch, angle, or nib shaped

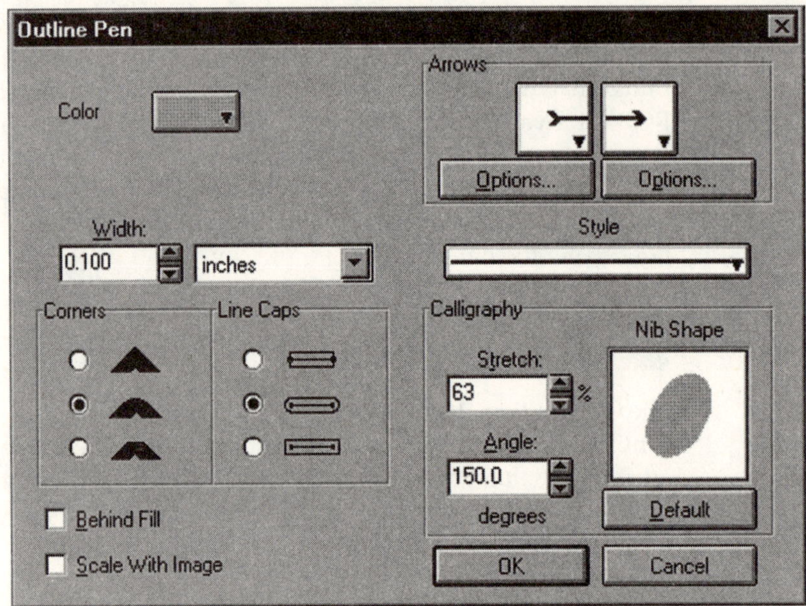

Figure 6-28: The Outline Pen dialog box offers a wide array of options.

You also can set the outline to be Behind Fill as well as to Scale With Image. These two options sound a bit cryptic but aren't difficult to understand. Behind Fill places the object's outline behind the object's fill color. Since the outline straddles an object's edges, Behind Fill cuts the visible outline width in half. Scale With Image scales the outline width proportionally if you enlarge or reduce the size of the object. If this option is not selected, the outline width remains the same if the object is resized—which can be less than desirable. You'll probably want to choose the Behind Fill and Scale With Image options for most outlined objects.

The Fill Tool

CorelWEB.DRAW's Fill tool lets you assign five different types of object fill. This delivers the flexibility to create vibrant and impressive graphics. The Fill tool fly-out menu (as shown in Figure 6-29) provides access to all the goodies. The top row features buttons for the Uniform Fill dialog box, the Fill roll-up, the Fountain Fill dialog box, the Two-color Pattern dialog box, the Full-color Pattern dialog box, and the Texture Fill dialog box. The bottom row allows one-click access for no fill, white, black, and 10, 30, 50, and 70 tints of gray fills.

The Fill roll-up (see Figure 6-30) puts all of CorelWEB.GRAPHICS's fill options at your fingertips as well. Buttons for Uniform Fill, Fountain Fill, Two-color Pattern, Full-color Pattern, and Texture Fill line the top. Click a button to configure the roll-up for the appropriate Fill option.

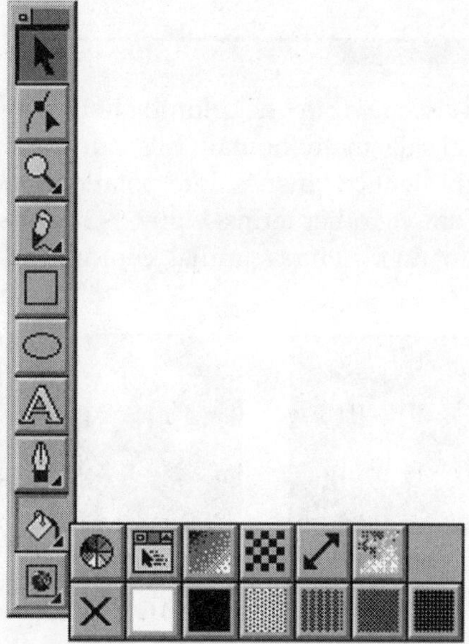

Figure 6-29: The Fill fly-out menu delivers the goods.

Figure 6-30: The five faces of the Fill roll-up.

Solid Color Fills

The Uniform Fill dialog box is identical to the Outline Color dialog box shown in Figure 6-27 and provides all the same flexibility. If your Web pages use a limited palette, you may want to build your own custom color palettes to save time and ensure that you're specifying the colors consistently. Chapter 10 discusses color palettes.

Fountain Fills

Fountain fills let you change from one color to another (or even more) within an object. Corel calls them fountain fills, but you may have heard them referred to as gradients, vignettes, interpolations, sweeps, degrad+s, or ramps, among other terms. Figure 6-31 shows the four different types of fountain fills: linear, radial, conical, and square.

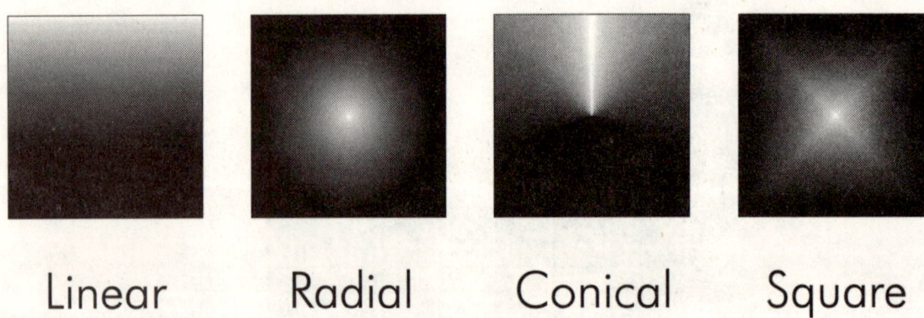

Figure 6-31: There's a fountain fill for every design situation.

To access the Fountain Fill dialog box, click on the Edit button on the Fill roll-up when the Fountain Fill button is clicked (or on the Fountain Fill button on the Fill fly-out menu). The Fountain Fill dialog box includes settings for every option. You'll learn how to create cool effects and take complete control over fountain fills in Chapters 8 and 9.

Two-Color & Full-Color Patterns

Two-color patterns let you fill objects with simple patterns from polka dots to architectural designs. These patterns are black and white by default, but you can change them to any colors you wish. You can import black-and-white bitmaps or create your own patterns from within CorelWEB.DRAW. Although two-color patterns may be of limited use in your Web page design work, we'll delve into their inner workings in Chapter 9.

Full-color patterns are, as you might imagine, similar to their two-color cousins. You can use the patterns that come with WEB.DRAW or import color bitmaps and CorelDRAW! files to create your own full-color patterns. Chapter 9 explores full-color patterns in depth.

Texture Fills

CorelWEB.DRAW's texture fills are one of the program's most intriguing features. They let you create synthetic textures that mimic those found in nature. These textures are infinitely modifiable and can be rendered in your choices of colors and sizes. You may have noticed the large number of wild-looking graphics included with CorelWEB.GALLERY; they were created with this feature. Chapter 10 goes into texture fills in depth.

The URL Drawing Tool

The URL (Uniform Resource Locator) drawing tool allows you to assign Web addresses to specific portions (or *hot spots*) of your artwork. Use this tool in one of three modes: rectangle, ellipse, and freehand. Draw a hot spot, then assign a URL to it by typing the address in the URL Location bar. The URL drawing tool is redundant with CorelWEB.DRAW's other drawing tools to some extent; it actually creates invisible objects with no outline or fill. Although WEB.DRAW allows you to assign a URL to any object, the URL drawing tool adds versatility and ease.

Moving On

In this chapter, you learned the basics behind CorelWEB.DRAW and got an overview of how you can use the program to create compelling images. In the next chapter, you'll learn about each of the effects you'll use to create your own cool artwork.

After that, in the next three chapters, you'll go hands-on with WEB.DRAW, using lively exercises, tips, and tricks to learn how to use the program in concert with CorelWEB.DESIGNER to create exciting Web sites (and sights!).

7

Getting Down to Business With CorelWEB.DRAW

In the last chapter, you learned the basics of CorelWEB.DRAW's toolbox and how to use its tools to create text and basic shapes. This chapter focuses on using the program's more advanced features to create incredible works of online art. We take a look at WEB.DRAW's Effects roll-ups as well as a number of the program's drop-down menus and dialog boxes. While there aren't any big exercises in this chapter, you'll find it handy to have WEB.DRAW up and running as you read through the text.

If you're an experienced user of CorelDRAW!, you may recognize that CorelWEB.DRAW is based on CorelDRAW! 5 technology. It's likely the company based the program on DRAW 5 (rather than Version 6 or 7) to ensure compatibility with the greatest number of systems: CorelDRAW! 5.0 works with Windows 3.x, Windows 95, and Windows NT; newer versions don't support Windows 3.x.

What Didn't Make the Cut?

Corel added plenty of Web savvy to WEB.DRAW. But many of DRAW 5's advanced features did not make their way into it, including:

- Contour effect
- Powerlines
- Lens effects
- Powerclip
- Clone
- Paragraph text
- Preset effects

Although you may be able to live without many of these features for Web page design, you can use some effects by creating the artwork in CorelDRAW! 5.0. Thankfully, WEB.DRAW can open 5.0 (.cdr) files. Object attributes such as lens effects and contours are actually supported in WEB.DRAW, although editing is inhibited. You can also save files created in CorelDRAW! 6.0 and 7.0 as 5.0 format files, and then open them with WEB.DRAW.

Let's get rolling with a look at the first of CorelWEB.DRAW's drop-down menus.

The File Menu: Open & Shut

The File menu, shown in Figure 7-1, is where you start and end your work with CorelWEB.DRAW. This menu lets you perform the most basic Windows file functions, that is, opening, saving, and printing files. In addition, it allows access to the program's file import, export, and publishing functions, as well as the Mosaic roll-up (for visual file management). Think of the File menu as a transportation center, where you bring files in from one format and send them out, Web-ready.

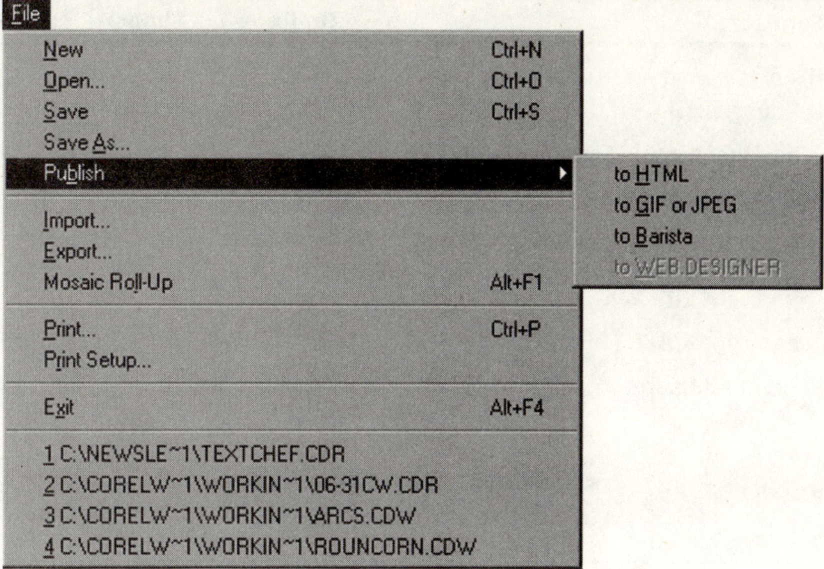

Figure 7-1: The File menu allows you to move files into and out of CorelWEB.DRAW.

File Import & Export Formats

CorelWEB.DRAW offers a subset of its big brother's file import and export capabilities. CorelDRAW! can work with files in a broad array of formats; WEB.DRAW uses the following formats common in Windows and on the Web:

Format	Suffix	Import	Export
Coordinate Position	MAP		x
CompuServe			
Graphics Interchange Format (GIF)	GIF	x	x
CorelDRAW! 5.0	CDR	x	x
CorelWEB.DRAW	CDW	x	x
Corel Presentation			
Exchange 5.0	CMX	x	x

Format	Suffix	Import	Export
HyperText Markup Language (HTML)	HTM		x
Joint Photographic Experts Group (JPEG)	JPG	x	x
TARGA Bitmap	TGA, VDA, ICB, VST	x	x
Tagged Image File (TIFF)	TIF	x	x
Windows Bitmaps	BMP, DIB, RLE	x	x
Windows Paintbrush	PCX	x	x
Windows Metafile	WMF	x	x

Table 7-1: Import and export capabilities.

Although the bitmap import choices cover the most common formats, vector import choices fall short without Adobe Illustrator (AI) and PostScript (PS or EPS) import capabilities. Most professional designers, illustrators, and publishers favor the Illustrator and PostScript formats. Again, you can get around this shortcoming by using WEB.DRAW in concert with a full-featured version of CorelDRAW!

The next few chapters discuss exporting GIF and JPEG files.

Drag & Drop Imports With Mosaic

Once upon a time, Corel had a nifty little file management utility called Mosaic. CorelMOSAIC was introduced in CorelDRAW! Version 2.0, back in the fall of 1990, as a way to manage files visually. This was approximately two years before NCSA Mosaic, the Web browser that started it all, first hit the streets, in 1992. When the ruckus over the World Wide Web (WWW) started to heat up in the summer of 1995, CorelMOSAIC morphed into Corel MULTIMEDIA MANAGER with the release of CorelDRAW! 6.0.

The CorelMOSAIC roll-up lingers unassumingly, in CorelWEB.DRAW's File menu. (It also can be summoned with the Alt+F1 keyboard shortcut.) Mosaic provides a cool way to preview (as shown in Figure 7-2) then drag and drop existing artwork into your creations. To bring an image into CorelWEB.DRAW from Mosaic, click on the image you want to use, then drag and drop it into your artwork. It's that easy!

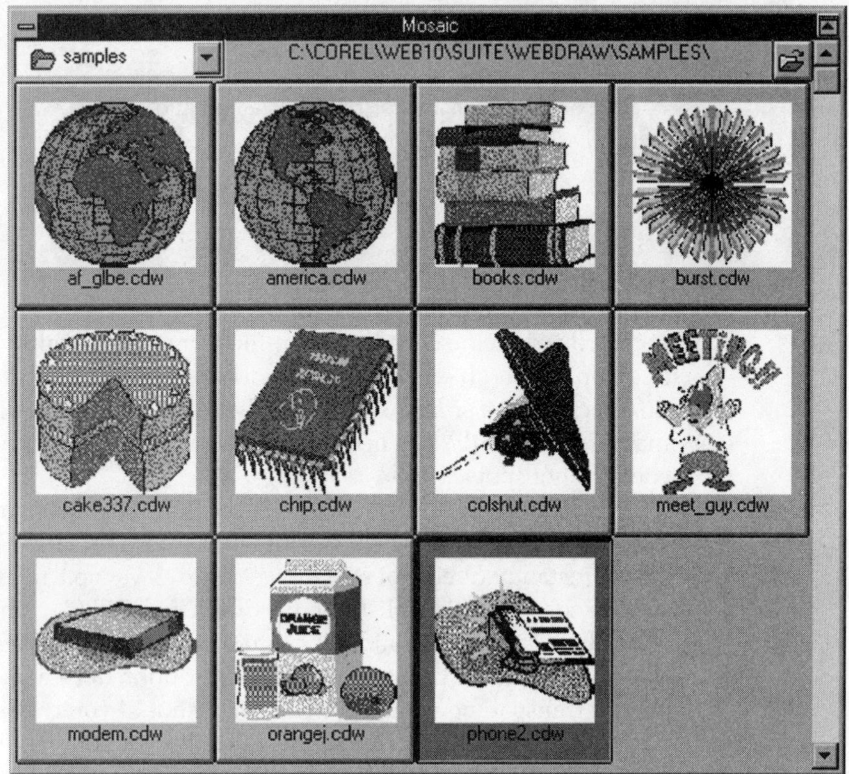

Figure 7-2: CorelMOSAIC lets you drag and drop existing images into your artwork.

Mosaic allows you to work with BMP, GIF, JPEG, PCX, TIFF, TARGA, and all of Corel's proprietary formats (CDR, CDW, CMX, and CMV). In addition, it provides access to Corel's older CLC catalog and CLB image libraries, although it only lets you pull images from your existing image catalogs and libraries; it does not let you add images or create new catalogs or libraries. If you need to build new image collections, investigate CorelGALLERY, which is detailed in Part VI of this book.

Publishing Files

The File menu includes the options to publish files to HTML, GIF, JPEG, Barista, and WEB.DESIGNER.

What's Barista?

Barista is Corel's fancy name for their implementation of Java, which saves images as vector files, rather than bitmaps.

Publishing CorelWEB.DRAW files to GIF or .JPEG simply exports your artwork in the chosen bitmap file format. Publishing to HTML goes one step further: It exports the artwork in your chosen format, in addition to creating a simple HTML file that contains a client-side image map. Consequently, you need to publish to HTML only if your artwork contains hot spots.

The CorelWEB.DESIGNER publish option is available only when you've launched WEB.DRAW from within WEB.DESIGNER. It allows you to instantly (well, not exactly *instantly,* as Version 1.0 is slow to process the request) publish your artwork as a GIF file, while automatically placing the image and image map into your open WEB.DESIGNER document. This may seem handy, but the option does not allow you to specify transparency or the JPEG format, should you choose to use it.

Publishing to Barista creates a Java version of your CorelWEB.DRAW document, complete with image map coordinates. Barista offers great promise, although this first implementation exhibits agonizingly slow performance. For simplicity's sake, we won't delve into Barista now. Instead, we'll save it for Parts III and VII.

The Edit Menu: Essentials

You'll find a few old friends on the Edit menu—such as Cut, Copy, and Paste—as well as a number of other familiar functions—such as Undo, Redo, Delete, and Duplicate. Rather than repeat the basics, we're going to assume that you've mastered the principles of Cut, Copy, and Paste.

Just Undo It!

Look at Figure 7-3. Undo, Redo, and Repeat listings change, depending on the most recent maneuvers. For example, if the last maneuver performed was to move an object, the menu will read "Undo Move." Redo provides the means to undo an Undo. The Repeat function is particularly helpful when creating a number of drag-duplicated objects. Repeatedly press Ctrl+R after drag-duplicating the first object and lay down an array of evenly spaced objects in a flash.

How Many Undos?

Undo can be set for up to 99 levels via the Preferences dialog box (more on that in Chapter 10).

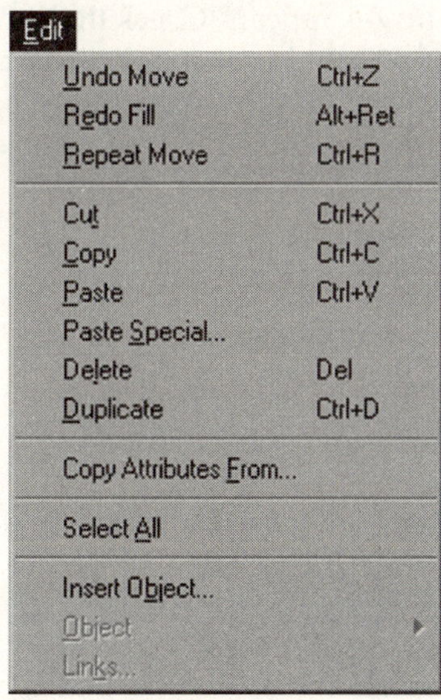

Figure 7-3: The Edit menu is chock full of keyboard shortcuts.

Paste Special

Paste Special is handy when you want to use the Windows clipboard to copy and paste objects from other programs while maintaining links to those programs. For example, you might use it to bring in a chart from Microsoft Excel or another charting program so that it can be updated quickly when the data change in the source program. Paste Special uses Windows's Object Linking and Embedding (OLE) features to maintain ties to the original source program. In the early days of OLE and Windows 3.x, the function was best used with extreme caution. With the advent of Windows 95 and Windows NT 4.0, however, it's delivered on its promise.

Swipe That Style!

Copy Attributes is another convenient time-saver. It lets you quickly copy fill, outline color, and pen characteristics from one object to another or copy text attributes from one text block to the next.

To use this function, select the object to which you want to copy attributes. From the Edit pull-down menu, select Copy Attributes From. A dialog box like that in Figure 7-4 appears. Check the attributes you want to copy and click on OK. When the fat arrow cursor appears, click on the object from which you want to copy attributes. As soon as you make the last click, the attributes are copied to the first object.

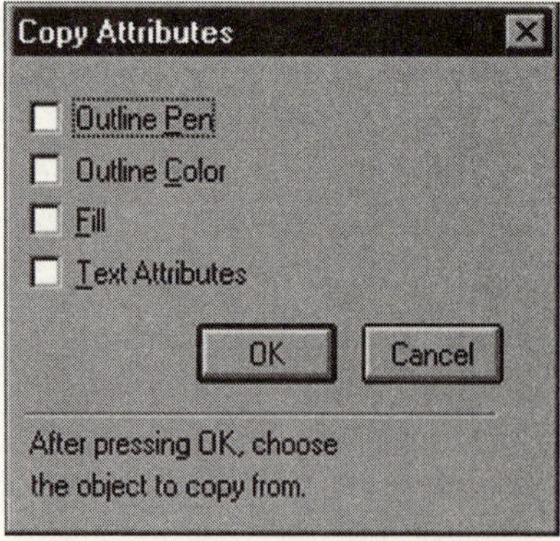

Figure 7-4: The Copy Attributes dialog box makes short work of copying fill, outline, and text characteristics.

Another Way to Copy Outline & Fill Attributes

You also can use the Update From buttons on the Outline and Fill roll-ups to copy these attributes from one object to another.

To select every object in the file you currently have open, choose Select All in the Edit pull-down menu. This function is helpful to remove the outline from all objects in one fell swoop or to scale everything up or down.

Insert Object

The insert object feature is similar to Paste Special. It allows you to place either a *linked* object or an *embedded* object into your artwork. A linked object is not stored within the CorelWEB.DRAW file; only a pointer is. When you change the original file (in its source application), the object is updated within WEB.DRAW. The Links dialog box keeps track of all the links in each file and provides complete control. Embedded objects are copies of the original object that are contained within WEB.DRAW. To edit an embedded object, double-click on it to launch its source application. The further you get into OLE, the more you'll appreciate its power. We'll look at using OLE to supercharge your work flow in Chapter 10.

The View Menu: Scope It Out

Want to change the way CorelWEB.DRAW looks onscreen? Look no further. The View menu, shown in Figure 7-5, is your key to changing the way the program appears. Here you turn on rulers, change the toolbox from floating to fixed, choose high-resolution bitmap previews, and access all the roll-ups. Some of the less-obvious features include:

- Color Palette—choose between Uniform and Custom Color palettes, or none at all. Palettes are covered in depth in Chapter 10.

- Wireframe—displays all objects in a black-and-white skeleton editing mode, without any outline or fill attributes. This provides the fastest screen refresh and is especially useful when working on complex artwork.

■ URL Fill—displays hatching to denote image map hot spots. You can alter the hatching style via the Preferences dialog box.

■ Bitmaps—affects only the screen preview, not the final artwork. Bitmap display can be set to high or low resolution in color editing mode, and can be turned off entirely in wireframe editing mode. These options are provided to speed up screen redraw.

■ Full-Screen Preview—toggles to a nonediting clean view of your artwork, sans windows.

■ Preview Selected Only—similar to Full-Screen Preview, except that only selected objects are shown. Once again, this is extremely useful when working on complex artwork and often is used in conjunction with the wireframe editing mode.

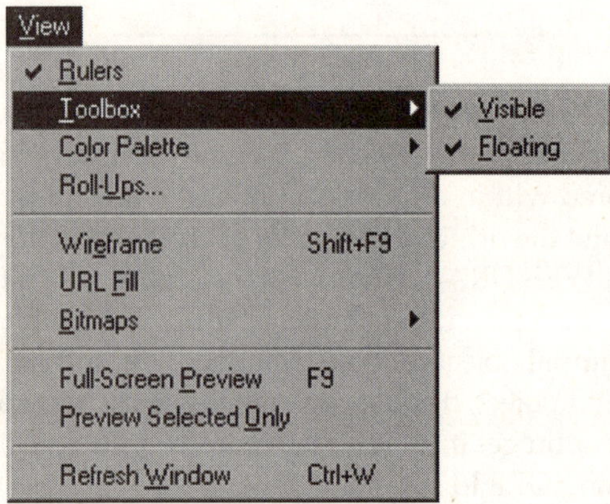

Figure 7-5: The View menu lets you take charge of CorelWEB.DRAW's screen appearance.

Is Your Screen Dirty?

Press Ctrl+W (or click on the scrollbar button) to refresh CorelWEB.DRAW's window and clean up all that "screen lint"!

The Layout Menu: Get Organized

The Layout menu, shown in Figure 7-6, is useful for its structural features. Notice that the menu includes a host of multipage functions, which may be better suited to the program's print-focused siblings. You won't need multipage illustration files as often when creating online materials as when you're creating those to be printed. Web artwork is usually a single page affair.

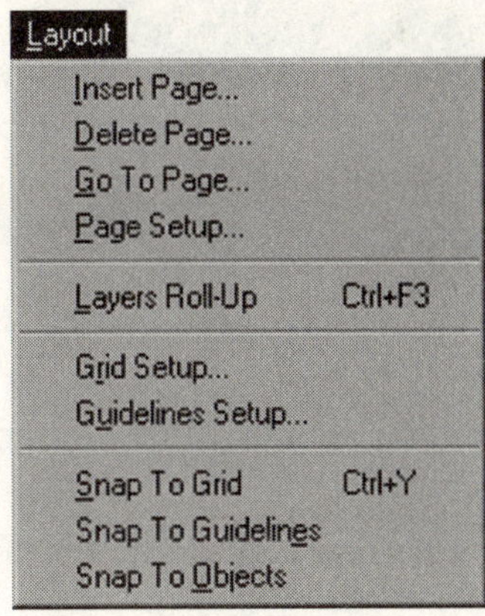

Figure 7-6: The Layout menu helps bring order to your artistic chaos.

The Layers roll-up, grid, and guidelines features are extremely useful when creating anything other than the most basic artwork. You'll put them all to work in the next chapter, as we create our own Web page graphics. You'll see how both the standard and *snap to* options are used to align and position objects.

The Arrange Menu: Slice & Dice

The Arrange menu, shown in Figure 7-7, contains a host of essential object controls and powerful special features that you'll find indispensable. Here are the keys to creating professional electronic artwork. They're not flashy, glitzy, or whizbang; they just do what has to be done.

Remember our Colorforms analogy in the last chapter? It's important to be able to easily move an object backward or forward through the object-stacking order. The five order commands—To Front, To Back, Forward One, Back One, and Reverse Order—quickly shuffle objects around. Group and Ungroup are important as well: To be effective, you need to move a group of objects in concert, rather than one by one.

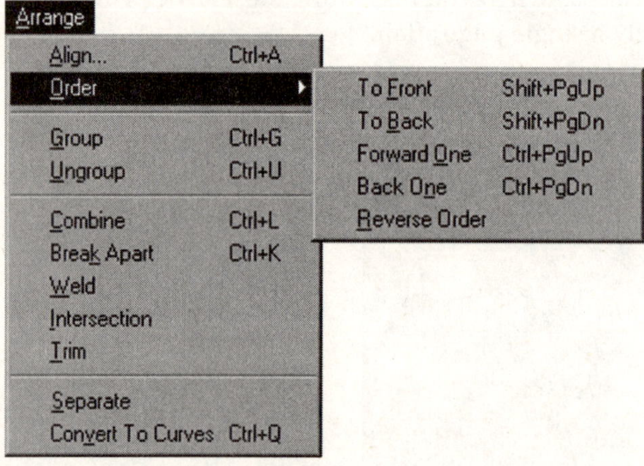

Figure 7-7: The Arrange menu lets you boss your objects around.

Get in Line With Align

The Align dialog box, shown in Figure 7-8, governs the spacing relationship between two or more selected objects. You may align selected objects along their vertical and/or horizontal axis or to the grid or the center of the page. The ducks in the bottom row of Figure 7-8 are aligned along their bottom horizontal axis. Remember as you Shift-click objects that they align to the last object selected.

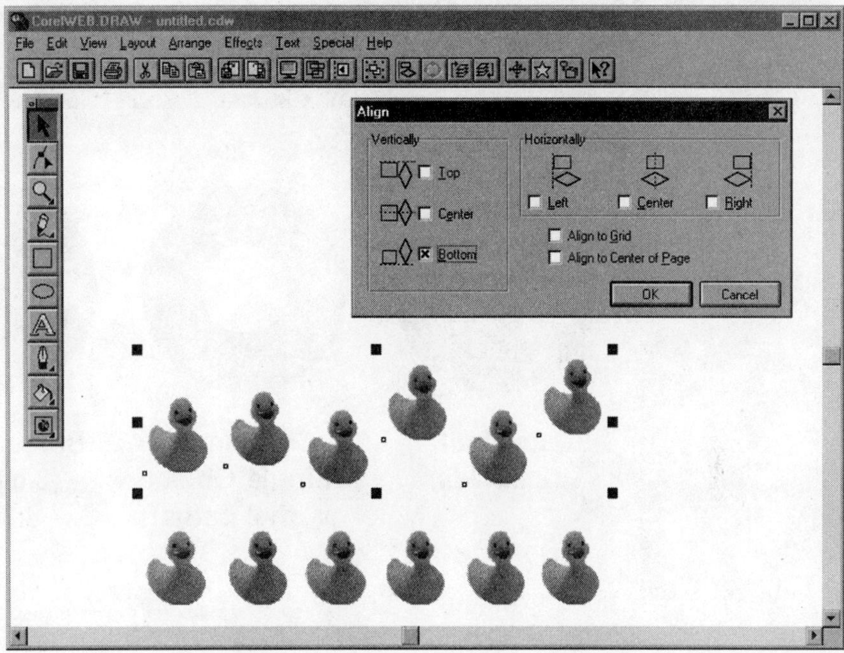

Figure 7-8: Want all your ducks in a row? Use the align feature!

Combine & Break Apart

If Homer Simpson wanted a metaphor for the Combine and Break Apart commands, he'd definitely use a doughnut. (But then again, Homer could probably use a doughnut for just about any metaphor.) Think of how a round doughnut (not jelly-filled) is put together and how you would draw it in a two-dimensional vector drawing program: as a combined-path object made up of two circular paths. If you simply created two circles on top of each other, you wouldn't be able to see through the hole (in other words, the inner circle) . . . unless you combined the two circles into one object using CorelWEB.DRAW's Combine command. See Figure 7-9.

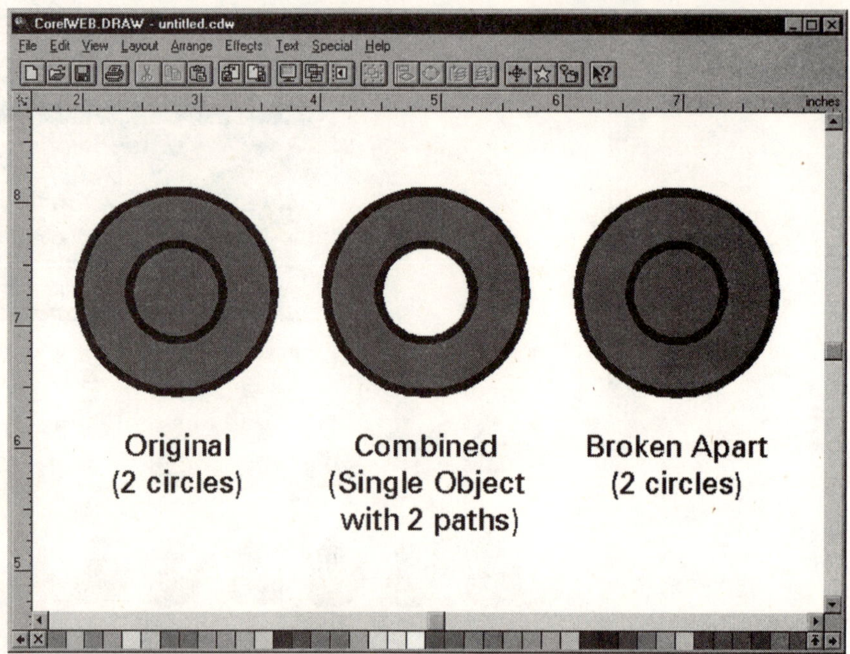

Figure 7-9: Mmmmmm . . . chocolate doughnuts.

To create a combined-path object, select the paths (more than two, if you like) and choose from the Arrange menu (or use the Ctrl+L keyboard shortcut). To break apart a combined path object into its component paths, select Arrange | Break Apart (Ctrl+K).

The Cookie Cutters: Weld, Intersection & Trim

Since we're on a snack food binge, let's talk about how weld, intersection, and trim—cousins of the Combine command—can be thought of as CorelWEB.DRAW's ever-so-convenient cookie cutters. Figure 7-10 illustrates the results of using these three functions on three identical pairs of objects.

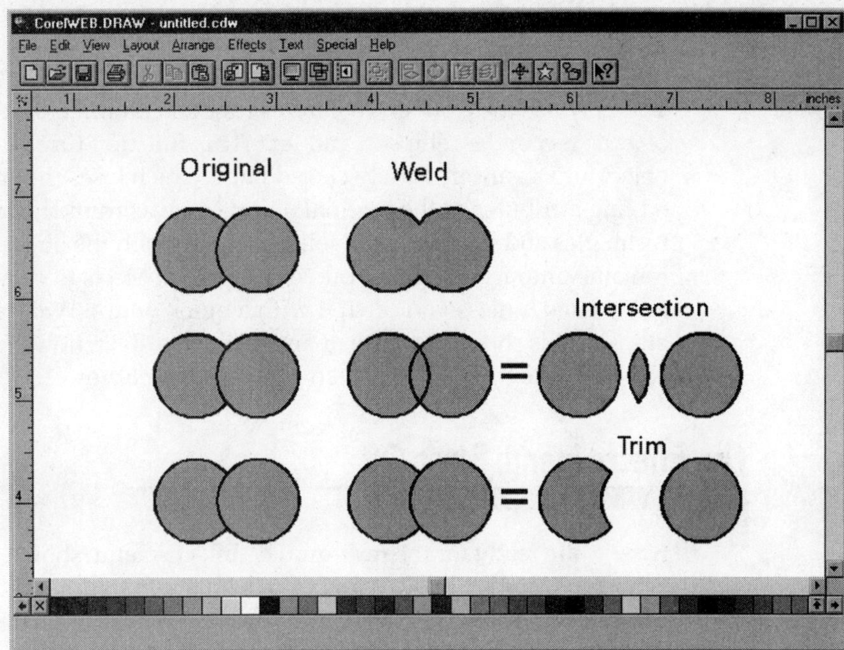

Figure 7-10: Weld, intersection, and trim let you bake up a tasty batch of objects.

- Weld—melds the objects together into one new object.

- Intersection—leaves the original objects untouched; creates a new object(s) from the overlapping portion of the original objects.

- Trim—leaves the topmost object untouched; cuts away the portion that overlaps the lower object.

Separate

The Separate command is used to chop up the results from a handful of high-level effects, thus allowing the separated pieces to be edited individually. Here's a quick rundown of when the Separate command comes in handy:

- Blend—breaks the starting and ending objects away from the intermediate (blending) objects.

- Extrude—breaks the original objects away from the extruded surfaces.

- Fit Text to Path—breaks the text away from the path.

Convert to Curves

You may use the Convert to Curves function on three different types of objects: rectangles, ellipses, and text. This function turns the original object into a garden-variety closed path, which loses the special node-editing attributes of the original object (such as rounded corners on rectangles and pie slices with ellipses), although the object's shape remains untouched. After you've converted objects to curves, there's no going back (unless you catch it with a quick undo). With rectangles and ellipses, this shouldn't present any problems. Text, however, is no longer editable as text after it has been converted to curves.

The Effects Menu: Blast Off

Now we're ready for the real fun. The Effects menu, shown in Figure 7-11, is host to CorelWEB.DRAW's famous image-manipulation effects—perspective, envelope, blend, and extrude—as well as its transformation features. Use these features to create exciting Web page graphics that seem to literally jump off the browser with the illusion of depth and space.

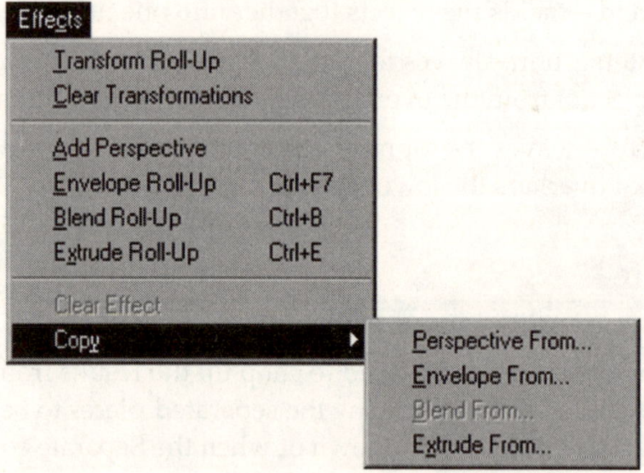

Figure 7-11: The Effects menu provides access to a world of powerful features.

Gain a New Perspective

The perspective effect allows you to create the illusion of depth, as illustrated by the roadside billboard in Figure 7-12. Select the object (or group of objects) to which you want to apply the perspective effect. Select Effects | Add Perspective. The cursor will change to the Shape tool, and a dotted-line bounding box will appear around the object. Click and drag on the appropriate perspective handle at a corner of the bounding box to apply the perspective. To make an object appear as if it is receding, pull the upper handle on the receding side of the object downward and the corresponding lower handle upward. Hold down the Ctrl key to constrain handle movement to a horizontal or vertical plane.

Figure 7-12: The perspective effect lets you set a vanishing point.

As you apply perspective to an object, the object's *vanishing point* moves in from the edge of the window. The vanishing point is the horizon position to which your object recedes. You'll achieve a more realistic appearance in artwork with perspectives if all objects share the same vanishing point. To copy a perspective from one object to another or clear a perspective altogether, use the Effects menu.

You'll find many interesting ways to apply this effect. You might even create a splash page for your Web site that recalls the prologue to *Star Wars*, as shown in Figure 7-13. You'll learn how to create this fun effect and other cool tricks in Chapter 9.

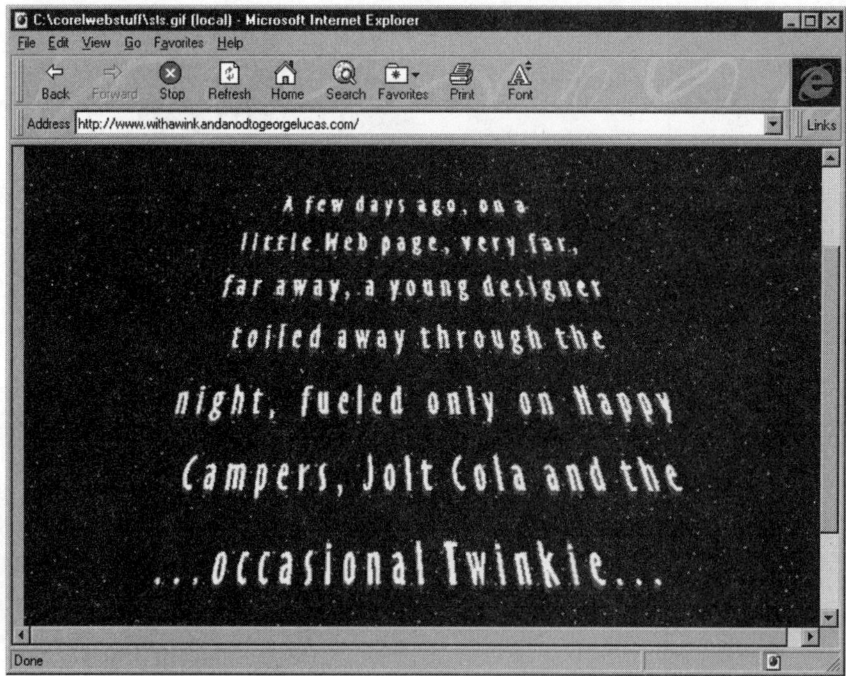

Figure 7-13: Typographical treatments like this are easy to achieve with the perspective effect.

Get Twisted With Envelopes

The envelope effect is great for twisting and turning text and other objects into new and interesting shapes. Figure 7-14 shows how easy it is to twist a piece of text into a ribbon-like three-dimensional design. The first example shows the original chunk of text and a preset envelope style being chosen from the roll-up. Once the style has been clicked, a preview bounding box appears over the selection, as shown in the second example. Click on the Apply button on the Envelope roll-up to execute the command, as shown in the third example. Once an envelope has been assigned to an object, you can tweak the shape to your heart's delight, as shown in the final example. Figure 7-15 shows old-time hand-lettered effects created with the envelope effect.

Figure 7-14: Applying the envelope effect is easier than it may first seem.

Figure 7-15: The envelope effect allows you to create elegant letterforms that would make a sign painter proud.

Blend: It's a Smoothie!

CorelWEB.DRAW's blend effect lets you meld two objects together to create new objects. The effect works on both the object's shape (as shown in Figure 7-16) and its color (as shown in Figure 7-17). This allows you to create a wide variety of special effects. They might be spooky, like the man-to-bat transformation, or so smooth they seem to have just come out of a Play-Doh Fun Factory. The vampire transformation was created with just five steps; the flower tube uses 200.

Figure 7-16: The blend effect morphs one object into another, as you can easily see with the blend steps set low.

Figure 7-17: With the number of blend steps set high, it can be difficult to discern where one object ends and the next begins.

Blends afford a wide variety of impressive design options. The flower tube is an example of a blend along a path. CorelWEB.DRAW gives you the option of running a blend along any path, including type characters that have been converted to curves! You'll see more cool blend effects in Chapter 9.

Extrude: Quick & Cheesy 3D

Have you ever wanted to create basic three-dimensional effects but were stymied by the extensive math and perspective issues? Well, hang onto your hat, because CorelWEB.DRAW lets you build pseudo-3D objects with relative ease. Although these are not true 3D objects (for which you'd need a real 3D modeling and rendering package), they're often all you need to create convincing 3D Web page graphics. See Figure 7-18. We'll go hands-on with the extrude effect in the next chapter as we build some way cool imagery.

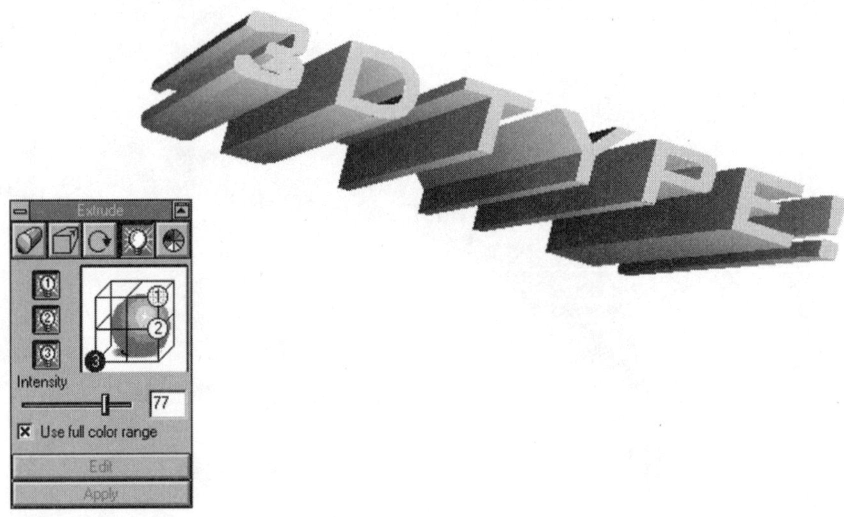

Figure 7-18: The extrude effect lets you create eye-popping 3D objects without those wacky red and blue glasses!

Transformation

While CorelWEB.DRAW's Pick tool lets you stretch, scale, move, rotate, and skew objects with interactive ease, its Transform roll-up (shown in Figure 7-19) lets you dial in your object transformations with numerical precision. This comes in handy when you know exactly how large you want to make an object or how far you want to move it. The Transform roll-up contains all the basic object manipulation functions in one handy device.

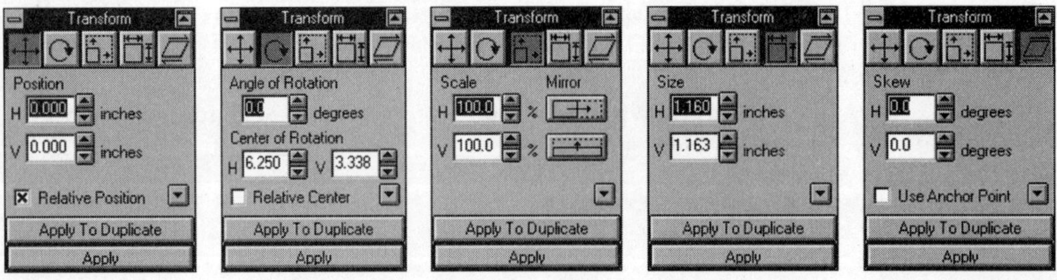

Figure 7-19: The Transform roll-up puts all the controls at your fingertips.

Moving On

In this chapter you learned how to take text and basic shapes to the next plane. By applying CorelWEB.DRAW's advanced effects, you create beautiful and effective Web page graphics quickly and with minimum hassle.

In the next chapter, you'll really get down to work, as you create a number of exciting Web page graphics and image maps with CorelWEB.DRAW. Subsequent chapters let you in on some cool tips and tricks, in addition to helping you make the most of vector graphics for Web page design.

8

Creating Structural Web Graphics

With the basics of CorelWEB.DRAW under your belt, it's time to put that knowledge to good use. The bulk of this chapter focuses on the methods used to build structural Web page graphics, such as backgrounds, buttons, navigation bars, horizontal dividers, and bullets. We discussed the basic principals behind these graphic elements in Chapter 2, learning how they're used with WEB.DESIGNER. This chapter goes hands-on, showing you how to create the individual elements necessary for a polished Web page. It ends with a discussion of image-mapping techniques. This chapter and the two that follow are crammed full of how-to methods, with plenty of exercises and examples. Get ready to crack the spine and dog-ear those pages!

Building Backgrounds

CorelWEB.DRAW provides you with many tools you need to create distinctive Web page backgrounds. Web page backgrounds were introduced in Chapter 2, but if you've just flipped to this page, it might be a good idea to quickly review the basics. Three key points to consider when designing a tiled background image follow:

- Ensure readability.
- Less is more.
- Never let them see your seams.

It's imperative to ensure readability. The information contained on your Web pages is more important than the electronic paper (the background) on which they are printed. Avoid overly complex designs—they may confuse your visitors. Strive for a clean, effective, and seamless presentation. Wild patterns can be fun, but they should only be used in situations where they do not obscure the text. Figure 8-1 breaks all three rules. It uses a pattern that is not only dense but seamy. Figure 8-2 is a slight improvement, in that the seams have been covered. However, it's still too busy to be used as a Web page background, in most cases.

Figure 8-1: This background was created from a WEB.DRAW texture fill.

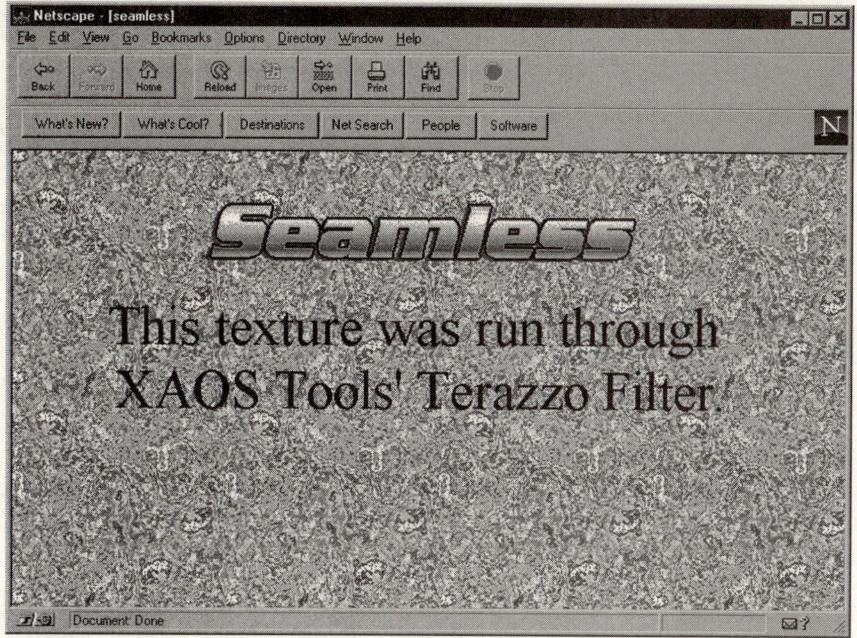

Figure 8-2: Here, we lost the seams (with some work in a paint editor), but the text is still difficult to read.

Figure 8-3 represents an improvement over both of the previous examples. It uses the same seamless texture used in Figure 8-2, but instead of covering the entire background of the page, it only covers a vertical accent stripe. This treatment is far more effective. The first exercise in this chapter demonstrates how easy it is to create a vertical striped background.

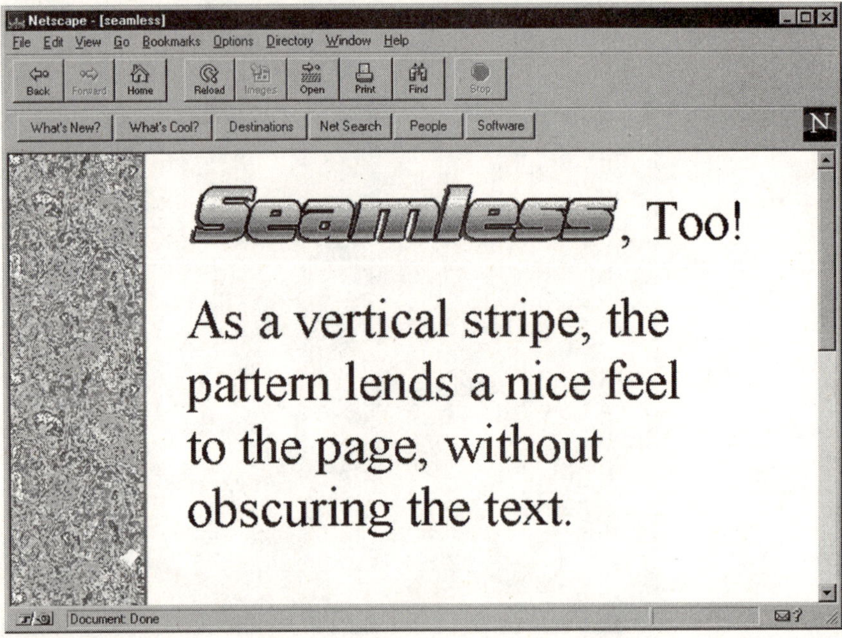

Figure 8-3: Now that's more like it!

Don't Forget to Check Out the CD!

The Comprehensive Guide to CorelWEB.GRAPHICS Suite CD-ROM includes more than 3,000 textures and hundreds of patterned backgrounds, from mild to wild!

We're going to jump right into a discussion of striped backgrounds, as they are a forte of WEB.DRAW. Backgrounds that tile out to symmetrically fill an entire window, such as the image shown in Figure 8-2 are really the province of the bitmap paint editors. Unfortunately, WEB.DRAW does not have the provisions to build this type of seamless background.

Vertically Striped Backgrounds

Simple, solid-color vertical stripes are one of the most popular Web page background styles. When properly executed, they are clean, effective, and fast. By constraining the image to several colors, you'll create a lightweight file. (The more colors in an image, the larger the file size.) A limited palette and small file size ensure rapid downloading and consistent display on a variety of platforms and browsers. The colored stripe is often used as the background for a vertically stacked navigation bar, as in the c|net Web site shown in Figure 8-4. A table controls the placement of text and graphics—in this case, the site ID and buttons—within the stripe. Advertising banners often overlap the vertical stripe, as does the example at the top of this page.

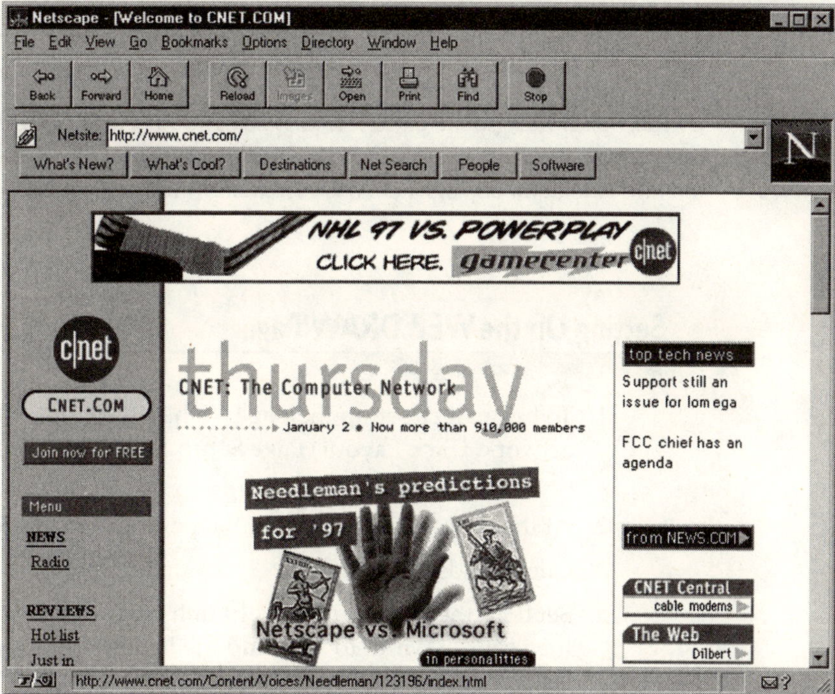

Figure 8-4: A vertically striped background provides a clean, uncluttered canvas for c|net's immensely popular Web site.

It's easy to create vertically striped backgrounds with WEB.DRAW. The key to fast backgrounds is to create a short and wide image that uses an extremely tight color palette. These images should be as wide as the widest browser window and (often) just a handful of pixels in height. When the image tiles down the browser window, it imparts a seamless stripe, as if being pulled by an invisible paint roller. The simplest backgrounds use just two colors: one for the stripe and one for the main body. In WEB.DRAW terms, that equates to using just two appropriately colored rectangles. However, Web page designers are not often satisfied with the flat appearance that this scheme presents. Fortunately, it doesn't take much effort to turn the flat stripe into something a bit more 3D-ish. If WEB.DRAW is not already running, it's time to launch it and get down to work!

How Wide Is Wide Enough?

A 1,024-pixel background pattern is as wide as you normally need to go; anything wider is overkill. If you make the pattern less than 800 pixels, however, it will repeat on high-resolution displays if the browser window has been pulled wide open.

Setting Up the WEB.DRAW Page

1. To begin, let's set up the page so that it's wide enough to fit the artwork. Click Layout | Page Setup to summon the Page Setup dialog box.

2. At the drop-down menu, set the page size to Custom.

3. Click Landscape.

4. Set both the Width and Height unit drop-down menus to pixels, then set the Width to 1024 and the Height to 768, as shown in Figure 8-5.

5. Click OK.

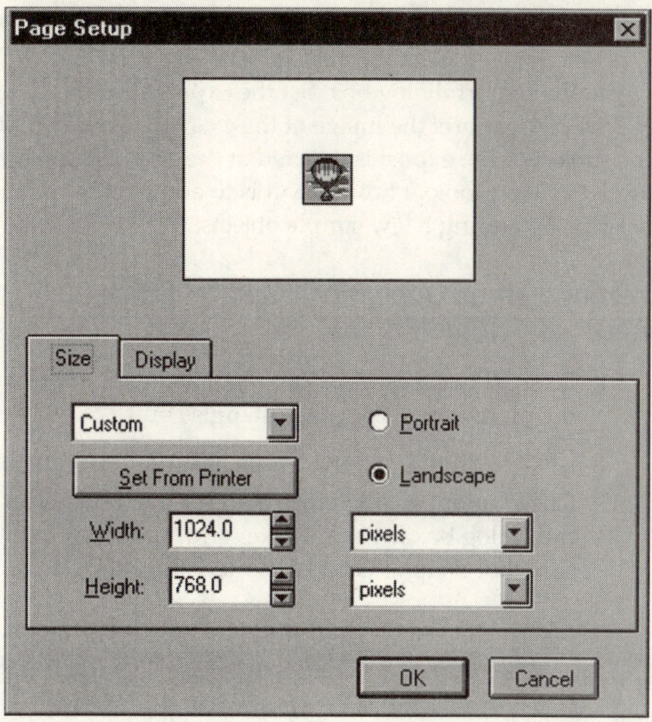

Figure 8-5: Page Setup is used to define the overall dimensions of the WEB.DRAW page. The dialog box can be summoned by double-clicking on the edge of the page.

Creating a Solid-Color Vertical Stripe

1. Click the Rectangle tool.

2. At the left side of the page, draw a rectangle 120 pixels wide by 10 pixels high. Set its color to Blue (R0/G0/B255) and its outline to None.

3. Click Layout | Snap to Objects to make the rectangle "magnetic."

4. Draw another rectangle 904 pixels wide by 10 pixels high. Butt it to the first rectangle, so that the left side of the new rectangle meets the right side of the first rectangle. Set its color to Yellow (R255/G255/B0) and its outline to None. (Although a white background is far more common, we're using yellow, so that the rectangle is visible for the purposes of this exercise.)

That's it! All you need to do is export the background. When you export the image, select the objects to be exported and click Selected Only in the Export dialog box. Set the export size to be 1 to 1, so that WEB.DRAW exports the image at the exact size at which it was created. (The subject of file export is covered at the end of the chapter.) Right now, let's take a look at how easy it is to add a bit of dimensionality to the stripe by adding a few simple objects.

Creating a Three-Dimensional Vertical Stripe

1. Press F2 to access the Zoom tool. Drag a tight marquee around the place where the two rectangles butt.

2. Click Layout | Snap to Objects to turn this feature off.

3. Click Layout | Grid Setup to access the Grid Setup dialog box. Set the dialog box for a one-pixel grid, as shown in Figure 8-6. Be sure that Snap to Grid is selected and click OK.

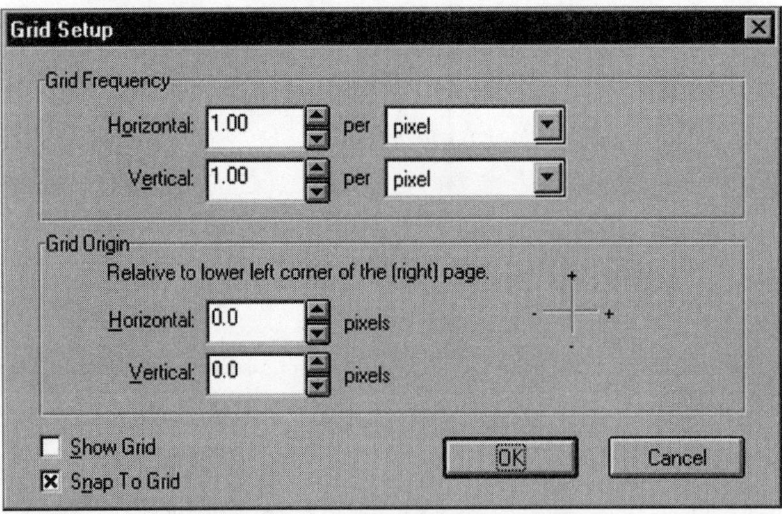

Figure 8-6: The Grid Setup dialog box provides total grid control, down to the pixel level.

4. Click the Freehand tool. Draw a straight vertical line, one pixel to the right of where the two rectangles butt. Make it 10 pixels high.

5. Click Edit | Select All to select all three objects.

6. Click Arrange | Align to access the Align dialog box. Click Top. Click OK. The line is now vertically aligned with the rectangles.

7. Press Esc to deselect all three objects.

8. Press Shift+F7 to summon the Pen roll-up.

9. Click the vertical line and assign it a pixel width of 1 and an 80% gray color, as shown in Figure 8-7.

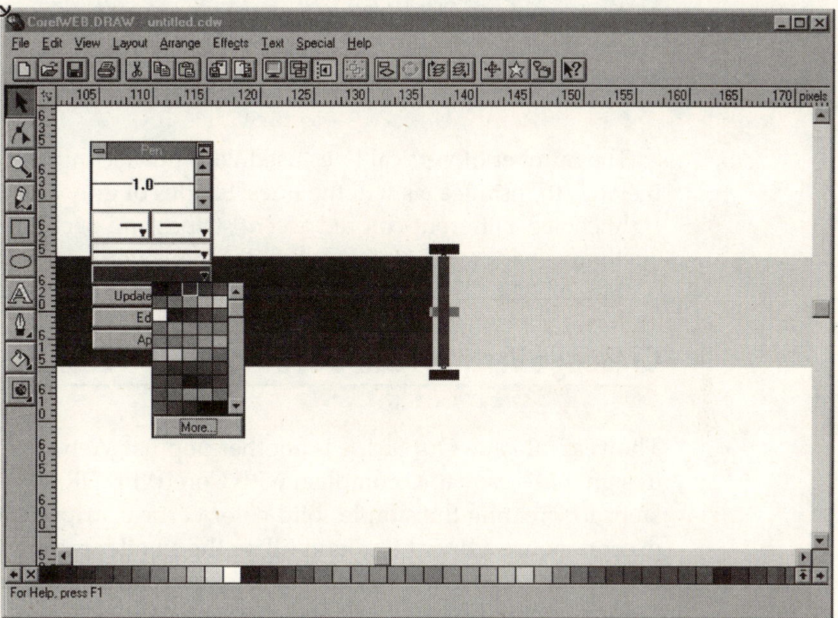

Figure 8-7: The Pen roll-up makes quick work of assigning outline widths and colors.

10. Drag the vertical line one pixel to the right. Click the right mouse button to duplicate the object and release. Repeat this drag-duplicate procedure to create a third and fourth line.

11. Use the Pen roll-up to assign a 60% gray outline color to the second line, a 40% gray outline color to the third line, and a 20% gray outline color to the fourth line.

12. Select all four vertical lines and drag them so that they appear as in Figure 8-8.

Figure 8-8: When viewed in a browser, these four little lines will blur together and impart a three-dimensional look to the background stripe.

The number of vertical lines used with this technique will vary from instance to instance, as will the hues. Shades of gray are often not the right choice. Different-colored accent stripes and backgrounds call for a customized approach. It is a good idea, however, to only specify colors within the Netscape 216-color palette, as covered in Chapter 10.

Creating a Vertical Fade-Out Stripe With a Fountain Fill

The Vertical Fade Out Stripe is another popular Web page background design that's easy to accomplish with CorelWEB.DRAW. Just follow the steps for creating the simple solid-color vertical stripe as above, with one exception: use a linear fountain fill on the smaller rectangle to achieve the fade-out. Let's see how easy it is to create a black background that fades to white on the left border.

1. Select the larger rectangle. Give it a black fill.

2. Select the smaller rectangle.

3. Press F11 to access the Fountain Fill dialog box. By default, it will be set to a 90 degree linear black-to-white fountain fill. Set it to –180 degrees (as shown in Figure 8-9) and click OK. When exported, the background image will appear as in Figure 8-10.

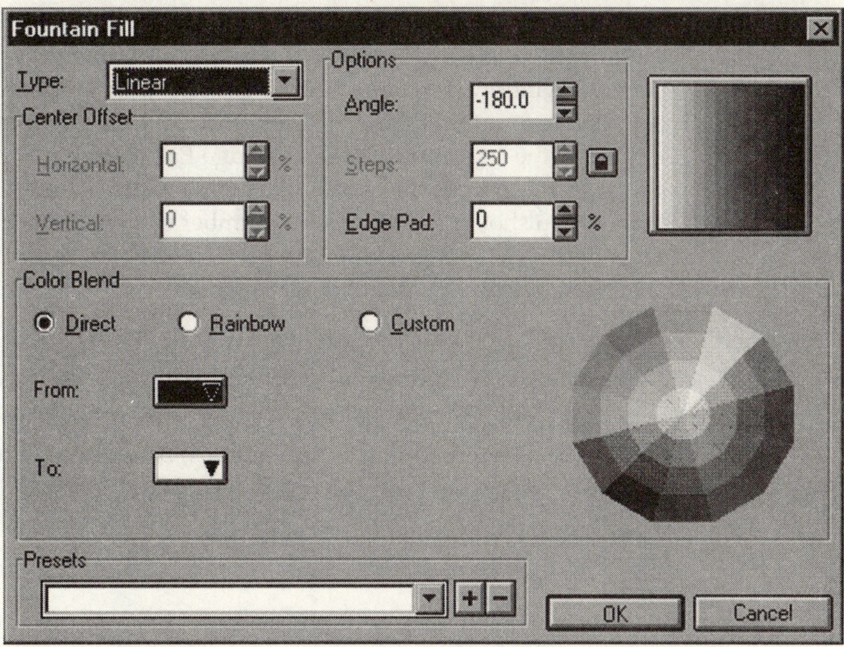

Figure 8-9: The Fountain Fill dialog box makes it simple to create smooth fades.

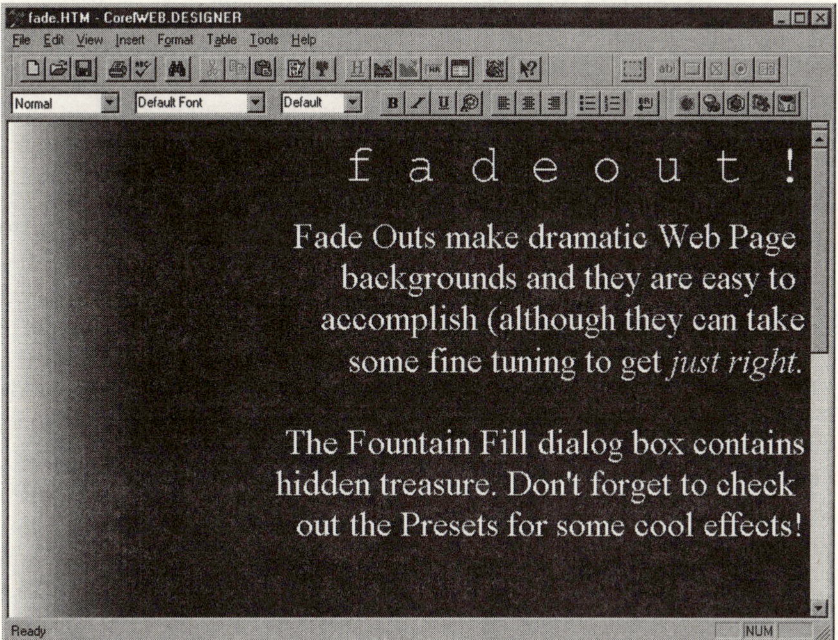

Figure 8-10: This one was way too easy! Try varying the fountain fill settings to achieve different effects.

Now try fooling around with the Fountain Fill dialog box. You can alter the fill angle by interactively clicking and dragging around the preview window. The Steps setting governs the number of transitional stripes in a fountain fill, to a maximum of 256 (the higher the number, the smoother the transition), while the Edge Pad setting will push the blend toward the center of the object. Each step creates an intermediate color. Hence, you should use the lowest number of steps necessary to achieve a smooth blend; the higher the number of steps, the larger the resulting file. There are three types of color blends:

- *Direct*—blends from one color directly to the next.

- *Rainbow*—blends from one color to the next while cycling through the color wheel in a clockwise or counterclockwise spiral.

- *Custom*—ping pongs (or transitions) between a number of colors.

Creating a Cylindrical Vertical Stripe

As mentioned in Figure 8-10, the Fountain Fill dialog box contains some nifty preset fills. You can use a number of these critters to quickly create some totally tubular background patterns. Start with the same two rectangles.

1. Select the smaller rectangle.

2. Press F11 to access the Fountain Fill dialog box.

3. At Presets, select Cylinder - Gold 01 from the drop-down list. Click OK. Hey, Web surfing dudes and dudettes, it's totally tubular!

Figure 8-11 shows the Fountain Fill dialog box in Custom mode. The little triangles along the blend denote the blending colors. To change the way a custom fountain fill fades, try sliding the triangles around. To change a blending color, click on the appropriate triangle to select it (the triangle will turn black). Then click on the color you want to use (from the palette), or click on the From color to access the full spectrum of color.

It's easy to add and delete color transition points. To add a triangle, double-click in the blend; the triangle will be assigned the color value of that position (which you can then alter at will). To delete a triangle, double-click on it. Figure 8-12 displays a unique effect that was created by placing three identically filled rectangles next to each other.

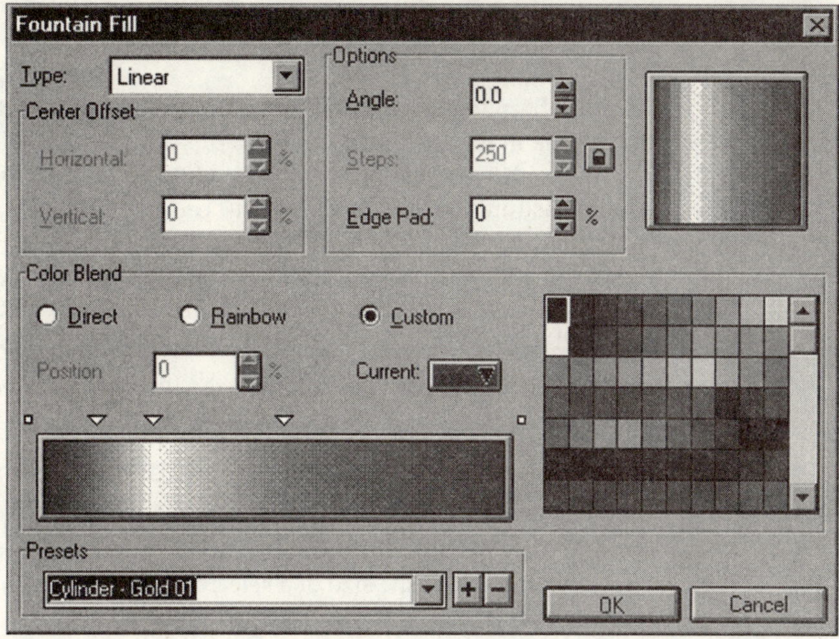

Figure 8-11: *Each triangle denotes a custom color blend transition point.*

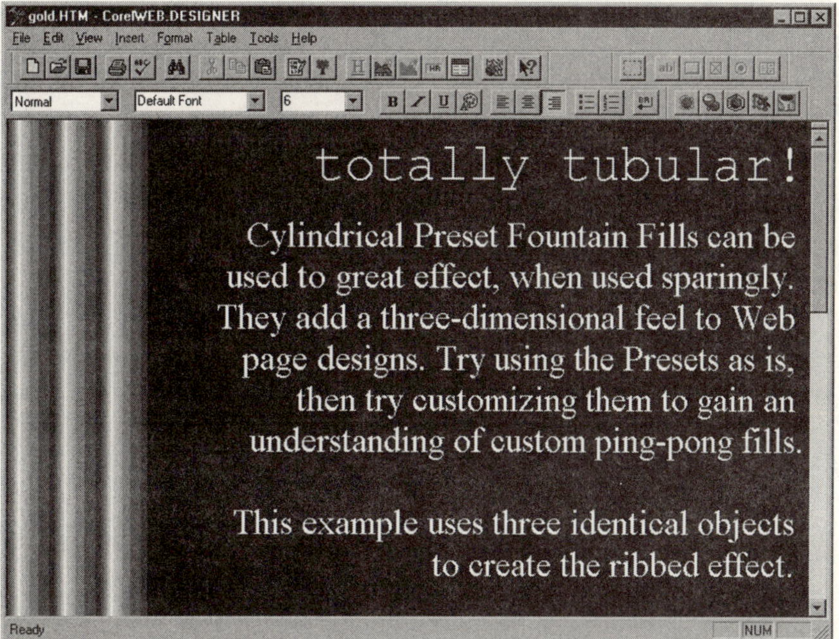

Figure 8-12: *By using more than two colors, custom cylindrical fills provide the illusion of 3D.*

Creating a Seamless Textured Vertical Stripe

Have you been wondering how the seamless textured vertical stripe shown back in Figure 8-3 was created? It's another simple trick; the key is to *start* with a seamless texture. You'll find more than 3,000 bizarre seamless textures on *The Comprehensive Guide to CorelWEB.GRAPHICS Suite Companion CD-ROM*. The "official" CorelWEB.GRAPHICS CD-ROM contains some cool photographic seamless textures as well. Let's build a seamless stripe from one of Corel's textures. With the "official" CorelWEB.GRAPHICS CD-ROM in your computer's CD-ROM drive:

1. Click File | Import to summon the Import dialog box.

2. At List Files of Type, click JPEG Bitmap (*.jpg).

3. At Directories, maneuver to your CD-ROM drive and select backgrds\stone.

4. Click the Options button to display the full Import dialog box. This displays the size of a selected file as well as other pertinent information, as shown in Figure 8-13.

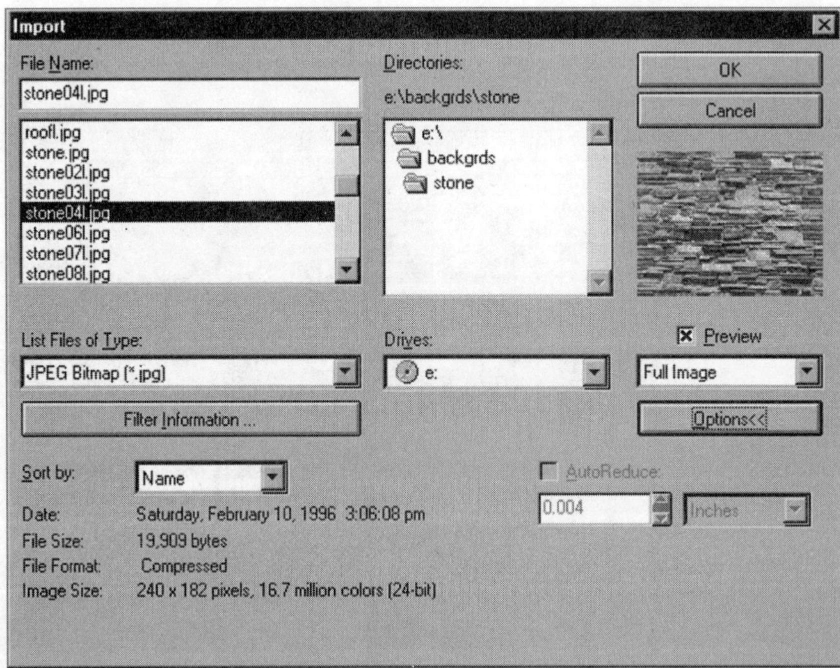

Figure 8-13: The Import dialog box allows you to visually identify images before you bring them into WEB.DRAW.

5. Scroll through the list of files. When you select a file, it will be previewed in the window at the right of the dialog box. Select stone04I.jpg and click OK to import the file.

Cropping Imported Images With the Shape Tool

When the stone texture comes into WEB.DRAW, it will be 240 pixels wide by 182 pixels high. While we will use the full height, it will be necessary to crop the width using the Shape tool.

1. Press F2 and drag out a marquee to zoom up on the imported stone texture.

2. Press F10 to access the Shape tool. If the stone texture is not selected, select it. The status line will report on the crop statistics, as shown in Figure 8-14.

3. Let's crop the image so that it's 120 pixels wide (50% of the original width). Click and drag the left side center handle toward the middle of the stone texture. Watch the status line and release the mouse button when it reports a 50% left crop. The cropped image will appear as in Figure 8-15. Notice how the status line reports on the cropping percentages.

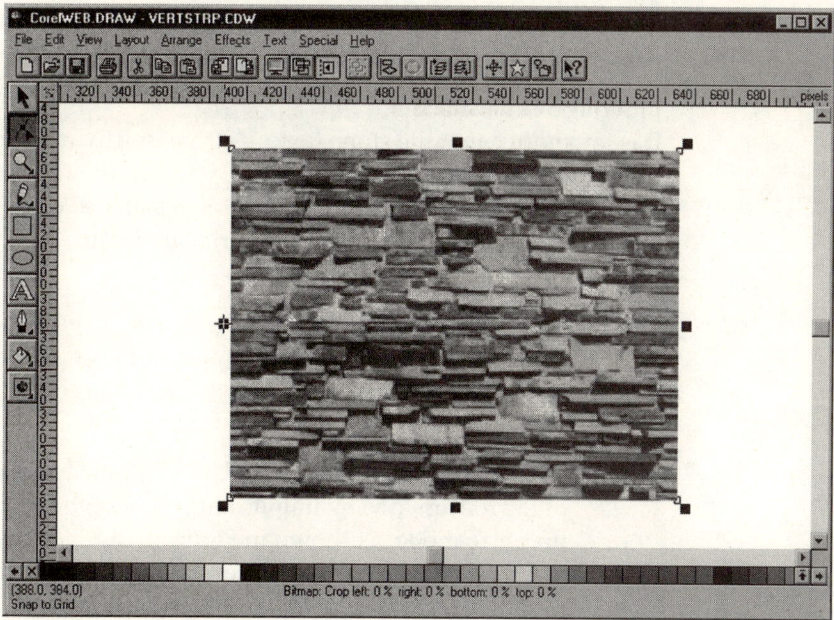

Figure 8-14: The status line provides you with the feedback you need to crop by percentage. For a more precise crop, you may want to drag out some guidelines.

4. Press Shift+F4 to zoom out to page view.

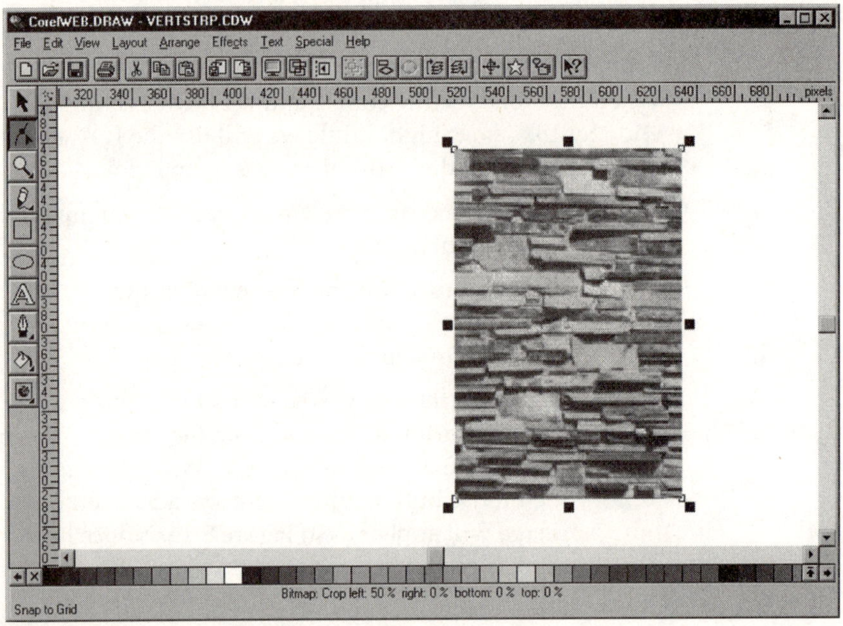

Figure 8-15: Cutting down stone walls has never been so easy!

Ensuring Seamlessness

It is imperative that the stone texture stripe exactly matches the overall background rectangle in height. If not, you will fail to create a seamless texture. Thus, you should make the large rectangle 904 pixels wide by 182 pixels high (the height being the critical measurement).

1. Click Layout | Snap to Object.

2. Press F6 to access the Rectangle tool. From the top right corner of the stone texture, draw a rectangle 904 pixels wide by 182 pixels high. If it's not exactly 904 x 182, don't fret. The next step will cure all.

3. Click Effects | Transform Roll-Up. Click the button at the bottom of the roll-up to view it in its entirety. Use the Transform roll-up's Size mode, as shown in Figure 4-16. Click the top left marker in the grid at the bottom of the roll-up to resize the rectangle from its top left corner. At H, enter 904. At V, enter 182. Click Apply.

4. Assign the rectangle an off-white fill (R255 G255 B204) and no outline.

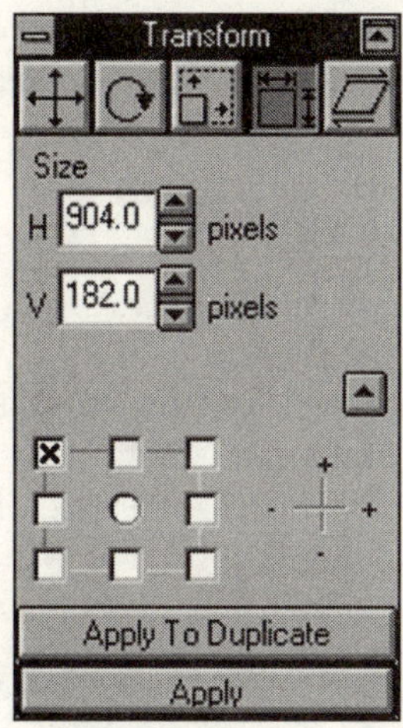

Figure 8-16: The Transform roll-up delivers precise control over sizing functions.

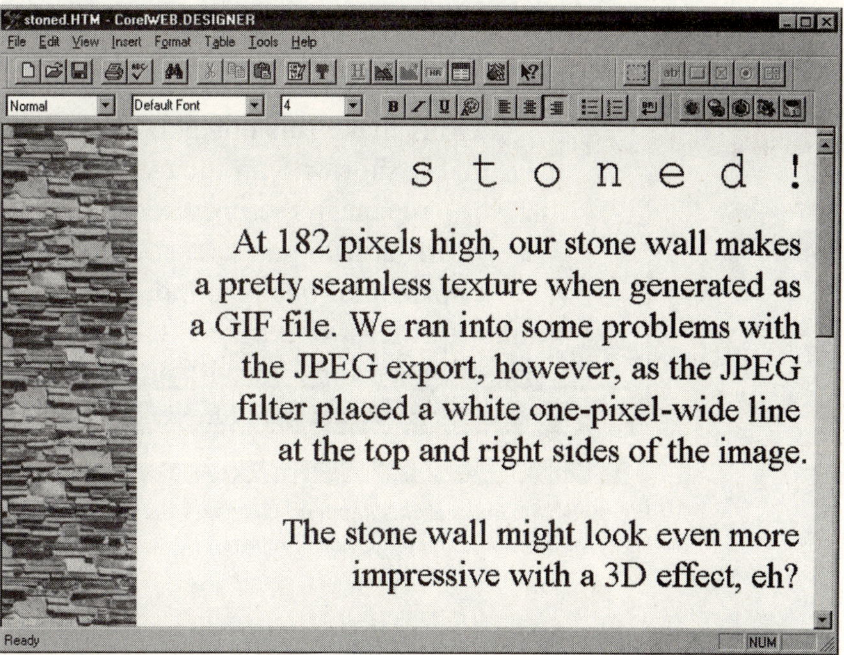

Figure 8-17: The photographic backgrounds that come with CorelWEB.GRAPHICS Suite provide many opportunities to create realistic background treatments.

When the file is exported, it creates a flawless GIF background, with nary a seam showing. As mentioned in Figure 8-17, however, the JPEG filter produced an unfortunate anomaly. The 256 color GIF file weighed in at 27K, which represents significant download time. Be kind to your audience: tweak and tighten those GIF palettes. In Chapter 10, you'll see how easy it is to optimize GIF images for fast downloads.

Horizontal Striped Backgrounds

Horizontally striped backgrounds are far less common than vertically striped backgrounds. However, the methods used to create them are similar, with one important difference: a horizontal striped image is tall and skinny while a vertical striped image is short and wide.

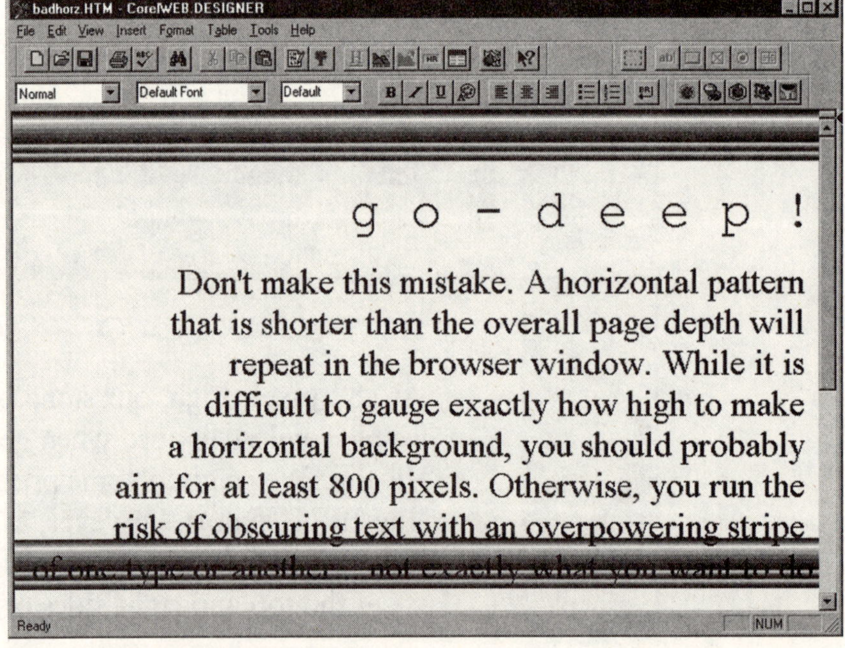

Figure 8-18: Don't let this happen: make sure that your horizontally striped backgrounds are tall enough not to repeat.

How Tall Is Tall Enough?

The trick with "stripe at the top of the page" horizontal patterns is that they must be tall enough not to repeat within the page. The page depth will determine the height of the pattern, as shown by Figure 8-18. This is far from exact, however, as individual browser text size settings can play havoc with your layout.

Creating a Solid Color Horizontal Stripe

1. Click the Rectangle tool.

2. At the top of the page, draw a rectangle 10 pixels wide by 36 pixels high. Set its color to Blue (R0/G0/B255) and its outline to None.

3. Click Layout | Snap to Objects to make the rectangle "magnetic."

4. Draw another rectangle 10 pixels wide by 732 pixels high. Butt it to the first rectangle, so the top side of the new rectangle meets the bottom side of the first rectangle. Set its fill color to off-white (R255 G255 B204) and its outline to None.

5. Bingo—it's an instant pattern! Try experimenting with some horizontal accent lines.

Creating a Deckled-Edge Horizontal Stripe

The following is just one example of a decorative horizontal stripe. Deckled edges are found on expensive writing paper and in some high-end documents, including corporate annual reports. An electronic deckled edge, such as that shown in Figure 8-19, is quick and easy to create. Start with the pattern created in the previous exercise.

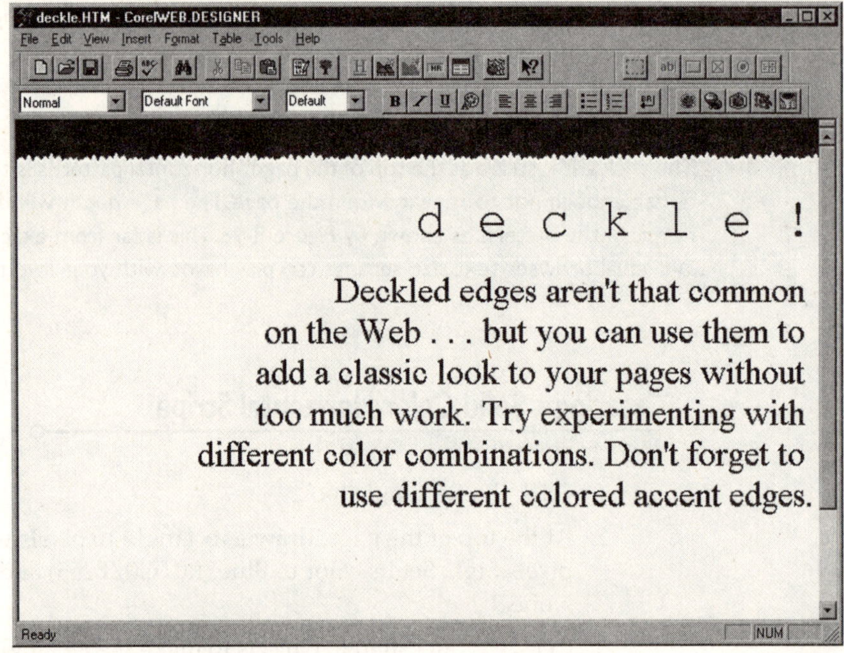

Figure 8-19: A deckled edge recalls the look of fancy paper.

1. Select both rectangles.

2. Use the Transform roll-up's Size mode to resize both rectangles to 60 pixels wide. This will provide enough room to create a nice jagged edge.

3. Press F2 and drag out a marquee to zoom up on the imported stone texture.

4. Press F5 to access the Freehand tool. Draw a jagged little object, as shown in Figure 8-20. It's important to keep the object from extending over the sides of the rectangles (otherwise, you will not create a seamless texture). Give the jagged object a white fill and no outline.

5. Click and drag the object down a few points. Hold down the Ctrl key to constrain movement to a vertical plane. Right-click to duplicate the object. Give the new object a fill identical to the bottom rectangle—off-white (R255 G255 B204).

6. Click Edit | Select All.

7. Press Ctrl+A to access the Align dialog box. Center all the objects horizontally and click OK. Deckle-rific!

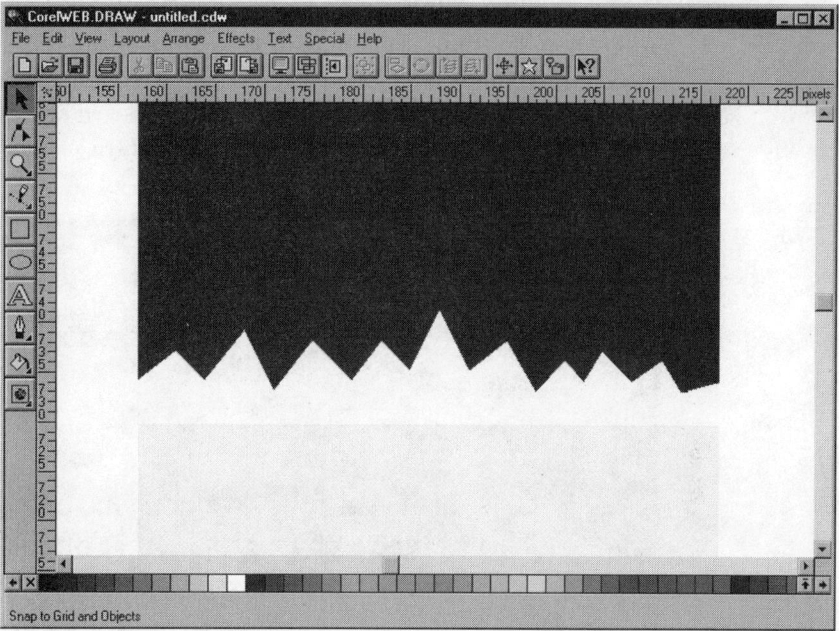

Figure 8-20: Everyone can use a jagged little edge once in a while.

Textured Backgrounds

If you've had the opportunity to fiddle with WEB.DRAW's bitmap texture fills, you may be eager to try using them as background images. Here's the bad news. Unfortunately, the program does not provide the means to make these cool bitmaps into seamless tiles. To make them seamless, you must import them into a paint program, such as Adobe Photoshop or Fractal Design Painter, to erase the seams. In fact, that's exactly what we did to turn the seamy texture shown back in Figure 8-1 into the smooth and seamless textures shown in Figure 8-2 and 8-3.

Truth be told, the lack of a real bitmap editor is, perhaps, the WEB.GRAPHICS Suite's biggest shortcoming. While WEB.MOVE contains a bare-bones paint editor, it can hardly be considered sufficient for professional-level graphics. Nonetheless, we'll cover CorelWEB.DRAW's two- and four-color patterns in the next chapter and its texture fills in Chapter 10.

Before the Web design community got too sophisticated for its own good, there were tons of Web page backgrounds similar to the example shown in Figure 8-21. It's easy to create embossed effects with CorelWEB.DRAW. Just don't overdo it. You'll learn how in the next chapter, which just happens to be chock full of tricks and tips.

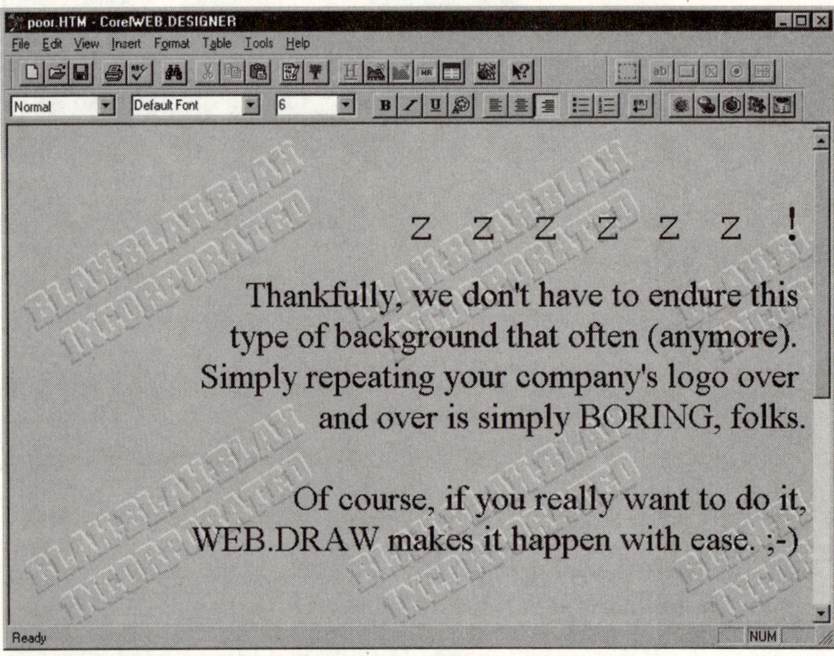

Figure 8-21: Pseudo-embossed backgrounds like this were fairly popular in the early days of Web page design.

Building Buttons

In addition to creating custom buttons from scratch, WEB.DRAW lets you quickly add text to the many prebuilt buttons that can be found on the "official" CorelWEB.GRAPHICS Suite CD-ROM. (The CD comes with both labeled and unlabeled buttons.) Let's start this section with a fast little exercise that demonstrates how easy it is to add text to a prebuilt button. Before you begin the next exercise, make sure that the CD-ROM is in your computer's CD-ROM drive.

Using Prebuilt Buttons

The prebuilt buttons can be great time-savers when you need to create buttons in a flash, but the selection runs the gamut. Some of the buttons are quite nice, while others are bizarre at best. We'll use one of the more pleasing designs for the purposes of this exercise.

1. Click File | Mosaic Roll-Up.

2. At the Mosaic roll-up, click the "open folder" button. At List Files of Type, click All Files. Maneuver to your CD-ROM drive and open the Buttons directory. Click OK.

3. Scroll through the buttons to find a likely candidate. You may note that the labeled buttons begin with "butt," while the unlabeled buttons begin with "buttn."

4. Click and drag buttn19a.jpg onto your WEB.DRAW page.

5. Press F2 and drag out a marquee to zoom up on the imported button.

6. Press F8 to access the Text tool. Click on the button and type **Home**.

7. Click Ctrl+spacebar to access the Pick tool.

8. Click Ctrl+F2 to access the Text roll-up. 24-point type (the default) should fit fine. Choose a typeface and apply it (we selected CastleT Bold, but you may have different fonts loaded on your computer).

9. Drag a marquee around the button and the type. Click Edit | Select All. Press Ctrl+A to access the Align dialog box. Center the objects vertically and horizontally and click OK. The button should appear, as shown in Figure 8-22. All you have to do is export the image!

Figure 8-22: A close look at our simple Home button.

To get a feel for how the button will look when exported, try zooming out to an actual size (1:1) view. Does the type get a bit lost on the patterned button? The best way to make the type pop off the button is to use a drop shadow (or two), along with a careful application of color. Figure 8-23 uses a dark purple drop shadow, set two pixels below and to the left of the base type, along with a light-green (somewhere between lime and pond scum) highlight, one pixel above and to the right.

Figure 8-23: This color combination may sound strange, but the contrast works to pop the type off the button!

Flat-Color Buttons

If none of the prebuilt buttons fit your bill (and there's a good chance they won't), you can create a set of simple flat-color buttons. Flat-color buttons are the most bit-economical graphics choice, since they use the fewest number of colors. This results in the ultimate compression (smallest possible file size) and the fastest download times. Flat-color buttons can be any shape you can think of, but the key is that they primarily use large areas of flat contiguous color, with no fountain fills, fancy textures, or blends. Vertical navigation bars are one of the most common uses (as you'll see, momentarily), while icons are the most playful way to use flat-color buttons, as shown by Figure 8-24. The Rectangle tool makes quick work out of simple flat buttons. Try creating some rectangular buttons now. Use the Shape tool to experiment with rounded corner rectangles, as explained in Chapter 6.

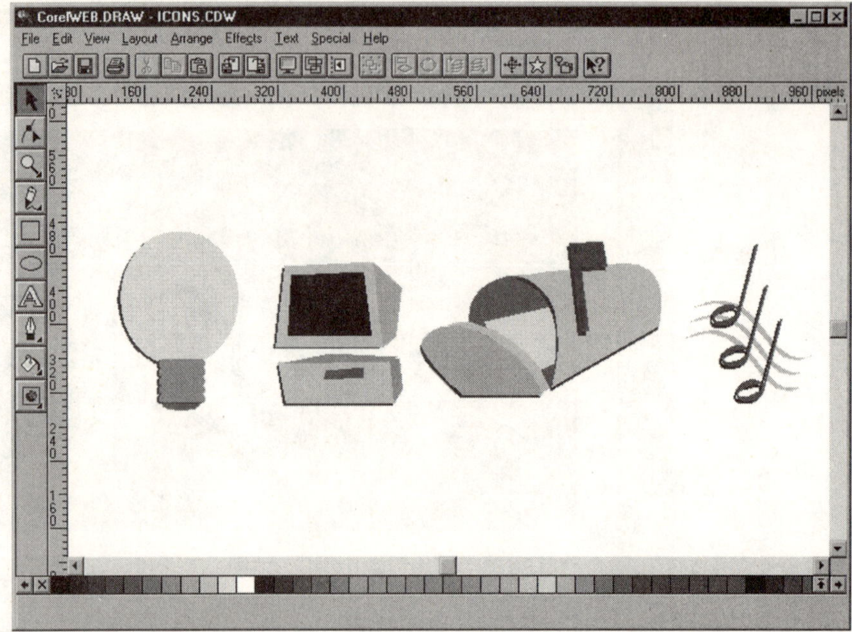

Figure 8-24: Flat doesn't have to mean boring. These goofy icons were all built from scratch with WEB.DRAW in a matter of minutes.

Has Anyone Seen My Symbols?

Don't forget WEB.DRAW's symbol libraries. They contain thousands of icon objects. The Symbols roll-up can be summoned via the Ctrl+F11 keyboard shortcut, by clicking the "star" button on the ribbon bar, or by clicking Special|Symbols Roll-Up.

Three-Dimensional Buttons

Okay, so flat buttons don't ring your bell. Perhaps 3D's the key? While three-dimensional buttons take a bit more work, and result in larger files (and longer downloads), they're not all that difficult to build in CorelWEB.DRAW. With a handful of the tricks you'll learn here, you'll soon be building 3D buttons with the best of them.

Opposite Ramps: Quick to Create

The fastest way to create a three-dimensional button is to use two rectangles with fountain fills that run in opposite directions. In the next little exercise, you'll see how easy it is to create quick-and-dirty 3D buttons using this method. To make things even faster, we'll work with WEB.DRAW's default black-to-white fountain fills. While we're working with a rather small size for the purposes of this exercise, it's likely that you'll create your Web site's buttons at a larger size. Consequently, this exercise stresses the concept behind the method, rather than the specifics:

1. Press F6 to access the Rectangle tool.

2. Draw a rectangle 60 pixels wide by 30 pixels high.

3. Click F11 to summon the Fountain Fill dialog box. Use the default Linear settings with one exception: set the angle to 45 degrees. Click OK.

4. If the Transform roll-up is not onscreen, click Effect | Transform Roll-Up. Click the fourth button on the Transform roll-up to put it in Size mode. Click the arrow button at the lower right to roll the menu out to its full size. Click the centerpoint on the Transform roll-up. At H, type **54**. At V type **24**. Click Apply to Duplicate. This will center a 54 x 24 duplicate object on top of the original, as shown by Figure 8-25.

5. Click F11 to summon the Fountain Fill dialog box. Set the angle to –135 degrees. Click OK.

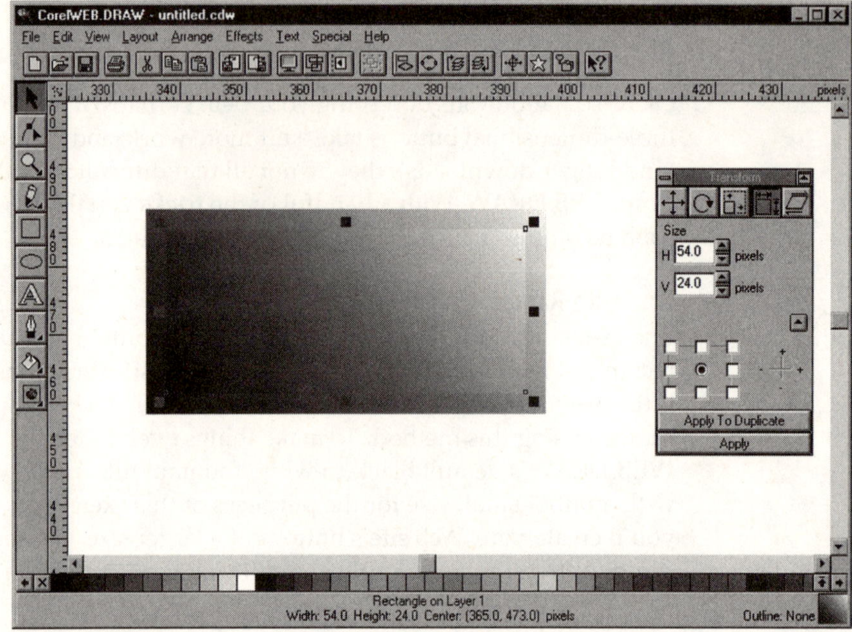

Figure 8-25: Using the centerpoint automatically centers the duplicate rectangle upon the original.

6. Now it's time to bring in the type. Press F8 to access the text tool. Click on the button and type **Home**.

7. Click Ctrl+spacebar to access the Pick tool.

8. Click Ctrl+F2 to access the Text roll-up. If you have it on your system, try 12-point Futura LtCn. Change its fill to black. Try opening up its letterspacing a tad.

9. Let's create a quick drop shadow! Press Esc to deselect all three objects. Click the word "Home" and drag it two pixels up and to the right. As you are dragging, press + (plus) on the numeric keypad (or press the right mouse button) to duplicate it.

10. Give the duplicate Home a yellow fill.

11. Drag a marquee around both Homes (but not the rectangles). Press Ctrl+G to group the text together.

12. Click Edit | Select All. Press Ctrl+A to access the Align dialog box. Center vertically and horizontally and click OK. The button should appear similar to Figure 8-26.

Figure 8-26: It's an instant pseudo-3D button! These critters look best with no outline (at least on the inner rectangle).

Accent Borders: Just Use Another Ramp!

You can quickly add a little more pizzazz with another cheap trick; use a third rectangle that falls halfway between the sizes of the other two. In this scenario, you might have 72 x 36, 68 x 32, and 64 x 28 rectangles. The inner and outer rectangles will have matching fountain fills while the middle rectangle will run in the opposite direction, as shown by Figure 8-27.

Figure 8-27: A third rectangle adds a bit more visual interest to our quick-and-dirty 3D button.

Ribbed Buttons: Just a Blend (or Two) Away

With three rectangles making up the button, there's another cool effect that's only a handful of keystrokes away. By using the Blend roll-up menu, you can create an even more convincing three-dimensional treatment. And since we're working with a low target resolution and a small image, it's not even necessary to use a large number of blend steps! Start with the button you just created:

1. Press Ctrl+B to summon the Blend roll-up.

2. Click the outer rectangle. Shift+click the middle rectangle.

3. At the Blend roll-up, change the Steps setting to 4 and click Apply to blend the middle and outer rectangles.

4. Shift+click the outer rectangle to deselect it. Shift+click the inner rectangle (so that it is selected, along with the middle rectangle).

5. At the Blend roll-up, click Apply to blend the middle and outer rectangles. The blends may seem crude when you're zoomed up, as shown in Figure 8-28, but when viewed at normal size, they look pretty slick. Remember, we're not working with very much resolution. A handful of blend steps go a long way!

Figure 8-28: Things are really starting to pop!

You don't have to blend between fountain fills to get a great 3D effect. Try setting the rectangles to various color fills to get a feel for the different effects you can achieve.

Hard Bevels: For the Chiseled Look

This next method takes a bit more work. The Hard Bevel method requires you to create an upper bevel object and a lower bevel object, which will sit behind a plain vanilla rectangle. This exercise uses

WEB.DRAW's Guideline layer to create a pair of custom rectangular guidelines. Objects drawn on the guideline layer appear with a blue dashed outline (by default). Their primary purpose in life is to help you draw with precision.

1. Press Ctrl+F3 to summon the Layers roll-up.

2. At the Layers roll-up, click Guides. This puts you on the Guide layer.

3. Press F6 to access the Rectangle tool.

4. Draw a rectangle 120 pixels wide by 60 pixels high.

5. If the Transform roll-up is not onscreen, click Effect | Transform Roll-Up. Click the arrow button and roll it out to its full size. At H, type **110**. At V type **50**. Click the center point. Click Apply to Duplicate. This will center a 110 x 50 duplicate object on top of the original, as shown by Figure 8-29.

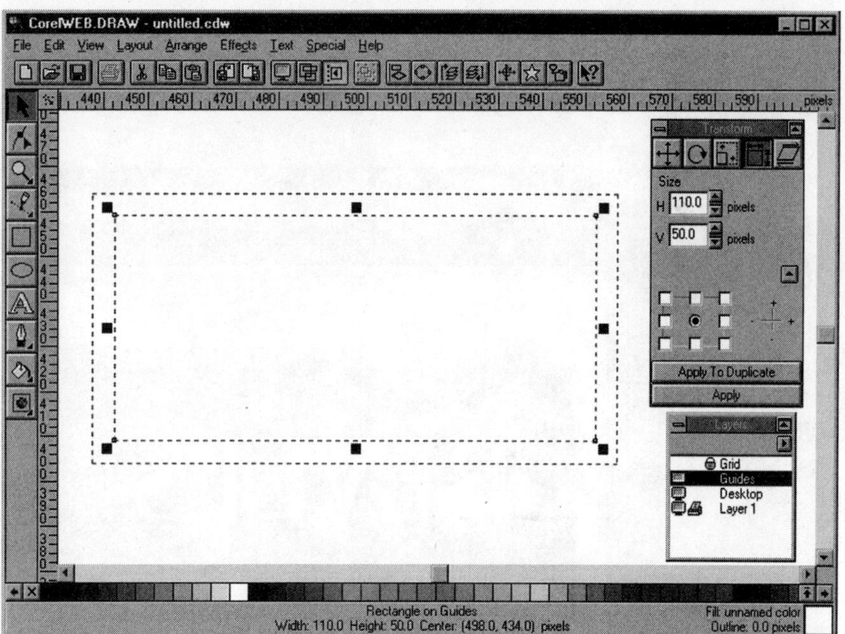

Figure 8-29: The guideline rectangles are in place.

6. At the Layers roll-up, click Layer 1. This will place you back on the visible drawing layer.

7. Make sure that Layout | Snap to Guidelines is selected.

8. Click the Freehand tool button and drag it down to select the Bezier tool (this will make it easier to draw the perfectly straight lines you'll need to create the top and bottom bevels).

9. Use the Bezier tool to draw two objects as shown in Figure 8-30. These will create a top bevel and a bottom bevel. The guidelines snap the Bezier tool to each corner. Follow this click-pattern to draw the first object: outer/upper left, inner/upper left, inner/lower left, inner/lower right, outer/lower right, outer/lower left, and outer/upper left (to close the path). Use this click-pattern to draw the second object: outer/upper right, outer/lower right, inner/lower right, inner/upper right, inner/upper left, outer/upper left, and outer/upper right (to close the path).

    Fill the top bevel with a light 20% gray tint, and fill the bottom bevel with a dark 60% gray tint. Set the outlines to None.

10. Press F6 to access the Rectangle tool.

11. Draw a rectangle 110 pixels wide by 50 pixels high, using the center guideline rectangle. It's a snap-to affair! Give it a 40% gray fill and set the outline to None.

Figure 8-30: Each bevel object will require seven clicks. The guidelines make it easy to hit each corner with precision.

As the complexity of your Web site grows, so too will its navigational requirements. Buttons may handle many of the simple needs, but you'll soon find them metamorphosing into full-blown navigation bars.

Creating Graphic Navigation Bars

Although we covered the subject of navigation bars back in Chapter 2, it's worth a recap. Graphic navigation bars come in both vertical and horizontal varieties and provide a number of ways to accomplish the same goal. Navigation elements can be created as individual objects (such as the buttons we've just created) or they can be built as solid bars. The individual buttons are assigned individual hyperlinks, while the solid bars (which are intended to jump to more than one location) are image-mapped.

Corel Corporation's home page, as shown in Figure 8-31, features a flat-color horizontal navigation bar running across the top of the layout. In addition, it uses a vertical button bar down the left side. The top bar is a high-level navigation tool, in that it enables visitors to surf the top layer of the Web site. The buttons running along the left side jump to specific product pages.

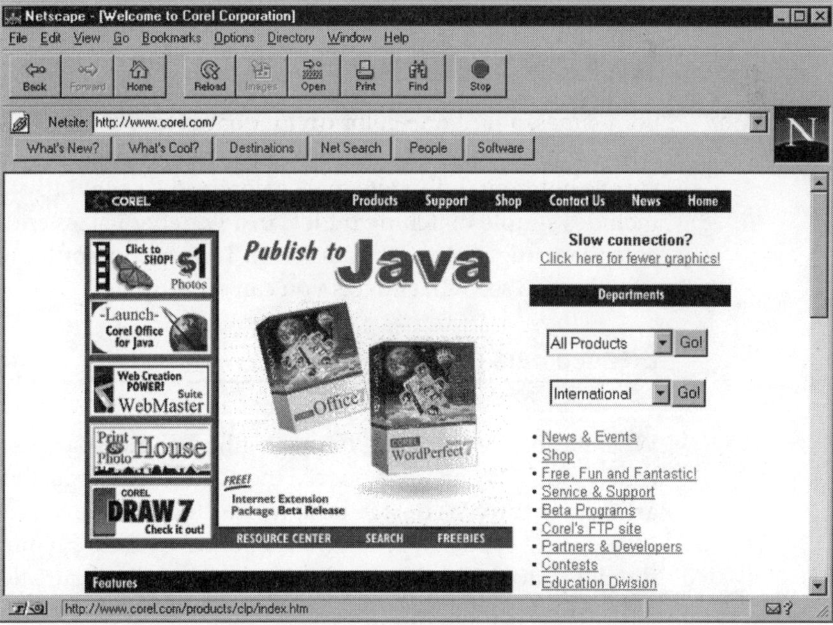

Figure 8-31: Corel's front door provides visitors with myriad choices. As you might have guessed, the horizontal navigation bar at the top of the screen uses an image map to jump to the various subsites.

Flat-color image-mapped navigation bars, such as the one used at the top of Corel's Web page, are perhaps the fastest way to go . . . short of a text navigation bar (which you should always provide, just to be polite). They're easy to create and fast to download. Just draw a rectangle, drop in some keywords, assign the URLs, export the file, and you're done. Of course, you can always use the techniques outlined in this chapter (in the sections that relate to buttons) to create three-dimensional navigation bars, should you desire that effect.

Want to try your hand at building a graphic navigation bar? The image-mapping section at the end of this chapter includes a complete exercise where you'll build a quick image-mapped graphic navigation bar.

Building Horizontal Dividers

Bored with the standard HTML horizontal dividers? You can create a wide range of graphic dividers, with little hassle. Custom graphic dividers can help to set your pages apart from the pack, and creating your own horizontal dividers is an easy task. At its simplest, all you need to do is draw a rectangle to the exact proportions you need, color it, and export the file.

Simple Colored Bars

Sometimes, a nice one-color divider bar is all you need. The *Comprehensive Guide to CorelWEB.GRAPHICS Suite Companion CD-ROM* includes simple horizontal dividers in 99 colors and three widths. The disk also includes simple matching bullets in a variety of sizes and shapes. One-color bars might not suit your fancy. Try experimenting with some two-color bars to see what effects you can cook up.

Blendee Bars

When tastefully executed, fountain-filled divider bars can add an interesting touch. When used poorly, they can ruin a page. One of the worst artifacts of early Web page designs was the "rainbow" horizontal divider. Nonetheless, you can achieve a cool effect by fading your horizontal dividers into the background color, as shown in Figure 8-32.

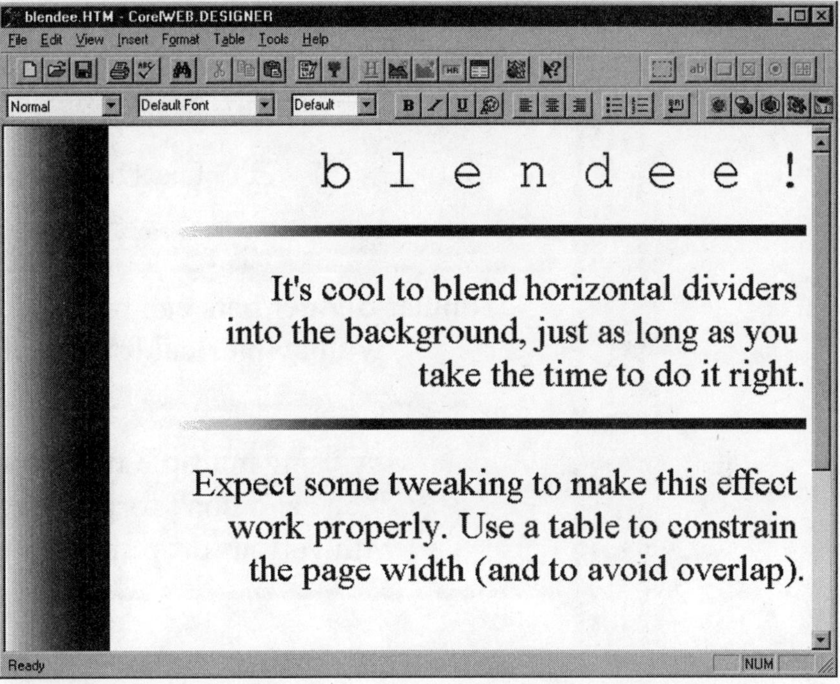

Figure 8-32: You may need to use a few rectangular objects side-by-side to achieve the perfect blendee effect.

Tubular Bars

Remember the cylindrical stripes earlier in this chapter? Take another look at Figures 8-11 and 8-12. You can use those same cylindrical fountain-fill presets to create some pretty nifty cylindrical divider bars. And when you use them in concert with a cylindrical stripe bordered background, your Web page could end up with a look that would do an old hot-rodder proud, as in Figure 8-33.

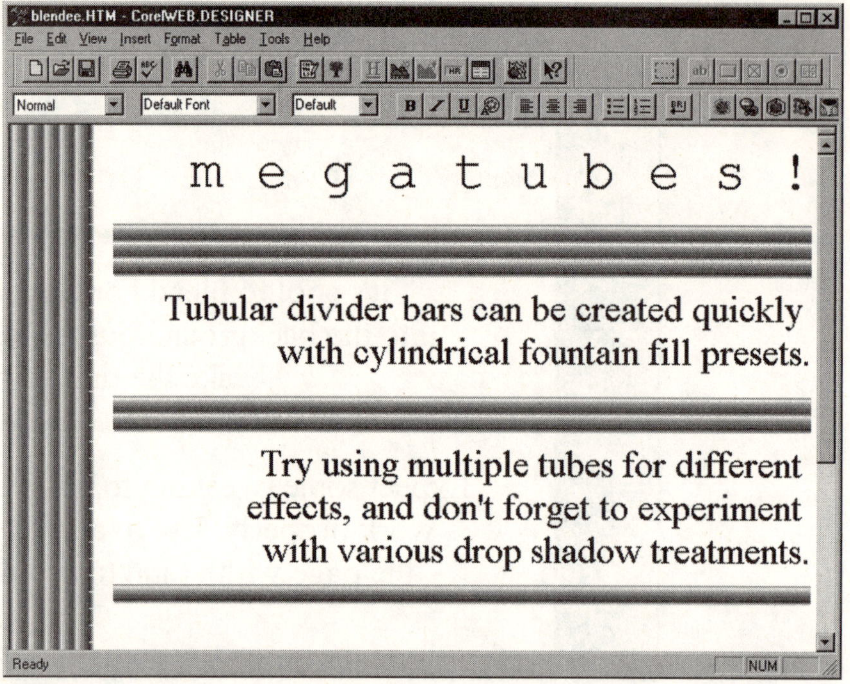

Figure 8-33: While these tubes are rather large and obvious (so that you might actually be able to see them printed at this small size), you'll do well to make your Web tubes a tad thinner.

Building Bullets

HTML bullets will get you only so far. Like custom horizontal dividers, custom graphic bullets are another small feature that can deliver a polished touch to your Web page designs. You can create simple bullets, or use three-dimensional effects, which were covered earlier in this chapter, to create your own custom bullets. Radial fountain fills are most useful for creating bullets that pop off a Web page like marbles from a shooter's fingers.

Watch That Transparent Color!

Round circles usually demand that you export with transparency. Consequently, you have to watch your colors carefully to avoid making a 3D highlight color transparent (the background color or image *could* show through)!

Simple Bullets

To create a simple bullet, all you need to do is draw your bullet object—be it round, square, or what have you—color it, and export. You should also try creating a selection of two-color bullets. But if you need a one-color jump start, check out the Companion CD-ROM: it includes simple bullets in 99 colors and a variety of sizes and shapes.

Three-Dimensional Bullets

There's no question about it—three-dimensional bullets are the rage. While there are a number of methods for creating three-dimensional bullets, here are a handful of examples.

Flat-Color 3D Bullets

This technique uses the Convert to Curves and Break Apart commands to slice a circle down the middle. Then, close each half with the Pencil tool, push them back together (but don't combine them!), and fill each half separately. By creating two equal parts, as shown in Figure 8-34, you can color the highlight and shadow objects with precision. This flat-color technique will yield the smallest file size of all the 3D bullets. While you wouldn't want to use this crude technique on a large bullet, it will give you all the dimensionality you need at smaller sizes.

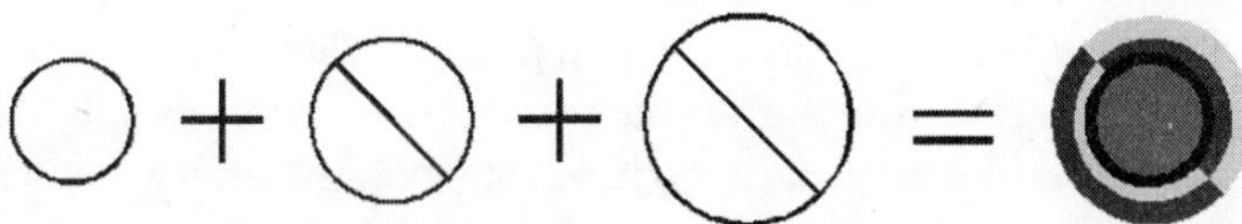

Figure 8-34: It takes five objects to build this circular flat-color bullet.

Ramp Bullets

Remember that quick technique we used to create opposite ramp rectangular buttons earlier in this chapter? You can use the same technique to produce three-dimensional bullets in a flash. The crowning touch is an offset radial fountain fill in the middle bullet, as shown in Figure 8-35.

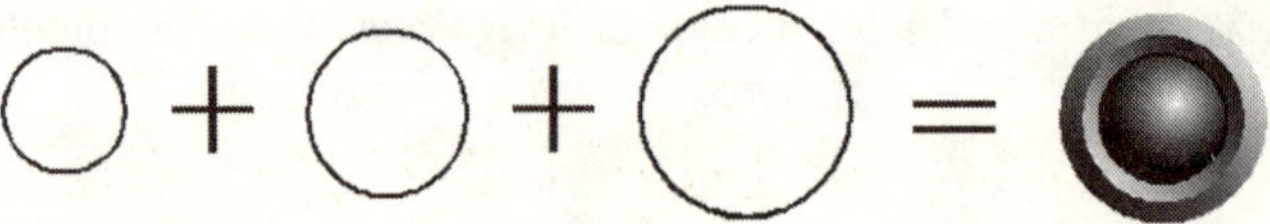

Figure 8-35: This opposite ramp bullet uses just three circles.

1. Press F7 to summon the Ellipse tool.

2. Draw three circles (hold down Ctrl for a perfect circle), 16, 12, and 8 pixels across.

3. Press Ctrl+A to summon the Align dialog box. Horizontally and vertically center the three circles.

4. Assign the circles an outline of none.

5. If the circles are not in the right order—largest at the back, smallest at the front—use the Arrange|Order commands.

6. Press Esc to deselect the three circles, then select the largest button.

7. Press F11 to summon the Fountain Fill dialog box. Use the default Linear settings with one exception: set the angle to 45 degrees. Click OK.

8. Select the middle circle. Press F11 to summon the Fountain Fill dialog box. Set the angle to –135 degrees. Click OK.

9. Select the smallest circle and assign it a colored fill. In the next section, you'll learn how to make it pop!

Lose Your Marbles?

This technique uses just one circle with a radial fountain fill. The key to success is to fiddle with the Fountain Fill dialog box, as shown in Figure 8-36. Try looking at some real marbles (or other shiny spherical objects) to get a feel for the highlight. You can also try fooling with the circular fountain fill presets to get a jump start on the effect. Let's try giving the center circle from the last exercise a highlight fill.

Select the smallest circle. Press F11 to summon the Fountain Fill dialog box. Set the Fountain Fill Type to Radial. Set the From: color to dark red and the To: color to white. Click OK to check it out . . . it won't look just right. Press F11 again. Set the Edge Pad to 15 percent, or so. Push the highlight to the top right quadrant of the preview window (or manually set the Horizontal and Vertical Center Offsets to 15 percent) and click OK. Cool!

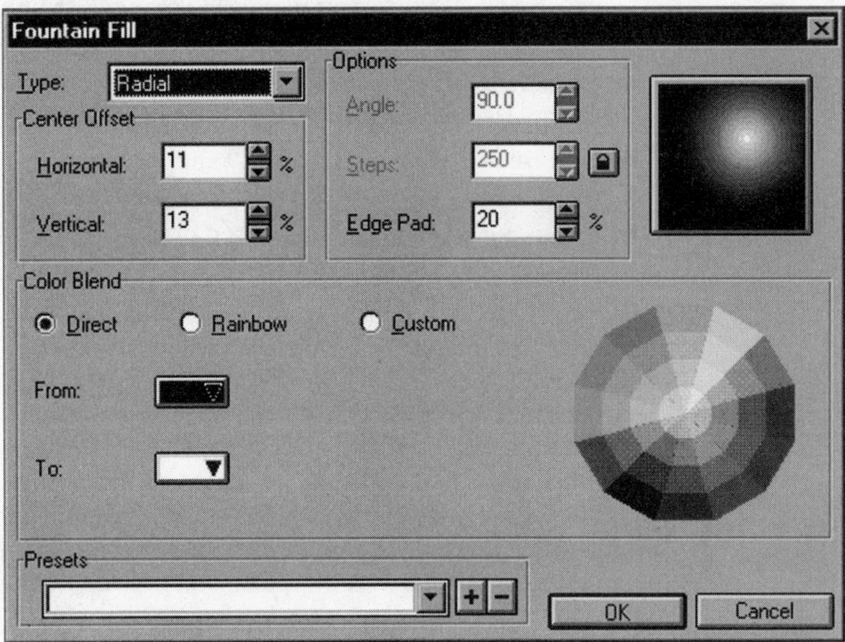

Figure 8-36: There's no secret to creating marbles: just use an offset radial fill and experiment with edge pad percentages until you get the result you want!

While marbles are fun as is, you can always spiff them up with a drop shadow, as shown in Figure 8-37. The middle example uses a solid color drop shadow, while the example at the right uses a "pseudo-soft" drop shadow, which was created with a blend between the background color (white) and a medium tone.

Figure 8-37: Drop shadows help to pop those marbles off the page.

Exporting Web Graphics

True Web design pros know the ins and outs of image export. The key to success when exporting WEB.DRAW graphics is knowing which format to use and specifying the proper settings in the Export dialog box. To recap from Chapter 2:

- Continuous tone photographic images should (almost always) be exported as JPEG format files. JPEG provides the highest-quality photographic image with the highest level of compression.

- Graphics with areas of flat contiguous color, such as logos, should be exported as GIF format files.

- Because the JPEG format doesn't support transparency, images that contain transparency must be exported as GIF format files.

- Images that contain an imported GIF image (including GIFized photographs) should be exported as GIF format files.

Before you export an image, you should select only those objects that you want in the final graphic. You don't want to export your images with the little chunks of graphic construction debris that may be lurking in your file. Drag a marquee around the "good" objects and group them (if they haven't already been grouped). Click File | Export and click the Selected Only option in the Export dialog box, as shown in Figure 8-38. This first Export dialog box lets you do three important things (in addition to specifying the Selected Only option): choose your export format, name the file, and select a directory for the file to be exported to. When you click OK in the first Export dialog box, a second Export dialog box will appear.

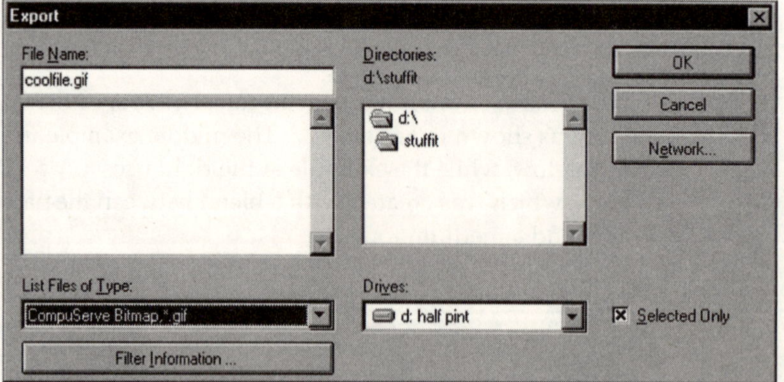

Figure 8-38: Don't leave room for surprises! Use the Selected Only option in the first Export dialog box to ensure that you're exporting only those objects you want to export.

Exporting as GIF Format

If you have chosen the GIF format, the Bitmap Export dialog box will appear, as shown in Figure 8-39. This is a critical step in the success of your export. This dialog box governs three important factors:

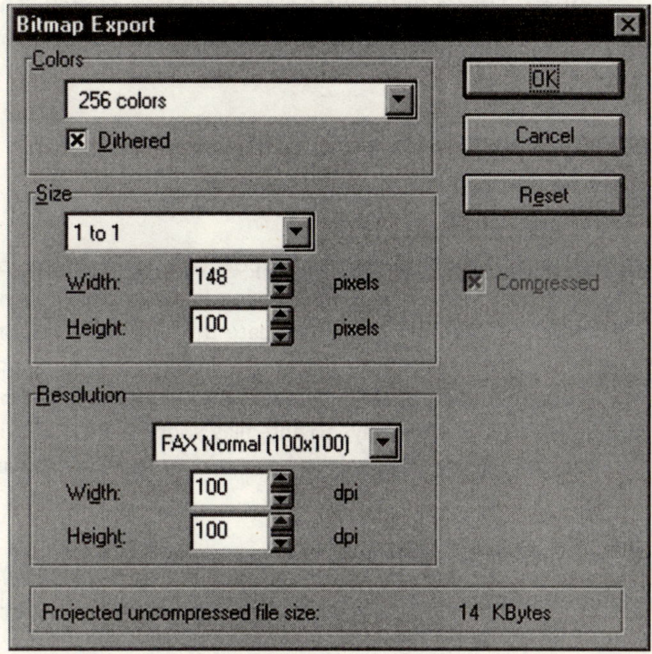

Figure 8-39: Set up the Bitmap Export dialog box to export your GIF files as 256 color images, with a 1 to 1 ratio, at 100 dpi. The dialog box has a good memory: it will remember its last settings.

What's Dithering?

Dithering is a graphic software technique that makes the most of a limited color palette. It makes a handful of colors seem like many, many more.

- *Colors*—Specify 256 colors. The Export filter will actually reduce the palette and throw out the unused colors.

- *Size*—Use the "1 to 1" option. This will export your graphics pixel for pixel. In general, you should be creating your artwork at exactly the size at which it will be placed on the Web page.

- *Resolution*—We achieved success with the Default (100 x 100 dpi) setting. The 75 dpi setting may work fine as well. There is no need to go higher than the 100 dpi setting for Web graphics.

What About Anti-Aliasing?

While CorelWEB.DRAW handles most export tasks with ease, it comes up short in one specific area: *anti-aliasing*. Anti-aliasing is a software technique used to soften the edges of a bitmap image to create the illusion of smoother lines and curves. Incredibly, the export filter does not offer an anti-aliasing option. This is a major oversight that will hopefully be addressed in a future version of the program. Nonetheless, there are ways to anti-alias your WEB.DRAW images. Chapter 10 covers anti-aliasing and explains how to optimize your exported graphics.

When you click OK, the Transparent Color dialog box will appear, as shown in Figure 8-40. This little dialog box controls two GIF characteristics, interlacing and transparency. Here's a quick rundown on these features:

- *Interlaced* GIF images appear in the browser in waves. They start out fuzzy and gradually come into focus as the image is downloaded.

- *Non-interlaced* GIF images only appear in the browser once they have been completely downloaded.

- *Transparency* lets you specify one color as a "see-through" color. In Figure 8-40, we chose the background white color to be transparent, so that the bullet would float on the Web page's background image. (Otherwise, we'd end up with a nasty white block around our nice marble bullet.) You can assign transparency by clicking on the image or by specifying the color from the palette.

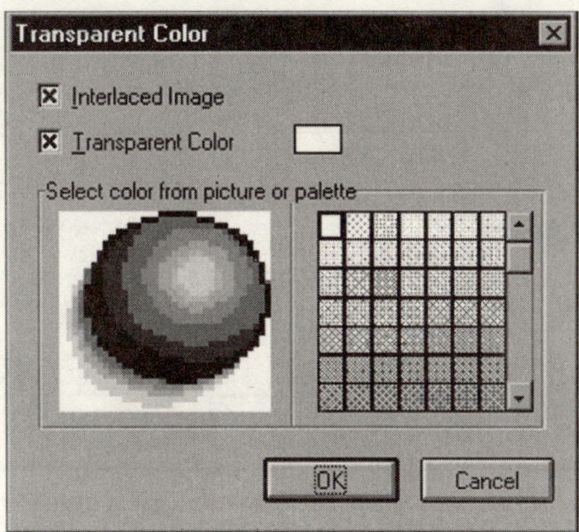

Figure 8-40: Be careful when specifying transparency, lest your background image (or color) show through in the wrong places!

Exporting as JPEG Format

When you specify a JPEG export in the first Export dialog box and click OK, WEB.DRAW summons its succinct little Export JPEG dialog box, as shown in Figure 8-41. This dialog box controls two important JPEG attributes. The Progressive option creates a JPEG file that fades into the browser window (some folks call it "the underwater look") in a manner reminiscent of an interlaced GIF. While Progressive JPEGs are cool and offer a nice degree of compression, they are not supported by the older Web browsers, so you should use this format with caution. In fact, WEB.DESIGNER 1.0 doesn't have the ability to preview Progressive JPEGs!

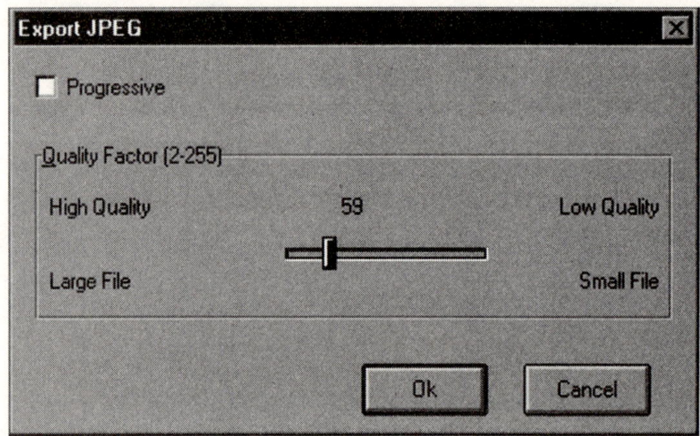

Figure 8-41: Just slide the knob to achieve your desired degree of JPEG quality and compression.

If the Progressive option is not chosen, you can specify the Quality Factor of the exported JPEG image, via the slider bar. The more compression you choose, the lesser the quality of the image. The best trade-off between image quality and file compression is to choose a higher (but not the highest) quality image. When you click OK, the Bitmap Export dialog box appears, as shown back in Figure 8-39. You should always export your JPEG images as 16 million color files.

Image Mapping With WEB.DRAW

Creating image maps in CorelWEB.DRAW saves you time and trouble—especially when it comes time to revise the graphic and image map! WEB.DRAW provides two means to create image map coordinates. You have the option of assigning a URL to any object, or you can drag out an invisible hot spot with the URL tool. In order to create an image map, you must have the URL Location Bar onscreen. If you can't find it, click Special | Preferences | View, and select Show URL Location Bar. Make sure that Show Alternate Text Bar is selected as well, and click OK.

Let's see what it takes to image-map a typical vertical navigation bar. Figure 8-42 shows a nav bar that was created from seven separate 120 x 30 pixel rectangles. We will be assigning a different URL and alternate text to each rectangle. Using the WEB.DRAW techniques you've learned, go ahead and create the seven separate rectangles. Create the first rectangle, and give it a dark-blue fill and a one-point medium-blue outline. Then, drag-duplicate the other six rectangles. Use 13-point Bank Gothic (or a similar typeface) for the text, and set it in a yellow or off-white color. Once you've drawn the graphic, save the file. It's time to start the image-mapping procedure!

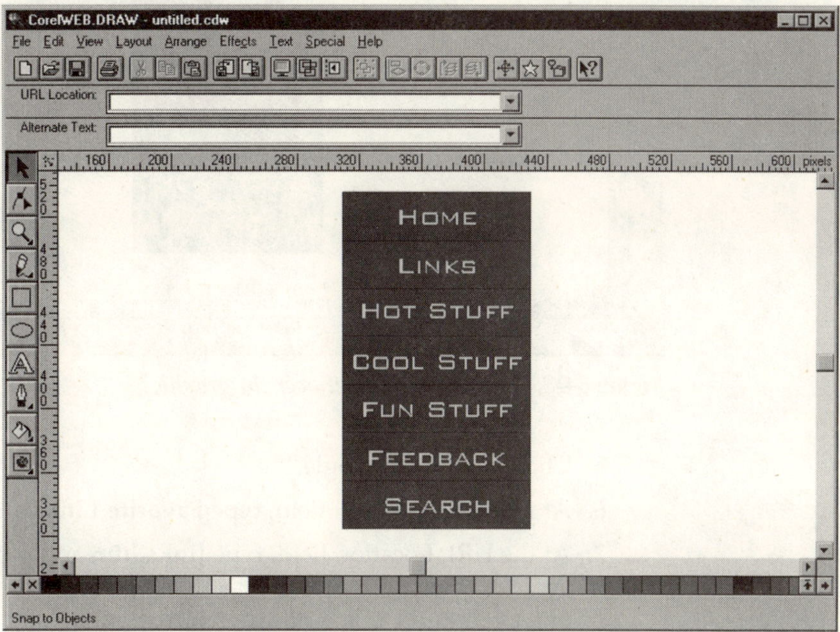

Figure 8-42: Our simple vertical navigation bar, before being image-mapped.

1. Click the Pick tool.

2. Click the uppermost rectangle in the navigation bar graphic.

3. At the Alternate Text field, type **Home** and press Enter.

4. At the URL Location field, type **index.htm** and press Enter. A mesh pattern will appear over the uppermost rectangle, to let you know that it has been hot-spotted, as shown by Figure 8-43.

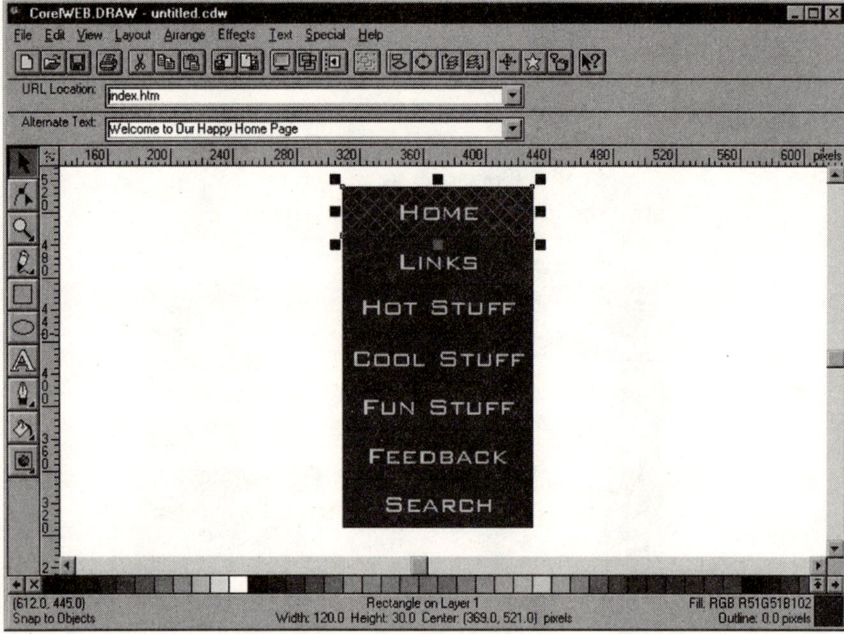

Figure 8-43: Who threw that net over the graphic?

5. Click the next rectangle.

6. At the Alternate Text field, type **Favorite Links** and press Enter.

7. At the URL Location field, type **links.htm** and press Enter. Once again, a mesh pattern will appear over the uppermost rectangle, to let you know that it has been hot-spotted.

8. Continue with this until you have hot-spotted the remaining five rectangles. When you're done assigning URLs, the graphic will appear as in Figure 8-44.

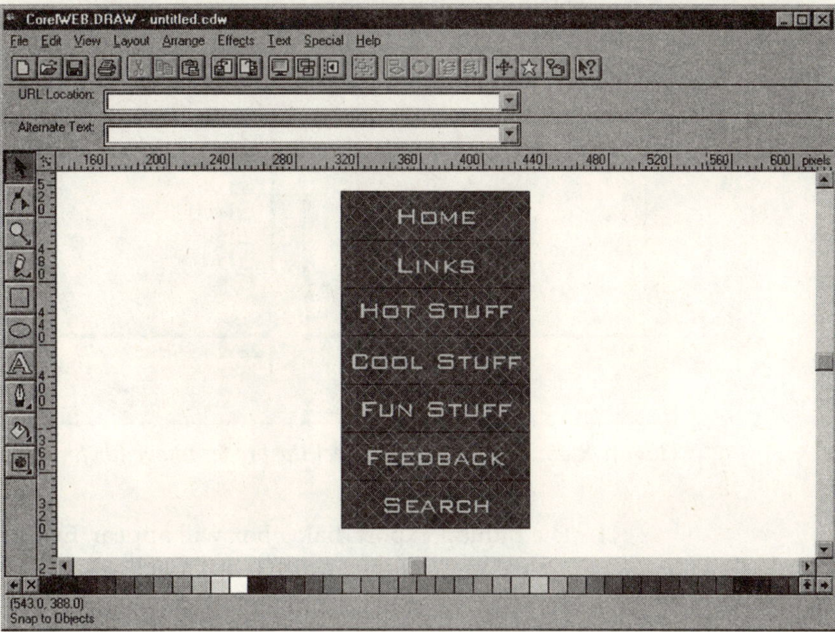

Figure 8-44: Don't worry . . . those webs won't appear in the exported graphic!

9. Drag a marquee around the entire navigation graphic. There should be 14 objects selected.

10. Click File | Publish | To HTML. The Publish to HTML dialog box will appear, as shown in Figure 8-45. Name the file "navbar.htm," and make sure that all the settings match the figure (with the exception of the drive and directories, of course). Click OK.

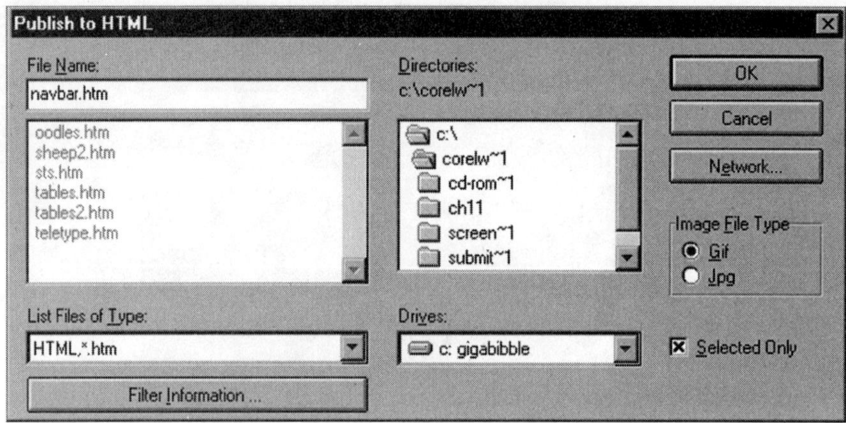

Figure 8-45: Don't forget to select the proper image file format.

11. The Bitmap Export dialog box will appear. Export this image as a 256 color, 1 to 1 image at 100 dpi. Click OK.

12. The Transparent Color dialog box will appear. Since this is a rectangular graphic, there's no reason to use transparency (so you can deselect Transparency if it is selected). Select Interlaced Image and Click OK.

CorelWEB.DRAW will create an HTML file that includes the image-mapped graphic. If you're curious, open this file up with WEB.DESIGNER's HTML edit mode to have a look at the HTML code that WEB.DRAW has generated. Figure 8-46 shows the HTML code, with seven lines of the image map that should be deleted. These NOHREF areas (generated by the text objects) are worse than wasted code: they'll make the image map practically worthless. Before you delete the lines, open the file up in a Web browser to see how it behaves.

Having found that CorelWEB.ANOMALY, we quickly wanted to take a look at WEB.DRAW's URL tool to see if it, too, produced the same quirky results. Much to our delight, the URL tool seemed to perform up to par, without the many NOREF lines. Start fresh: open up the nav bar graphic file again and try image-mapping it with the URL tool. We found the results to be more consistent.

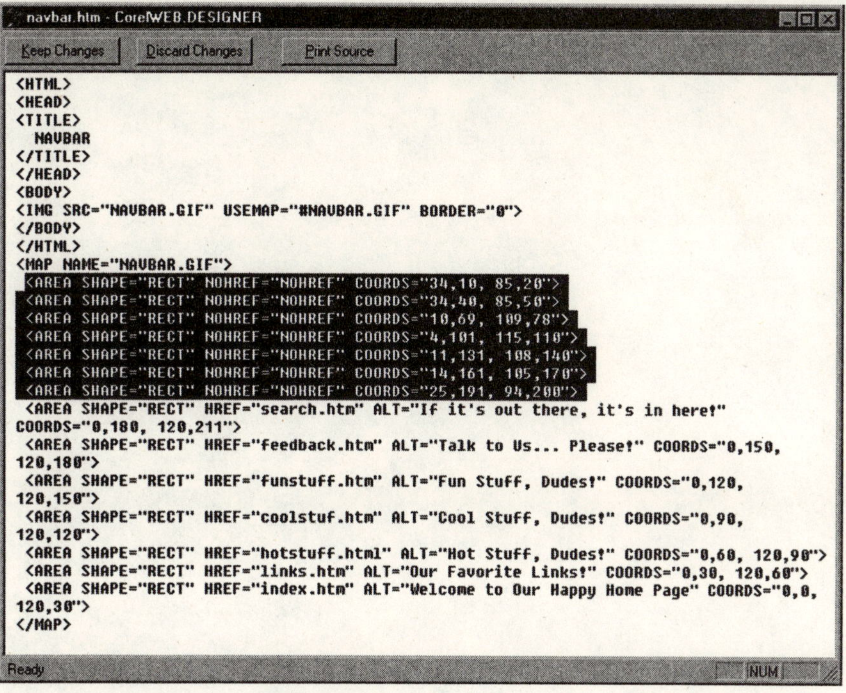

```
navbar.htm - CorelWEB.DESIGNER

  Keep Changes      Discard Changes      Print Source

<HTML>
<HEAD>
<TITLE>
   NAVBAR
</TITLE>
</HEAD>
<BODY>
<IMG SRC="NAVBAR.GIF" USEMAP="#NAVBAR.GIF" BORDER="0">
</BODY>
</HTML>
<MAP NAME="NAVBAR.GIF">
<AREA SHAPE="RECT" NOHREF="NOHREF" COORDS="34,10, 85,20">
<AREA SHAPE="RECT" NOHREF="NOHREF" COORDS="34,40, 85,50">
<AREA SHAPE="RECT" NOHREF="NOHREF" COORDS="10,69, 109,78">
<AREA SHAPE="RECT" NOHREF="NOHREF" COORDS="4,101, 115,110">
<AREA SHAPE="RECT" NOHREF="NOHREF" COORDS="11,131, 108,140">
<AREA SHAPE="RECT" NOHREF="NOHREF" COORDS="14,161, 105,170">
<AREA SHAPE="RECT" NOHREF="NOHREF" COORDS="25,191, 94,200">
 <AREA SHAPE="RECT" HREF="search.htm" ALT="If it's out there, it's in here!"
COORDS="0,180, 120,211">
 <AREA SHAPE="RECT" HREF="feedback.htm" ALT="Talk to Us... Please!" COORDS="0,150,
120,180">
 <AREA SHAPE="RECT" HREF="funstuff.htm" ALT="Fun Stuff, Dudes!" COORDS="0,120,
120,150">
 <AREA SHAPE="RECT" HREF="coolstuf.htm" ALT="Cool Stuff, Dudes!" COORDS="0,90,
120,120">
 <AREA SHAPE="RECT" HREF="hotstuff.html" ALT="Hot Stuff, Dudes!" COORDS="0,60, 120,90">
 <AREA SHAPE="RECT" HREF="links.htm" ALT="Our Favorite Links!" COORDS="0,30, 120,60">
 <AREA SHAPE="RECT" HREF="index.htm" ALT="Welcome to Our Happy Home Page" COORDS="0,0,
120,30">
</MAP>

Ready                                                                      NUM
```

Figure 8-46: Why does WEB.DRAW generate bogus lines in its image maps? Don't ask us!

Moving On

In this chapter you learned how to use a slew of cool techniques to create compelling Web page graphics. These methods will help you to design exciting backgrounds, bullets, buttons, rules, navigation bars, icons, and illustrations. But they're only a jumping off point. In the next chapter, you'll find tips and tricks that will enable you to create a wide range of cool effects. The fine points of node-tweaking and pattern fills are covered as well.

9

CorelWEB.DRAW Tips & Tricks

CorelWEB.DRAW provides the tools you need to create exciting and compelling Web page images. It's not always easy, however, to figure out how to execute the graphic treatment you have in mind. And many times it's difficult to come up with a creative new treatment at all! This chapter's intent is to provide you with a creative "jump start." By demonstrating how to create a slew of effects, you'll learn how to quickly move those images from your mind's eye onto your computer screen.

This is a chapter for the true tweaker. In addition to all the fun stuff, it covers the subjects of node-tweaking, WEB.DRAW patterns, and program preferences.

Type Tricks

Typefaces set the tone for your Web page designs as much as any other graphical element, be it a subtle background texture or a snazzy illustration. The proper choice of typefaces will help to distinguish your site from all the others. And the consistent use of a core set of typefaces will help to ensure continuity from page to page.

The nomenclature of the type world can be a bit bewildering for graphics greenhorns and journeymen alike. People have taken to referring to a specific *font*, such as Garamond Bold Italic, as either a typeface *or* a font. The two terms are now pretty much interchangeable, although this wasn't always the case.

There are a number of type classes—for example, serif and sans-serif typefaces. *Serifs* are the fancy doodads and little feet that adorn faces such as Garamond and Times Roman. A *sans-serif* face, such as Helvetica or Futura, is (sans) without serifs. There are many types of *decorative* and *display* faces, including fancy *scripts* and way-cool (and some not-so-cool) trendy designs.

The CorelWEB.GRAPHICS Suite gives us a big leg up; the CD-ROM generously contains 500 fonts, in a wide variety of styles. Corel has traditionally packed a huge font load with its flagship program, CorelDRAW! The current version, DRAW 7, comes with 1,000 fonts. Now that may seem like a lot of fonts to most folks but not to us font freaks! The true typophile can never have enough fonts. Thankfully, there is an incredible array of type available on the World Wide Web, with some free samples just for the asking (or is that downloading?), as well as a huge assortment of shareware fonts. Scores of servers deliver scads of choices for every taste and budget. As you troll for type in this chapter, it will become apparent how vast (and immediate) your online typographic resources truly are. You're bound to pick up some great ideas and a few gratis typefaces as well.

Typeface selection is a crucial decision in any serious graphic design, and it is not to be taken lightly. This is not to say that the act of choosing a typeface is a tense and stuffy affair. On the contrary, it can be a wonderfully creative experience! Finding the right font for a design after an exhaustive search is akin to finding a long-lost piece of a puzzle. If the fonts on the WEB.GRAPHICS CD-ROM fail to satisfy your appetite for type, here is a list of places to search for additional fonts:

Font Sources

Adobe Systems
http://www.adobe.com

Agfa
http://www.agfahome.com

Attention Earthling
http://www.attention-earthling.com/

Bitstream
http://www.bitstream.com/

comp.fonts home page
http://jasper.ora.com:80/comp.fonts/index.html

designOnline
http://www.dol.com/

Digiteyes Multimedia TypeArt Library
http://www.typeart.com/

Emigre
http://www.emigre.com/

Fonthead
http://www.fonthead.com/

Garage Fonts
http://www.garagefonts.com/

House Industries
http://www.houseind.com/

Image Club
http://www.imageclub.com/

International Typeface Corporation (ITC)
http://www.esselte.com/itc/

Letraset
http://www.letraset.com

Linotype
http://www.linotype.com

MindCandy
http://www.mindcandy.com/

Monotype
http://www.monotype.com

NIMX
http://members.aol.com/nimx001/index.html

OptiFont
http://www.castcraft-software.com/

Phil's Fonts
http://www.philsfonts.com

Psy/Ops
http://www.psyops.com/

P22
http://www.p22.com/fonts/index.html

SynFonts
http://members.aol.com/coolFonts/index.html

Tiro Typeworks
http://www.portal.ca/~tiro/

Treacyfaces/Headliners
http://www.treacyfaces.com/

T-26
http://www.t26font.com/

And for the ever expanding complete list of type on the Web, be sure to check out the ever cool Internet Type Foundry Index at http://users.aol.com/typeindex/index.html/.

Once you've found the font of your dreams, you must determine how it will be treated on the Web page. In the following section, you'll learn how to create a wide variety of type effects.

Drop Shadow & Emboss Effects

The most common type effects on the World Wide Web are *drop shadows* and their siblings, the *embosses*. The intent of a drop shadow is to impart a three-dimensional look that makes the type pop off the page (or appear as if it is floating). Drop shadows are merely duplicate chunks of type that have been placed behind the original. The duplicates are offset by a number of pixels, both horizontally and vertically. The amount of offset depends upon the size of the type. Smaller type might only be offset by a pixel, while larger type may be offset by half a dozen pixels. It can take some experimentation to make a drop shadow look just right. Once you've determined the exact offset, you can dial those numbers into the Duplicate setting in the Preferences dialog box, as outlined later in this chapter. Let's take a look at some options.

Simple Drop Shadows

Figure 9-1 demonstrates a variety of simple drop shadows. The examples at the top of the figure have their shadows offset upward, while the examples at the bottom of the figure have their shadows offset downward. If your base type is a light color, you'll probably want to use a dark drop shadow. Consequently, if your base type is a dark color, you'll most often use a lighter shadow. Color choices are determined by the color behind the type, whether it's sitting on top of a colored background, a button, or some other graphic element.

Figure 9-1: Drop shadows are the most basic type effect; they are often combined with more intricate maneuvers.

Instant Drop Shadows?

The CorelWEB.GRAPHICS Suite CD-ROM contains a number of typefaces, such as Decorated 035 and Horndon, that feature built-in (albeit monochromatic) drop shadows.

To create a drop shadow:

1. Select the word(s) with the Pick tool.

2. Press + on the numeric keypad to duplicate the word(s).

3. Use the cursor keys to nudge the duplicate word(s) up and to the right by a few pixels.

4. Assign an appropriately colored fill to the shadow.

5. Use the Align | Order commands to rearrange the objects, if necessary.

Simple Emboss

Embosses are similar to drop shadows, with one major difference. They use two duplicates behind the original type: one darker and one lighter than the background color. Figure 9-2 shows a simple emboss that uses the same color for both the background and the base type, for a subtle effect. Of course, you can always use a fourth color for the base type.

Figure 9-2: This effect mimics a traditional printer's blind embossing technique.

Embossed Type for the Lazy at Heart

Check out the aptly named Buxom font on the WEB.GRAPHICS CD-ROM.

To create an emboss:

1. Select the word(s) with the Pick tool.

2. Press + on the numeric keypad to duplicate the word(s).

3. Use the cursor keys to nudge the duplicate word(s) two pixels, up and to the right.

4. Press + on the numeric keypad to duplicate the duplicate word(s).

5. Use the cursor keys to nudge the second duplicate word(s) two pixels, up and to the right.

6. Press Shift+PgDn to send it to the back.

7. Assign a light-colored fill to the highlight and a dark-colored fill to the shadow.

8. Select the center word(s). Give it the same color fill as the background, for the appearance of a blind emboss.

Blended Drop Shadow

You can take the drop-shadow effect one step further by using a blended shadow, as shown in Figure 9-3. This requires that you use two duplicate objects. The first duplicate should be a dark color placed exactly behind the original (or offset by just a pixel). The second duplicate should be the background color; it is offset by the distance you want the shadow to travel. Select both duplicate objects and press Ctrl+B to summon the Blend roll-up. Set the number of blend steps down to the width of the shadow and click Apply.

Figure 9-3: Although WEB.DRAW allows you to make blended shadows, these blends fall short of what's possible with a bitmap paint program. The softer the shadow, the more realistic it will appear.

Blended Emboss

You can apply the same blended effect to embosses as well. Figure 9-4 demonstrates how a blended emboss imparts a softer, rounded look. Use the technique outlined above to accomplish this effect. You'll want to create a pair of duplicates for the shadow and a pair of duplicates for the highlight.

Figure 9-4: Blended embosses can be more realistic than hard-edged embosses, but the payoff only comes when you apply the effect to large objects.

Inline/Outline Effects

You can create scores of different effects by overlapping duplicate objects with varying outline widths and colors. This is accomplished with a simple trick: in order to let the outlines show through, none of the objects is assigned a fill, except for the backmost object. The following section shows you how to create four treatments that will send you back on a sentimental typographical journey.

Varsity Sweater

Looking to relive your glorious high school or college sports career? This fun effect uses the squarish City Bold typeface to approximate the look of your old moth-eaten varsity sweater. The example shown in Figure 9-5 consists of three chunks of 48-point City Bold. The backmost object has a 12-point black outline. The middle object has a 4-point gold outline. The topmost object has a green fill and no outline. Try one for your alma mater . . . just apply your school colors and go!

Figure 9-5: Is that a bonfire I smell, or did a transformer just blow?

Team Jacket

If you're an old jock, there's a good chance that you joined your local watering hole's sports team after you graduated. Whether it's softball, bowling, or soccer, here's an effect that mimics the all-important team jacket. It uses the Brush 455 typeface and WEB.DRAW's Fit Text to Path effect to create a smoothly arced logo; it follows the same concept as the Varsity Jacket effect, with overlapping outlines of varying widths.

Figure 9-6: Get ready to use this effect for the corner bar's Web page.

Sloppy Print (or Bad Trap)

We've all seen this effect on a bad print job. It harkens to a poorly registered printed piece, where all the colors just don't meet up. The example shown in Figure 9-7 was created with magenta- and cyan-filled objects with no outlines. These were offset and overlapped by a black-outlined object with no fill. Process print purists will want to throw in a fourth, yellow-filled object just for kicks. The typeface was grunged up by converting it to curves and changing all the curved lines to straight lines with the shape tool.

Figure 9-7: On a printed piece, this looks bad. Online, it looks edgy.

Hand-Tooled

Here's a cool inline/outline effect that takes a little work to pull off. Not a whole lot of work, mind you, just a bit more than the previous three examples. Do this one right and you'll have a chunk of type that'll look as if it's just popped off a jar of hot sauce. You'll do best to start out with a nice big fat typeface: we used 58-point Bremen Black for this example. Here's a rundown on how the effect in Figure 9-8 was created:

Figure 9-8: This hand-tooled type effect takes less work than you might imagine.

- The backmost object has a purple fill and no outline.
- The next layer consists of the lime-green sawtooth pattern, which was created by duplicating a single triangular object. The curve in the G was accomplished by applying an envelope to the group of six triangles.
- The next object uses a six-pixel magenta outline with no fill, so that it overlaps the sawtooth pattern.
- The topmost object uses a three-pixel black outline.

Likely Candidates for the Hand-Tooled Look

Check out Castle Ultra, Clarendon Black, Incised 901 Compact, and Informal 011 Black, among others.

High-Contrast Effects

As we've hammered home throughout this book, fast Web graphics use limited palettes. This section demonstrates four effects that create bit-stingy, high-impact artwork. Although we're obviously showing them in black-and-white here, you can come up with your own high-contrast color combinations from the magic 216 color nondithering palette, as discussed in the next chapter. And to stretch things a bit (if you'll pardon the pun), you can try these effects with a soft drop shadow for even more drama.

Two Color

The simple two-color effect shown in Figure 9-9 was created by using two rectangles of identical height and outline. Start by drawing the black rectangle and applying the outline width and color. Then, use the Pick tool to stretch out the second rectangle while pressing the right mouse button to create it as a duplicate of the original. Apply a white fill, and place it behind the original using Ctrl+PgDn. Set the type in two separate chunks, using a white fill for the type that runs over the black background and a black fill for the type that runs over the white background. We used City Medium for this example. You may want to experiment using two different typefaces to heighten the effect.

Figure 9-9: Clean, simple, and fast.

Chopped Off

Looking for a quick way to add an edgy feel? The chopped-off effect
shown in Figure 9-10 couldn't be much easier to accomplish. Just fill the
type with the same color as the background (don't use any outline) and
size it so that it bleeds off the edge of the object it sits astride. The right
type choices will make all the difference here. In general, clean sans-serif
fonts will work better than frilly serif fonts. And if you've got any grunge
fonts in your repertoire, this is where you'll want to try 'em for size.

Figure 9-10: It's cheap. It's cutting edge. It's yours.

Squared

And speaking of edgy design, it shouldn't be too tough to figure out
what techno-trendy magazine flag inspired Figure 9-11. The trick to
making this effect work is to set each character as a separate object. This
allows you to space everything out properly, and with the least possible
hassle. Let's take a step-by-step look to see how this effect was accomplished.

Figure 9-11: Two hints: day-glo ink and a botched IPO.

1. Start by drawing the first rectangle.

2. Click Layout | Snap To Objects (to magnetize the rectangle).

3. While holding down Ctrl (to constrain movement to a horizontal
   plane), drag-duplicate the rectangle to the right, until the left
   side of the duplicate snaps to the right side of the original.
   Repeat this step until you have a rectangle for each of the letters.
   Give them all a gray fill with no outline.

4. Deselect Layout | Snap To Objects (to turn off the magnetic effect).

5. Create each character as a separate object. Give each a black fill
   with no outline.

6. Center each character horizontally within its own rectangle. Drag out a horizontal guideline and make sure the baselines align.

7. Group the rectangles together, then Group the characters together.

8. Shift-click the group of rectangles (so that it is selected, along with the group of characters).

9. Press Ctrl+A to summon the Align dialog box. Vertically align the group of characters with the rectangles.

10. Ungroup the rectangles and delete every other one.

11. Assign a white fill to the characters that sit astride the rectangles. Assign a black fill to all the rectangles.

That wasn't so tough (just a little tedious). Try adding a soft drop shadow to add the illusion of depth. Figure 9-12 demonstrates a couple of skewed variations on the theme.

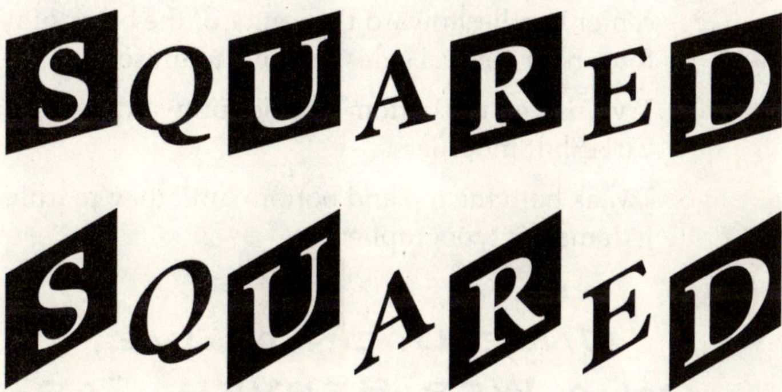

Figure 9-12: Group all the characters and rectangles, summon the rotation handles, and skew away.

The Magic See-Through Die Cut

The see-through effect shown in Figure 9-13 was created by combining (Arrange | Combine) the type and the rectangle, so that the background shows through the cutout. Nifty yet simple to achieve. A heightened sense of dimensionality was added by using a blended drop shadow, as detailed earlier in this section.

Figure 9-13: This die cut effect seems to float eerily above the background.

Sci-Fi Perspective

Here's the effect you've wanted to create ever since you saw the first *Star Wars* movie.

1. Set your type centered, with open leading.

2. Click Effects | Add Perspective.

3. While holding down Ctrl and Shift, click and drag one of the top center handles toward the center of the block of type. This will force both vertical sides to move in unison.

4. Try pushing the bottom handles outward, using the same Ctrl+Shift modifiers.

5. Tweak both the top and bottom until they're truly worthy of a Jedi master typographer.

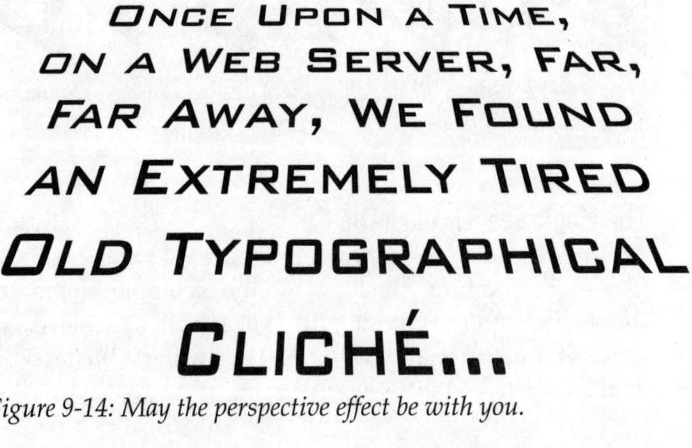

Figure 9-14: May the perspective effect be with you.

Licking the Envelope

CorelWEB.DRAW's envelope effect can be tons of fun, though it's easily abused. Here are two common effects you can create with the Envelope roll-up. The first example is created from scratch, while the second example uses an envelope preset.

Sign Painter's Arcs

1. Start by setting the type and assigning a proper typeface. We used Flareserif 821.

2. Press Ctrl+F7 to summon the Envelope roll-up.

3. At the Envelope roll-up, click the Single Arc button (the rightmost button at the center of the palette) and click Add New.

4. Click Layout | Snap to Guidelines.

5. Click and drag the bottom left handle downward. Drag out a guideline to meet the bottom handle's new position. Click and drag the bottom right handle downward to meet the guideline.

6. At the Envelope roll-up, click Apply. Tweak the handles until it looks right. (You may want to try pushing the bottom center handle upward.

7. Drag-duplicate a drop shadow and fill as shown in Figure 9-15.

Figure 9-15: While this effect was inspired by a bottle of gin, it's not our brand. Really.

Waving the Flag

The Envelope roll-up's preset shapes can speed up the application of an envelope effect, and they're extremely useful when repetitively applying the same effect to more than one object. There's a wide variety of shapes, including octagons, stars, ovals, and even seasonal favorites including a heart and a pine tree. In the following exercise, you'll use a simple banner.

WAVING FLAG

Figure 9-16: Preset shapes can expedite your enveloping chores.

1. Start by setting the type and assigning an appropriate typeface. We used Bernhard Bold Condensed.

2. At the Envelope roll-up, click Add Preset and select the wavy banner from the drop-down menu.

3. Just click Apply and you're done! (Of course, you can always fine-tune the effect by tugging on the handles.)

Can't Find the Right Envelope Shape?

You can create an envelope based upon any object. With the object you want to envelope selected, click Create From (on the Envelope roll-up). A big fat arrow will appear. Click the object you want to use as the envelope shape and it will be transferred to the original object. Click Apply to administer the effect.

More Blended Effects

Earlier, we used the blend effect to create soft drop-shadow and embossed effects. Now, let's take a look at how we can use a blend to create a pair of glowing effects. Cool neons are easy to accomplish. All you have to do is blend two objects. The object in back has a fat outline (in the same color as the background), while the object in front has a skinny outline (in the glowing color).

Neon Glow

The Flopping Fish Lounge sign, shown in Figure 9-17, uses a simple neon glow effect, as outlined above. We used Balloon Bold for the type and reeled in the fish from Letraset's DF Diversities icon font. This example was created in an extra-large size. Hence, the back (black) outlines were a whopping 33 pixels in width. The fat outlines blended down to single-pixel neon-colored outlines, in only 10 steps. The fonts you choose and the size you generate in the final artwork will determine the proper outline widths. To achieve more "pop," use a hairline color that is slightly different from the fill.

Figure 9-17: Nope, we didn't spend time at the bar researching how to create this effect. Honest.

Which Fonts Make Nice Neon?

Stick with the skinny sans-serifs. Here are some additional fonts to try: Bank Gothic Light, Bernhard Fashion, Circle Round, Dextor, Freehand 575, Futura Light, and Horatio.

X-Cellent

Watch out . . . it's another logo rip-off! This time, we're modifying the neon glow effect to knock off everyone's favorite Fox Television Sci-Fi drama. The X-Cellent effect shown in Figure 9-18 uses the same technique as the neon glow, with the only difference being that the top object is filled with black (the background color). This makes the type appear as if it is a backlit shadow. Try this effect with various typewriter-style fonts—the grungier the better.

Figure 9-18: It's got to be a conspiracy, Agent Sculley . . . this effect is too easy to achieve.

More Timeless Typographical Clichés

What's old is new, what's new is over in fifteen minutes, and what will be "in" next week is practically unfathomable. Typographic styles and trends get recycled and regurgitated at an alarming pace. Internet time has heightened this phenomenon to the point where most designers are sitting with their noses five inches away from the side of a speeding bullet train. They never read the writing until the back end of the caboose has passed them by.

With that in mind, here are a few old favorites you might consider for special Web page graphics.

Big Old Quotes

No doubt you've seen this one a dozen times. The trick here is to find the right combination of typefaces and sizes for the quotes and text. The example shown in Figure 9-19 uses 90-point Normandie quotes with 36-point Normandie Italic text. Notice the tight leading and careful fit between the two lines of type. When this effect works right, it delivers an elegant yet playful feel.

Figure 9-19: Just take a pair of giant quote marks and sandwich a snippet of text between them. Yum-Yum!

Cartoon Balloon

Ever want to put words in someone's mouth? The cartoon balloon effect, as shown in Figure 9-20, is a sure way to lighten up a Web page. Choose a whimsical typeface, such as Balloon Light. It shouldn't take too much effort to create a balloon shape with the Freehand or Bezier tool.

Figure 9-20: It's always fun to stick one of these in a photo with the big cheese. Just make sure that you get the approvals before going online or you may be joining the freelance ranks.

Superhero

The heroic effect shown in Figure 9-21 was created with a combination of an envelope and an extrude effect. Rotate the extrusion and fiddle with the lights until it looks right. Use a shaded extrusion to add the most depth. You may want to click Arrange | Separate to break the front face away from the extrusion in order to tweak its fill and outline without affecting the extrusion.

Figure 9-21: Extruded type can be tons of fun.

Spin-A-Rama!

Have you ever wanted to create an object that contained spokes that radiated from a central core, such as a star, snowflake or flower, as shown in Figure 9-22? The Pick tool's rotation mode makes this a quick trick, by simply moving the center of rotation. The next little exercise will demonstrate how easy it is to create radiant symmetrical objects. While this example uses a simple oval as its base object, you can start with a wide variety of objects—even type characters! Figure 9-23 will help guide you through this nifty little procedure.

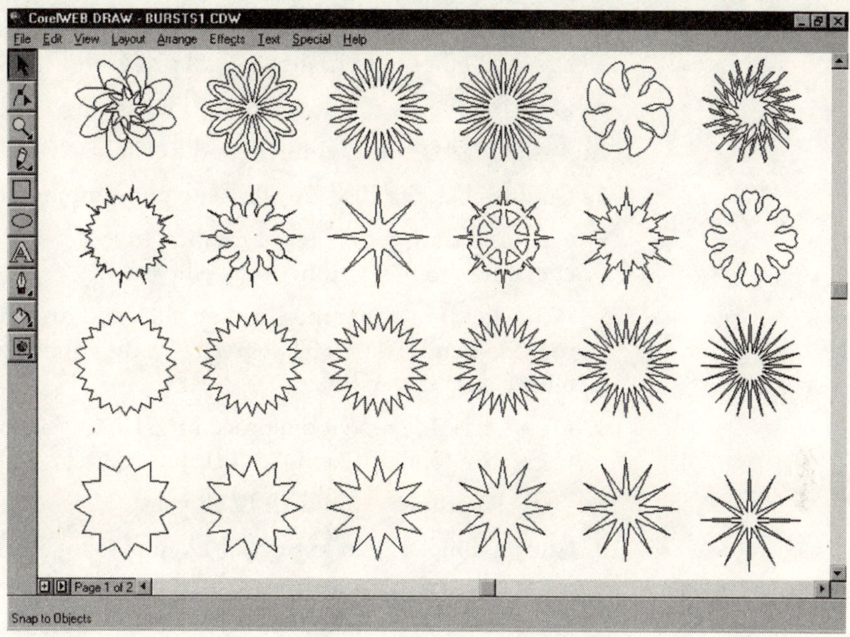

Figure 9-22: Spin yourself a flower, star, burst, or snowflake . . .

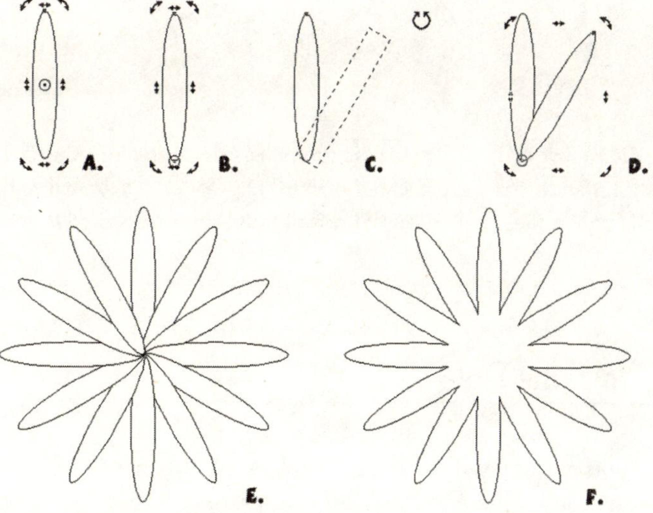

Figure 9-23: . . . just follow these steps!

1. Press F7 to access the Ellipse tool.

2. Draw an ellipse approximately 20 pixels wide by 120 pixels high.

3. Press the spacebar to activate the Pick tool.

4. Assign the ellipse a white fill and a thin black outline.

5. Double-click the 20 x 120 ellipse to put it into rotation mode (A).

6. Click and drag the center of rotation (it looks like a little bull's eye) down to the bottom of the ellipse (B).

7. While holding down the Ctrl key, click and drag the upper right rotation handle down 30 degrees (C). Right-click to duplicate the ellipse and release (D).

8. Press Ctrl+R to repeat the procedure. Do this a total of 10 times to create a total of 12 ellipses (E).

9. Drag a marquee around all 12 ellipses.

10. Click Arrange | Weld to fuse all 12 ellipses together (F). Cool!

11. There's one more step. Take a close look at the flower to see if it has a tiny path at its center. If so, click Arrange | Break Apart, then Shift-click the flower to deselect it and press delete to remove the extra path.

Look for the Bursts!

CD-ROM

The Companion CD-ROM that accompanies this book includes dozens and dozens of cool shapes that were created in WEB.DRAW with the Spin-A-Rama technique. Look for the files named burst1.cdw, burst2.cdw, burst3.cdw, and burst4.cdw.

Node-Tweaking Tips

If you never have the need to create an illustration with WEB.DRAW, you'll never have the dubious pleasure of tweaking nodes with the Shape tool. But if your work entails more than just rectangles, ellipses, and type, you're bound to spend some time learning the ins and outs of one of the program's most involved procedures. Remember your first taste of beer? You probably didn't care for it very much. Node editing is like that—it's an acquired taste. You might end up liking it, but then you might not.

There are a number of ways to change the appearance of a line with the Shape tool. The simplest method is to just click on the line and push it around. If that doesn't do the trick, you can click and drag the nodes around. But if that doesn't meet your needs, you have little choice other than to jump in with both feet and start node-tweaking. Soon you'll be pulling on those knitting needles like a pro!

Choose the Correct Node

Curved nodes come in three different varieties: smooth, symmetrical, and cusp. When you lay down a line with the Freehand tool, WEB.DRAW decides what types of nodes to use. It doesn't always make the right choice. Figure 9-24 displays the three curved node types. As you can see, the node type influences the lay of the line. Changing between smooth, symmetrical, and cusp types can greatly affect the manner in which a line enters and exits a node.

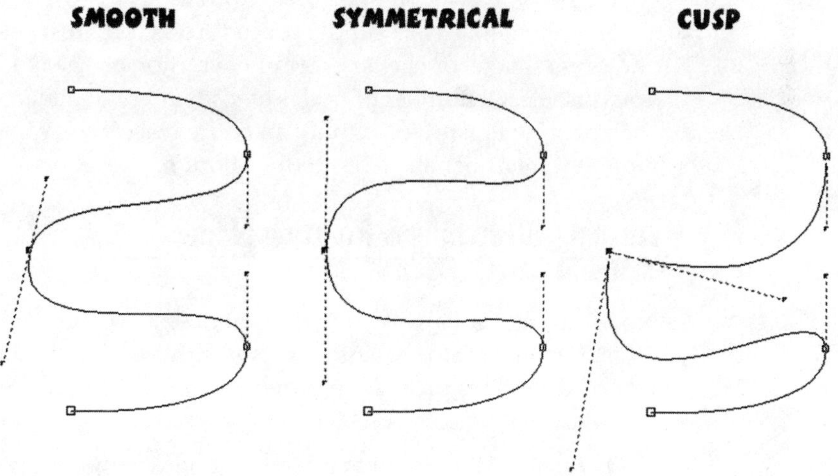

Figure 9-24: Choosing the correct node type—whether it's smooth, symmetrical, or cusp—is one of the most important node-tweaking steps.

- *Smooth nodes*—The node and both control points run on a common plane. The control points can be at different distances from the node; the distance from the node affects the fatness of the curve.

- *Symmetrical nodes*—Like smooth nodes, the node and both control points run on a common plane. The difference is that both control points are exactly the same distance from the node. If you push one control point in, the other control point will automatically follow.

- *Cusp nodes*—These critters are most often used for sharp changes in direction. The control points are completely independent of each other.

Adding & Removing Nodes

Need to make a sharp change of direction? Just add an extra node! All you have to do is use the Shape tool to click on the line in the exact place where you want the new node to appear. Then click the + (plus) button on the Node Edit roll-up. To make sure that the node is added in precisely the right place, you might want to drag out a couple of guidelines from the onscreen rulers to mark the spot. Then, click Layout | Snap to Guidelines and click on the crossing point.

Removing nodes is a simple procedure as well. Just select the node and press Delete, or click the – (minus) button on the Node Edit roll-up. You can select a number of nodes by dragging out a marquee or by Shift-clicking. If you want to simplify an entire object, you can drag a marquee around it then click the AutoReduce button.

Aligning, Stretching & Rotating Nodes

Node editing isn't always a tedious node-by-node procedure. Quite often, you'll want to save time by editing several nodes in harmony. The Node Edit roll-up provides a number of convenient features to make this happen.

- *Align*—Allows you to align two nodes, either vertically or horizontally, while subsequently allowing you to align the control points to create an exact match.

- *Stretch*—Select a number of nodes, click the Stretch button, and you can stretch or scale the selection in a manner similar to that of the Pick tool.

- *Rotate*—As with the Stretch feature, Rotate works like its Pick tool cousin . . . just click and drag!

Getting Elastic

Just say boing! Perhaps the best way to explain the Node Edit roll-up's elastic mode is to liken it to (as you might guess) a rubber band. This magical feature places all the selected nodes on a springy line that's anchored just to the outside of the selected nodes (or to a starting or ending node if all the nodes are selected in an open path). This one really has to be experienced to be fully understood. Create a curved line now, and try using the Node Edit dialog box in both elastic and nonelastic modes.

Working With Pattern Fills

Although we briefly touched on the subject of two-color and full-color patterns back in Chapter 6, they're well worth a closer look. While these patterns date back to CorelDRAW's print-based roots, they still have some relevancy in the world of Web design.

Two-Color Patterns

The Two-Color Pattern dialog box, as shown in Figure 9-25, can be summoned from the Fill fly-out (the button looks like a little checker-board) or roll-up menu (press the checkerboard button, then click Edit). Two-color patterns are selected from a drop-down menu. They can also be created pixel by pixel or imported from various bitmap formats or Corel files. While you can set these patterns to any two colors you wish, you'd be wise to stick to colors within the magic 216 palette (more on that in the next chapter). In addition to color, there are a number of tweakable settings:

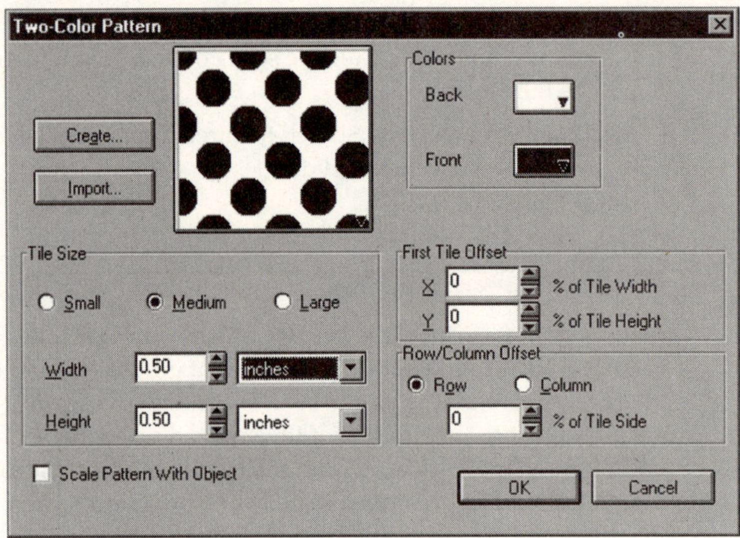

Figure 9-25: The Two-Color Pattern dialog box provides total control over simple motifs.

- *Tile Size*—Can be set to Small, Medium, Large, or a specific width and height.

- *Scale Pattern With Object*—Causes the pattern to be proportionally sized up or down when scaling or stretching a pattern-filled object.

- *Offsets*—These control the tiling pattern. If you're working with a seamless pattern, you'll want to leave these settings at their defaults.

Creating Two-Color Patterns

Want to try bitmap editing at its crudest 1-bit level? The Two-Color Pattern Editor, as shown by Figure 9-26, is about as raw as it gets. You have the option of working with bitmaps of 16 x 16, 32 x 32, or 64 x 64 pixels or pens 1 x 1, 2 x 2, 4 x 4, or 8 x 8 pixels wide. A left click will turn a gray pixel black, while a right click will turn a black pixel gray. The guidelines help to ensure seamlessness. Once you click OK, the new bitmap will be placed on the Two-Color Pattern dialog box's drop-down menu. The black pixels will become the front color and the gray pixels will become the back color. These patterns cannot be reopened with the Two-Color Pattern Editor. Consequently, two-color pattern creation can be a hit-or-miss procedure.

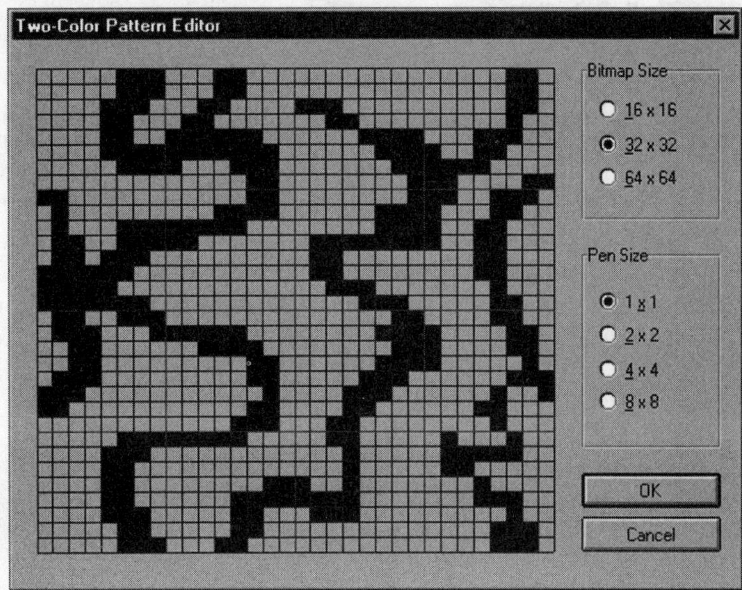

Figure 9-26: Bitmap editing doesn't get any more basic than this.

It's also possible to create two-color patterns from any artwork you have onscreen in WEB.DRAW by clicking Special | Create Pattern. This summons the Create Pattern dialog box, which allows you to specify a two-color pattern in low, medium, or high resolution. When you click OK, a crosshair cursor is displayed. Just drag out a marquee, click the OK button, and the pattern will appear on the Two-Color Pattern dialog box's drop-down menu. This procedure works best when you use uncomplicated high-contrast originals.

Importing Two-Color Patterns

Although it's possible to import two-color patterns, you shouldn't get your hopes up too high. This procedure only works well with the simplest of files. It's important to remember that there are only two colors to work with. Attempting to convert intricate artwork into a two-color pattern is a tedious procedure at best. The most favorable results will occur when you use a real bitmap editor before importing the pattern into WEB.DRAW.

Full-Color Patterns

You've probably noticed that the Full-Color Pattern dialog box, as shown in Figure 9-27, looks a lot like the Two-Color Pattern dialog box. Thankfully, it is far more applicable for Web design use than its bicolor sibling. All of the same Tile Size and Offset controls are there, but there's also a lot more utility. You can load CorelWEB.DRAW .PWG pattern files or import real images. This allows you to create WEB.DRAW graphics with the scrumptious full-color seamless patterns that can be found on the CorelWEB.GRAPHICS Suite CD-ROM, as well as on the Companion CD-ROM that accompanies this book (not to mention out on the Web)!

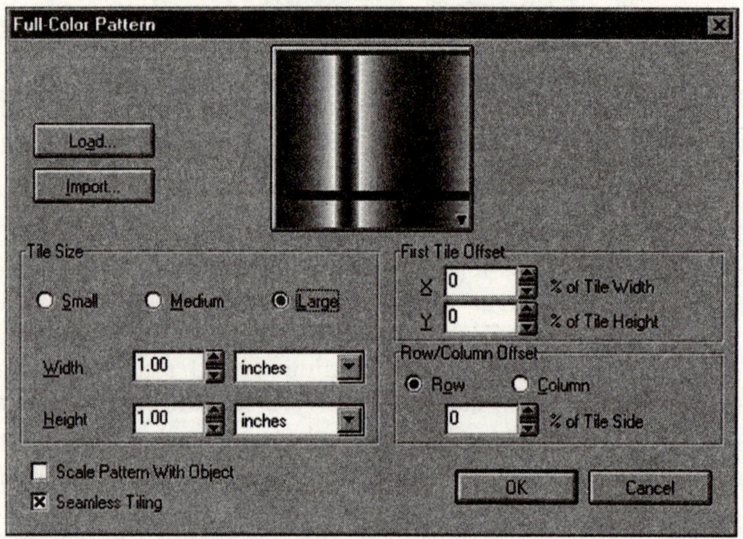

Figure 9-27: Full-Color Patterns can pack a wallop!

You also can create a full-color pattern from any part of a WEB.DRAW image, by clicking Special | Create Pattern. In addition to creating two-color patterns, as outlined above, the Create Pattern dialog box allows you to capture artwork as .PWG format pattern files.

Hot Spot Tips

Here are a handful of tips that should shed some light on the URL tool:

- Don't assign a URL to a grouped object—it will create a separate hot spot for each object within the group. Consequently, the image map will be huge. Draw a hot spot with the URL drawing tool instead.

- Avoid assigning URLs to freehand objects. When CorelWEB.DRAW exports the GIF or JPEG image, it will consider all the space around the image—including the control points—to be part of the exported image. This can result in empty white bars around your exported image. Try to draw your hot spots with straight rather than curved lines to avoid this (remember: straight lines don't have control points, only nodes).

- Limit the number of nodes in a freehand hot spot. You should strive to make them as simple as possible to keep the image map a lean-and-mean piece of code. Don't be sloppy: kill all the superfluous nodes.

Changing WEB.DRAW Preferences

Do you want to increase your productivity with WEB.DRAW? This section explains how Preferences dialog box settings affect your work patterns; it also suggests making a number of changes to the default settings. These minor tweaks will make your WEB.DRAW life far more pleasant and productive. Once you make a change to the Preferences dialog box, it will "remember" the settings and use them (rather than the default settings) each time you launch the program.

The Preferences dialog box is summoned by the Ctrl+J keyboard shortcut, or by clicking Special | Preferences. It is a six-tabbed affair, with General, URL, View, Curves, Text, and Advanced modes. In the following section, we'll point out the highlights of each mode and explain how different settings can increase your productivity. We won't describe every setting, just those most important in day-to-day operations.

General Preferences: The Basics

The General tab, as shown by Figure 9-28, controls seven basic
WEB.DRAW settings that physically affect the manner in which you
create artwork. Since you're creating Web graphics, which are always
measured in pixels, the first thing you should do here is change the
Duplicate and Nudge measurement systems to pixels. Here are a handful
of suggestions for the other settings:

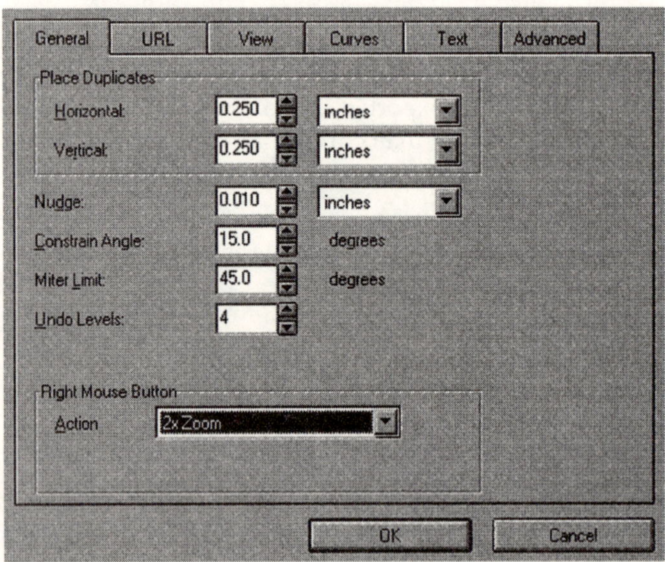

Figure 9-28: The General tab is the first place to start your WEB.DRAW tune-up.

■ *Place Duplicates*—Are you creating lots of drop shadows? Set this
option to three pixels horizontal and vertical (or whatever your
exact distances are), and you'll save tons of time.

■ *Nudge*—Do you like to move objects "just a tad"? Set this for one
pixel for the highest precision when moving objects with the
cursor keys.

■ *Constrain Angle*—The default setting of 15 degrees is fine for most
circumstances. You may want to change it when creating a series of
rotations, as in the Spin-A-Rama exercise shown earlier in this
chapter.

- *Miter Limit*—Affects the manner in which outline corners are joined. The default setting of 45 degrees is usually all you need.

- *Undo Levels*—Here's where you can save your hide. The default setting of four undos is pretty skimpy. Dial this one up as you see fit, but be warned that this setting is memory-dependent. You won't get all 99 levels of Undo unless your system has plenty of RAM (not that you'd need that many levels of Undo!).

- *Right Mouse Button*—This setting can make things run really smooth! Choose between 2X Zoom, Character, Edit Text, Full Screen Preview, and Node Edit, depending upon your working style. For example: if you're working with a lot of text graphics, choose Character or Edit Text. And if you're doing a lot of node-tweaking, choose Node Edit.

URL Preferences: Image Map Ease

If you've done any hot-spotting with WEB.DRAW, you may have noticed that the hot spots can be quite ugly. Fear not: there's an easy cure! The URL tab, as shown by Figure 9-29, controls the appearance of URL hot spots as well as the default URL. It allows you to choose from half a dozen different hatched patterns, and it also provides control over the color of the hatching. Here are a few tips:

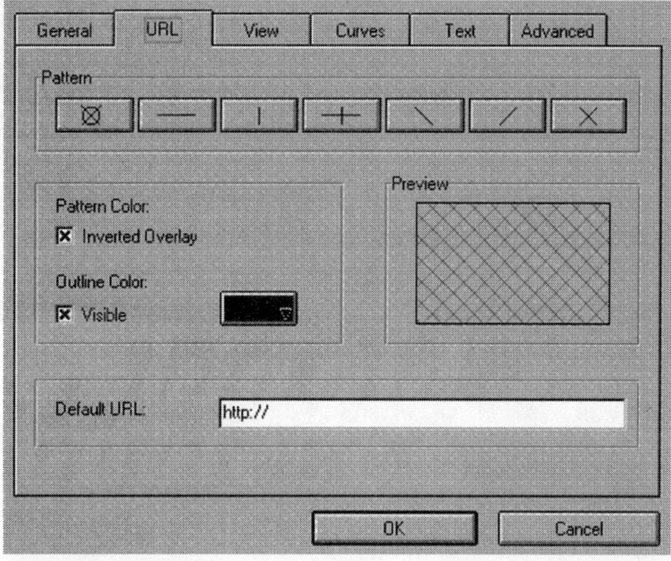

Figure 9-29: The URL tab makes your hot-spotting chores a more pleasant experience.

- Choose one of the single-line patterns rather than the cross-hatched patterns; the single-line patterns are a bit easier on the eyes.

- To ensure contrast, use a pattern color that is not used in your graphics. Selecting Inverted Overlay will change the color of the hatched lines in relation to the color of the objects they overlie. This can make the hatching even more obtrusive.

- For the cleanest preview, turn Outline Color off.

- Set the Default URL to your Web site's home page.

View Preferences: Take a Gander

Want to take charge of your WEB.DRAW windows? The View tab delivers the goods, as shown by Figure 9-30, allowing you to tweak the screen settings to your heart's delight. Let's touch on some of the most important productivity enhancers:

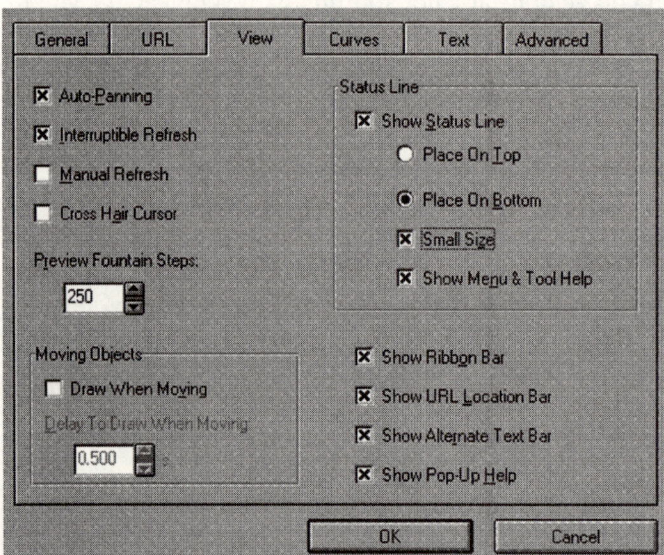

Figure 9-30: The View tab provides total control over WEB.DRAW's appearance.

- *Auto-Panning*—Selecting this option allows you to automatically pan beyond the WEB.DRAW window. When you drag off to the side of the window, the image scrolls with your cursor.

- *Interruptible Refresh*—Definitely leave this setting on. It allows you to stop the screen redraw by pressing any key or clicking a mouse button.

- *Manual Refresh*—While some folks might consider this to be a feature in search of a purpose, we can think of one good reason to use it: cruel practical jokes. Sneak into a buddy's Preferences dialog box and turn this feature on. The screen will not redraw until your buddy click's on a scrollbar button or presses Ctrl+W. Other than that, you should always leave this option off!

- *Cross Hair Cursor*—For folks who need clinical precision. This option extends cursor lines all the way to WEB.DRAW's onscreen rulers.

- *Preview Fountain Steps*—This setting controls the smoothness of fountain fill previews and exports. The higher the setting, the smoother they'll be. But there's a price to pay: the more steps, the longer they'll take to display. If your system isn't the fastest (and if you have a slug of a video card), you'll probably want to dial this down . . . otherwise, you'll spend a lot of time waiting for the screen to redraw. But if you're lucky enough to have a killer video card, such as a Number Nine Imagine 128, go for it!

But Before You Export ...

If you're exporting fountain-filled objects, you may want to adjust the Preview Fountain Steps setting. Low settings result in banded fountains. Check Chapter 10 for further details.

- *Moving Objects*—Once again, unless you have a fast system and a decent accelerated video card, you'll probably want to leave this setting off.

- *Status Line*—For the most part, you should run with the status line on. It's your personal preference as to whether it appears at the top or the bottom of the WEB.DRAW window. Select Small Size to maximize your workspace.

- *Ribbon Bar*—Once you learn the keyboard shortcuts (and perhaps before), the Ribbon Bar is a waste of onscreen real estate. Turn this option off to maximize your workspace.

- *URL Location and Alternate Text Bars*—Turn these options off, until you need to create an image map, as they also waste far too much workspace.

Curve Preferences: Drawing Aids

If you create a lot of artwork with WEB.DRAW's Pencil tool, you'll probably want to take a look at the Preferences dialog box's Curves tab, as shown in Figure 9-31. Otherwise, you can just as well leave this one at its default settings. The Curves tab governs how the Pencil tool operates, with regard to tracking, curves, nodes, and control points.

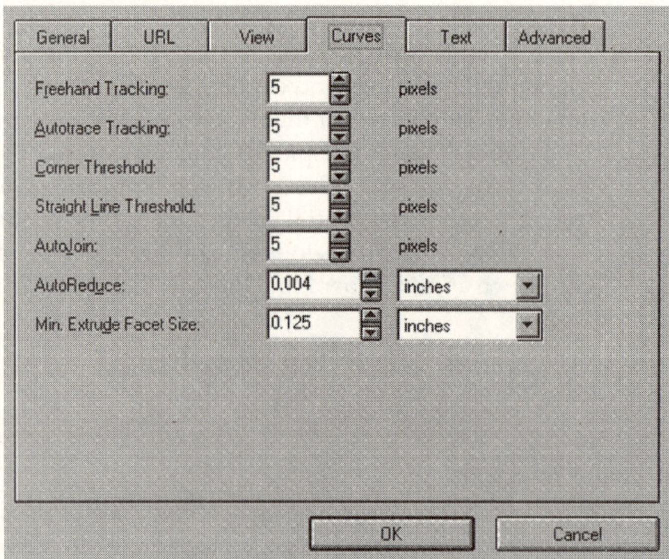

Figure 9-31: The Curves tab helps you take charge of the Pencil tool.

- *Freehand Tracking*—This governs the precision of your freehand drawing. With higher settings, you'll have smoother lines and fewer nodes. With lower settings, the opposite will occur.

- *Autotrace Tracking*—This setting is designed to govern the precision of the Autotrace feature. Lower settings should produce more accurate traces. Unfortunately, we were not able to test this feature in WEB.DRAW 1.0, Build 152 because Autotrace did not function as promised.

- *Corner Threshold*—Lower settings produce more cusps than smooth nodes, while higher settings result in a greater number of smooth nodes.

- *Straight Line Threshold*—Lower settings produce more curves rather than straight lines.

- *AutoJoin*—Governs the "magnetic" quality of starting and ending nodes when drawing. The higher the setting, the more sticky they will be and the easier it is to close an object. Use a lower setting for the most precision.

- *AutoReduce*—Governs the amount of spurious nodes that the Node Edit roll-up's AutoReduce button removes. The higher the setting, the more aggressive. Lower settings are more faithful to the original object.

- *Minimum Extrude Facet Size*—Set this to a higher setting to speed up screen redraw when working with extruded objects. For the highest-quality image, ratchet it down when you're ready to export the graphic.

Text Preferences: Type Control

Unless you have something special in mind, the Text tab, as shown in Figure 9-32, can be left alone. The default settings should cover most situations. For example, it's hard to imagine why you would not want to be able to edit text onscreen or see a font sample in the Text roll-up. You may want to use the Greek Text Below setting when working with large amounts of small text, although this won't happen very often when creating Web graphics. The PANOSE settings govern how WEB.DRAW handles font substitution when opening up files created with fonts that are not presently loaded on the system. This feature is worth a look only if you are passing a lot of files back and forth between machines with dissimilar font loads.

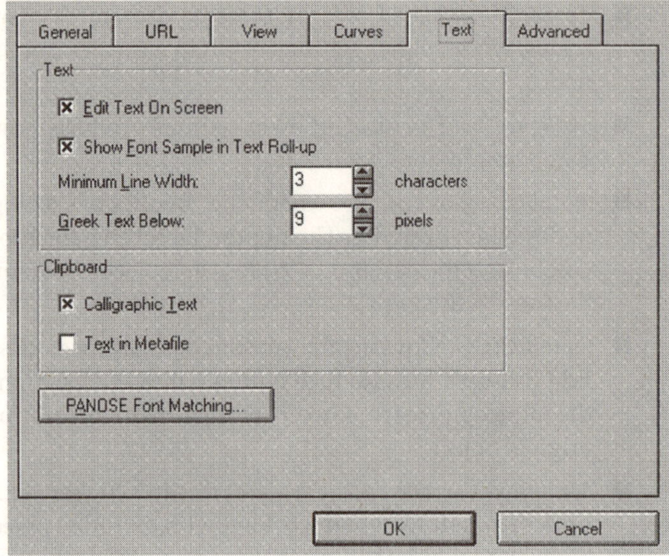

Figure 9-32: The Text tab won't get much traffic, but some of its settings may be worth looking into.

Advanced Preferences: Whatever's Left Over

It's tough to say what's really advanced about the Advanced tab. Suffice it to say that Corel popped in all the preferences that didn't fit into the other tabs. The Advanced tab, as shown by Figure 9-33, merely controls a number of backup and preview settings. It's good working practice to leave the Make Backup on Save and Auto-Backup settings on. The regular backups will have the same name as your original file but will have a .BAK file extension. If you ever need to open up a backup file, just change its extension from .BAK to .CDW.

Auto-Backup automatically saves WEB.DRAW files while you are working. It can be set to perform its function according to your schedule—anywhere from once every minute all the way up to once every 120 minutes, in one-minute increments. If the default setting of once every 10 minutes is too frequent for you, just dial it up. Auto-Backup files are named with the .ABK file extension.

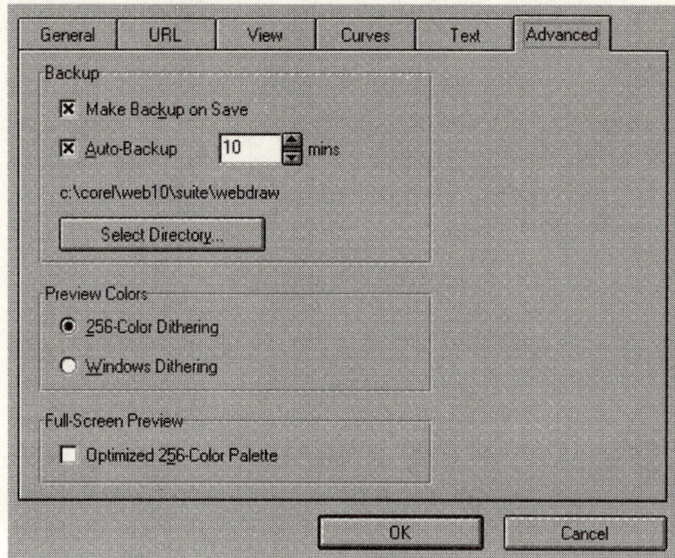

Figure 9-33: The Advanced tab covers backup and preview settings.

The Preview Colors settings you use depend on the way your system is set up. Different video cards and color depths produce different effects. What looks right on a 256 color display may not be the best solution when working on a 24-bit display. Try fiddling around with these settings to see what works best on your computer.

Moving On

This chapter should give you a jump-start, in creativity and productivity. The techniques explained here will help you build fun, effective artwork in a flash. In the next chapter, you'll learn how to make the most of vector-based illustration in your Web page designs and help you choose what works best when converting vector artwork into GIF and JPEG images. We'll cover bitmap optimization, palette reduction and Corel's Barista technology.

10

Optimizing Web Graphics

Right out of the box, CorelWEB.DRAW provides a range of powerful tools for building Web graphics. But we'd be the first to admit that the program falls short in certain places. Thankfully, these shortcomings are easily overcome. This chapter explains where WEB.DRAW can be tweaked and when it can use a helping hand. You'll see how other applications can be used in conjunction with WEB.DRAW to achieve the best possible results. By following the advice in this chapter, you'll be assured that the Web graphics you create will look great on any platform.

Getting It Right For the Web

Before you launch headfirst into the world of online graphics, you must acknowledge that the World Wide Web is by no means a Microsoft franchise. The browsers that sit on the other end of the wire are not all running on the same kind of machine; they can be Macintosh, Sun, Silicon Graphics, or Hewlett-Packard UNIX workstations. The types of machines will vary in percentages from industry to industry. For example, printers and publishers will tend to have a higher percentage of Macs, while engineers and scientists will have more UNIX boxes. The Web, by its very nature, is a cross-platform community.

You must also consider the type of browser software being used, without committing yourself (and your Web site). Each brand and version has its own little quirks. Generally speaking, you should avoid coding your pages or creating your graphics to look best in one particular browser. The Web moves far too quickly.

What's Dithering?

Dithering is often used when preparing GIF images. When you dither an image, the original RGB (red, green & blue) color value of a pixel is swapped for the closest color in the indexed palette. The reduction in the number of colors is monumental: from 16.7 million RGB colors down to 256 indexed colors. When properly done, the dithering process fools the eye into perceiving more color. It does this by placing pixels of various colors together to simulate an entirely different color. Dithering isn't always a good thing, however. Dithered colors can appear spotty or uneven. That's one reason why you should use pure (nondithered) colors whenever possible.

The Magic 216-Color Netscape Palette

While the GIF format supports 256 indexed colors, one shouldn't get the wild idea that it's possible to use all 256 colors! This is due (in part) to the fact that the Windows operating system eats up 20 colors just to display its graphical user interface. For that reason, Netscape had to make some concessions when it designed Navigator's color palette.

The *Netscape palette* (as it's referred to in some circles) is a nondithering combination of 216 colors that are designed to appear consistently across platforms within Netscape Navigator. (The same 216 colors are used by Microsoft's Internet Explorer.) When specifying colors with the Netscape palette, you can be assured that the colors will look similar whether they're viewed on a Macintosh, Windows 95, Silicon Graphics, or Sun workstation. To this end, we've posted a Corel palette file (216color.cpl) that matches the Netscape colors. You can find the palette file on this book's online update: http://www.vmedia.com/updates/.

When you design your GIF graphics, try to stick to the colors in the Netscape palette, to avoid dithering. And as mentioned in Chapter 2, if you are converting photographs for use on your Web pages, don't bother with the GIF format at all. The best way to display color-rich images (such as photographs) is to use the JPEG format.

Avoiding Palette Clash

Web browsers load palette colors on a per-page basis. The colors that come in first are the colors that are used to display all the GIF images on a page. That is, if a Web page includes a number of images whose color palettes use a total combination of colors higher than 256, the images that come in late (after all the slots are filled) may suffer from a distorted display as the browser converts the orphaned colors to their closest match.

In short, you need to proceed with caution when indexing colors. While we all want the smallest possible image file sizes, the safest method for preparing GIF images may be to first create them using the Netscape palette, then save them with the smallest number of possible colors. By using the 216color.cpl palette, you'll achieve this goal.

Loading Custom Palettes in WEB.DRAW

Loading custom palettes is a cinch. To load the 216color.cpl palette, you'll have to first download it from the Ventana Web site. Once you have it on your system, launch WEB.DRAW and follow these steps:

1. Draw an object.

2. Press Shift+F11 to summon the Uniform Fill dialog box.

3. Click the Custom Palettes button. Click Open (as shown in Figure 10-1).

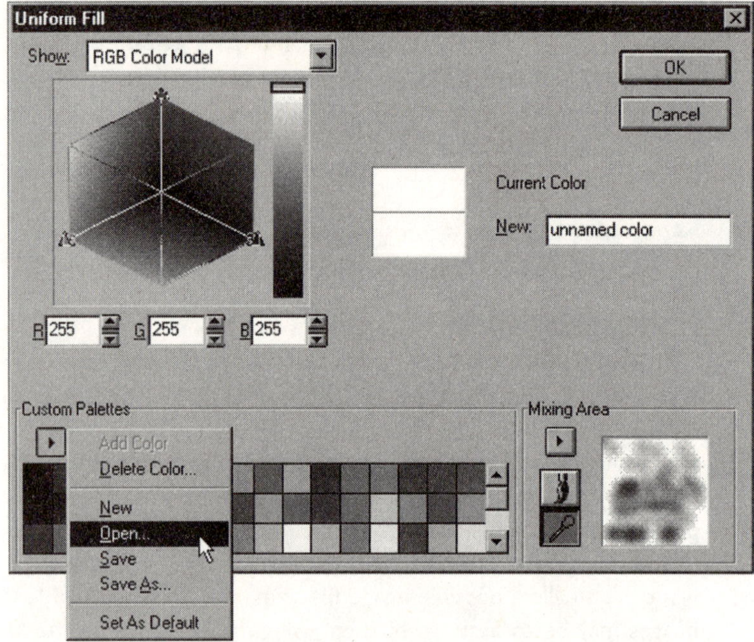

Figure 10-1: You're just a few clicks away from nondithered Web graphics!

4. Use the Open Palette dialog box to maneuver to the palette you want to load. When you locate the file (in this case, 216color.cpl), double-click on it. The palette will load, and its name will be displayed under the Custom Palette listing.

5. Click the Custom Palettes button again. Click Set as Default to ensure that the 216 color palette always comes up as the default palette.

A Palette Productivity Pointer

You can rearrange the order in which the palette colors appear by clicking and dragging a color to a new location in the palette. This is extremely handy when you develop a tight color scheme for your Web site. By dragging your most commonly used colors to the front of the list, they'll always be right there when you need them. Try dragging some colors around now, just to get the hang of it. When you've tweaked the palette order to perfection, save it with a new name.

Where's the Anti-Aliasing Option?

Arguably, CorelWEB.DRAW's biggest shortcoming as a Web graphics editor is that it does not provide an *anti-aliasing* option. Anti-aliasing is another bitmapped graphic trick that fools the eye. Unlike dithering, whose primary goal is to simulate more color, anti-aliasing's aim is to make images look smooth. Anti-aliasing is often used when setting type, to eliminate the chunky, jagged edges that appear in curved characters. Figures 10-2 and 10-3 demonstrate the difference between a typical WEB.DRAW GIF export and the same graphic that has been anti-aliased. These two images have been zoomed up, in order for you to see the big (pixel) picture.

Figure 10-2: *Right out of WEB.DRAW, this GIF graphic is jagged, especially when viewed at 300 percent of its original size.*

Figure 10-3: *The same graphic with anti-aliasing applied (in another program) is far smoother.*

Figure 10-4 demonstrates how the two images appear when viewed at their intended viewing size within Netscape Navigator. While the grayscale screen shot shown here may not convey all the subtleties of anti-aliasing, the truth becomes readily apparent when it's viewed online. In particular, anti-aliased type will blend smoothly into its background color.

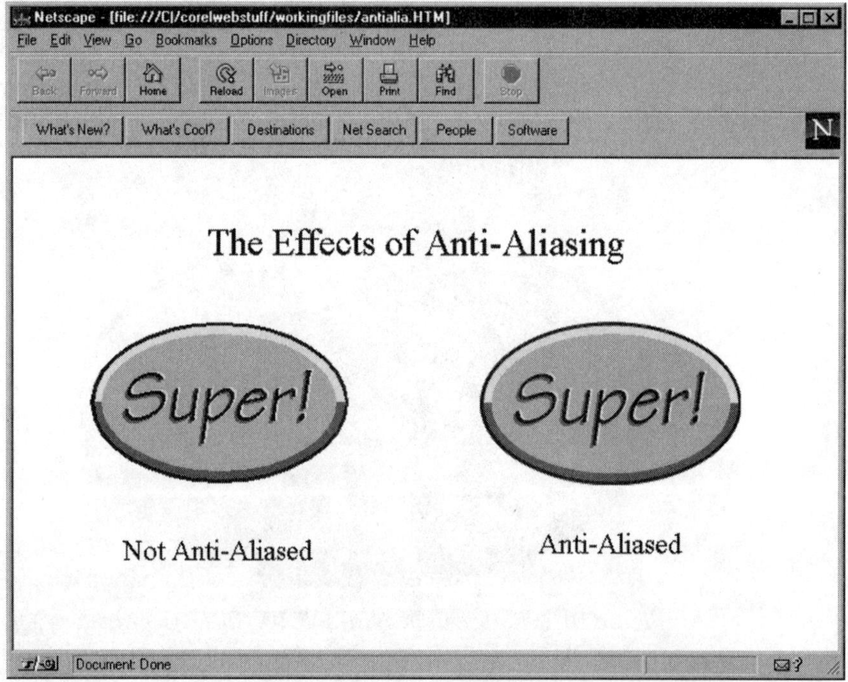

Figure 10-4: When viewed in the browser, the anti-aliased graphic looks slick, while the nonanti-aliased graphic looks chunky.

Although CorelWEB.DRAW does not offer an anti-aliasing option, there are a number of ways to achieve this effect. The following sections will show you how you can use CorelPHOTO-PAINT or Ulead's GIF/JPEG SmartSaver to anti-alias your WEB.DRAW graphics.

Anti-Aliasing With CorelPHOTO-PAINT

If you're serious about creating high-quality Web graphics, a bitmap paint editor is not merely an accessory, it is essential. There are a number of highly competent bitmap editors on the market today, including Adobe Photoshop, Fractal Design Painter, Macromedia xRes, and Ulead PhotoImpact. CorelPHOTO-PAINT has one big advantage over these other programs: it can open up native WEB.DRAW (CDW or CDR) files. Although PHOTO-PAINT was left out of the CorelWEB.GRAPHICS Suite, it's been wisely included in the new CorelWebMaster suite.

We used CorelPHOTO-PAINT 7 (part of the CorelDRAW 7 suite) to tweak the anti-aliased graphic shown in Figures 10-3 and 10-4. The importing and anti-aliasing process is fairly straightforward, with only a handful of options. PHOTO-PAINT's Import Into Bitmap dialog box, as shown in Figure 10-5, provides all the settings you'll need to create smooth images. Take a close look. This dialog box is remarkably similar to WEB.DRAW's Bitmap Export dialog box, with the addition of the anti-aliasing options. Ah, if only Corel had been kind enough to include those last few tidbits in WEB.DRAW!

There are three anti-aliasing options when importing WEB.DRAW graphics into PHOTO-PAINT. You can set anti-aliasing to None, import with the Normal setting, or use Super-sampling. The Normal mode is designed to be used mostly with images composed of straight lines, while the Super-sampling mode is intended for images with lots of curves and text. Once an image has been *rasterized* by PHOTO-PAINT's import filter, you can really go to town. Rasterization is what turns the vector artwork into a bitmap, enabling you to edit the image, pixel by pixel. This precise yet tedious editing method ensures the cleanest possible Web page images.

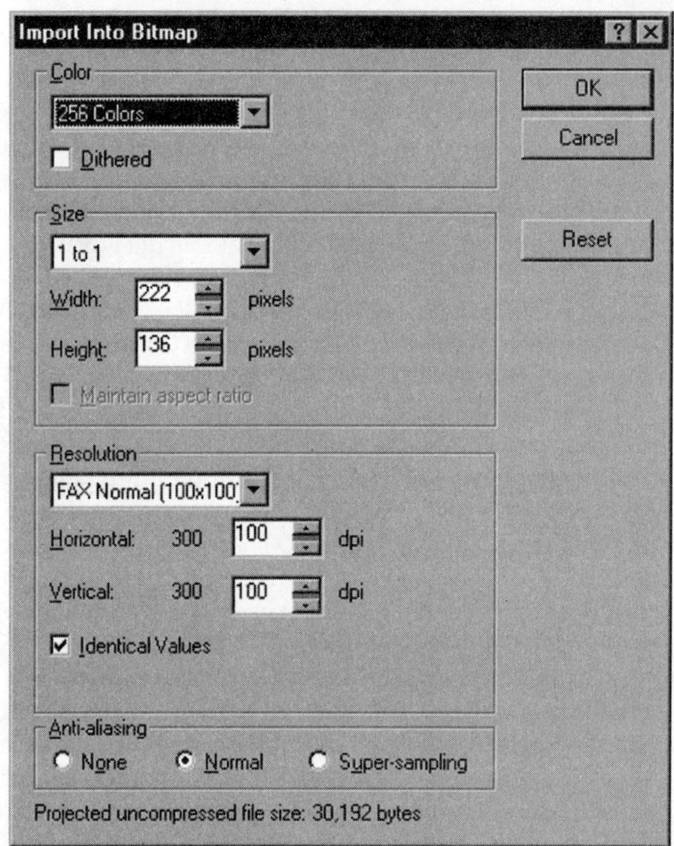

Figure 10-5: PHOTO-PAINT's Import Into Bitmap dialog box is the key to creating anti-aliased images from WEB.DRAW.

Anti-Aliasing With Ulead GIF/JPEG SmartSaver

Do you want to smooth out your WEB.DRAW graphics without having to get bogged down with individual pixel-tweaking? Ulead's GIF/JPEG SmartSaver offers a number of interesting capabilities. This program operates as a stand-alone image-optimization utility and can be used as a Photoshop export plug-in as well. It is also part and parcel of the Ulead PhotoImpact image-editing application. Figure 10-6 demonstrates how the SmartSaver's Smooth controls can be used to anti-alias GIF images that have been exported from WEB.DRAW. The program offers a host of other important features, including palette conversion and color reduction. You can zoom up on an image and pan around with its convenient grabber hand to get a closer look.

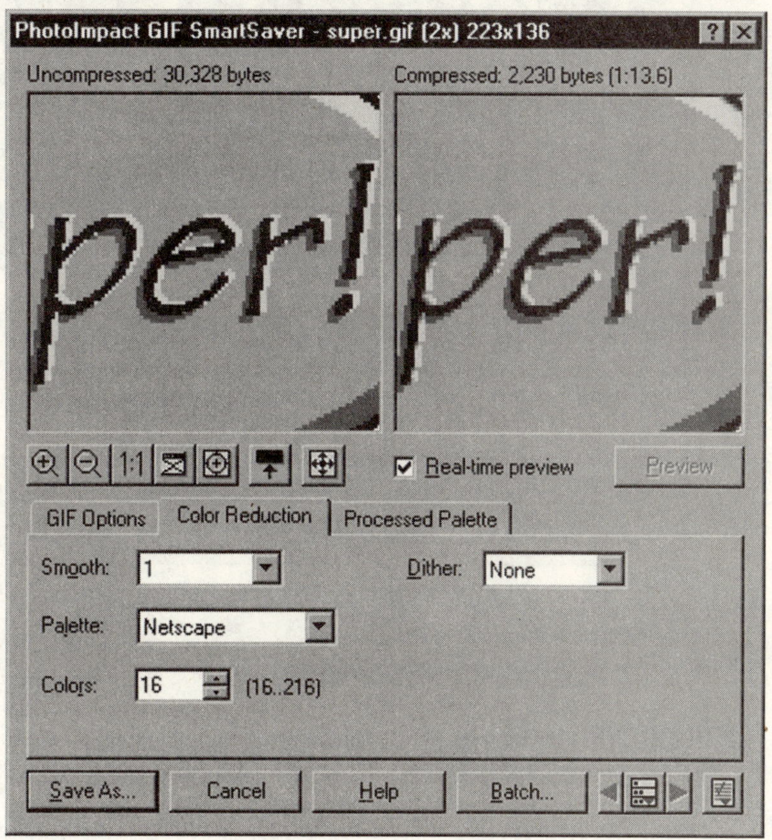

Figure 10-6: A Smooth setting of 1 does a nice job of anti-aliasing this graphic.

SmartSaver is easy to work with and is a champ at creating the smallest possible images. Its handy batch mode lets you apply a range of palette size options to an image, as shown in Figure 10-7. When you find the best trade-off of image quality and file size, you can quickly save the file. A fully functional demo version of GIF/JPEG SmartSaver is available on Ulead's Web site, at http://www.ulead.com/.

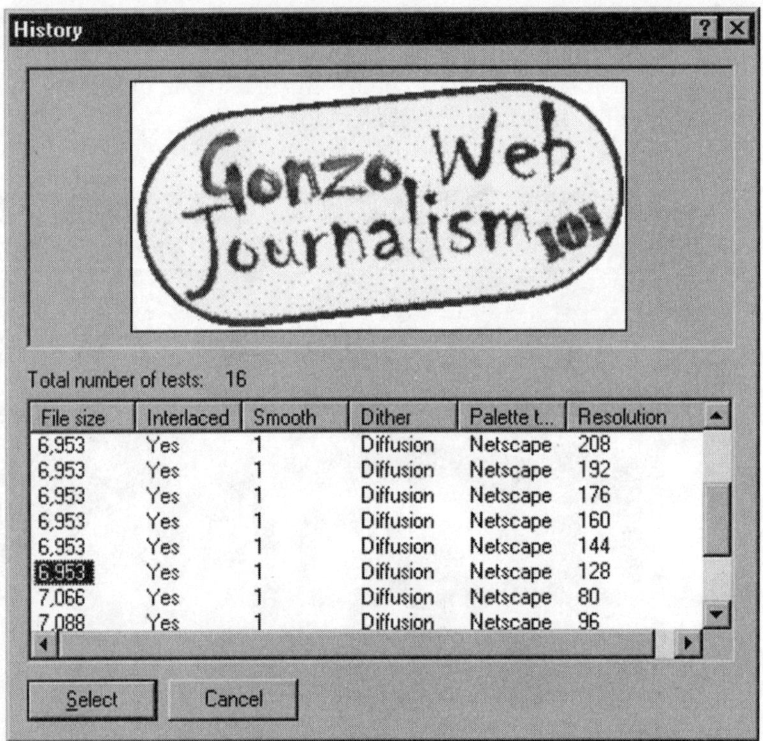

File size	Interlaced	Smooth	Dither	Palette t...	Resolution
6,953	Yes	1	Diffusion	Netscape	208
6,953	Yes	1	Diffusion	Netscape	192
6,953	Yes	1	Diffusion	Netscape	176
6,953	Yes	1	Diffusion	Netscape	160
6,953	Yes	1	Diffusion	Netscape	144
6,953	Yes	1	Diffusion	Netscape	128
7,066	Yes	1	Diffusion	Netscape	80
7,088	Yes	1	Diffusion	Netscape	96

Figure 10-7: Pick and choose the best image with SmartSaver's batch history window.

Using Advanced Fills

Although CorelWEB.DRAW delivers some impressive object fills, the real trick is getting all that beauty onto your Web page. What looks great on your computer (while in WEB.DRAW) won't always look great in the browser. It's essential to choose the correct options when creating and exporting fountain and texture fills. The following section provides a number of helpful pointers.

Fooling With Fountain Fills

It takes forethought to achieve the smoothest fountain fills. Bad fountain fills will appear *banded*, with visible stripes. There are two major factors at work: the number of fountain steps and the number of colors afforded by the export file format. While you can set WEB.DRAW's overall Fountain Steps setting in the Preferences | View dialog box, as mentioned in Chapter 9, you can override it on a per-object basis in the Fountain Fill dialog box. Figures 10-8 and 10-9 demonstrate the differences between a fountain fill with 40 and 256 bands (the maximum), in both GIF (256 color) and JPEG (16.7 million color) formats.

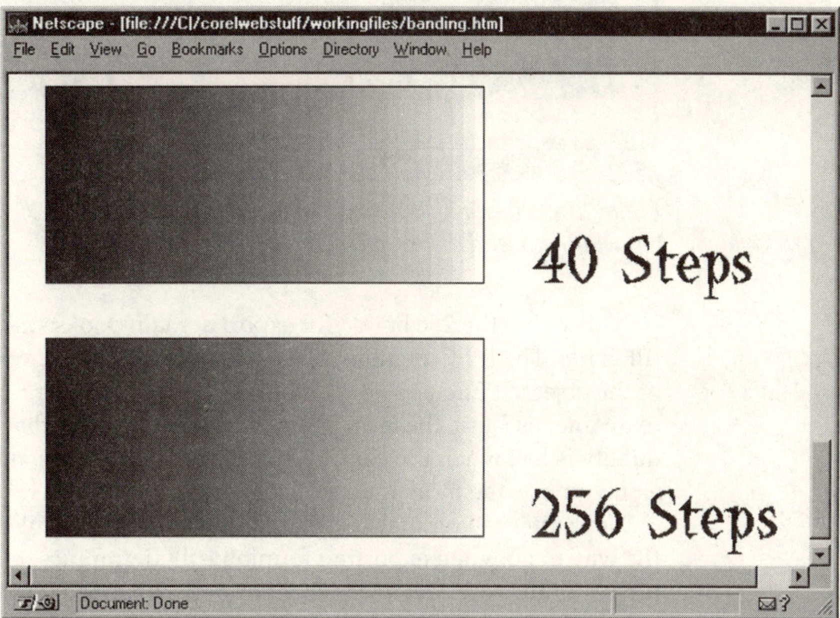

Figure 10-8: Here's our fountain fill exported as a GIF file with 40 and 256 bands.

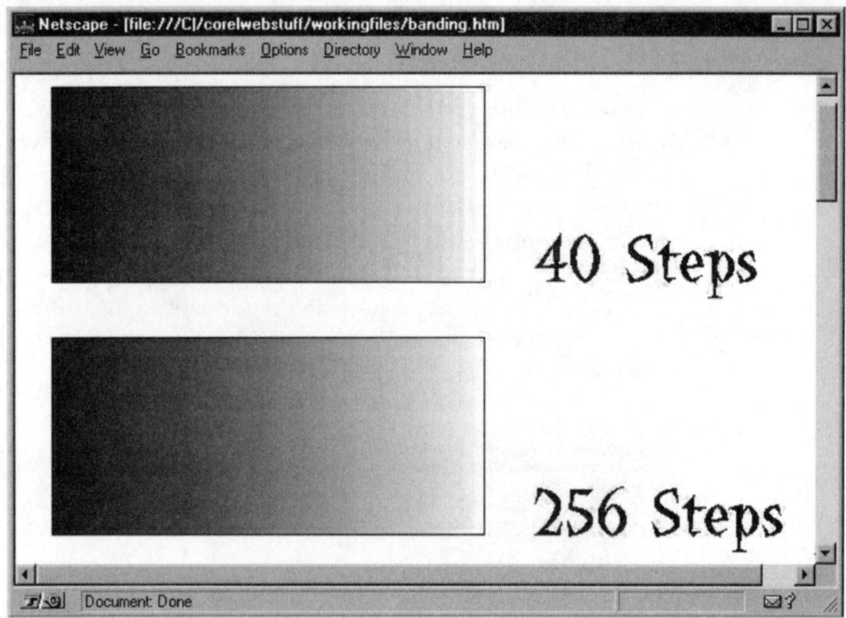

Figure 10-9: Take a look at the same image exported as a JPEG file. What's going on with that weird distortion?

Notice that the 256 band GIF export actually looks smoother than the JPEG file. The JPEG demonstrates some distortion at the top and bottom of the object. JPEG uses *lossy* compression. While you might think that really means *lousy*, the term actually refers to the fact that some image quality is lost when the compression is performed. The more compression you use, the more image quality you will sacrifice.

Now, after seeing that last example, you may be thinking that GIF is the way to go when exporting fountain-filled graphics. But that's definitely not the case. Let's see what happens when we throw a whole bunch of fountain fills into the mix. Figures 10-10 and 10-11 use nine different fountain fills, in a variety of colors. The intent behind this experiment is to max out the number of indexed colors available. Notice how the GIF graphic shown in Figure 10-10 loses its smoothness in the vertical fountains. The JPEG graphic shown in Figure 10-11 maintains its smoothness (although it exhibits those same irritating JPEG compression artifacts). The strongest case is made by the file sizes: the GIF file weighs in at 57K while the JPEG file (with a medium-high quality level) weighs in at 31K.

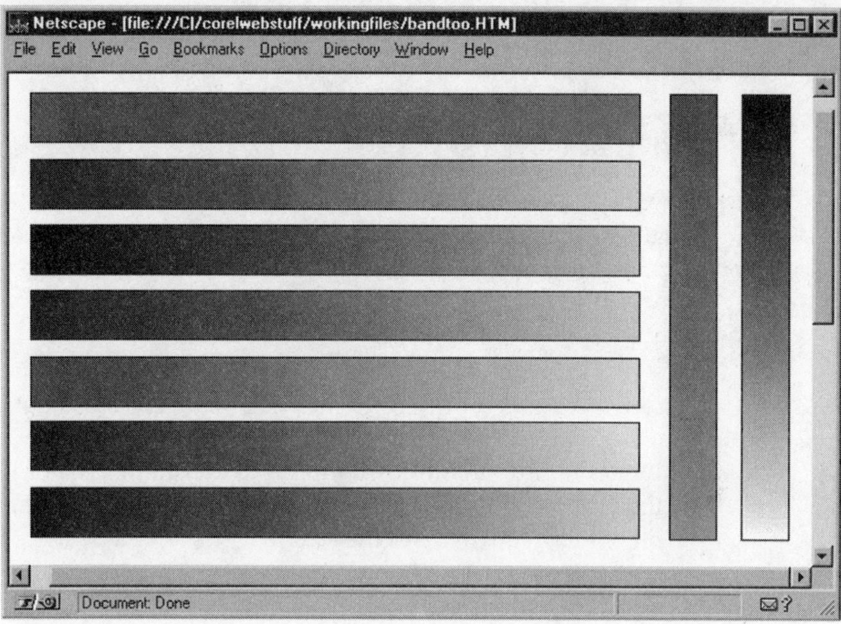

Figure 10-10: Take a look at the banding and pixelating in the vertical fills. The GIF file has run out of indexed colors.

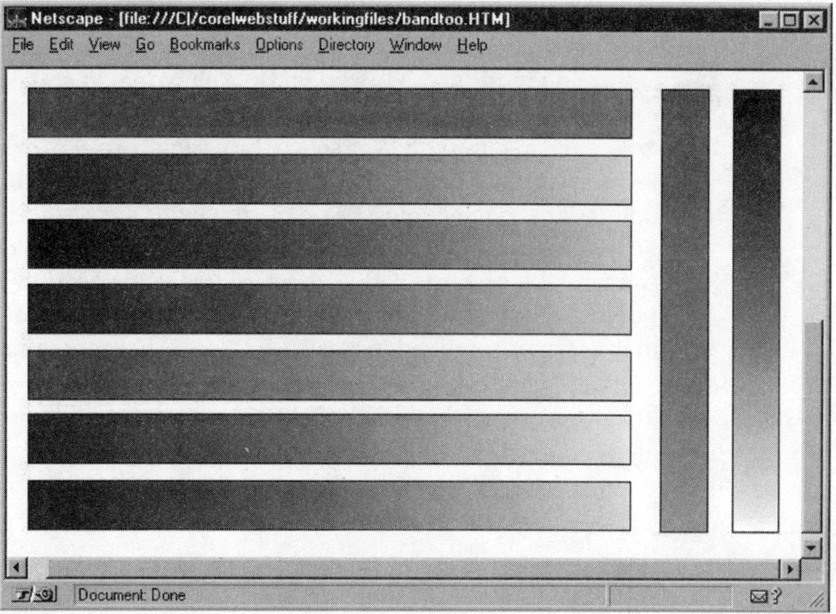

Figure 10-11: Although the JPEG file exhibits some anomalies, it presents the best compromise of image quality and file size.

Want to See How It Really Looks?

If truth be told, the grayscale figures in this book are not the best way to illustrate the GIF/JPEG dilemma. That's why we have our Online Update! Just point your Web browser at Ventana's Web site at http://www.vmedia.com/updates/ to check out how the images look online.

For the smoothest fountain fills, use the highest practical number of steps. Long sweeps of color may call for all 256 steps but you can get away with far fewer steps when creating fills that cover a short distance. Export multifountain-filled images as 16.7 million color JPEG files. Experiment with the level of JPEG compression to achieve the best trade-off of image quality and file size.

Tweaking Texture Fills

CorelWEB.DRAW's texture fills offer an infinite variety of design possibilities. The textures are generated by means of fractal mathematics, which thankfully we are not required to master. While there's no need for a doctoral dissertation on the subject, the Texture Fill dialog box, as shown in Figure 10-12, is well worth a close look. Lets see if we can uncover a few of its intricacies!

Be prepared to spend some time browsing here, as CorelWEB.DRAW's textures can be the black hole of time. Once you start fiddling with all the settings, it's tough to quit. Begin by drawing a simple rectangle. Click the fill tool, then click the Texture Fill button on the fill fly-out menu to summon the Texture Fill dialog box. WEB.DRAW ships with three Texture Libraries. Each of these libraries contains many individual textures, which in turn can be modified to create countless more variations.

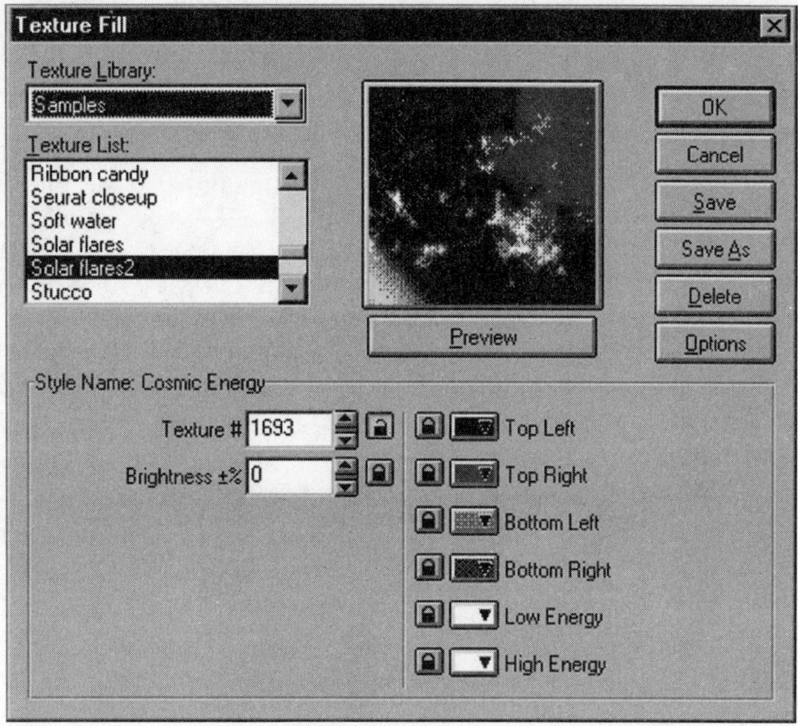

Figure 10-12: The mysteries of the world of fractal textures await those who take command of this dialog box.

256 Color Displays Just Don't Cut It

The first piece of advice for texturenaughts is to abandon your computer's 256 color display. If you want to create great texture fills, your computer should be running a 16-bit (high-color) or 24-bit (true-color) display. 256 color displays will only show a disgusting, grainy representation of what the texture *actually* looks like. 16- or 24-bit displays will show the textures in their true glory.

In order to run at these higher color depths, a video card with at least 2MB of video RAM is mandatory. And to get both high resolution (800 X 600 or more) and lots of color, you should look for a 4MB card. If you're in the market, check out Number Nine's Imagine 128. In addition to delivering a beautiful display, this card is a snappy performer, with blazing acceleration.

Customizing Texture Fills

Try clicking on some texture names now, to see how they look. As you select different textures, notice how the Texture Fill dialog box is reconfigured to show the different settings available with each selection. Cosmic Clouds, for example, allows you to set Red, Green, and Blue Softness, as well as Density and Brightness. Cosmic Energy, on the other hand, offers settings for Brightness and six specific colors: Top Left, Top Right, Bottom Left, Bottom Right, Low Energy, and High Energy. Plug in some different color settings and click Preview to see the results. Once you've created a gorgeous texture, you might want to save it to use again at a later time. Click Save As to summon the Save Texture dialog box. You can name the new variation and create your own custom texture library, as shown in Figure 10-13.

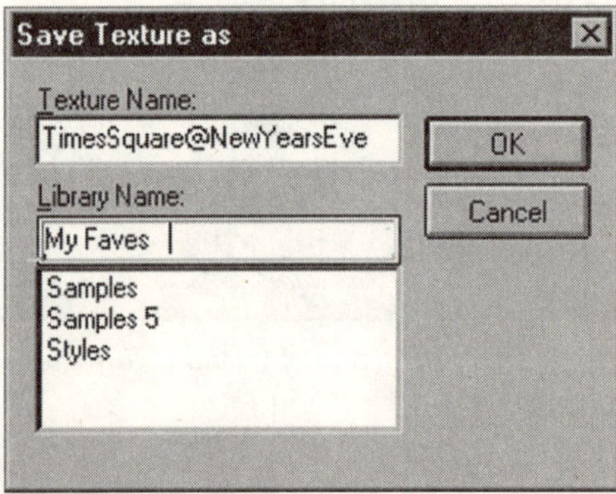

Figure 10-13: If you've spent an hour creating the perfect texture, don't forget to save the settings, or you may lose the recipe forever!

Clicking the Options button summons the Texture Options dialog box. This device governs the Bitmap Resolution and Texture Size Limit. The 100 dpi setting should give you all the resolution you need for Web graphics. You may want to experiment with different texture sizes to see how they affect the image.

Exporting Texture Fills

When exporting texture fills, many of the same caveats apply. JPEG exports can produce the smallest file sizes. However, GIF exports will be truer to any solid colors used in the image. Once again, the best way to see these effects is on the Web. Tune in to http://www.vmedia.com/updates/ to check out The Comprehensive Guide to CorelWEB.GRAPHICS Suite Online Update!

Combining Images to Shave Download Times

Remember the "Too Rich, Too Thin" exercise from Chapter 4, where you dragged a bunch of images from WEB.GALLERY into WEB.DESIGNER? In this section, you'll see how you can incrementally shave download times by combining images. If you recall, we used two images at the top of the page, modela1.gif and modmala1.gif. These files weighed in at 3,290 and 3,672 bytes, respectively. By combining the images into one WEB.DRAW image, you will be able to trim the total number of bytes.

With WEB.DRAW running, launch WEB.GALLERY:

1. Select \albums\objects.gal from the Bookshelf drop-down menu and click on the Open button (the button right next to the menu). A dialog box appears, informing you that the gallery file is read-only (since it's on the CD-ROM).

2. Click on OK. Double-click on the 180 album to open it.

3. With the 180 (-pixel-wide) album open, scroll over to the images named modela1.gif and modmala1.gif. Click on modela1.gif and drag the image into WEB.DRAW. Then click modmala1.gif and drag it into WEB.DRAW.

4. Line up our two happy prospects with some white space between them.

5. Draw a rectangle around the images to denote the boundaries of the image. Give the rectangle a white fill, set its outline to none, and set it behind the images with a Ctrl+PgDn.

6. Export the image as a 256 color, nondithered GIF file.

We came up with an exported file size of 6,581 bytes, which doesn't save that much over the combined total of 6,962 (for the separate files). Now, try adding the "Too Rich, Too Thin" heading, in the Bernhard Fashion typeface. With the type added, our total file size came in at 7,904 bytes. Remember, however, that it's not just the total of the file sizes that affects download times: the more files the browser has to download, the longer it will take for the complete page to display. That's why whenever possible it's a good idea to minimize the number of separate graphic components on each page. And just as important, using a single file allows you to precisely position each graphic element with regard to the other elements.

Exporting to Barista

Albert Einstein once said, "I never think of the future. It comes soon enough." While Corel's Barista technology offers an intriguing look into the next generation of Web graphics, it was just not ready for prime time when the CorelWEB.GRAPHICS Suite originally shipped. As we began writing this book, we hoped that Barista would percolate in time for our press date. Although we're putting this to bed in early 1997, the dialog box shown in Figure 10-14 is due for an update. Nonetheless, we'll be taking a closer look at Barista in the next section, as we tackle the topic of Web animation.

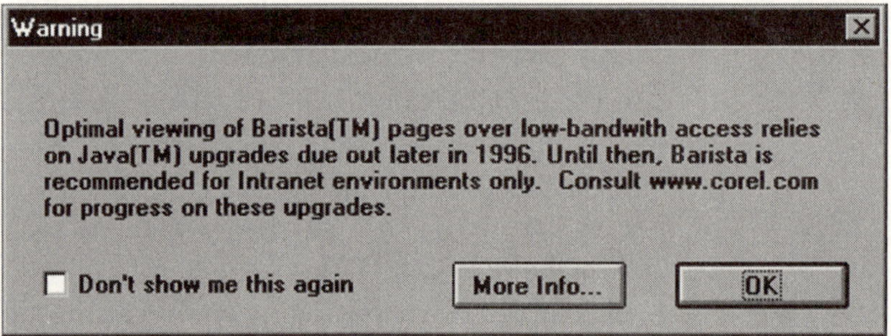

Figure 10-14: This dialog box says it all. When the WEB.GRAPHICS Suite shipped, Barista was more a demonstration of technology than a viable mechanism for graphical information delivery.

Barista offers the promise of a completely faithful rendition of CorelWEB.DRAW artwork, with typefaces intact. The same vector wizardry that appears in WEB.DRAW should appear in the Web browser. While Corel recommends that this initial release of Barista be used only on intranet applications, we had trouble getting it to perform on a stand-alone machine, much less a network. Does this mean that you shouldn't experiment? Of course not! If you have the time to play, try exporting a few of your WEB.DRAW creations to Barista files, then open up your Web browser and take a look at the resulting HTML files. You'll be amazed . . . and disappointed, all at once. But don't fret—the fix will come "soon enough."

Moving On

In this chapter, we wrapped our coverage of CorelWEB.DRAW with a review of graphics optimization techniques. Whether it be the fine points of dithering, palettes, or anti-aliasing, the best advice is to fine-tune those images until you get them right. Just don't forget to document your procedures! Writing down those all-important settings can save you countless hours each and every time you have to create a similar image.

Get ready to make your Web pages come alive. In the next section, we'll jump into the wild world of Web animation with CorelWEB.MOVE.

CorelWEB.MOVE

Introduction to CorelWEB.MOVE & Multimedia on the Web

This chapter introduces you to CorelWEB.MOVE and its place in developing *multimedia content* for use on the World Wide Web (WWW). WEB.MOVE is unique among the applications in the CorelWEB.GRAPHICS Suite, because it creates files that incorporate moving pictures and sounds. Learning to use WEB.MOVE is easy, and the payoff for the few hours you'll invest in mastering it is a Web site that stands out from the sea of dull, dry, boring HyperText Markup Language (HTML) pages that languish on Web servers around the world.

We start with basic history of what is loosely termed *multimedia*—and how it has impacted the WWW. That should help those who are new to the whole Web experience. Then, a segue into CorelWEB.MOVE's heritage which should help you to understand the "why" behind the way it works. The last part of the chapter explains the basic concepts of *animation* that you need to know and connects WEB.MOVE's way of creating multimedia files with the established, traditional world of animation.

When the Web Was Young

If you're a Web newcomer, you may not realize that a few years ago most World Wide Web documents were text-based. Over thousands of years, text has proven an efficient way to disseminate information to vast numbers of people, but it pales in comparison to works that incorporate pictures (moving and still), sound, and music.

Let's face it: text-based documents get really boring really fast—especially considering our daily multimedia environment. Documents with elements, other than words, which you can see and hear stimulate many more areas of the brain. Not only does the audience remember more information, they enjoy the learning experience. While "a picture is worth a thousand words" is truer than ever, a moving picture is even better.

Five years ago there were many applications on the market to create files that incorporated multimedia content, but there was a missing link in the Internet world. Even when a Web site offered a document in a graphical format, Web browsers couldn't display it. You had to download the file, then run another application to view its multimedia contents. At best, this was inconvenient, and inconvenience is something computer users despise. Things needed to change.

Some of the most dramatic changes in the way we use computers have been spurred by revolutionary advancements in operating systems. With the growing popularity of Windows and Mac operating systems, as well as the various flavors of UNIX, computers have totally embraced the world of multimedia. The developers of these operating systems have convinced us all of the importance of the *graphical user interface (GUI)*. A GUI enables a computer to display information in a graphical form rather than just text. This allows the user to interact with the computer by way of pictures or icons, pop-up menus, and cascading dialog boxes. Further improvements to these operating systems came with improving integrated sound technology.

The incorporation of these advancements in operating system designs caused a flood of affordable commercial applications that could create multimedia content. In the mainstream computer world, multimedia content sped ahead at a feverish pace. It was inevitable that more and more of it ended up on the Web. There was a dire need for a truly graphical rather than text-based Web browser. Enter NCSA's Mosaic. Others followed: Cello, Navigator, and Explorer, to name just a few. The newest Web browsers communicate with other computers and display the contents of remote graphics, animation and sound files, as well as character-based documents, with ease.

The evolution of the Web hasn't been as simple as these few paragraphs imply. It would take many pages to detail the technical networking developments that got us where we are today. Maybe this brief history puts into perspective how remarkable it is that you can sit at your desktop PC and not only create but also broadcast your multimedia productions. This book's focus is on Web graphics and getting you up to speed to produce pages that fulfill your goals. So let's move on in that direction.

Where does CorelWEB.MOVE fit in for a person developing documents to be published on the WWW? Simply put, it's a key application that provides the tools and framework needed to add multimedia-type content to your Web pages. It's a one-stop shopping center for animation, sound, and interactivity. It gives you the means to make your Web pages come to life. Indeed, lively and interesting pages will keep your audience coming back for more.

The Life & Times of WEB.MOVE

WEB.MOVE is not a new application exactly. It existed several years ago as part of the CorelDRAW! 4 and 5 packages. Originally called CorelMOVE!, it was designed to be a full-featured animation editor and was tightly integrated with CorelDRAW! This allowed the budding animator to take full advantage of DRAW's powerful and easy-to-use vector-based drawing tools, a unique approach at a time when reasonably priced animation-authoring programs were simply evolutions of traditional manual animating. These paint-type programs made every movement of a hand, blink of an eye, or change of color by pushing individual pixels around. How slow and tiring! Thank goodness for the innovative design of CorelMOVE.

WEB.MOVE has changed somewhat over the years but happily has retained its greatest strength: tight integration with CorelDRAW!, the world's most popular Windows-based vector illustration program. This incarnation of MOVE is very Web-focused and closely tied to its WEB.GRAPHICS suitemate, WEB.DRAW—a slightly modified Web-centric version of CorelDRAW! 5 (see Part II). If you are a past or present user of CorelDRAW! 5 and CorelMOVE! 5, you'll be right at home with most of the tools and animation techniques used in WEB.MOVE.

The Basics of Animation

Blinking lights, bouncing balls, moving text, and cavorting cartoon characters—are all examples of animation. Animation is the process of making something inanimate come to life.

Although animation has its complexities, its basic principles are simple. Fortunately, we don't need a thorough knowledge of animation or computer science to master WEB.MOVE.

Work Smart—Aim for Simplicity

Although WEB.MOVE can produce pretty fancy animation, Web animations should be kept simple. Even when you incorporate some type of interactivity with the user, you still should strive for simplicity. Why? Because animation files grow in byte count *very* quickly. Pictures and sounds are not economical in terms of file structure. This may not be a concern when the files reside on your local hard drive or CD-ROM. But remember that your audience will likely use a modem and phone line to move large files over the Internet, slowing down almost any computer. Your fancy animations and your intended message will go for naught if your audience stops downloading in impatience and surfs off elsewhere.

So don't aim to create full-length cartoons or computer-based training modules (CBTs) that incorporate sound and programmable branching like hyperlink jumping. Instead, use WEB.MOVE in simpler ways. Most pages that incorporate moving images keep animations small and simple; sound is used sparingly. Don't make the mistake of creating pages that use every bell and whistle that WEB.MOVE has to offer. This will only inflate the size of your Web page files and at least irritate your Web site visitors, if not lose them.

Tip

It certainly doesn't hurt to dissect the work of Web animation pros. Examining animated GIFs from other Web pages will help you learn valuable techniques. When you find a cool animation out on the Web, it's easy to grab it and do a bit of reverse-engineering. If you are using Netscape's Navigator 2 or higher as your browser, you can quickly save most animations or images contained in HTML documents you view.

Click on the image with the right mouse button and choose Save Image As from the menu. If you are using Microsoft's Internet Explorer 2 or higher, the procedure is similar. The only difference is that the menu item is called Save Picture As.

Once you've saved the image to your hard drive, you can use a bitmap editor or animation utility to open the file and see how it was constructed.

Now that you've taken the vow of simplicity, let's get into animation basics. You need to understand a few important concepts whose roots extend to the traditional world of animation. Then we'll see how those concepts have carried forward into the age of microcomputing, especially in WEB.MOVE.

Animation Frames

The first basic we'll tackle is frames. A frame is nothing more than a snapshot, a static image that is projected or displayed somehow. Displaying many different frames in quick succession creates the illusion of movement or change. This occurs in all forms of animation. Have you ever studied a movie filmstrip? Each frame is a picture of a scene that is just slightly different than the previous frame. When the film is played on a movie projector, the still images fit together to produce a lifelike image.

You can see the concept of frames in action by playing a videotape with your VCR. Press Pause to stop the video. Most VCR remote controls have buttons that allow you to step through a video one frame at a time. Try it. The picture may not be too clear, depending on the quality of your machine, but you should be able to see the slightly different positioning of objects moving through the scene.

What . . . no VCR? Here's an even easier way to see frames in action: Use the Windows Media Player application to play an AVI file. If using Windows 95, you should have plenty of AVI files in your WIN95\HELP subdirectory. (If you can't find one, use the search tools in Explorer or File Manager.) Double-click on the AVI file; Media Player launches and loads it automatically. Use the Stop button, then the Scroll Forward or Scroll Backward arrow buttons to the right of the Time/Frames counter control to step through individual frames. If you have Microsoft's Active Movie software, which comes with Explorer 3.x, you can stop the AVI and use the left and right arrow keys on your keyboard to advance or move backward, one frame at a time.

So, now you know the secret of creating the *appearance* of movement, motion, or change in an animation. As Figure 11-1 illustrates, animation depends on the following steps:

- Break movements down into discrete, static snapshots.
- Render the snapshots (perhaps the most difficult part for most people).
- String the static images together in the right sequence.
- Play them back at a fast speed.

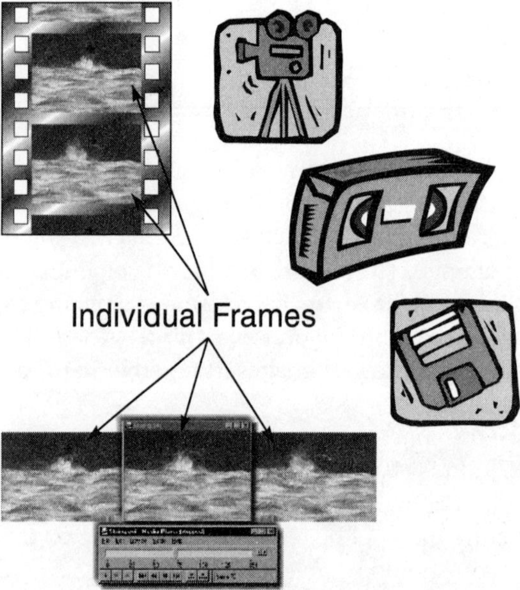

Figure 11-1: Whether movement is captured on film, on videotape, or in a digital computer file, animation is built on frames.

WEB.MOVE provides the tools to create complex moving images that can incorporate sound and interactivity, and we'll discuss all of WEB.MOVE's tools in the next few chapters. But for this discussion of the basics of animation, let's focus on much simpler images that you are likely to use in everyday Web projects.

You may not realize it, but you see examples of simple animations all the time in the Windows environment. Every time you press a button control on a dialog box or toolbar you are watching an animation that consists of three frames and only two images. One image depicts the button in the "up position" while the other depicts the button in the "down position." To animate a button, the following sequence occurs:

- Frame 1: Before mouse is clicked, the "up position" image of the button is displayed.

- Frame 2: As mouse is clicked, the "down position" image replaces image from Frame 1.

- Frame 3: When mouse is released, original image of the "up position" button is displayed again.

This whole sequence of events is shown in Figure 11-2. These are the simpler kinds of moving images that you can start with and quickly learn to expand on.

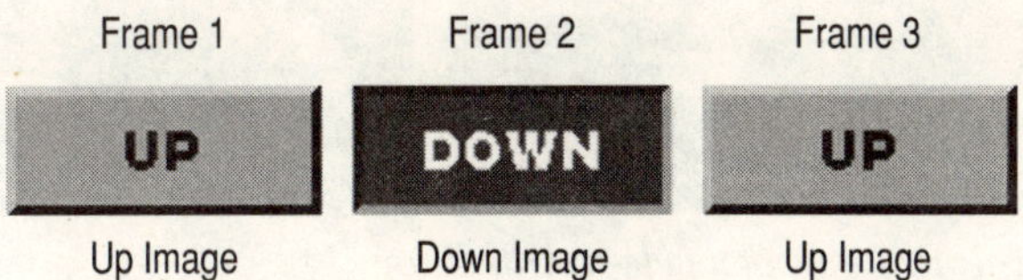

Figure 11-2: The three frames of images used to show a button being pressed.

This three-frame/two-image animation technique is great for objects that have only two states: up or down, on or off, one color or another. There are plenty of situations in which this technique is used very effectively on Web sites—blinking headlines or bullets, for example. The next step is to add more frames. What images do you put on these added frames? If you copy the first image to several subsequent frames, the image appears to stay onscreen longer. Alternate the frames with various images, and the animation cycles through all the images. This "barrage of images" style was popularized by MTV.

Another suggestion: Copy an image to successive frames but make it progressively lighter each time; this calls for a bitmap editor like PhotoPaint or Photoshop. The result is a visual effect that is known as a *fade-out*.

The next logical step: Apply the same technique to another image— only this time, work the effect backward, starting with the lightest image and building to the full-strength image. This effect is called—you guessed it—a *fade-in*. Examples of a fade-out and a fade-in are shown in Figures 11-3 and 11-4. Figure 11-5 shows a hybrid of the two effects, merging the last frames of the fade-out with the first frames of the fade-in. This is called a *cross-fade*. As a whole, these types of special effects are called *transitions*. WEB.MOVE includes several built-in transition effects that preclude the need to painstakingly create each frame of a transition effect, one image at a time.

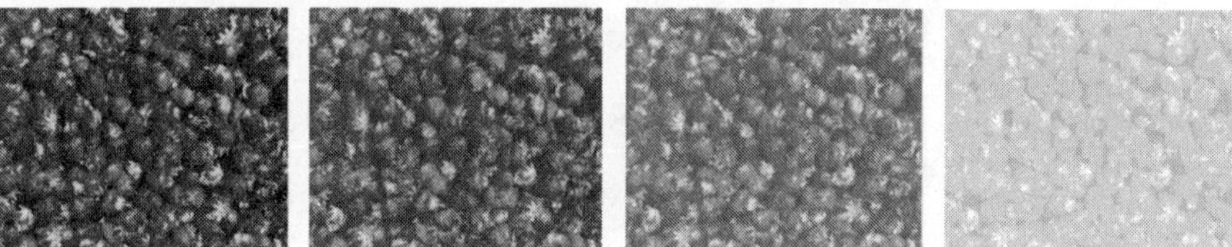

Figure 11-3: The sequence of images in a fade-out transition.

Figure 11-4: Example of a fade-in transition.

Figure 11-5: Notice how frames 3, 4, 5, and 6 are made up of some portions of both the fade-out and fade-in effects.

You may have noticed that the fewer frames in a particular sequence, the faster the motion or change appears. Obviously, not all natural actions occur at a herky-jerky pace. If you want the movements in an animation to be slow and smooth, you must break the motion down into more intermediate steps and render more images. Look at the two sequences of drawings in Figures 11-6 and 11-7. Each portrays a walking motion. The two sequences have an equal number of frames and will take the same amount of onscreen time.

The big difference between the two sequences is the number of different renderings used to illustrate the walking motion. Figure 11-6 uses only three different drawings (marked A, B, and C). When this series is played back, the character's movements appear very stiff and jerky. Figure 11-7, on the other hand, breaks the walking motion down into six different poses (A, B, C, D, E, and F). Played back, this animation sequence looks smoother and more natural. In summary, if a quick, jerky motion is desired, use fewer frames. For a more fluid look, use more frames and more intermediate renderings.

Figure 11-6: Walking motion achieved with only three renderings.

Figure 11-7: A much smoother rendition of the walking motion is created by using more intermediate drawings.

Animation Cels

Cel is a carryover term from the world of animation that existed long before the digital revolution. In traditional animation, in which everything is drawn or painted by hand, objects that will show motion are rendered on a clear piece of celluloid. That's where *cel* comes from.

Every change in pose needed to depict the steps in a particular movement requires a new image painted on a new cel. Just like the frames of the movie, video, and AVI file we looked at earlier, the position and pose of the character rendered on the new cel is slightly different than the one on the previous cel.

Why are the images painted on a clear material? So that each image can be laid over a background painting to create a composition. Click—the composition is shot with a camera, and there's your first frame. The next cel in the sequence is lined up precisely on the background, the camera's film is advanced, and—click—frame two. And on the process goes: next cel, click; next cel, click . . . tedious, huh?

How many frames does it take to make up a minute of broadcast-quality animation? In the vicinity of 1,400. Since we promised to keep this simple, let's get back to how WEB.MOVE uses cels.

WEB.MOVE borrows the concept of cels direct from traditional animation and provides the tools to create objects that consist of multiple images. You create these various images in WEB.DRAW or WEB.MOVE's own Paint Editor. Special controls allow you to add as many cels as you wish to your animated object. There is even functionality to automatically morph one cel's image to another. Done properly, morphing can really knock the socks off your audience. You'll find out more about creating morph effects in Chapter 13, "The CorelWEB.MOVE Editors," and Chapter 15, "CorelWEB.MOVE Tricks & Tips."

Props & Actors

WEB.MOVE generates four kinds of objects: *actors*, *props*, *sounds*, and *cues*. Sounds and cues are discussed thoroughly in Chapter 12, "Getting Down to Business With CorelWEB.MOVE," and Chapter 13, "The CorelWEB.MOVE Editors." Because actors and props are fundamentally the same kinds of objects—graphic images—now is a good time to discuss what sets them apart.

Props

Props are static images; they don't move. They are not made up of cels. Because a prop is a single image, motion cannot be depicted. A good example of a prop is a background image. Props aren't as boring as they may first seem. For one thing, you can make a prop appear or disappear (this is called *entering* and *exiting* the scene) at any frame of an animation. You also can do something to props that you can't do to actors: You can apply transition effects to props. With a little experience and thought, you'll soon find many creative ways to use WEB.MOVE's prop objects.

Actors

Actors are fundamentally different from props in that they are made up of one or more cels. Actors are very versatile objects, the virtual work-horses of WEB.MOVE. As mentioned earlier, you can use WEB.DRAW to create the images that make up an actor's cels or use WEB.MOVE's Paint Editor to do the job. We'll discuss both of these options in detail in the next two chapters.

Actors can't have transition effects applied to them, as props can, but WEB.MOVE offers other special built-in effects just for actors. These effects are controlled from the Cel Sequencer roll-up. You use the Cel Sequencer, which we'll explore in later chapters, to change in various ways the order in which an actor's cels appear.

It's important to establish the correlation between frames and an actor's cels. One cel is displayed for every frame. What happens when the number of an actor's cels and the number of frames is not the same? Simple. If an actor has 10 cels and is set to enter the scene on frame 1 of a 20-frame animation, the actor will run only through its 10 cels—1 cel displayed per frame. On the 11th frame, the actor disappears, or exits the scene.

But what if you want the actor to stay in the animation for all 20 frames? One solution is to edit the actor, adding 10 more cels. If the actor's movements are to be different than those of the first 10 cels, this is the best solution. However, if the actor needs only to repeat the sequence of the 10 original cels, you can take a much simpler approach: Extend the *timeline* of the actor to last all 20 frames. You accomplish this miraculous feat with the Timelines roll-up, which you'll learn all about in the next few chapters.

Where did we leave off in our cels-to-frames correlation discussion? And did I ever tell you the one about how simple this would be? Now I remember!

Let's assume we've taken the second approach. So far, we have a 20-frame animation with an actor of 10 cels, and we've extended the actor's time onscreen to last all 20 frames. What cels are going to be displayed for the last 10 frames? Elementary, really: the actor starts displaying its sequence of cels all over again, starting from cel 1 and proceeding as normal. If there's ever a mismatch between the number of cels and number of frames left in an animation, remember that the actor will cycle continually through its series of cels. What happens when the animation reaches the last frame but the actor is in the middle of its cel sequence? The last frame in the animation is equivalent to the final curtain in a play: no matter how great the desire to continue, the actor's done! Fini!

Figure 11-8 shows several examples of a simple 3-celed actor with different timelines and demonstrates which cel is displayed in each frame, depending on the length of the animation.

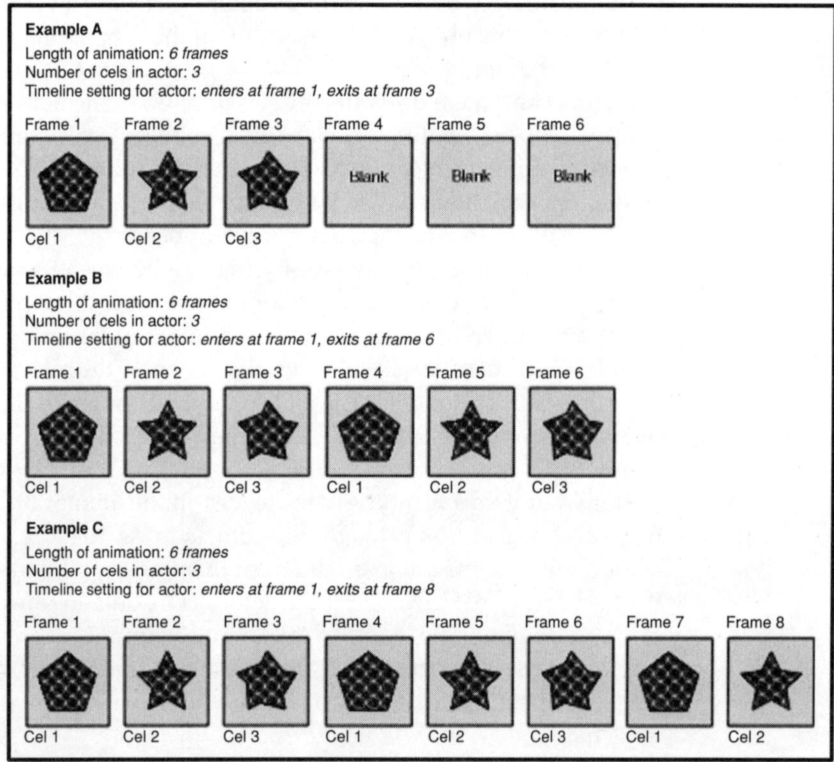

Figure 11-8: Example A shows how a 3-celed actor disappears from the scene when its timeline is shorter than the amount of frames. Example B shows what happens when the same actor's timeline is extended to match the frame amount. Example C shows what happens when the actor's timeline is extended but the amount of frames is not a multiple of the actor's cel count.

Paths

One final basic that needs explanation is *paths*. In traditional animation, if you want an object to move from left to right across a scene, the first cel must show the object on the left side. Each subsequent cel shows the object moved slightly to the right. Finally, it makes its way to the right side of the last cel.

If the object is a ball that is bouncing from left to right, each cel must show an up-and-down bouncing motion as well as the left-to-right action. What if the ball is rotating as it bounces along? Indeed, you must do quite a bit of tedious rendering just to animate a bouncing ball that moves from left to right.

How much easier animation would be if you only had to draw the different stages of the ball rotating and then just tell a computer to move the cels in an up-and-down and left-to-right motion. Guess what? With WEB.MOVE it's just that simple! You can assign the up-down, left-right motion in MOVE as a path. Figure 11-9 illustrates how this dramatically cuts down the number of cels you must draw.

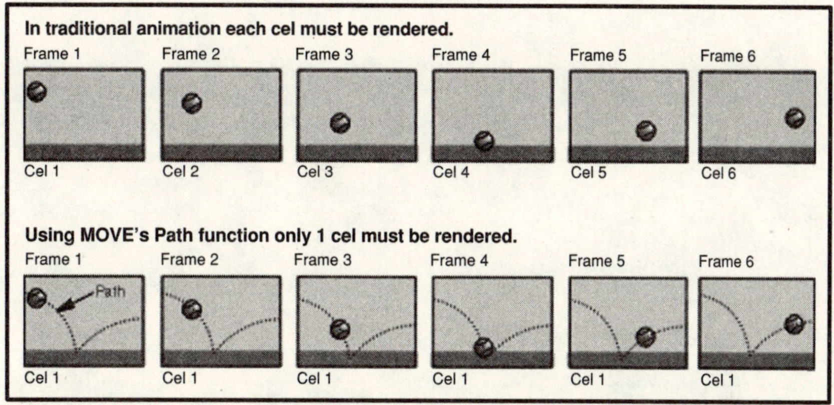

Figure 11-9: These two illustrations show how assigning a Path to create movement cuts down on the number of cels.

Herein is another key difference between actors and props: Only actors can have paths assigned to them. In the next chapters you'll be thoroughly introduced to the Path Edit tool and what it can do for your actors.

Moving On

So, the hard part's done. Your lessons on Web and multimedia advancements are over. You understand the fundamentals of animation and will never again look at a cartoon, video, push button, or flashing Web graphic the same way. You've been introduced to several of WEB.MOVE's tools and functions, such as actors, props, frames, and paths. Now it's time to get intimately acquainted with WEB.MOVE and all its features.

In the next chapter, we'll take an in-depth look at each of MOVE's various tools, as well as the interface in which you'll be working. Soon you'll have all the information you need to start making moving pictures to incorporate in your Web pages. So hang on to your hat: we're off on a *moving* experience!

12

Getting Down to Business With CorelWEB.MOVE

Now that you have a good sense for CorelWEB.MOVE's potential to create multimedia content, it's time to get acquainted with the tools WEB.MOVE provides to create really cool animations. This chapter discusses WEB.MOVE's tools, menus, and roll-ups. The next chapter discusses the three editors that create and modify WEB.MOVE actors, props, and sounds.

First, a distinction about file formats: WEB.MOVE creates files in several file formats. WEB.MOVE's native file format is CMV, and you should save your project in the CMV format before publishing the animation for use on the Web, which will be done in either Graphics Interchange Format (GIF) or Barista format (CJW). Unfortunately, WEB.MOVE cannot load or modify an existing GIF or Barista file. More information about Corel's Barista format is found under "The File Menu" later in this chapter.

Now let's start our guided tour of the interface and tools that make up the WEB.MOVE environment.

Introduction to MOVE's Interface

From an interface point of view, CorelWEB.MOVE is a very rich program. In fact, WEB.MOVE can be quite appropriately described as an *authoring* tool. Like a book author who gathers material and research data from many different sources and then assembles everything in one place for publication, so WEB.MOVE incorporates source files produced in other programs. The ultimate goal is to create a composite file. This one file can be either a Barista Java applet or a GIF file. It's this file that you will reference in your HyperText Markup Language (HTML) documents and that, in due course, will be displayed to your audience on a network like the World Wide Web.

WEB.MOVE lets you create and edit objects, such as images and sounds. The program also allows you to play back, at any time during the creation process, the composite animations assembled. This lets you see how things are shaping up and tweak any element to get things just the way you want them. All the tools you need to develop multimedia content for Web pages plus this valuable preview capability are available within CorelWEB.MOVE.

When you start WEB.MOVE, the screen should appear as it does in Figure 12-1. The Arrange menu is grayed out and its options inaccessible because there are no objects currently in the animation that can be arranged. As soon as we add an actor or prop, the Arrange menu, with all its functions, becomes available.

Figure 12-1: WEB.MOVE as it appears when first started.

The Animation Window

The white rectangle in the center of WEB.MOVE's window is the animation window, which represents the *live area* of your composition. Anything contained inside its borders displays when you play back your animation. However, an object placed in the gray area surrounding the animation window is not lost or truncated. This feature is useful for making objects enter and exit your scene. Take note: this special feature applies while working in WEB.MOVE only. When you publish the project to a GIF or Barista file, everything outside the animation window's borders is cut off. This is another good reason to save all your projects as CMVs first.

Think of the animation window as the stage for your production. You don't actually draw on this surface, like a canvas in a paint program; rather, you place and arrange objects on top of it. Typically, you first place background scenes, then add props and, finally, actors. For all practical purposes, you can place as many of these objects as you like in the animation window. WEB.MOVE utilizes something called a *stacking order*. This makes it possible to place objects on top of one another and then rearrange that order if you need to. An example of this stacking order is shown in Figure 12-2.

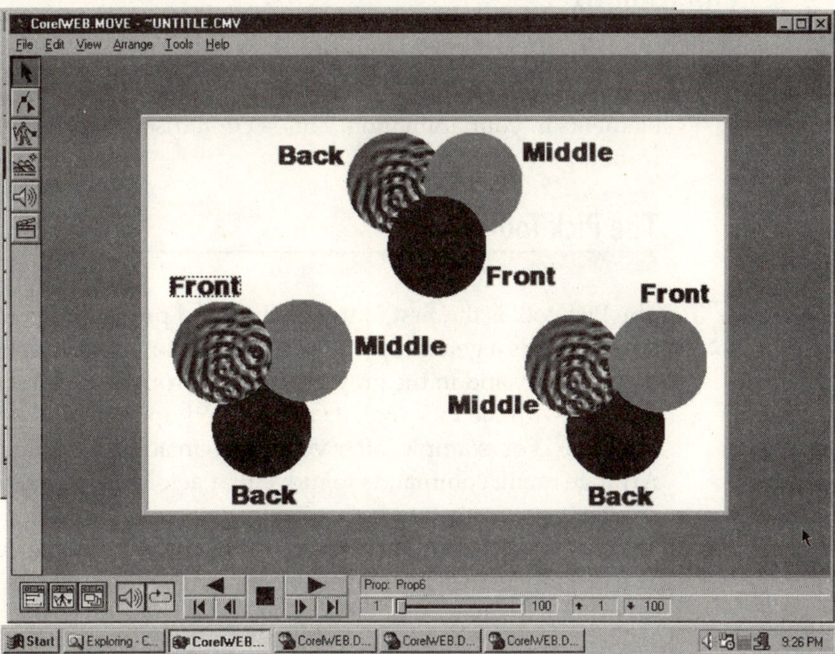

Figure 12-2: The stacking order in WEB.MOVE determines which objects are covered. You have complete control over the order of your props and actors.

The animation window can be sized to fit the needs of your project, in a measurement based on pixels. This is appropriate because your images probably will display on a computer monitor, and a pixel is the basic unit of measurement for any cathode-ray tube (CRT). It's easy to calculate how big your image will appear on a Web page when everything figured in pixels.

For instance, if you are designing a Web page to fit a common monitor resolution of 640 pixels wide by 480 high and you want an animation to run the entire width of the page, you might set the width of the animation window to be 560 pixels wide (560 pixels will allow room for the Web browser's window borders and scroll bars). Hmmm, that doesn't seem to work. Corel has set the maximum animation size at 550 pixels wide by 360 high, with the minimum size 30 by 30.

Tip

If you are a CorelMOVE 5 user, you can get around these arbitrary maximum and minimum limitations. See Chapter 15 for the secret to creating very large or very small animations.

The Toolbox

The six tools in the toolbox are most commonly used to place or modify elements in your animation. This section discusses each tool, working from top to bottom.

The Pick Tool

The Pick tool is the first in the toolbox and probably the most used of all the tools. It is a general-purpose tool used to select objects in the animation window and in the gray area that surrounds it. After an object is selected with the Pick tool, it can be acted upon by one of WEB.MOVE's functions. For example, after you select an actor, you can select any of the Arrange menu commands to move that actor behind or in front of another actor in the scene.

A dotted rectangle encompasses the selected object (see Figure 12-3). You can move a selected object by clicking and dragging; when it's repositioned where you want it, release the mouse button. Or use the keyboard cursor keys to move a selected object: Press a key once to move it 1 pixel in the indicated direction. This technique is very useful to get your actors and other graphic elements positioned just right. You cannot use the arrow keys to move an object when the Snap to Grid setting is turned on. This setting is discussed in "The Edit Menu," later in this chapter.

Figure 12-3: An object selected with the Pick tool is bordered by a dotted line.

The Path Edit Tool

You'll use this tool almost as much as you do the Pick tool. The Path Edit tool affects only one type of WEB.MOVE object: an actor.

Before we go into the details of the Path Edit tool, let's discuss paths and how they are used in WEB.MOVE. A path—which is made up of a series of points—designates the movement of an actor. By default, the first point is always the top left corner of your actor. You draw all successive points with the Path Edit tool. This means that every actor has at least one *path point*. The left side of Figure 12-4 shows an actor with just one path point; the actor on the right has a path with four points. These four points will make the actor appear to move from left to right.

With every advance of the frame counter, the actor moves to the next path point. If the actor is made up of more than one cel, the next cel in the sequence displays in the next frame—at the next path point. The basic rule: next frame, next cel, next path point.

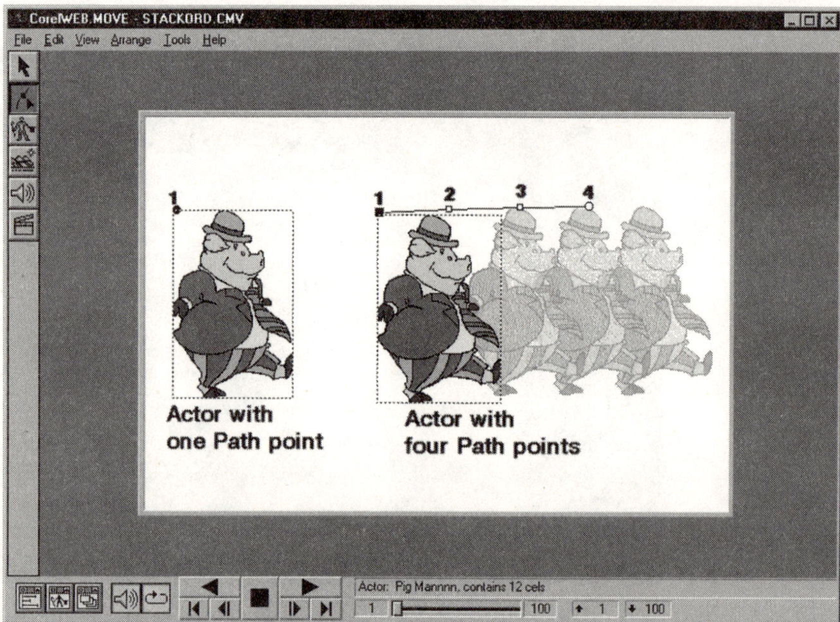

Figure 12-4: The actor on the left has only one path point as designated by the circle in its top left corner. The actor on the right has a path with four points, which enable the actor to move from left to right.

Paths are very versatile elements in WEB.MOVE and can save you lots of time creating extraordinary animations that would otherwise require a lot of painstaking rendering. WEB.MOVE offers special functions with the Path Edit tool that make modifying paths a very quick process.

When the Path Edit tool is active, as shown in Figure 12-5, a special *roll-up* window appears. The cursor also changes shape to indicate that you are in path editing mode.

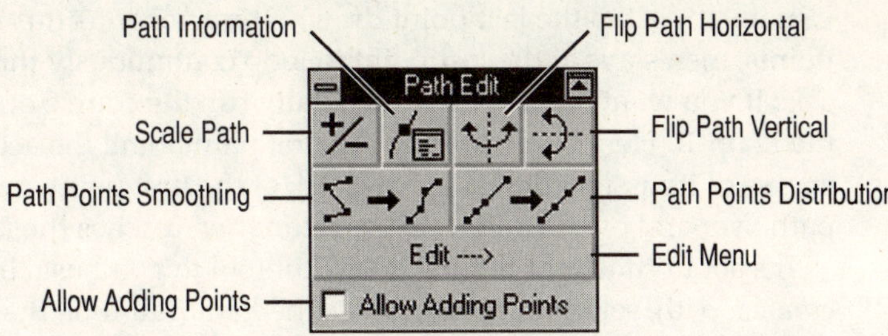

Figure 12-5: The Path Edit roll-up contains all the tools you need to designate an actor's movements.

The Path Edit roll-up shows seven buttons and one check box option. If no object is selected when you switch to the Path Edit tool, all buttons on the roll-up will be grayed out and inactive. If an object is selected but has no path assigned, the only active button will be the Point Information button. When you click on this button, the Point Information dialog box, shown in Figure 12-6, appears. From it, you precisely locate this particular path point on the screen. To change the position of the point, enter new coordinates in the Horizontal or Vertical fields and click on OK. The dialog disappears and the actor has changed position.

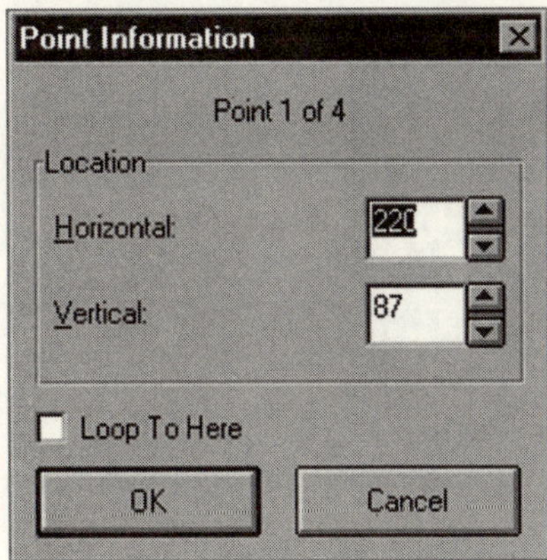

Figure 12-6: Use the Point Information dialog to change the location of any point on a path.

The Loop To Here option in the Point Information dialog box can be set for only one point on a path. It tells WEB.MOVE to which path point an actor should return *after* visiting all the points in the current path.

Usually it's set to the last point drawn: the actor runs through its path points, then stays at the last point to loop continuously through all its cels. If you want the actor to continually run the course of its path, check the Loop To Here check box for the first path point: the actor runs the course of its assigned path, starts back at the first point, and travels the path over and over again until the animation reaches the last frame.

It's about time you put the Path Edit tool to good use. In order to create a path, select an actor, choose the Path Edit tool, then check the Allow Adding Points option at the bottom of the roll-up. Once turned on, it adds a new path point wherever you click with the mouse, either inside the animation window or in the surrounding gray area. If you click far enough into the gray area that your actor disappears, you still see the path, its points, and the rectangular selection marker for the actor.

When an actor has a path of more than one point, the rest of the buttons on the Path Editing roll-up become operational. Click on the Scale Path button to learn the number of points that make up the current path and to add or delete points. This is handy if you have established the basic direction and course of an actor's path already but want to add more points to make movements appear slower or smoother. Also use it to reduce the number of points on a path to make the actor move more quickly or erratically.

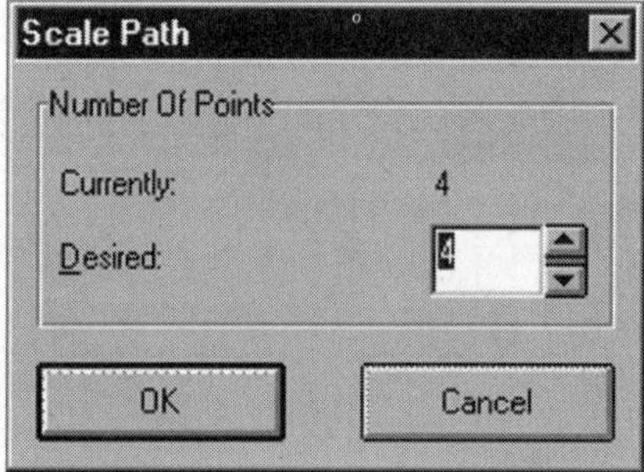

Figure 12-7: The Scale Path dialog lets you control the number of points on an actor's path.

Adding & Deleting Points

To change the number of points, simply plug in a new number in the Desired text box. WEB.MOVE adds or removes the appropriate number of points so that the total number equals the number you desire. This can lead to some unexpected results if your path is complicated and you set the number much lower than the previous one. WEB.MOVE randomly deletes points and sometimes discards what you consider key points. For that reason, be careful when deleting points this way.

Adding points to an existing path is an easy, two-step process: First, select the path point *just before* the path segment where you need the new point, then click on the spot where you want the new point. Bingo, a brand new path point, just where you need it.

To reposition any path point, just select it with the Path Edit tool and drag it to a new spot.

To remove a path point, select it, then press the Delete key.

Flipping Paths

The basic function of the Flip Path Horizontal tool is pretty self-explanatory: it repositions points horizontally in a mirror image of their original locations. This tool does not call up any additional dialogs; rather, it acts on an entire path or a selected number of path points. To select more than one point, click on the first node, then hold down the Shift key and select the last node. All nodes in between the two will be highlighted and affected by the Flip Path Horizontal tool.

The Flip Path Vertical tool performs the same path/point mirroring function, except that it flips the points in a vertical direction. Figure 12-8 shows the results of using the two Flip Path tools on entire paths.

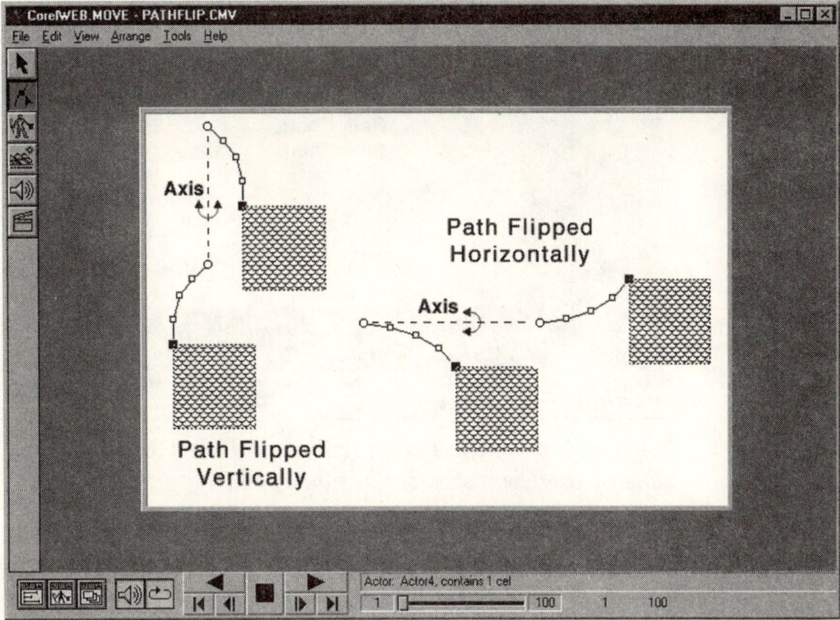

Figure 12-8: Some before-and-after shots demonstrate what you can expect when using the Flip Path tools on an entire path.

Smoothing & Redistributing Path Points

Click on the Path Points Smoothing tool to cause the current path or selected nodes on the current path to conform to a straighter line. Dramatic changes take place with paths whose points are connected at severe angles. As the angles are flattened out the path becomes less erratic giving the actor a more fluid movement. Apply this function more than once to progressively modify the path; the effect is cumulative. The Path Points Smoothing tool tries to preserve varying amounts of space between path points.

To redistribute path points and make the spacing between them even, use the Path Points Distribution tool, which also affects an entire path or just selected nodes. It, too, can be applied more than once, with the effects progressive and cumulative. Figure 12-9 shows the results of using the Path Points Smoothing and Path Points Distribution tools on selected path points.

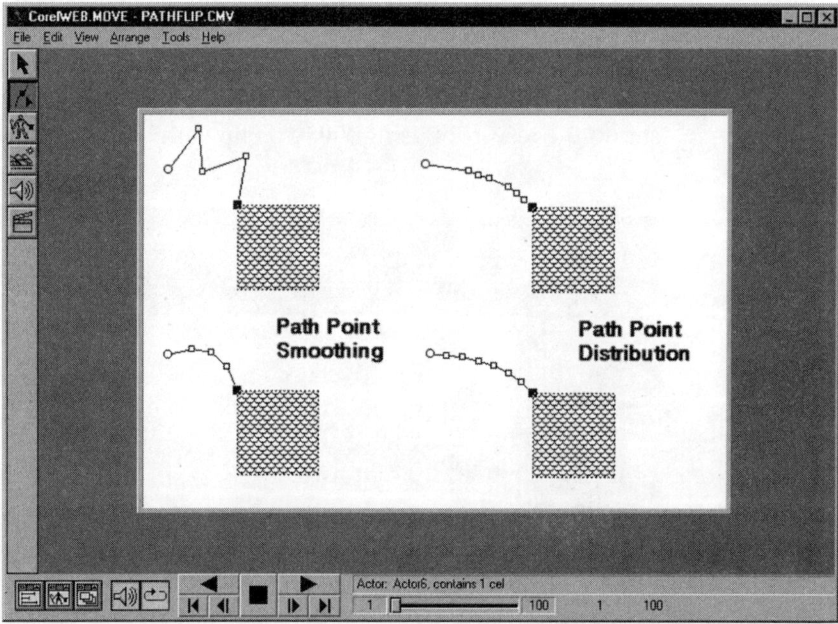

Figure 12-9: The effect of using the Path Points Smoothing and Path Points Distribution tools several times on a path.

Editing Paths

Pressing the Edit button causes a menu to appear, which offers the following seven selections:

- Undo Path Operation reverses the last operation that was performed on the selected path. For example, if you deleted points, they reappear. If you added points, they are removed.

- Cut Point(s) removes the selected path points somewhat differently than when you use the Delete key to do so. Use the Delete key; permanently lose the points. Use the Cut Point(s) selection, and the points go on the clipboard and can be retrieved via the Paste Point(s) selection, also on the Edit menu.

- Copy Point(s) pastes a copy of the selected nodes onto the clipboard and makes them available from the Paste Point(s) function.

- Paste Point(s) inserts any path point information that is on the clipboard into the current path, just *after* the currently selected point. Make sure you have the right node selected before issuing the Paste Point(s) command.

- Clear Whole Path leaves your actor with just one point.

- Select All Points is very useful when you want to apply an effect to an entire path. If you unintentionally do something to ruin your entire path, just reach for the trusty Undo Path Operation function, and you're back in business.

- The final menu option is Move Frame With Point. This toggle switch affects what displays in the animation window as you select various points along a path. By default, this option is turned off. You'll know when it's turned on because a checkmark appears next to the menu item. When Move Frame With Point is turned on and you select a path point, the animation window advances to display the frame that corresponds with the selected node. In this way, you see what's happening to your actor and your scene while you change its path. If you don't want the animation window to change to the corresponding frame while working on an actor's path, just toggle this switch off.

Now you can see how the Path Editing tool is very versatile—one you'll do well to get familiar with. With just a little practice, you'll be using this tool to spice up your Web animations. Now it's time to move down the toolbar to the next tool.

The New Actor Tool

 The New Actor tool is the primary way to add actors to your scenes. Select it for the New Actor dialog box, shown in Figure 12-10.

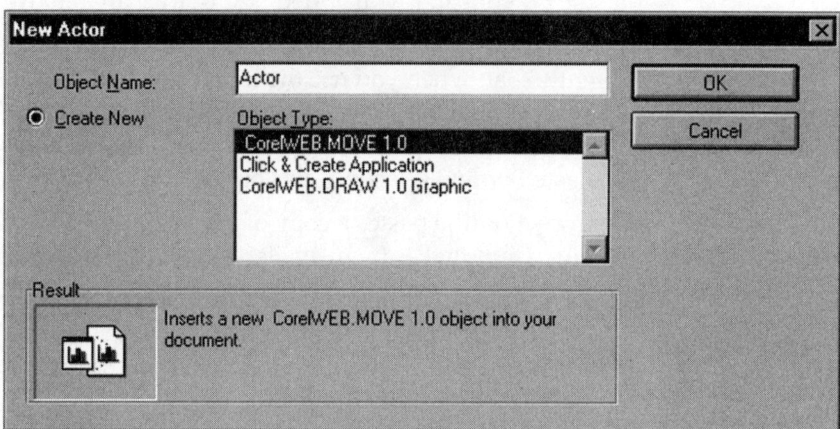

Figure 12-10: The New Actor dialog.

Your first option is naming actors. WEB.MOVE offers the generic name Actor for the first actor brought into a scene, and names subsequent ones Actor2, Actor3, and so on. This sounds convenient, until you have several actors in your project and discover you can't keep them straight. It's wiser to insert more meaningful names for your actors in the Object Name text box.

The Object Type section presents the applications that can create actors for WEB.MOVE. The two choices most likely to show up are CorelWEB.MOVE 1.0 and CorelWEB.DRAW 1.0 Graphic. Select either to bring up an editor designed specifically to create images to serve as actors in a WEB.MOVE animation. WEB.DRAW creates graphics using vector-based drawing tools, while WEB.MOVE—the internal editor— is a paint-type program, like Corel's PhotoPaint or Adobe's Photoshop.

The Create New radio button serves no purpose; it's a remnant of MOVE's previous life as CorelMOVE 5. You also may see some additional application names in the Object Type area. At present, this appears to be a bug. However, in the past, CorelMOVE 5 was endowed with the ability to use other applications, like CorelPHOTOPAINT, as object editors. Will today's bug become tomorrow's feature? Will Corel revise other apps, opening the way for their use as object editors? We can't say for sure. But these are possibilities which could affect the list of Object Type applications in the New Actor dialog box. In any event, if you find that another Corel application appears, try it out. The worst that can happen is you'll get an error message or be brought into WEB.MOVE's own editor instead.

The New Prop Tool

The New Prop dialog parallels the New Actor dialog. The default naming convention calls for Prop, Prop2, and so on. This works if you only have one or two props. If you have more, come up with more meaningful names for your images.

Notice that you have the same choice of applications for prop creation as for actor creation. Remember: the only difference between an actor and a prop is that props have no cels and cannot have paths assigned to them; otherwise they are created in exactly the same manner as actors.

The New Sound Tool

A multimedia authoring application would not be complete without the capability to add and modify sounds. Corel uses the generic term "Wave" for any sounds created in WEB.MOVE because the default file format used to save such sounds is WAV (pronounced "wave"). The New Wave dialog box is very similar to the dialog boxes for creating actors and props. Change the default name of Wave if you like. The biggest difference you'll notice is that you have no choice about the application to be used to record your new sound object; CorelWEB.MOVE 1.0 is the only option. Click on OK and the Wave Editor, shown in Figure 12-11, appears. If you have no sound board installed in your computer, you'll receive an error message indicating there was a problem creating the requested Wave file.

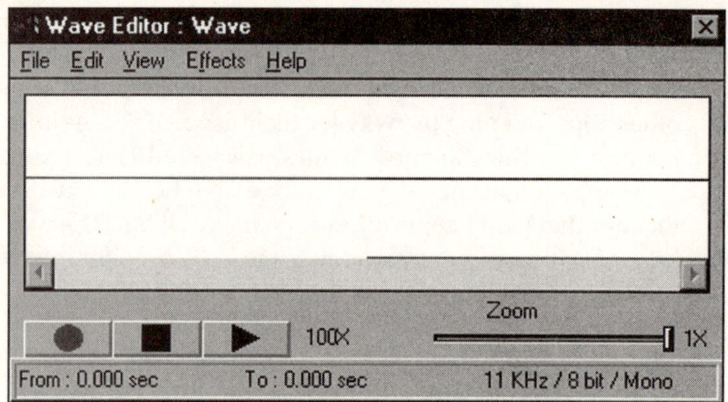

Figure 12-11: The Wave Editor allows you to record a sound file, if you have a sound board and microphone installed.

New Sound will record only a new sound file. To begin recording, click on the button with the red circle. To stop recording, click on the button with the black square. Play back your sound with the button with the black triangle. We'll cover Wave Editor and its many additional features in detail in Chapter 13.

You cannot open existing Wave files for modification from the New Sound selection. To bring in a previously recorded sound file, select File | Import | Sound. The Import command is discussed thoroughly under "The File Menu," later in this chapter.

The New Cue Tool

Select New Cue for the rather large Cue Information dialog box, shown in Figure 12-12. It gives you control over a WEB.MOVE object that, although invisible to the naked eye, is extremely powerful. Cues are the key to creating interactivity in your projects. A cue is a signal for some action to start, at a specific point in your project. The action may be a pause in animation until the mouse is clicked on a particular object or until a specific time period elapses. A cue may demand that a sound be played or that the rate at which the animation is playing should change.

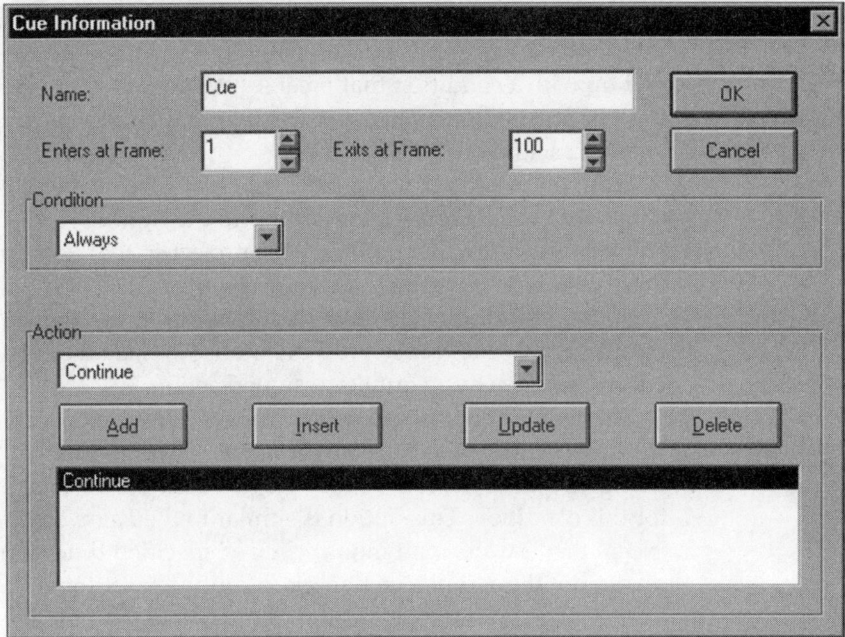

Figure 12-12: The Cue Information dialog contains the controls you need to provide user interactivity in your project.

Setting a Cue's Condition

You may keep the default name Cue or type a more descriptive name into the box. The two controls—Enters at Frame and Exits at Frame—inform you of the frames when the cue becomes active and inactive and can be changed. The boxed Condition section lets you tell WEB.MOVE what type of condition will spark a cue into carrying out the task assigned in the Action section.

The default condition is *Always*. This means that the cue is always going to carry out its action. Coincidentally, the default action is set to *Continue*. So, the default cue will "always continue," and this pretty much assures that nothing will interfere with the playing of the animation. The other conditions besides Always are *Pause Until/For* and *If/After*, which appear from the down arrow of the Condition list box.

Select pause Until/For, and two more controls appear to the right. The first is another list box, which defaults to *Time Delay Of*. The next control is a time interval control set at 1.0 seconds. The trick to deciphering

WEB.MOVE's condition statements is to combine the phrases set in the various controls. For example, string these statements together and you end up with a condition that means: "When you get to the frame where this cue enters the scene, pause for 1 second and then carry out the assigned action."

From the down arrow on the *Time Delay Of* control, select *Mouse Click On*. WEB.MOVE changes the control to the right to read *Anything*. The box lists any actors or props in your project so that you can choose one of these objects as the trigger for your condition. Leaving the control set to *Anything* would translate into the following condition: "When you encounter this cue, pause until the mouse is clicked on anything in the animation, then carry out the assigned action."

For the final condition setting, from the down arrow in the *Pause Until/For* control, select the *If/After* option. The controls to the right don't change, because the same time delay and mouse click options are valid for this condition. This option is similar to the *Pause Until/For* condition, except that it waits for a mouse click or specified time delay before it carries out the assigned action. So, a condition setting of *If/After, Time Delay Of, 2* would mean: "At the frame where this cue is set, wait for 2 seconds, and then carry out the assigned action.

Those of you with some programming experience will see the logic of cues pretty readily. However, if you're a "nontechy," like many people using Corel products, it probably will take some experimenting to get used to the way each cue will affect your project. But that's only part of the power of cues. Let's tackle the Action portion of the dialog now.

Setting a Cue's Action

The Action section contains a drop-down list of all the possible tasks MOVE can carry out when a cue is triggered. The drop-down list is context-sensitive: it changes depending on the kinds of objects contained in your WEB.MOVE project. For instance, if you have imported a sound file, two additional actions are listed that apply only to sound objects. Here are the eight possible actions:

- *Continue* is the default action and in many cases really has no effect on your project. It is most useful to restart an animation interrupted by using the *Pause Until/For* condition.

- Selecting *Goto Frame* displays a frame counter control to the right of the Action list box. This lets you jump to a particular frame in the animation when the cue is triggered. Use this if you want to start an animation over from frame 1 or end it by jumping to the last frame.

- *Pause Until Above Condition Occurs Again* refers to the condition trigger set in the Condition area. Therefore, if you have a condition set to *If/After*, *Mouse Click On*, *Anything*, and the user clicks on any object, the animation pauses until another mouse click signals it to resume. This is a great way to give the user the ability to start and stop an animation at will.

- *End Animation* is pretty self-explanatory—the animation simply ceases to run. Beware! You cannot revive an animation that has been terminated with this setting by calling another cue that is set to continue. If you want to be able to start and stop an animation, use Pause Conditions and Actions.

- The *Change Frame Rate to* option is another that displays a counter control in the Action section. This action controls the rate at which the animation plays. The range is from 1—the slowest—to the fastest setting of 18. If you want your audience to be able to slow an animation down, place objects in the animation that act as triggers to change this option.

- *Play a Sound* shows up only if your project has a Wave sound incorporated. If you have more than one Wave file in the animation, the drop-down list shows them all. This action lets you play a particular sound when the user carries out some specific action, such as clicking on a button.

- The counterpart to playing a sound is *Stop a Sound*. This, too, appears only if a sound has been introduced into the project previously. This is handy if you have a particularly long Wave file that may become irritating. One caveat: If the animation is set to loop over and over, cutting the sound short will stay in effect only for the duration of the loop in which the cue is triggered. On the next loop through the animation, the sound will play, unless the user intervenes again.

- *Goto URL* (Uniform Resource Locator) is very important for Web page designers. Use this setting to make any object a hyperlink. This effectively makes WEB.MOVE capable of creating animated image maps. This setting offers a text box in which to enter any URL. It can be that of another Web page on your site or even that of another Web site entirely. We'll give you some tips on how to enter URLs in Chapter 15.

Managing Multiple Actions

The last few items in the Cue Information dialog are controls to help manage the actions you set. Because it is possible to stack or combine cue actions, there needs to be a way to manage multiple cues. The text box at the bottom contains any actions set in the Action drop-down list. By default, the currently selected action is placed in the text box. If you want to add more than one action, select the first item and click on the Add button. Select the next action and click on Add again. The difference between Add and Insert is where the action is placed in the text box. Add places the selection at the bottom of the list, while Insert places the new item just above the selected item. For example, if you have three items in the text area and the third is highlighted when you click on Insert, the new item will be inserted into the third position, while the previously highlighted item is pushed into the fourth slot.

Why such a big deal about the order in which these actions are stacked in the text box? Because the actions are carried out in order, from top to bottom. Being able to reorder and manage actions in the text box is vital. You can remove an item with the Delete button. Or you can modify or completely change an action: highlight it, choose a new setting from the action list or its associated controls, then click on the Update button. The highlighted item will be replaced with the new settings.

Before you stack cue actions, test each one out. It is possible to make combinations that create unexpected results. The Cue Information dialog houses a wealth of functions, doesn't it? Let's move on to the portions of WEB.MOVE that control the playback of your multimedia creations.

The Playback Controls

There are several pieces of WEB.MOVE's interface that govern how your animation plays back.

The VCR Controls

The most frequently used playback controls are styled after VCR controls. Table 12-1 lists the controls and their functions.

Icon	Control Name	Function
■	Stop	Stops the animation playback
▶	Play	Plays the animation
◀	Reverse	Plays the animation in reverse
▷‖	Next frame	Moves forward one frame with each click on the button
◀‖	Previous frame	Moves backward one frame with each click on the button
◀	First frame	Moves to frame number 1
▶‖	Last frame	Moves to the last frame in the animation
↩	Loop	Plays the animation continuously
◀))	Sound	Plays back sounds

Table 12-1: CorelWEB.MOVE playback controls & functions.

Tip

If you want GIF or Java animations embedded in your Web pages to loop continuously, make sure the Loop button is active when you publish the file.

If you haven't already, play with each of the controls to get a feel for the way they work.

Frame & Status Controls

To the right of the VCR controls are other useful tools to help you build your animations. One that is very important to playback is the Frame slider. Drag the slider's knob right or left to move to any frame in the animation. Watch the objects in the animation window move about, forward or backward, depending on how you move the knob. The number to the left of the slider changes to tell you exactly which frame you are viewing. This is the current frame counter. The counter to the right of the slider is the total frames counter. It stays the same until you change the total number of frames in your project.

The status line, located above the Frame slider, displays useful information about a currently selected object. It informs you of the object's type and name. If the object is an actor, it also displays the number of cels that make up the actor.

Enter and exit frame counters are located to the right of the total frames counter. The counter with the up arrow identifies the first frame at which the currently selected object enters the scene. Conversely, the counter with the down arrow, tells you in what frame the currently selected object exits the scene.

We've come to another crossroads in our tour of MOVE's interface. We're about to move on to three very special controls that call up specially designed window palettes, called roll-ups. Each roll-up is discussed, at length, in the next section.

The Roll-Ups

At the bottom left of WEB.MOVE's application window are three special buttons that call up palettes from which you interactively control the objects in your projects. Because these special palettes stay on top of WEB.MOVE, Corel built in the ability to collapse these windows into just a title bar. That's how they got the name "roll-ups." If a roll-up is in the open or down position, pressing the up arrow in the upper right corner of the title bar causes it to roll up. In this state, the arrow is flipped to point downward: pressing it now reopens the roll-up so its controls are readily accessible.

Without the Timelines, Library, and Cel Sequencer roll-ups, you'll have trouble fine-tuning your projects. Details about each follow.

The Timeline Roll-Up

The Timeline roll-up is very powerful. From it, you can perform varied functions on every object in your project: reposition an object in the stacking order, control the frame at which it enters and exits the scene, even turn an object on or off. This roll-up is so useful that you'll probably have it onscreen much of the time you're working on an animation project.

Click on the Timeline roll-up button in the lower left corner of WEB.MOVE, and the roll-up appears. Only a portion of the roll-up displays, by default. Click on the button with the right arrowhead just under the title bar, and the roll-up expands toward the right. Both the collapsed and expanded views of the roll-up are shown in Figure 12-13. In the expanded view, you see not only the objects but also each object's corresponding timeline.

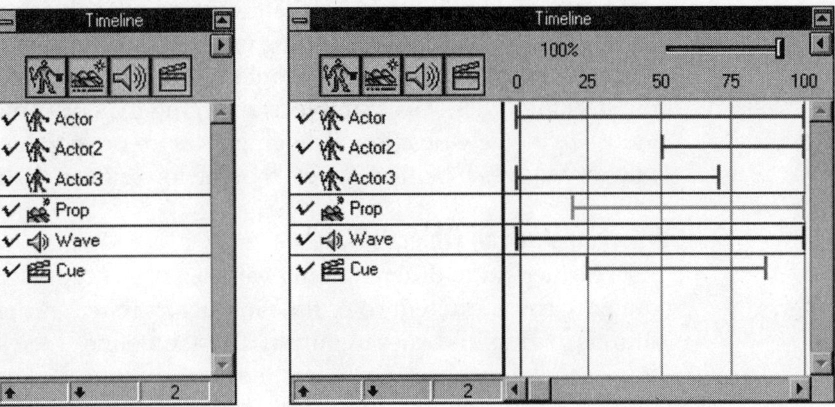

Figure 12-13: The Timeline roll-up in its collapsed (left) and expanded (right) states.

Object Categories & the Stacking Order

At the top of the roll-up are four buttons that are depressed (turned on) by default. They represent the four types of WEB.MOVE objects contained in an animation: actor, prop, sound, and cue. All four object types are shown in the roll-up until you click on a button to turn it off. Those object categories are not deleted from the current project, just temporarily shut off or hidden. This means that they do not display during playback, nor will they be exported if the project is published as a GIF or Barista file. Hiding objects is very useful while developing your animations. In this way, you can remove specific elements to make it easier to focus on those that need fine-tuning.

Each object name has a blue checkmark to its left, which allows you to hide specific objects. If you want to hide just one object—not the entire object category—click on the object's checkmark, and it will be removed from the scene. The name of the object you hide is highlighted in gray.

There is design logic behind the order in which objects display in the roll-up. Actors are always at the top, props next, sounds third, and cues last. Each category is separated from the others by a horizontal black line. The notion of the stacking order, which WEB.MOVE imposes, is reinforced in this roll-up. Objects of different types must stay together. Objects of the same type can be repositioned in the stack, relative to other objects of the same type. Further, no matter how you arrange the order of actors, they always display on top of any props in the scene. Another way to think of this is that actors are on one layer—the topmost—and props are on a lower layer. You can rearrange the objects within each layer, but you can't make anything on a lower layer display in front of an object on a higher layer. If you want to move an object higher or lower in the stacking order, it's as simple as dragging the object name with the mouse to the new position. Dragging an actor or prop higher in its group category moves it behind objects that are lower in the listing.

Working With an Object's Timeline

As a further aid to differentiating between object types, each object category has a different color timeline: actors in red, props in green, sounds in blue, and cues in purple. These timelines correspond to the frames in your project. Each timeline has a starting and ending position designated by a short vertical bar. This vertical bar designates the frames at which the object enters and exits the scene. The vertical bars are connected by a horizontal line. The entire timeline is a graphical representation of the total number of frames that an object is onscreen. Remember: an object can be hidden; it won't display in the animation window yet its timeline is still visible, so you can still modify the timeline. You can interactively modify an object's starting or ending frame or even its duration onscreen: Place the cursor over the timeline and drag. If you place the cursor over the left end of a timeline, the cursor changes to a left-pointing arrow; hold down the mouse button and drag on the timeline's starting vertical bar to adjust its position. You can do the same with the vertical bar at the end of a timeline. If a timeline is set to the correct length but you want to move it as a complete unit, click the mouse over the horizontal bar connecting the two vertical bars. The cursor changes to a double-headed arrow. You now can drag the entire timeline to reposition it.

Near the top of the Timeline roll-up are numbers that designate the frames in your animation. Above them is the Zoom slider. Because the Timeline roll-up is a nonresizing window, you can't grab its borders and make it larger in order to zoom in on an area of the timelines and adjust them. This is where the Zoom slider comes in handy. By default, the slider is all the way to the right at 100 percent. This causes the roll-up to show all—100 percent—of the frames in the allotted space. Move this slider to the left to zoom in on and view a smaller area of the timelines.

This enables you to set timelines with much greater precision. Move the slider all the way to the left for a 10 percent glimpse of your timelines. In other words, if your project has 100 frames, you will see 10 frames worth of timeline information. If your project contains 50 frames, you will view 5 frames worth of timeline area. Scroll bars at the bottom of the timeline area become active when you move the Zoom slider from the 100 percent position, so that you can view any timeline area that is currently offscreen. If your project contains more objects than can fit inside the Timeline roll-up, scroll bars appear on the far right, so that you can scroll up or down to access all the project's objects.

At the roll-up's bottom left, a status bar area shows a highlighted object's enter and exit frame numbers. To the right of the two indicators is the current frame counter. The thin blue line that cuts vertically through all the object's timelines is another version of the current frame counter. Click on the play button of the VCR controls, and watch the blue line travel across the roll-up and the frame counters in the status areas progress.

Remove the Timeline roll-up from your screen in any of the following ways:

- Click on the Timelines button you used to activate the roll-up.

- Click on the control menu in the left corner of the roll-up's title bar and choose Close from the drop-down menu.

- Double-click on the control menu button to instantly remove the roll-up.

- Choose the Tools | Timeline Roll-Up menu option.

The Library Roll-Up

The middle roll-up button is for the Library roll-up. Click on it to bring up a special palette that gives you access to collections of actors, props, and sounds that come bundled with CorelWEB.MOVE or to libraries of WEB.MOVE objects that you assemble. This convenient tool also previews the objects in each library. So you can preview an actor's entire cel sequence or hear a sound *before* you place it into your current animation.

As shown in Figure 12-14, the Library roll-up has three buttons at the top similar to the four buttons on the Timeline roll-up. Click on a button, and the roll-up displays objects of that type. When the button is in the up position, those object types are hidden from view.

Figure 12-14: The Library roll-up contains controls to access and preview collections of MOVE objects— actors, props, or sounds.

Working With MOVE Libraries

The first time you call up the Library roll-up, it may present you with the Open Library dialog box. Tell WEB.MOVE which library you want loaded. Libraries are stored as MLB files. If you are not already there, use the dialog's controls to navigate to the directory where WEB.MOVE is installed and then select the SAMPLE.MLB file. After you click on OK, the roll-up will look like Figure 12-14. The roll-up can visually display an object in the preview window. Because props are made up of only one image, they are easily represented in this preview area. If the object is an actor, the first cel in its sequence displays. If the object is a sound, a waveform—represented by a pattern of dots—appears. The object name assigned to the library item displays under the preview window.

Below the object name is a scroll bar used to move through the various objects contained in the library file. Press one of the arrows at the end of the scroll bars to view each library item, one by one, or drag the scroll button to move to an arbitrary position in the library file. When you are previewing an actor, you can click on the Play button and watch it run through its cel sequence. The actor will keep playing until you click on the button again (now labeled Stop Playing). The same actions apply to sound objects.

When you find library objects that you want to include in your animation, click on the Place button. The currently previewed object moves into the animation window. The object is inserted into the animation at the frame designated by the current frame counter on WEB.MOVE's status bar.

Using the Pop-up Menu

This roll-up contains a pop-up menu used to access several other functions that pertain only to libraries. Click on the right arrow button located just under the title bar in the upper right corner of the roll-up. When you let go of the button, a menu of six items displays. The first two items are used to maintain MLB files.

Choose the first item in the menu to call up the New Library dialog box, which asks you to provide a subdirectory and name for the new MLB file you are creating. When you click on OK, the Library roll-up preview area goes blank, indicating that you now have an empty library. To add items, select an object in the animation window or from the Timeline roll-up, press the pop-up menu button on the library roll-up, and select Add Member to Library from the menu. Use the Delete Member menu option to remove the currently previewed library object from the MLB file. And should you want to give a library object a different name, use the Rename Member option.

The second item on the menu, Open Library, brings up the same Open Library dialog discussed earlier in this section. Use this dialog to locate and open additional library files.

The final menu selection is a toggle switch called Visual Mode. This switch replaces the preview window with a list of all object names found in the library. You'll still be able to visually preview actors and props and hear sounds by selecting a name and pressing the Play button. Click on the Visual Mode button again to return to the preview window.

The Cel Sequencer Roll-Up

As you may have guessed from the name, the Cel Sequencer roll-up affects only WEB.MOVE actors; they are the only objects that have cels. Invoked with no actor selected, this roll-up contains no information. Select an actor, and numbers fill both rows of small boxes, as shown in Figure 12-15. This roll-up is simple in design because it serves only one purpose: to change the normal sequence of an actor's cels. With this in mind, let's take a look at its different features.

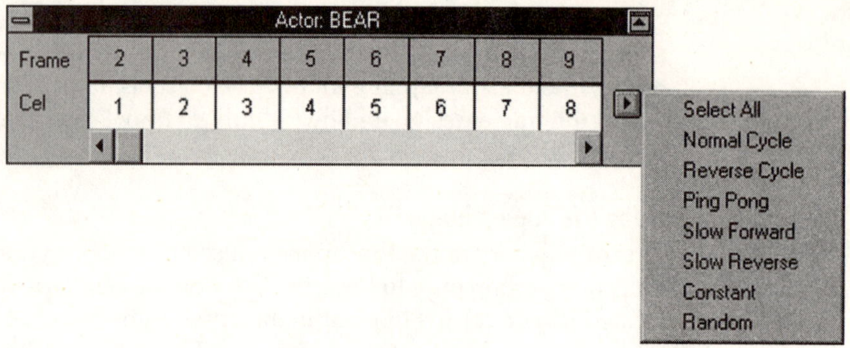

Figure 12-15: Use the Cel Sequencer roll-up and its pop-up menu to change which cel of an actor displays at any given frame in the animation.

The title bar of the roll-up displays the object name of the actor, so there can be no mistake about which actor you are modifying. In the first row, labeled Frame, the numbers correspond to the frames in which the selected actor appears in the animation. If an actor enters a scene at frame 24 and exits at frame 50, the numbers in the top row start at 24 and end with 50.

In the second row, labeled Cel, the numbers identify exactly which cel of an actor displays when a specific frame number is reached. Click on any cel number: the number highlights and the image from that cel displays in the animation window. If the number of frames is more than can be displayed at one time in the roll-up, a scroll bar allows you to move to any frame not currently visible.

By default, the cel numbers follow in the order originally designed for the actor. In other words, if an actor has 5 cels and was set to appear onscreen from frames 1 to 10, the cel numbers would be 1, 2, 3, 4, 5, 1, 2, 3, 4, 5. The beauty of the Cel Sequencer roll-up is that you can change the number of any cel and replace it with any other cel number: Double-click on a cel number: the number moves up and to the left. Type in a new cel number and either press Enter or select another cel number with the mouse. There, it's done! You've modified the normal sequence of your actor.

Modifying its sequence is a very powerful technique for getting the most out of an actor. For example, you can make an actor appear to move slower by changing the cel numbers to show the same cel twice rather than once: The sequence would be changed to 1, 1, 2, 2, 3, 3, 4, 4, 5, 5. This is less work for you and the computer than going back and adding twice the number of cels to the actor.

Here's another example of how handy reordering cel numbers can be: You can make an actor run backward by changing the cel numbers to run from the highest to the lowest, like 5, 4, 3, 2, 1. You can even make the actor go a little crazy by totally mixing up the numbers, like so: 3, 1, 4, 2, 5. With a little imagination, you soon will utilize the cel sequencer to really spice up the movements of your actors.

Changing Cels With the Pop-Up Menu

The roll-up has a pop-up menu to help you make wholesale changes to the cel numbers. See Figure 12-15. Before applying these changes you must select a range of cels. To select a group of cels, click the first cel to be affected, hold down Shift, and click on the last cel. All the cels in between are highlighted and ready for modification. Here's what each of the options found on the pop-up, located to the right of the Cel number row, does:

- Select All selects all the cel numbers for all the frames in the animation.

- Normal Cycle resets an actor's sequence to its original state, starting at cel 1 and proceeding to the highest cel number. If there are additional frames to fill, the sequence starts all over again. This option is useful after you've made extensive changes to an actor's sequence and then choose to discard them and start from scratch.

- Reverse Cycle changes the cel number order to start with the highest cel number and proceed toward the lowest. For example, an actor which has 5 cels and stays onscreen for 10 frames would be changed to: 5, 4, 3, 2, 1, 5, 4, 3, 2, 1. Obviously, this is the natural choice to make an actor move in reverse.

- Ping Pong is an interesting variation. This option renumbers cels to run through the first iteration in the natural order but proceed in reverse order on the second iteration. This forward, reverse, forward, reverse pattern is followed until the number of frames is exhausted. An example is 1, 2, 3, 4, 5, 4, 3, 2, 1, 2, 3, 4, 5, 4, 3, 2, 1. If you are familiar with the cat food commercial in which the cat prances forward, then backward, you'll pick up on this effect pretty quickly.

- Slow Forward repeats an actor's cels to make the actor move slower. An example is 1, 1, 2, 2, 3, 3, 4, 4, 5, 5. Because twice as many cels (and therefore frames) are being used to display this motion, the actor moves at half-speed.

- Slow Reverse performs the same doubling of cels but reorders the cels in reverse. An example is 5, 5, 4, 4, 3, 3, 2, 2, 1, 1. Choose this option to make your actor move at half-speed in reverse.

- Constant makes all selected cels the same number. In effect, this stills the animation, as the same cel displays over and over. This is best used selectively to make an actor pause for a few frames. Note that the number of the first selected cel is inserted into each subsequent cel box. For example, selecting all frames and then choosing Constant will make all the cels display 1. If you select cels that show 11, 12, 13, 14, they will be changed to 11, 11, 11, 11. If you want all frames to display a specific cel number, say 3, change the first frame's cel number to 3. Next, choose Select All, then Constant, and all cel numbers change to 3.

- Random throws concern to the wind. If you just don't really care in what order the cels display, choose Random and that's what you'll get. Try it and see if you like it.

We've come a long way in our tour of WEB.MOVE's interface; there are only a few more areas to touch on. Next, let's look at useful features found under WEB.MOVE's various menus.

The Menus

As we've seen, much of WEB.MOVE's functionality can be accessed through interactive controls such as buttons and controls on toolbars and special palettes. But in the Windows world, there are always two or more ways to accomplish the same task. Menus have become a universal and convenient way to access almost all the functions and commands of a program. Many of the selections found under WEB.MOVE's menus are duplications of those we've already discussed. However, there are a few functions accessible only by way of the menus. In this section we'll run through each menu and its commands, quickly touching on those that have been introduced in earlier sections and spending ample time explaining anything new.

The File Menu

The commands discussed in the following section control various aspects of WEB.MOVE's file functions. Some commands are applicable to WEB.MOVE's native CMV format, while others affect a host of different file types.

New

Choose New to start a brand new project that is completely empty. If you have an animation file open that has not been saved yet, MOVE will prompt you to save it before continuing.

Open

Open loads an existing CMV file into WEB.MOVE's authoring environment. When the Open Animation File dialog box appears, use the navigational controls to move to a disk and subdirectory that contains CMV files and they will display in the files list. Click on a file. If the Preview option has been turned on, a low-resolution thumbnail image depicting the first frame of the animation displays, to help you decide if you selected the file you wanted. Click on OK; the selected CMV file loads.

Save

Save and Save As are closely related and, in fact, call up the same dialog box: Save Animation File. Use either of these two selections to save your project to disk as a CMV file. If you have not saved it previously, a dialog requests a name and subdirectory for storing this file. Type a name (it must conform to the DOS 8.3 convention) into the File Name text box and click on OK. WEB.MOVE adds the CMV extension for you. If you have previously saved your project, the Save command updates the stored file with any changes made since the last save operation.

Save As

Save As stores an already-saved file under a new name. If you invoke Save As and use a file name already in use, WEB.MOVE asks if you want the older file overwritten by this new file. Click on Yes to replace the existing file with the new CMV information or No to go back to the dialog and type in a new file name.

Import

Import is your key to getting MOVE to bring in images and sounds that already exist in files created in other applications. Choose Import for a submenu of four items. Here's what each does:

Actor From Animation File   The Import Actor dialog box allows you to negotiate your disk drives to find animation files from which WEB.MOVE can extract images. Select the drop-down list under the List Files of Type text box for the four different kinds of animation files that WEB.MOVE can decipher: AutoDesk Animator formats (.fli, .flc) head the list, followed by CorelWEB.MOVE (.cmv), MPEG Movie (.mpg), and QuickTime for Windows (.mov).

Each file format allows you to make a multiceled image of its contents; however, importing actors from a CMV is the most flexible situation. When you select a CMV, all actors contained in that file are displayed in the Select an Actor to Import dialog box, shown in Figure 12-16. Choose an actor's name from the list on the left and the Information section displays data on the actor's physical size in pixels, number of cels, and size in bytes. Turn on the Preview option to see the selected actor run through its sequence of cels, much like the preview function of the Library roll-up. When you have found the actor you desire, click on OK, and it is placed into your current project. If the imported actor's name duplicates one that already exists in your project, the Duplicate Imported Actor dialog box will pop up and ask you to give the imported actor a unique name.

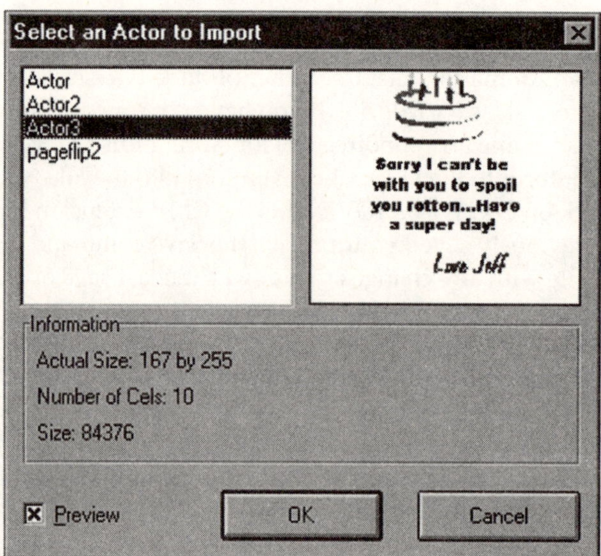

Figure 12-16: The Select an Actor to Import dialog shows you a lot of information about all the actors in a given CMV file.

Actor From Bitmap File   This option lets you import single images to become MOVE actors in your project. When the Import Actor From Bitmap File(s) dialog appears, you can access the list of different types of image formats from which WEB.MOVE can extract information. They are

Windows Bitmap (.bmp, .dib, .rle), CompuServe Bitmap (.gif), JPEG Bitmap (.jpg), Paintbrush (.pcx), Targa Bitmap (.tga, .vda, .icb, .vst), and TIFF Bitmap (.tif, .sep, .cpt)—all the common bitmap formats.

Prop   The Import Prop dialog is, for all intents and purposes, the same as the Import Actor From Bitmap File(s) dialog. The same image file types are supported for importing props as for actors, with the addition of WEB.MOVE's own CMV format. Again, importing props from a CMV offers an additional dialog that allows you to preview and select any prop object that exists in that file.

Sound   From the Import Sound dialog, you can bring in sounds that are contained in the following types of files: CorelWEB.MOVE (.cmv), Wave files (.wav), QuickTime for Windows (.mov), and SoundBlaster Audio (.voc). As with actors and props, importing sounds from a CMV gives you the added flexibility to choose and preview any sound from that file by way of the Select a Sound to Import dialog.

Publish

The next command in the File menu is Publish. Publish is equivalent to the more commonly used term *export*. In actuality, you are really saving your animation in a format other than a CMV file. Like import, publish offers a submenu. It is a good idea to make sure that your project is saved in CMV format before publishing to another file format. The six items on the menu are discussed in the following subsections.

To Java   Choose this command if your project contains sounds and cues you want operable in your Web pages. When you select the Java option from the Publish menu, the Publish To Java dialog box, shown in Figure 12-17, displays. The only file type shown in the drop-down list is CorelWEB.MOVE HTML (.htm). WEB.MOVE creates an HTML page that is just a wrapper for the Java applet that contains your WEB.MOVE animation. Navigate to a subdirectory where you want to save your HTML file and type a name into the File Name text box.

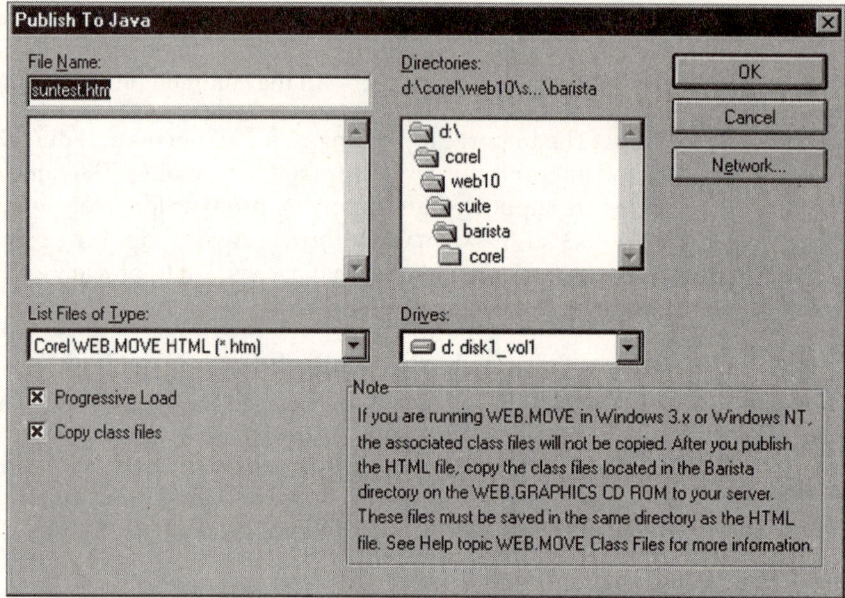

Figure 12-17: The Publish To Java dialog lets you save your animation as a Java file, which can be included in or referenced from any HTML document.

Tip

As far as CorelWEB.MOVE is concerned, Java and Barista are interchangeable. Beware though: Outside the scope of Corel WEB.GRAPHICS Suite applications, Java refers to a program language that has become very popular, especially for writing applications that operate over the World Wide Web. Barista is Corel's name for the strategy it has come up with to make Java applets out of your CorelWEB.GRAPHICS drawings and animations.

Before you click on OK and send WEB.MOVE off to convert your multimedia masterpiece into a stunning Java applet, there are two options in the lower left portion of the dialog you should note. Progressive Load refers to what your Java applet will look like when it is called by an HTML document. Because it can take a considerable amount of time for an image to appear, MOVE gives you the option of showing a partial image of your animation or simply showing a white box with a message saying that a CorelWEB.MOVE animation is loading. Try both options and determine for yourself which better suits the needs of your project.

Underneath Progressive Load is Copy class files. What's a class file? As we stated a few paragraphs ago, Java is really a programming language. A Java program, or applet, relies on certain files that contain libraries of code that enable it to function properly. These libraries are the class files referred to here. So quite a few files are needed to display Web pages that contain Java components. To ensure that you can view the Java-enabled pages on your local computer, always select this option. If you are developing Web pages or HTML documents that are going to be accessed from another computer, like an Internet Service Provider (ISP) or your company's Web server, make sure these class files are uploaded to the proper place on that computer. We'll explain that process in depth in Chapter 15.

To Animated GIF   Chose this publishing choice if you want to capture only animated images. This option produces a CompuServe GIF file that cannot contain any information regarding sound or interactivity. As you'll see in the Export To Animated GIF dialog, GIF is the only file format supported. Even if it is limited in functionality, GIF is by far the most popular animation file format encountered on the Web. Besides being ubiquitous, it offers the advantage of being easy to incorporate into HTML documents. Unlike Java applications, there is only one file to worry about.

To Animated Movie   This selection brings up the Export To Movie dialog box, which lets you convert your project into any of the following formats: Video for Windows (.avi), MPEG (.mpg), and QuickTime for Windows (.mov). This option isn't really a first choice if you want to get your WEB.MOVE files onto the Web. Although there are plug-ins that allow browsers to display these file types, none of these can retain the cue information that publishing to Barista/Java supports. In practice, exporting to a Video for Windows AVI file and embedding it in an HTML page has proven the most reliable for video and sound playback in both Navigator and Explorer.

To Individual Files   If you want specific frames of your project exported as single images, choose this option to call up the Export To Individual Files dialog box. As you can see in Figure 12-18, this dialog has special controls to export specific ranges of frames. The choices of bitmap file formats will sound very familiar by now: Windows Bitmap (.bmp, .dib, .rle), CompuServe Bitmap (.gif), JPEG Bitmap (.jpg), Paintbrush (.pcx), Targa Bitmap (.tga, .vda, .icb, .vst), and TIFF Bitmap (.tif).

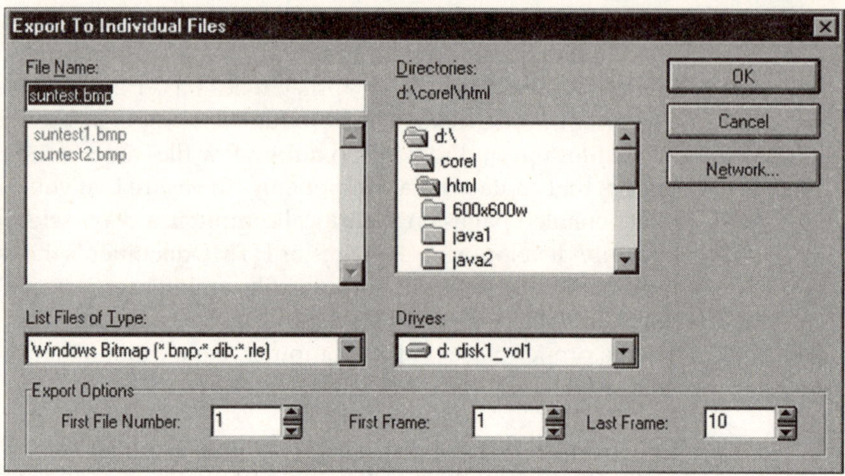

Figure 12-18: Use the frame controls on the Export To Individual Files dialog box to save specific frames as individual bitmap files.

Notice the counters in the Export Options section at the bottom of the dialog. The First File Number counter controls the starting number appended to the file name you type into the File Name text box. The default is 1, although you can go up to 10,000. The other two controls, First Frame and Last Frame, determine which frames in your animation are captured. When you click on OK, WEB.MOVE saves the first requested frame into a file that is of the type you requested from the List Files of Type drop-down list. The name of the file will be whatever you typed into the File Name text box, with a number appended. Subsequent frames are captured with the file number appendage incremented by one. For example: if you request a file name of MOVETEST, with the First Frame number set to 1, and are capturing two frames, the resulting file names will be MOVETE01 and MOVETE02. Because WEB.MOVE has inherited DOS's old 8.3 file-naming convention, it must truncate the requested file name in order to add on the sequential frame numbers.

To Sound When you want to export sounds from your WEB.MOVE project, call up the Export To Sound dialog. The only two file format choices are Wave File (.wav) and SoundBlaster Audio (.voc). Choose the type and directory location, type in a file name, and click on OK. If you have more than one sound object in your project, each will be saved as a separate file with a number appended. For Wave files, the number starts at 1 and is incremented by 1 for each subsequent sound file. For VOC files, the initial appended numeral is 0, then 1, then 2, and so forth.

To WEB.DESIGNER   This last choice is available only if you launched CorelWEB.MOVE from within WEB.DESIGNER. To do so, click on the WEB.MOVE button on DESIGNER's toolbar or select CorelWEB.MOVE from DESIGNER's Tools menu.

Publishing to WEB.DESIGNER is another route to creating a Barista/ Java applet. The dialog box that comes up, Publish to WEB.DESIGNER, asks you to set only the two options already discussed in the earlier "To Java"section. WEB.MOVE and WEB.DESIGNER automatically name and save your Java applet.

Exit

Exit shuts down WEB.MOVE. If you have a CMV file that has not been saved, you will be prompted to save it before WEB.MOVE terminates.

Most Recently Used Files

The last part of the File menu lists the last four files that were saved, to give you quick access to your most recently worked-on WEB.MOVE projects. It's time to move over to the next menu, Edit.

The Edit Menu

Under this menu you'll find commands that affect various aspects of your project. These functions include adding, removing, and modifying objects in the animation.

Cut

Cut removes a selected object from the project and places it on the clipboard for retrieval with the Paste As command.

Copy

Copy places a copy of a selected object on the clipboard for later retrieval but does not remove it from the project.

Copy Frame

Copy Frame takes a snapshot of all the items displayed in the current frame and places this bitmap image on the clipboard so that it can be pasted back into the project at some other position. This command does not copy separate elements; everything displayed is lumped together as one picture.

Paste As

Paste As copies objects from the clipboard and inserts them back into your WEB.MOVE project. Three choices—Actor, Prop, and Sound—appear on a submenu.

If the item on the clipboard is an actor, paste it back in as an actor and its cels remain intact. Paste an actor back as a prop object and only its first cel inserts at the current frame.

If the object copied or cut is a prop, you can paste it back into the animation as either a prop or an actor. This is a pretty quick way to change the object type of any item.

It the object on the clipboard is a sound element, the Sound menu option is active and you can paste the sound into the project wherever you desire.

Be careful! Every use of the Cut or Copy function erases whatever is currently on the clipboard. If you cut or copy an object that you want pasted back into your project, do it *before* you use Cut or Copy again.

Delete

Delete removes a selected object from the project without making a copy—it's gone for good. You also can use the Delete key on the keyboard to carry out this command. Because this is a permanent deletion, you are prompted to make sure that you really want to remove the object.

Duplicate

Duplicate combines Copy and Paste As into one step. Select an object, select Duplicate, and WEB.MOVE prompts you to confirm the duplicate object's new name; the default is the original name with a number appended. If you want the name changed, type a new one into the text box and click on OK. The new object appears a little lower and to the right of the original object.

Clone

Clone is an interesting variation of the Duplicate function. Everything that applies to the Duplicate function goes for the Clone function. However, cloning an object sets up a relationship between the original item and its clone. Any change that you make to either one automatically applies to the other. For example, change a color in a cloned actor, or add a cel to it, and the original actor will be updated with the same changes, simultaneously. Give this command a try; it's very useful.

Select All

Select All is pretty self-explanatory. All objects in the current project are selected and ready to be acted upon by whatever command you issue next.

Insert New

The Insert New | Actor, Prop, Sound, or Cue menus are equivalent to pressing the corresponding buttons in the toolbar. They call up the same dialog boxes that we discussed in the previous sections devoted to each tool.

Object

The Object menu option opens the editor that created the selected object. This could be WEB.DRAW (WEB.MOVE's internal paint editor), the internal sound editor, or the Cue Information dialog box. These different editors are discussed in detail in Chapter 13.

Object Properties

When you select Object Properties, a dialog box related to the type of item selected opens. If the item is a cue, then the familiar Cue Information dialog appears to allow you to review and change any aspect of a cue's function.

Sound Information Dialog   If the selected item is a sound object, you see the Sound Information dialog, shown in Figure 12-19.

Not only can you change the name of the object and its enter or exit frame, you also can use the Volume slider control to increase or decrease its volume. This is helpful when you want to tone down one sound that is much louder than others in the project. There is another slider control labeled Priority. This helps WEB.MOVE sort out which sound object should be played when several overlap. If you definitely want a sound to be heard, set its priority to high.

The Channel section gives you control over which speaker(s) will deliver the sound—Left, Right, or Both. Under the Channel box is the recorded sound's total length of time and the Repeat Sound option box. If a sound's timeline extends for a longer period of time than its recorded length, you can turn this option on to have the sound repeated over and over until the timeline duration is reached. If you want the sound to play only once, turn this option off.

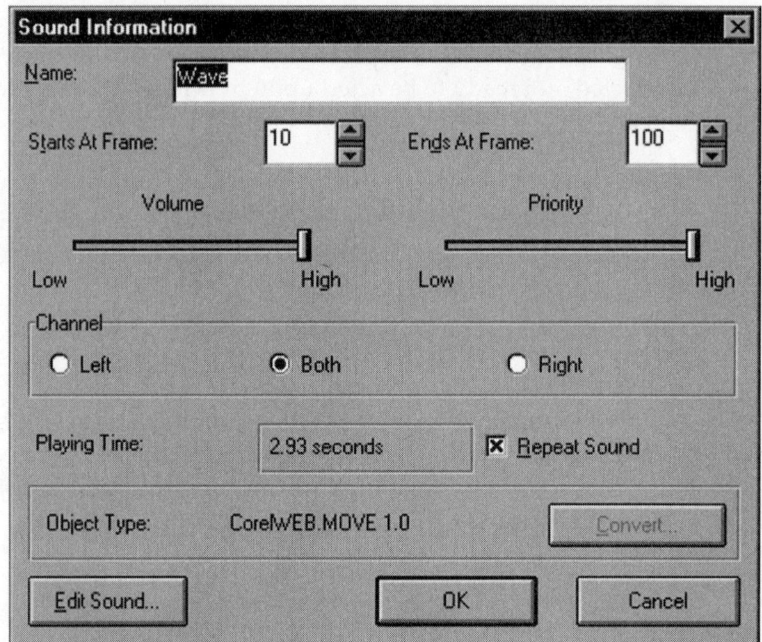

Figure 12-19: Many basic aspects of a sound object can be modified from the Sound Information dialog box.

Click on the Edit Sound button at the bottom left to bring up the sound editor to add special effects, change characteristics, or even re-record a sound file. The sound editor is discussed in detail in Chapter 13.

Actor Information Dialog   If the object selected before you selected Object Properties was an actor, the Actor Information dialog, shown in Figure 12-20, appears.

As with the other object information dialogs called by the Object Properties menu command, from the Actor Information dialog box you can change common aspects such as object name, enter and exit frames, and even the start position of an actor. But this dialog has several unique controls that affect aspects of an actor object not found anyplace else in WEB.MOVE.

The first unique control is the Locked option box to the right of the Name text box. If you don't want an actor to be repositioned after you've got it in place, turn this option on. Should you find that you need to reposition this actor or change any aspect of its timeline, you must come back to the Actor Information dialog and turn off this option.

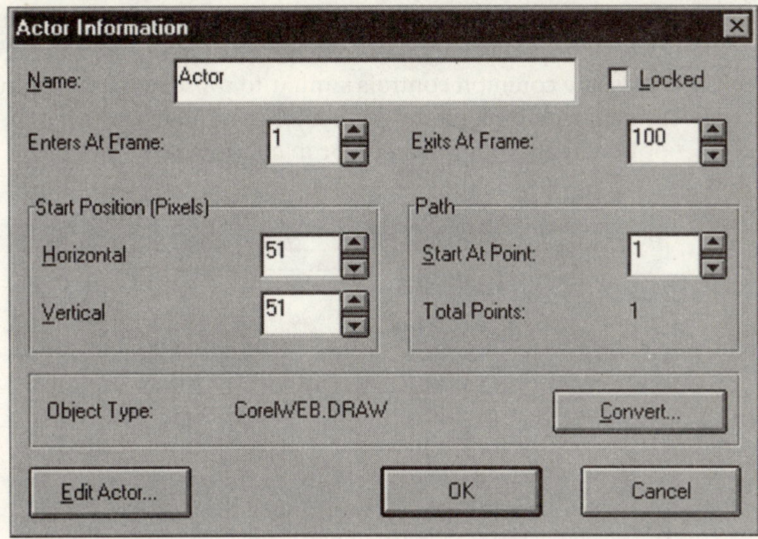

Figure 12-20: In addition to modifying the standard aspects of an actor from the Actor Information dialog box, you also can lock its position.

The next control found only on this dialog box is the Path area. It reports how many path points the actor has, but more importantly gives you a control to modify at which path point the actor starts to display. This is useful when you want an actor to start in the middle of its path for the first run-through. You can team this up with setting the first path point as the Loop To Here node in the Point Information dialog: The actor starts in the middle of its path but loops back to point 1 and then continues to cycle through all its path points normally.

The Object Type region may at first glance seem to contain mundane information, but remember that you can create actors in both WEB.DRAW and WEB.MOVE's internal paint editor. So this information is noteworthy, especially if the object was created in WEB.DRAW. Why? Because only then will the Convert button to the right become operational. Click on this button to change a WEB.DRAW object to be editable by WEB.MOVE's internal paint editor. Be very careful about doing this, because it completely separates the link the object had with WEB.DRAW, and WEB.DRAW has special features for object creation that the internal paint editor does not. The differences between the two editors are discussed in Chapter 13.

Prop Information Dialog   The final dialog that can be accessed from the Object Properties menu is Prop Information, shown in Figure 12-21. It has some common controls similar to those in the Actor Information dialog, including name, enter and exit frame, and even the position lock option. It also offers unique prop controls.

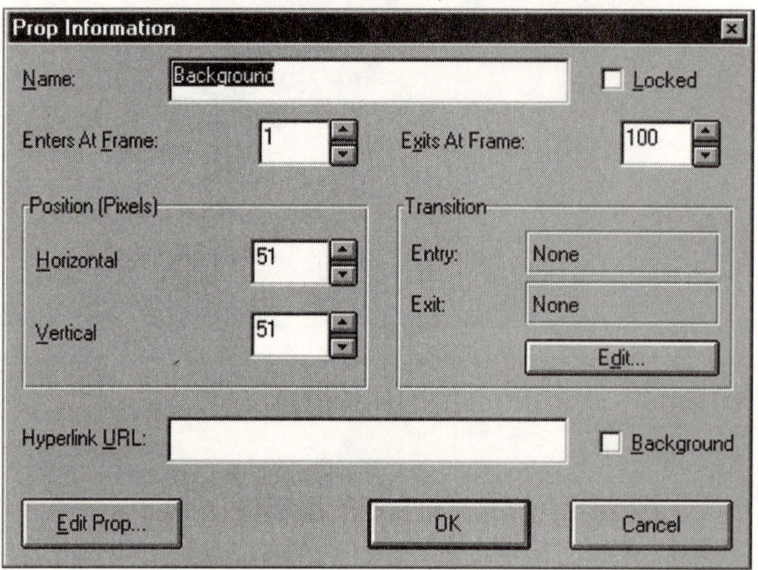

Figure 12-21: Many attributes of a prop can be modified from the Prop Information dialog box. The Hyperlink, Background, and Transition options are only accessible from this dialog box.

Let's tackle the easy ones first. Just above the Cancel button is an option marked Background. Enabling this feature forces a prop to take on certain characteristics. The first is that the image will be made to fit the entire animation window area. If the prop is smaller, it will be stretched as needed (this produces a poor image if applied to a prop that is very small). Conversely, if the prop is larger than the animation window, it will be shrunk to fit. The second characteristic change concerns the timeline duration. No matter what length of time you have set for the timeline, it will be overridden in order to keep the background prop present throughout the entire animation. Last, by default, a background prop is always locked in position.

The Hyperlink URL option is very similar to the Goto URL cue action in the Cue Information dialog. Type any valid URL in this box and, every time a user clicks on the prop, the Web browser jumps to the specified link. For instance, type in **http://www.corel.com** and the user is taken automatically to the Corel Web site.

One of the most powerful features of a prop object is available only from the Prop Information dialog in the Transition boxed area. By default, no transitions are set, so both the Entry and Exit controls display None. Click on the Edit button, and the Transitions for Prop dialog, shown in Figure 12-22, appears. The prop's name is enclosed in quotes and displayed in the title of the dialog box.

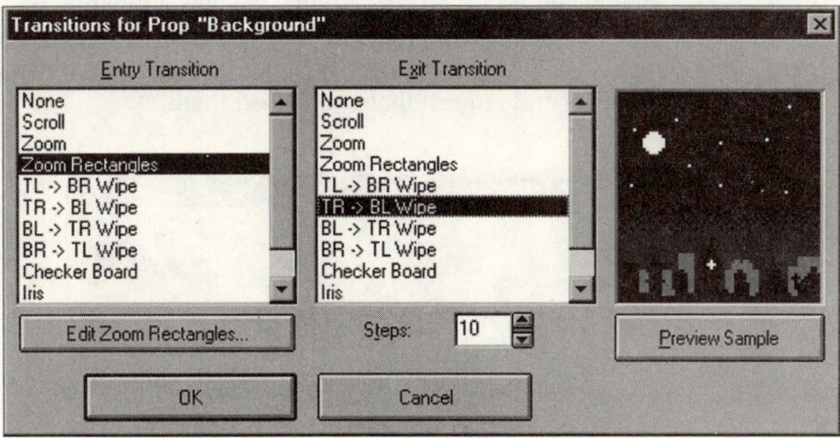

Figure 12-22: The two lists on the Transitions for Prop dialog allow you to set various transition effects for the entry and exit of a prop in a scene.

The two lists—Entry Transition and Exit Transition—in the Transitions for Prop dialog offer 12 identical choices of transition effects, including a setting of None. This allows for really interesting visual effects, because a prop can have different entry and exit transitions. As you click on an item in the list, different buttons or controls which modify aspects of the transition may appear. For most effects, a counter is provided to allow control of the number of steps a transition uses to create its effect. Sometimes—as with the Scroll and Zoom transitions—a button opens another dialog with still more settings to modify. To see how a transition will look, click on the Preview Sample button. You won't see the effect applied to your actual image, but rather a generic demonstration of what the particular transition resembles.

Some words to the wise regarding the application of transitions: Use them judiciously and test them thoroughly. Transitions slow down the frame in which they appear, so your actors will seem to pause. This slowdown can be drastic when viewed in a Web browser. Setting the number of steps lower minimizes this effect to some degree. Also, transitions are supported only when publishing to a Java applet; they are lost if published to GIF or any of the movie file formats.

Animation Information

To change the size of the animation window for the project at hand, you need the Animation Information dialog box, shown in Figure 12-23. Enter the new dimensions for the animation window, in pixels, in the Height and Width boxes to define the new animation window size. If you accidentally put in a number that is not within the predetermined range, WEB.MOVE will notify you of any problem it has with the numbers and request that you correct them.

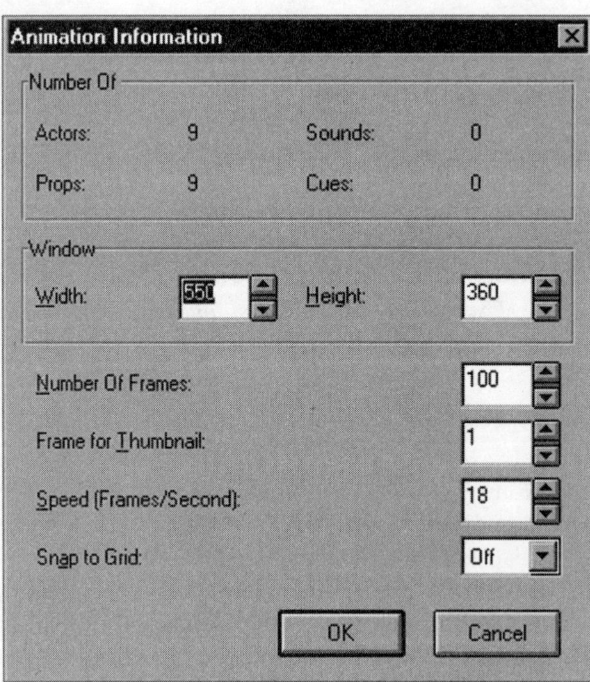

Figure 12-23: You can view and change many aspects of your animation project from the Animation Information dialog.

The Number Of area summarizes how many of each object type are in the project. This is for information only; you cannot change any aspect of these items from this dialog area. However, the dialog has four controls with which to make adjustments, some of which will profoundly affect your WEB.MOVE project.

The Number Of Frames setting lets you control the total number of frames in your MOVE project, ranging from 1 to 9,999. An animation of only one frame makes no sense, of course, since you need at least two images to show any change.

And what's with 9,999 frames? That large a number is very impractical. This seems to be a holdover from the days of CorelMOVE 5, which was designed for making animations that were to be part of large presentations. Bear in mind our general rule: Keep it small and simple. This means that you want to stick with the fewest possible number of frames. The default for a new animation is 100 frames, and even that is more than you'll ever use for most animations that will end up on the Web.

The Frame for Thumbnail setting lets you choose which frame in your project is captured as the low-resolution image displayed in the preview window of the Open Animation File dialog box. Any number that does not exceed the number of frames in your current animation is valid.

Speed (Frames/Second) controls the speed at which your animation plays back. The range for this control falls between 1 and 18, 18 (the default) being the fastest and 1 the slowest. Although the title of the setting makes it sound as if an animation can be synchronized to a specific increment of time (a second), this should not be taken literally. Every system will play back an animation as fast as it can, but not all systems are equal. This means that a system with a very fast hard drive, CPU, and video subsystem will play back an animation much quicker than a computer system with slower components. If you attempt to synchronize sounds and graphics by timing out every detail of your animation, you'll be very disappointed the first time you view it on a different computer.

Even though the Speed (Frames/Second) setting is relative because every system is different, it does have a real effect on the animation. A setting of 9 frames will always run at half the speed of a setting of 18.

By default, Snap to Grid is off, which means that you are free to place or position objects anywhere in the animation window. If you need to move or place objects by a specific number of pixels, use the drop-down list to set the incremental number of pixels you want any movable object to jump. For example, if you change the grid setting to 10, any object positioned with the mouse will move 10 pixels at a time, in whatever direction you specify.

The View Menu

Under the View menu, you will find commands that affect WEB.MOVE's interface or play back the current animation.

Control Panel

Control Panel is a toggle switch to hide or display the entire control panel area—the roll-up buttons, sound and looping controls, VCR playback buttons, frame slider, and status indicators—beneath the animation window. All their functions, except those controlled by the frame slider and object status indicators, can be executed with keyboard or menu commands. A complete list of all keyboard shortcuts is provided in Chapter 15.

Toolbox

The Toolbox option offers a submenu of two toggle switches—Visible and Floating. If you don't want the toolbox to show, uncheck the Visible option and it disappears. If you want the toolbar closer to your animation instead of docked in the upper left corner, select Floating, and the toolbox turns into a free-floating palette you can drag anywhere on the screen.

Frame

Frame also sports a submenu, which allows you to control playback of the animation window contents. This is another way to carry out the functions of the VCR buttons. Choose First to go to frame 1 and Last to move to the last frame. Choose Previous or Next to move forward or backward through the animation sequence, one frame at a time. If you want to jump to a particular frame number, choose Specific. When a small dialog box pops up, plug the frame number into the counter control and click on OK or press the Enter key. Presto, you're at your destination!

Play & Stop

Play and Stop are the final items on the View menu. They, too, control animation playback and are equivalent to clicking on the Play and Stop buttons on the VCR control panel.

The Arrange Menu

The Arrange menu has only four items under it, all of which modify the stacking order of actor and prop items.

To Front

When you issue the To Front command, the selected item moves to the top of the object stack. If the item is an actor, it displays on top of all other elements in the animation. If the selected element is a prop, it covers other props in the scene but does not obscure any actors. Actors always display on a layer above props.

To Back, Forward One & Back One

Select To Back to push a selected object to the bottom of its object category stack. All other items in the same object category display on top of it. Choose Forward One and Back One to make an object move one position at a time in the relative stacking order. To get a better feel for the way these commands work, open the Timeline roll-up and watch each selected item change position in the list as you use each of these commands.

The Tools Menu

This menu allows access to various roll-ups and the Options dialog.

Timeline, Cel Sequencer & Library Roll-ups

Choosing one of these items has the same effect as clicking on the corresponding button on the control panel: the appropriate roll-up displays. However, these menu items toggle: If the Timeline or Cel Sequencer roll-up is already onscreen, selecting the menu item removes it from view.

Options

The Options dialog has three tabs with settings that affect different areas of WEB.MOVE. The topmost tab, Playback Options (Figure 12-24), removes items from view when you play back your animation. Turn on Hide Tools, Hide Menu Bar, and Hide Cursor if you want a pristine viewing area during playback. Because you won't have any onscreen controls to stop your animation, use the Escape key to terminate playback. Checking Enable Sounds and Auto Replay is equivalent to clicking on the Sounds and Loop buttons next to the VCR playback controls.

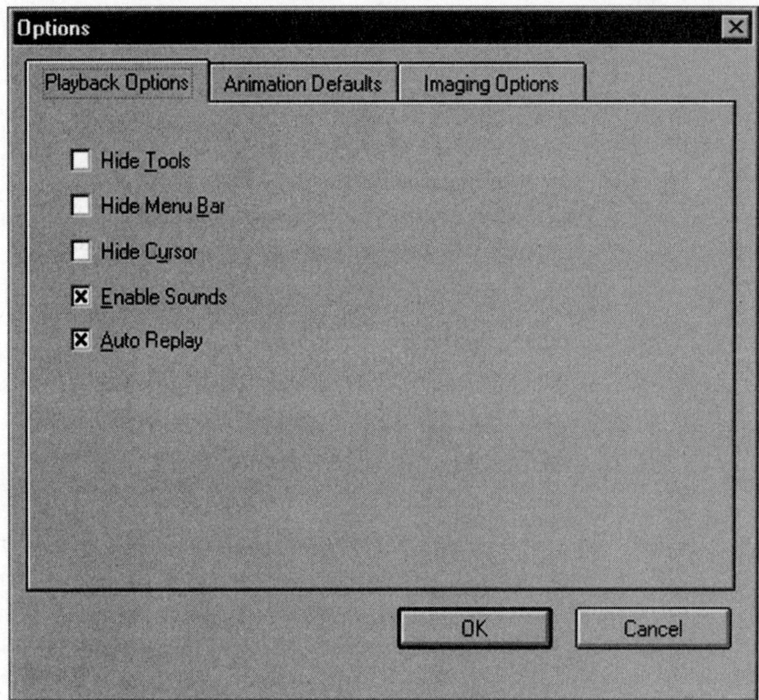

Figure 12-24: The Options dialog Playback Options tab.

The Animation Defaults tab (Figure 12-25) lets you set many default features of WEB.MOVE projects. Ever wish you could make WEB.MOVE start a new project with an animation window other than 200 X 200 pixels? Well you can—by entering new sizes in the Width and Height text boxes in the Window Size area of this dialog tab. Is 100 frames way too many for most of your animation projects? Then use the Number Of Frames control to lower it to a number that suits your needs. If you want to change the frame that is captured as a thumbnail image and displayed in the preview window of some of the dialogs, do so with the Thumbnail Frame control. If the default of 18 frames per second is too fast for most of your projects, set the Speed control to a lower number. And finally, if you want to establish a different Snap to Grid default, this is the place to make the change. After closing the dialog, all new animation projects will start with your new default settings.

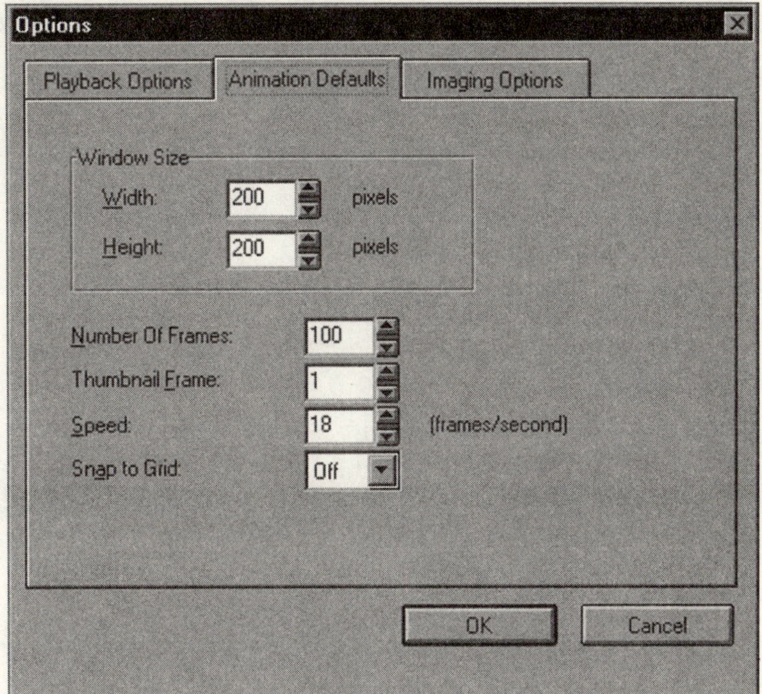

Figure 12-25: The Options dialog Animation Defaults tab.

The Imaging Options tab (Figure 12-26) affects images and animations being imported into WEB.MOVE. Turn on Always prompt for imaging options for the Import Imaging Options dialog to appear every time you import a graphic image into your project. That small dialog offers the same controls found on the Imaging Options tab; however, instead of applying the image options to all incoming images, you customize them to suit the needs of each image you import. A discussion of the various imaging options follows.

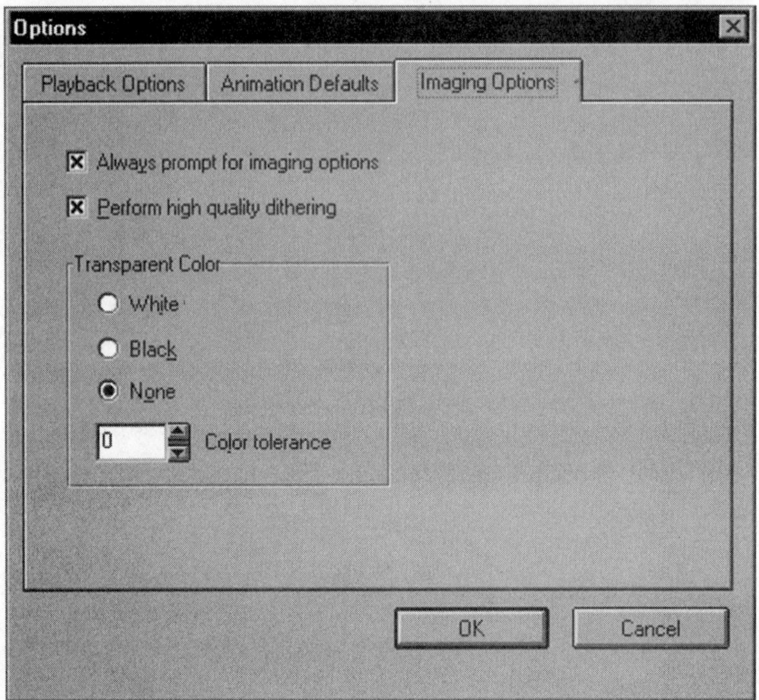

Figure 12-26: The Options dialog Imaging Options tab.

The Perform high quality dithering option is turned on by default. Experiment with this setting, but for the most part, you'll probably leave it on. It tells WEB.MOVE to do its best when converting images made up of colors that WEB.MOVE can't duplicate. WEB.MOVE has only 255 colors, including black and white, with which to display all graphics. Other graphics applications can create images using a palette of 255 colors, but they might be 255 different colors altogether. Dithering is an effective conversion scheme applied to images to approximate colors not reproducible with the available palette. Again, if in doubt, it is best to leave this option on.

The Transparent Color area lets you choose a color in your imported graphics—either white or black —that will allow images underneath to show through. If you prefer that no areas appear transparent in your objects, select None.

The Color Tolerance setting works in tandem with the White and Black options. This numerical control determines how close to black or white a color has to be before it becomes transparent. If you have gray shades in your images and want them to be transparent, try different tolerance settings to see how they affect your images.

Moving On

In this chapter, you learned how to change the size of an animation, how to set and lock objects in position, and how to establish an element's duration onscreen. You've been introduced to all the roll-ups with which WEB.MOVE controls object timelines and actors' paths and cel sequences. You discovered the key to importing objects from libraries and other programs, as well as how to get the most out of WEB.MOVE when exporting images and sounds.

CorelWEB.MOVE is a full-featured multimedia authoring environment, and we've only begun to scratch its surface. The next chapter is devoted exclusively to discussing the three content editors that enable CorelWEB.MOVE to produce actors, props, and sounds.

13

CorelWEB.MOVE's Object Editors

The Great Editors

When I think of great editors, at least two come to mind: Perry White and J. J. Jameson. What, you've never heard of them? How can it be that aspiring animators are not familiar with cartoon classics like Superman and Spiderman?

Cartoons Aren't Just for Children

OK, your next assignment is to put this book down, turn on the TV and watch some cartoons. Study them from an illustrator's and animator's perspective. Notice how they use backgrounds over and over again. Watch for techniques that make objects appear to move closer to or farther away from the viewer. In no time at all, you'll be "seeing" a lot more going on in cartoons than you ever realized. And you'll be applying these observations to your own animations.

In the publishing world, an editor takes raw material, a manuscript, and refines it. Authors soon learn to trust their editors. Editors keep track of the "big picture," not just the details of grammar, and make sure the whole project comes together effectively.

WEB.MOVE has its own "editors": the Wave Editor (for sound objects), the Paint Editor (for image objects), and CorelWEB.DRAW (for image objects).

There are, of course, other applications that that can be used to create images to incorporate into WEB.MOVE animations. Like a book editor working with a chapter from a freelance writer, WEB.MOVE may take some liberties with an imported object to ensure that the entire project works properly.

WEB.MOVE's editors can create objects and modify objects imported from other programs. In this chapter, we'll take an "up close and personal" guided tour of each WEB.MOVE object editor. We'll start with the Wave Editor and then proceed to the image editors: Paint and WEB.DRAW. So crank up WEB.MOVE and get ready for a whirlwind tour of the three greatest editors—from a WEB.MOVE user's point of view, that is.

The Wave Editor

In this chapter, we're assuming that you have a properly installed sound board. Let's get started. When you press the New Sound button on the toolbar, you're presented with the New Wave dialog. To begin, type in a name for your sound, and click OK. This brings up the Wave Editor dialog, shown in Figure 13-1. This editor was introduced in Chapter 12, but now we'll look at each aspect of it in greater detail.

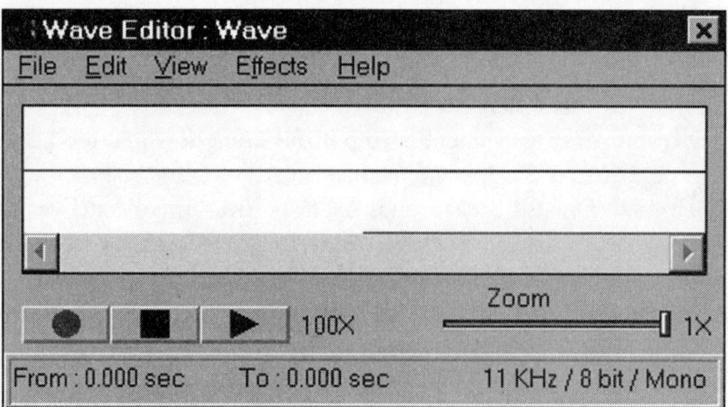

Figure 13-1: The Wave Editor contains special controls and menus full of features and options.

The Wave Editor consists of several parts: menus, editing window, playback controls and status bar. We'll discuss each item in the following sections.

Installing Sound

If you don't have a sound board and microphone installed in your computer system, you can't *create* custom sound objects. You can import sound files, but you won't be able to hear them during playback. Overall, it's not a bad idea to install a sound card. A reliable name-brand, 16-bit audio card is not very expensive. Try to find one that comes with a microphone and some software for playing audio CDs. You'll also need to think about getting speakers. Most of the cheap ones will disappoint you when you turn up the volume. Your home stereo may have a jack that allows you to hook up an auxiliary input and play through the stereo's amplifier and speakers. Or perhaps you have an old pair of speakers in a closet somewhere. In either case, you'll need the right audio cable to connect the stereo or speakers to the sound card. We're sure you'll be pleasantly surprised with the sound quality of this arrangement.

The Editing Window

First, let's load the Wave Editor with a sound file. Select File | Import | Sound from WEB.MOVE's menu bar. Use the navigational controls in the Import Sound dialog to move to a subdirectory that contains WAV files. If you are running Windows 3.x, the Windows subdirectory is a good place to start. If you are running Win95, then take a look in the Windows\Media subdirectory. If you can't find a WAV file, use the Search tools in Explorer or File Manager and look for anything that matches the *.WAV mask. For the purpose of this exercise, I'll use the CHIMES.WAV file (usually located in the Windows or Windows\Media subdirectories).

Nothing appears to have happened, because you can't see a sound object in WEB.MOVE's Animation window. The only way to select a sound object for editing is to access the Timeline roll-up. Click on the Timeline Roll-Up button at the bottom left corner of WEB.MOVE or select the Tools | Timeline Roll-Up menu option. You will see all your WEB.MOVE objects listed in the roll-up, including the WAV file you just imported. At this point, there are three ways to get to the Wave Editor. First, double-click on the object's name in the roll-up. This should bring up the Sound Information dialog, click the Edit Sound button in the lower left corner and the Wave Editor will appear. The second way uses the Edit | Object Properties menu item to access the same Sound Information dialog (with your sound selected in the Timeline roll-up). Last, a more direct approach is to select your sound and choose Object from the Edit menu. This technique immediately brings up the Wave Editor with the WAV loaded.

Just below the menus is a rectangular area that spans the entire width of the editor; this is the editing window. The editing window displays a graphical representation of the sound object currently loaded in the editor. These dots are actually plot points that map out a sound. A sound lasts for a specific time period. In the editing window, the beginning of the sound is at the left and the end of the sound is on the right (in between are the components that make up your particular sound object). The dots farther away from the black line, which horizontally bisects the editing window, represent sounds that are louder than those closer to the line. So the dots plot a sound according to time (horizontally) and volume (vertically). Initially, the Wave Editor displays the entire wave file in the editing window, no matter how much time it spans. If you cram a minute's worth of sound information into this area, it's going to look like a real jumble. The Wave Editor provides a way to zoom in on a smaller portion of the waveform.

The Zoom Control

The Zoom control is located under the editing window on the right side of the editor. This control is a slider. In its default position, the knob is all the way to the right. You'll notice the label 1X next to it. This means you are viewing the entire waveform. Drag the slider knob to the left slightly and release the mouse: the dots move. Keep dragging and releasing the knob, gradually moving it all the way to the left. It might remind you of an army of marching ants. By dragging the slider, you increase the scale at which you view the waveform. Now the 100X label, way off to the left of the slider, makes some sense. So if the waveform is 100 times larger, how come you can't see it? Well, at the same time the Wave Editor was zooming in, it also moved the view to the beginning of the sound.

Because most sounds start off low in volume, there are no plot points to see. Use the scroll bar and buttons under the editing window to move to the right: plot points will soon appear. Figure 13-2 shows the CHIMES.WAV file in the Editing window at 100X zoom.

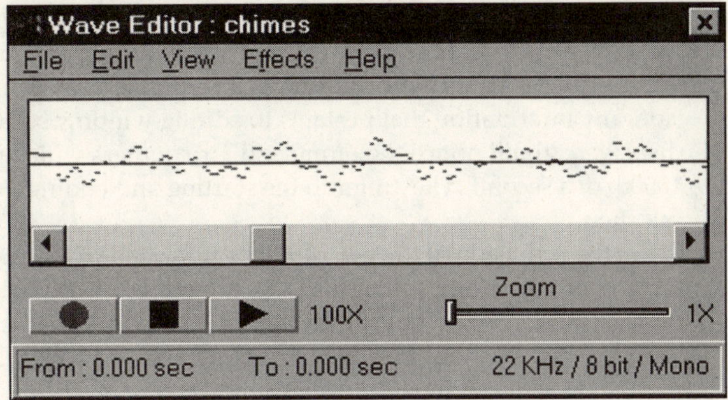

Figure 13-2: When you use the Zoom control you can magnify a waveform in order to edit it with greater precision.

When you modify a sound by changing a characteristic or adding a special effect, you are not limited to affecting the entire sound. You use the editing window to select portions of the waveform to apply your changes. If you want to work on just a small section of the sound, use the Zoom control to get in very close. Now, click your mouse in the editing window at a starting position and drag it right or left to an ending position, then release the mouse. A specific time period of the sound object has now been selected and will be acted upon by other Wave Editor functions. For instance, if you press the Play button, only the selected portion of the sound will play back. This is a useful technique for testing out what portion of the sound you have selected.

Tip

Setting the Zoom control at the 100X position may be overkill. At this magnification, selecting the entire contents of the editing window may amount to such a minute part of the waveform that it will play back like a simple clicking noise. Nothing's wrong with the Wave Editor: adjust the Zoom control's slider to a position closer to the middle and try your selection again.

Wouldn't it be helpful if you could tell exactly where you are when you click and make selections in the editing window? The Status Bar will let you do just that.

The Status Bar

At the very bottom of the Wave Editor you'll find the status bar. The Wave Editor's status bar contains two types of information. On the left side, any information that pertains to editing window selections is displayed. You'll notice the From: and To: counters which read out to 1000th of a second. They refer to the starting and ending points of a selection.

On the right side of the bar, you'll be informed of the specific characteristics of the loaded sound file. There are three characteristics displayed, each separated by a forward slash. The first characteristic is the Sample Rate, which can be one of three settings: 44 KHz, 22 KHz, or 11 KHz. KHz is the abbreviation for kilohertz, which is a way of measuring sound waves. Usually, the higher the sample rate, the more accurate the sound reproduction.

The second item, in between the two forward slashes, is the *Sample Size*. This will be either 8- or 16-bit and refers to the volume "resolution" of the sound. The higher the Sample Size, the more accurately the changes in volume can be reproduced, resulting in a higher quality of sound reproduction.

The final characteristic displayed is the *Channel* setting. Your sound object can be either *Mono* or *Stereo*. A mono sound file has only one channel of information, whereas a stereo file has two channels in which to store and deliver sound information to your sound card, which in turn sends this information to your speakers. Stereo is generally considered better, but only if the sound file was originally recorded in this mode. Consider also that a stereo file is storing two times more information than a mono sound file. This means the stereo file is taking up two times more disk space, too. As you'll see later in this chapter, it's easy to switch from stereo to mono. If you find you really don't notice much difference between the two, go with mono. Figure 13-3 shows the positions of the various items found on the status bar.

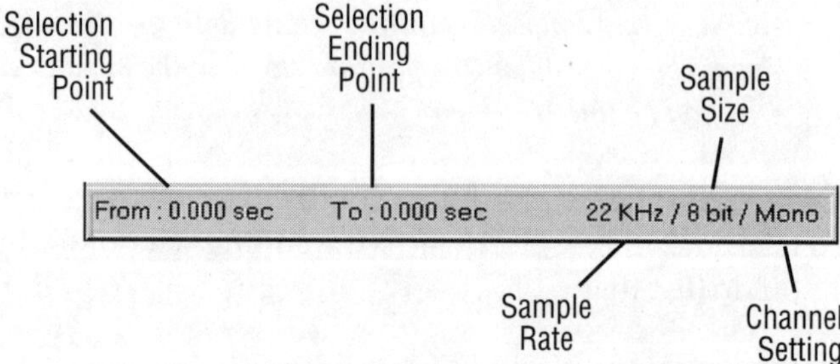

Figure 13-3: The status bar reveals much information about a sound object.

The Playback Controls

The last three controls on the Wave Editor are shown in Figure 13-4.
These are handy buttons used to facilitate playback or recording of
sounds. The three controls are off to the left of the Zoom slider and right
above the status bar. The first button, with the red circle on it, is the
Record button. If you have a microphone hooked up to your sound card,
then turn it on (most mikes have an on/off button on them) and press
Record. Speak directly into the mike for a few seconds—"testing 1, 2,
3"—is pretty universal if you can't think of anything else to say. As soon
as you are finished speaking, press the *Stop* button, the one with the
black square on it. To hear the recording you just made, press the last
button for *Play*.

*Figure 13-4: The playback controls are simple yet effective. With them you
record, stop, and play a sound object.*

That's it for the visual controls on the Wave Editor. Let's have a look at
what's hiding under those four menus at the top.

The File Menu

Under the File menu are four options. Each is explained below.

Apply Changes

When you modify a sound file, your original sound file is not overwritten until you choose Apply Changes. At this point, your original sound
object is permanently altered. Reserve using this option until you are
sure that the modifications are exactly as you desire.

This option has the same effect as pressing the Play button.

Stop

This menu choice causes the playback of the sound file to cease. It is
identical in functionality to pressing the Stop button.

Exit

When you have finished modifying your WAVE file, choose Exit. If you have made changes that have not been saved by using the Apply Changes selection, you will receive a message notifying you of this fact. Choose Yes if you want all current changes saved. Select No when you want to discard any modifications made and retain the original WAVE object. If you wish to continue editing the WAVE in the Wave Editor, choose Cancel.

The Edit Menu

All five choices listed under the Edit menu assist you in working with the waveform in the Editing window.

Undo

If you alter a WAVE file and decide you don't like the results, immediately choose Undo to remove the effect of the last command. This is true for all functions, except selecting the entire waveform and choosing Cut or Delete. If you accidentally make this error, choose File | Exit and press No at the request to save changes to the WAVE object. If you have issued the Apply Changes command, your sound will include all modifications made to that point. Otherwise, your sound will revert to the state it was in before invoking the Wave Editor.

Cut

Using the Cut option removes any currently selected portion of the WAVE from the editing window and places it on the clipboard. You can then use the Paste function to add the cut portion back into the editing window at another location.

Copy

Copy works much like Cut, except that it doesn't remove any portion of the sound object from the editing window. Any part of the WAVE copied to the clipboard can be pasted back into the Editing window wherever desired. Every time you use the Copy command, you are replacing the previous contents of the clipboard.

Paste

Use Paste to take any sound information stored on the clipboard and place it back into the editing window at another location. The pasted material will be inserted into the editing window to the right of the cursor position.

Select All

When you want to apply a special effect or perform a function on the entire sound file, use the Select All command first. The entire waveform will be highlighted.

The View Menu

There are only two choices available on the View menu. They are available when you have a stereo sound file loaded. They control what waveform information is displayed in the editing window. Both are toggle-switch options—they are either on or off.

Left Channel

Select this option to see the waveform information recorded on the left channel.

Right Channel

Turn this option on to see the sound data stored in the right channel of the WAVE file.

Neither of these settings has any effect on how changes are applied to the sound. If only the right channel is visible and a characteristic is changed, that change will be applied to the left channel as well.

The Effects Menu

All of the options under this menu are used to modify or enhance your sounds.

Change Characteristics

It was mentioned in the previous section discussing the status bar that a WAVE file has specific characteristics that define its dynamic range and inherent quality. These characteristics can be altered through settings found on the *Change Wave Characteristics* dialog, shown in Figure 13-5.

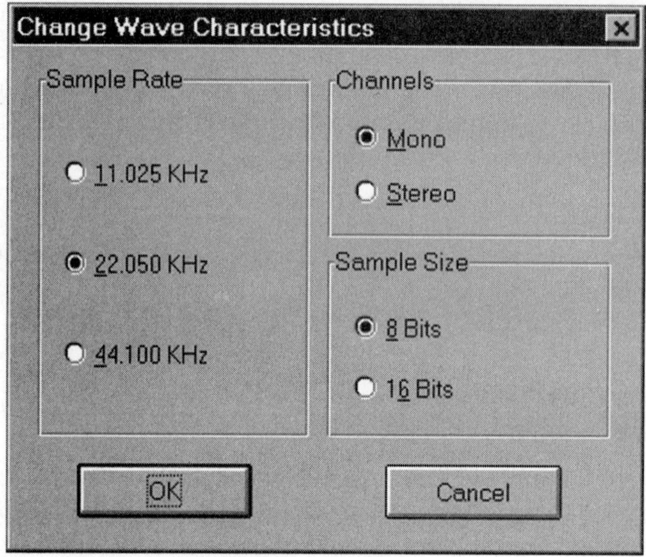

Figure 13-5: All the basic characteristics of a sound can be altered in the Change Wave Characteristics dialog.

The boxed area labeled Sample Rate refers to the frequency range of the particular sound file. The three choices are 44.100 KHz, 22.050 KHz, and 11.025 KHz. Although the larger number indicates that more data is being captured, recording through a microphone and common sound board negates any advantage of using the higher Sample Rates. Stick with 11 or 22 KHz, unless you have special recording equipment.

In the section marked *Channels*, you can choose to save your sound in Mono or Stereo format. Unless you have special sound equipment, setting the Channels selector to Stereo will not provide any advantage in sound quality.

The final setting in this dialog is titled Sample Size. The options are either 8 Bits or 16 Bits. This setting controls the amount of "resolution" available for a sound's volume range. 16 bits provides twice the amount of data to capture detailed sound than 8 bits does. However, we were unable to record anything with the Wave Editor when set to 16 Bits.

When in doubt, it's best to leave all the settings at their default values of: 11.025 KHz, Mono, and 8 bits.

Silence

This is a great way to remove some sound data and create silence in its
place. Basically, you're creating a pause. Select a portion of the sound
wave in the editing window and select Silence to wipe out any sound
data in the selected area. If you do not make a selection, the Silence effect
will be applied to the entire sound, and you'll end up with no sound at
all. To get your sound back, immediately select Edit | Undo.

Fade Up

Selecting this option calls the Fade Selection Up dialog box, shown in
Figure 13-6. There is only one parameter requested: Maximum Level.
This effect takes the selected sound data and lowers the volume level at
the left end of the selection to zero, gradually raising the volume to the
level you set. The range for this setting is 0 to 100, with the default set to
100, or full volume. If you do not make a selection before invoking this
command, the entire sound will be affected. Use this effect to make
sounds increase in volume as they play.

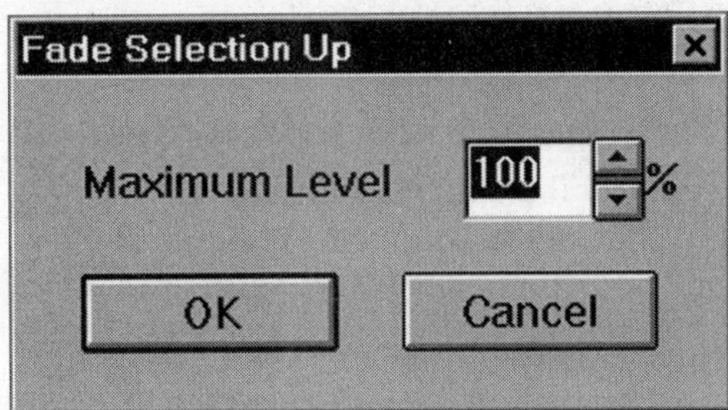

*Figure 13-6: Set the Maximum Level for the Fade Up effect in the Fade Selection
Up dialog box.*

Fade Down

This command is the opposite of Fade Up. It takes a sound and gradually
fades it out to the Minimum Level you set in the Fade Selection Down
dialog. The range for this setting is 0 to 100. The default is 0, which
means no sound. As with most effects, if you do not make a selection in
the editing window first, the entire file will be altered.

Amplify

When a sound is not loud enough (and this is usually the case when using a basic sound card and microphone for recording), use the Amplify menu option to access the Amplify Selection dialog shown in Figure 13-7. By changing the Amplification control to a number higher than 100, you are raising the volume. A number below 100 acts to lower the sound's volume.

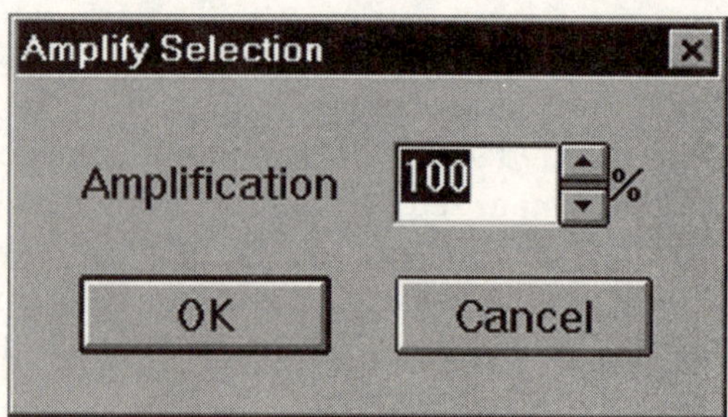

Figure 13-7: Raise the volume of a sound by setting the Amplification level higher than 100.

The range for this setting is 0 to 10,000. You will find that numbers higher than 400 or so will cause the sound to become very distorted. If you don't want to change the volume level of the entire sound object, select the portion you want to alter in the editing window first.

Reverse

Reverse is very cool. It takes the highlighted sound and flips it, so that it plays in reverse. Great for making normal sounds into spacey sound effects.

Echo

This effect adds a tinge of echo to your selected sound. If you want your WAVE to sound like it was recorded in a big empty room, add some echo. This effect is a little subtle, so you may have to apply it several times before you get it just right.

This brings us to the close of our Wave Editor tour. Now you are familiar with all the tools needed to record and modify your own sound objects. The next section turns attention to MOVE's own Paint Editor.

The Help Menu

Use the options under this menu to access various parts of the online Help.

The Paint Editor

CorelWEB.MOVE comes equipped with its own bitmap editor for creating actors and props. Compared to full-fledged bitmap editors, like Corel's PHOTO-PAINT, WEB.MOVE's editor contains rudimentary tools for drawing and selection. However, the editor offers some tools that other paint programs don't. The first is the ability to link more than one image into a sequence and allow you to edit each image. The second is the famous *morphing* function. Morphing allows you to take two images and create intermediate images, which gives the appearance that the first image is "melting" into the second.

There are two ways in which the Paint Editor is invoked. The first is by selecting Insert New | Actor or Prop from the Edit menu. The second is to press either the New Actor or New Prop tool. Next, choose CorelWEB.MOVE 1.0 as the Object Type in the New Actor or New Prop dialog.

The Paint Editor consists of two distinct parts: the Painting window and the toolbox. The Painting window, shown in Figure 13-8 is the area where you create your actors and props. Let's first focus on the many elements of the toolbox.

The toolbox is a persistent window which contains various tools used to paint on or select items within the Painting window. If you are experienced with bitmap editors, most of the tools will be familiar. The top portion of the toolbox contains 13 drawing and 2 selection tools, 3 color selectors, and a line width selector. Under these items is a palette of the 12 most recently used colors, and below that the cel counter and scroll bar. Figure 13-9 shows the toolbox with these major items labeled. Each of these tools and selectors is discussed in the next section.

Figure 13-8: The Painting window is like an artist's canvas: you create your images on it.

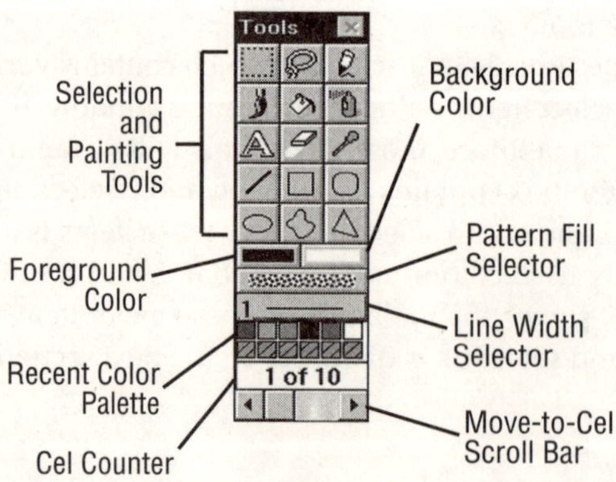

Figure 13-9: The toolbox houses the most commonly used tools needed to create images.

Marquee Tool

The Marquee tool is one of two tools used to make selections in the Painting window. Once you have made a selection, you can then perform some action, such as moving, copying, or applying an effect.

The Marquee tool makes rectangular-shaped selections. Simply place the cursor into the Painting window and select it by dragging diagonally across the area you want to select it. The perimeter of the selection area will be highlighted by a dotted line. The status bar will now display the X and Y coordinates of the upper left corner of the selection. Also included is the selection width and height, in pixels. Both statistics are enclosed in parentheses.

To reposition a selection, move the pointer inside the selection area: the cursor changes to a four-headed arrow. Click and drag the selection, releasing the mouse button when you are happy with the new position. To deselect an area and merge its contents with the underlying image, click on any white space outside the dotted line.

Lasso Tool

The Lasso is the other selection tool. Use it for free-form selections. To use the Lasso tool, click and drag around the area you want selected. When you release the mouse button, the Lasso tool will automatically complete the selection area by drawing a straight line that connects with the starting point.

All the functionality of the Marquee tool also applies to the Lasso tool.

Pencil Tool

The Pencil tool is used to draw free-form lines. It's simple to use: click and drag in the Painting window. If you use the left mouse button, you draw pencil lines using the current foreground color; if you draw with the right mouse button, you create lines in the current background color. You can change the width of the lines drawn with the Line Width Selector button. These settings are explained further on in this section.

Brush Tool

The Brush tool is very versatile. This tool paints lines using various shaped *brushes*. You can choose between square, round, or other shapes. These brushes come in various sizes, so the Line Width Selector will have no effect on this tool.

To select a brush's shape, double-click on the Brush tool button. The brush shape pop-up palette, shown in Figure 13-10, will appear. Click on a brush shape and draw in the Painting window. Like most of the drawing tools, dragging with the left button creates brush strokes in the foreground color; dragging with the right button gives you brush strokes in the background color.

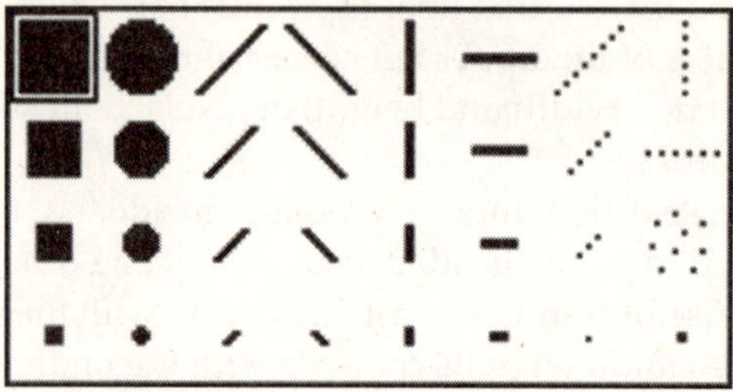

Figure 13-10: Double-click the Brush tool and choose from the preset selection of brush shapes in the pop-up palette.

Paint Bucket Tool

The Paint Bucket tool fills solid areas of an image with the currently selected color and pattern. After the Paint Bucket tool is pressed, the cursor changes to a bucket spilling over. The active area of the cursor is the lowest point of the spilling paint; click this anywhere in the Painting window and that area will fill with color. You can use either the right or left mouse button to vary the fill color.

When a fill is applied, it affects all contiguous pixels of the same color as the one you clicked. To illustrate, draw a complete circle in the center of the Painting window, select the Paint Bucket tool and click in the white area surrounding the circle. The color will flood the area but not fill the inside of the circle. Press Ctrl+Z to remove the fill color. Now remove a small portion of the circle outline with the Eraser tool (this tool is discussed further on in this section). Reapply the Paint Bucket fill and notice that the inner area of the circle also floods with color. This is because there were no pixels of another color to "hold off" the fill. To further illustrate the Paint Bucket function, click on the pixels that make up the circle outline: all the pixels that make up that outline will change to the fill color.

Spray Can Tool

The Spray Can tool is similar to an airbrush. You use either the left or the right mouse button to spray color in the Painting window. The size of the spray and the rate of color applied are controlled by settings found in the *Air Brush Settings* dialog, shown in Figure 13-11. To access the dialog, double-click on the Spray Can tool in the toolbox.

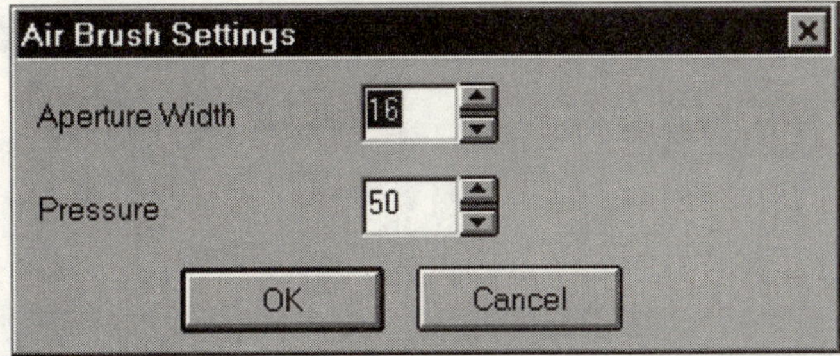

Figure 13-11: The Air Brush Settings dialog contains controls used to change the effect of the Spray Can tool.

The two settings in this dialog are Aperture Width and Pressure. Aperture is the size of the spray. This is measured in pixels. The shape of the spray is always a circle; the number you choose is the radius of that circle. Aperture width has a range of 1 to 300.

The Pressure setting affects the density of color sprayed on the image. This is also measured in pixels. If you set the pressure to 10 and click once, there should be approximately 10 colored pixels sprayed within the area of the circle, whose radius is determined by the Aperture Width setting. The longer you hold the mouse button, the more color will spray into the circle. If you continually hold the button down, without moving it, eventually the entire area of the spray circle will become filled with color pixels.

The range of the Pressure setting is between 1 and 750. You can use either the right or the left mouse button to control whether the foreground or the background color is sprayed.

 Text Tool

There are many situations when adding text to an animation is necessary. The Text tool can use any font installed in Windows to create text in the Painting window. You can change the font, size, or other aspects of the type style that is used in the image. All of these changes are made from the Font dialog, shown in Figure 13-12.

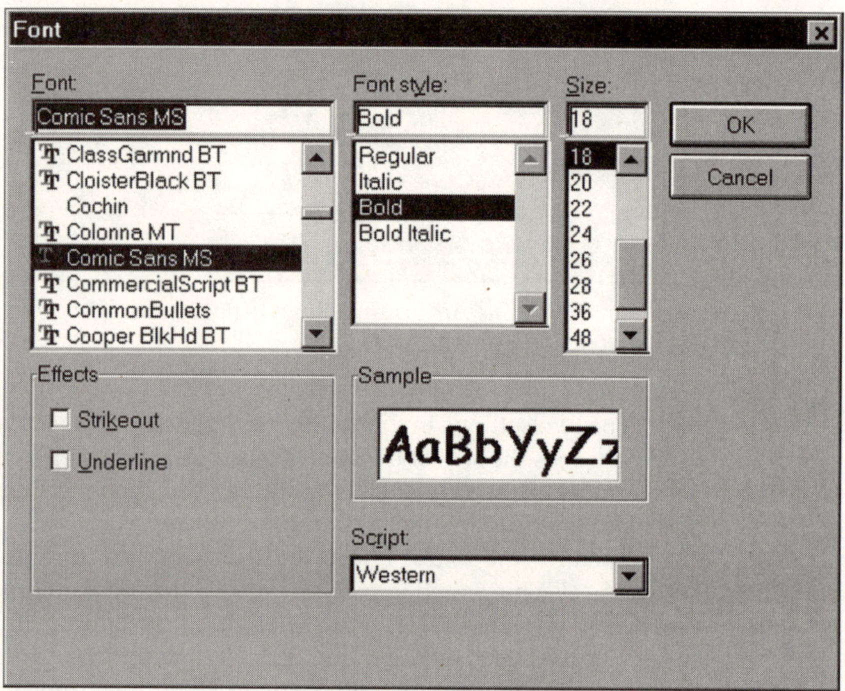

Figure 13-12: Within the Font dialog you can choose the font, the style, and other options of the text applied to an image.

There are two ways to gain access to the Font dialog. The first method involves double-clicking the Text tool icon. For example, click an insertion point in the image and type your text. Do not move the cursor or click anywhere else in the window. Immediately, double-click the Text tool icon. The Font dialog box appears. Any changes made to font attributes are applied to the text immediately after pressing OK in the Font dialog box. If you double-click on the Text tool before you plant the Text tool in the Painting window, all changes made in the Font dialog will be applied the next time you use the text tool. The second way to access the Font dialog is to select Options | Font.

While the dialog is open, you can choose a new font from the Font listing or apply an attribute, such as Bold or Italic, from the Font Style list. Changing the size is as easy as changing the number in the Size list. Additionally, you can select Strikeout or Underline from the Effects options. As you work in the Font dialog, the Sample window will display an example of the text with all currently selected attributes.

The color of text is determined by the current foreground color. You can change the color of text while you are entering it in the Painting window by changing the current foreground color. When you are happy with your text, click anywhere in the Painting window and the text will be permanently merged into the rest of your image.

 Eraser Tool

Click the Eraser tool and drag in the Painting window to remove parts of your image. The color that the Eraser leaves behind is always white. To remove only a particular color used in the Painting window, hold down the Ctrl key while dragging: the Eraser toggles into Color Eraser mode. As long as the Ctrl key is held down, the Color Eraser removes only the current foreground color. All other colors remain.

You cannot change the size of the Eraser tool. It always stays the same size, even when you're working at higher zoom levels. When you want to make smaller erasures, as small as four pixels at a time, work in x8 zoom view. Be careful not to double-click on the Eraser tool! This is a shortcut that clears the entire contents of the Painting window.

 Color Pick-Up Tool

The Color Pick-Up tool resembles an eye dropper and is used to select colors from the image in the Painting window and assign them to the foreground and background colors. When you click with the left button, the chosen color becomes the foreground color. Click on a color using the right mouse button: the chosen color becomes the current background color.

 Line Tool

The Line tool is used to draw straight lines. Simply click a starting position in the Painting window, drag the mouse button, and release it when you have reached the desired end position. The Paint Editor will create a straight line between the two points.

Holding down the Shift key constrains the tool to make vertical or horizontal lines. Using the left mouse button creates lines in the foreground color; using the right mouse button draws lines in the current background color. To change the thickness of the line, use the Line Width control, explained further on in this chapter.

Rectangle Tool

All the rest of the drawing tools in the toolbox can be classified as *closed shape* tools. They draw complete shapes which can be either filled or not. Additionally, the width of a shape's outline can be modified with the Line Width Selector. The first of these tools, the Rectangle tool, draws rectangles or squares. To start a rectangle, click a point in the Painting window for the first corner. Drag the crosshair pointer diagonally to the position of the final corner and release the mouse button. To draw a square, hold down Shift while drawing. To create rectangles filled with the currently selected color and pattern, double-click the Rectangle tool icon in the toolbox. You will see all the closed shape tools change to reflect the *fill* state.

Rounded Rectangle Tool

The Rounded Rectangle tool works the same as the regular Rectangle tool, except it draws rectangles with rounded corners. The radius of the round corners cannot be changed.

Oval Tool

The Oval tool is used to draw ovals and circles. Start an oval by positioning the cursor where you want the oval to start, then drag diagonally and release the mouse when the oval is the size and shape you desire. To make perfect circles, hold down Shift while dragging with the Oval tool. Changing borderline width, colors, and pattern fills is the same as with the Rectangle tool.

Curve Tool

You draw free-form shapes using the Curve tool. This tool is used very much like the Lasso selection tool: simply click and drag out a shape. When you release the mouse button, the Paint Editor draws a straight line connecting the ending and starting points. As with most of the other tools, you can use either mouse button to draw curves. Double-clicking will toggle the Curve tool between filled and unfilled modes.

Polygon Tool

The Polygon tool creates shapes with straight lines. Click a starting point, then click anywhere you want a corner for your shape. When you are finished, double-click the mouse to draw a line between the first and last corner points. All the options that apply to the other closed shape tools also apply to the Polygon tool.

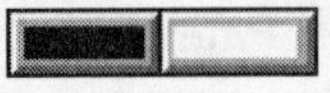

Color Selectors

There are two Color Selector buttons, which are side by side. The left-hand button determines the Foreground color; the right-hand button controls the Background color. When you press and hold down either of these buttons, the Color Palette pop-up window is displayed. (See Figure 13-13.) Drag the cursor over to the palette and release the mouse button over any of these colors. This action selects that color and places it on the appropriate Color Selector control.

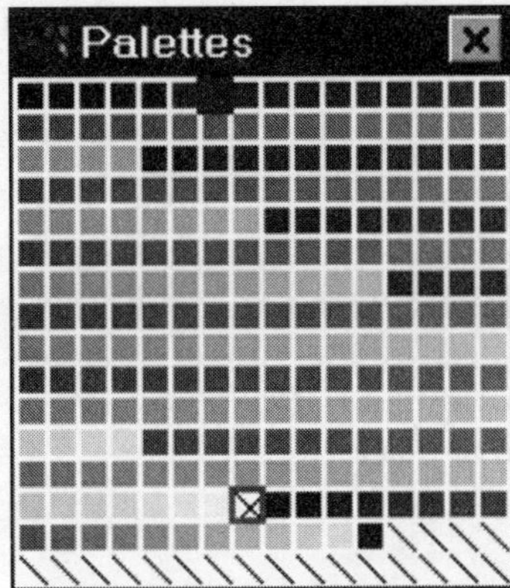

Figure 13-13: The Color Palette pop-up presents all the colors that can be assigned as a foreground or background color.

The Color Palette is detachable from the toolbox. To detach it, drag the cursor across any one of the four edges of the pop-up window. You will see a hollow rectangle when the palette is separated from the toolbox. Drag the palette to a convenient position and release the mouse button. The Palettes window will now persist onscreen, allowing you to select colors more quickly.

With the Color Palette visible, you can easily select a new foreground color by clicking on a color with the left mouse button. To select a new background color, click with the right button. Look closely at the Color Palette: you will see that the current foreground color is highlighted with a blue border and the background color is highlighted with a red border.

In the upper left corner of the Color Palette is the Control Menu which activates a drop-down menu. The Move command allows you to reposition the window, although dragging it by the title bar is certainly easier and more convenient. Selecting the Close command will remove the

Palettes window from the screen. The final menu item is Sort Palette; it has a submenu with three choices. Sorting the palette does not change the colors contained on the palette. There is no way to add or delete colors in the Paint Editor's Color Palette. The Sort option simply displays the colors in different orders so that it is easier for you to find a particular color. The three sorting schemes are based on different color models, explained below:

- RGB—This stands for Red, Green, and Blue. These are the three primary colors used to display all colors on a computer monitor. Every color you see is made from various combinations of the three primaries.

- Gray Scale—This arranges the colors according to the percentage of black the colors contain. Black is the first color and white is the last.

- HSB—This stands for Hue, Saturation, and Brightness. Hue is a pure base color. Saturation is a measure of how much gray the color contains, thus how dull it is. Brightness is a measure of how close a color is to white or black.

 ### Pattern Fill Selector

Closely related to the Color Selectors is the Pattern Selector. It, too, offers a pop-up palette when pressed and held down. You can drag this palette and tear it off to separate it from the toolbox. As shown in Figure 13-14, it offers a choice of 36 patterns that can be used for painting and filling. The default pattern is solid color. The other patterns range from simple lines: diagonal, vertical, and horizontal; bricks and checkerboards; and others that resemble tile roofs and tire treads.

The patterns are two-color schemes. The two colors used are those of the current foreground and background. As you change these colors, the pattern changes and the Pattern Selector also reflects the changes. Of interest is the difference that using the left or right mouse button has on filled shapes when a pattern is selected. Try it out. You'll have fun experimenting with all the patterns and color variations.

Figure 13-14: The Pattern Fill pop-up offers a variety of patterns that can be applied in the Painting window.

Line Width Selector

We have mentioned that the thickness of straight lines and border strokes for closed shapes can be altered via the Line Width Selector. Press and hold down this icon to call up the Line Width pop-up menu, shown in Figure 13-15. Unlike the previously discussed pop-up windows, this one does not tear away from the toolbox. Select from one of the nine preset line widths. They are numbered 0 through 8. The number denotes how many pixels wide a line is. Although Corel says line number 0 is supposed to be a one-pixel-wide dotted line, we were not able to create any dotted lines with this setting.

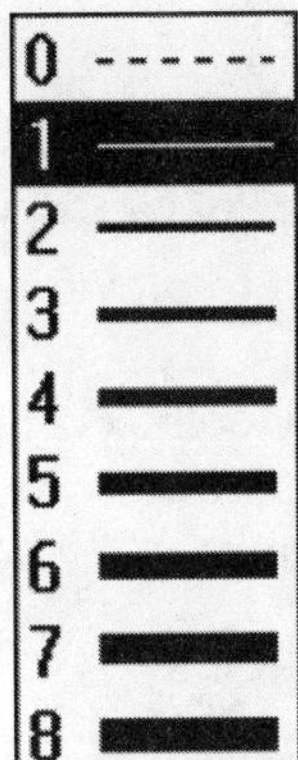

Figure 13-15: The Line Width Selector serves up a choice of preset line widths that affect straight lines and shape borders.

Recent Color Pick-Up

These two rows of squares make a convenient place to select colors you have recently used in the Painting window. Each time you select a color from the color Palette or by using the Color Pick-Up tool, that color is added to the first position in the first row. Should you need a color you know you have already used, look to the Recent Color Pick-Up and click on it with the left or right mouse button. This will load the color as the foreground or background color.

The Recent Color Pick-Up adds each successively chosen color to the palette. If you should pick the same color twice but not in succession, Paint Editor will not add a duplicate swatch of the same color to the palette. Rather, it will rearrange the color swatches and always place the last selected color into the number 1 position. When you fill the palette with 12 different colors and select a 13th, it is inserted into position 1 and all the other colors slide over one slot, pushing out the color in position 12 to make room.

Cel Counter

The Cel Counter displays the current cel number and the total number of cels in the actor. When you have a new actor, this area will display *1 of 1*. This means you are working on cel 1 of a one-celed actor. Referring to this counter is the only way to keep track of where you are in a multiceled actor project. If you are in the Paint Editor working on a prop, this area is blank.

Move-to-Cel Scroll Bar

Click on this scroll bar to move to the next or previous cel in the actor. If you want to preview what your actor will look like when played back, hold down the right arrow button. If you want to preview it in reverse, hold down the left mouse button.

And so, our dissection of the Paint Editor's toolbox comes to an end. But there's still a consideration of the Painting window to go. Plus, there are some real goodies hiding under those menus.

The Painting Window

The title bar of the Painting window displays the name of the object you are working on. Under the title bar are various menus that allow access to many options and functions. Each of the menus and their submenus are discussed thoroughly in this section. At the very bottom you'll see a status bar that displays the X and Y coordinates of your drawing or selection tool and the current zoom level.

The File Menu

Apply Changes   When you modify an actor or prop, your original images are not overwritten until you choose Apply Changes. At this point, your original object is permanently altered. Reserve using this option until you are sure that the modifications are exactly as you desire.

Page Setup   Selecting this option calls up the Set Size dialog. There are two controls: Horizontal and Vertical. Use these to set the desired width and height of the image area of the Painting window. The range of acceptable numbers is 100 to 1000, in either of these text boxes. Setting these much larger than the size of your Animation window is usually not recommended. The only case might be when creating a prop to be used as a background. In this case, you want the image to be larger than the Animation window's image area.

Apply & Exit   This option is grayed out until the Paint Editor recognizes that you have made a change in the Painting window that needs to be saved. Choose this when you are finished in the Painting window and want to return to the Animation window. This immediately saves the current state of the image and places the object you were working on into the Animation window.

Exit   Use Exit when you want to leave the Paint Editor. If you have made modifications to the image that have not been saved by using the Apply Changes command, then you will see the Close Paint Window dialog. This prompts you to save the changes made. Press Yes if you want the current state of the image saved and placed into the Animation window. Click No to revert the image to the last saved state, or select Cancel to return to the Paint Editor and continue working on the object.

The Edit Menu

Undo   Undo removes the effects caused by the last action applied to the image. Beware! There are some instances where Undo is not available—such as applying any of the functions found under the Effects menu to all the cels rather than to a selection. Another instance where Undo is ineffective is after merging a selection area to the underlying image. If you make a mistake and find the Undo command is not operable, exit from the Paint Editor without applying any changes. If you have issued the Apply Changes command, your image will include all modifications made to that point. Otherwise, the image reverts to the state it was in before invoking the Paint Editor.

Keep Paint   Keep Paint is a way of saving the image in the Painting window, up to the point when you issue the command. This may sound a lot like the Apply Changes command but is technically different. Apply Changes saves all the changes made to the object and prepares to transfer your object back into the Animation window. Keep Paint merely saves the image in the Painting window and has no effect on what is actually saved and later transferred to the Animation window. Think of Keep Paint as a temporary place-marker. When you have something you like, choose Keep Paint. You'll see the usefulness of this command when teamed with the capabilities of the next item found on the Edit menu.

Revert Paint   If you have used the Keep Paint command to save a particular state of the image and wish to discard any subsequent changes, use the Revert Paint command. This returns your image to the state it was in when the Keep Paint command was performed.

Cut   The Cut command is only enabled when you have made a selection. Issuing this command removes the selection from the Painting window and places it on the clipboard. The clipboard contents can be retrieved and placed back into the window by using the Paste command.

Copy   Copy is also grayed out unless you have made a selection first. Selecting Copy will place the contents of the selection area onto the clipboard where it can be retrieved later. The contents of the selection area in the Painting window are left intact. Every time you use the Copy command, you are replacing the previous contents of the clipboard.

Paste   To retrieve image data that is on the clipboard, choose Paste. The pasted information will be placed as a selection in the middle of the Painting window. Move it where you desire and click anywhere outside of the selection to merge it with the rest of the image.

Delete   Delete is very similar to Cut, except the contents of the selection are not placed on the clipboard. Delete permanently removes the selected material. If you delete something by mistake, immediately select Undo.

Insert Cels   To create a multiceled actor, choose Insert Cels. This calls up the Insert Cels dialog, shown in Figure 13-16. This command, along with the following two on the Edit menu, only apply to actors. They are not applicable when editing prop objects.

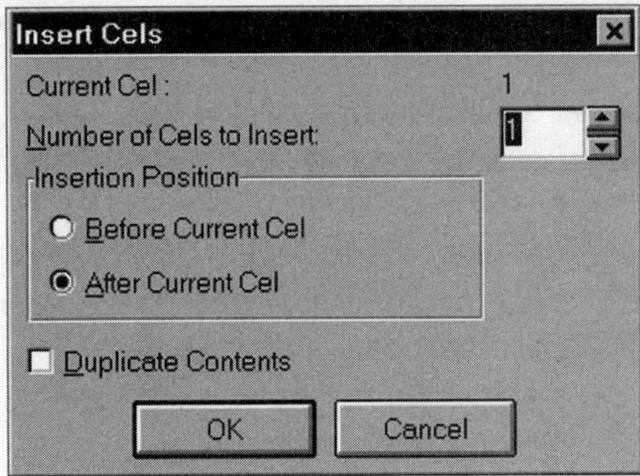

Figure 13-16: Use the Insert Cels dialog to control the insertion of more cels into an actor object.

The first item on the dialog identifies the number of the Current Cel. The current cel is the cel you were on when you selected the command. Insert the number of additional cels into the Number of Cels to Insert text box. You can control where these cels are inserted, relative to the current cel, by choosing Before Current Cel or After Current Cel in the Insertion Point boxed area. The final control is a check box option labeled Duplicate Contents. Turning this on causes all the inserted cels to contain the same image as the current cel. This is very useful if the new cel's images are very similar to the contents of the current cel.

After you have made your choices and pressed OK, you are returned to the cel you were working on in the Painting window. Check out the Cel Counter on the toolbox; it has been updated with the new total of cels in the actor.

Delete Cels   To delete cels from your actor, move to the first cel to be removed and select Delete Cels from the menu. The Delete Cels dialog appears and informs you of the Current Cel number. This dialog allows you to enter the total number of cels to be removed in the Number of Cels to Remove text box. When you press OK, the number of requested cels will be deleted, including the cel you were on at the start of the process. Beware, this is one area where the Undo command cannot save you!

Reverse Cels   This command reorders the cels in the reverse direction. This is useful if you want an actor's movements to appear backward.

Select All   When you want to select everything on the current cel, use this command. You can then Cut, Copy, Delete, Move, or apply one of the functions from the Effects menu to the selection.

Registration   The Registration Point is the spot on an actor used as the Path point. By default, it is in the upper left corner; however, you can change it with the Registration command. The Registration menu selection is a toggle switch; as long as the option is on, you can move the registration point anywhere you click the mouse. When you have the point in the location you desire, reselect Edit | Registration to complete the process. If you are completely finished editing your actor, you can also choose Apply & Exit.

The Effects Menu

This menu houses lots of hidden treasures that are very useful in creating cool effects. Except for Morph Cel, all the rest can be applied to all the cels in the actor or just to a selection area. If you have chosen an area first, then the menus will change to read "selection" rather than "all cels." Remember that Undo is only available if you apply an effect to a "selection" and not to "all cels."

Morph Cel   Morphing is perhaps the coolest of all the effects the Paint Editor performs. Morphing takes two images, we'll call them the *source* and the *target*, and creates a predetermined number of intermediate cels. These in-between cels contain gradual and progressive blends of the two images.

In order to use the Morph Cel command, you must have an actor that consists of two or more cels. If your actor only has one cel, use the Insert Cels command (discussed earlier in this section) before selecting Morph Cel. Before we delve into the Morph dialog, a few words about source and target images is in order.

I like to think of the Morphing process as a sandwich: the source and target are the bread, and the blended cels WEB.MOVE generates are the meat in the middle. With this delicious picture in mind, you'll always remember that the source and target images are the first and last images in your morphed sequence. The cel you are viewing when you choose the Morph Cel command is always the source image. The very next cel in your actor will be the target image. It's important to set your actor's image sequence up *before* you choose the Morph command. When the target image is blank, the actor is morphed into invisibility. If your actor has no target image, you can copy one from the Animation window (or another bitmap editor) and use the Painting window's Paste command to insert it into the actor. Now, it's time to tackle the mighty morphin' dialog box, shown in Figure 13-17.

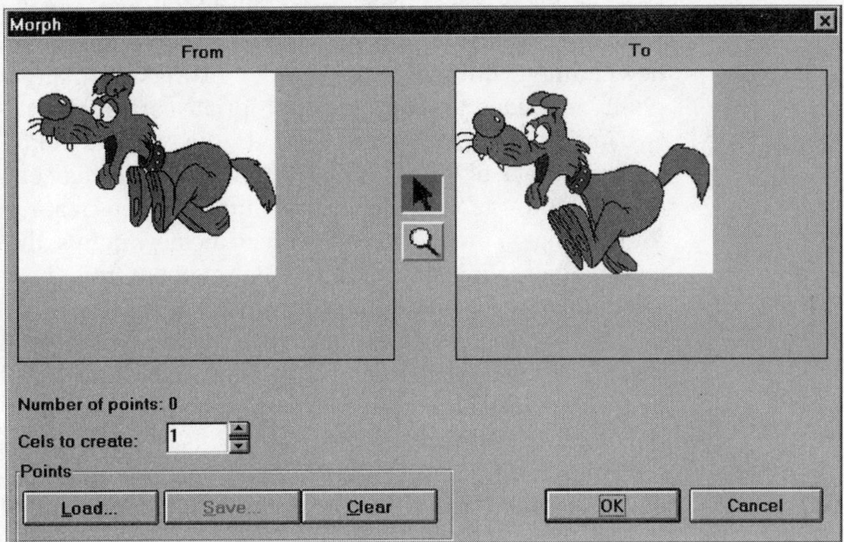

Figure 13-17: The Morph dialog displays the source and target images and offers options to control the morphing process.

The source and target images are displayed in the From and To picture boxes. The two tools between the images are the Pick tool and the Zoom tool. To keep from getting confused with the Pick tool in the Animation window, I like to call this the Control Point tool. You'll see why in the next few paragraphs. The Zoom tool allows you to zoom in or out of either the From or To image. Click with the left mouse button to zoom in and with the right button to zoom out. The Zoom tool also allows you to pan the image by dragging the cursor around in either image. This is useful when you've zoomed in and need to bring parts of the image not currently visible into the picture frame.

Select the Control Point tool and click in the From image. A red square appears. A corresponding red square appears in the To image. A readout of the X and Y coordinates for the point is displayed in the lower left of each image. These matched pairs of points set up a correspondence between the two images. They tell WEB.MOVE which pixels should be blended. As you can see from the X, Y readout, the default is that the same pixels in the same position of each image should be morphed. You can create more exciting morphs by varying the position of the control point in the To image. This causes WEB.MOVE to actually distort and warp the intermediate images. To move any control point, drag it to a new location with the Control Point tool. Make as many sets of control points as needed to set up the appropriate correspondences between the two images. As you set control points, the Number of Points indicator will keep track of the amount. Up to 1,000 points may be applied, although this is a very impractical number when creating small images for viewing on the Web. When you create new points, the color of existing pairs turns green, differentiating them from the currently selected control points, which are always red.

Don't be afraid to experiment with placing control points; this is the best way to understand them and create interesting morph effects. To help you manage and recreate complex control point layouts, the Morph dialog contains three buttons in the Points boxed area. To save a set of control points for reuse later, press the Save button. A dialog box appears allowing you to save a file containing information WEB.MOVE uses to recreate your points. Choose a subdirectory to store the file in and give it a name. WEB.MOVE will automatically add an .MPH extension to your file name.

To apply a set of saved control points, use the Load button. Another dialog appears requesting the name and location of an MPH file: select one and press OK. If the physical dimensions of the original image used to set up the control points was different than the new image, the points will be scaled to fit into this new image. Should you already have control points set when you press the Load button, WEB.MOVE asks if you want these discarded. If not, press Cancel, save these points to a new MPH file, then start the Load procedure again. If you decide that the current set of points just isn't working out, press the Clear button to remove all control points.

The final setting needed is the number of cels you want inserted to create the morphing effect. Enter this number into the Cels to Create control. WEB.MOVE allows a maximum value of 200, but, again, this is far too many to ever utilize in Web graphics. Try to keep the number in the single digits if possible. When everything is set, click OK to start the morphing process.

When you have the Always Prompt for Imaging Options feature turned on in the Animation window's Tools|Options menu, you will be presented with the Import Imaging Options dialog. At this point, you can make further choices regarding the rendering of the morphed images. (See the Tools Menu section in Chapter 12 for details on the Import imaging options.) Next, a window with a progress indicator appears. This window informs you of the progress of the morphing function. Remember that keeping things simple will help speed up the morphing procedure. The lower the number of control points and requested cels, the quicker things will move along. When the morphing process finishes, you are returned to the Painting window, and the Cel Counter will be updated to reflect the new total of cels. To preview the actor's morphing sequence, hold down the right scroll button to quickly cycle through all the cels.

Presto! The magic of morphing is revealed. Not only will you be the envy of your block, but you'll also have some really cool animations to use in your Web pages. But wait, there are more special effects ahead — read on!

Tint All Cels   Tinting, either all the cels or just a selected area, is the process of adding a color to the image in the Painting window. This selection offers a submenu of two choices: Toward Foreground and Toward Background. Choosing the first option causes the currently selected foreground color to be added to your image. Selecting the latter choice adds the current background color to the image. The process doesn't add much color to the image, so it may be necessary to choose this option several times to get the exact effect you desire.

Anti-Alias All Cels   Painting with pixels often causes a noticeable jaggedness in your images. A common technique to mitigate this undesirable look is adding pixels to the harsh edge of an object. These new pixels are varied in color. The colors are determined by averaging the background and image color. Strategically adding these pixels fools the eye into seeing softer or smoother edges. Remember to make a selection first or you will apply Anti-Alias to all your actor's cels—this cannot be undone!

Rotate All Cels   Rotating cels or selections is a common task in the course of animation chores. For your convenience, WEB.MOVE offers a submenu of five choices: 90° Clockwise, 90° Counterclockwise, 180°, Free, and Custom. (If you have not made a selection, the Free choice is grayed out.) The first three are pretty self-explanatory.

The Free option causes WEB.MOVE to display a bounding box with four corner handles around your selection. Grab one of the handles and drag it in a circular motion to adjust the angle of rotation. Release the button when you want to redraw the selection with the new rotation applied. The selection will not be merged with the underlying image until you click somewhere off the selection.

Selecting Custom brings up the Rotate By dialog box, shown in Figure 13-18.

Figure 13-18: The Rotate By dialog allows you to rotate "by the numbers."

This dialog offers numerical control over the rotation process. You insert the amount of desired rotation in the Degrees text box and then choose whether you want the rotation direction to be clockwise or counterclockwise. Click OK, to perform the rotation, or Cancel if you've changed your mind.

Tip

Using the Free and Custom options will cause a degradation around the edges of small objects. Choosing Anti-Alias several times may help to lessen the problem.

Mirror All Cels   Flipping images and selections is child's play with the Mirror function. You have two choices presented on the submenu: Vertically and Horizontally. Mirroring vertically flips the image from top to bottom; mirroring horizontally causes the image to flip from left to right.

Scale All Cels   You can resize the images on your cels by choosing the Scale menu option. If you have made a selection, there are two ways to resize that selection: Free and Custom. Free displays four corner handles that allow you to drag the selection to a new size. Release the button when you reach the desired size. Holding down Shift while dragging causes a proportional resize. Otherwise, you are free to resize the selection more or less in one direction than the other.

The Custom choice presents you with the Scale By dialog. It has two numeric controls: %Vertically and %Horizontally. You can insert any number from 5 to 200 in these text boxes. Putting 200 in each box would make the object grow twice its original size in each direction. If you want the image to be scaled more in one direction than another, enter different numbers in each control.

Be careful when scaling images larger—they will become very jagged. Depending on the image, using Anti-Alias may help. Also, reducing an image's size will cause it to lose detail because pixels must be discarded during the process (which means that once you scale an image down, you should leave it that way and not try to enlarge it again).

The Options Menu

Zoom   To make more detailed edits to your image, like erasing small imperfections left after using the Rotate or Morph effects, you'll need to see the pixels enlarged as much as possible in the Painting window. This is where the Zoom menu saves the day. The submenu offers four zoom levels: x1, x2, x4, and x8. The default is x1, or actual size. Each succeeding choice displays the pixels two times larger than the preceding. You can resize the Painting window while in any view other than x1 to see more of the image. If you still can't see all your image, use the scroll bars on the bottom and the right side. Should you forget what zoom level you are at, look to the status bar under the scroll bar to remind yourself.

Font   This is another way to access the Font dialog box shown earlier in Figure 13-12. Review the preceding section on the Text tool to get the lowdown on using this dialog.

Onion Skin   Don't cry! This option has nothing to do with onions. It refers to a type of translucent drawing paper called onionskin. You might be more familiar with the term *tracing paper*. Because it's important for an animator to see the preceding or following drawing in an actor's sequence, tracing paper comes in very handy.

WEB.MOVE offers a digital version of this important viewing capability. By default, this feature is turned off. Using the submenu you can turn it on and decide whether to view the Previous Cel or Next Cel in the sequence. When Onion Skin is enabled you not only see the contents of the current cel but also a very light copy of the previous or next cel—whichever you have chosen from the flyout menu. Selecting None turns the feature off once again.

The end has finally come. Not only for the features of the Painting window but also for the entire WEB.MOVE Paint Editor. Congratulations, you are now ready to go on to the last of the editors: WEB.DRAW.

The WEB.DRAW Editor

The last editor that can be used inside of the WEB.MOVE authoring environment is CorelWEB.DRAW. There are many more drawing and editing features available in WEB.DRAW than in WEB.MOVE's Paint Editor, and the good news is that all these powerful tools are at hand for creating actors and props. Because WEB.DRAW's feature set and capabilities are covered in Chapters 6 and 7, there are only a few areas regarding WEB.MOVE and DRAW's special interaction that need to be considered here.

When you select CorelWEB.DRAW 1.0 as the object creator for props and actors, you are launching a version of WEB.DRAW that is slightly different than the one you see when launching it under other circumstances. In fact, there are even minor changes in WEB.DRAW depending on whether you are creating a prop or an actor. As you see in Figure 13-19, the most significant difference is the presence of the Cel Select roll-up. This special-purpose roll-up is not present when you create a prop. There are other differences, too. They are found under the File and Edit menus. But, let's start off taking a closer look at the roll-up.

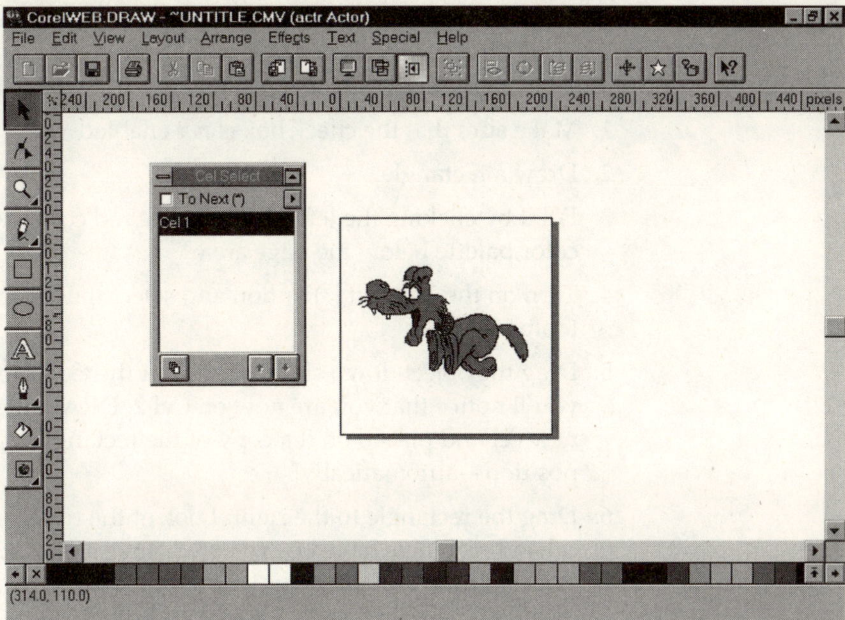

Figure 13-19: The Cel Select roll-up is used for making multiceled actors in WEB.DRAW.

The Cel Select Roll-Up

This roll-up is the key to creating multiceled actors. It works like all the other roll-ups discussed in Chapter 12, with the exception that it cannot be removed from the screen.

The first item you'll notice is the *Cel List* window: it always contains at least one cel, and the currently selected cel is always highlighted. To move from one cel to another, click on the cel's name in the cel list, or use the Up or Down arrow button, in the lower right corner. When there are too many cel names to fit in the window, scroll bars will appear, allowing you to access any cel in the list. The Actor Preview button, in the bottom left corner, brings up a previewing window. This window runs through your actor's cels so that you can see how it will appear when placed in WEB.MOVE's Animation window. When you are finished previewing, press the OK button.

At the top left corner of the roll-up you'll see a check box labeled To Next (*). This little gem comes in handy for automating small animation projects. Starting with a one-celed actor, here's how it works:

1. Make sure that the check box is *not* enabled.

2. Draw a rectangle.

3. Fill it by clicking the left button on the red color swatch in the color palette below the page area.

4. Turn on the To Next (*) option and select the Pick tool from the toolbox.

5. Drag the object down slightly. Look at the Cel Select roll-up and you'll notice that you are now on Cel 2. DRAW has created a new cel and placed on it a copy of the rectangle in the new position—automatically!

6. Drag the rectangle to the right. Look at the roll-up. Another new cel and rectangle have been created. Take a moment to look back at Cels 1 and 2 to see the trail of red rectangles that has been left.

7. Go back to Cel 3 and select the red rectangle with the Pick tool. Left-click on the yellow color swatch in the color palette. A yellow rectangle is now placed, in the exact position of the previous rectangle, on Cel 4.

8. Select the Shape tool from the toolbox and click on the yellow rectangle: small corner nodes will appear. Grab any node and drag it to create a round-cornered rectangle. When you release the mouse button, Cel 5 (with the modified rectangle) will be created.

9. Again, select a node with the Shape tool and drag it to the midpoint of one of the rectangle's sides. This will produce a perfect circle. Release the mouse button and Cel 6 (with a yellow circle) is created.

10. Now press the Preview button and see what you've created in just a few minutes. Your red rectangle should move down to the right, turn yellow, and then change to a circle. The To Next function is too cool! Just make sure you turn the option off before modifying any of the objects you have created. If not, you'll automatically be making lots of new shapes and cels.

Tip

If you can't see the color fills while working in WEB.DRAW, press Shift+F9 or select View | Wireframe.

The Pop-Up Menu

The majority of this roll-up's power comes from functions found on the pop-up menu in the upper right corner. The menu contains 10 options. The first four options deal with adding or deleting cels in the cel list.

New

Selecting this menu option causes the Append New Cels dialog to appear. Enter the number of new cels desired into the Number of Cels text box. Press OK, and the specified number of cels will be added at the *end* of the cel list. You can add from 1 to 100 new cels.

Insert Before

This option brings up the Insert New Cel dialog box. Enter the desired number of new cels you wish into the Number of Cels text box and press OK. The new cels will be placed into the cel list *before* the cel on which you were working when the command was issued.

Insert After

This option also calls the Insert New Cel dialog box. The difference here is that the new cels will be placed into the cel list *after* the cel on which you were working.

Delete

To remove cels from your actor, select Delete from the menu and enter the amount you wish to remove in the Number of Cels text box. The currently selected cel, and as many after it as are needed to fulfill the requested amount, will be deleted from the cel list. WEB.DRAW will not allow you to delete all the cels—you must have at least one.

Move to

Any selected objects can be moved from the current cel to any other cel in the list. After you have chosen the Move to command, the cursor will change to an arrow with "To?" on it. Click on the cel where you want the objects moved and the objects will disappear from the current cel and be transferred to the requested cel.

Copy to

Selected objects can also be copied from the current cel to any other cel in the list. After you have chosen the Copy to command, the cursor will change to the familiar "To?" arrow. Click on the cel you want the objects copied to and the objects will be transferred to that cel—leaving behind the originals.

Make Common Before

This function makes special copies of selected objects and places them on as many cels, *before* the current cel, as you specify. You enter the desired number of cels to be affected in the Make Common Object dialog. For example, if you are on cel 9 and enter 2 cels to affect, WEB.DRAW will place copies on cels 8 and 7.

These special copies are "clones" of the original object. If you change the color of the original object, the clones will change, and vice versa. You can sever the "parent-child relationship" of a clone by changing either its position or its color.

Make Common After

This command performs in the same way as Make Common Before, except that it creates cloned copies on the specified number of cels after the current cel. WEB.DRAW keeps track of the number of cels before and after the current cel. It will not allow you to enter an invalid number into the Number of Cels text box.

Options

The ability to view objects on cels before and after the current one was noted in the Paint Editor section dealing with the Onion Skin feature. WEB.DRAW has an improved implementation of Onion Skin; it's controls are found on the Cel Options dialog, shown in Figure 13-20.

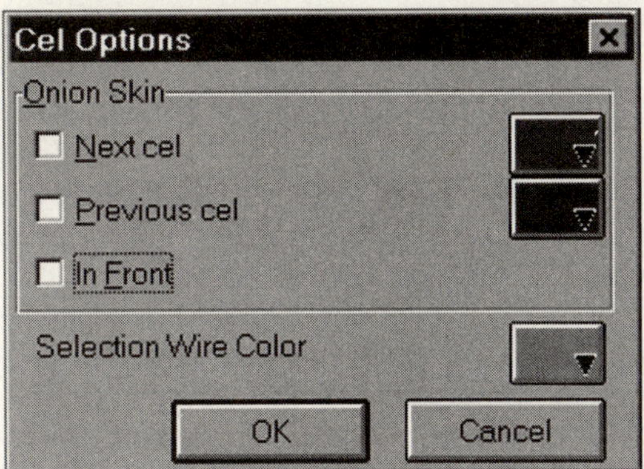

Figure 13-20: The Cel Options dialog controls the Onion Skin feature of WEB.DRAW.

WEB.DRAW allows you to see objects on the Next Cel, Previous Cel, or both. This is definitely a nice touch. DRAW does not show a tinted rendering of the next or previous cels, as the Paint Editor does. Rather, it shows a wireframe version of objects on adjacent cels. This could get pretty confusing; however, you can control the color of these wireframe objects. Press one of the color selector pop-up controls on the right side of the dialog and click on any color in the palette: the wireframe of the appropriate cel will change. You will also notice that the colors of the cel names in the Cel Select roll-up change to match. There is another option in the Onion Skin area of this dialog: In Front. When you set this on, the entire wireframe outline of shapes from the adjacent cels appears in front of objects drawn on the current cel.

The last control on the Cel Options dialog is Selection Wire Color. This setting helps to identify when the selected object is not on the current cel. If this sounds confusing, it is—until you realize that WEB.DRAW offers the capability to keep objects selected after moving to another cel. At this point, any changes you make are being applied to the object on the previously active cel—not the one you have moved to. To help you sort this all out, Corel allows you to assign a color for displaying a wireframe rendition of a selected object that is not on the current frame. By the way, this feature only works when you are in editable preview mode.

Preview Cels

This has the same effect as pressing the Preview button on the Cel Select roll-up. Check out the section on the Preview window, earlier in this section.

This covers all the visual differences in WEB.DRAW's interface when used as an object editor for WEB.MOVE. Now let's turn attention to the differences on the File and Edit menus.

The File Menu

There are only three items that are different on the File menu. They are discussed below:

Update

Update is equivalent to the Paint Editor's Apply Changes command. One difference is that the actor or prop is immediately rendered and placed into WEB.MOVE's Animation window. WEB.DRAW is not shut down—it is still running behind MOVE's window. This is a two-edged sword. On the one hand, you have quicker access to DRAW when you want to edit the object. But on the other hand, each running copy of WEB.DRAW eats up Windows's memory resources. At some point, your system will get unstable and possibly crash, because there are too many copies of WEB.DRAW running.

Save Copy As

At any point, you can save the work you have created in WEB.DRAW to several file formats. When the Save Drawing dialog appears, you can choose from CorelWEB.DRAW File (*.cdw), CorelDRAW! File (*.cdr), or Pattern File (*.pwg).

If you Save As a CDW file or a CDR file, the individual cels are saved as separate pages. The neat thing about these multipaged CDW or CDR files is that you can import them into a WEB.MOVE-launched instance of WEB.DRAW and each page will create individual cels again. Saving as a PWG file is useful only if you want to use the currently selected cel's image as a Full Color Pattern fill in WEB.DRAW.

Exit & Return To

This renders all of your cels, shuts down WEB.DRAW, and places your actor or prop back in WEB.MOVE's Animation window. WEB.DRAW will always ask you if you want your object updated. Yes is generally the right answer, unless you want to discard the modifications you have made to the object. In that case, press the No button. Cancel will return you to WEB.DRAW to continue your editing session.

The Edit Menu

There is one menu choice that is unique to WEB.DRAW while creating an actor:

Select Across Frame

This is very similar to the regular Select All option, except that it selects every object on every frame. When you want to move or delete everything from every cel at the same time, this is a handy option to have around.

Moving On

At last, all there is to know about CorelWEB.MOVE's interface and its Object Editors has been told. The mysteries of the Wave Editor have been revealed, including how to record your own Wave files. You know how to cut and paste portions of sounds and add special effects, like echos and fades. You can even turn a sound into Martian-speak by applying the reverse command.

You've seen just about every nook and cranny of the Paint Editor and the many tools and functions that can be applied to bitmap objects. And let's not forget that ever popular Morph command.

You now know how to harness WEB.DRAW's powerful feature set to create quick and easy multiceled actors. You've gone through all the basics and nailed all the fundamentals. So it's time to flex your WEB.MOVE muscles and get some hands-on experience with all the tools you've learned about. Turn the page and let's get started creating Web graphics.

14

Creating Animations— Three Projects

The moment of truth has arrived! It's time to put the knowledge you've amassed about CorelWEB.MOVE to work. In this chapter, you'll find three "real-life" exercises that make use of a variety of WEB.MOVE's features. As you work through each exercise, you'll gain hands-on experience using actors, paths, and .Move library files; importing groups of files; and publishing to Corel's Barista format. You'll use the Timeline, Cel Sequencer, and Library roll-ups. Not only do these exercises demonstrate WEB.MOVE's tools and features, they also illustrate practical techniques you can easily modify to create unique animations for your own Web pages. The instructions for the three lessons are arranged in numbered steps. Intermingled with the instructions are comments that explain why we must undertake certain steps.

What You'll Need

The primary item you'll need for completing the exercises in this chapter is knowledge of WEB.MOVE. The instructions are written as if you are familiar with WEB.MOVE's tools and interface. This helps to move along at a pretty good pace. If you find some terms or instructions confusing, go back to the previous chapters that discuss WEB.MOVE's tools and interface to refresh your memory.

Additionally, you will need access to a CD-ROM drive. The first two exercises—the Web Page Banner and the Spinning Globe—use files contained on this book's Companion CD-ROM. The last exercise calls for two .MLB files found on the CorelWEB.GRAPHICS Suite CD. The last exercise, which incorporates Barista, assumes that you are familiar with CorelWEB.DESIGNER. This is necessary, so that you can create some simple HyperText Markup Language (HTML) documents. If you're not sure about this process, review the chapters in this book that discuss WEB.DESIGNER to learn the simple steps required to complete the exercise.

Without further ado, let's bring on our first group of actors. Let's give a big WEB.GRAPHICS round of applause to the guys and gals from GalacticMall.com: "The out-of-this-world source for all your space-age computer gadgets!"

Web Page Banner

Many Web pages use banners. These are generally small graphics—very often animated—used to quickly capture viewers' attention. The idea behind these little gems is that viewers will be intrigued enough by the flashy banners to follow hypertext links to other Web pages or sites. The following exercise demonstrates one way to develop such a banner.

This Web page banner project contains one prop and two actors. This project is intended to be published as an animated GIF file, but publishing to Barista will work, too. However, there are no special effects that warrant the use of Barista and the "higher overhead" it requires.

Are you ready to blast off for GalacticMall.com? Put on your crash helmet (just in case we encounter subspace GPF fields). Here we go:

1. Start WEB.MOVE, then choose Edit | Animation Info from the menu bar. In the Animation Information dialog box, change the Window Width to 350 and Height to 84. Change the Number Of Frames to 16. Then click OK.

2. Choose Tools | Options and click on the Imaging Options tab. Make sure the two boxes—Always prompt for imaging options and Perform high-quality dithering—are checked. Keep the other settings at the defaults and click on OK.

3. Put this book's Companion CD-ROM into your CD-ROM drive. In WEB.MOVE, choose File | Import | Prop. When the Import Prop dialog appears, navigate to the XXX\BANNER subdirectory. Select CompuServe Bitmap (*.gif)from the List Files of Type drop-down list, click on the file named GALACTIC.GIF, then click on OK.

4. When the Import Imaging Options window appears, make sure the box Perform high quality dithering is turned on and None is marked as the Transparent Color option, then click on OK.

5. After the prop has been imported, click on the Timeline Roll-Up button (or choose Tools | Timelines Roll-Up). Your screen should look like Figure 14-1. To keep this prop from being moved, you must set a special property option. Double-click on the prop's name in the Timeline roll-up.

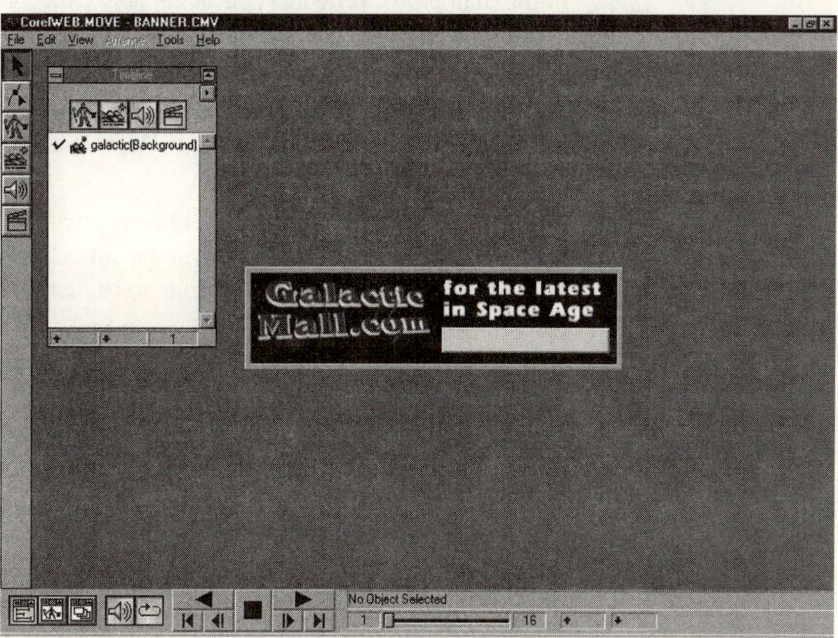

Figure 14-1: After the prop has been imported and the Timeline roll-up displayed, here's how your animation window should look.

6. In the Prop Information dialog, turn on the Background option located just above the Cancel button, then click on OK. Although it isn't readily apparent, this prop can no longer be repositioned. Try moving it and see what happens.

Next we're going to add the actors to this scene. As you can see so far, this is going to be an advertisement of sorts. The yellow rectangle at the bottom will display the word *software*. The word will spell itself out—one letter at a time, pause, and then march off the right side of the scene. If you want the animation to play over and over again, be sure to turn on the loop button at the bottom of WEB.MOVE's window.

Notice in step 1 we set the number of frames to 16. This will give us just the right number of frames to allow the word (which is 8 characters long) to spell out, go through its paces, and then disappear before starting the sequence over again. Let's add the first actor.

7. Move to frame 2. Choose the New Actor button from the toolbox. In the dialog box, type in **Type** as the new Object Name, and select CorelWEB.MOVE 1.0 from the Object Type list. Click on OK.

8. When the Paint Editor appears, double-click on the Text tool; the Font dialog displays. Select Courier or Courier New from the list and Bold from the Font style menu. Also, change the Size to 12, and click on OK.

If you don't have either of these fonts, choose an alternative. If nothing else seems appropriate, choose the System font. You may have to experiment with different sizes to get things to fit just right.

9. Back in the Paint Editor, click the text tool anywhere in the editing window and type the word **software** in lowercase. It should resemble Figure 14-2. Choose File | Apply, then File | Exit from the Paint Editor's menu bar. The actor will transfer into the Animation window. Use the cursor to position the word in the yellow rectangle, near the left side. We'll fine-tune the position a little later.

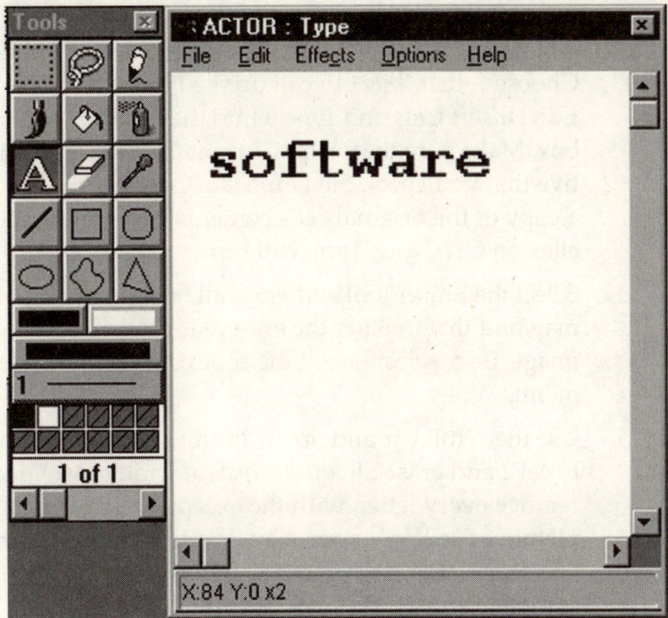

Figure 14-2: After setting the font and size in the Font dialog and then typing **software,** *here's how the Paint Editor should look.*

The next step is to make a copy of this actor. Why do you need two actors? That will make it simple to localize the two different movements of the word *software*. The first actor will handle the spelling out portion, and the second actor will carry out the marching duties.

10. Select the actor, then choose Edit | Duplicate. When the Duplicate Actor dialog appears, change the name to **TypeMove** and click on OK. A copy of the actor appears a little lower and to the right of the original.

Now the tricky part: The original actor, Type, must be transformed into a multiceled actor so that we create the spell-out effect. After that, the duplicate actor, TypeMove, needs a path to send it offscreen. Along the way, you'll adjust the positions and timelines of the two actors so they appear to be one. First, let's create our multiceled actor.

11. Select the Type actor. If this is difficult to accomplish in the Animation window, click on the name in the Timeline roll-up. Choose Edit | Object to call up the Paint Editor. Next, choose Edit | Insert Cels and type **8** into the Number of Cels to Insert text box. Make sure that After Current Cel is turned on. It is imperative that you check the Duplicate Contents option; this will place a copy of the original cel's contents on each new cel. When ready, click on OK. Now, Type will be made up of 9 cels.

12. Select the Eraser tool and erase all the letters, except the *s*. You may find that making the erasure is easier if you zoom in on the image. If so, select one of the choices from the Options | Zoom menu.

13. Use the scroll bar and arrow buttons under the toolbox to move to cel 2 and erase all letters, except *s* and *o*. Move to cel 3 and remove every letter, with the exception of *s, o,* and *f.* You get the picture now. Work your way through the cels, each time leaving one more letter than in the previous one. You should have the complete word *software* when you arrive at cel 8. Cel 9 also will contain the complete word; this is necessary to create the pause effect. When you have finished all the erasing, cycle through the cels to make sure everything is correct and then choose File | Apply and Exit from the editor's menu bar.

14. You're ready to set this actor's timeline. Expand the Timeline roll-up using the button under the right side of the title bar. Double-click on Type. When the Actor Information dialog appears, set the Exits At Frame counter to 10, and set the Start Position coordinates as follows: Horizontal 188, Vertical 54. Click on OK and notice that Type's timeline has been adjusted to end at frame 10.

15. Now we turn our attention to the TypeMove actor. Double-click on its name in the Timeline roll-up and set its Enters At Frame counter to 10 (the Exits At Frame counter should already be set at 16; if not, do so). Set the Start Position coordinates to: Horizontal 188 and Vertical 54. Click on OK.

You've set TypeMove to enter the scene at frame 10 (the last one for Type) and placed it on top of the Type actor. Having two identical actors share the same position, on the same cel, removes the chance of any "hiccup" in the animation as the first actor exits and the second enters. Play back your animation. At this point, you will see the word *software* spell out and then sit motionless, until the animation loops again. On subsequent passes, the word is erased before the sequence starts again. The next task is to set a path for TypeMove.

16. If your animation is moving, click on the stop button and move to frame 10. Click on TypeMove in the Timeline roll-up; the actor is highlighted with a dotted line around its perimeter. Click on the Path tool from the toolbox. Turn on the Allow Adding Points option on the bottom of the Path Edit roll-up. Click on the Edit button and turn on Move Frame With Point from the menu.

17. Move to frame 16 (use the Last Frame button). Click the mouse cursor in the black area, just to the right of the yellow rectangle. Figure 14-3 shows the path that is created.

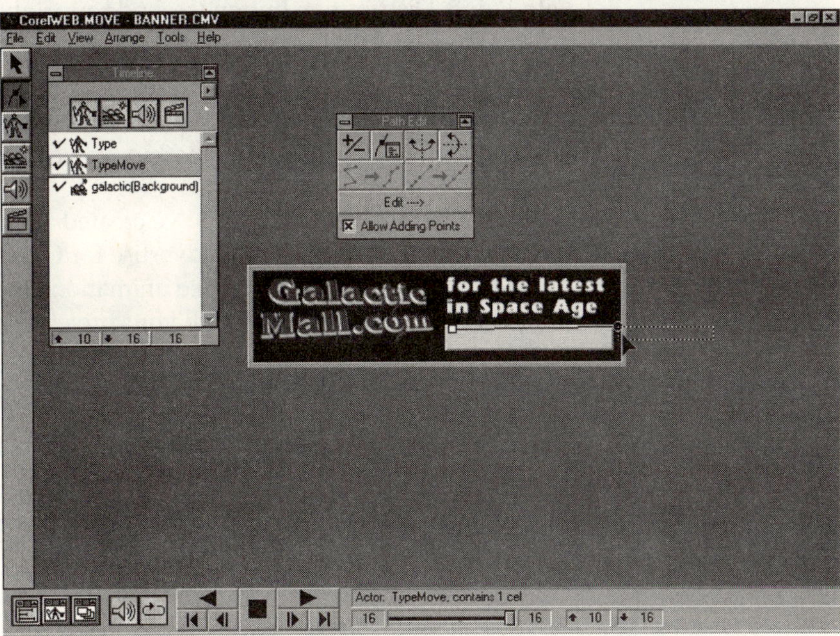

Figure 14-3: Move to frame 16 and click the mouse to create a path like this.

18. Click the Point Information button on the Path Edit roll-up (top row, second from the left) and set the Horizontal location to 344 and the Vertical to 54. Also, make sure the Loop To Here option is turned off, then click on OK.

Although TypeMove has disappeared from the screen, you should be able to see the dotted rectangle that indicates the actor has exited the scene and is out of frame. At this point, you have created a path that consists of two points. When you play your animation, the actor just jumps out of view. To rectify this, we have to add some intermediate points to the path.

19. With the Path tool active and TypeMove selected, click on the Scale Path button (top row, first on the left). Enter 7 in the Desired text box of the dialog and click on OK. Your path now has 7 unevenly spaced points.

20. To get the points distributed evenly across the path, click on the Path Points Distribution button (second row, right), several times. When you are happy with the spacing, play back your animation.

If your animation is running too fast, use the Animation Information dialog to change the Frames speed to something lower than the default of 18.

There you have it. In 20 easy steps, you've created a banner to adorn the page of any Web site that wishes to advertise for GalacticMall.com. We have included a copy of this completed animation on our Companion CD-ROM, so that you can compare it with your project. Look for BANNER.CMV in the subdirectory for this exercise.

The last thing to do is export to an animated GIF. (Make sure you save the file as a CMV before you export.) Choose File | Publish | to Animated GIF and save the GIF someplace convenient. When the export is completed, you can include the GIF file in any HTML document. Exactly how you accomplish this feat is covered in the previous chapters devoted to WEB.DESIGNER.

The Spinning Globe

Guess what? GalacticMall.com loves your ad banner! They want you to create a huge animation to include on their corporate Web site. You've made the big time, at last. They have this great concept: their logo floating in the middle of space. Now get this, circling around the logo they want the earth spinning in orbit. Cool, huh? What do you mean you can't pull it off? It's easy, all you need are three actors and one prop. Watch, we'll show you:

1. Start a new animation by choosing File | New. Press Ctrl+A to access the Animation Information dialog. Change the Animation window's size to 333 pixels wide and 333 high. Set the number of frames to 24 and click on OK.

2. Choose Tools | Options and click on the Imaging Options tab. Make sure that the boxes Always prompt for imaging options and Perform high quality dithering are turned on. Keep the other settings at the defaults and click on OK.

3. Start WEB.MOVE, then put this book's Companion CD-ROM into your CD-ROM drive. In WEB.MOVE, choose File | Import | Prop. When the Import Prop dialog appears, navigate to the XXX\GLOBE subdirectory. Select CompuServe Bitmap (*.gif)from the List Files of Type drop-down list, click on the file named SPACE.GIF, and click on OK.

4. When the Import imaging options window appears, make sure that Perform high quality dithering is turned on and None is marked for the Transparent Color option, then click on OK.

5. After the prop has been imported, press the Timeline roll-up button (or choose Tools | Timelines Roll-Up); your screen should look like Figure 14-4. To keep this prop from being moved, double-click on the prop's name in the Timeline roll-up. In the Prop Information dialog, turn on the Background option, then click on OK. There's our one prop. Now let's get that logo actor brought into the scene.

Figure 14-4: After the SPACE.GIF file has been imported, here's how your Animation window should look.

6. Choose File | Import | Actor from Bitmap File(s). When the Import Actor dialog appears, navigate to the XXX\GLOBE subdirectory. Select CompuServe Bitmap (*.gif)from the List Files of Type drop-down list, and click on the file named: GALACTYP.GIF. Select the Preview option on the right side of the dialog, and a low-resolution image of the GIF file displays. The background is black, but we want it to be transparent so that we can see the stars of the background around the logo. This is where the Import Imaging Options dialog comes in handy. Now click on OK.

7. When the Import imaging options window appears, make sure that Perform high-quality dithering is on. Make sure that the Transparent Color option is set to Black this time. Then click on OK. The object has been added to the scene in the upper-left corner and its name, *galactyp*, has been added to the Timeline roll-up.

8. Double-click on the name in the roll-up to access the Actor Information dialog. Let's change the name to something more meaningful; type in **GalacticLogo**. Change the Horizontal Start Position to 62 and the Vertical coordinate to 87. Confirm that the Enters at Frame is set to 1 and the Exits at Frame is set to 24. When all settings are correct, click on OK.

We're ready to add the spinning globe. We need two actors to accomplish the job of orbiting the floating logo. We'll call one GlobeSmall; the other we'll name GlobeLarge. Each actor will share half the duties in our project. GlobeSmall will portray the part of the earth spinning away and halfway back toward the audience. GlobeLarge will portray dear Mother Earth spinning right toward the audience and then getting smaller as she returns to her original size and position.

We've already prepared separate bitmap images of each of the cels needed to show all these changes in size; there are 24 altogether. Each actor will be made up of 12 cels. We'll first bring in the images needed to create GlobeSmall.

9. Choose File | Import | Actor from Bitmap File(s). When the Import Actor dialog appears, navigate to the XXX\GLOBE subdirectory. Select CompuServe Bitmap (*.gif) from the List Files of Type drop-down list. You see a list of GIF files starting with EARTHS01 and proceeding through EARTHS24. Click on the file named EARTHS01.GIF, and select the Preview option on the right side of the dialog. Notice that the background of this file is black. We want each black background to be transparent so that we can see the stars of the background around the globe. Here comes the neat part: With the first file highlighted, hold down the Shift key and scroll down the file list until you can see EARTHS12.GIF. Select it. All the files between EARTHS01 and EARTHS12 are now highlighted. Click on OK.

10. When the Import Imaging Options window appears, make sure that Perform high quality dithering is on. Make sure that the Transparent Color option is once again set to Black. Then click on OK. Each of the separate images is imported and a 12-celed actor named Imported Actor is added to the scene. Its name has been added to the Timeline roll-up. Click on the play button, and watch the actor spin halfway around while it gets smaller and then larger.

11. To position this actor, double-click on the name in the Timeline roll-up and set the Horizontal Start Position to 6 and the Vertical to 129. Let's take the opportunity to change the name to GlobeSmall and set the Exits at Frame setting to 12. Confirm that the Enters at Frame counter is set to 1 and then click on OK. Your animation should look like Figure 14-5.

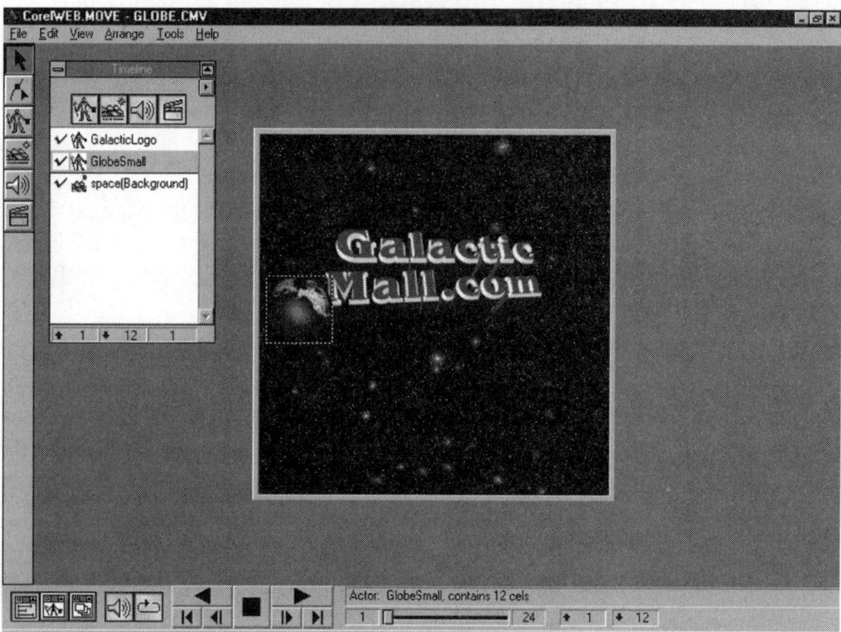

Figure 14-5: After your actor has been imported, renamed GlobeSmall, and positioned correctly, the Animation window should look like this.

The time has arrived to set GlobeSmall on its path: half of the orbit around the back of the GalacticMall.com logo. We're going to use the Path tool extensively for the next few steps. In order to help you get the orbiting motion right, we've provided a table of the path points and their coordinates.

12. Move to frame 12. Select the GlobeSmall actor, then select the Path tool. On the roll-up, turn on the Allow Adding Points option. Click on the edit button, and make sure that Move Frame With Point is turned on.

13. In the Animation window, click the cursor near the right side of the word *Galactic*. In the Path Edit roll-up, click the Path Point Information button and set the Horizontal position to 266 and the Vertical to 71. Also, make sure the Loop To Here option is turned off, then click on OK.

14. With the Path tool active and GlobeSmall selected, click on the Scale Path button. Enter 12 in the Desired text box of the dialog, then click on OK. Your path will now have 12 points spaced out across a straight path. Now it's time to select each path point and enter the coordinates from Table 14-1. Let's do the first together.

15. Move the frame slider to frame 2. You see the globe move with you and the path node that corresponds with frame 2 highlight. Click on the Path Point Information button. The dialog should read Point 2 of 12. Enter 15 for the Horizontal setting and 103 for the Vertical, then click on OK. This moves path point 2 up and to the left. Move to frame 3 and enter the coordinates from the table. Continue until you've got all the points set up as indicated. Your path should look like that shown in Figure 14-6.

Frame Number	Horizontal	Vertical
1	6	129
2	15	103
3	30	83
4	52	66
5	79	52
6	106	43
7	134	36
8	163	32
9	193	29
10	227	35
11	252	48
12	266	71

Table 14-1: GlobeSmall path coordinates.

Figure 14-6: The correct path for the GlobeSmall actor.

Take some time to play the animation through. Look at it frame by frame. Depending on your system, you may want to change the Speed setting in the Animation Information dialog. When you're done admiring your handiwork, let's move along to a point about the stacking order of your actors.

We talked a little about stacking order in Chapter 12. To see exactly how this feature works, move to frame 1. GlobeSmall covers the lower-left edge of the logo. Because we want this actor to display *behind* the logo, we have to move it lower in the stacking order. Here's how to do it:

16. Look at the Timeline roll-up; it lists GlobeSmall under GalacticLogo. Drag GlobeSmall and drop it above the GalacticLogo name. The two change places! Look at the animation window and see that the logo is now on top of the globe. The stage is now set for the final actor to make its entrance.

17. Choose File | Import | Actor from Bitmap File(s). When the Import Actor dialog appears, navigate to the XXX\GLOBE subdirectory. Select CompuServe Bitmap (*.gif) from the List Files

of Type drop-down list. Scroll down through the file list until you find EARTHS13.GIF; select it. Hold down the Shift key and scroll down the file list until you see EARTHS24.GIF; select it. All the files between EARTHS13 and EARTHS24 are now high-lighted. Click on OK.

18. When the Import imaging options window appears, make sure that Perform high quality dithering is on. Set the Transparent Color option to Black, and click on OK. The separate images are imported, creating another 12-celed actor, which is deposited in the upper-left corner of the Animation window. This time the actor is named: Imported Actor2. You'll find that its name has been added to the Timeline roll-up. Click on the Play button, and watch this actor spin halfway around while it gets larger and then smaller.

19. This actor needs to enter the scene where GlobeSmall leaves: at the right side of the animation. To position this actor, double-click on Imported Actor 2 in the Timeline roll-up and use the controls in the Actor Information dialog to set the Horizontal Start Position to 261 and the Vertical position to 117. We need to change the actor's name to GlobeLarge and set the Enters At Frame counter to 13 and the Exits At Frame setting to 24. Click on OK.

When you move the Frame slider to frame 13, you see your newest actor on the right side of the scene. Because this actor is supposed to move in front of the logo, its default position—lower in the list, therefore higher in the stacking order—does not need to be altered. Next comes the tedious task of making a path and setting its points. We'll follow the same basic procedure with GlobeLarge as we did with GlobeSmall.

20. If you're not already there, move to frame 13. Click on GlobeLarge and select the Path tool. On the roll-up, turn on the Allow Adding Points option. Click on the Edit button and confirm that Move Frame With Point is turned on.

21. In the Animation window, click the cursor near the left side of the word *Mall*. In the Path Edit roll-up, click on the Path Point Information button and set the Horizontal Location to 1 and the Vertical to 149. Make sure that the Loop To Here option is off, then click on OK.

22. With the Path tool active and GlobeLarge selected, click on the Scale Path button. Enter 12 in the Desired text box of the dialog and click on OK. Your path now has 12 points spaced out across a straight path. It's time, once again, to use the Path Point Information dialog and enter the coordinates from Table 14-2 for each point. When you have all the points altered, your path should look like that shown in Figure 14-7.

Frame Number	Horizontal	Vertical
13	261	117
14	253	146
15	236	172
16	212	190
17	184	204
18	156	215
19	125	220
20	89	221
21	56	216
22	26	199
23	8	175
24	1	149

Table 14-2: GlobeLarge path coordinates.

At last, the moment we've all been waiting for: Click on the Play button and let 'er rip! Magnifico! Bravo! A masterpiece! As a director, you may want to fine-tune your creation. If your animation is running too fast or too slow, experiment with changing the frame rate until you are pleased. If you want, compare your results with a copy of the completed space animation included on our Companion CD-ROM. Look for GLOBE.CMV in the subdirectory for this exercise.

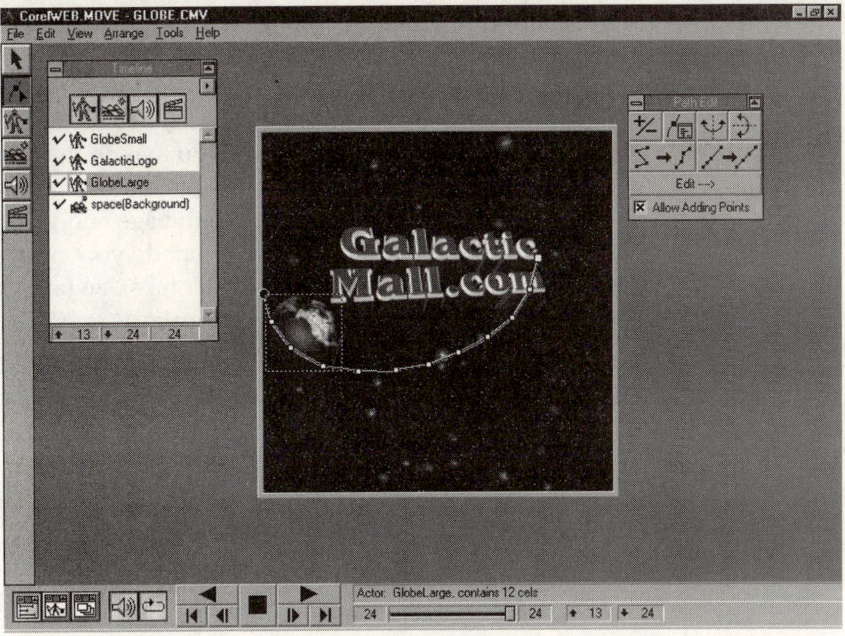

Figure 14-7: The correct path setup for the GlobeLarge actor.

I told you it would be easy! Just 22 steps, and you've created an out-of-this world animation destined to become the centerpiece for GalacticMall.com's corporate Web site.

As far as exporting this animation, you can make a .GIF or even try an Animated movie format, such as .AVI. These export choices are found under the File | Publish menu. But please, before you export, save the file as a .CMV.

A few words of warning regarding the way your exported files may display in a Web browser: An .AVI will play faster than a .GIF, but the user must click on the image each time to set it in motion; it does not loop continuously without the user's intervention. The .GIF file loops continuously, but it will be noticeably slower. There are ways to speed up a sluggish .GIF; one way is to cut down on the size of the images. If you really want to keep the image as large as possible, other strategies can improve matters; however, they are accomplished with third-party applications and utilities not included in the CorelWEB.GRAPHICS bundle. Check out Chapter 15 for more information on how we made the images used in this exercise and ways to optimize animated .GIF files.

Barista-Driven Navigation Buttons

Your last production was a stunning success. The folks at GalacticMall.com have commissioned you to redo their entire Web site. The CEO of Galactic visited a Web site with animated buttons that allowed Web surfers to jump from page to page and would really like something like that on Galactic's site. What do you mean you don't know? This is a perfect situation to use Corel's newfangled Barista technology. This is going to be a piece of cake; watch:

1. Start CorelWEB.DESIGNER and make three HTML files. The first should be named PREVIOUS.HTM and should contain two lines of text. Make sure to press the Enter key after the first line. The text should read as follows:

   This is the Previous Page
   Go to SPINNING BUTTONS

   Highlight the second line and assign a hypertext link to SPINNING.HTM, then save the page.

Tip

Although we present the names for all files in these exercises in all-capital letters, care should be taken with the exact capitalization you use in the Save and Save As dialogs. Computers that run under Windows don't have a problem with inconsistent capitalization in file names, but other computers on the World Wide Web do. Those running under the UNIX operating system are very picky. For example, a UNIX computer reads PREVIOUS.htm as different than Previous.HTM or previous.htm. The lesson here is to be careful about how you name your files and to be consistent. We prefer to type the whole name, including the extension, in lowercase.

2. Now change the first line to read:

   This is the Next Page

   Use the Save As command to save this file as NEXT.HTM.

3. Delete all your text and use Save As to name this file SPINNING.HTM. Choose Tools | CorelWEB.MOVE from the menu to launch WEB.MOVE. Alternatively, you can choose View | Applications Toolbar to display a toolbar of buttons that launch the five applications that work hand in hand with DESIGNER. Click on the first button on the left to launch WEB.MOVE. In either case, in the resultant dialog, click Open CorelWEB.MOVE.

4. When WEB.MOVE appears, press Ctrl+A to access the Animation Information dialog. Change the size of the Animation window to 52 pixels wide by 53 pixels high. Also, set the number of frames to 5.

5. Insert the CorelWEB.GRAPHICS Suite CD into your CD-ROM drive. Select Tools | Library Roll-Up or click on the Library Roll-Up button at the bottom of WEB.MOVE. When the Open Library dialog appears, proceed to step 6. If the dialog doesn't appear, continue to the next paragraph.

   If you have previously used the Library roll-up, the last .MLB file you accessed is loaded and displayed. For this exercise, we need to load a new .MLB file from the CD: Press the pop-up menu button at the upper-right corner of the roll-up and select Open Library from the menu. Now you are presented with the Open Library dialog.

6. Navigate to the CD-ROM drive, and use the controls to access the WEBMOVE\LIBRARY\3D subdirectory. Select the BUTN_#-E.MLB file and click on OK. After the file loads, the Library roll-up displays the first object in the library—1Way Down—as shown in Figure 14-8. If you don't see this object, use the pop-up menu to open the correct library file.

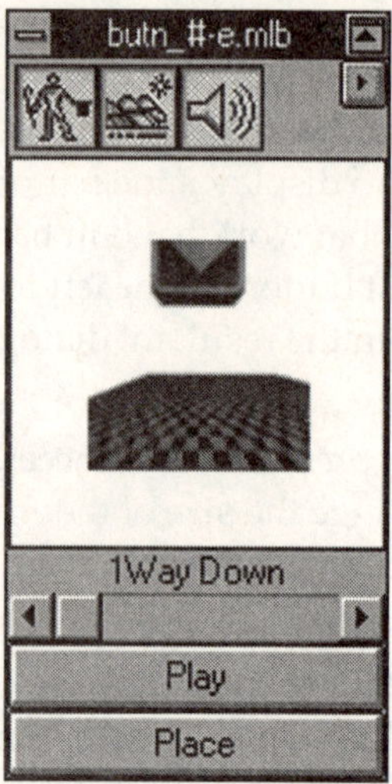

Figure 14-8: When the Library roll-up is loaded with the BUTN_#-E.MLB file, the 1Way Down object will be the first element in this library.

7. Use the scroll bar and arrow buttons on the Library roll-up to find the Cube Left actor object (it's near the end of the library). When you find it, click on Play and watch the blue button with the little house on it spin around and around. After you're satisfied that you have the right object, click on Stop Playing, then click on Place. The actor is placed in the Animation window.

8. Choose Edit | Object Properties and position Cube Left at 2 Horizontal and 2 Vertical. Because we don't want to move this actor inadvertently, turn on the Locked option, also. After you click on OK in the Actor Information dialog, your project should look like Figure 14-9.

When you look to the status line above the Frame slider, you notice that this actor is 20 cels long. However, the same 5 images play 4 times. That's why we have set the number of frames for our project to only 5 frames. When we publish our animation, the 15 hidden cels will be truncated.

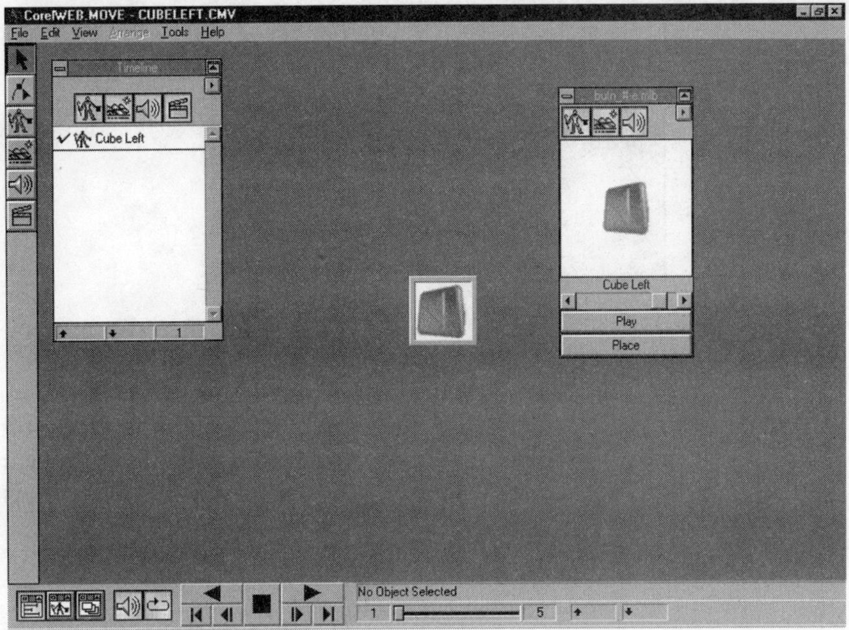

Figure 14-9: After Cube Left has been positioned properly, the Animation window looks like this.

In frame 1, Cube Left is turned slightly, and we want the animation to start with the cube facing head on. Move to frame 5, the cel we want to display in frame 1. To make the adjustments, we'll call on the services of the Cel Sequencer roll-up.

9. Make sure Cube Left is selected, then choose Tools | Cel Sequencer Roll-Up or press the Cel Sequencer Roll-Up button. When the roll-up appears, the name of the actor is in the title bar. If it isn't, click on the actor to select it. The top row of Frame numbers reads 1, 2, 3, 4, 5. The bottom row of Cel numbers matches. Click on cel number 1 to select it, then double-click on it. The number is positioned in the upper-left corner of the box. Type in **5** and click on cel number 2. The cel number under frame 1 now reads 5. Use this technique to change the cel numbers of each frame to match Table 14-3.

Frame Number	Cel Number
1	5
2	1
3	2
4	3
5	4

Table 14-3: Cube left cel sequence order.

10. Move to frame 1 to be sure it displays the head-on image of Cube Left. Now to add a cue: Click on the New Cue button in the toolbox. When the Cue Information dialog appears, change the name to **GoToPrevious.** Set the rest of the options in the dialog as follows:

    - Enters at Frame: 1

    - Exits at Frame: 5

    - Condition: If/After | mouse click on | anything

    - Action: Goto URL

    - Type: **file:///previous.htm** into the field that appears.

    Note: Double-check in Explorer or File Manager for the exact capitalization you used when you saved these files earlier. The names must match for this URL to work on servers that are running UNIX.

    When you are satisfied that all the settings are correct, press Update and then OK.

11. At this point, it is very important to choose File | Save and name this file CUBELEFT.CMV. Make sure that you remember where you store it, as we will recall it later in the project.

As long as we're in WEB.MOVE and Cube Left has been saved, we can save time and start on the next navigation button. It helps not to have to wait for WEB.MOVE to launch every time we create an object. Plus, the objects in this project share many of the same settings, so you don't have to set everything up from scratch. The easiest button to make next is a mirror image of Cube Left. We'll call it Cube Right. It will be used to call up the NEXT.HTM document.

12. Select File | Save As and name this file CUBERITE.CMV. Choose Edit | Object Properties and change the actor's name to Cube Right, then click on Edit Actor. The Paint Editor appears, with the actor displayed in the upper left corner.

13. We are going to mirror the image, but because we don't need any of the cels past number 5, let's delete those first: Move to cel 5 and select Edit | Delete Cels. Type **15** in the Number of Cels to Delete text box. Click on OK. Check the remaining 5 cels to see that everything worked properly.

If something goes wrong while you're deleting cels, select File | Exit and click on No to the request whether to update this actor in the Close Paint Window dialog. Your actor will not be altered. Double-click on the actor in the Animation window to enter the Paint Editor and start over again.

14. While still in the Paint Editor, choose Effects | Mirror all cels | Horizontally from the menu bar. Watch as each cel flips in succession. Select File | Apply and Exit. When you are back in the Animation window, click on Play and watch the button spin from left to right.

15. Once again, we have to change the order of the cels using the Cel Sequencer roll-up. Refer to step 9, if necessary, and make the changes shown in Table 14-4.

Frame Number	Cel Number
1	5
2	1
3	2
4	3
5	4

Table 14-4: Cube right cel sequence order.

16. We need to change the cue information for Cube Right. Access the Timeline roll-up and double-click on the GoToPrevious cue. Rename it **GoToNext**. Change the Goto URL text box to read **file:///next.htm**. Click on Update and then on OK. The cue's name changes in the Timeline roll-up.

17. Choose File | Save from WEB.MOVE's menu bar. Now for the last button: Select Cube Right in the Animation window with the mouse and press the Delete key. Click on OK when asked to confirm the deletion.

18. Click on the library roll-up and use the left arrow button to display the actor named Cube Home. When you have found it, click on Place. Cube Home appears in the Animation window.

19. Double-click on Cube Home in the Timeline roll-up. Change the Start Position to 2 Horizontal and 2 Vertical. Turn on the Locked option and click on OK.

20. Once again, we have to change the order of the cels using the Cel Sequencer roll-up. Refer to step 9, if necessary, and make the changes as shown in Table 14-5.

Frame Number	Cel Number
1	5
2	1
3	2
4	3
5	4

Table 14-5: Cube home cel sequence order.

Here's where we depart from the other buttons in this project. This button could call an HTML document named HOMEPAGE.HTM or something like it. However, we're going to set up a cue that's a little more exciting. This cue will play a sound file, then call up a window allowing the user to send an e-mail message through the Internet. The first step is to find the sound file we want in one of the supplied libraries.

21. On the Library roll-up, use the Open Library command to access the WEB.GRAPHICS Suite CD and find the WEBMOVE\LIBRARY\SOUND subdirectory. Click on the SOUND.MLB file. After it loads, move to the object named WOW.WAV (next to the last item). Click on Play to get an idea how the file sounds. When ready, click on Place. WOW.WAV shows up in the Timeline roll-up.

If the Loop and Sound buttons are turned on, you hear an incessant, clipped version of the WOW sound file. The reason for the clipped sound is that there is not enough time in the animation to play the entire sound. Try boosting the number of frames to 15. That number won't disturb our animation, because 15 frames is equally divisible by 5 frames: Instead of just one rotation, we'll see three complete rotations of Cube Home. Now that our sound file's incorporated, it's time to set up the cue for this actor.

22. Access the Timeline roll-up and double-click on the GoToNext cue. Rename it **WowMail.** Leave all the settings the same, except for the Actions section. Change the Goto URL text box to read **mailto:phoenix@ifu.net**. Click on Update. Next, choose the Action drop-down list and select Play a Sound. Confirm that sound WOW.WAV shows up in the drop-down list to the right. (If you had more than one sound file in your project, you could choose which you wanted to associate with this action.) Click on Insert and then on Play a Sound: WOW.WAV is added as the first item in the Actions window. Goto URL: **mailto:phoenix@ifu.net** is last. Click on OK. The cue's name changes in the Timeline roll-up.

23. We don't want the WOW.WAV file to sound until the user clicks on the button. To accomplish this, access the Timeline roll-up and click on the checkmark to the left of the WOW.WAV object. After the checkmark disappears, click on the play button; there'll be silence—until you click on the animation! Now it's time to choose File | Save As and name this file CUBEWOW.CMV.

All the actors that make up your navigation buttons are complete. It's time to get them back into the SPINNING.HTM document you created in WEB.DESIGNER. Although it's fairly easy to rearrange objects in WEB.DESIGNER, we're going to import these buttons in the order in which we want them to appear on the page. From left to right, that will be CUBELEFT, CUBEWOW, and CUBERITE. As soon as you're sure the current .CMV is working correctly and has been saved, proceed to the next step.

24. Select File | Open from WEB.MOVE's menu bar. Locate CUBELEFT.CMV (it is probably on the list of most recently used files at the bottom of the File menu) and load it. Select File | Publish | to WEB.DESIGNER. Turn on the Progressive Load and Copy class files options. Read the information in the Note area of this dialog to see if the information about copying class files pertains to you; whether it does depends on your operating

system. Details about this note are explained further in Chapter 15, under the Barista section. Click on OK. WEB.MOVE disappears as the publishing process starts. After the process finishes, a static image of the CUBELEFT button appears at the top of the HTML document.

25. Click the cursor to the right of CUBELEFT and launch WEB.MOVE again. Choose File | Open and locate CUBEWOW.CMV. Load this file, then publish to WEB.DESIGNER as you did the previous animation. Back in WEB.DESIGNER, CUBEWOW has taken its place beside the first button. Make sure the cursor is on the right side of the new button, and launch WEB.MOVE one more time.

26. Choose File | Open and locate CUBERITE.CMV. Load this file, then publish to WEB.DESIGNER as you did the previous two animations. Back in WEB.DESIGNER, CUBERITE has joined the other two buttons (see Figure 14-10).

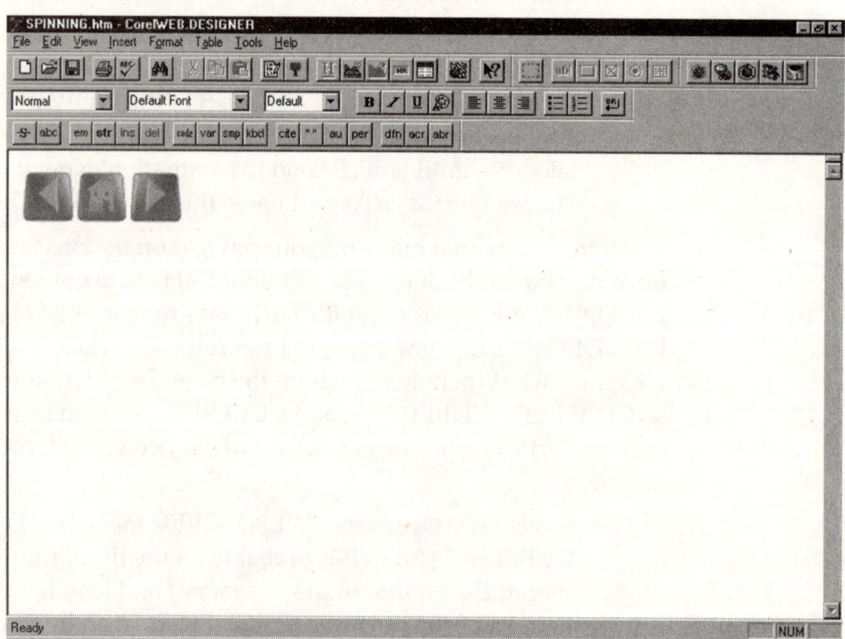

Figure 14-10: The finished HTML document in WEB.DESIGNER with the three navigation buttons.

27. One final touch: Choose File | Page Properties. In the Customize Background area, there's a drop-down menu of color swatches next to the Background Color label. Click on the color swatch, and choose the white one. Click on OK to accept the change and exit the dialog. Now you are ready to issue WEB.DESIGNER's File | Save command and save this updated document.

Does it work? We won't know until we load it into our Web browser and try it out. Fire up Netscape Navigator and select File | Open File. Move to the directory where you saved SPINNING.HTM and load the file. After a short time, the background of the page turns white and the three spinning buttons appear.

Click on either of the two outer buttons. If you have set everything up properly, you jump to either NEXT.HTM or PREVIOUS.HTM. Each of these pages has been set up to provide a hypertext link back to SPINNING.HTM. When you press the middle button, you hear the familiar WOW sound effect (a little distorted, I'm afraid), and then a preaddressed e-mail message form appears. If you have an open connection to the Internet, fill in the subject line, write a short message to let us know you completed the exercise, then send the message. If at all possible, we'll reply.

If things don't work correctly, wait a few seconds. Barista is a new technology, and it takes a little longer to get all the elements loaded and displayed. If you get the sound and e-mail form when you click on the middle button but don't jump to either the NEXT or PREVIOUS HTML file, you may have one of the following problems: First, check that the NEXT and PREVIOUS files are in the same subdirectory as SPINNING.HTM. Also, check that the name of each file is spelled correctly. If this doesn't fix the situation, open DESIGNER, load SPINNING.HTM, and delete the button(s) that doesn't work. Launch WEB.MOVE, open the original .CMV files you saved, and check the URLs you entered in the cues. Make sure you have spelled the file names correctly and that **file:///** precedes each file name.

If you still can't get your buttons and pages to work, check out the section on Barista in Chapter 15. There may be a piece of information there to shed some light on your problem.

Moving On

And so, the final curtain drops on our three WEB.MOVE productions. We trust you've learned many important lessons while producing your first WEB.GRAPHICS animations with WEB.MOVE. Just take a moment to reflect on some of the tasks accomplished while completing the exercises in this chapter. Here's a list of just a few:

- Imported images made in other applications to use as props
- Imported single and multiple images to use as actors
- Set the transparency color and other image options when importing images
- Created simple and complex paths for actors
- Used the Paint Editor to add and delete cels in actors
- Changed attributes like object names, background and locked options, and starting position coordinates
- Added and set cues, for both single and multiple actions
- Added sounds that fire on cue
- Created Barista/Java applets

You have certainly accomplished a lot. But don't think your lessons end here. When you're finished enjoying the fruits of your labors and examining the images you just created with WEB.MOVE, turn the page. You'll find some tricks and tips we think every WEB.MOVE-Meister can benefit from in the next chapter.

15

CorelWEB.MOVE Tricks & Tips

In this chapter, we offer a compilation of shortcuts that allow you to work more efficiently and we share some of the tricks we learned while preparing the exercises found in the preceding chapters. We also identify some of WEB.MOVE's rough edges. Even though WEB.MOVE has grown out of the more mature and stable CorelMOVE 5, it is really a 1.0-version application.

Remember, when CorelMOVE 5 was a current offering from Corel Corporation, the explosion of the World Wide Web wasn't even a rumble yet. Consequently, there's plenty of new code in WEB.MOVE 1.0, including its new Barista technology. Along with this new code has come some "unanticipated limitations and shortcomings." That's corporate marketing speak for "poor design and bugs." Some of the tips in this chapter alert you to these problem areas. Where possible, we offer workarounds to help you attain your goal of producing interesting, yet functional, Web pages.

The tricks and tips have been arranged by subject to make it easier to find valuable information while working with particular features of WEB.MOVE. Scan the various subheadings in this chapter for an overview of the many topics covered.

WEB.MOVE's Tools

This section deals with the tools in WEB.MOVE's main interface. You'll find tips and keyboard shortcuts that apply to the content editors mentioned in Chapter 13.

Keyboard Shortcuts

The following tables will help give your mouse finger a break.

Main Workspace

Main workspace shortcuts are in Table 15-1.

Shortcut Key	Action Performed
Help	
F1	Help Contents page
Shift+F1	Help for screen elements or menus. Press Shift+F1, then click on the element you need help with.
Ctrl+F1	Search for Help topics
Objects	
F5	New Actor dialog
F6	New Prop dialog
F7	New Wave dialog
F8	Cue Information dialog
Roll-ups	
F10	Path Edit roll-up
Playback controls	
F9	Forward playback
Shift+F9	Reverse playback
Esc	Stop playback
Shift+F5	First frame
Home	First frame

Shift+F6	Last frame
End	Last frame
Shift+F7	Previous frame
PgUp	Previous frame
Shift+F8	Next frame
PgDn	Next frame
MOVE's main window	
Ctrl+N	New Animation
Ctrl+O	Open Animation File dialog
Ctrl+S	Save Animation As dialog (If the animation has already been saved as a .CMV file, the file will be updated with the current animation information.)
Ctrl+D	Duplicate object
Ctrl+X	Cut object
Ctrl+C	Copy object
Ctrl+A	Animation Information dialog
Ctrl+J	Options dialog
Del	Delete
Alt+F6	Toggles between the last two active roll-ups
Alt+F4	Exit MOVE
Animation window	
Up arrow	Move selected object 1 pixel up
Down arrow	Move selected object 1 pixel down
Left arrow	Move selected object 1 pixel to the left
Right arrow	Move selected object 1 pixel to the right
Shift+PgUp	Move selected object to the top of the stacking order
Shift+PgDn	Move selected object to the bottom of the stacking order
Ctrl+PgUp	Move selected object toward the top of the stacking order 1 layer
Ctrl+PgDn	Move selected object toward the bottom of the stacking order 1 layer

Table 15-1: Main workspace shortcuts.

Paint Editor

Paint Editor shortcuts are in Table 15-2.

Shortcut Key	Action Performed
Help	
F1	Help Contents page for the Paint Editor
Shift+F1	Help for screen elements or menus
Ctrl+F1	Search for Help topics
Zoom	
Alt+1	No zoom, actual size
Alt+2	2X zoom
Alt+3	4X zoom
Alt+4	8X zoom
Editing functions	
Ctrl+Z	Undo
Ctrl+X	Cut
Ctrl+C	Copy
Ctrl+V	Paste
Del	Delete
Ctrl+T	Insert cels
Ctrl+R	Change Registration point
Alt+F4	Exit the Paint Editor

Table 15-2: Paint Editor shortcuts.

Sound Editor

Sound Editor shortcuts are in Table 15-3.

Shortcut Key	Action Performed
Help	
F1	Help Contents page for the Sound Editor
Shift+F1	Help for screen elements or menus
Ctrl+F1	Search for Help topics
Editing functions	
Ctrl+Z	Undo
Ctrl+X	Cut
Ctrl+C	Copy
Ctrl+V	Paste
Del	Delete
Sound playback controls	
Ctrl+P	Play
Ctrl+S	Stop
Alt+F4	Exit the Sound Editor

Table 15-3: Sound Editor shortcuts.

All Roll-Ups

Select the control menu in the top left corner of any roll-up and choose from the following actions. You also can access any roll-up's control menu by pressing F10 when the roll-up's title bar is highlighted.

- Roll Up or Roll Down—toggles any roll-up between the up and down states.

- Arrange—collapses the roll-up and moves it into either the upper left or upper right corner.

- Arrange All—collapses all open roll-ups and moves them into either the upper left or upper right corner.
- Help—brings up the Help topic for the selected roll-up.
- Close—closes the selected roll-up.
- Close All—closes all open roll-ups.

Timeline Roll-Up

Double-click on the title bar to collapse or expand the roll-up.

Select an object in the roll-up to select the object in the Animation window.

Double-click on an object's name to open the object's Information dialog box. Click on the Edit button to launch the appropriate object editor.

The Animation Window

Double-click on an object to access the object's editor.

Press Ctrl+Shift and drag to move the Animation window around in the gray workspace area. Repositioning the Animation window will allow you to keep several roll-ups open while working on an animation.

You can open more than one Library roll-up. Simply click on the Library roll-up button again and locate another .MLB file using the Open Library dialog.

The Paint Editor

The following tips and tricks pertain to the Paint Editor.

Text Tool Paint Window

To create a block of text, activate the Text tool and hold down the Ctrl key. Drag the cursor to mark out a region for the text. As you type, text will wrap at the right side of the text block region.

To merge the text block into the image, click outside of the text block. If you make a mistake, choose Undo from the Edit menu.

Eraser Tool

Double-click on the Eraser tool to erase everything in the Paint Editor window.

Color Pickup Tool

Hold down the Ctrl key and click on a color area in the image to change all instances of that color to the currently selected foreground color. Use Undo to reverse the change.

Paint Editor Window Size

By default, the size of the Paint Editor window differs depending on how your video is set up under Windows. For example, when Windows is set at 1024 X 768 using Large fonts for display, the default Paint window will be 333 X 333 pixels. If you keep the same resolution settings but select Small fonts, your default Paint window size will be 250 X 250 pixels.

You do not have to use the File | Page Size menu selection to enlarge the image area of the Paint Editor window. It's much easier to drag the border of the window to resize the image area. You cannot make the image area smaller by dragging the window border: you must use the File | Page Size dialog to make this change.

Selection Tool

Double-click on the Selection tool to select the entire image area of the Paint window. This is the same as choosing Edit | Select All on the Paint Editor's menu bar.

Morphing Tips

If you cancel the Morph dialog to make changes in the source or target images and then find you can't get the Morph dialog to show the revised images in the To and From picture areas, try the following: Go to the Paint window; make changes; choose Edit | Keep Paint or File | Apply Changes. The revised images will show in the Morph dialog.

You can use the clipboard to insert bitmap images into an actor's cels. First, copy or cut a bitmap image from an application like PHOTO-PAINT, Photoshop, or CorelXARA to the clipboard. Next, use the Paint Editor's Edit | Insert Cels menu option to add a new cel to your actor. Move to the new cel and choose Edit | Paste. After the bitmap has been pasted into cel 2, position it and move back to cel 1. Now you are ready to choose Effects | Morph.

Depending on the source and target images, Morph may create intermediate frames that contain stray pixels, especially near the edges of the images. Make sure you check each Morph-created frame carefully and use the Paint Editor to remove any errant pixels.

How Morphing Works

WEB.MOVE's Morphing function is pretty neat but isn't very sophisticated when compared to newer programs that perform the same type of special effect. The following information explains how Morph works, which will help you use the command effectively.

First off, if you have not applied any control points in the Morph dialog, the function will create a transition similar to the cross-fade effect demonstrated in Chapter 11 (see Figure 11-5). As Figure 15-1 shows, this combination of lightening and blending the source and target images is the initial modification applied.

Figure 15-1: This sequence of cels shows the result of the Morph effect when no control points have been defined.

The most interesting aspects of Morphing come into play when control points are defined to set up correspondences between the source and target images. These matching sets of points tell MOVE to push the pixels from one area of the image toward the area designated by the matching control point. The best way to demonstrate what occurs when the Morph command is applied is to take two simple bitmap images, define two sets of control points, then closely examine the resulting frames. Figure 15-2 shows the simple source and target images used in the demonstration. The locations of the two sets of control points are shown as numerals on the bitmap.

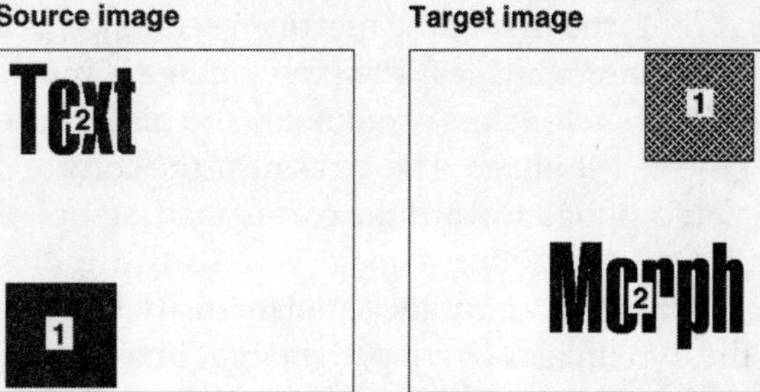

Figure 15-2: We'll use these two images to demonstrate what happens during the Morphing function when control points have been defined. Two sets of control points have been set and are labeled with the numerals 1 and 2.

After setting the control points, we specified 3 in the Cels to Create text box and clicked on OK. Figure 15-3 shows the entire five-frame sequence consisting of the source image, three frames created by the morph function, and finally the target frame.

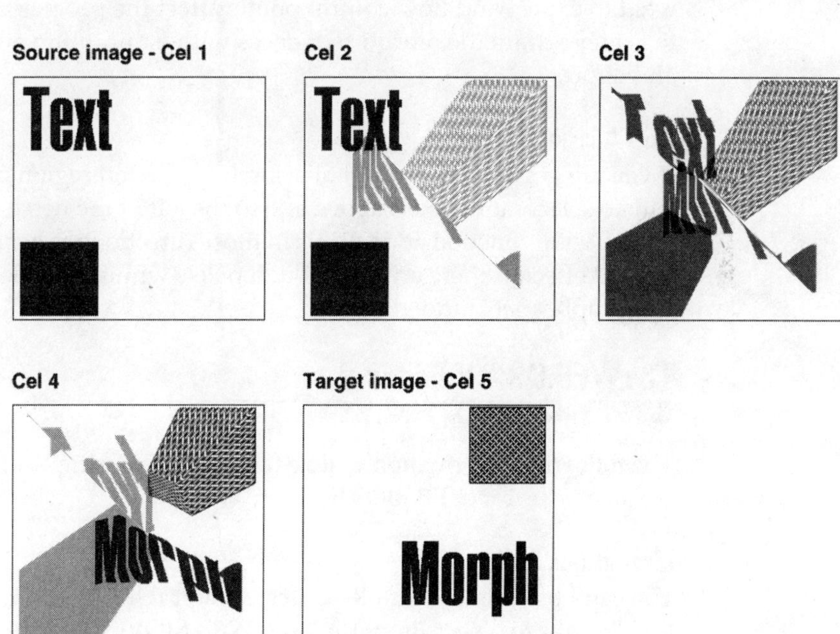

Figure 15-3: This five-cel sequence shows very clearly how the Morph function works its magic.

Notice that cel 2, the first of the morphed sequence, is a combination of the source and target images. The target image is much lighter than the source and is therefore less prominent. You also can see the severe distortion of the target image. The areas near the control points have been pinched and pulled toward the corresponding points set in the source image. As yet, the source image is unscathed.

In cel 3, each image is about the same intensity level; however, in any area where the two images overlap, the target image is more intense. Also, it's now the source image's turn to get pinched and pulled toward the control points set in the target image.

Cel 4 clearly shows severe distortion and loss of intensity in the source image. The target image is much darker and the distortion is comparatively mild, making the word *Morph* easily recognizable. The fact that the target image is more prominent sets up a natural progression to the unadulterated target image in cel 5.

Now that the mystery of WEB.MOVE's morphing abilities have been revealed, we are sure you'll be able to use it more effectively. Knowing what to expect and how control points affect the process will help you to achieve dramatic morph sequences with a minimum amount of time and effort.

Anti-Aliasing

If you are going to apply anti-aliasing to a selected region of an image, be sure to select more pixels above and to the left of the needed image. The anti-aliasing function adds pixels in those directions to achieve the desired effect. If there are not enough pixels within the selection area, the image appears truncated.

The WEB.DRAW Editor

The following information will be helpful when using WEB.DRAW to create images for WEB.MOVE.

Limitations & Bugs

You can't use the Uniform Resource Locator (URL) tools in WEB.DRAW to add links to objects imported into WEB.MOVE. To work around this, after an object is imported to WEB.MOVE, set up a cue with a Goto Action and publish to Java.

WEB.DRAW objects import into WEB.MOVE at half-size. To get around this inconsistency, use WEB.DRAW's Page Setup dialog and set the dimensions of the page to twice the size needed in MOVE. The downside of this technique is the entire contents of the page will not be displayed in the Preview window.

No Anti-Alias Feature

Without anti-aliasing, images likely will display very jagged. One workaround involves converting the WEB.DRAW object to a WEB.MOVE object by choosing Edit | Object Properties from the WEB.MOVE menu bar. In the object's Information dialog, select Convert, then click on OK in response to the "are you sure" message. Back in the Information dialog, click on the Edit button in the lower left corner. The Paint Editor opens with the newly converted object loaded. Choose Effects | Anti-Alias from the Paint Editor's menu bar. After the object has been modified, choose File | Apply and Exit to bring the object back into the Animation window.

WEB.MOVE's anti-aliasing capabilities are not that sophisticated. An alternative workaround is to save WEB.DRAW objects to bitmap files: Choose Export from WEB.DRAW's File menu. Open the resulting files in a bitmap editor that can apply anti-aliasing and resave the modified files. Use either WEB.DRAW's or WEB.MOVE's File | Import menu options to bring the files back into WEB.MOVE.

Missing Outlines in MOVE

If your outline is too thin, you probably will lose some of the outlines when you exit WEB.DRAW and import your image into WEB.MOVE. To avoid this problem, set your default outline in WEB.DRAW at 2 pixels. To accomplish this:

1. Make sure no object is selected.

2. Click on the Pen tool and access the Outline Pen dialog from the fly-out menu.

3. A dialog appears asking which objects you want the default outline applied to. Select Graphic. If you plan to include outlines around text, also choose Artistic Text and click on OK.

4. When the Outline Pen dialog appears, set the measurement system to pixels and set the Width to 2. You also can choose a new default color and line style if desired. When the attributes are set the way you wish, click on OK.

All new objects are drawn with a 2-pixel outline and survive the import process back into WEB.MOVE.

Cloning a Square Into a Circle

Here's a quick way to use the Clone function in WEB.DRAW to make a rectangle into a circle:

1. Click the Add Actor button and choose Corel WEB.DRAW as the creator type. Once WEB.DRAW appears, hold down the Ctrl key and use the Rectangle tool to draw a square on cel 1. Fill the square.

2. Access the pop-up menu on the Cel Select roll-up and choose Insert After. Type 3 into the Number of cels text box and select OK.

3. Click on the square to make sure it is selected. Access the Cel Select pop-up menu and choose Make Common After. Type 3 into the Number of cels text box and click on OK. A clone of the filled square will be inserted on every cel.

4. Go to cel 4. Choose the Shape tool from the toolbox and grab any corner node. Drag the node to the center of any side. This will create a perfect circle.

5. Go to cel 3 and use the same technique to create a round-cornered square. Go to cel 2 and make the square into a round-cornered square that is in between a perfect square and the shape on cel 3.

Make sure you reselect each shape when you move from cel to cel. Otherwise, the last selected item on the previous cel will be altered. Figure 15-4 shows the shapes you should create on each of the frames.

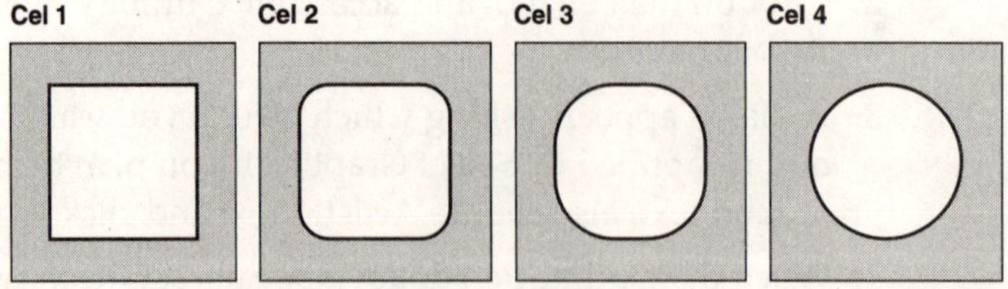

Figure 15-4: Use the Shape tool to modify the square cloned from cel 1 into round-cornered squares and a circle.

Morph Shapes With the Blend Tool

The following exercise demonstrates use of the Blend tool to attain results resembling the Paint Editor's Morph effect:

1. Click the Add Actor button and choose Corel WEB.DRAW as the creator type. Once WEB.DRAW appears, use the Pen tool to draw a star on cel 1. Fill the star.

2. Access the pop-up menu on the Cel Select roll-up and choose Insert After. Type 1 into the Number of Cels text box and select OK.

3. On cel 2, draw a circle and fill it with any color.

4. Access the pop-up menu on the Cel Select roll-up and choose Insert Before. Type 3 into the Number of Cels text box and select OK.

5. Choose Edit | Select Across Frames. The status bar should now read "2 Objects Selected Across Multiple Layers."

6. Choose Effects | Blend Roll-Up. The Steps text box on the roll-up will already be filled in with a 3; this matches the number of cels available. Click on the Apply button.

Figure 15-5 shows the resulting shapes created with the Blend function. Experiment with blending two pieces of text to create unique effects. Also, slight changes in the Rotation, Color, and Node Mapping settings will make very dramatic changes in the effect.

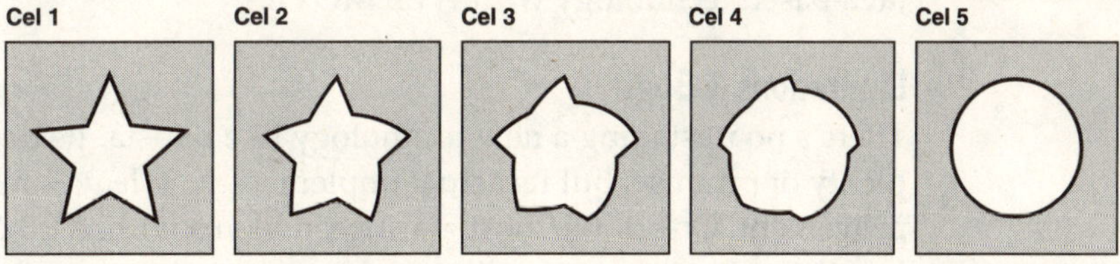

Figure 15-5: The resulting sequence of shapes created by using the Blend roll-up to change a star into a circle.

Using CorelMOVE 5 to Create .CMV Files

WEB.MOVE's file format is so similar to CorelMOVE 5's, you can create .CMV files in the latter to get around limitations in the former. For instance, CorelMOVE 5 allows you to set the animation size smaller than the 30-pixel square allowable in WEB.MOVE. Conversely, you can make a much larger animation window than the 500 X 360 pixels WEB.MOVE allows. These "out-of-range" sizes will be honored when the .CMV file is opened in WEB.MOVE.

Also, in the Cel Sequencer CorelMOVE 5 offers several special effects not found in the WEB.MOVE version. These effects change the size of cel contents and cel order.

After creating and saving a CorelMOVE 5 .CMV that uses a Cel Sequencer special effect, open the .CMV in WEB.MOVE and publish to an animated Graphics Interchange Format (GIF) file. You can include this GIF in any HyperText Markup Language (HTML) document. If you publish to Java, the special animation sizes will be honored, but the CorelMOVE 5 special effects will not.

Barista

Barista is Corel's latest brainchild for bringing content to the World Wide Web. The following are observations regarding our experience using this Java-based technology with WEB.MOVE.

Limitations & Bugs

There's no mistaking a new technology like Barista. Its description holds plenty of promise, but its actual implementation leaves room for improvement. One of the most glaring problems with WEB.MOVE's Barista functionality concerns multiple cues not being processed correctly. For example: You set up two actors—animated buttons—in the same .CMV file, and each has a cue assigned. One might have a Stop sound action, the other a Play sound action. The problem is only one of the buttons will work and only one of the cues will fire. Also disturbing is that the cue assigned to the working button is not necessarily the cue that will be triggered.

The workaround for this problem is to create separate .CMV files for each actor that has a cue assigned. This is the approach we took when building the navigational button bar example in Chapter 14.

We also encountered some problems trying to view Barista/Java applets in Web browsers. For one thing, the Web browser's status bar indicated the page had loaded completely yet the animation did not display. If this happens, try clicking on the browser's Reload button. In some cases, we had to close the browser and then restart it to clear the problem completely.

Overall, we found that Explorer 3.0 doesn't much care for Barista. On a few occasions, Explorer just disappeared while trying to load a Barista-enabled page. Other times, it took a very long time to load a page. For these reasons, we can't wholeheartedly endorse using Barista. By the time you read this, Corel may have fixed these problems, or the browser developers may have released new versions that eliminate the problems. Take the time to search the Web sites of Corel, Netscape, and Microsoft for fixes to these problems.

All in all, Netscape's Navigator had fewer problems digesting and displaying Barista components. On rare occasions, we did have to press the Reload button to jump-start a stalled applet.

Barista Files Needed

If you decide to incorporate WEB.MOVE Barista applets in your Web pages, it is important to understand what files WEB.MOVE creates and uses. You'll also need to know where it saves these files so you can transfer and set them up properly on your Web server.

When you publish to WEB.DESIGNER, WEB.MOVE automatically creates one directory containing at least one file. The directory is created under the server root directory you specified when setting up WEB.DESIGNER. The new directory name always starts with "MOVE*x*", where *x* is a numeral, with the series starting with 0. Every time you publish to WEB.DESIGNER, WEB.MOVE checks the server root directory for any existing directories starting with MOVE. If it finds any, it notes the trailing number, increments the number by 1, and creates a new directory.

Within this new directory, a file with a name matching the directory and having a CJW extension is created. This file contains the actual Java code executed by the receiving Web browser. If you turn on the Progressive Load check box when you publish your animation from WEB.MOVE to WEB.DESIGNER, then another file is created in the same directory. This file is always named STARTUP.GIF. It's a single-image GIF file that WEB.DESIGNER displays in its WYSIWYG authoring window. If a STARTUP.GIF file is not available, WEB.DESIGNER displays a generic question mark icon instead.

If you have incorporated sound objects in your animation, WEB.MOVE also creates files with the extension AU and places them in the same directory. The first sound object will be named S0.AU, with subsequent sounds being named S1, S2, and so on. Now that you know what files are generated by WEB.MOVE, you will be able to determine what files to transfer to your Web server. Remember that you are trying to construct a mirror image of the directories and files that WEB.MOVE creates, under the server root of your local computer, on your Web server.

Besides the files generated by WEB.MOVE and unique to each animation project, you must make several other files available on the Web server. These files are known as Java *class* files and have a CLASS extension. These class files contain instructions that can be carried out when a .CJW file requires it. Corel designed the Barista technology to support all the applications that come in the WEB.GRAPHICS Suite. However, WEB.MOVE Java applets require the services of only four CLASS files. They are:

- AR.CLASS
- EFFECT.CLASS
- LOADER.CLASS
- WEBMOVE.CLASS

When you transfer your files to the Web server, it is important to copy these four files to the same directory as the .CJW, STARTUP.GIF, and any AU files.

Tip

Windows 3.X Users: See the following section, Can't Run Under Windows 3.1x, for important information regarding Barista class files.

Java Applet Parameters

When a WEB.MOVE-generated Java applet is embedded in a Web page, it is necessary to pass it certain parameters. These are included in the Web page's HTML code between the <APPLET CODE> and </APPLET> tags. A section of HTML code that shows the parameters of a Barista applet follows:

```
<APPLET CODE="webmove.class"
WIDTH="53" HEIGHT="52" CORELCOPY="MOVE33/">
<PARAM NAME="INPUTFILE" VALUE="MOVE33/MOVE33.CJW">
<PARAM NAME="THUMBNAIL" VALUE="MOVE33/Startup.GIF">
<PARAM NAME="LOADING" VALUE="Loading CorelWEB.MOVE Anima-
tion">
<PARAM NAME="PROGRESSIVE" VALUE="true">
</APPLET>
```

Changing any of these parameters affects your Web page's functional-ity. Depending on which parameter you modify, the effect on the page can range from cropping an image to completely breaking the Java applet. A list of each parameter and what it does follows:

- APPLET CODE="webmove.class"—This refers to the class file that allows WEB.MOVE Barista files to function. If you change this to any other CLASS file name or leave it out entirely, the applet will not work.

- WIDTH="xx" HEIGHT="xx"—These parameters accept numerical values that define how many pixels wide and high the Web browser will display the Java applet. If you increase these values, more space will be allotted around the right side and bottom of the applet. Despite what WEB.DESIGNER may show, the image will not be stretched to fill the enlarged space when displayed in a Web browser. Instead, you will see a larger white background around your applet. Decreasing these values causes the image area of the Java applet to be cropped. The image is reduced to fit the newly defined area.

- CORELCOPY="directory_name/"—This sets the name of the directory, under the server root, where the particular Java applet looks for the files it needs to carry out its functions.

- "INPUTFILE" VALUE="directory_name/file_name.CJW"—This parameter's value is set to the directory and name of the WEB.MOVE-generated .CJW file to be run and displayed in the allotted space. Now you can see why it is so important to main-tain the filename and directory structure on a Web server. If you decide to rename .CJW files or place them in a different directory on the server, make sure you change the code in this field to match your changes.

- "THUMBNAIL" VALUE="directory_name/Startup.GIF"—This parameter is a pointer to the directory and file that will display when constructing Web pages in WEB.DESIGNER. If the path or file name is not valid, WEB.DESIGNER will display a generic icon instead. You can move or rename the STARTUP.GIF file, but make sure you update the values of this parameter in the HTML code to match the changes you make.

- "LOADING" VALUE="Loading CorelWEB.MOVE Animation"— The parameter is a string of text displayed in the applet's image area if there is no graphic to display. This text string is usually displayed as a result of not selecting the Progressive Load option when publishing from WEB.MOVE or because of a time delay in downloading the graphic data from the Web server. You can change the text string to any message you like; just make sure it's enclosed in quotes.

- "PROGRESSIVE" VALUE="true_or_false"—The setting for this parameter can be either "true" or "false." This value is determined at the time of publishing from WEB.MOVE to WEB.DESIGNER by the Progressive Load option. However, you can override it by changing the HTML code directly. When "true" is set, each frame of the animation appears in the Web browser as an interlaced GIF. Although this gives the user something to look at, it may steal some of the impact of your animation. When the parameter is set to "false," the browser displays the text string defined by the Loading parameter scrolling through a white rectangular area.

No Transparency

Barista/Java applets do not support transparency as the GIF 89a file format does. This means all applets will display in a white rectangular area. The easiest workaround is to set the background of the Web page to be white also.

Can't Run Under Windows 3.1x

This one is not really Corel's fault. Responsibility for the fact that Java applets need instructions contained in files whose names have five-character extensions lies at the feet of the designers of Java. This causes a severe problem for WEB.GRAPHICS Suite users running Windows 3.1x, because the operating system doesn't recognize any file that has extension with more than three characters.

If you are using Windows 3.1x, this means you can't view Java-enabled Web pages on your local computer. You are able to create Barista/Java files because they are created with .CJW extensions. It is the .CJW file that needs to locate and call on the services of the files that have the longer CLASS extensions.

Corel's workaround is to supply WEB.GRAPHICS Suite users with two compressed files that contain all the needed Java component files. Each file contains the same contents, the only difference is they were created with different archival/compression programs. One file is named BARISTA.ZIP and the other is BARISTA.TAR. Both can be found in the BARISTA directory, under the directory where the WEB.GRAPHICS Suite is installed. Or you can find both files in the BARISTA directory on the WEB.GRAPHICS Suite CD. If you upload either of these files to your Web server, you can ask your server's system administrator to expand it in the directory where you upload your Java applets.

Creating the Images for the Globe Exercise

Some programs, such as 3D applications, make light work of projects that would be nearly impossible to accomplish using WEB.MOVE's native drawing tools. For example, to create the images used in the Spinning Globe exercise in Chapter 14, we called on the services of four programs in addition to WEB.MOVE. The first two— CorelDREAM and CorelDEPTH—are 3D programs. The other two applications we used were CorelPHOTO-PAINT and CorelDRAW 7. Here are the steps we took to create the images:

The Globe

1. In CorelDREAM we opened a 3D clip art file supplied with DREAM. We added a black background to the scene.

2. Next, we set up a camera and rendered 24 different views of the earth, saving them as RGB tagged image file format (TIFF) bitmaps. After each rendering was completed, we rotated the earth 15 percent counterclockwise.

3. We used CorelPHOTO-PAINT to crop, resample, and resize each of the 24 images. We set the resolution to 72 dots per inch (dpi) and made sure each image was 64 X 64 pixels. The images were converted to palleted, 8-bit images with the pallet options set to Uniform and Error diffusion. (These settings worked best with WEB.MOVE's Import imaging options set to use a transparent black color and to perform high-quality dithering.) We saved each image as a GIF file.

4. To create the appearance of an object moving away in space, the object must be made progressively smaller. Conversely, something that appears to come forward in space grows progressively larger. An orbiting object requires a combination of both these effects. Figure 15-6 shows how we mapped out the orbit of the planet. This layout helped us determine the size of each image in the planet's cel sequence. The following is a table of the 24 images and the percentage of reduction or enlargement applied:

Image Number	% of Enlargement or Reduction
1	100
2	92
3	84
4	76
5	68
6	64
7	66
8	72
9	79
10	86
11	93
12	100
13	115
14	130
15	145

16	160
17	175
18	190
19	200
20	183
21	166
22	149
23	132
24	115

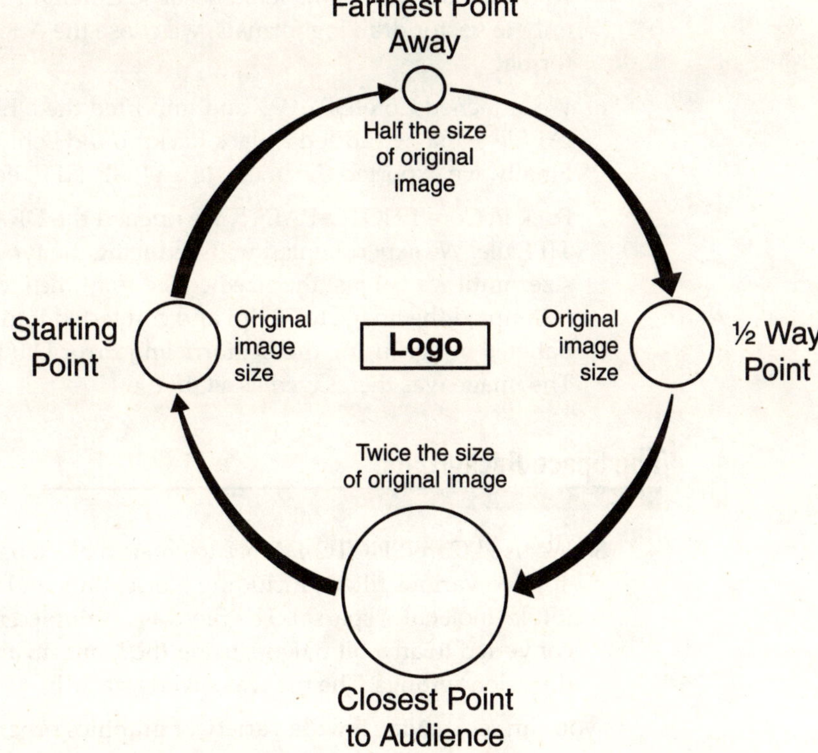

Figure 15-6: This bird's-eye view of the planet's orbit shows what size the individual images need to be at specific points in the actor's cel sequence.

In a perfect circular orbit, the image farthest away from the viewer should be 50 percent, or exactly half the size of the original. After viewing the assembled scene, a 50 percent reduction just seemed too small. We opted to lessen the amount of reduction for the images depicting the back half of the orbit (images 6 and 7). That's why the reduction percentages don't fall below the mid-60s.

The Type

5. We started CorelDEPTH and set the words *Galactic Mall.com* on two lines and arranged them. We experimented with setting the perspective, colors, bevel size, extrusion depth, and lighting until we were happy with the look. Because CorelDEPTH exports only to vector drawing formats, we chose the Adobe Illustrator format.

6. We launched CorelDRAW 7 and imported the DEPTH-generated .AI file. Next, we added a black background behind the type. Finally, we exported the image to an RGB TIFF file.

7. Back in CorelPHOTO-PAINT, we opened the DRAW-generated TIFF file. We experimented with reducing the type to different sizes until we got just the size needed to fit the scene. We resampled the image to 72 dpi and converted it to an 8-bit, palleted image, using the Uniform and Error Diffusion settings. The image was then saved as a GIF file.

The Space Background

8. We used CorelPHOTO-PAINT to create a black background. We applied various filters, including Noise, Blur, and Paint Alchemy (Style: molecules sparse). The file was resampled to 72 dpi, converted to an 8-bit palette, using the Uniform and Error diffusion settings. The file was saved as a GIF.

As you can see, having a wide variety of graphics programs allows you to create eye-catching images for your Web pages quickly and easily. Thanks to Corel, simply adding CorelDRAW! 6 or 7 to your software library provides just about every tool any Web Meister could want.

Running Under NT 4.0

When the WEB.GRAPHICS Suite was being developed, Windows NT 4.0 had not been released and so was not available for testing. However, we have been running the suite under NT 4.0 (with Service Pack 1 and then 2) and have found it to be very stable. We have encountered a few problems, as follows:

- The Paint Editor window cannot be resized by dragging the window border with the mouse. Use the File | Page Setup menu option to resize the window.

- The Paint Editor image area is not redrawn properly when using the x2, x4, and x8 Zoom levels. If you must use Zoom, you can force a redraw of the paint window. Use the scroll bars to move the affected area of the image out of and then back into the viewing area.

- We had no success recording sounds under NT 4.0 with Creative Lab's AWE 32 sound board. No matter what settings we tried, the resulting sound file was either garbled, truncated, or both.

Moving On

This chapter wraps up the discussion of CorelWEB.MOVE. Even though we've pointed out some of WEB.MOVE's rough edges, we've also demonstrated that WEB.MOVE has a lot to offer those desiring to add animation or sound to their Web pages.

What's next? More multimedia! Yes, more sounds, more animation, and more 3D! You don't have to own CorelDEPTH or CorelDREAM to experience the world of 3D. Read on to see how the WEB.WORLD application included in the CorelWEB.GRAPHICS Suite can add the excitement of virtual reality to your Web site.

PART IV

CorelWEB.WORLD

16

Introduction to CorelWEB.WORLD

In recent years Corel has stretched its ever-lengthening software arms in diverging directions, one of which is the world of 3D applications. The CorelDRAW! 6 package was the first offering to include graphics applications that went beyond the two dimensions in which illustrators and designers have traditionally toiled. Corel licensed two applications from the RayDream company and, after making mostly cosmetic changes, recommissioned them CorelDEPTH and CorelDREAM. Additionally, they gathered another product—CorelMOTION—into the DRAW 6 fold.

By late 1996, 3D applications had gained a firm foothold in the commercial software world, and Corel Corporation continued to provide easy-to-use, inexpensive 3D for the masses. One proof of Corel's commitment was the updating of CorelDEPTH and CorelDREAM for inclusion in the CorelDRAW! 7 suite of graphics applications. However, even before DRAW 7 was delivered, Corel had enhanced its presence in the 3D marketplace with the release of another 3D authoring tool: CorelWEB.WORLD.

Why, you ask, would Corel offer so many 3D applications? The simple answer is that each application is aimed at serving a particular need. CorelDREAM provides the user with a way to create photo-realistic renderings of 3D scenes. These renderings are output as bitmap files. CorelDEPTH is well suited for simpler projects, consisting of text and simple shapes. DEPTH's finished product is not output as bitmaps but rather as vector format files, like Adobe Illustrator and Windows Metafile. CorelMOTION is unique in its ability to create animation files.

As with these other products, CorelWEB.WORLD has its particular area of focus: virtual reality. Creating artificial environments in cyberspace where humans can interact with computer generated 3D objects. Technically speaking, the images that WEB.WORLD generates are an interesting combination of bitmap and vector. Bitmap images can be applied to entire surfaces of 3D objects as textures or as discreet pictures. But the 3D objects themselves are described with mathematically—which classifies them as vector-based graphics.

The designers of WEB.WORLD figured that people surfing the Internet weren't interested in walking around table-top scenes of tea cups and salt shakers—the kinds of images that CorelDREAM excels at. Instead, they chose a simple metaphor for creating virtual environments, one easily recognizable to most humans: buildings. Consequently, WEB.WORLD is endowed with tools that construct basic building elements, such as rooms with walls, ceilings, and floor surfaces. As Figure 16-1 illustrates, with WEB.WORLD you can create very elaborate rooms. You can make structures with several levels, or create scenes with many structures. Literally—the sky's the limit!

This chapter introduces you to the CorelWEB.WORLD application included in the CorelWEB.GRAPHICS Suite. We'll start with a nostalgic look at 3D graphics and its evolution on the Web. You'll be introduced to the Virtual Reality Modeling Language (VMRL)—a protocol that has revolutionized creating and viewing 3D worlds on the Web. Along the way, we hope to stir your imagination with the many possibilities WEB.WORLD offers to Web authors entering the world of 3D.

3D & the World Wide Web

Several decades ago, I remember pumping quarters into an arcade game that held me spellbound. Inside the goggle-shaped viewer, I was entranced by visions of battle tanks. The simply crafted vehicles roamed a bleak landscape of eerie-green see-through cones and rectangles. Alas, I was usually defeated in the skirmishes with the sure-shot opposing tank commanders. But still, I derived great fun from learning to navigate around the glowing-green geometric shapes that littered the flat battle-field floor. This was my first experience with 3D graphics. How times have changed!

Figure 16-1: WEB.WORLD's tools are well suited for constructing virtual worlds that represent rooms, buildings, and cities.

Compared with the computer of two decades ago, the power of today's home PC is definitely immense. The images created by today's 3D programs are so realistic, they engulf the user in a quick-moving, richly textured world where anything can happen. After all, it's completely fabricated—a virtual reality.

There is no mystery to why 3D images captivate computer users: humans live in a 3D world. 3D images are natural to our senses. So why shouldn't more of our computing experiences be based on a 3D metaphor, complete with images that resemble our real world? By the late '80s several software developers were already leveraging their expertise with high-end 3D graphics systems, trying to bring affordable solutions to the PC market. Then the playing field expanded dramatically when the

World Wide Web began to explode in the early 1990s. The next logical question was how to get 3D on the WWW. The answer arrived in 1994; it was spelled *VRML*. The Virtual Reality Modeling Language was designed as a cross-platform solution for publishing and viewing 3D simulations over the Web.

VRML (pronounced *vermal*) is a scene description language that standardizes how 3D environments (also known as *worlds* or *spaces*) are represented on the Web. A VRML file, usually having a .WRL file extension, is similar to an HTML file in several respects. First, it is written in ASCII format. This means just about any computer can read the file and understand its contents. Second, the contents of the file get parsed—that is, they are read in character by character, gradually assembling program instructions and associated parameters. As these are found, they are interpreted and converted into images that are displayed by the Web browser. (The foregoing assumes that the user has a VRML-enabled Web browser.) Some browsers have VRML capabilities built in. However, the two most popular for Windows users—Navigator and Explorer—need add-on programs, called plug-ins, to handle the interpretation and display of WRL files.

Because the VRML file is not compiled, some programmers would call it a scripting language. But however you classify it, VRML is like a fast-moving forest fire—catching on and growing in intensity, daily. In fact, the first version of the VRML file specification, finalized in May 1995, has already been supplanted by Version 2.

Many seeking to add 3D worlds to their Web sites might be tempted to launch their favorite ASCII editor and start typing VRML commands. After all, this is the approach quite a few have taken in producing HTML documents. However similar HTML and VRML seem at first glance, don't be fooled into thinking VRML is simple to *learn*. Below is the WRL code generated by CorelWEB.WORLD for a simple 3.5 meter cube.

```
#VRML V1.0 ascii
#     This file was created with
#     CorelWEB.WORLD (tm).
#     According to License Agreement,
#     you may not remove or modify this notice.

Separator{
   ShapeHints {shapeType SOLID vertexOrdering COUNTERCLOCK-
WISE}
   SpotLight  {on FALSE}
```

```
PerspectiveCamera{
    orientation 0 1 0 0.29262
    position 4660 1074 -3091
    heightAngle 1.58358
}
DEF BackgroundColor Info{
    string" 0.643137 0.784314 0.941176"
}
Coordinate3{
    point[
      3456 0 -5120, 3456 0 -4224, 3456 896
-4224, 3456 896 -5120, 4352 0 -5120, 4352 896 -5120,
      4352 0 -4224, 4352 896 -4224,
    ] # 8 points
}
MaterialBinding {value PER_FACE_INDEXED}
Material{
    ambientColor 0.2 0.2 0.2
    diffuseColor 0.8 0.8 0.8
    emissiveColor[
      0 0.737255 0.737255, 0.109804 0.470588 0.376471,
0.737255 0 0.737255, 0.188235 0.580392 0.988235,
      0.109804 0 0.392157, 0.0627451 0.423529 0.0627451,
    ] # 6 colors
}
Separator{
    IndexedFaceSet{
      coordIndex[
        0, 1, 2, 3, -1,
        4, 0, 3, 5, -1,
        6, 4, 5, 7, -1,
        1, 6, 7, 2, -1,
        2, 7, 5, 3, -1,
        1, 0, 4, 6, -1,
      ] # 6 faces
      materialIndex[
        0, 1, 2, 3, 4, 5,
      ]
    }
  }
}
#EOF
```

We certainly don't want to discourage anyone from delving more deeply into the VRML language. Really, we encourage such an effort. But, the fact remains that the quickest route to constructing 3D virtual worlds for the Web is to use an authoring tool like CorelWEB.WORLD.

CorelWEB.WORLD & the Web

A unique aspect of WEB.WORLD is its ability to write two different types of 3D description files. Not only can it write VRML 1.0 files but it can also save your 3D world in the more robust .MUS file format. When you issue the Save or SaveAs command, WEB.WORLD saves your project in .MUS format. When you want to save it as a WRL file, pick File | Publish to VRML and your scene will be saved in a directory you choose. At the same time, an updated .MUS file is written to the same directory. How's that for convenience?

VRML Versus MUS

Why do we say that the .MUS file format is more robust than VRML 1.0? The designers of WEB.WORLD realized that they could add more multimedia features to their product than the VRML 1.0 specification recognized. Rather than leave all these features out of the application, they envisioned users creating feature-rich 3D environments and then offering both types of files to their audience. If the viewer has access to the Web browser plug-in for .MUS files or the CorelWEB.WORLD Viewer, they can enjoy all the features included by the author. Should they decide that .WRL files are all they wish to view, they can experience the same 3D world right within the confines of their Web browser but with many of the bells and whistles stripped out. Like they say: "Choice is good."

When you publish your WEB.WORLD scenes as WRL files, the following features are supported:

- paints
- wallpapers
- pictures
- links to URLs

When a user views a published .MUS file, all of the features supported by WRL are included, plus the following special ones:

- movies
- albums
- moving wallpaper
- attached text
- sounds
- background MIDI music
- walking shows

By comparing the list of supported features, you can see that .MUS files offer rich multimedia features that really spice up your Web site. All of these premium features are discussed in the next two chapters.

Note: These .MUS-only features don't come without some price to be paid. WRL files are generally more compact because they don't need to support the associated sound, movie, and album files that must be transmitted with an .MUS. The natural consequence is that .MUS files are larger and so they download slower.

Tip

Here's where to get the various plug-ins and viewers. If you are using Netscape Navigator 2.0, download Netscape's Live3D VRML plug-in. Go to http://home.netscape.com/ and follow the links to the 3D plug-ins. Live3D is built into Netscape 3.0, so you do not need to download anything.

The Internet Explorer VRML 1.0 plug-in is available at http://www.microsoft.com/ie/. You'll need to follow the links to the software library.

The .MUS plug-in for Navigator and Explorer can be found at http://www.corel.com/corelweb/webworld/plugin.htm or http://www1.paragraph.com/vhsb/mhsv/download/. Although the plug-in is the same, the file found at Paragraph's Web site is 100K larger because it includes an installer that automates installing the plug-in.

The CorelWEB.WORLD Viewer, a Windows .MUS viewing application, can be found in the \PROGRAMS subdirectory under the directory where the WEB.GRAPHICS Suite is installed. It is also on the WEB.GRAPHICS Suite CD in the \WEBWORLD\PROGRAMS directory. The file is named: WRLDVIEW.EXE. See chapter 17 for more information on this file and several support .DLLs also needed.

Determining Your Site's 3D Needs

There's no doubt that the .MUS format offers tremendous features, but do you really need them? To answer that question you must consider *why* you are using a 3D interface for your Web site. You must also consider the likely audience you will be attracting to your site. Are they going to be users who need the multimedia features and will they have the components, both hardware and software, to fully experience your 3D environments? Assembling the needed software is something you can help with. You can alert Web surfers to the requirements necessary to view your 3D site, and provide links to sites that offer VRML and .MUS plug-ins for their browsers. Besides browser plug-ins, you can also freely distribute and make the .MUS file-viewer application, CorelWEB.WORLD Viewer (WRLDVIEW.EXE), available from your site. The CorelWEB.WORLD Viewer is a stand-alone Windows program—it looks and feels like WEB.WORLD, but doesn't include the authoring portions of the program. Chapter 17 contains more information on this viewer.

But there are some factors beyond your control. What can you do about users' hardware components? They will need, at the very least, a 14.4K modem and a computer with a fast 486 chip. Any setup that is slower than this is likely to be a waste of time for the viewer. In reality, a Pentium with a fast video card and a 28.8K modem are much more realistic for viewing and navigating 3D spaces online. If you have included MIDI background music or attached .WAV files to objects, your audience will need sound capabilities in order to benefit. It would be a courteous gesture to post these recommended requirements on your home page.

Finally, you have to assess why you want or need to provide an online 3D environment. You must ask why your audience will want it. In some cases, the answer will be very obvious, For example, if you are a developer of 3D software, it makes overwhelming sense to use 3D to display your wares. If you are an illustrator or designer, then a 3D simulation of an art gallery is irresistible and you know it's going to knock the socks right off visitors who are potential customers or clients. On the other hand, if you determine that the visitors coming to your site aren't likely to appreciate the added hassle and overhead needed to download and navigate your 3D Web site, then it would be foolish to hitch your Web wagon to the 3D-horse.

Don't get dejected just yet. If you really want to offer 3D but aren't sure whether it will be a plus or a minus to your audience, there is a solution: compromise. Give your audience the choice of viewing your site in traditional HTML pages or taking the scenic route via 3D virtual space. Basically, your home page would present two links: one for HTML-only viewing and the other for those ready, willing, and able to experience the depth of 3D Web browsing. The only drawback to this strategy is that you'll have to carry out a lot more work. If your site is pretty static—the content doesn't change much—this shouldn't pose too much of a problem. Compromise is an elegant solution. Remember: "Choice is good."

WEB.WORLD Basics

WEB.WORLD goes beyond simply building 3D structures; it gives you the tools to adorn any surface with wallpaper, paint, and pictures. Some of these decorating tools are space age—like animated wallpaper and pictures that change. You can even "hang" digital movies on your virtual walls. If you want to present information about an item contained in your virtual space, you can make text messages appear when an item is double-clicked with a mouse. Or, you can have the item "speak" for itself by attaching a sound file to the item. Additionally, most items have the ability to act as hyperlinks to any URL on the WWW. This could be another site, document, or 3D virtual world. With so many possibilities available, the idea of creating virtual spaces in WEB.WORLD is definitely exciting!

When it comes to navigating in a 3D environment, remember that the structures you create in WEB.WORLD are always stationary; you're the one who does all the moving. You wander around the WEB.WORLD space like a tourist viewing the world through a video camera. Your camera has different lens settings; you have a telephoto lens so that you can zoom up closer to items or pull back and get a panoramic view with a wide-angle lens. Just like a real camera, you can tilt it up or down. Last but not least, in cyberspace you can hover above the surface of the ground to reach and view new heights.

Simple & Easy to Learn

Many 3D authoring programs possess tools that create exotic shapes and structures. WEB.WORLD's tools create simple, basically flat objects. You can draw boxes or cubes of any size and walls of varying thickness and height. These walls can have corners, but they must be at right angles to each other. If you want to make a wall on an angle, WEB.WORLD has a special tool that creates *faces*. Faces are paper-thin walls. These basic building materials are shown in Figure 16-2.

Besides tools that create surfaces and faces, there are tools that cut away portions of boxes and walls. These are handy for carving out windows, doors, and room interiors. There is also a tool that removes face surfaces. These faces may be segments drawn with the Face tool or portions of walls that make up the sides of a box object.

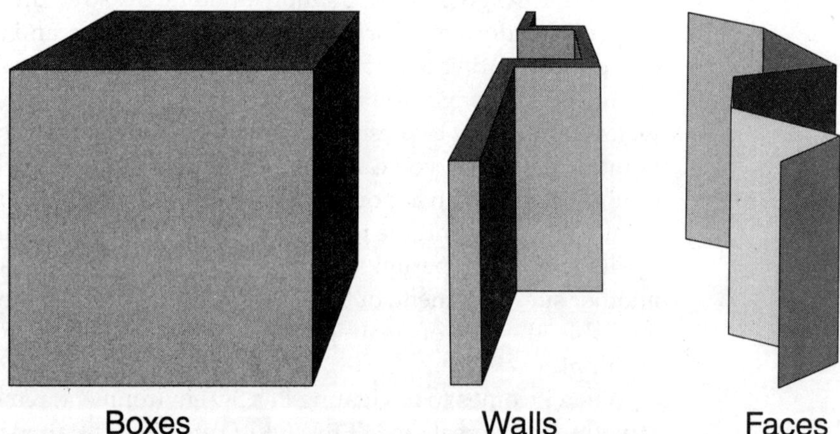

Figure 16-2: The three basic building materials in WEB.WORLD are boxes, walls, and faces.

Because WEB.WORLD's tools create simple shapes, they are very easy to learn. When designing your virtual scenes, try not to think in terms of round objects. WEB.WORLD is quite brain dead in this regard. That's right—no spheres, pipes, or cones. Also, you can't rotate the flat primitive shapes you create. This means you can't even create a pitched roof for a house. These limitations don't lie with the VRML 1.0 spec. They were design decisions made to keep the product simple—so that users new to 3D can start creating virtual worlds quickly and easily.

Moving On

At this point, we're sure you can see that as a WEB.WORLD author you must wear many hats. Not only are you the designer and architect, you're the entire construction crew, the painter, the wallpaperer, the interior decorator, the art collector, and even the videographer.

You've learned the differences and advantages of VRML 1.0 and .MUS files. You've seen that the bandwidth needed to broadcast virtual reality worlds is much greater than simple HTML pages. You're also aware that special viewing software for browsers is needed. And you have been given a cursory introduction to the basic tools and navigation features contained in WEB.WORLD.

The next chapter explains, in detail, the interface and tools that make up the WEB.WORLD authoring environment. After that, Chapter 18 walks you through using each tool to create virtual buildings and decorate them with cool materials only available in cyberspace.

17

Getting to Know CorelWEB.WORLD

Creating an effective interface is the biggest challenge for developers of 3D software applications. The trick is to create a working environment that expresses three dimensions while displaying it on a two-dimensional device—the monitor. This formidable task has led to many different interface styles, some of which are much better than others. Just look at the varying interfaces of the three Corel applications mentioned in the previous chapter: CorelMOTION, CorelDREAM, and CorelDEPTH.

And now, WEB.WORLD enters the scene—with its own way of looking at the world of 3D. In comparison with the other Corel 3D applications mentioned, WEB.WORLD creates simple shapes, making its interface relatively easy to learn and use. This means you'll be creating 3D virtual environments in no time flat. As Figure 17-1 illustrates, there are relatively few components to WEB.WORLD's interface.

This chapter is divided into three main sections, which introduce you to every part of WEB.WORLD's interface. The first section discusses the three windows you'll use for all building and decorating chores. The second section describes the buttons on the various toolbars. The last section covers the menu selections and options. You might find it helpful to start CorelWEB.WORLD and follow along onscreen as each component is discussed. Although there will be some discussion of how to use each tool in this chapter, look to Chapter 18 for hands-on lessons in building, decorating, and adding multimedia to 3D worlds.

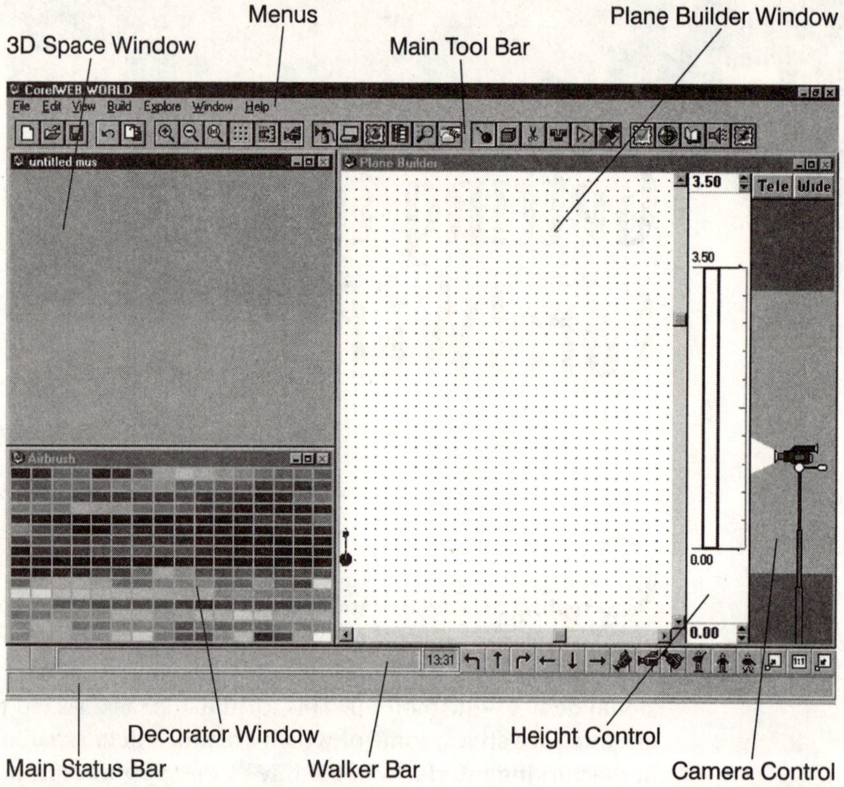

Figure 17-1: Various windows, toolbars, and menus make up WEB.MOVE's 3D virtual reality authoring environment.

Three Windows on the World

The most noticeable portion of WEB.WORLD's interface is made up of three windows: Plane Builder, 3D Space, and Decorator. These windows allow you to build, decorate, and view your 3D worlds. Each of these windows can be expanded, minimized, or moved about inside the larger WEB.WORLD window. Unlike many other Windows applications, only one .MUS file can be opened and worked on at a time, and there are no facilities for cutting, copying, or pasting 3D elements from one file to another.

The Plane Builder Window

Figure 17-2 shows the Plane Builder window and the different controls attached to it. All building work takes place in this workspace. The white area is the terrain in which you place boxes, walls, and faces. This window gives you a birds-eye, or aerial, view of your world. If you are familiar with architectural floor plans for houses and buildings, this will seem very natural.

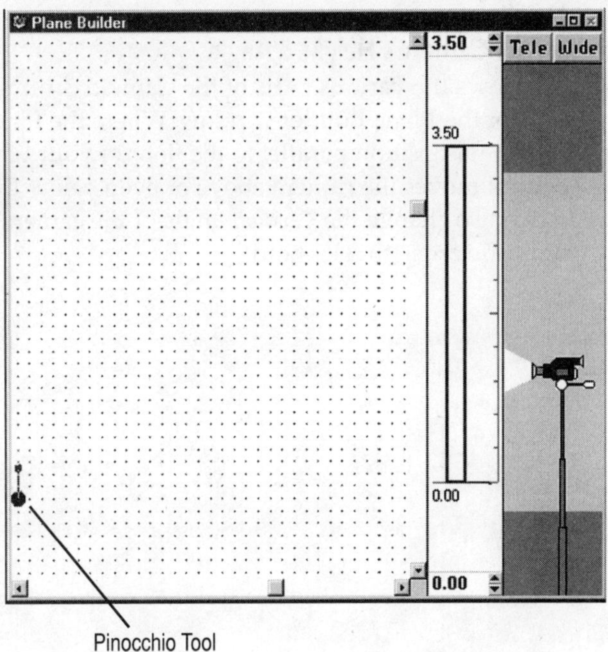

Figure 17-2: The Plane Builder window provides a birds-eye view of your virtual world. Note the Pinocchio tool, the Height and Camera controls.

Working & Moving in the Plane Builder Window

By default, a Grid is visible and the Snap to Grid option is turned on. This makes it easier to line up objects in the Plane Builder. More details on this grid system are discussed later in this chapter in "The Edit Menu."

To place or modify an object in the Plane Builder window, you select one of the Build tools, click a starting point, and drag the tool. With some tools, you click once to finish the object; with others, you double-click.

Each tool's behavior is described in detail under "Build Tools," later in this chapter. There is one special tool always present in the Plane Builder window—the Pinocchio tool.

Yup, you heard right. The name makes a little more sense after further explanation—which you'll get in the following section devoted to the Build tools. WEB.MOVE uses the metaphor of viewing the 3D space through a video camera: the Pinocchio tool represents that camera. To change the camera's position, drag the tool around the Plane Builder window with the mouse. All changes in view are reflected in the adjacent 3D Space window.

Controlling the Camera's Height & Angle

Figure 17-3 shows the various parts of the Camera control, found on the far right side of the Plane Builder window. Where the Pinocchio tool moves the camera position parallel to the floor of your virtual world, the Camera control moves the camera above or even below the level of the floor. You can also change the vertical angle of the camera and its field of vision from wide angle to telephoto.

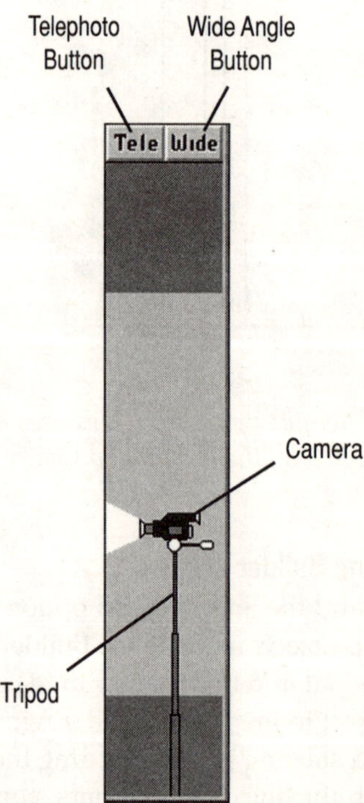

Figure 17-3: The Camera control comprises several elements, including the image of a video camera, which can be set interactively with the mouse.

Modifying the camera's height and angle can be accomplished in several ways. The easiest way is to grab the video camera icon with the mouse and interactively change its position. There are only two spots on the camera icon that activate its interactive nature. Figure 17-4 shows where to click the mouse if you want to drag the camera up and down or tilt its angle toward the floor or sky. At first, finding the exact spot can be a little tricky. Figure 17-4 also illustrates how you'll know when you've found it—the cursor will change to the shape of a hand as you hold down the mouse button.

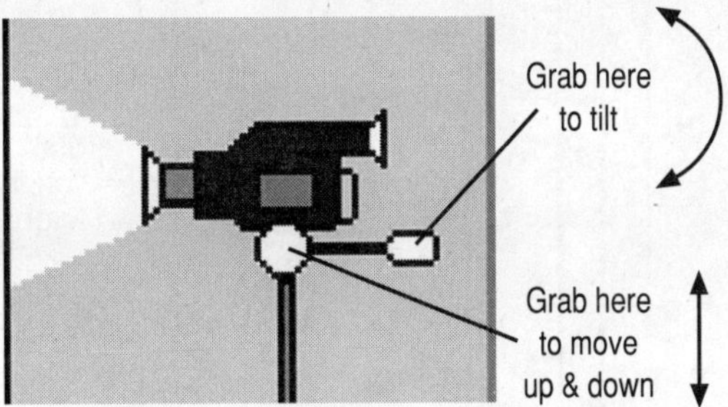

Figure 17-4: Click on the white circle just below the camera to drag the camera to a different height setting. Click and drag the tripod handle to tilt the camera up or down.

You change the camera's field of vision using the two buttons at the top of the Camera control. Pressing the Tele (short for telephoto) button, causes the view to zoom in on the scene, thus narrowing the field of vision. The Wide button allows you to view more of the surrounding space and objects. As you hold down either of these buttons, watch the 3D Space window: the view is constantly updated to correspond with the changes in camera settings. Additionally, there are nine buttons on the Walker toolbar that correspond to the camera changes you can make interactively, and these are described later in this chapter.

The Height Control

The Plane Builder work area only shows two dimensions of an object. From the birds-eye view this would be the width and length. From the camera's point of view they are the width and depth. So how do you control the height of the elements you build in the Plane Builder? The answer is: the Height control. This control is sandwiched between the right side of the Plane Builder window and the Camera control. Although it isn't as flashy looking as the Camera control, it is an interactive piece of the interface. Figure 17-5 shows the control with all its parts labeled.

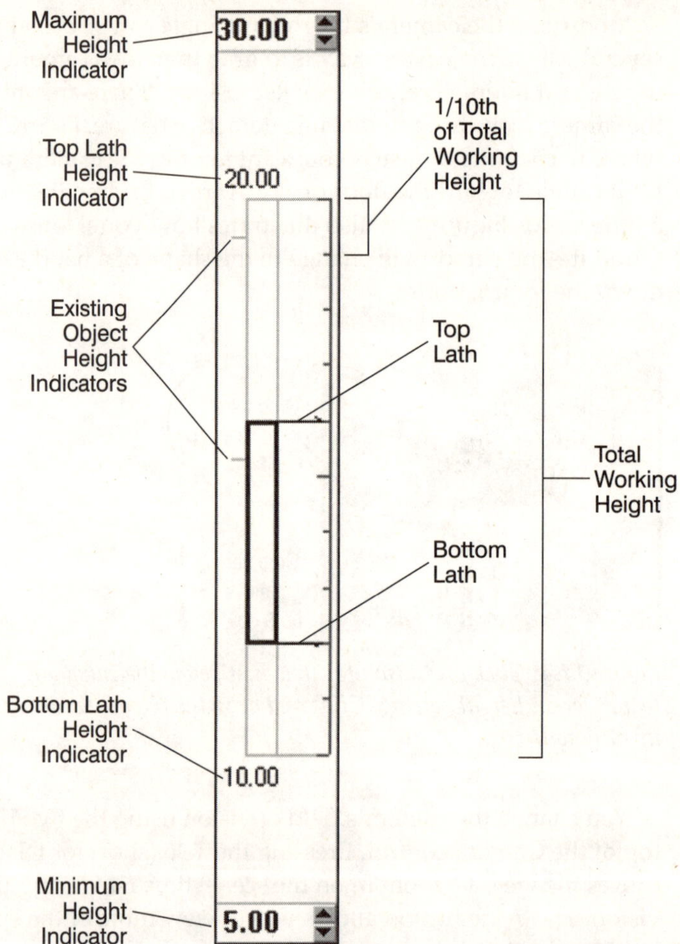

Figure 17-5: The Height control is made up of several key components that control the height and vertical placement of all objects created with the building tools.

At the very top and bottom of the Height control is a number with two arrows next to it. The top number is the Maximum height and the bottom is the Minimum. By default, the minimum is set to zero, which always denotes the floor of the virtual world. You can raise the number in either of these two text fields by pressing the up arrows: the number will increase by 0.05 with each click. Alternatively, you can click on the numbers and type any decimal numbers you choose, up to 127. By changing these values, you are setting the extreme limits for subsequent operations of any building tool. For instance, if you change the Minimum height indicator to 0.05, the lowest position any 3D object could occupy is 0.05 units above the floor of the virtual space. To create a 3D object that sits on the floor of the virtual space, you would have to set the minimum height control to 0.00 again.

This scale, with its minimum and maximum numbers, is like the speedometer of your car—just because it reads from 0 to 120 doesn't mean you *have* to drive only one speed or the other. You drive at differing speeds, within that range. The clever thing about the Height control is that you change the range when you modify the Minimum and Maximum indicators. The red tick marks on the right side never change—there are always 10 divisions. The fifth mark is slightly longer to denote its being the halfway point. No matter what your Min and Max height settings are, each tick mark represents one tenth of the total range. For example, if the Minimum is set to 10 and the Maximum set to 30, the working range is 20 units (30 minus 10). Each tick mark now represents two units (20 divided by 10). In this case, the fifth tick mark represents ten units (5 times 2), or twenty units above the floor of the virtual space.

Now that you understand how to set the working limits of the Height control, it's time to learn how to set the height of objects created with the building tools. The red scale has two thin black bars called laths. These indicate the top and bottom of any new objects created with the building tools. There are also smaller numbers close to the ends of the red height scale. The smaller numbers display the lath settings numerically. Click on either lath, drag it to a new position, and you'll see these numbers change. You'll also notice there is a heavy black outline that corresponds to the new height settings. You can click inside the border and drag the outline up or down within the range set by the Maximum and Minimum settings. Remember: you must make all height, top, and bottom changes *before* using a building tool.

Just to make sure you get the sense of how the various indicators work, here's an example: Set the Minimum height control at 5 and the Maximum at 30. Move the top lath to 20 and the bottom to 10. Any object you create will be 10 units high. The base of the object will be 10 units above the floor, with the top of the object at 20 units above the floor. If you want to create another 10 unit high object that sits directly on top of the first, set the bottom lath to 20, the top lath to 30, and create the object. Figure 17-6 illustrates this process.

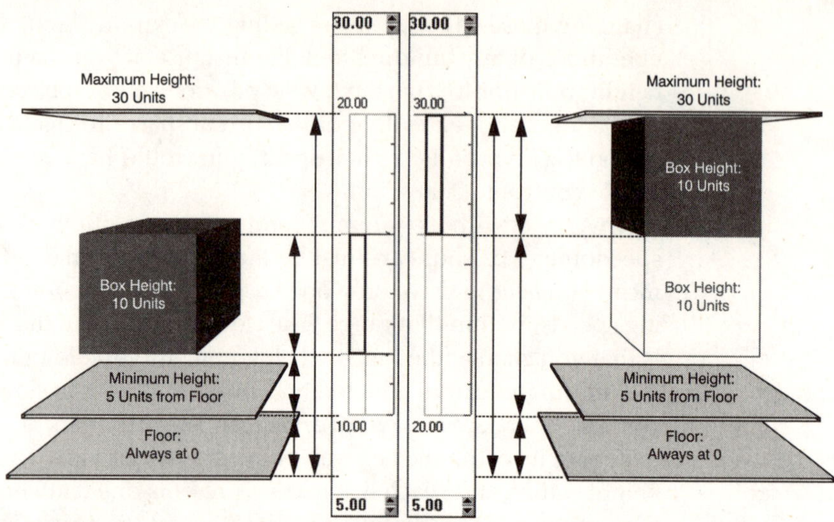

Figure 17-6: On the left, a box has been created 10 units above the floor. On the right, another box has been created above the first—20 units above the floor.

There is one more subtle feature of the Height control left to consider, this has to do with determining the height of any previously drawn object. When you click on an object in the 3D Space window, you will see two red tick marks appear on the left side of the height scale: these are top and bottom indicators for that object. These indicators are handy references when creating and positioning new objects that must correspond in some way with existing objects. If you click on an object and one or both of the height indicators do not appear, it is most likely that the extremities of the existing object do not fall within the currently set maximum and minimum height range. You will need to increase the range of the height scale by adjusting the minimum and maximum settings in order for the tick marks to be displayed.

At first glance, the Height control appears to be pretty insignificant, yet it holds the key to unlocking WEB.WORLD's third dimension. One final note: there is a logical reason for the Camera control being positioned next to the Height control. The two are coordinated. It is possible to position the camera so far above or below your working range that your 3D objects cannot be seen. But don't worry, with a little practice you'll soon get the hang of using the camera and the Pinocchio tool to get just the right point of view for your 3D worlds.

The 3D Space Window

The 3D Space window displays a view of your scene as it looks from the perspective of the camera. The camera's position is set with a combination of the Pinocchio tool and the Camera control. As Figure 17-7 illustrates, the 3D Space window also provides two background elements: a floor and a sky (by default, green and blue, respectively).

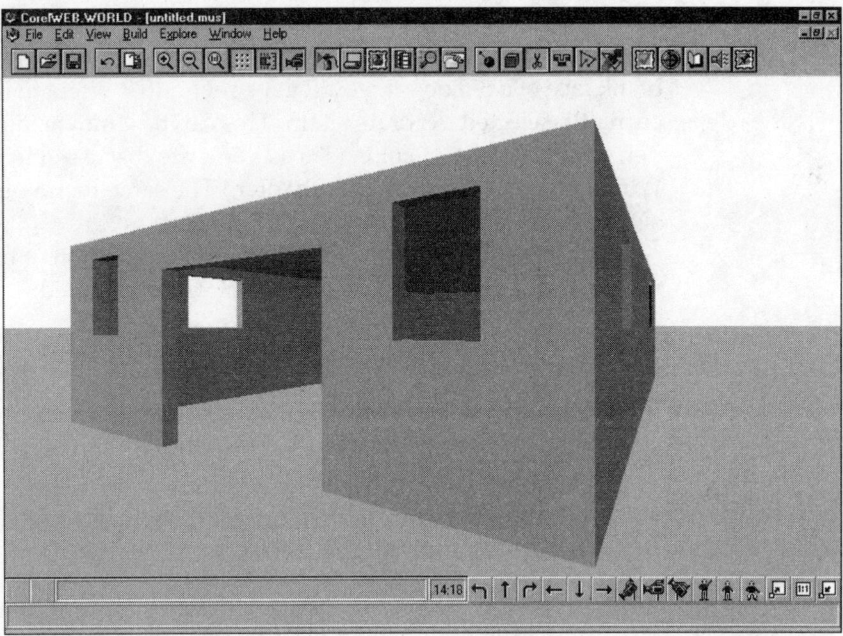

Figure 17-7: This screen shot of the 3D Space window shows a room with a door and windows. Note the floor and sky elements are always added to your scenes.

The 3D Space window contains several interactive features. One, already mentioned, gives you the ability to click on objects and have their top and bottom measurements displayed by the Plane Builder window's Height control. Another is its essential role in the decorating process, as described below.

Drag-&-Drop Decorating

You can decorate your 3D objects by dragging images and colors from
the Decorator window and dropping them on object surfaces displayed
in the 3D Space window. Another way to accomplish this task is by right-
clicking an object to display a menu option that applies the currently
selected item in the Decorator window. At certain times, the right mouse
button menu offers other options.

The Right Mouse Button Menu

The right mouse button menu is context-sensitive; that is, the menu
contains only options appropriate to the selected item. If you click on a
blank face of a 3D object, you'll get a menu that offers to apply the
currently selected decorator item. This can be a movie, picture, wallpaper, or airbrush paint color. (These items are discussed in the "Decorator
Window" section later in this chapter.) The same menu offers options to
switch to one of the other decorator modes.

If the selected item is a picture, album (a collection of pictures), or a
movie, a menu with the following choices is presented:

- Edit Attachment—Calls up the Attachment dialog box. This is
  discussed under the "Attachment Tools" section of this chapter.

- Move/Resize—Allows repositioning and resizing of an item.
  Discussed further in the "Decorating With Pictures" section.

- Direct View—Changes the view so that the selected item fills the
  3D Space window. Also discussed in "The Edit Menu" later in this
  chapter.

- Delete—Removes the selected item from the scene. Also found
  under the Edit menu. Note: the delete key will not remove selected
  items.

- Display Attached Text—If text has been entered, via the Attachment dialog box, it will be displayed in a pop-up box. These boxes
  are similar to the yellow pop-up help labels displayed when the
  cursor is over a toolbar button.

- Play Attached Sound—If a sound file has been attached, via the
  Attachment dialog box, it will be played.

- List Album—If the item consists of a stack of pictures, the next
  picture in the sequence will be displayed. Albums are discussed in
  the "Decorator Window" section.

Note, it's possible that some of these options will be grayed out. For instance, if the object has no sound or text attached, these menu items are not available for selection.

How to Copy & Paste

Although you can't copy and paste any 3D objects, WEB.WORLD does allow you to copy and paste decorator items—with some keyboard and mouse gymnastics.

First, position the cursor over the decorator item you wish to copy. This can be a movie, album, picture, wallpaper, or even a paint color. Next, hold down Ctrl and click the mouse, the cursor will change to a basket (I know, it's a pretty funny-looking basket) with an arrow pointing into it. This signifies that the item has been copied to WEB.WORLD's internal clipboard. To paste the item elsewhere, position the cursor over an object, hold down Shift and click the mouse. The cursor will change again: this time the basket will have an arrow pointing away from it and the item will be pasted into the 3D Space window.

Tip

WEB.WORLD's clipboard is completely independent of the Windows clipboard. This means you can't copy items to and from other Windows applications or even from one WEB.WORLD file to another.

At this point we've established that the operations performed in the Plane Builder window affect what's displayed in the 3D Space window. We've also gotten a small glimpse at the integration between the 3D Space window and the Decorator window. It's time to finish the discussion of WEB.WORLD's three windows by examining the Decorator Window in detail.

Decorator Window

The Decorator Window is a multi-faceted, interactive workspace. It's main purpose is to act as a repository for items used to decorate walls, ceilings, floors—any flat surface—created by WEB.WORLD's building tools. This window serves up four different types of decorator elements. But, as Figure 17-8 shows, it only has two distinct looks. This is because three of the four decorator types look the same when displayed in the Decorator window.

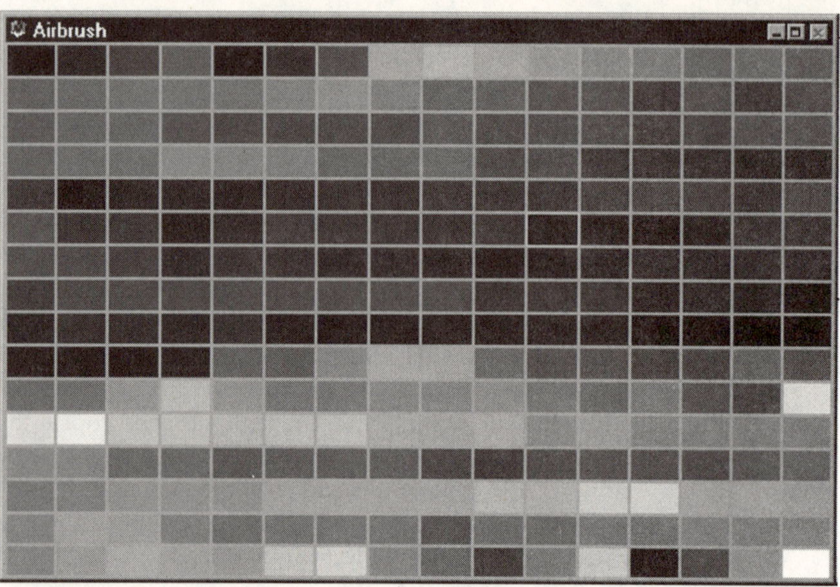

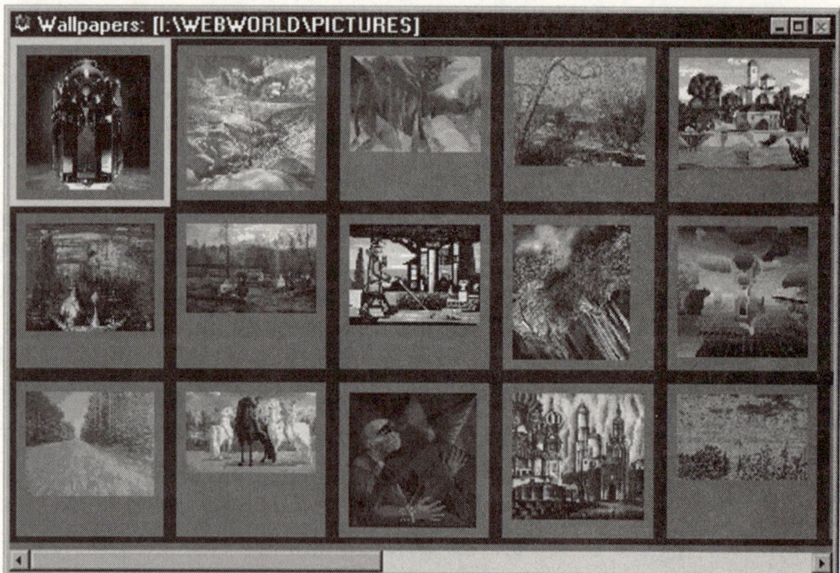

Figure 17-8: The two faces of the Decorator window: the Airbrush paint pallet and the collection of thumbnail images that display available wallpaper, picture, and movie items.

To apply a decoration, you click on it with the mouse and drag it into the 3D Space window, dropping it on the surface of a 3D object. Alternatively, you can apply a decoration by selecting the decorator item in the Decorator window, right-clicking the mouse over a surface in the 3D Space window, and choosing Apply from the pop-up menu.

At this point, we need to make clear what's meant by a *surface* of a 3D object. This refers to any flat, contiguous panel that is part of a 3D object. For example, drawing a box creates a 3D object with six surfaces: a top, a bottom, and four sides. When you apply a decoration that covers an entire surface—like airbrush paint or wallpaper—the color or image only covers the selected panel. If you want an entire cube to be one color, all six sides must be selected and the color applied. This principle applies to Wall objects as well. Every time you create a corner, you are starting a new surface, and each surface must be decorated separately.

The Different Decoration Types

As mentioned, there are four *basic* types of decorations the Decorator window can display. These are:

- Airbrush paint colors
- Wallpapers
- Pictures
- Movies

Each of these decoration types is discussed below. There is one more decorator type: *albums*. An album is a collection, or stack, of images that can be viewed one at a time. You use the Decorator window's picture mode to compile albums in the 3D Space window.

There are three ways to switch the Decorator window to a different type of decoration. First, choose the View | Decorator menu option to access a submenu that offers the following choices: Pictures, Wallpapers, Movies, and Airbrush. Second, choose one of the Decorator tools on the toolbar. Last, you can click the right mouse button over an undecorated surface in the 3D Space window. A context-sensitive menu pops up with choices to switch to another decorator mode.

Once you've switched the Decorator window to display a different type of decoration, you need to direct it to different locations where appropriate files are stored. This is accomplished by using the Select Directory dialog box, shown in Figure 17-9. You access this dialog in one of two ways: select the View | Decorator | Directory menu option, or press the Directory button on the toolbar.

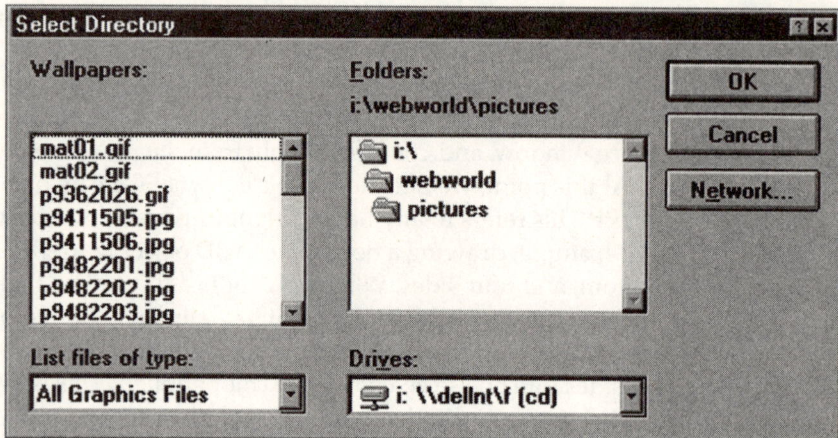

Figure 17-9: Access the Select Directory dialog box to tell the Decorator window where to look for bitmap files to use as wallpaper, pictures, and movies.

Decorating With Airbrush Paints

As seen in Figure 17-8, the airbrush paint mode of the Decorator window is simply a pallet of 256 colors. The airbrush metaphor is a little misleading, if you are used to an airbrush tool that gradually sprays paint on a surface. The action of this WEB.WORLD tool is more like a Fill tool—it floods the entire surface with one flat color.

There is no way to change the pallet of colors or reorder them. This could be a severe limitation for users who need more flexibility in color choice. Unfortunately, the only solution in this situation is to acquire a more sophisticated 3D virtual reality authoring application.

Decorating With Wallpapers

Wallpapers are bitmap images used to cover an entire surface of a 3D object. Wallpapers are far more interesting than the flat colors offered by the airbrush paints. You can create and use your own bitmaps or any of those provided on the CorelWEB.GRAPHICS Suite CD. The following bitmap image file types can be used as wallpapers:

- .BMP
- .DCX
- .DIB
- .EPS
- .GIF

- .JPG
- .PCT
- .PCX
- .RLE
- .TGA
- .TIF

Wallpapers can be tiled—multiple copies of the image are repeated across the width and height of a surface—or not. When not tiled, the bitmap image is stretched as needed to cover the entire surface. Depending on the shape of the surface and the size of the bitmap, this stretching may cause considerable distortion of the graphic image. You'll need to experiment to determine the best size and shape for a particular surface. To turn the tiling capability on, access the WallPaper Detail dialog box, shown in Figure 17-10. To open the dialog, choose the Detail button from the toolbar or select the View | Decorator | Detail menu option.

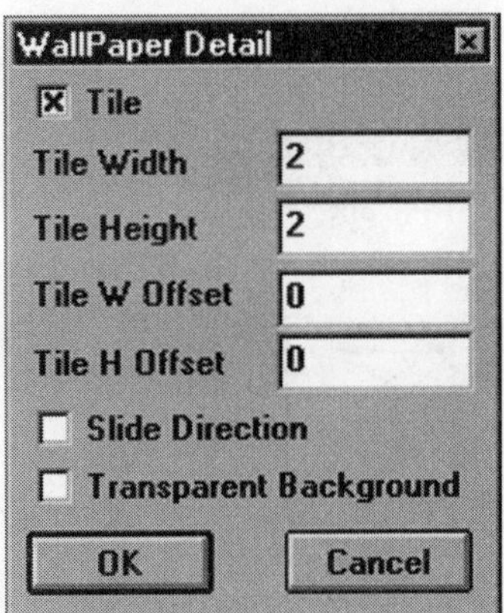

Figure 17-10: The WallPaper Detail dialog contains options for changing many aspects of wallpaper images, including tiling the image to cover an entire surface.

The WallPaper Detail Dialog Box   In conjunction with setting the Tile option on or off, you use the Tile Width and Tile Height options to control how many copies of the image are used to cover a surface. You can enter a number from 0.1 to 100. The smaller the number, the greater the number of repeat images. Of course, each image will become smaller. Conversely, the larger the number, the larger the image will appear.

You'll probably be disappointed in the effect you get by setting either of these two settings in the double digits. Although it depends on the resolution of the bitmap image, you are effectively stretching the image to such a point that you will see the actual pixels of the image. However, if this is the effect you're after, you now know how to achieve it. By experimenting with these options you can create some very interesting tiled patterns.

The Tile W Offset and Tile H Offset options are used to fine-tune the repeat pattern of wallpaper. Normally, the first complete image in a tiled wallpaper pattern is positioned in the lower left corner of a surface. Subsequent images are added above, and to the right, until the surface is completely filled. By changing the numbers in these two controls the position of the first image can be adjusted vertically or horizontally. The usefulness of this feature is demonstrated in the "Working With Wallpaper" section in Chapter 18.

A very clever wallpaper feature is Slide Direction. This creates moving wallpaper. After selecting this check box, the dialog will expand, as shown in Figure 17-11. This new control allows you to set the direction and speed at which the wallpaper moves.

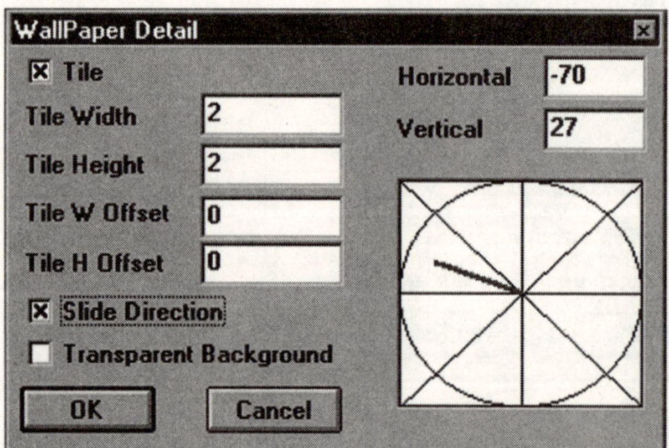

Figure 17-11: After selecting Slide Direction, the WallPaper Detail dialog box expands to display the direction and rate control.

To determine the wallpaper's movement, you can type numbers into the Horizontal and Vertical text boxes. An easier way is clicking inside the circle and dragging the red line to a new position. This automatically updates the numbers in the two text boxes. The farther away from the center of the circle the end of the red line is, the faster the wallpaper moves. After making the changes, any newly applied wallpaper will slide as set. When you want to apply wallpaper that does not move, you will need to access the WallPaper Detail dialog and turn off the Slide Direction option.

Tip

Static Wallpaper can be viewed in an .MUS or .WRL file. However, moving wallpaper is displayed only in an .MUS file.

The last option in the WallPaper Detail dialog is Transparent Background. This option tells WEB.WORLD to apply the wallpaper, so that any pure black areas of the image appear transparent. This allows the original airbrush paint color to show through. Corel's documentation states this option will not work for all wallpapers. We experimented with 256 color: .BMP, .TIF, .PCX, .TGA, and .JPG files all honored the transparency setting.

Decorating With Pictures

Pictures are also bitmap images; however, they do not cover entire surfaces of objects, so they cannot be tiled either. You can use the very same bitmap images for pictures that you use for wallpapers.

Moving, Resizing & Deleting Pictures   After dragging a picture onto the surface of a 3D object, the item stays selected until you click the mouse off the picture item. Up until the time you deselect the picture, you can move or resize it. If a picture has been deselected, click on it with the right mouse button and select Move/Resize. The cursor changes to a small picture with two arrows to denote that you are in Move/Resize mode. To move the picture anywhere on the surface, drag with the mouse, releasing it when it is positioned properly. You cannot move a picture off the surface it was originally placed on.

Resizing is a little trickier. First, make sure you are in Move/Resize mode. Click the upper right corner of the picture and drag it in any direction. When the picture is the desired size, release the mouse button. WEB.WORLD does not allow you to use a keyboard modifier to resize a picture proportionally. This is lamentable but not without remedy. You can change the default resize behavior for all images used as pictures and movies. Choose the File | Settings menu option and turn on the Keep Aspect Ratio While Resizing Picture check box found in the CorelWEB.WORLD Settings dialog box.

Deleting is accomplished by selecting a picture and choosing Edit | Delete from the menu bar, or right-clicking the item and selecting Delete from the pop-up menu. You cannot use the Delete key to remove selected items from the 3D Space window.

Creating Picture Albums   There is no Picture Detail dialog box, because there are no attributes for this type of decoration that can be changed. However, you can create albums of pictures. To accomplish this:

1. Drag a picture to the 3D Space window and drop it on a surface.

2. Drag another picture and drop it on top of the previously placed picture.

3. Continue to place as many pictures as desired, each time dropping them on the previously placed picture.

4. To cycle through the series of pictures, right-click and choose List Album. Or press the List Album button on the toolbar.

The pictures that comprise an album do not have to be the same dimensions or bitmap type. WEB.WORLD makes all the adjustments necessary to display each picture properly. While working in WEB.WORLD you'll be able to differentiate an album from a regular picture by looking for the Album Indicator icon displayed on the status line below the Decorator window. This looks like a book with pages being turned.

Decorating With Movies

Movies take picture and album decorations to a higher level. The best thing is that you don't need any special programs, like Macromedia's Director or Adobe's Premier, to make movies in digital formats such as AVI, MPG, or .FLI. WEB.WORLD can take a series of static bitmap images—the kind made by standard paint programs—and make a movie out of them. All you need to do is:

1. Name the bitmaps properly.

2. Put them in the same directory.

3. Switch to the Decorator window to Movie mode and tell it what directory the images are stored in.

The trickiest part of preparing bitmap files for use as a movie is naming them properly. What WEB.WORLD looks for is a series of names that have the same beginning characters, followed by a sequence number. For example, the following files stored in the same directory will be recognized by WEB.WORLD as a movie:

- movie01.gif
- movie02.gif
- movie03.gif
- movie04.gif

Each bitmap file becomes one frame of the movie. If you need a primer on animation and frames, check out Chapter 11. If you have created animations with CorelWEB.MOVE, you can use these in WEB.WORLD by publishing to sequential bitmap files. See Chapter 12 for the scoop on this technique.

Tip

The images used do not have to be the same size, although they do have to be the same file format. For this reason the Select Directory dialog box does not contain the All Graphics Files selection in the List Files of Type drop-down listing. You must select one type of bitmap file format, so that WEB.WORLD knows what type of file to expect when it imports a whole series.

The Movie Detail Dialog Box   As shown in Figure 17-12, the Movie Detail dialog box contains a cornucopia of options that control everything from the direction and the amount of time each frame displays to changing the animation into an album or sliding wallpaper. You'll recognize that some of these options are related to those that apply to pictures and wallpaper.

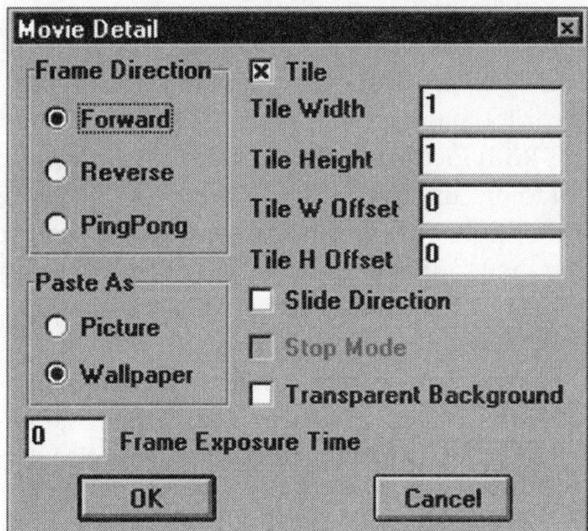

Figure 17-12: The Movie Detail dialog box is chock full of options that modify how movie images are displayed in the 3D scene.

You can set one of three options contained in the Frame Direction area. Forward plays the frames of the movie from the lowest sequence number to the highest. Reverse displays the frames in the opposite direction. Ping Pong switches between playing the frames in forward direction and playing them in reverse.

The Paste As area offers two settings: Picture places the image as a single movie on the surface of the 3D object; Wallpaper creates tiles of the movie to fill the entire surface.

Frame Exposure Time controls how long each frame of the movie is displayed. The higher the number, the longer each frame displays and the slower the movie appears. The range for this option is 0 to 9999. We didn't have the patience to sit and find out exactly how long 9999 was—suffice it to say it was too long!

You'll recognize the Tile check box from the WallPaper Detail dialog. Basically, it carries out the same functions, along with its associated options Tile Width and Tile Height. As noted earlier, the Tile W Offset and Tile H Offset options are inoperable at this point in time.

Slide Direction creates moving and animated wallpaper. As in the WallPaper Detail dialog, choosing this check box causes the dialog to expand and reveal the Slide Direction controls. These work exactly the same as the wallpaper options.

Tip

If the Paste As option is set to Picture, the Tile and Slide Direction options will be unavailable.

Stop Mode transforms a movie into an album of pictures. This means you must manually cycle through each picture item using the List Album menu selection or toolbar button. See the earlier section on albums under the "Decorating With Pictures" heading for more information.

The last item to discuss in the Movie Detail dialog box is the Transparent Background option. This works the same as the corresponding feature found in the WallPaper Detail dialog box. Basically, any pure black areas of the movie's frame will become transparent, allowing the original airbrush paint color to show through.

Remember that changing any of the above options will affect any movies subsequently applied to objects. You cannot change the attributes of movies that have already been placed—these movies must be replaced.

The True Image Viewer

There is one more window that is closely tied to the Decorator window and image-based decorator items. This is called the True Image window. It is used to get the best possible view of an image—at its original size and proportion, if the object has been resized in the 3D Space window. You can also change an image's brightness, contrast, and gamma factor. Figure 17-13 shows the True Image window opened with a picture item loaded.

Figure 17-13: The True Image window is a convenient way to view an image without the distractions of the rest of the 3D scene.

To open the True Image window, right-click an image object in the 3D Space window and choose True Image from the pop-up menu. Or select the image and choose the Explore | True Image menu option. Or press the True Image button on the toolbar.

Tip

You can also use the True Image window to view any image displayed in the Decorator window by double-clicking its thumbnail.

At the top of the window is a row of icons that activate the various functions of the True Image window. The first one represents a door: click on this to close the True Image window. If you have made any changes to an image's attributes, you will be asked if you want to save the image to disk. If you answer yes, you will be presented with the Save Image File dialog box. Give the file a name and a directory and select the file format type before pressing OK.

You can click the Save Image icon to access the Save Image File dialog box and save the current image under a new filename.

The next three icons represent the Zoom tools. The one with the plus mark is the Zoom In function. Each time you press the icon, you view the image at twice the original size. The icon with the minus sign on it is the Zoom Out tool. Pressing this displays the image at one-half the original size. If you want to view the image at its original size, press the Actual Size icon. Zooming does not affect the image file you are viewing, unless you invoke the Save Image command. If so, the image will be saved at the current zoom state. The next button, with the 1:1 image, activates only if you zoom an image. Clicking this button will automatically return the image to its original size.

The Image Attributes Dialog

The final icon, Change Image Attributes, calls up the Image Attributes dialog box, shown in Figure 17-14. This dialog box contains controls to adjust the brightness, contrast, and gamma factor of the image. These settings should be very familiar to those who have used bitmap editors, such as CorelPHOTO-PAINT and Adobe's Photoshop.

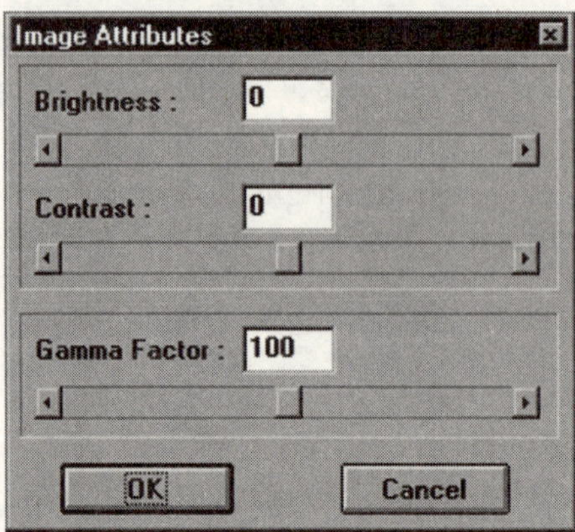

Figure 17-14: The Image Attributes dialog contains three controls that dramatically affect your image.

The first scroll bar, Brightness, adjusts the amount of black in an image. Moving the button to the left makes the image darker; moving it to the right makes it lighter. The second scroll bar is labeled Contrast. Moving this button to the left reduces the amount of visual contrast within the picture. Moving the button to the right increases the contrast, heightening the differences between the colors of the image. The last scroll bar controls the Gamma Factor. This affects only the middle range of colors in an image. Changing the gamma factor will not affect the shadow or highlight areas of the image.

If you change an image's attributes, you will be asked to save the image before exiting the True Image window. If you decline to save the changes, your image will revert back to its original settings. If you choose to save the edited image under the original filename rather than saving with a new filename, and you have the Fast 3D Space Images Loading option enabled, you must reapply the image to the 3D object to view the changes.

Tip

If you save any changes under a new filename in the same directory, press F5 to refresh the Decorator window and the new image's thumbnail will be displayed.

Thus far, our introduction to the WEB.WORLD interface has covered the majority of features used to construct and view your 3D environments. However, there are still some areas we have not touched upon. The next section focuses entirely on the tools found on the various toolbars.

The Tools of the 3D Trade

The WEB.WORLD interface contains several toolbars and status lines. These make it easier to carry out repetitive functions. The Main toolbar, across the top of the application, can logically be divided into the following five sections:

- File Tools
- Plane Builder Window Tools
- Decorator Window Tools
- Building Tools
- Attachment Tools

The following sections discuss the individual tools found in these five groups. Many of the tools have been mentioned previously in this chapter, so we won't dwell on these—unless there is supplemental information to present.

The File Tools

These tools deal specifically with WEB.WORLD's file functions. Figure 17-15 shows each of the five tools that make up this grouping.

Figure 17-15: The File Tools buttons.

New

Pressing this button starts a new, empty WEB.WORLD scene. If you have an unsaved scene currently open, you will be given the opportunity to save this.

Open

The invokes the Open 3D Space File dialog box, shown in Figure 17-16. Use this dialog to navigate to a directory where .MUS files are stored.

When WEB.WORLD finds .MUS files in a directory, it presents them in the list directly below the File Name text box. When you select a file with the mouse, the 3D Space Info button is enabled. Press the button to open the 3D Space Info dialog box, shown in Figure 17-17.

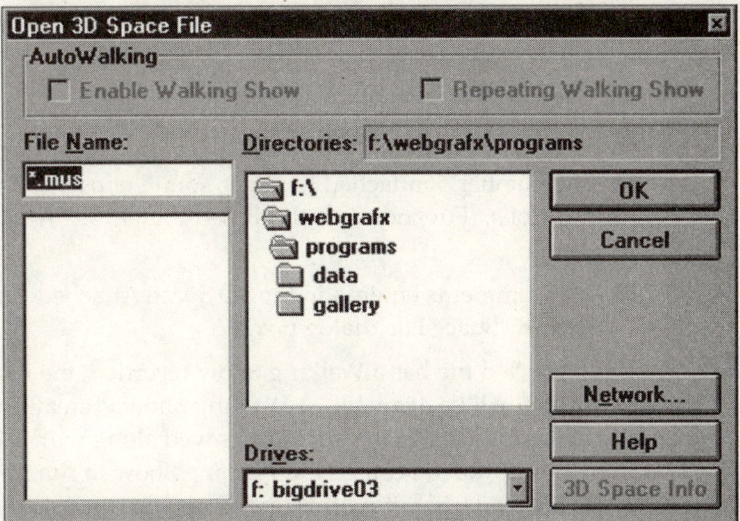

Figure 17-16: The Open 3D Space File dialog box.

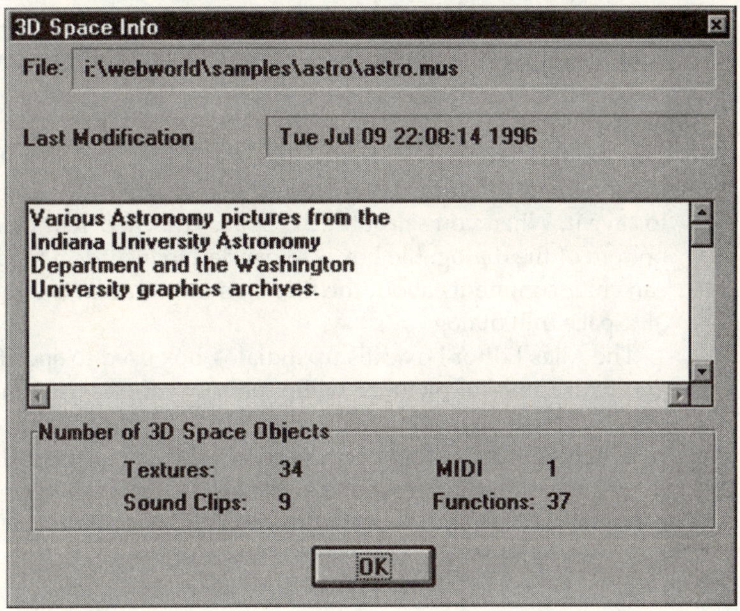

Figure 17-17: The 3D Space Info dialog displays the vital statistics of a selected .MUS file.

The 3D Space Info dialog box presents information about the location and makeup of the selected .MUS file. This includes:

- The exact location of the file.

- The date and time the file was saved.

- The number of attached textures, sound clips, MIDI files, and functions. (Functions are discussed under the "Attachment Tool" section.)

- Text comments entered in the 3D Space Attached Text area of the Save 3D Space File dialog box.

If the selected file has a Walking Show recorded, the Enable Walking Show option will be available. A Walking Show is an automated tour of the virtual world that is recorded and saved along with the .MUS file. Turning this option on causes the Walking Show to run immediately after the file loads. Selecting this option enables the Repeating Walking Show option. Selecting this option causes the Walking Show to run continuously rather than just once. This is a great way to show off your 3D scene, even if the computer is unattended. A Walking Show can be interrupted by moving the camera with the Walker buttons or keyboard controls. The Walker buttons are discussed later in this chapter.

Save

This invokes the Save 3D Space File dialog box, shown in Figure 17-18. Enter a name for your .MUS file and pick a drive and directory in which to save it. When you select the 3D Space Attached Text Box option at the bottom of the dialog, the box is expanded to include a field where you can enter comments about the file. This information is displayed in the 3D Space Info dialog.

The Alias Editor box calls up a dialog box used to specify the directory and path names of pictures, wallpapers, or movies used in your world. When publishing an .MUS file on a network, you may have to change the path names of these files because some servers require full references. If you're encountering problems publishing your .MUS files on your network, contact your server administrator and ask which of the following types of references your network requires:

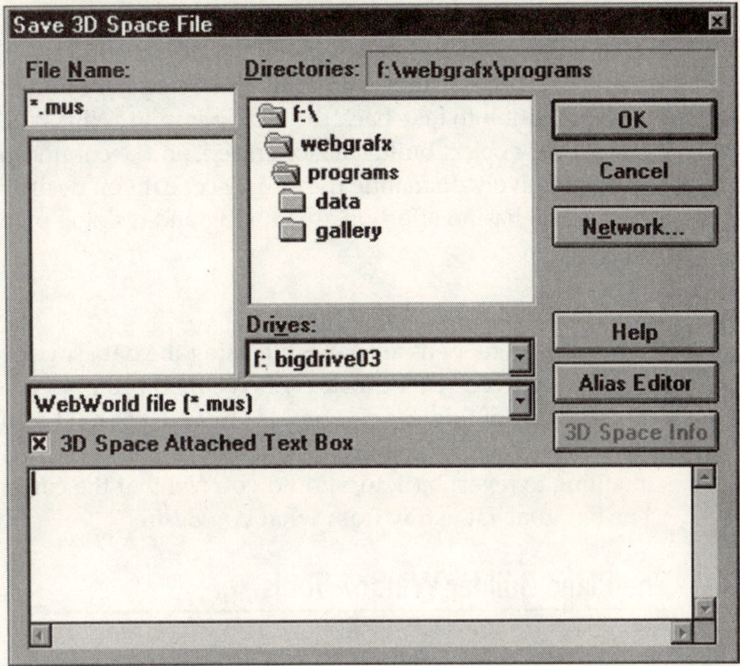

Figure 17-18: Besides using the Save 3D Space dialog to name and save your file, you can enter comments into the 3D Space Attached Text Box field.

- Full (includes drive, directory, and file name with extension)
- Absolute (includes full directory—starting from the root—and file name with extension)
- Relative (includes file name with extension)

Should you need to change the path statement of any decorator image used in your .MUS file, select the item from the Texture File Name list: the file name is displayed in the Alias text field. Now that you know which type of reference is needed, select it from the File Access Mode list and press the Correct Alias for Selected Textures button. The corrected file reference is displayed. If your server administrator directs you to include a prefix to all file references (perhaps a network drive or proxy server string), you can input this into the Alias Prefix text field and it will be added to the beginning of each corrected alias.

Undo

Pressing this undoes the last operation performed in the Plane Builder or 3D Space window. There is no limit to the number of times you can press the Undo button to take back the last operation. WEB.WORLD keeps track of every object built, surface erased, and decorator item applied. It can progressively dismantle the entire scene if you desire. The only operations it has no effect on are moving and resizing pictures and movies.

Revert to Saved

This operation reopens an .MUS file using the data saved to disk. All changes not saved will be lost. WEB.WORLD prompts you to make sure you are aware of this. It's a good idea to save your 3D scenes periodically, just in case your system locks up or crashes. It also gives you something to revert back to, should you feel that the current state of the scene has gone far astray from what you desire.

The Plane Builder Window Tools

The following tools all pertain to items related to the Plane Builder window. Figure 17-19 shows the name of each tool button.

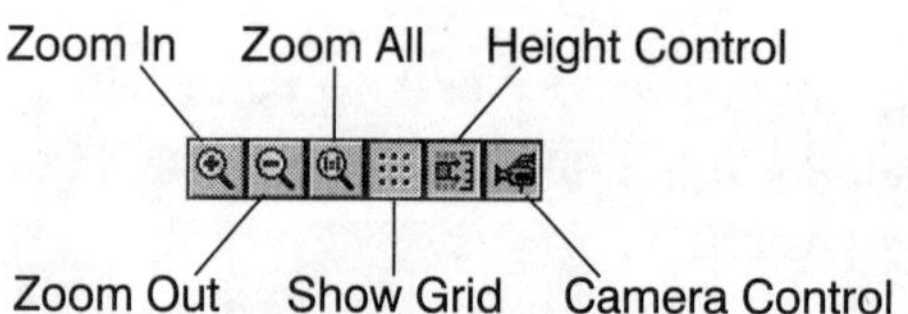

Figure 17-19: These six buttons make up the Plane Builder window tools.

Zoom In

Press this button to progressively zoom in on the contents of the Plane Builder window. This is useful when performing detailed building or erasing work.

Zoom Out

Press this button to progressively zoom out and view more of the contents of the Plane Builder window. This is useful when you need to see an overview of your entire virtual space.

Zoom All

Press this button once to zoom out and view all the contents of the Plane Builder window. This is the quickest way to see all the objects in your 3D scene.

Show Grid

If this button is depressed, the grid is displayed in the Plane Builder window. To remove the grid from view, press the button. This button has no effect on the Snap to Grid feature.

Height Control

The Height control is displayed, by default. If you wish to remove it from view, press this button. As there is no other way to set the height of 3D objects, you will probably want this control active. To redisplay it, press the button once again.

Camera Control

By default, the Height control is displayed at the far right of the Plane Builder window. If you wish to remove it from view, press this button. To redisplay it, press the button once again. There are other controls for the camera; these are found on the Walker bar, which is discussed later in this chapter.

The Decorator Window Tools

Figure 17-20 shows the names of the six tools categorized as the Decorator window tools. These tools simply switch the mode of the Decorator window.

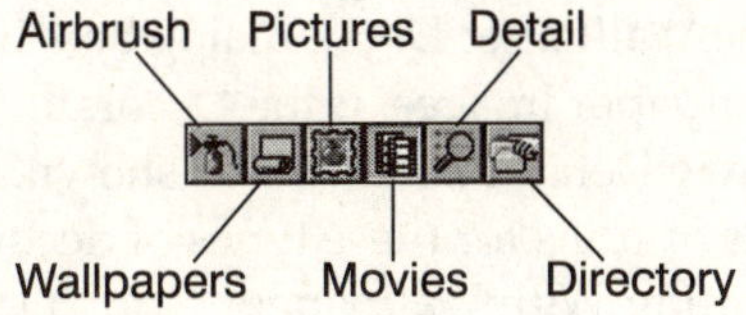

Figure 17-20: The six buttons that make up the Decorator window tools.

Airbrush

Press this button to display the pallet of 256 colors which are used to paint the surfaces of 3D objects. See the earlier section on "Decorating With Airbrush Paints" for further information.

Wallpapers

Press this button to change the Decorator window mode and display images that can be used as wallpaper decorations. If there are no images in the currently selected directory, the Decorator window will be empty. Use the Directory button to point WEB.WORLD to a directory with valid bitmap images. See the earlier section on "Decorating With Wallpaper" for more details.

Pictures

This button switches the Decorator window into picture mode and displays images that can be used as picture items. If there are no images in the currently selected directory, no thumbnail images will be displayed in the Decorator window. Use the Directory button to locate a directory with valid bitmap images. See the earlier section on "Decorating With Pictures" for more details.

Movies

This button causes the Decorator window to display thumbnail images of files that can be used as movie decorations. If there are no valid movie images in the currently selected directory, no thumbnail images will be displayed in the Decorator window. Use the Directory button to locate a directory with valid movie images. See the earlier section on "Decorating With Movies" for all the information on creating movie files.

Detail

This button will call up the WallPaper Detail dialog box, if the Decorator window is set to show wallpaper images. If the Decorator window is in movie mode, then the Movie Detail dialog will be shown. Use these dialog boxes to set various options for these types of decorations. See the earlier sections on "Decorating With Wallpapers" and "Decorating With Movies" for more information on these options.

Directory

Use this button to call up the Select Directory dialog box and locate directories with valid bitmap files for use as pictures, wallpapers, and movies.

Tip

WEB.WORLD remembers the last directory selected for each of the three decorator categories by recording them in the WEBWORLD.INI file. This file is saved in the Windows startup directory. The directory entries will look similar to the following:

[Chooser]
Picture=D:\EXPLOR~1
WallPaper=D:\COREL\HTML
Movie=D:\EXPLOR~1

The Building Tools

The following six tools all pertain to drawing or viewing 3D objects. They are only active within the Plane Builder window. Figure 17-21 puts a name to each tool's button.

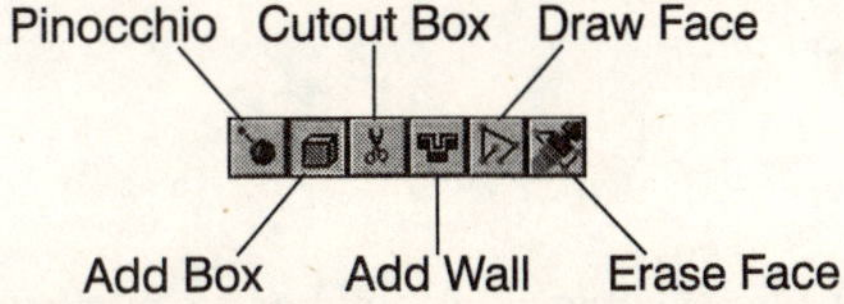

Figure 17-21: The six tools used in the Plane Builder window to create or view 3D objects.

Pinocchio

You've just got to love this tool! Although it has a kooky name and looks a wee bit weird, it does one heck of a job. Pressing this button activates the Pinocchio tool.

The Pinocchio tool represents the camera, through which you view the 3D scene. The larger circle part of the tool (called the body) represents the actual location of the camera, while the smaller circle at the end of the stick (the nose) determines the direction in which the lens is pointing. You can grab the body and drag the tool to different locations within the Plane Builder window. Or, you can drag the nose of the tool to simultaneously move and rotate the camera.

The Pinocchio tool can be operated by buttons on the Walker bar and various keys on the keyboard. The following is a list of the keys that control movement of the Pinocchio tool:

Keypad	Keyboard	Action
7	Home	Rotate left
9	Page Up	Rotate right
8	Up arrow	Move forward
2	Down arrow	Move back
4	Left Arrow	Move left
6	Right Arrow	Move right
Hold down the CTRL key to double the speed.		

Tip

Double click the mouse anywhere in the Plane Builder window to move the tool to that location.

Add Box

The box is one of the basic 3D objects. A box has six surfaces: top, bottom, and four sides. To create a box, press the Add Box tool, click the mouse in the Plane Builder window, and drag out a rectangle. Release the mouse button when you have a rectangle of the desired size and shape. The box's width and depth are determined by the shape you drag out in the Plane Builder window. The height is determined by top and bottom lath settings in the Height control. See the previous section under "The Plane Builder" heading for more information on creating 3D objects.

The Add Box tool will stay active until you select another Building tool. A quick way to deactivate any tool is to right-click in the Plane Builder window. This instantly switches to the Pinocchio tool.

Cutout Box

The Cutout Box tool doesn't really create anything. It actually removes sections of any 3D object. Think of it as destroying any object it touches. The shape and size of a Cutout Box are determined the same way as the regular box; drag out the length and depth in the Plane Builder window, and set the height with the top and bottom laths of the Height control.

The Cutout Box tool is exceedingly useful for carving out the insides of boxes to create rooms, and for removing portions of walls to create openings that serve as windows and doors.

Add Wall

The Add Wall tool is used to create walls that have thickness. Walls can only be drawn as straight horizontal or vertical lines. You can create corners, but they will always be perfect right angles. To create a wall, select the Add Wall tool, click a starting point in the Plane Builder window, and double-click a point for the end of the wall. The wall will be drawn as a straight line between the two points. To create multisectioned walls with corners, follow the same procedure—except click every place you want a corner that starts a new section. Straight lines are drawn to connect each corner. Double-click to finish creating the wall.

The height of a wall is determined by the top and bottom lath settings in the Height control. The thickness of a wall can be changed with the Wall Width control found in the Builder Settings dialog box. This dialog is found under the Build | Builder Settings menu. You can set widths for walls as thin as 0.02 and as thick as 127.99. Although an ultra-thin wall may be advantageous, a very thick wall will cut into itself at corners, and this will definitely cause some problems.

Draw Face

A face is similar to a wall, except is has no thickness. A face is inherently different from a wall because it can be drawn on angles, rather than being constrained to right angles. You create faces the same way you create walls: click a starting point, click at each corner, and double-click to end the object. A face's height is controlled like all other 3D objects: by adjusting the top and bottom laths of the Height control.

A word of warning: do not overlap face objects. This creates bizarre surfaces. This strange behavior does not affect walls that intersect themselves.

Erase Face

The Erase Face tool is a destruction tool in the same vein as the Cutout Box tool. This tool removes entire surfaces of any 3D objects. Drag out a rectangular shape that completely encompasses the face of a 3D object. When you release the mouse button, the surface is removed from the scene.

Unlike the Cutout Box tool, the Erase Face tool is not affected by the Height control. This tool takes out the entire surface of any object it engulfs. If you erase a surface unintentionally, press the Undo button to resurrect it.

The Attachment Tools

This set of five buttons aids in working with the images and multimedia content of your WEB.WORLD scenes. All but one of these buttons activate some hidden attribute of the various decorator items. The fifth button is used to call up a dialog box that allows control over specific attributes of attached decorator items. WEB.WORLD knows when a selected item has a particular attribute turned on; it signals this by displaying the corresponding button's icon in color. Otherwise, the icons are represented in black and white.

True Image

If this button is active, it signals that the image item can be displayed in the True Image window. Details regarding the features and capabilities of this special window are discussed in "The True Image Viewer" section earlier in this chapter. You can also access the True Image window by right-clicking on the object and selecting this choice from the menu.

Direct View

When this button is depressed, the camera is moved to a position directly in front of the selected item. The selected object will fill the 3D Space window area no matter what size that window happens to be at the time. This assures that the viewer will have the best view of the object. You can also activate Direct View by right-clicking on the object and selecting it from the menu.

List Album

An album is a series of picture items. However, only the first picture is displayed. To view the rest of the series, press this button repeatedly. Alternatively, you can cycle through albums by selecting List Album from the object's right mouse button menu. Albums are discussed in the "Decorating With Pictures" section.

Play Sound

Although we have not discussed it up to this point, you can attach WAV
sound files to picture and movie decorations. You accomplish this feat
with the help of the Edit Attachment dialog, discussed next. When a
sound has been attached, pressing this button activates playback. As you
might expect, you can activate sound playback by right-clicking on the
object and selecting Play Sound from the menu.

Attachment

Depending on the type of object selected, this button calls up one of three
versions of the Attachment editors shown in Figures 17-22 a–c.

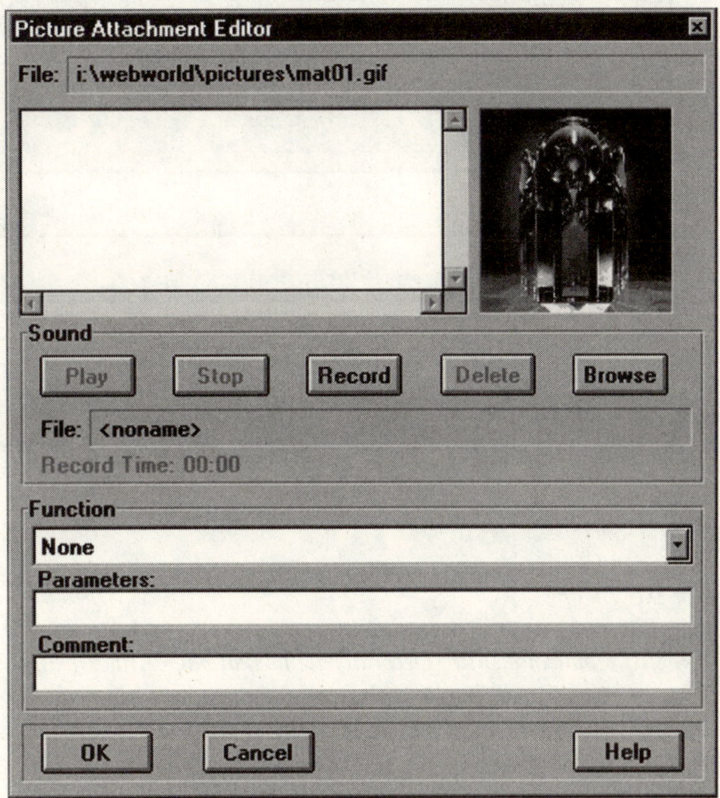

*Figure 17-22a: There are slightly different Attachment Editor dialog boxes for
pictures, albums, and movies.*

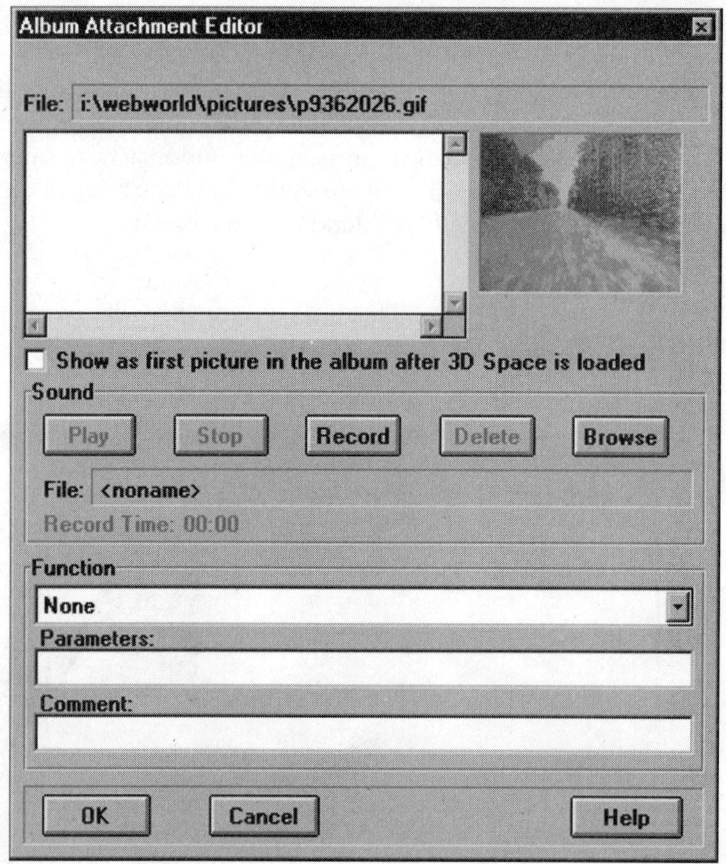

Figure 17-22b.

Tip

You can identify Decorator items that have Attachments because the cursor will change to the shape of a hand.

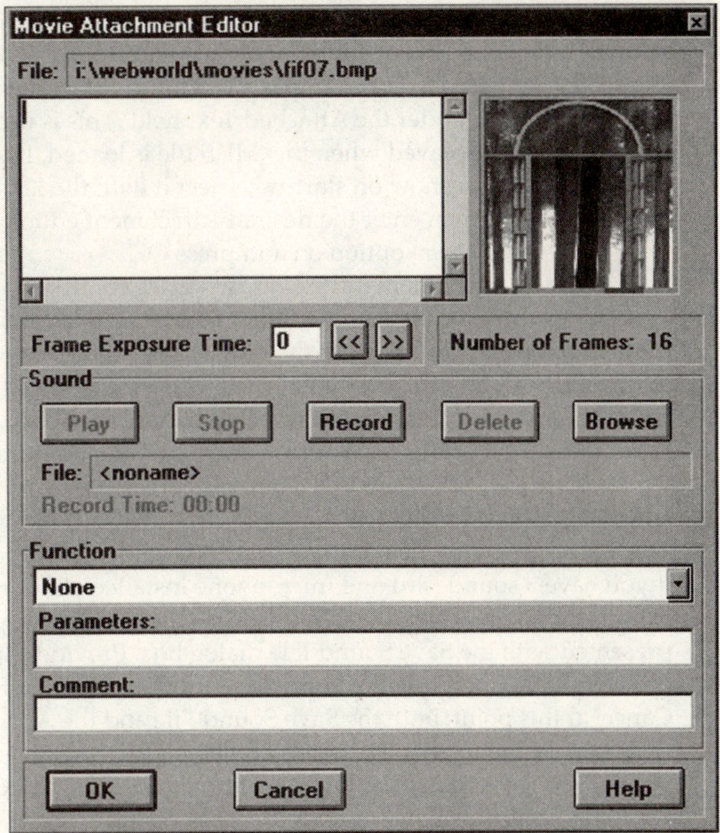

Figure 17-22c.

Each of these dialog boxes share many of the same options. These are listed below:

- File name, including the full path to the file.

- Text field to enter text comments displayed using the Display Attached Text option, found on the right mouse menu.

- A picture of the particular decoration object.

- An area for recording, playing, and attaching sound files.

- A Functions area, used to assign actions carried out when the object is double-clicked.

Differences in Attachments

Although the Attachment editors look very similar, there are some significant differences. For example, the Album Attachment Editor has a special check box under the Attached Text field. This is used to change the first image displayed when the .MUS file is loaded. If you want a different picture to show on start-up, select it with the List Album toolbar icon and then enter the desired Attachment editor. Turn the *Set as first picture in the album* option on and press OK.

The Movie Attachment Editor has two extra controls not found in either of the other Attachment editors. The first control displays the number of frames contained in the movie. The second control, Frame Exposure Time, controls how long each frame is displayed. A setting of 0 is very quick. You can set the Frame Exposure Time up to 999, but having an animation that takes forever to change is a little pointless.

Attaching Sounds to Objects

The Sound area provides controls to record, play, and stop a .WAV file—if you have a sound card and microphone installed. After recording your sound clip and pressing the OK button on the dialog box, you will be presented with the Save Sound File dialog box. Provide a filename and directory to save your newly recorded sound. Be careful: if you press Cancel at this point, both the Save Sound File and the Attachment editor will close, and the recorded sound will be lost. If you have no microphone, you can still use the Browse button to attach any existing .WAV file to the object.

Assigning Functions to Objects

Functions are actions automatically carried out when an object is double-clicked in the 3D Space window. There are a host of functions available to attach to pictures, albums, and movies. The 23 in the following list are available to all three object types.

- None—No functions are carried out. This is the default setting.

- Activate Publish to VRML Dialog—Opens the Select Destination Path and File Name dialog box. Use this dialog to give the .MUS file a name and save all of the files needed to reconstruct your 3D scene into a single directory. If you've already used the Publish to VRML option once, you will be presented with the Select Destination Path dialog. This dialog allows you to save the .MUS and associated decorator object files but not change the name of the .MUS file. If you choose to save into the original directory, WEB.WORLD displays prompts to let you know you are overwriting existing files.

- Activate Open 3D Space Dialog—Invokes the Open 3D Space dialog box to allow loading another .MUS. If the current 3D scene has not yet been saved, WEB.WORLD prompts you to save it.

- Activate Save 3D Space Dialog—Invokes the Save 3D Space dialog box. You can save the current .MUS file under any name or directory. This is the same as selecting the Save toolbar button.

- Activate True Image Window—Opens the True Image window and displays the selected image.

- Exit: Conditional—Presents a dialog that allows you to Exit CorelWEB.WORLD. If you want to continue, press No.

- Exit: Unconditional—Exits CorelWEB.WORLD but does not offer a dialog to confirm the shut-down. However, if your .MUS file has not been saved, you will be prompted to save it. Selecting Cancel in the Exit dialog allows you to continue working on the present file.

- Link to URL—Activates a link to an assigned URL. When you select this item from the drop-down list, the Input URL dialog appears. Type a valid URL, such as, http://www.corel.com, into the text field and press OK. When the item is double-clicked, WEB.WORLD will attempt to launch the program you have associated as your Windows default Web browser and connect to the specified URL. If you wish to change an existing URL, simply type it into the Parameters text field rather than trying to invoke the Input URL dialog again.

- Load 3D Space File—Selecting this function calls up the Select 3D Space File dialog. This dialog is basically the same as that displayed by the Open toolbar button. Find the file you wish to load and press OK; the file's name and path will be inserted into the Parameters text field. When the object is double-clicked, the current .MUS file will close (you will be prompted to save it, if necessary) and the specified .MUS file will be loaded.

- Load Any Document—Calls the Select Any Document dialog box. Use this dialog to chose any file on your system. After selecting OK, the document file and path are inserted into the Parameters text field. When the object is double-clicked, the application associated with the file type is launched and the specified document is loaded. If there is no Windows association assigned to the file type you have specified, you will receive an error message stating this.

■ Load Any Program—Displays the Select Application to Load dialog box. Specify a program with an .exe, .pif, .com, or .bat extension and press OK. You can enter applicable command line parameters in the Parameters dialog box. When the object is double-clicked, the program will be launched and any parameters passed to it for execution.

■ MIDI List: Start Playing—WEB.WORLD allows you to assemble and play a list of MIDI music files. This is done by selecting the Edit | MIDI Play List menu option and choosing files in the Select MIDI File dialog box. These MIDI files are automatically played when the .MUS file is loaded or when the MIDI List: Start Playing function is triggered. If no list of MIDI files has been configured in the Select MIDI File dialog box, nothing happens.

■ MIDI List: Stop Playing—Stops playing the MIDI file play list mentioned above.

■ Multifunction—Opens the Multifunction Editor dialog box, shown in Figure 17-23. This is an extremely powerful tool for setting up functions that have multiple actions.

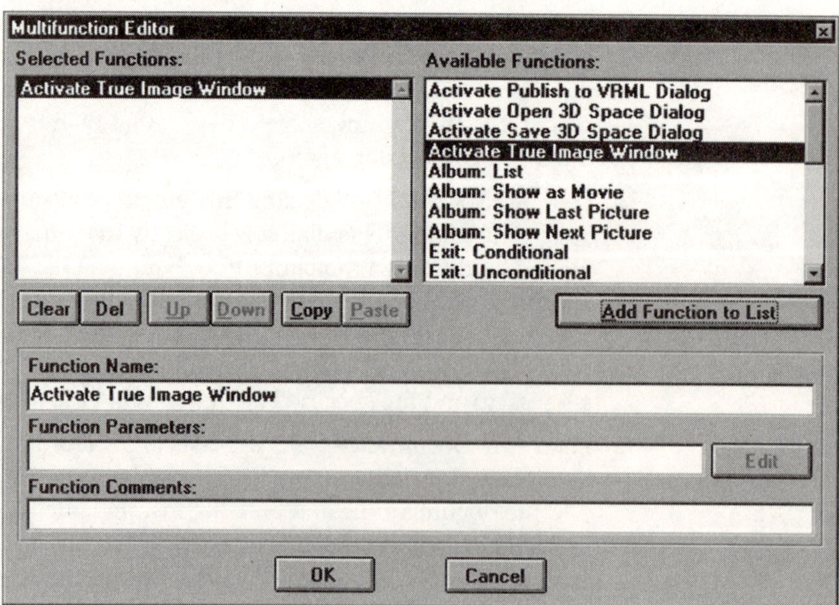

Figure 17-23: The Multifunction Editor dialog box allows you to create lists of multiple functions.

On the right side of the dialog is the Available Functions list. Select the first function you want executed and press the Add Functions to List button. The function is now displayed in the Selected functions list on the left. You can enter any applicable command line parameters in the Function Parameters text field. Continue choosing functions and configuring them in the Selected Functions list. Use the buttons under the Selected Functions list to reorder, delete, copy, or paste functions within the listing.

The last item in a list must always be Multifunction Stop Executing. Don't worry if you forget it—WEB.WORLD will prompt you to include it when you press the OK button. The Multifunction Editor is too cool for words—you've got to try this out to believe it.

- Multifunction: Delay Executing—Pops up the Set Delay dialog that allows you to enter a number of seconds to delay the execution of a multifunction list. We could not get this to actually trigger a previously defined Multifunction list. However, Multifuntion: Delay Executing is on the listing of Available Functions in the Mutifunction Editor. Place it at the top of your Selected Functions list, set the delay, and it will work as expected.

- New 3D Space—This performs the same function as the New toolbar button: it starts a blank 3D scene. If the current scene has not been saved, you will be prompted to save it first.

- Play AVI or FLI files—Invokes the Select Video File dialog, allowing you to choose an .AVI, .FLI, or .FLC file. When the object is double-clicked, the Windows multimedia player is launched and the specified file is displayed.

- Sound: Play—If a sound card is installed, this function plays the sound file that is attached to the object.

- Sound: Stop—If a sound file is playing, this function stops it.

- Start Walking Show—Selecting this function brings up the Select Walking Show Mode dialog. You can choose to play the Walking Show once or keep repeating it. When the object is double-clicked, the Walking Show will start. If no Show has been recorded, nothing happens.

Functions Unique to Albums

There are four functions that only apply to albums:

- Album: List—When the album is double-clicked, all of the pictures are displayed, in succession.

- Album: Show as Movie—Turns the album into a movie—a continuous display of all images in the album.

- Album: Show Last Picture—Displays the last picture in the album.
- Album: Show Next Picture—Displays the next image in the album.

Functions Unique to Movies

There are only two functions that pertain specifically to movie objects:

- Reverse Movie—Displays the frames of the movie in reverse order.
- Stop Movie—Double-clicking causes the movie to stop. This pretty much transforms the movie into an album. The List Album functions will now be operational; however, it takes two clicks of the Album button to cycle to the next picture. Beware: there is no way to restart a movie once the Stop Movie function has been called.

That does it for the buttons contained in the top toolbar. But there are plenty more items of interest found on the bottom toolbar. We'll tackle each one of these in the next section.

The Walker Bar

The Walker bar contains tools used to control the camera—to walk it around the Plane Builder window. There are 15 buttons on the Walker bar, located under the Plane Builder window. The first six, shown in Figure 17-24, control the movement of the Pinocchio tool. For a complete discussion of the Pinocchio tool, see "The Building Tools" earlier in this chapter. All of the following actions can be accelerated by holding down the Ctrl key.

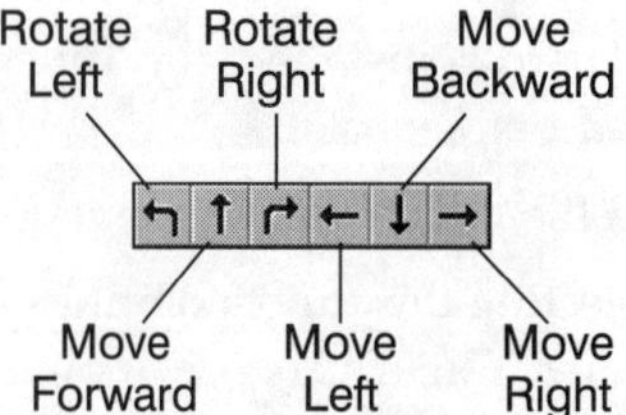

Figure 17-24: These button, located on the Walker bar, manipulate the Pinocchio tool's movements.

Rotate Left

Press this button to spin the Pinocchio tool around to the left.

Move Forward

Causes the Pinocchio tool to move in the direction in which the nose is pointed.

Rotate Right

Pressing this button spins the Pinocchio tool around to the right.

Move Left

Causes the Pinocchio tool to move to the left of the direction in which the nose is pointed.

Move Backward

Moves the Pinocchio tool in the opposite direction from which the nose is pointed.

Move Right

Causes the Pinocchio tool to move to the right of the direction in which the nose is pointed.

The next 9 buttons on the Walker bar control the height, angle, and field of vision for the camera. When you press each, keep your eye on the Camera control. Figure 17-25 shows each button and its name.

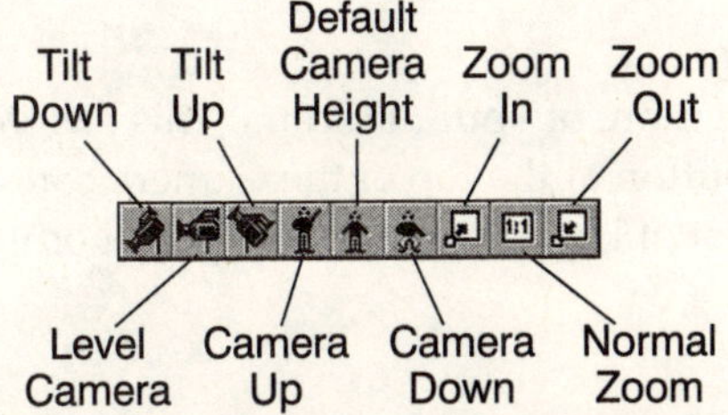

Figure 17-25: The nine buttons that control WEB.WORLD's camera.

Tilt Down

Pressing this button changes the angle of the camera; pointing it toward the floor of the 3D scene.

Level Camera

Pressing this button changes the orientation of the camera to horizontal level. Apply this if you have used either the Tilt Up or Tilt Down button and need to revert the camera to level.

Tilt Up

Pressing this button progressively changes the angle of the camera, pointing it toward the sky of the 3D scene.

Camera Up

Pressing this button progressively changes the height of the camera. You will see the tripod on the Camera control extend.

Default Camera Height

Resets the Camera control to the default height.

Camera Down

Press this button to gradually lower the height of the camera. You will see the tripod on the Camera control shorten.

Zoom In

Press this button to change the camera's field of vision. This has the same effect as pressing the Tele button at the top of the Camera control.

Normal Zoom

When this button is pressed, the camera reverts to the default field of vision.

Zoom Out

Press this button to see more of your 3D scene. This has the same effect as pressing the Wide button at the top of the Camera control.

The following is a list of keyboard shortcuts that modify the Camera control:

Keyboard	Action
+ (plus on the number keypad)	Camera Up
– (minus on the number keypad)	Camera Down
Insert	Tilt Up
Delete	Tilt Down
Home	Rotate Left
Page Up	Rotate Right
Holding down the Ctr; key doubles the speed of camera movements (including the Camera tilt controls).	

The Status Bars

There are two status bars at the bottom of WEB.WORLD. One is attached to the Walker bar, while the other is part of the main WEB.WORLD window. Together they provide information about various features or object attributes.

As shown in Figure 17-26, the Walker bar status line displays information about attachments to decorator objects. If a picture object contains more than one image, the Album Indicator icon is displayed. Should the object have a sound file attached, the Sound Indicator displays an icon that resembles an ear. If text has been attached, the text is displayed on the status line. To the far right, the system time is displayed in military time.

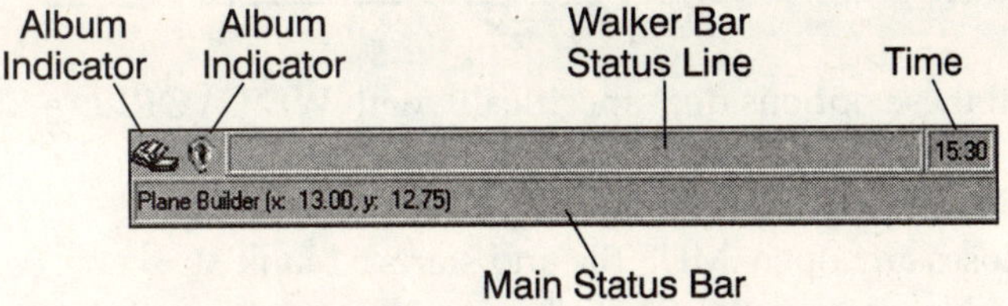

Figure 17-26: There are two status bars; together they display information about decorator items, attachments, and cursor position.

The main status bar is constantly updated to show which tool or window the cursor is currently over. While working in the Plane Builder, coordinates for cursor position and object size are displayed. Also, the name and path of images stored in the Decorator window are displayed when selected.

At last, we've covered every button that WEB.WORLD sports on its various toolbars. No doubt, you've been impressed by the fact that you can perform the same task in several different ways. The next section deals with yet another way of carrying out tasks in WEB.WORLD—the menus.

May I See a Menu, Please?

Menus are an essential element of any Windows application. However, considering the amount of mouse movements needed to activate them, they aren't the most efficient way for performing repetitious tasks. Thank goodness for the toolbars and right mouse button menus. At any rate, knowing what functions are found under what menu headings is important. Because most of the selections on the menus are repetitions of functions and commands already discussed, we won't dwell on these again. However, there are some dialog boxes that can only be accessed from menus. These are explained thoroughly in the following sections.

The File Menu

All these options deal specifically with WEB.WORLD's file functions.

New

Closes any open .MUS file and starts a blank 3D scene. Same as pressing the New button on the toolbar.

Open

Invokes the Open 3D Space File dialog. This is the same as pressing the Open button on the toolbar.

Save

Invokes the Save 3D Space File dialog. The same as pressing the Save button. If your file has already been saved but has been modified, the original file is overwritten with the new information.

Save As

Invokes the Save 3D Space File dialog. Choose this when you want to save a .MUS file under a different name or in a different directory.

Publish to VRML

This is different from the Save function because it saves all the files associated with your WEB.WORLD scene—decorator images, .WAV, .MID, .MUS and .WRL—into one directory. At the same time the .MUS's internal pointers to all these images are updated. If you have previously used the Save command, the Select Destination dialog box appears. This is because the file already has a name assigned. Select a directory to save to. If your file was not previously saved, you will see the Select Destination Path and File Name dialog box, shown in Figure 17-27. Except for the File Name text field, the two dialogs are functionally the same.

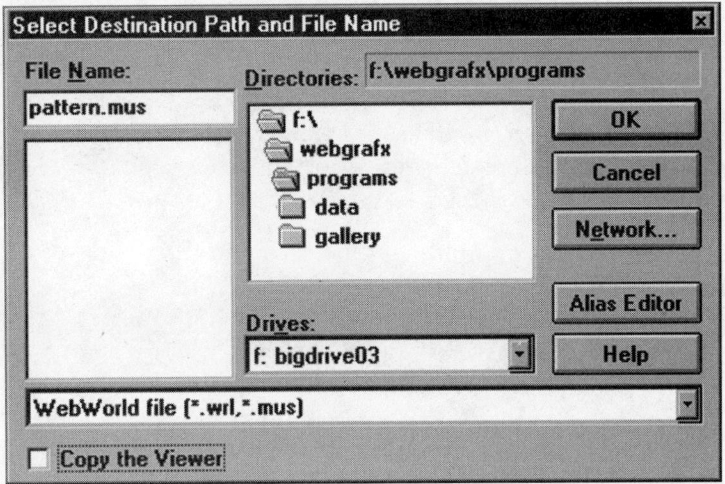

Figure 17-27: If your file has not been saved previously, the Publish to VRML command calls the Select Destination Path and File Name dialog.

The Copy the Viewer option, at the bottom, refers to the CorelWEB.WORLD Viewer. As Figure 17-28 shows, this is a stand-alone application that is used to view your 3D scenes. The Viewer can display all wallpapers, albums, pictures, and movies, as well as play sounds and MIDI background music. Distributing the CorelWEB.WORLD Viewer, along with all the component files, is the route to go if you want visitors to experience your 3D worlds in all their glory. Because the Viewer also needs some .DLL files to function, the following are copied to your destination directory:

- WRLDVIEW.EXE
- TREGION.DLL
- NS16.DLL
- ACCUSOFT.DLL

Figure 17-28: The CorelWEB.WORLD Viewer application is a scaled-down version of WEB.WORLD. Notice all the familiar navigation buttons on the Walker bar.

You can provide a .ZIP archive of the above files along with your .MUS and other resources (basically every file that WEB.WORLD copies to the destination directory) on your Website. Instruct visitors to download the file, unzip the contents into a directory, and double-click WRLDVIEW.EXE. CorelWEB.WORLD Viewer starts with a dialog box that requests an .MUS file; point it at the unzipped .MUS and they're off. Of course, the WEB.WORLD Viewer is a Windows-only application. Persons running other types of computers will need to use their Web browser, with a VRML plug-in, to view the .WRL version of your 3D scene. They will, unfortunately, not experience movies, albums, sounds, and background music.

Publish to WEB.DESIGNER

This menu selection is only available if you have launched WEB.WORLD from within WEB.DESIGNER. This command saves a copy of your 3D world in both .WRL and .MUS format. All the requisite resource files mentioned in the previous section—except those associated with the WEB.WORLD Viewer application—are copied to a directory under the

Server Root directory set in WEB.DESIGNER. This directory will be named: WORLDx, where x is a number starting at zero. Each subsequent Publish to DESIGNER request will add another directory; incrementing the trailing number by one.

Publish to WEB.DESIGNER also saves a static image of your 3D scene in .GIF format. This file is displayed as a placeholder in the HTML document until the complete .WRL file is downloaded and operational in the visitor's Web browser. All a visitor needs to do is click on the .GIF image to let the browser and its VRML plug-in take over.

Embedding a .WRL file into an HTML Web page is the only way to publish your 3D worlds for visitors who can't use the WEB.WORLD Viewer application. It's a good idea to explain to your visitors what files and viewers will be needed to display the 3D worlds you make available on your site.

Workspace

There are three selections offered on the Workspace submenu:

Lock

Selecting this option keeps the three main windows—Plane Builder, 3D Space, and Decorator—from being resized or moved. To unlock the windows, reselect the Workspace | Lock option. When the workspace is locked, the toolbars, Camera control, and Height control can still be turned on or off.

Restore

If you have moved or resized any of the windows in WEB.WORLD, selecting this causes them to be resized and moved to the default arrangement. If you have used the Save command, mentioned below, Restore returns the workspace to the Saved arrangement—the defaults are lost. One way to restore the defaults is to make a copy of the original WEBWORLD.INI file (found in the same directory as WIN.INI) before you issue the Save command. You'll be able to compare the contents of the revised WEBWORLD.INI (the one recorded after the Save command) with the copy of the original and remove any entries referring to the nondefault arrangement. Look for entries like these:

```
px=0
py=0
dx=529
dy=422
```

You can remove these. There will be four coordinates under each of the three window sections labeled [Chooser], [Space], and [Builder]. Save the WEBWORLD.INI file, restart WEB.WORLD, and the default workspace will have returned. It's a good idea to always make a backup copy of any .INI file before making modifications. If you're a little squeamish about playing around in .INI files, see the Window menu section near the end of this chapter for a simpler way to restore the defaults.

Save

Use this option to save the arrangement of the WEB.WORLD workspace after customizing it. All the window sizes and toolbar states will be recorded. Every time you start WEB.WORLD or issue the Restore command, the workspace will revert to the states recorded in the WEBWORLD.INI file.

Settings

From the CorelWEB.WORLD Settings dialog box, shown in Figure 17-29, you have control over several global settings that affect the WEB.WORLD environment.

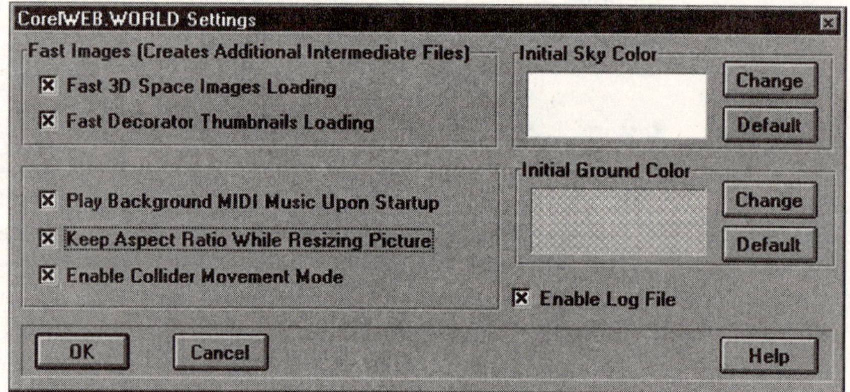

Figure 17-29: The CorelWEB.WORLD Settings dialog allows control over many of the application's global variables.

- Fast 3D Space Images Loading—Decreases the time it takes to open WEB.WORLD files by saving uncompressed copies of the decorator image files in the same directory as the image. These uncompressed files have the same filename but have a .V##

extension. If you run low on hard drive space, you can delete these files. Alternatively, turn off the option and live with the slightly slower load times.

- Fast Decorator Thumbnails Loading—Speeds up the time it takes to display wallpapers, pictures, and movies in the Decorator window by creating thumbnail image files in the same directory as the images. These files have the same filename with a .S## extension.

- Play Background MIDI Music Upon Startup—If a playlist of MIDI files has been configured, these are automatically played each time the file is loaded. If an incessant MIDI tune is becoming annoying, turn this option off. The next time you reload the file, the MIDI files will not play. This will affect all .MUS files opened thereafter.

- Keep Aspect Ratio While Resizing Picture—When turned on, any pictures, albums, or movies maintain their original proportions when resized. We don't know why this isn't on by default. We recommend turning it on first thing.

- Enable Collider Movement Mode—When this is enabled, the camera will not move through walls and faces. This only applies to moving the camera with the Walker bar controls and the keyboard. You are still able to move the Pinocchio tool through walls with the mouse.

- Initial Sky Color—The default color for the sky in your 3D scene is blue. If you want it to be otherwise, click the Change button and choose another color from the Color dialog box. To change the sky color back to the original blue, click the Default button. Making this change affects the sky for all new WEB.WORLD scenes—not for the current one.

- Initial Ground Color—The default color for the ground in your 3D scene is green. If you want to change this, click the Change button and choose another color from the Color dialog box. To change the ground color back to the original green, click the Default button. Making this change affects the ground for all new WEB.WORLD scenes—not for the current one.

- Enable Log File—When this is turned on (it's off by default), CorelWEB.WORLD writes a log file containing a list of the image files used as decorator items that the program could not find while loading. This log file is saved in the same directory as your .MUS file. If you have black rectangles where images should be, use a text editor to open the .LOG file. The contents will be similar to that below:

```
CorelWEB.WORLD Log file.
3D Space Name: d:\corelw~1\webworld\todesign\images2.mus
Creation Time: Thu Jan 23 16:01:10 1997

Can't find file: p9482201.jpg
```

The last line shows an error entry describing what image file could not be found. Use this information to search for the missing file and replace it in the proper directory.

The reason for "black holes" in your scenes is usually because the original image file was moved, renamed, or deleted. WEB.WORLD does not swallow up image files into one big .MUS file; rather, it records only the name and path of the images. When these path "pointers" get tripped up, because images aren't where they are supposed to be, then black holes are born. This should help you understand why the Publish to VRML option copies all files to one directory—and at the same time updates the .MUS's internal pointers.

Exit

This option shuts down WEB.WORLD. If a file is open and has not been saved, you will be prompted to save it.

The Edit Menu

The following menu items have all been discussed in previous sections of this chapter.

Undo

Undoes the last operation. See the previous section on the File tools for more information.

Revert to Saved

WEB.WORLD discards the current 3D scene and reloads the .MUS file from the information recorded on the hard drive. See the previous section on the File tools for more information.

Move/Resize

This selection is only available when a picture, album, or movie is selected in the 3D Space window. More information on moving and resizing objects is found in the "Decorating With Pictures" section.

Delete

This is another selection that is only available when a picture, album, or movie is selected in the 3D Space window. More information on deleting objects is found in the "Decorating With Pictures" section.

Attachment

This is enabled when a decorator item is selected in the 3D Space window. It is the same as pressing the Attachment button on the toolbar. See the previous section on the Attachment tools for more information.

Grid

The Grid is a feature of the Plane Builder window. It is a series of points that allow you to easily line up 3D objects. By default, the grid is turned on—you see little dots in the Plane Builder window. When you click a building tool in the window and start to drag, the object's starting point jumps to the nearest grid point. Every time you click your mouse to finish your object or create a corner, the cursor will snap to the nearest grid point. Although the grid is convenient, there are times when you will want to turn it off or modify its attributes to better suit your needs. The following options, found on the Grid submenu, assist in that task.

- Show Grid—Makes the grid visible or invisible. This is the same as pressing the Grid button on the toolbar. The distance between one grid point and the next is determined internally by WEB.WORLD. The default is simply referred to as "1 unit." You can change the frequency of the grid, so that there are more grid points to snap to, by selecting one of the Snap options described below:

  - Snap Off—Disables the ability to automatically snap the cursor to the nearest grid point. The Grid and Snap features are not mutually exclusive: Snap can be on while the Grid is invisible, or vice versa.

  - Snap To Grid—Turns the Snap feature on if it is currently off.

  - Snap To $1/2$ Grid—Makes the grid finer by allowing twice the number of grid points.

  - Snap To $1/4$ Grid—Makes the grid even finer by allowing four times the number of grid points.

  - Snap To $1/10$ Grid—This is the finest setting (you'll probably be working at a high zoom level in order to distinguish the grid points). Creates ten times more grid points than the default setting.

There is another setting that affects the above grid options, found under the Build I Builder Settings menu. It will be discussed shortly.

MDI Player

MIDI files are compact sound files, suited to music rather than sound effects. Although the playing of a MIDI file can be triggered by a function attached to a decorator item, a MIDI file can also be played as background music when the .MUS file loads. This is accomplished by using the Select MIDI File dialog box, shown in Figure 17-30.

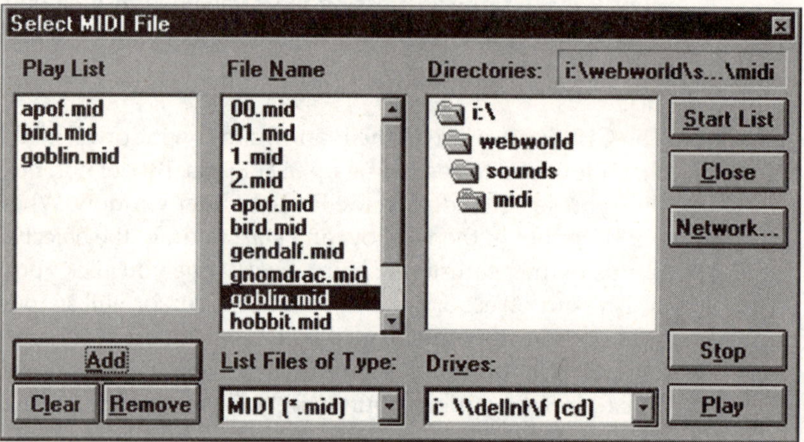

Figure 17-30: Use the Select MIDI File dialog box to assemble lists of MIDI files and play them as background music.

Use the Directories list to navigate to a drive and directory that contains MIDI files. When WEB.WORLD locates a MIDI file, it is displayed in the File Name list. To listen to the file, select it in the File Name list and press the Play button. When you are satisfied, press the Stop button. To add the selected MIDI file to your 3D scenes playlist, press the Add button: the file is added to the Play List window. Continue this process to add as many MIDI files as you like.

If you want to remove all the files from the Play List, press Clear. To take one file out of the list, select it, and press Remove. To close the dialog and start playing the MIDI files, choose Start List. To cancel the whole process, select Close.

Record Walking Show

A Walking Show is a guided tour through your 3D scene. Basically, you take the metaphorical camera and record a trip through your world—showing off all the goodies you've built in. The Walking Show can be played at any time by those viewing the .MUS file.

To start recording your Walking Show, position the Pinocchio tool where you want the tour to begin and select Record Walking Show from the Edit menu. From this point on, do not touch the Pinocchio tool—all navigation must be accomplished with the Walker bar buttons or the keyboard. (You know you're really good when you can use a combination of the two and cruise around your world at high speed.) The only exception is selecting and double-clicking decorator items to activate their attachments.

When you are finished, select the Edit menu, the Record Walking Show option has changed to Stop Recording. Select this. WEB.WORLD saves one Walking Show per file; it is saved with the same name as your WEB.WORLD file, with a .WLK extension. As mentioned in the discussion of the Open toolbar button, you can make the Walking Show play automatically when the file opens. Or you can start a Walking Show with the Explore | Walking Show menu selection.

The View Menu

The View menu contains several items that control the way WEB.WORLD appears on screen. All these items have been discussed in previous sections.

Tool Bar

This is a toggle switch that removes the main toolbar. Select it again to make the toolbar reappear.

Walker Bar

This is another toggle switch. Selecting it causes the Walker bar to disappear. Select it again to make the Walker bar reappear.

Status Line

Selecting this option causes the status bar to vanish. Select it again to make the Status bar return.

Decorator

The Decorator menu contains a submenu of items that control various aspects of the Decorator window. The first four selections toggle the Decorator window to display one of the following decorator types:

- Pictures
- Wallpapers

- Movies
- Airbrush

The next two selections call up dialog boxes already discussed in the section on the viewing tools earlier in this chapter.

- Detail—Calls up the appropriate dialog box, depending on what mode the Decorator window is in.
- Directory—Calls the Select Directory dialog box used to change where WEB.WORLD looks for image files to display in the Decorator window.

Height Control

Toggles the Height control on and off. This control is discussed at length in "The Plane Builder Window" earlier in this chapter.

Camera Control

Toggles the Camera control on and off. This control is also discussed at length in "The Plane Builder Window."

Zoom Floor Plan

The Zoom Floor Plan selections control the view in the Plane Builder window. Select from the following choices found on the submenu.

- Zoom In—Zoom in to get a closer look at small items in the Plane Builder window. This is the best way to work on small objects.
- Zoom Out—Zoom out to see more of your objects in the Plane Builder window.
- Zoom All—Select this option to see all of your scene's objects at one time.

The Build Menu

This menu allows you to activate the various tools operable in the Plane Builder window. All but the Builder settings have been previously discussed under "The Building Tools" earlier in this chapter.

Pinocchio

Activates the Pinocchio tool. See the previous sections for full details on how this tool functions.

Add Box

This is one of WEB.WORLD's main building tools; it creates six-sided rectangular objects.

Cutout Box

Used to create six-sided boxes that are subtracted from other 3D objects.

Add Wall

Use this tool in the Plane Builder window to draw perfect horizontal or vertical partitions with corners that are always right angles. The thickness of a wall is set in the Build | Builder Settings dialog mentioned later in this chapter.

Face

Face objects are partitions, like walls. For the whole story on faces, see the previous section on the Build tools. The submenu offers the following choices:

- Draw Face—The tool used to create face objects.
- Erase Face—Use this tool to remove face objects and surfaces of box objects.

Building Settings

Select this option to call the Builder Settings dialog box, shown in Figure 17-31. From this dialog you can set three different Plane Builder features.

Figure 17-31: The Builder Settings dialog box contains controls for the grid, building levels, and wall thickness.

The first items in the dialog deal with grid spacing options. You can change the default unit from one to any decimal number between 0.01 and 127.99. These limits are impractical; anything below 0.1 or above 70 are virtually ineffective. The Grid X text field controls the horizontal spacing between grid points, while Grid Y controls the vertical spacing. If Isotropic is turned on, the Grid Y text field will be inactive. This is because Isotropic sets Grid Y to the same value as Grid X.

Only one of the next two items can be turned on at a time. Show All Levels displays all 3D objects in the Plane Builder window. Show Only Current Level allows you to exclude certain 3D objects from displaying in the Plane Builder window. Only those objects with heights falling within the range specified by the maximum and minimum height controls of the Height control tool are displayed.

This is a good way to reduce the clutter in the Plane Builder window when you are working on scenes that have multiple levels. This setting only affects the Plane Builder window. The 3D Space window always displays every object within the camera's view.

The final item is Wall Width. Refer to the Building Tools section for the complete story on this setting.

The Explore Menu

Select a decorator object, and the appropriate menu selection will become active. All the items on this menu may be inactive if an object is not selected and a Walking Show has not recorded.

True Image

Opens the True Image window and loads the selected item. This window is discussed under the earlier section entitled "The True Image Viewer."

Direct View

Direct View fills the 3D Space window with the selected decorator item. This is discussed in the Attachment Tools section.

List Album

List Album is only enabled when an album item is selected. Choose this selection to view each picture in the album, one at a time. This is also discussed in the section on Attachment tools.

Walking Show

This selection can only be accessed if a Walking Show has previously been recorded. If so, a dialog requests that you choose between running the Walking Show once or repeating it continuously. You can interrupt a Walking Show by clicking any of the Walker bar buttons, pressing a camera keyboard shortcut, or grabbing the Pinocchio tool in the Plane Builder window.

The Window Menu

The following menu selections control the placement of WEB.WORLD's three main windows.

Cascade

Makes all three windows the same size and positions them on top of each other in an overlapping, cascading arrangement.

Tile

This sets the three windows back to the original, default arrangement.

Tip

If you've saved a custom workspace arrangement, then you've also lost the ability to use the Restore command to set everything back to the default sizes and positions. Rather than muck about in the WEBWORLD.INI file, chose Windows | Tile. This reverts the windows to the default arrangement. Finally, choose File | Workspace | Save to save the arrangement.

Arrange Icons

If any of the three windows are minimized, selecting this option arranges them neatly along the bottom of the WEB.WORLD window.

The Help Menu

The Help menu can be invaluable in refreshing your memory on WEB.WORLD's features and tools. The following items function according to standard Windows behavior.

Contents

Launches Help and presents the Contents page. Select a hyperlinked text item or use the buttons above to find the subject you are interested in. You can also use the F1, Shift+F1 or Ctrl+ F1keys and combinations to access Help's contents page.

Search For Help on ...

When you choose this menu item, the Search dialog appears. Enter a word or phrase into the text field to receive a list of topics related to those you are searching for displayed. Double-click a topic to have subtopics displayed in the bottom area. Double-click a subtopic or select it and press the Goto button. A page with the subtopic is displayed.

About WEB.WORLD

Brings up the About CorelWEB.WORLD window. This displays some important information, like the WEB.WORLD version number and your registration number.

Moving On

This is the end of the line for the grand tour of CorelWEB.WORLD. You've peered into ever nook and cranny of this 3D virtual reality authoring application. No toolbar button, dialog, or menu selection was left unturned. Do you think you're ready to start using some of this gear?

The next chapter takes a hands-on approach in demonstrating how to build and decorate your own 3D environments. So strap on your tool belt and roll up your sleeves, because we've got some heavy-duty construction to do.

18

Creating Virtual Worlds With CorelWEB.WORLD

Creating virtual worlds with CorelWEB.WORLD can be very simple or very tricky, depending on the magnitude of the world you want to create. A room is much less difficult to construct than a building, and a building less so than a whole city block. The general rule of starting out small and learning the basics before moving to bigger and more ambitious projects holds true for learning WEB.WORLD. The goal of this chapter is to get the fundamentals down while keeping the exercises simple and easy to follow.

The first step is learning how to build objects using the only 3D shapes WEB.WORLD makes—rectangles and boxes. Next, you'll learn a technique called carving and apply it to making rooms with windows and doors. After that, you'll build a piece of furniture to go in your room. Before moving on to decorating the room, you'll finish the construction phase of the project by adding some walls and then learn how to fix mistakes by removing surfaces.

After the construction phase is complete, it's time to do some decorating with paints and wallpaper. WEB.WORLD makes this step painless by supplying a wide selection of these items on the *CorelWEB.GRAPHICS Suite Companion CD*. Make sure you have the CD handy when we get to this stage of the project.

Once the walls get the basic treatments, you'll move on to the finer points of decoration with various types of paintings. Here's where you'll leave the real world behind and blast off into the "unreality" of cyberspace. Some of the decorating materials available in WEB.WORLD are "cutting edge"—they combine the best (and worst) of the multimedia phenomenon. Pictures can have pop-up text captions, they can be animated, and they can even talk to your visitors. Speaking of sounds, the final mood setter, music, can be piped into your scene easier than Muzak finds its way into an office building's elevator.

All the principles and techniques you'll learn from this simple project can be readily applied to projects of much larger scope. As you work through the exercises in this chapter, you may need to refresh your memory regarding the names and locations of certain tools and dialog boxes. If so, refer to Chapter 17 for a complete discussion of every part of the WEB.WORLD interface.

Plan Ahead

The starting point for any building project is always back at the planning stage. If you think you don't have much in common with a group of architects who sit at drawing boards, you probably will after working with WEB.WORLD. Architects are trained to take a wish list of ideas and transform them into real three-dimensional structures. After accomplishing this feat, they have to convert the 3D images in their minds to detailed two-dimensional drawings, so that others can build the actual structures.

As a creator of virtual reality spaces, you not only think up the wish list of features, but you also take on the chores of the architect. Not only do you have to think in 3D, but you've got to convert these ideas into 2D drawings that are laid out in the Plane Builder window. As mentioned in the previous chapter, the Plane Builder window gives a birds-eye view of your scene. Trying to visualize an entire three-dimensional scene from this viewpoint is very hard. That's why architects, draftspersons, and designers commonly render objects from three different views: the top, the front, and the right side. But sometimes, as Figure 18-1 demonstrates, even this technique isn't as effective as seeing the object in 3D.

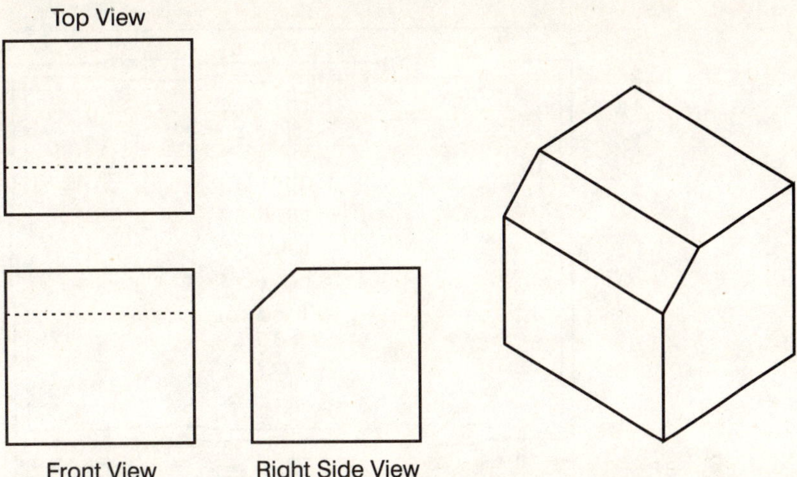

Figure 18-1: A typical blueprint for an object (left) may convey enough detail to manufacture it, but it's still easier to visualize the object in three dimensions.

The point is, drawing from the top down is no easy task. If you don't start by planning your scenes on paper—in 2 D and 3D—you'll make more mistakes than necessary. A useful by-product of this planning stage is breaking down a large project into its smaller components. This will help you evaluate the best approach to take when actually constructing your scene. With this in mind, Figure 18-2 shows a floor plan for the room you'll construct in the following exercises. Next to the floor plan is a perspective drawing of what we *think* the floor plan will look like in 3D.

During the course of making plan drawings, you'll probably notice some details you hadn't previously taken into consideration—details that could make a lot of difference in how you construct your scene. It's far better to make alterations in the planning stage than to get to the end of your scene and find that something like a staircase that connects the two already finished floors of your house doesn't fit. Also, you may notice that WEB.WORLD slows down as you accumulate more objects in your scene. In a complex scene, the time it takes to add a wall—or delete one, if it's drawn wrong—can be considerable. So, take ample time to plan your scene out in great detail.

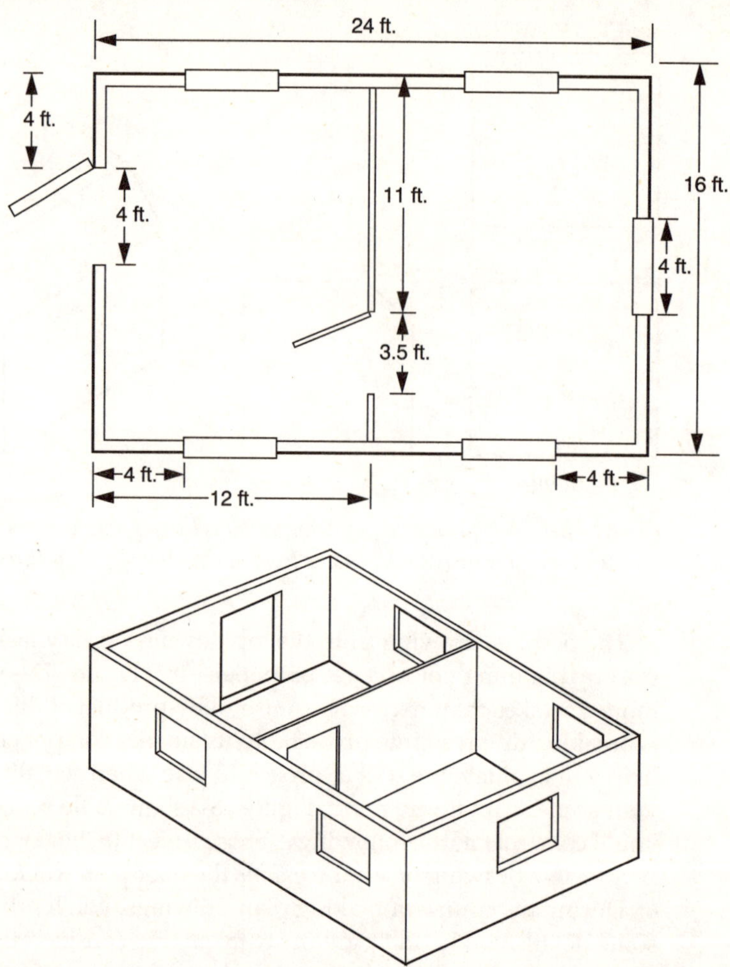

Figure 18-2: Start any WEB.WORLD project with a floor plan and a perspective drawing of the floor plan.

Setting Up Your Workspace

WEB.WORLD is designed with several features that make building 3D scenes easier. One feature is the Grid; another is Snap. By default, the grid is turned on, and, for the most part, it's a good idea to keep it on. The grid is an evenly spaced series of points, displayed in the Plane Builder window, that give you reference points for lining up your objects. When necessary, grid settings are modified in the Builders Settings dialog located under the Build menu. However, the default settings will be fine for the projects in this chapter.

By default, the Snap to Grid is also turned on. This feature ensures that any building tool operation is constrained to a grid point. Using Snap to Grid makes it easy to butt objects to one another or keep them lined up in nice neat rows. When this is not what you want, you can turn off the Snap to Grid option by selecting Edit | Grid | Snap Off. When Snap is turned off, you have the flexibility to place a building tool anywhere in the Plane Builder window. There are three other Snap settings found on the Grid submenu: Snap to $1/2$, Snap to $1/4$, and Snap to $1/10$. These modify the snap to allow for more snap points. Figure 18-3 illustrates how the Snap to $1/2$ setting allows for twice the number of snap points, Snap to $1/4$ creates four times the default points, and Snap to $1/10$ makes for the finest snap configuration of ten times the normal points.

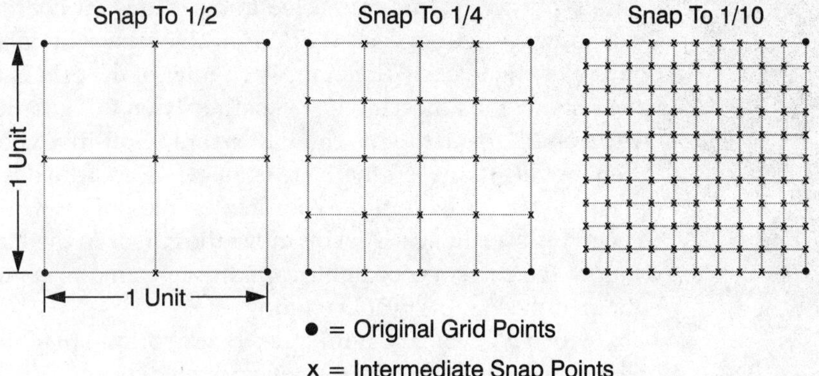

Figure 18-3: By using finer snap settings, you create more intermediate snap points between grid points.

Another item that's related to the grid and snap is the basic unit of measure. This is related to the grid because the default spacing between each grid point is one *unit*. This unit is also closely related to the Height control. Notice that the default setting for the Height control is 3.5 units high. What's a unit? Basically, it's any system of measurement you decide to make it. If you are familiar with the metric system, then a unit can represent a meter.

If you are more comfortable with inches and feet, as we are, then the unit can be a foot. In that case, the default height would be 3.5 feet and the distance between each grid point represents 1 foot. By using the $1/2$ setting, the building tools snap every six inches. When set to $1/4$, the tools jump every 3 inches. If you desire a higher degree of precision, set the snap to $1/10$ or turn off Snap to Grid altogether. Throughout the exercises presented, you'll change the grid snap and turn snap on and off. We'll start with the $1/2$ setting.

Tip

If you want to convert inches into meters or decimal inches, we've included a handy conversion utility called Cubit Meister on the accompanying CD. Cubit Meister converts inches into centimeters. To determine meters, just move the decimal point over one more place to the right.

An important feature connected to the grid is the coordinate system. By default, the floor of each WEB.WORLD scene is divided into 128 grid points running in each direction. The center of the grid is the 0,0 coordinate. Initially the Pinocchio tool sits directly on this coordinate. Moving away from the center to the right, there are 64 positive coordinates. When moving to the left there are 64 negative coordinates. Moving upward, there are 64 positive coordinates; moving downward, there are 64 negative coordinates. As you move the cursor in the Plane Builder window, the current coordinates are displayed in the status bar at the bottom of the WEB.WORLD window.

Now that we have the mundane, yet important, planning phases out of the way, it's time to start the construction work.

Building With Boxes

We've stated that boxes and rectangles are WEB.WORLD's basic building blocks—everything you build is one of these two geometric shapes. Actually, from WEB.WORLD's point of view, there isn't a whole lot of difference between a rectangle and a box. A box is simply made up of six rectangles placed at right angles to each other. Figure 18-4 illustrates this concept.

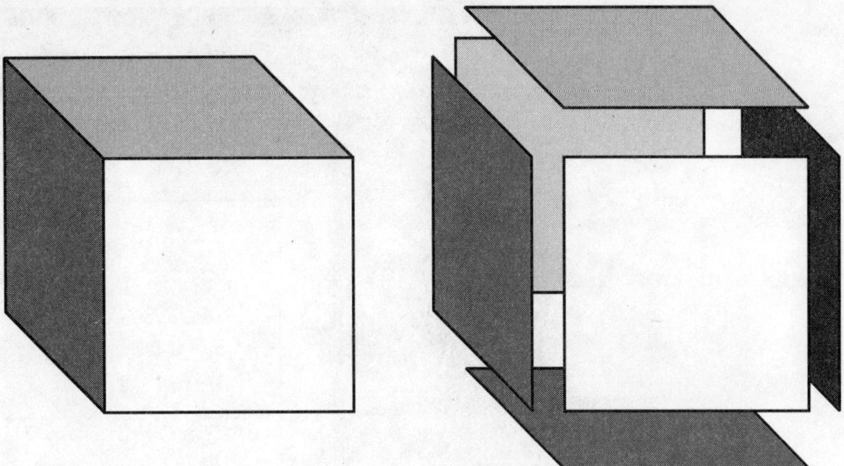

Figure 18-4: Although the box is a basic shape, it is simply six rectangle shapes placed at right angles.

Let's start constructing the room shown in the floor plan shown in Figure 18-2.

1. First, set the Height control to eight feet—this is a standard height for most interior rooms. To accomplish this, click in the Maximum height control, type in **8**, and press enter. The top lath of the Height control should automatically adjust itself to 8 units high.

2. Click on the Add Box tool in the main toolbar. Locate the Pinocchio tool and move it off the 0,0 grid point. Starting at 0,0, drag right 46 units and up 16 units. If necessary, click the Zoom Out tool several times to display enough grid marks in the Plane Builder window. When you reach coordinate 24.0, 16.0, click once to finish the box. Move the Pinocchio tool around to view the box. It should look similar to that shown in Figure 18-5.

Figure 18-5: Your 24 x 16 x 8 box should look like the one shown in the figure above.

Learning to Carve

Now that we have the perimeter of our room, it's time to create the insides. The way to do this is by subtracting an area of space out of the inside of the solid box. This technique is called *carving*. We use the Cutout Box tool to subtract box-shaped areas from other 3D objects. Basically, you set up the area to be removed the same way you set up adding a regular box. The height of a Cutout Box is set with the Height control, while the width and depth are drawn out in the Plane Builder window. Now is when you'll have to switch gears and put on your 3D thinking cap.

The walls of a room have thickness, right? There's also thickness to the ceiling and floor. So we need to allow for the floor and ceiling thickness by moving the top lath down and the bottom lath up.

Note: the resolution of your video settings determines how precise the laths of the Height control can be set. You may not be able to set your laths to the exact numbers specified in the exercises. For example, 7.86 may be specified, but you may only be able to set your lath at 7.88. This is nothing to be concerned over. The main thing is to be consistent with the settings you use.

1. As shown in Figure 18-6, set the top lath to 7.86 and the bottom lath to 0.13.

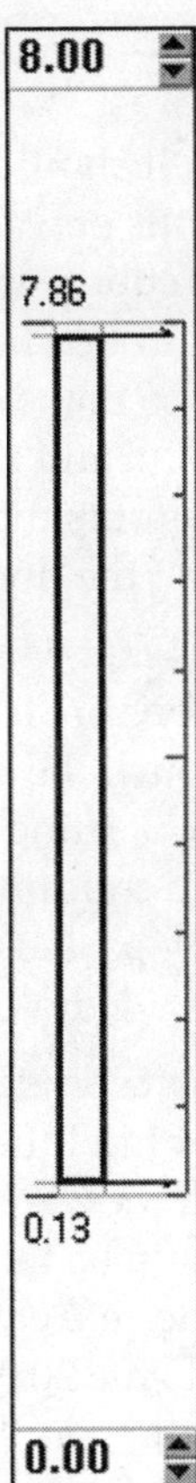

Figure 18-6: Set the top and bottom laths as shown to allow for a ceiling and floor thickness.

2. Click on the Cutout Box tool and click the cursor at coordinate 0.50, 0.50. Drag a rectangle up and to the right to coordinate 23.50, 15.50, and click once to finish the Cutout Box.

At this point, you can't see anything different. Move the Pinocchio tool into the center of the rectangles and spin it around. You should be able to see all four interior walls, the floor, and the ceiling of your hollowed out room. When you're finished walking around in circles, you can move on to carving out a door and windows.

Creating Doorways & Windows

Now that you understand the concept of carving, it should be pretty simple to transfer this idea into subtracting portions of walls to make a door and windows. The only difference with this subtraction process is that you need to extend the boundary of the Cutout Box beyond the inside and outside of each wall. This is necessary to make sure you carve out the entire width of the wall. Study the floor plan and the measurements in Figure 18-2 to get acquainted with the cutouts that need to be made. The next steps take you through carving out the door.

1. The dimensions of our door opening are 4 feet wide by approximately 6 feet 8 inches high. We want the bottom of the door to be flush with the inside floor, so we won't touch the bottom lath of the height control. Set the top lath to 6.70. Starting at coordinate −1.00, 12.00, drag down and to the right to coordinate 1.00, 8.00. This will delineate an area that completely passes through the thickness of the wall and leaves a 4-foot-wide hole.

2. Next, you'll make the window at the top left corner. The windows are 4 feet wide and high, and they sit 3 feet from the floor. Set the bottom lath at 3 and the top lath at 7. Click the Cutout Box tool at 4.00, 17.00 and drag to 8.00, 15.00. Click to finish the window carving. Move to coordinate 16.00,17.00 and make your first Cutout Box corner. Finish the box at coordinate 20.00, 15.00. Use the Pinocchio tool to move about and admire your handiwork.

3. Apply the skills you've just learned to carve out two more windows on the opposite side of the room. Refer to Figure 18-2 and carve a window on the right side of the room. When you are done, your room should look similar to Figure 18-7.

Figure 18-7: Congratulations! You've just built your first 3D home with a front door and five windows.

When the thrill of being a first-time virtual homeowner wears off, it's time to start improving your humble abode. You'll start by building a wall.

Building Walls

A wall is another type of box. Like a box, it's made entirely of rectangular surfaces connected at right angles. There are two convenient features to wall objects. The first is that their thickness is automatically set. By default, this thickness is set at .25 of the basic "unit." In our case, that equates to 3 inches—a good average thickness for interior walls. If you want to change the Wall Width setting, you do so in the Builder Settings dialog box.

The second convenience of walls is the ease of creating corners. To start a wall, click the Add Wall tool and click at the starting point for the wall, then click at the point for the first corner. The span between each click of the tool will be connected by a wall section. When you are finished with your wall, double-click the tool at an end point. As you see, the only down side to wall objects is that they must follow straight lines, and the corners must always be perfect right angles. If you need a wall that runs on an angle, you can't use the Add Wall tool.

To create a wall that fits properly in your room, you need to set the laths of the height control to the same height settings of the interior walls. In case you've forgotten what the settings for the floor and ceiling were, WEB.WORLD has a feature that makes determining these settings very easy. Click on any surface in the 3D Space window and look over at the Height control. On the left side you will see two red lines that correspond to the top and bottom settings of the surface you clicked on. To see this in action, click on an area of the wall to either side of a window. Notice where the red marks are in the Height control. Now click on an area of the wall directly below a window: the red marks have moved to indicate this surface's measurements.

So, anytime you need to match an existing wall's height measurements, you know how to do it. Once you've got the red marks, simply move the top and bottom laths to match. The next step in our project is to create a wall that bisects the middle of our house.

1. Click a wall section that extends from floor to ceiling and set the height for the wall accordingly.

2. Click the Add Wall tool and click on coordinate 12.00, 15.50, drag down to coordinate 12.00, 0.50, and double-click to finish the wall. The wall should completely separate the two rooms.

3. Get the measurements from the front door to create the same height door opening in the wall. This door will only be $3\,^1/_2$ feet wide. Start your Cutout Box at coordinate 11.00, 6.00 and finish it at 13.00, 2.50. Your interior wall should look similar to Figure 18-8.

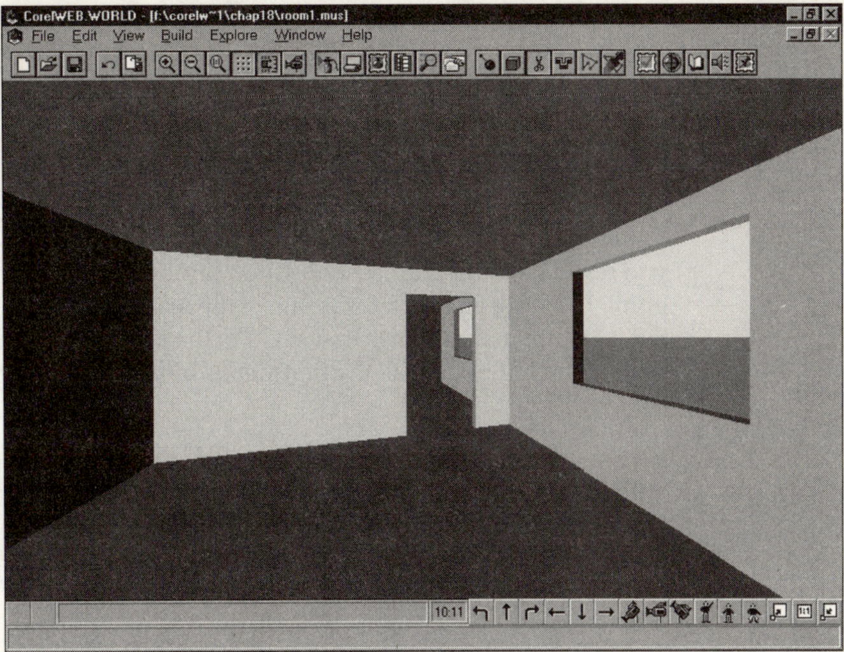

Figure 18-8: After creating the interior wall and carving the door, your scene should look this.

Creating Faces

WEB.WORLD provides another type of building material called *faces*. This is really a shortened form of the word surfaces. Faces are fundamentally different from walls in two respects:

■ A face can be placed on an angle.

■ A face has no depth—it is paper thin.

Don't let these differences lead you to think that faces aren't related to walls. Actually, it's the wall objects that are related to faces. Here are some similarities:

■ Faces have two sides; each can be decorated with paint, wallpaper, and pictures.

■ You can automatically create corners.

■ You set the height of faces with the top and bottom laths of the Height control.

Let's use the Draw Face tool to add a door to the interior wall's door opening. Remember to double-click to end your face object. If you forget and start drawing an additional face segment, click the right mouse button. This automatically ends the face—up to the last corner point. If you really get fouled up, just hit Undo until you are back to your starting point. Drawing angled faces is one of the few times when turning off the Snap feature makes things easier. Go to the Edit menu and select Grid | Snap Off. As usual, the first step is setting the laths of the Height control.

1. Position the Pinocchio tool so that you can see the entire doorway. Click on the area of wall directly over the top of the doorway opening. This will give you red indicators for the top of the opening. Set the bottom lath to the floor height and the top lath to the bottom red indicator.

2. As shown in Figure 18-9, set the first point of the face object right at the corner of the door opening. Drag out a line whose length corresponds to the width of the door opening (this should be 3 $1/2$ feet) and double-click to end the face. You can make it any angle you desire; however, leaving it open at least halfway will make it easier for visitors to navigate between rooms.

That's all there is to making the door—now you can have some privacy when company arrives. Faces are very useful for any partition that must be angled. Because faces are paper thin, they can be a little disorienting when viewed near an edge, but it won't take long for you and your visitors to get accustomed to this. A word of caution regarding face objects: Don't cross face segments over themselves and form intersections. You won't blow the program up or corrupt your file, but you will confuse WEB.WORLD and cause it to create some very peculiar perspectives.

In this next exercise, we'll demonstrate how the rectangular surface is the basic component of all WEB.WORLD objects. This will require using the Erase Face tool. The Erase Face tool is related to the Cutout Box tool in that it removes parts of 3D objects. However, instead of cutting out a certain volume of area, it removes whole rectangular surfaces. Now it becomes important to understand what WEB.WORLD considers a *surface*.

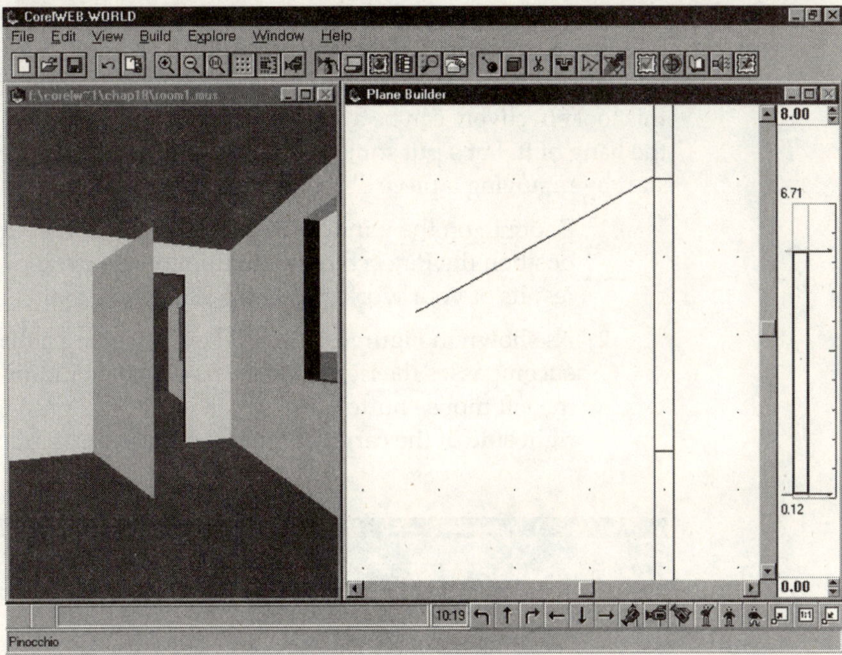

Figure 18-9: By drawing a face object as shown, you can easily create a door.

You've already seen one way to determine what a surface is: by clicking in the 3D Space window to measure a wall. Remember how clicking in different areas produced different measurements? This is because WEB.WORLD doesn't see a wall with a hole in it as a contiguous surface anymore. The interior wall with a window carved out of it becomes four surfaces: a rectangular section above the window, one below the window, and one to each side of the window. Now take a closer look at the window opening. How many surfaces make up the interior panels that represent the wall thickness? That's right, four. Next, take the Pinocchio tool outside and look at the exterior of the wall. How many rectangular surfaces can you count from this viewpoint? You can see why we say that the rectangle is the fundamental shape in WEB.WORLD. This also helps you to understand why WEB.WORLD slows down as you create more objects—simply carving out a window creates many more rectangles for WEB.WORLD to keep track of.

Now we have to apply this knowledge to using the Erase Face tool. The Erase Face tool will remove any surface it completely encompasses. This is the one Plane Builder tool that is not affected by the laths on the

Height control—it's power to delete surfaces is applied from the top down to the bottom of your scene. You have one means of control for this tool: dragging out rectangular areas in the Plane Builder window. Using this tool effectively can be a little tricky, but with some practice you'll get the hang of it. Let's put some of this information to practical use. We'll start by removing a piece of the window opening.

1. Zoom in on the window in the lower left corner and then position the Pinocchio tool in front of it, so you can see the results of your work. Select the Erase Face tool.

2. As shown in Figure 18-10, drag out a rectangle that completely encompasses the right side surface of the window opening. Click the left mouse button and watch in the 3D Space window as the right side of the carved window disappears.

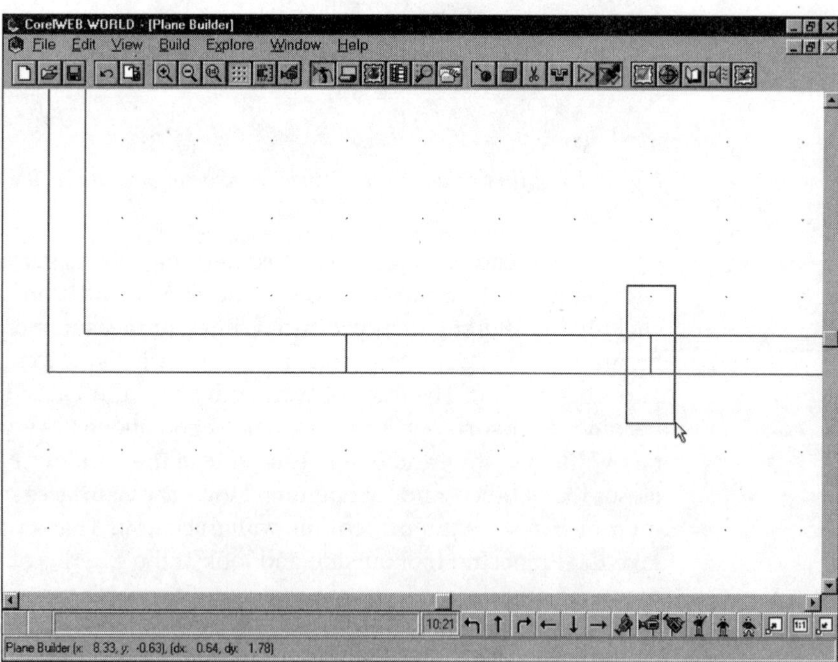

Figure 18-10: Drag out a rectangle, like the one shown above, to remove the window opening surface.

At this point, move the Pinocchio tool to survey the damage you've done. Place the Pinocchio tool right on the window sill and peer straight down the length of the wall section in both directions. Move outside and see what things look like from that perspective also. You'll notice that looking from the inside out, the side with the window surface removed appears to be missing the exterior surface of the wall. However, when viewed from the outside, the wall exterior is intact. This proves another point about surfaces: not all are the same type! For instance, those used to construct solid objects, like boxes and walls, have only the exterior side visible. Yet face objects are unique because both sides are visible. There will be times when you mistakenly remove a surface and expose the invisible side of a face. Now that you know the cause, you'll be ready to fix these situations when they arise.

Creating Furniture

Next, you'll apply the carving and building techniques to create smaller objects, like furniture. As with rooms, detailed planning for furniture is just as essential. If you start creating your furniture and find there isn't enough room to finish it, you can't just pick it up and move it. You'll need to press Undo until all remnants of the furniture are removed and start all over. With this in mind, Figure 18-11 illustrates the kind of plan drawings needed to create a table. Notice it is in the same "one unit equals one foot" scale, so it fits properly in your newly constructed room.

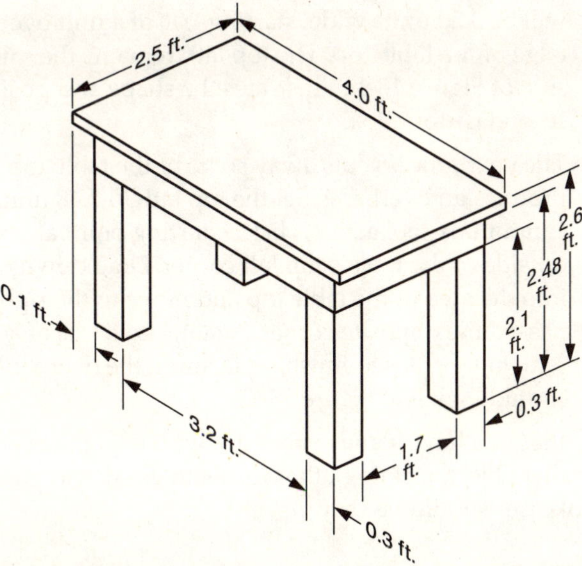

Figure 18-11: Detailed plans and measurements guarantee that your furniture will fit properly in your scenes.

The following sections provide step-by-step instructions for creating a simple table. The first shape you'll create establishes the extremities of the table. According to the measurements in Figure 18-11, the highest point is 29 inches; the widest point is 48 inches; the deepest point is 30. Pick a spot in the center of the room, giving yourself plenty of space to create an object of this size. You'll want to set the Snap to $^1/10$. (Note: when converting from fractions of an inch to tenths of a unit, we have taken some liberties in rounding off to make things easier. The amount of difference is negligible for our purposes.)

1. Set the bottom lath to match the floor height. Set the top lath to 2.60 (approximately).

2. Activate the Add Box tool and drag out a rectangle 2.5 units deep by 4 units wide. Click to finish creating the box.

3. Next you'll carve out the space under the table, between the legs. To accommodate for the width of the table top overhang and the width of the table legs, you'll need to draw a Cutout Box that is 1.70 units deep, starting $^4/10$ of a unit down from the top edge of the table top. This Cutout Box must start outside the left edge of the table and pass completely through the right side. The top lath should be set to 2.10 units. The left side of Figure 18-12 illustrates the shape and position of this Cutout Box.

4. The next carving gives shape to the table legs. This Cutout Box will be 3.20 units wide, starting $^4/10$ of a unit over from the left edge of the table top. The top lath remains the same. The right side of Figure 18-12 illustrates the shape and position of this second Cutout Box.

5. The next process cuts away some of the table top's thickness to produce an overhang. Set the top lath to 2.48 units. With the Cutout Box tool active, click a starting point at least $^1/10$ of a unit outside of the table's top left corner. Drag down $^1/10$ of a unit into the area of the table top and move to the right until you've passed the opposite corner. Again, carve $^1/10$ of a unit out of the remaining sides to finishing forming the overhang. Your table should look like Figure 18-13.

Now that you have some experience with using the carving technique on a smaller object, tackling other furnishings such as chairs, counters, and bookcases should be easy.

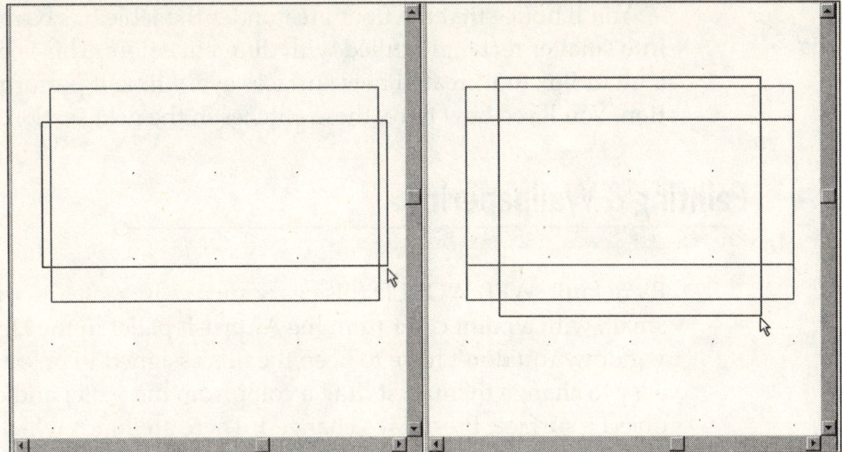

Figure 18-12: On the left, the shape and position of the horizontal Cutout Box is shown. The shape and position of the vertical Cutout Box is shown on the right.

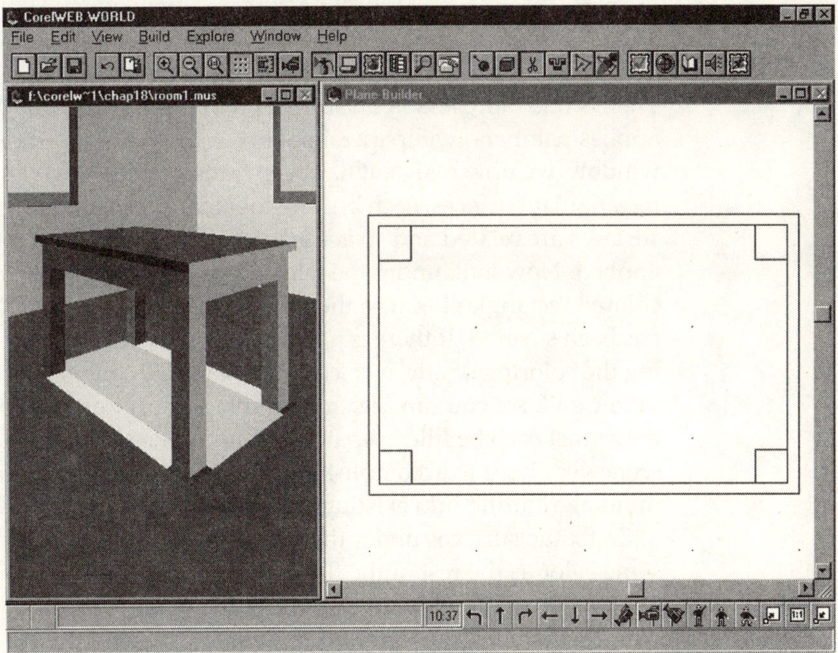

Figure 18-13: The finished table.

You'll notice that the floor area under the table has been broken up into smaller rectangles filled with different colors. This is because the Cutout Box tool created new surfaces every time it performed its function. You'll see how to fix these patches in the next section.

Painting & Wallpapering

By default, WEB.WORLD fills every surface it creates, no matter how small, with a paint color from the Airbrush pallet in the Decorator window. You don't have to keep the fills assigned to objects—it's quite easy to change them. Just drag a color from the pallet and drop it on an object's surface. Presto! It's changed. There are times when a surface is too small to use this method. In this case, select the desired color in the pallet and right-click on the surface in the 3D Space window. Select Apply Airbrush from the pop-up menu.

How Surfaces Are Covered

There's one more lesson on surfaces that deals with how WEB.WORLD applies paint and wallpaper. Looking at the wall with the carved-out window, we now realize it has been transformed into many different rectangular surfaces, each butting together precisely. However, these surfaces are related and so act as a whole when paint and wallpaper are applied. Now look under the table again. It's a patchwork of various-colored rectangles because the relationship to the original floor surface has been severed. If there is a relationship between surfaces, then changing the coloring of any surface in the "family" causes all the surfaces to follow suit. As you can see, once "orphan" surfaces have been created they must each be filled separately. This makes wholesale changes to a scene very hard to accomplish. The trick is to think ahead and try to minimize cutting into existing surfaces as much as possible.

To fix the surfaces under the table, you'll need to fill each with the same color as the rest of the floor. You'll notice that some of the rectangles still retain relationships with each other. This is good, because it cuts down on the number of times you must apply the Airbrush tool. You will need to move the Pinocchio tool around and use the Tele button on the Camera control to get in close to the small rectangles. Also, don't forget about the ability to right-click and apply paint.

Working With Wallpaper

The principles regarding the application of Airbrush paint also apply to covering surfaces with wallpaper images. The more surfaces you create, the more times you'll need to drag the particular wallpaper from the Decorator window and drop it into the 3D Space window.

Wallpapers are very versatile, much more so than Airbrush paints. You can create them from almost any bitmap image, and there are hundreds of images available on the WEB.GRAPHICS Suite CD. You'll **CD-ROM** have tons of fun exploring the PICTURES, PICTURE2, SAMPLES, and TEXTURES subdirectories under the WEBWORLD folder. There are also hundreds of home-brewed textures to be found on the CD accompanying this book. For the next exercise, direct the Decorator window to look for images in the WEBWORLD\TEXTURES\DALLE folder.

Grab any of the thumbnail images from the Decorator window and drop them on a wall. We chose DALLE03.GIF. Now it's time we took a closer look at some of the more interesting features of wallpaper. Click the Details icon on the main toolbar to access the WallPaper Detail dialog box.

Tip

If error messages rather than thumbnails show up in the Decorator window, don't panic. These images are probably still fine to use, so give them a try. We have found a small number of images that just resist being used as wallpaper. If you run across this problem, press the F5 key to refresh the Decorator window and try again. If you still have no success, load the file into a bitmap editor, like PHOTO-PAINT, and resave it. (If you load the image from a CD, you'll need to save it to a directory on another drive.) This may resuscitate the image.

Reducing the Tile Width and Height settings to a smaller number makes the repeated image smaller. This is useful in creating realistic scenes where patterns are mostly small and unobtrusive. However, the digital wallpaper hanger shares one of the same nightmares that real-world paperhangers face: matching patterns in the corners. As the image on the left side in Figure 18-14 illustrates, matching the patterns in corners can be troublesome. But the image on the right shows how we used the Tile W Offset setting to make a perfect match. Each image is different, so you'll have to experiment with this option to find the best settings for your particular pattern. Remember, you have to repaste your wallpaper after changing any of the Tile options.

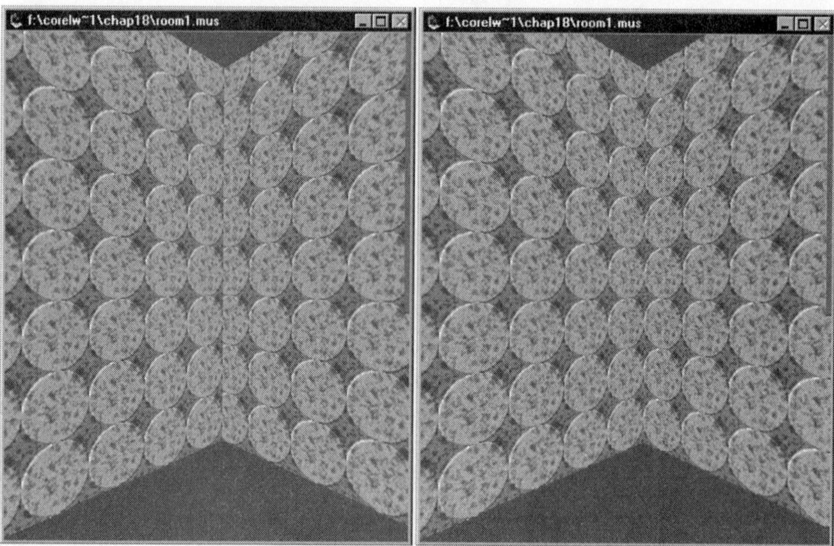

Figure 18-14: The corner on the left shows a mismatched pattern. After changing the Tile W Offset setting, the image on the right shows the perfectly matched pattern.

Let's go from the realistic to the outrageous. One of the wildest wallpaper options is activated by selecting Slide Direction. This feature allows your wallpaper to move. You control the rate of speed at which it moves and what direction the pattern travels in. After selecting this option in the WallPaper Detail dialog, the box will expand to include the Slide controls. Just click inside the circular control to set the rate and direction. The farther away from the center the end of the red line is, the faster the wallpaper will move.

Moving wallpaper's a real eye popper. You can't miss it. But be careful not to overdo it. Besides the risk of making your viewers dizzy, it slows down the computer.

Picture Perfect

After you've covered your walls with a basic paint or wallpaper, it's time to spruce things up a bit. There are three different types of images you can hang on your walls: Pictures, Albums, and Movies. Again, there are plenty of images available on the WEB.GRAPHICS Suite CD. Many can be found in the individual directories under the WEBWORLD\SAMPLES folder.

Once you've read the previous chapter, Pictures are pretty self-explanatory. There are no options for Pictures. One interesting thing you can do with Pictures is combine them into groups called albums. Your visitors can flip through the series of pictures by selecting List Album from the right menu. The neat thing about albums is that the individual pictures don't have to be the same size or bitmap format type. WEB.WORLD takes care of all those mundane details. Creating an album is easy: drag your first picture and drop it onto a surface. With the first picture still selected (you can tell it's selected because there are handles at the corners), drag and drop another picture onto the first. Follow this procedure until you have compiled a collection of all the images you want in the album. That's all there is to it.

Movies are animated Pictures and they can really grab a viewer's attention. The previous chapter explains how to make your own movies, so we won't dwell on that aspect. Instead, we'll look at a few of the options found in the Movie Detail dialog box. One we have a lot of fun with is Paste as Wallpaper. When you select this option, you can choose to turn on Tiling, just like regular Wallpaper. After you've played with this feature for a while, select the Slide Direction option. You guessed it. This is the same Slide Direction feature found in the WallPaper Details dialog box. Now you can really inflict motion sickness on your virtual visitors.

There are some nicely done movies—many of opening and closing doors and windows—included in the WEBWORLD\MOVIES folder on the WEB.GRAPHICS Suite CD. However, we want to direct your attention to one very interesting use of Movies. There is a series of .MUS files, with names that start with DWARF, found in the WEBWORLD\SAMPLES\LEGEND subdirectory. Not only do these files show off a unique approach to incorporating Movies, but they also make use of Attachments—and these just happen to be the next area for discussion.

Getting Attached to Multimedia

Whether it be a Picture, an Album, or a Movie, each can have attributes attached to it. These attachments are hidden aspects of the item, and they can be triggered by the viewer of your world. The attachment can be simple text that explains what the user is looking at, or it can provide instructions for navigating through your world. But Attachments go far beyond simple captioning.

If you want, save your room and table project. Then open the DWARF7.MUS file, found on the WEB.GRAPHICS Suite CD, under the WEBWORLD\SAMPLES\LEGEND subdirectory. After the file loads, move around and explore. Check out all the sleeping dwarfs and right-click on them to read any text attachments. You'll discover that one has a surprise—it snores!

So you see how attaching sound files can spice up an otherwise ho-hum virtual world. There are plenty of .WAV files to use on the WEB.GRAPHICS Suite CD. Many are in the WEBWORLD\SOUNDS\WAV directory but dozens more are strewn throughout the various WEBWORLD\SAMPLES folders.

The Power of Functions

Let's get back to the little underground world of Dwarfs. This particular file holds another surprise: it can automatically load another .MUS file. However, the exact mechanism for doing this is purposely obtuse. (Do you want me to tell you the secret to getting out of this world? Nah, I'm sure you love a challenge. If you get stomped, I'll leave a clue at the end of this chapter.) When you double-click on the hidden item, you will be brought into another virtual world. This next one, DWARF8.MUS, will really have you asking "How'd they do that?"

The DWARF series is a good example of what you can do with Functions. These are found on the Attachments dialog box you access by clicking the Attachments tool icon in the main toolbar. A complete rundown of all available Functions and what they do is found in Chapter 17. But what you've just experienced (you did find the passage, right?) demonstrates quite nicely WEB.WORLD's power to weave together multiple worlds and scenes so that they appear as parts of a whole. And you're not limited to connecting to other .MUS files. At any place on the Internet, you can use the Link to URL function to jump out of your 3D world into another. You can even start running applications or digital movie files, like .AVIs. The powerful combination of Attachments and Functions is awesome!

Playing MIDI Files

Music is very important for setting the mood in your virtual world. MIDI files are a great way to include very long passages of music, because they are very compact. This means they'll download over a network or modem connection pretty quickly. After you've gotten your feet wet with WEB.WORLD, you'll soon appreciate that speeding up virtual worlds is always a concern for 3D virtual world architects.

Refer to Chapter 17 for a detailed discussion on using the MIDI Play List dialog box to add MIDI tunes to your 3D scenes. There are some MIDI files, not a huge selection, on the WEB.GRAPHICS Suite CD. All but one are in the WEBWORLD\SOUNDS\MIDI directory. There's a soothing 4-minute 39-second classical selection entitled OPUS27.MID found in the WEBWORLD\SAMPLES\ASTRO folder.

3D sights, sounds, and interactivity—what more could you want from an application? WEB.WORLD has it all and it's easy to learn to boot. We're sure that this hands-on tutorial has piqued your interest and given you the skills and encouragement to start creating your own 3D worlds.

Moving On

Most people will admit that working and playing in a 3D virtual environment is a blast. Comparatively speaking, there aren't that many Web sites that offer this kind of exciting Internet experience. But you can bet that 3D is the wave of the future. With CorelWEB.WORLD in your toolkit, you already have the needed tools to be right up front—riding the crest of that wave.

Sadly, not every Web assignment calls for working in 3D. In many cases, Web authors are called on to make previously published information into HTML pages. In the next chapter, you'll learn about CorelWEB.Transit and how you can quickly convert word processor documents to HTML pages.

If it's the secret passage you long to see,
    "look in the corner," is the key.

Get close to the ground
    and the door will be found.

PART V

CorelWEB.Transit

19

An Introduction to CorelWEB.Transit

Have you ever gone through the tedious procedure of converting a word processing document into HTML? Have you ever longed for a quicker, easier way? If so, your wait is over. CorelWEB.Transit makes fast conversions from word processing to HTML a reality. WEB.Transit automatically converts source files in Lotus AmiPro, Microsoft Word, WordPerfect, and Rich Text Formats (RTF) into HTML—even if you don't have the source application! And, it will also convert placed graphics into GIF or JPEG format. Once the files have been converted, they are completely editable within CorelWEB.DESIGNER (or any other HTML or text editor).

This chapter provides a quick overview, while walking you through the basic steps necessary to complete a simple conversion.

When & How to Use WEB.Transit

CorelWEB.Transit offers amazing potential. Whether you need to convert your company's policies and procedures manual for your corporate intranet or transfer a manuscript to post on your personal Web site, you'll find that there's no better way to approach the task. The key to success with WEB.Transit is to start with a document that has been properly prepared in the word processing program. The document must use *style names* to completely define elements, rather than using individual typeface and size attributes. Styles provide the means to logically format a document. WEB.Transit's power is based upon its ability to convert these word processing styles into HTML coding.

If you start with a word processing document that has not been properly styled, the conversion process will not be effective. While WEB.Transit can identify and convert individual text attributes such as bold, italic, and underscore, these are minor elements when compared to heading levels, which give a document its structure. Here are a few examples:

- Styles can be used to break long documents into smaller chunks. WEB.Transit allows you to chop large, unwieldy word processing files into smaller, more manageable Web pages (ten pages, max.).

- Headings can be used to build a *Local Table of Contents (TOC)*. The TOCs are automatically placed at the top of each Web page, providing a convenient jump list. WEB.Transit takes care of all the anchor tagging.

- Styles can call specific graphics, icons, or horizontal separators to provide visual structure.

The Conversion Process: An Overview

The CorelWEB.Transit interface is simple, although it can be daunting to the uninitiated. Don't get frightened away! All you do is let the program walk you through a series of dialog boxes to prepare the conversion template, before you hit "go," by pressing the Translate Publication button. The more carefully you fill in the information, the cleaner the subsequent conversion. Figure 19-1 shows the basic window from which the dialog boxes are summoned.

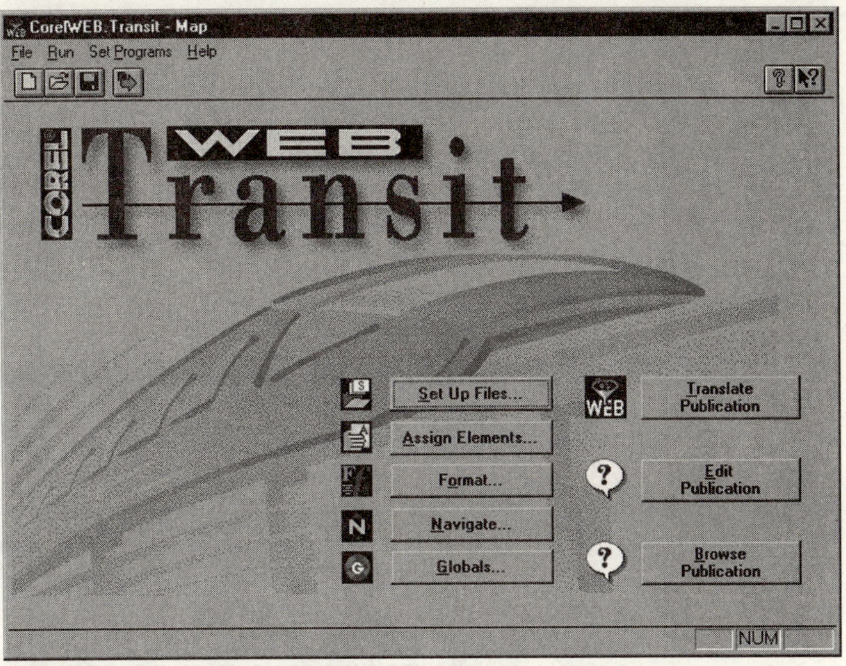

Figure 19-1: CorelWEB.Transit's simple interface packs a powerful punch. Just follow along, and you'll be whipping through word processing-to-HTML translations in no time at all!

There are five categories to define when preparing a file for conversion:

- Setting Up Files—Where are the files are coming from and where are they going?

- Assigning Elements—Which elements will be used and how will they be associated?

- Formatting—How will each element appear?

- Navigating—How will visitors jump between pages?

- Setting Globals—Which colors and elements will appear on each page?

Setting Up Files

The Set Up Files dialog box, as shown in Figure 19-2, controls the basics of file import and export. It tells WEB.Transit which word processing file to convert and where to place the translated HTML file. While files can be placed anywhere on your system, the HTML filename is limited to 12 characters in length. The dialog box also provides the ability to insert a Web page title. Remember that the title is what will show up in the search engines. (Refer back to Chapter 5 for the lowdown on search engines and page titling.)

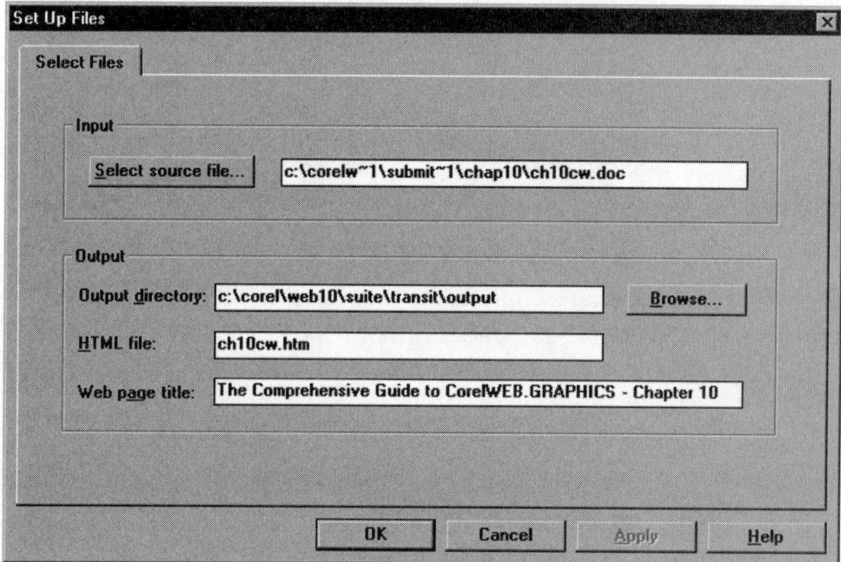

Figure 19-2: To set up a translation, begin by selecting your input file. Don't forget to add a Web page title.

As you can see in Figure 19-2, we're experimenting with an HTML conversion of the manuscript of this book's Chapter 10. The HTML filename is automatically based upon the original filename, with an HTM extension substituted for the DOC extension. The Web page title is complete, if a tad lengthy.

Assigning Elements

The Assign Elements dialog box is broken into two tabs: Place Elements and Assign Tags. The Place Elements tab, as shown in Figure 19-3, lets you decide which word processing elements you want to use in the final HTML. You'll want to go through the entire list of Translator Elements (styles) to decide whether they should be included in the Body of the Web page(s), and whether they should be used in the Local TOC on each page.

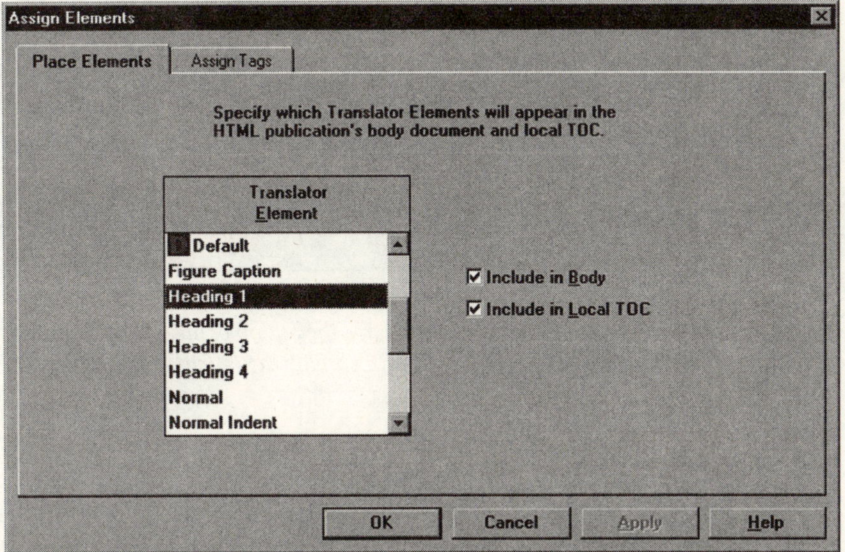

Figure 19-3: The Assign Elements tab gives you the ability to automatically weed out extrinsic text elements (such as production notes) from the finished HTML file(s).

The Assign Tags tab, as shown in Figure 19-4, ties the "live" Translator Elements to their associated tags. By default, the program assumes that most styles should be converted to the HTML <P> paragraph format— with a handful of exceptions. WEB.Transit is smart enough to know that Heading 1 is an <H1> command, Heading 2 is an <H2> command, and so forth. It also knows about certain list formats. Regardless of what the program assumes, you should go through the entire list of Translator Elements to ensure that they are associated with the proper HTML tags. If you remove a Translator Element in the Place Elements tab, it will not appear in the Assign Tags tab.

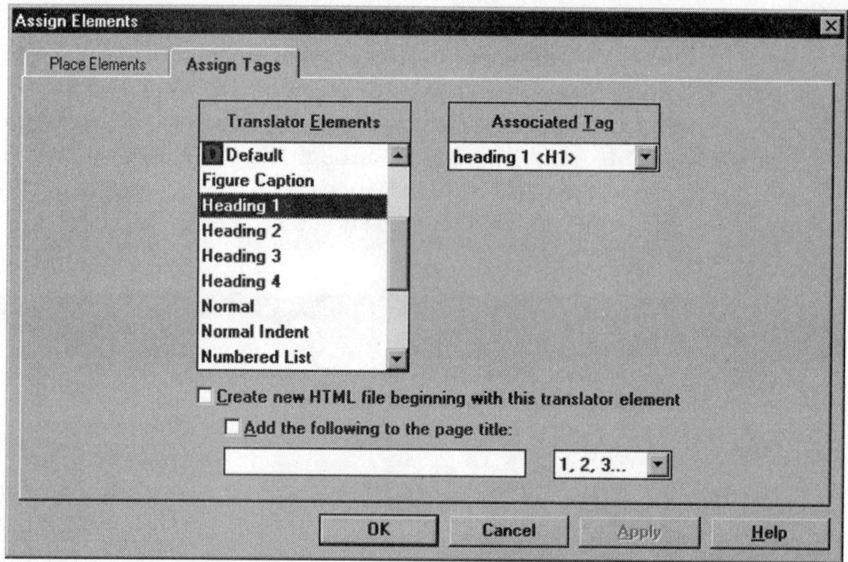

Figure 19-4: The Assign Tags tab lets you tie the word processing style to an associated HTML tag. You have the option of automatically breaking a big file up into smaller pages each time a specific tag (such as a Heading 1) is encountered.

If you want to break a big word processing file up into smaller HTML pages, this is the place to initiate the process. Just select the Translator Element where you want to break the pages, and select the *Create new HTML file . . .* check box. You have the option of adding additional text and numbers to the sliced and diced pages.

Formatting

Once you've decided upon which Translator Elements to use in your finished HTML file(s), you have the happy task of assigning a wide variety of attributes. The Format dialog box is broken into two tabs: Body and Local TOC. The Body tab, as shown in Figure 19-5, lets you tie each Translator Element not just to text attributes but to specific graphic elements as well, if you wish. If you remove a Translator Element when you're making choices in the Assign Elements dialog box, it will not appear in the Format Body dialog box.

You'll want to go through the entire list of Translator Elements again, to ensure that each style is converted to your exact specifications. While this may seem a bit tedious, a little work here goes a long way—especially when converting a large number of pages! The Paragraph - Format Body dialog box, as shown by Figure 19-6, is used to assign alignment and intraparagraph spacing attributes.

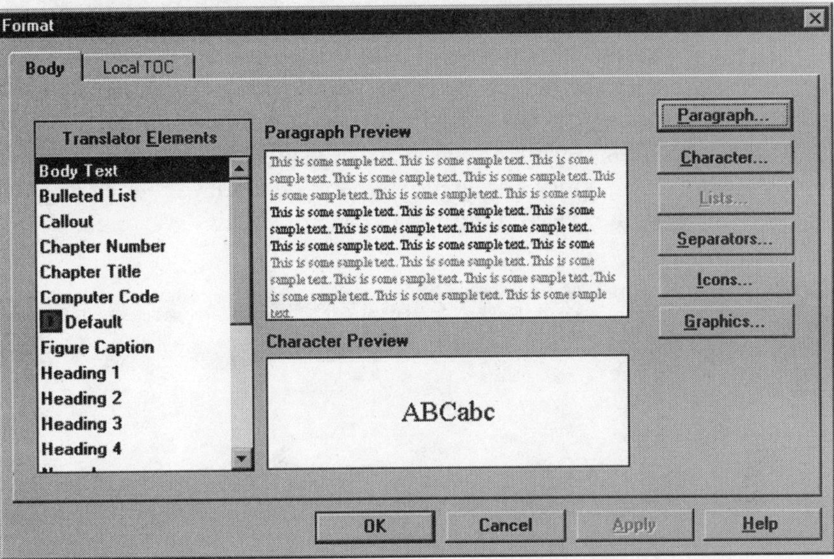

Figure 19-5: The Format Body dialog box allows access to the complete range of text and graphic controls.

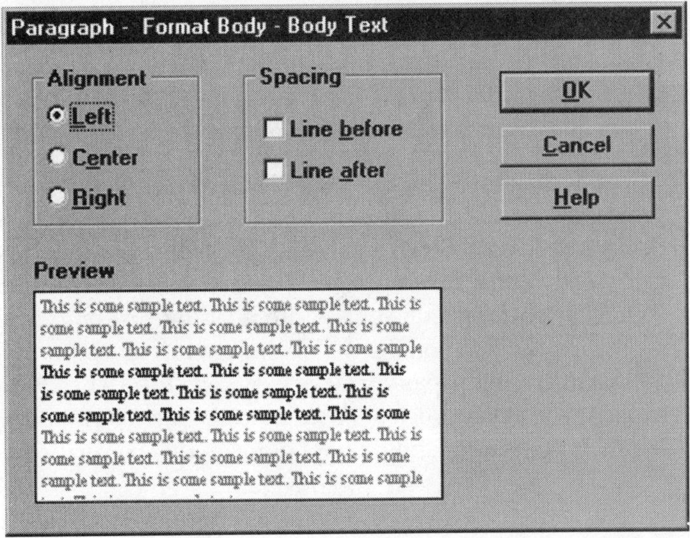

Figure 19-6: The Paragraph - Format Body dialog box defaults to left alignment with no extra space.

The Character - Format Body dialog box, as shown in Figure 19-7, lets you take total control over text attributes. If your Web pages use other than the default text size, you'll want to pay careful attention to how this dialog box is configured. You can specify Font Size in specific or relative sizes, control Effects Mapping, and choose text color. The Effects Mapping options are handy when you want to change, say, a bold command to the HTML Emphasis <EM> or <STRONG> tags.

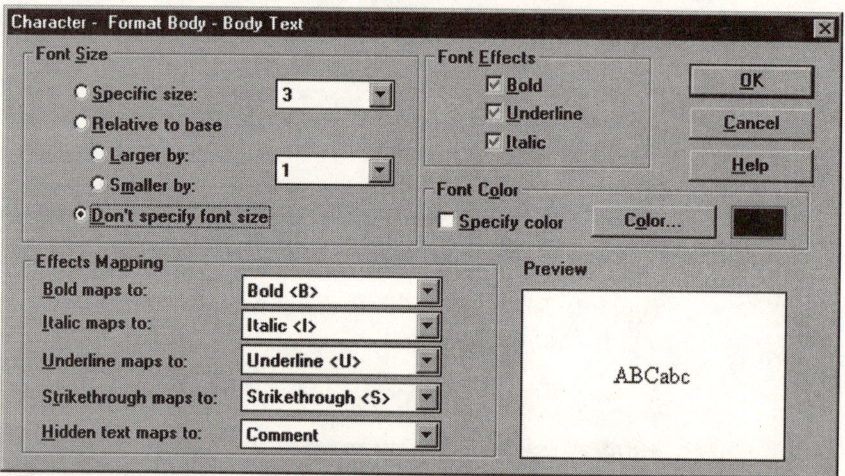

Figure 19-7: The Character - Format Body dialog box takes charge of every possible text attribute except typeface (which is controlled by the FONT FACE tag).

The Separators - Format Body dialog box, as shown in Figure 19-8, provides a powerful device for structuring Web pages. By telling this dialog box to add a horizontal separator before or after a specific style, you can quickly enhance your pages. You can choose HTML separators (with complete control over height, width, shading, and alignment) or graphic separators. Clicking on the Gallery button brings you to WEB.Transit's gallery of graphic separators (not to CorelWEB.GALLERY, as you might expect). The Icons - Format Body dialog box, as shown in Figure 19-9, is handy for placing graphic icons before or after a specific style.

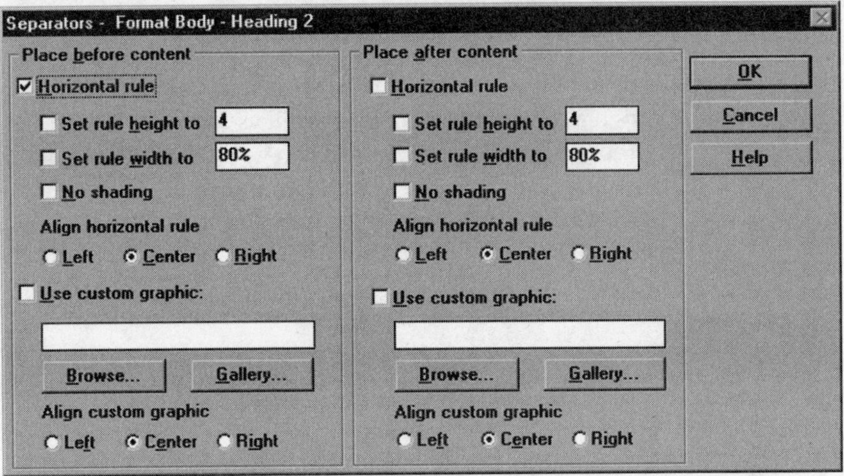

Figure 19-8: The Separators - Format Body dialog box allows you to place a horizontal rule before or after specific content. You can use HTML rules or custom graphics.

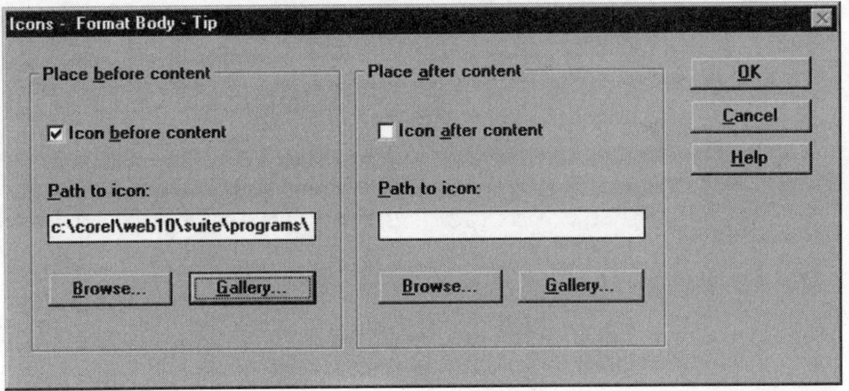

Figure 19-9: The Icons - Format Body dialog box lets you drop in an icon before or after a specific style. In this instance, we might drop in a "Hot Tip" icon.

The Graphics - Format Body dialog box, as shown in Figure 19-10, packs a powerful punch. Graphics placed in the original word processing file can be automatically converted into GIF or JPEG format. You can assign alignment attributes as well as alternate text to the graphics (although you'll probably want to go in and edit the alternate text tags in the finished HTML file in order to accurately represent each image). But perhaps the most amazing feature of this dialog box is its ability to produce linked thumbnails in 32-, 64- , and 96-pixel squares or $^1/_{16}$, $^1/_{36}$, and $^1/_{64}$ scales.

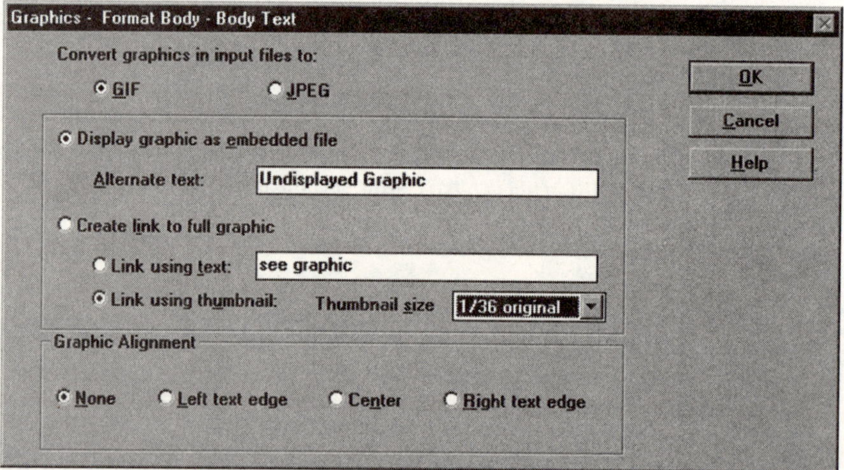

Figure 19-10: The Graphics - Format Body dialog box includes settings for GIF or JPEG exports, as well as alternate text settings, thumbnails, and alignment options.

WEB.Transit has the ability to translate a wide variety of placed graphics:

- AutoCAD (.DXF)
- Windows Bitmap (.BMP)
- CompuServe Graphics Interchange Format (.GIF)
- Computer Graphics Metafile (.CGM)
- CorelDRAW! (.CDR)

- Hewlett-Packard Graphics Language (.PLT)
- JPEG - Joint Photographics Experts Group (.JPG)
- Micrografx Designer (.DRW)
- Microsoft Paint (.MSP)
- Paint (.PCX and .PCC)
- TIFF - Tagged Image File Format (.TIF)
- Windows Metafile (.WMF)
- WordPerfect Graphics (.WPG)

The Format dialog box's Local TOC tab, as shown in Figure 9-11, controls the appearance of the TOC at the top of each page. In order for a Translator Element to appear in this list, it must be specified in the Place Elements tab of the Assign Elements dialog box. The Local TOC tab allows you to assign levels and list types (bulleted or numbered). Long TOC entries can be trimmed down by selecting the Truncate option.

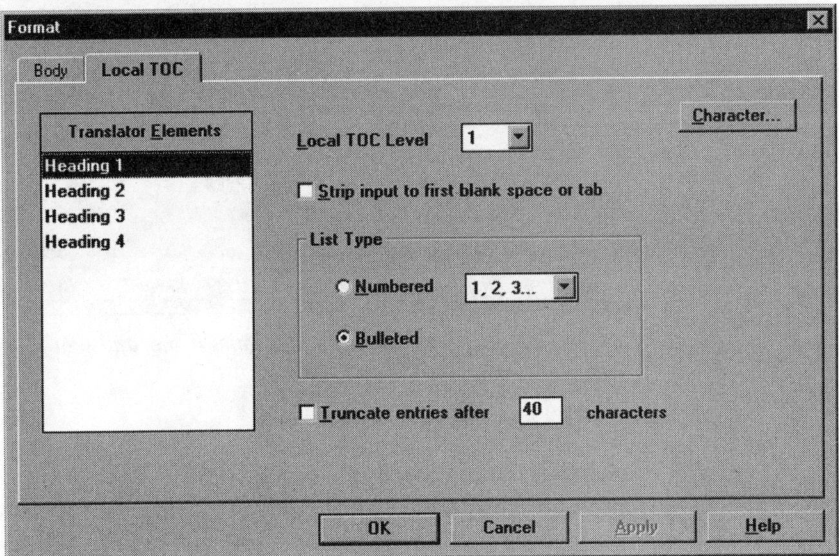

Figure 19-11: The Local TOC can be set up to meet specific requirements, including bulletted or numbered lists.

Navigating

If you break up a large word processing file into smaller HTML chunks, you'll have to provide a means of navigation for your visitors. The Navigate dialog box, as shown in Figure 19-12, controls the manner in which CorelWEB.Transit places its hyperlinked navigational icons. By default, WEB.Transit will automatically set up the proper forward (Next page) and backward (Previous page) links at both the top and bottom of each page. You have the option of linking to a specific page instead of the default. WEB.Transit includes a number of tasteful navigational icons.

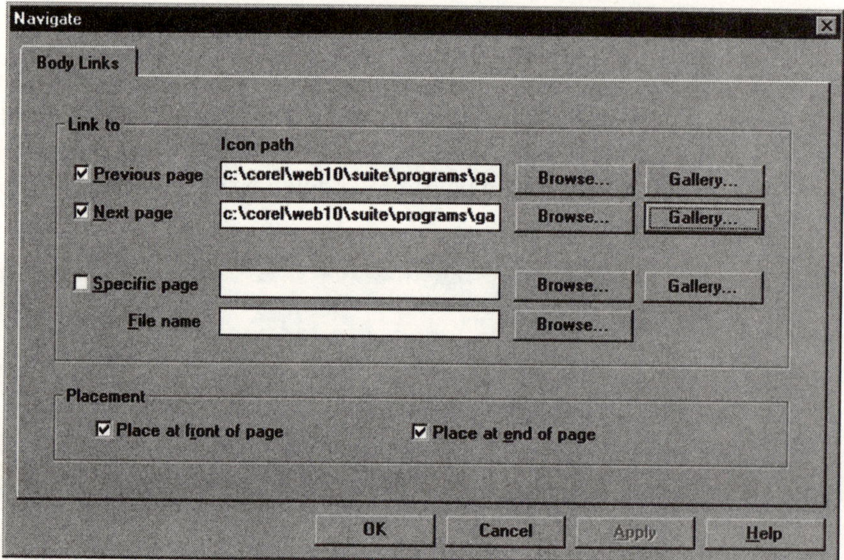

Figure 19-12: Just pick a set of navigational icons, and you'll be on your way!

Setting Globals

The Globals dialog box, as shown by Figure 19-13, is your last step before translating. This dialog box controls the global attributes for the HTML pages, including background, text, link, visited link, and active link colors. (Global text colors are overridden by individual Translator Element colors.) The Titles tab lets you add a title to the body of each Web page, while allowing the option of adding separators around both the Body and the Local TOC. The Address tab lets you add an address, as well as an e-mail address and prompt. This makes it easy to include a line that directs all e-mail inquiries to your Webmaster.

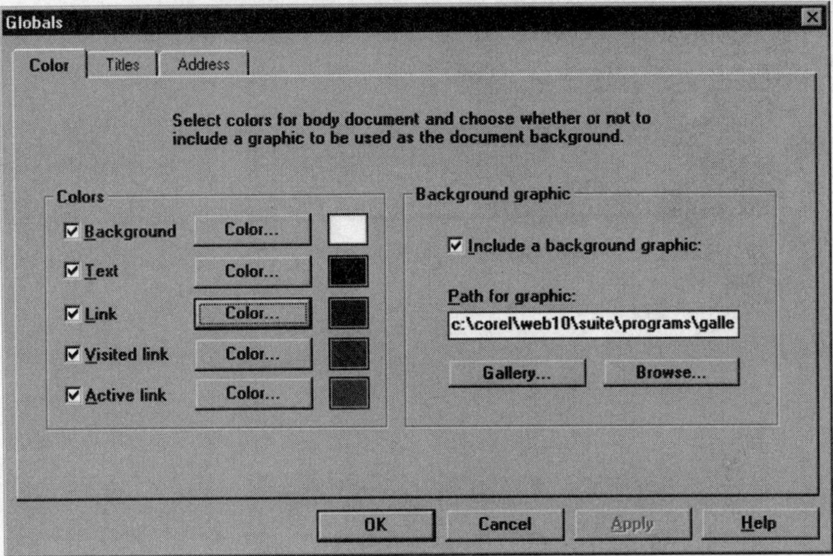

Figure 19-13: The Globals dialog box allows you to assign a background graphic. Don't overlook the WEB.Transit Gallery; it includes a nice array of elegant textures.

Translate!

Once you've filled in all the dialog boxes, you should Click File | Save As to save your custom translation template. After the template has been saved, you can click the Translate Publication button, sit back, and watch WEB.Transit go to work. The Translation Progress dialog box, as shown in Figure 19-14, provides feedback as the translation is running.

When the translation is complete, you can take a look at your handiwork in a Web browser. Figure 19-15 shows how our draft of Chapter 10 might look with a nice leather background. Once you've skimmed through the finished file, you can go back in and tweak the results with CorelWEB.DESIGNER. If the translation wasn't up to snuff, you can fine-tune the template and rerun it.

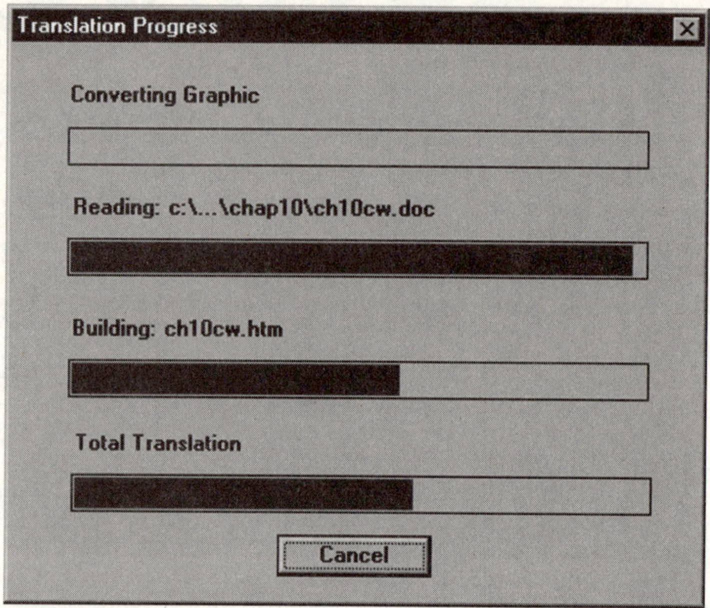

Figure 19-14: Watch those progress gauges . . . they move pretty fast.

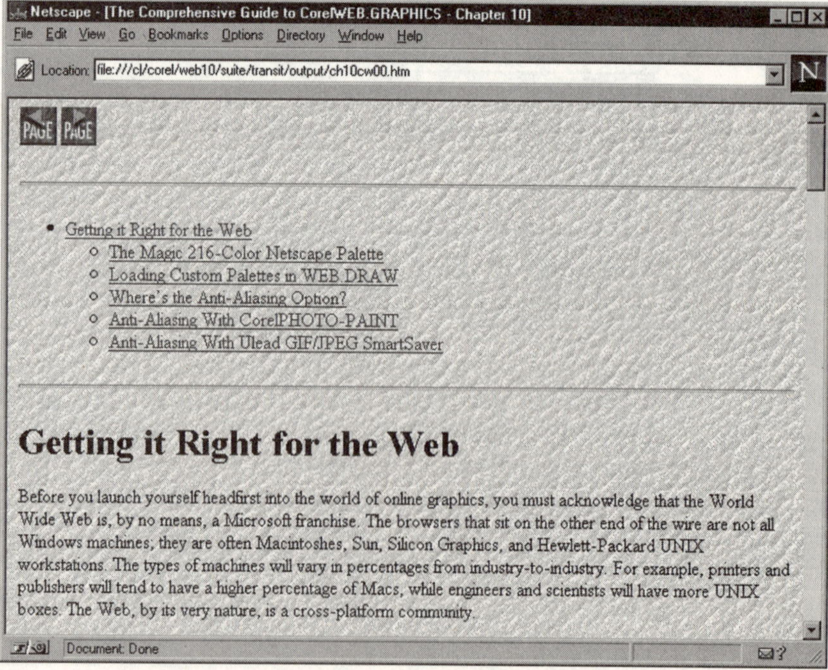

Figure 19-15: Here's the first Level 1 heading. Check out that cool table of contents!

Moving On

In this chapter, you learned how CorelWEB.Transit can make short work of converting word processing to HTML. Once you get the hang of WEB.Transit, this formerly tedious procedure actually becomes fun! By automatically converting AmiPro, Word, WordPerfect, and RTF files, you'll save countless hours, turning insurmountable tasks into child's play.

CorelWEB.GALLERY

An Introduction to CorelWEB.GALLERY

We first encountered CorelWEB.GALLERY way back in Chapter 4, while building the Too Rich, Too Thin Web page with WEB.DESIGNER. In this chapter, we'll investigate WEB.GALLERY to see how the program provides a simple interface to access the graphic elements you'll use while building your Web site. WEB.GALLERY's powerful tools and multiple-document interface enable you to organize and customize your graphics files and cure the "Now *where* did I see that?" syndrome.

Corel Corporation has long been known for bundling huge graphics libraries with their products. Longtime users of Corel products will remember what a thrill it was to open CorelDRAW! and instantly have a collection of hundreds of fonts and thousands of graphics. This time out, Corel has blessed us with yet another awesome assemblage of images. CorelWEB.GALLERY contains more than 7,500 Web-ready images to enliven your Web pages. Thankfully it's not just a library of images; it's also an image management application. This ensures that the blessing of backgrounds, icons, pictures, buttons, and bars do not become a curse.

Main Features—An Overview

WEB.GALLERY is fairly intuitive. Just a little tooling around in the Gallery window will make its features apparent. Here is a quick list of the major topics that are covered in this chapter:

- File Management

- Creating Albums

- Adjusting Windows

- Printing Thumbnails

- Archiving

- Using Keywords & Search

- Automatic Slideshows

- Scanning to Albums

The Graphics—or Button, Button, Who's Got the Button?

. . . and the banner . . and the bar, the arrow, the square, and much more? CorelWEB.GALLERY does! What a great collection of everything from an oil spill texture (one of our favorites) to tutmask (another favorite). The images are well ordered and ready to go, with most icons and bullets provided in several colors. You may not even need to open WEB.DRAW—only if you have to customize a button or banner.

As mentioned back in Chapter 4, the themesets alone are outstanding. These include 120 design elements (banners, bullets, dividers, round buttons, and square buttons) in matching themes—rainbow, marble, clouds, granite, and so on—which can pull together a site in a snap. Lest we forget, this package also contains more than 150 fonts plus hundreds of drop caps, floating objects, maps, and flags, and thousands of clip art images. Just perusing all these yummy images can really get your creative juices flowing.

File Management = Time Management

Every successful Web designer has long since learned the importance of being organized. In the fast-paced world of computer design, there is little time to spend looking for a misplaced image file in the middle of a project. And with hard disks in the gigabytes, there is a *lot* of space in which to lose those files!

Fortunately, the drag-and-drop, graphic album, thumbnail, and bookshelf features in WEB.GALLERY make organizing your graphics files an easy task. Unfortunately, you *will* need to spend a little time up front, analyzing how you work. WEB.GALLERY provides a marvelously customizable management system, but you still need to decide what best fits your design projects and make a game plan.

Read It & Weep

The CD-ROM galleries are read-only—as you will be informed every time you open a gallery window. Annoying as it is, there doesn't seem to be any way to disable this reminder—after all, it *is* read-only!

Starting Out

Take the time to familiarize yourself with the tools. By understanding how they apply to your work, you will be able to assemble professional Web pages quickly and easily. Let's open WEB.GALLERY and walk through this process. First, make sure the Corel WEB.GRAPHICS Suite CD-ROM is in your CD drive so you can access its libraries.

1. Double-click on the CorelWEB.GALLERY icon. This summons the welcome dialog box with a list of libraries and some brief instructions, as shown in Figure 20-1.

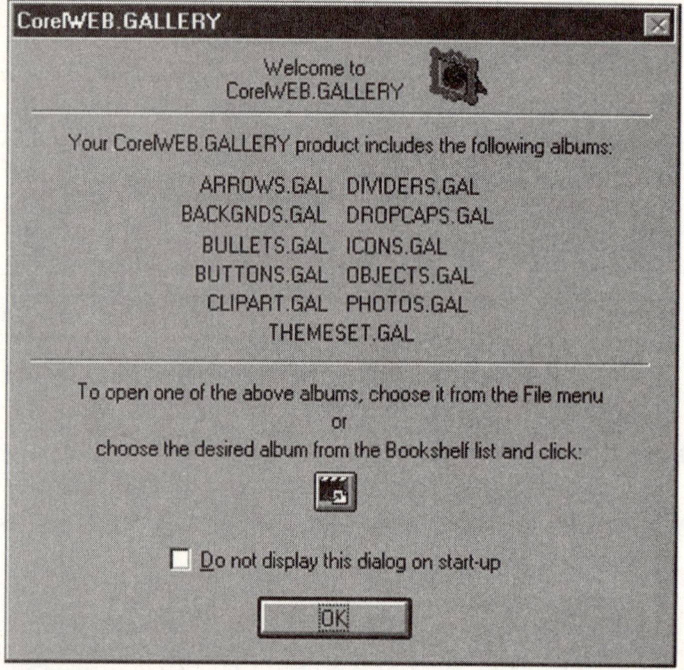

Figure 20-1: WEB.GALLERY upon launch.

2. You can disable the nagging welcome message by selecting the "Do not display..." check box. Click on OK. CorelWEB.GALLERY opens. The Bookshelf will have a path listing, such as, e:\albums\arrows.gal.

3. Click on the down arrow beside the path and scroll down to \albums\themeset.gal in the Bookshelf fly-out, click on this path and then on the Bookshelf icon. This will open the themeset gallery libraries, as shown in Figure 20-2. These basic themeset libraries contain many of the images that you'll need to create professional-looking Web pages.

Dust Off That Bookshelf!

Get yourself in the habit of using the Bookshelf. It is the backbone of CorelWEB.GALLERY's graphics file management tools.

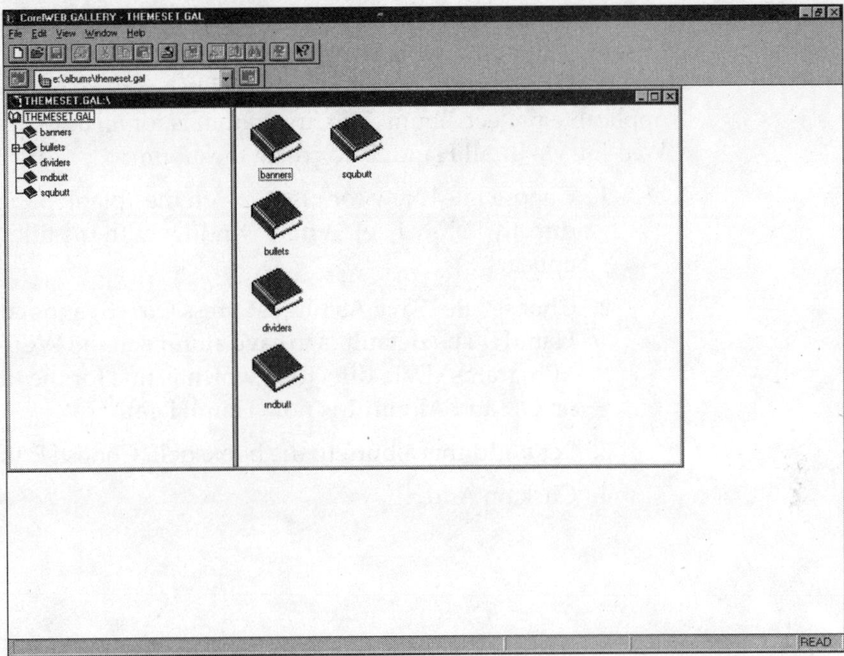

Figure 20-2: Themeset gallery libraries.

Using Albums

The graphic *albums* are really just subdirectories and files (or folders and files if you prefer). The advantage of albums is that the graphics are saved as image thumbnails; these can be chosen visually without having to remember an exact file name. You just click on a thumbnail image and drag it into another album or drop it into your Web application. Thumbnail items also may be cut or copied and pasted.

Make Your Play Pay

Warning: You can easily spend the whole day scrolling through these images! This is fun stuff, and there's no reason not to play (really, it's required to stay sane in this business). The trick is to make your play pay. If you consider your current and possible future projects, you can build a simple base of graphic element albums that will save you time in the long run.

It's a good idea to create albums before you begin browsing the images. This allows you to organize your current Web site project files, set up files for future projects, and quickly drag any images into the applicable project album. The first album is for an auto insurance agency Web site we'll call HandH. To create the album:

1. Choose File | New (or just click on the "blank paper" icon directly below File). A new window with the title "Album 1" appears.

2. Choose File | Save As (or just press Ctrl+S) and name the new file HandH. The default is to save albums in the WEB.GALLERY \Programs\Data directory, which is fine for the time being. Click on OK and Album 1 is now HandH.gal.

3. Let's add this album to the bookshelf. Choose Edit | Bookshelf.

4. Click on Add.

Now Where Did I Put That?

You also have the option of viewing the contents of the Bookshelf (which also includes the files on the CD) or opening an existing album. If you do not specifically add the album to the Bookshelf, you will not be able to access it through the Edit|Bookshelf Contents menu. Bookshelf operates from a list of all the Gallery files that have been added to it—wherever they reside on your hard drive.

Creating an Album With Cut & Paste

To create an album by copying and pasting files, follow the previous steps and then:

1. Choose the drive and directory from the Drive window at the bottom of the Gallery window. If the Drive window is not visible, click View | Drive Window.

2. Select the file and choose Edit | Copy.

3. Click to activate the album window and choose Edit | Paste.

Note: You can copy from the WEB.GALLERY files or graphic files you have created in other programs on your hard drive.

Adjusting Windows

Create three more albums until you have four new empty album windows and the original themeset gallery cascading on the desktop (go ahead and select the banner album from the themeset, if you haven't already). These cascading windows make dragging and dropping fairly problematic since only the top window is visible. Choose Window | Tile Horizontally to clean things up, as shown in Figure 20-3.

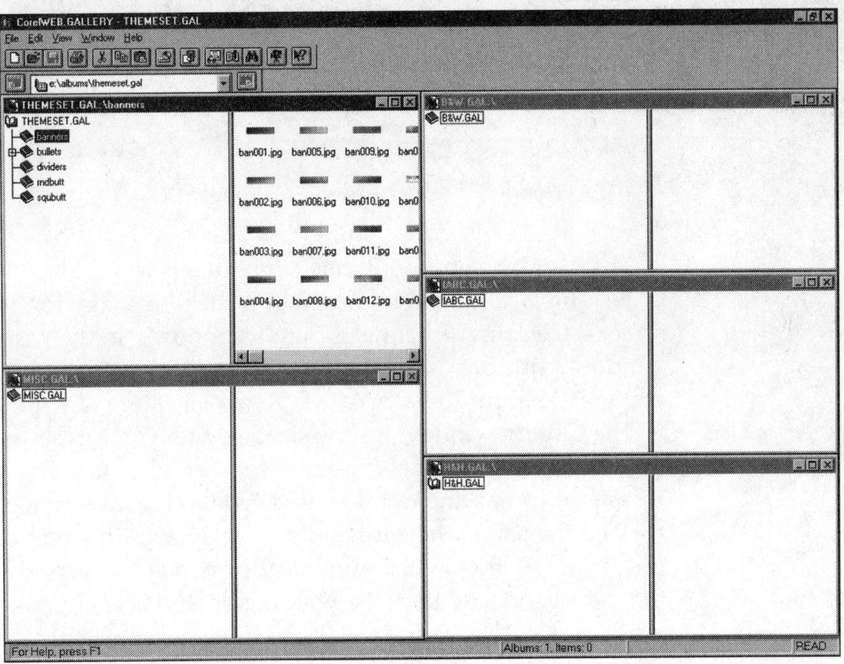

Figure 20-3: Gallery albums tiled horizontally.

That's a little better, but there is still a lot of wasted space. Go ahead and modify the Gallery window sizes individually to arrange the screen in a more efficient manner, as shown in Figure 20-4.

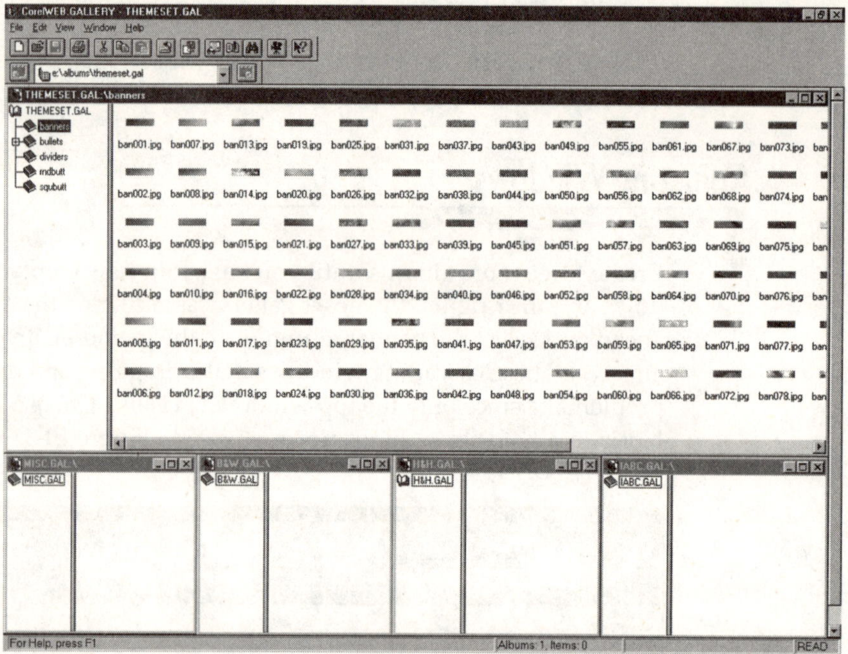

Figure 20-4: Gallery albums retiled individually.

That's much better! But those thumbnails could blind you in short order. Thankfully, Corel thought of those of us who don't have 28-inch screens! Click in the banner album's window—in the window, not the window's title bar. From the View menu, choose Thumbnail Size | Large and voilà! Figure 20-5 displays a view you can read without squinting.

The Gallery window is now sized so that you can see what you're doing. The other windows remain smaller, since you will use them for sorting purposes and don't really need to view the contents. When you click on the list on the left-hand side of the window on the galleries in this themeset, they will automatically open at the large thumbnail size on the right-hand side until the window default is changed.

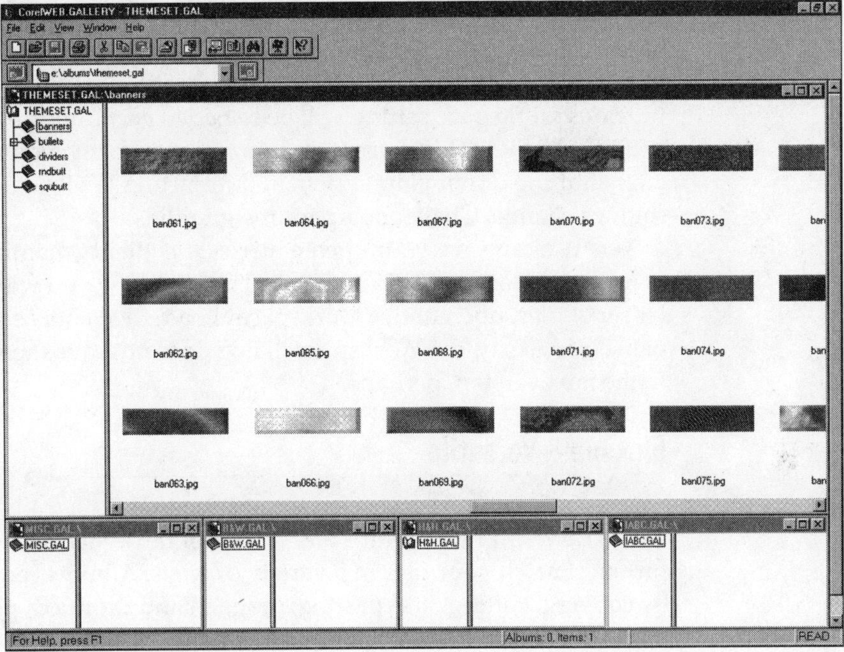

Figure 20-5: Gallery albums sized to fit the eyes.

Fine-Tuning Album Fonts

CorelWEB also gives you the ability to change the font style and size
independent of the thumbnail size. Choose View | Font, and the dialog
box displays the fonts available. Scroll down to view the font names. To
quickly jump down to a specific typeface, type the first letters of its name
in the appropriate field. Click to select type style options, such as bold
and italic, and change point sizes from the drop-down size list.

Preserving Your Workspace

Customizing the window sizes went quickly, but it's bothersome to have
to re-create this screen each time you work with these particular galleries. Corel's engineers have thought of us again! To maintain a consistent

workspace, just make a quick change to your WEB.GALLERY preferences. Click File | Preferences, and select the Workspace tab. Under Initial Workspace, make sure [Last Workspace Used] is selected. This way, your previous workspace setting will be reloaded each time you invoke WEB.GALLERY. This doesn't always work perfectly: you may find that after shutting down your system and restarting WEB.GALLERY, the settings change. Chalk one up for the gremlins.

You also can save your open galleries together by naming and saving your screen under File | Workspace. The next time you want that particular set of files, open under Workspace | Load, then choose the workspace name. Sad to say, the Workspace dialog does not save the window sizes. In the next version, perhaps?

Flexible & Versatile

The WEB.GALLERY albums are models of flexibility, allowing you to mix and match your files in a variety of ways. Albums can be transferred by copying, cutting, and pasting; dragged and dropped; printed on pages by item or album; and compressed in archives. They can even be printed as Adobe Acrobat PDF files!

Printing Thumbnails

Corel has incorporated options to easily assemble your WEB.GALLERY albums on printed pages. Formatting album thumbnails to print is a snap.

To format pages of your albums, open an album, select the thumbnails you want to print, and Ctrl+click on each item. Shift+click to choose by row. To print all thumbnails, select the album icon.

1. Choose File | Print to open the Print dialog.

2. Click on Options. (With a large album, it can take a few minutes for the options to appear.)

3. Click on the Options tab.

4. Select the Preview Image check box to view the changes as you make them.

5. Click to enable the Print Thumbnails radio button.

6. Click on the down or up arrows for the number of columns you want to print (the default is 2).

7. Now select each element as shown in Figure 20-6 (Print frame, Print name, Regenerate, Print border, etc.).

   You can also click on Font to customize your type style options for printing.

8. Click on OK.

   The Print dialog box reappears. (If the correct printer is not shown in the Printer window, click on Setup to install the correct printer.)

9. Click on OK.

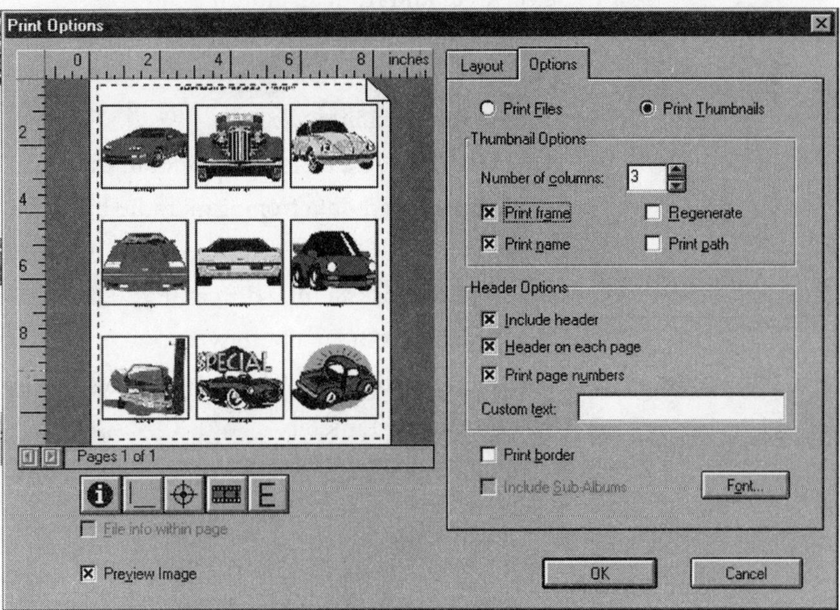

Figure 20-6: Thumbnail options in the Print Options dialog.

Archiving Albums & Files: Take a Smaller Byte!

Remember when a gigabyte-size drive was considered *big*? Amazing how no matter how many bytes on the system drive, the "disk full" message still shows up! Looks like compression schemes will always be a necessary evil, but at least WEB.GALLERY makes the process simple.

To save precious disk space and streamline the distribution of files to other WEB.GALLERY users, you can compress, or archive, your albums or items from them on an individual basis. If you're working on a specific project and using images from the CD-ROM, you can copy the files into a new album on your hard drive. When you're done with the project, you can archive the album. The archiving process works somewhat like that old favorite PKZip. The compressed items and albums are a copy of the original graphics files, and you do have to remember to delete the originals from your hard disk if you are archiving to save space.

To archive an album:

1. Select an album from an album window.

2. Choose Edit | Batch Edit. The Batch Property Edit dialog box opens.

3. Click on the File Links tab.

4. In the File Data box, enable the Update Data check box.

5. Enable the Embed data from Link radio button.

6. Click on OK.

Archiving by item works a little differently:

1. Select an item from an album window.

2. Choose Edit | Properties. The Properties dialog box opens.

3. Click on the File Link tab.

4. In the File Data box, select the Update check box.

5. Select Create Link from radio button.

6. Click on OK.

Just to be safe, you should check the archive before deleting any original files or albums.

Using Keywords & Search

Many a budding Web site designer has discovered that having a huge cache of graphics is a constant drain of time and energy without the means to access them easily. CorelWEB.GALLERY provides every feature you could wish for to put the *right* image at your fingertips. But there's a catch to these features: You have to *use* them!

Now that you've created your custom images and albums, don't forget to apply this valuable productivity tool: *keywords*. Keywords are words and/or phrases that describe a graphic item. Keywords can be assigned to one item or a group of items and are crucial to a successful search of your files. Custom notes, links, and descriptions are also worthy additions to aid in identifying your files.

Let's say you've come across the perfect graphic for a Web page. Even if you're not creating the page at the moment, it can be tagged with a keyword or two for easy retrieval later. To assign the keyword (or phrase) to a graphic as shown in Figure 20-7:

1. Select an item from an open album window.

2. Chose Edit | Properties to open the Properties dialog box.

3. Click on the Keywords tab.

4. Click in the New Keyword window and type a keyword or phrase.

5. Click on Add. Repeat if you want to add several words or phrases.

6. Click on OK.

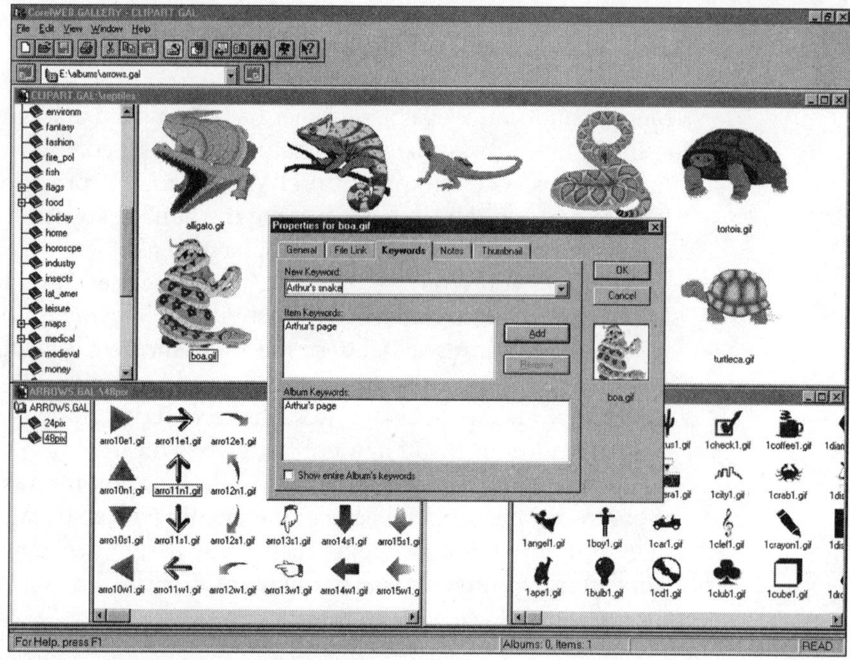

Figure 20-7: Graphic used for Arthur's Web Page.

Quick Searchin' for More Surfin'

The CorelWEB.GALLERY Search function allows you to find graphic items or albums by looking for keywords, labels, descriptions, notes, link names, and link paths. You can search an entire drive or narrow your path to a directory, album, or subalbum to search more efficiently. To search your albums by the keywords you have assigned:

1. Click to select an album or hold down the Shift key and click to select multiple albums if you are unsure which album your graphic file may be in.

2. Choose Edit | Search, and the Item Search dialog box opens.

3. Designate a search by label, keyword, notes, link name, or link path in the first drop down menu.

A Freebie!

The option you are searching (such as keywords) may very well still come up under the other options.

4. Designate a logical operator to define the search (like, not like, exactly like, not exactly like) in the second drop-down menu.

5. Click in the text field and enter a keyword, label, etc.

6. Click on Include Sub-Albums to extend your search.

8. Click on Add.

9. If you wish to search for multiple criteria, for instance, a graphics with the label "snake" and the keyword "Arthur," you may enter new criteria by simply specifying them in the Search for area, then clicking Add. When searching for more than one item, select the Or box to change the default (And).

10. Click on OK.

All the files matching your search will be listed in the Search Results window. These files can be selected individually or as a group and copied, printed, exported, batch-edited, or viewed in a slide show.

Automatic Slideshows

Perhaps you want to take a closer look at your graphic choices. Slide Show allows you to do this automatically. Select an album or individual graphic, or use the results generated by a search to scroll through your images in full-screen mode automatically. Once again, WEB.GALLERY furnishes a wealth of options. For your viewing pleasure, you can alter the defaults for Slide Show (automatic versus manual, delay time, etc.) by choosing File | Preferences and clicking on the Slide Show tab as shown in Figure 20-8.

Start the popcorn and:

1. Choose Select All in the Search Results window.

2. Click on Slide Show.

3. Sit back and enjoy!

To create a slide show of albums or files:

1. Click to highlight an album or choose specific files.

2. Choose File | Slide Show.

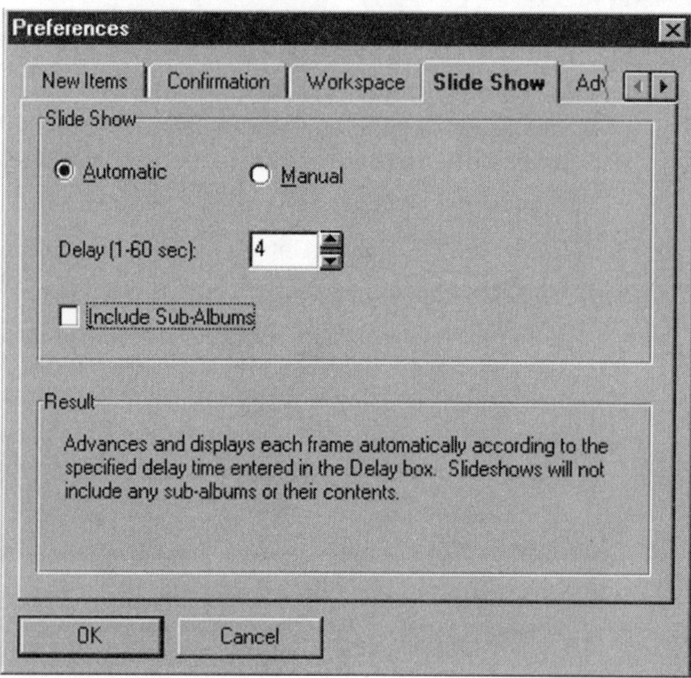

Figure 20-8: Slide Show options in the Preferences dialog box.

Scanning to Albums

If you are scanning images to add to your graphic libraries,
CorelWEB.GALLERY adds the convenience of scanning through the
Acquire command. Using a TWAIN-compliant scanning interface, it
places your scans in the Images directory as bitmap graphic files. To add
a scanned image:

1. Choose File | Acquire Image.

2. From the fly-out menu, choose Acquire. (The Corel Image Source
   dialog box options can vary according to your scanner.)

3. Click on Prescan to view the entire image.

4. Drag the marquee corner handles to select an area to scan.

5. Click on Scan.

6. Click on OK.

Moving On

As we've seen in this chapter, CorelWEB.GALLERY is a valuable component of the Corel WEB.GRAPHICS Suite. Although easily overlooked, WEB.GALLERY provides the graphics, the tools, and the inspiration to produce awesome Web sites. Once you're familiar with how the program works, your productivity will skyrocket as you drag and drop your way to a whole new world of Web page design. With all the goodies onboard, WEB.GALLERY helps you quickly pull it all together.

Appendix A

About the Companion CD-ROM

The Companion CD-ROM included with your copy of *The Comprehensive Guide to CorelWEB.GRAPHICS Suite* contains software programs, graphics, textures, and other goodies to aid in your exploration of the book.

Installation   Each software program resides in its own directory on the CD-ROM. To use the software on the CD-ROM, first go to Windows Explorer (for Windows 95 and Windows NT users) or File Manager (for Windows 3.x users) and copy the desired directory from the CD-ROM to the hard drive. Then follow the instructions in the readme that comes with each program on how to install.

Most of the programs are trial versions that require registration and payment of a fee after the trial period. Please consult each program's readme file for more information about this.

Software on the CD-ROM

ASAP WebShow

Folder   ASAP WEBSHOW

Description   ASAP WebShow is a presentation viewer that runs either as a Netscape Navigator 2.0 Plug-in or as a helper application for all other Web browsers. ASAP WebShow lets anyone download and view graphically rich reports and presentations from the Web that were created by SPC's award-winning ASAP WordPower. For more information, visit http://www.spco.com on the World Wide Web.

Calendar Quick 1.1

Folder   PLUGINS

Description   A plug-in ideal for publishing schedules of events on the Web. With features like calendar embedding, appointment lists, timelines, and project schedules, Calendar Quick makes browsing easier. For more information and the latest downloads, visit http://www.logicpulse.com on the World Wide Web.

Collage Complete 1.1 Demo

Folder   COLLAGE COMPLETE

Description   Screen capture and bit-mapped image handling for Windows and DOS. Everything a user needs to capture, crop, edit, annotate, print, convert, size, flip, rotate, and combine images for multimedia presentations and documentation. Supports many standard image formats and all image types for black and white to grayscale up through 24-bit color. Users can build thumbnail catalogs for image browsing and batch operations. Supports Twain scanners and Kodak Photo CDs. Screen captures for this book were created with Collage Complete by Inner Media, Inc. 60 Plain Road, Hollis, NH 03049 (603) 465-3216.

Cubit Meister

Folder   CUBIT MEISTER

Description   Cubit Meister 1.04 effortlessly converts decimal and fractional inches, millimeters/centimeters, picas/points, and points. Enter a number in any of the supported measurement systems and all the conversions are displayed simultaneously. Copy and paste results into your favorite Windows programs. Cubit Meister also provides an electronic Proportion Scale that calculates proportions between Original and Target sizes. Cubit will automatically convert and calculate proportions even when the Original and Target measurements are entered in different measurement systems.

Folder   Exercise

Description   This folder contains two exercises called Banner and Globe.

Fractal Design Painter 4.0 Demo

Folder PAINTER

Description Fractal Design Painter is the world's leading paint program. Painter's astounding Natural-Media features simulate the tools and textures of traditional artist's materials. From crayons to calligraphy, oils to airbrushes, pencils to watercolor, Painter turns your computer into an artist's studio. For more information and the latest uploads, visit http://www.fractal.com on the World Wide Web.

Goldwave

Folder GOLDWAVE

Description Goldwave is an editor for audio files.

Graphics

Folder GRAPHICS

Description The GRAPHICS folder contains a bunch of graphics files including but not limited to textures, backgrounds, buttons, bullets, hrules, bubbles, stucco, summer, and grayz.

ImageGen 2.1a2

Folder IMAGEGEN

Description ImageGen is a freeware Windows program that produces HTML Web pages consisting of small inline GIF images. For the latest download, visit http://www.canuck.com/~thivier1/imagegen on the World Wide Web.

MouSing

Folder MOUSING

Description Use your mouse as a musical instrument, to create eerie music and sounds, similar to a Theremin. Moving the mouse left to right changes the pitch and moving it up and down changes the volume. MouSing is a product of Sagebrush Systems, Inc.

PROZip Extract-Only 1.2

Folder   PROZIP

Description   PROZip is a Windows-based compression utility that uses a true drag-and-drop interface. Open/use multiple archives simultaneously, copy/move files between archives, create self-extracting, multi-volume and encrypted files, add comments, view/launch files, and make new Windows associations. For more information and the latest download, visit http://www.prozip.com on the World Wide Web.

Macromedia's Shockwave

Folder   PLUGINS

Description   A plug-in for various Macromedia tools that allows interactivity in Web pages. For more information about Macromedia's Shockwave, visit http://www.macromedia.com on the World Wide Web.

TextPad 2.2

Folder   TEXTPAD

Description   TextPad is a simple text reader/writer.

Virtual Home Space Builder

Folder   VHSB

Description   Paragraph International's Virtual Home Space Builder is a 3D rendering program. For more information and the latest download, visit http://www.paragraph.com on the World Wide Web.

WaveSong

Folder   WAVESONG

Description   WaveSong is an audio-generator that creates relaxing sounds of nature, including crickets, thunder, surf, rain, white noise, and more. For more information, visit http://www.sagebrush.com/~sells on the World Wide Web.

WinChime

Folder   WINCHIM

Description   Relax to the sound of windchimes. WinChime uses the MIDI capabilities of your sound card to produce a soothing sound environment. For more information, visit http://www.sagebrush.com/~sells on the World Wide Web.

WS_FTP Limited Edition

Folder   WS_FTP

Description   WS_FTP Limited Edition is a Windows file transfer client application that is used to transfer files between a user's local PC and another, remote computer system. Known for its speed and intuitive Windows interface, WS_FTP is the tool of choice for Internet users who require power and performance to minimize time online and maximize available bandwidth. A software program from Ipswitch, Inc.

Technical Support

Technical support is available for installation-related problems only. The technical support office is open from 8:00 A.M. to 6:00 P.M. Monday through Friday and can be reached via the following methods:

Phone: (919) 544-9404 extension 81

Faxback Answer System: (919) 544-9404 extension 85

E-mail: help@vmedia.com

FAX: (919) 544-9472

World Wide Web: **http://www.vmedia.com/support**

America Online: keyword **Ventana**

Limits of Liability & Disclaimer of Warranty

The authors and publisher of this book have used their best efforts in preparing the CD-ROM and the programs contained in it. These efforts include the development, research, and testing of the theories and programs to determine their effectiveness. The authors and publisher make no warranty of any kind expressed or implied, with regard to these programs or the documentation contained in this book.

The authors and publisher shall not be liable in the event of incidental or consequential damages in connection with, or arising out of, the furnishing, performance, or use of the programs, associated instructions, and/or claims of productivity gains.

Some of the software on this CD-ROM is shareware; there may be additional charges (owed to the software authors/makers) incurred for their registration and continued use. See individual program's README or VREADME.TXT files for more information.

Index

C

M

N

X

Y

Z

VENTANA
VENTANA
http://www.vmedia.com

VENTANA

Interactive Web Publishing With Microsoft Tools

$49.99, 818 pages, illustrated, part #: 462-6

Take advantage of Microsoft's broad range of development tools to produce powerful web pages, program with VBScript, create virtual 3D worlds, and incorporate the functionality of Office applications with OLE. The CD-ROM features demos/lite versions of third party software, sample code.

Web Publishing With Microsoft FrontPage 97

$34.99, 500 pages, illustrated, part #: 478-2

Web page publishing for everyone! Streamline web-site creation and automate maintenance, all without programming! Covers introductory-to-advanced techniques, with hands-on examples. For Internet and intranet developers. The CD-ROM includes all web-site examples from the book, FrontPage add-ons, shareware, clip art and more.

Microsoft Internet Studio Publishing

$49.95, 500 pages, illustrated, part #: 358-1

Harness the power of Microsoft's versatile multimedia publishing system! Learn to deliver dynamic interactive applications across multiple platforms. Features enhanced design techniques, content linking and onscreen title creation. The CD-ROM features include titles, graphics, sound files, templates, free utilities and more!

VENTANA

Looking Good in Print, Deluxe CD-ROM Edition

$34.99, 416 pages, illustrated, part #: 471-5

This completely updated version of the most widely used design companion for desktop publishers features all-new sections on color and printing. Packed with professional tips for creating powerful reports, newsletters, ads, brochures and more. The companion CD-ROM featues Adobe® Acrobat® Reader, author examples, fonts, templates, graphics and more.

Looking Good Online

$39.99, 384 pages, illustrated, part #: 469-3

Create well-designed, organized web sites—incorporating text, graphics, digital photos, backgrounds and forms. Features studies of successful sites and design tips from pros. The companion CD-ROM includes samples from online professionals; buttons, backgrounds, templates and graphics.

Looking Good in 3D

$39.99, 400 pages, illustrated, part #: 434-4

Become the da Vinci of the 3D world! Learn the artistic elements involved in 3D design—light, motion, perspective, animation and more—to create effective interactive projects. The CD-ROM includes samples from the book, templates, fonts and graphics.

VENTANA

3D Studio MAX f/x

$49.99, 552 pages, illustrated, part #: 427-8

Create Hollywood-style special effects! Plunge into 3D animation with step-by-step instructions for lighting, camera movements, optical effects, texture maps, storyboarding, cinematography, editing and much more. The companion CD-ROM features free plug-ins, all the tutorials from the book, 300+ original texture maps and animations.

Microsoft SoftImage|3D Professional Techniques

$69.99, 524 pages, illustrated, part #: 499-5

Create intuitive, visually rich 3D images with this award-winning technology. Follow the structured tutorial to master modeling, animation and rendering, and to increase your 3D productivity. The CD-ROM features tutorials, sample scenes, textures, scripts, shaders, images and animations.

LightWave 3D 5 Character Animation f/x

$69.99, 700 pages, illustrated, part #: 532-0

Master the fine—and lucrative—art of 3D character animation. Traditional animators and computer graphic artists alike will discover everything they need to know: lighting, motion, caricature, composition, rendering ... right down to work-flow strategies. The CD-ROM features a collection of the most popular LightWave plug-ins, scripts, storyboards, finished animations, models and much more.

Net Security: Your Digital Doberman

$29.99, 400 pages, illustrated, part #: 506-1

Doing business on the Internet can be safe . . . if you know the risks and take appropriate steps. This thorough overview helps you put a virtual Web watchdog on the job—to protect both your company and your customers from hackers, electronic shoplifters and disgruntled employees. Easy-to-follow explanations help you understand complex security technologies, with proven technologies for safe Net transactions. Tips, checklists and action plans cover digital dollars, pilfer-proof "storefronts," protecting privacy and handling breaches.

Intranet Firewalls

$34.99, 282 pages, illustrated, part #: 506-1

Protect your network by controlling access—inside and outside your company—to proprietary files. This practical, hands-on guide takes you from intranet and firewall basics through creating and launching your firewall. Professional advice helps you assess your security needs and choose the best system for you. Includes tips for avoiding costly mistakes, firewall technologies, in-depth reviews and uses for popular firewall software, advanced theory of firewall design strategies and implementation, and more.

VENTANA

TO ORDER ANY VENTANA TITLE, COMPLETE THIS ORDER FORM AND MAIL OR FAX IT TO US, WITH PAYMENT, FOR QUICK SHIPMENT.

TITLE	PART #	QTY	PRICE	TOTAL

SHIPPING

For orders shipping within the United States, please add $4.95 for the first book, $1.50 for each additional book.
For "two-day air" add $7.95 for the first book, $3.00 for each additional book.
For orders shipping to Canada, please contact our Nelson Canadaat 800/268-2222 to place your order:
For orders shipping outside the United States and Canada, phone 800/332-7450or
Email: vorders@kdc.com for exact shipping charges.
Note: Please include your local sales tax.

SUBTOTAL = $ _______________

SHIPPING = $ _______________

TAX = $ _______________

TOTAL = $ _______________

Mail to: Media Group Customer Service • International Thomson Publishing • 7625 Empire Drive • Florence, KY 41042
☎ 800/332-7450 • fax 606/283-0718

Name ____

E-mail __________________________________ Daytime phone __________________________________

Company ____

Address (No PO Box) ____

City _______________________________ State __________ Zip __________

Payment enclosed ___ VISA ___ MC ___ Acc't # _______________________________ Exp. date __________

Signature _______________________ Exact name on card _______________________

Check your local bookstore or software retailer for these and other bestselling titles, or call toll free:

800/332-7450

8:oo am - 6:oo pm EST